interpersonal communication

3e

KORY FLOYD

University of Arizona

Mc
Graw
Hill
Education

INTERPERSONAL COMMUNICATION, THIRD EDITION

Published by McGraw-Hill Education, 2 Penn Plaza, New York, NY 10121. Copyright © 2017 by McGraw-Hill Education. All rights reserved. Printed in the United States of America. Previous editions © 2011 and 2009. No part of this publication may be reproduced or distributed in any form or by any means, or stored in a database or retrieval system, without the prior written consent of McGraw-Hill Education, including, but not limited to, in any network or other electronic storage or transmission, or broadcast for distance learning.

Some ancillaries, including electronic and print components, may not be available to customers outside the United States.

This book is printed on acid-free paper.

1 2 3 4 5 6 7 8 9 0 DOW/DOW 1 0 9 8 7 6

ISBN: 978-0-07-352390-3 (Student's Edition)
MHID: 0-07-352390-9
ISBN: 978-0-07-776825-6 (Instructor's Edition)
MHID: 0-07-776825-6

Senior Vice President, Products & Markets: *Kurt L. Strand*
Vice President, General Manager, Products & Markets: *Michael Ryan*
Vice President, Content Design & Delivery: *Kimberly Meriwether David*
Managing Director: *David S. Patterson*
Senior Brand Manager: *Nancy Huebner*
Director, Product Development: *Meghan Campbell*
Lead Product Developer: *Lisa Pinto*
Senior Product Developer: *Noel Hohnstine*
Senior Marketing Manager: *Laura Kennedy*
Senior Market Development Manager: *Sally Constable*
Director, Content Design & Delivery: *Terri Schiesl*
Program Manager: *Jennifer Gehl*
Content Project Managers: *Lisa Bruflodt, Samantha Donisi-Hamm, Judi David*
Buyer: *Jennifer Pickel*
Design: *Matt Diamond*
Content Licensing Specialists: *Shawntel Schmitt, DeAnna Dausener*
Cover Image: *seamartini/Getty Images*
Compositor: *SPi Global*
Printer: *R. R. Donnelley*

All credits appearing on page or at the end of the book are considered to be an extension of the copyright page.

Library of Congress Cataloging-in-Publication Data
Floyd, Kory.
   Interpersonal communication / Kory Floyd, University of Arizona. — 3 Edition.
     pages cm
   Revised edition of the author's Interpersonal communication, 2011.
   ISBN 978-0-07-352390-3 (alk. paper)
   1. Interpersonal communication.   I. Title.
BF637.C45F56   2016
153.6—dc23

          2015030914

The Internet addresses listed in the text were accurate at the time of publication. The inclusion of a website does not indicate an endorsement by the authors or McGraw-Hill Education, and McGraw-Hill Education does not guarantee the accuracy of the information presented at these sites.

mheducation.com/highered

To those who communicate
for the betterment of us all.

Name: Kory Floyd

Education: I got my undergraduate degree from Western Washington University, my master's degree from the University of Washington, and my PhD from the University of Arizona.

Current jobs: Professor at the University of Arizona, researcher, writer

Favorite job growing up: Singing busboy

Worst childhood memory: Getting sent to the principal's office in third grade. (It's possible I haven't told my parents about that.)

Best childhood memory: The birth of my sister and brother

Hobbies: Playing piano, singing, reading, traveling, playing Wii tennis

Pets: I have a dog named Cruise and a puppy named Buster.

Favorite recent book: The Language of Life by James Lull and Eduardo Neiva

Favorite TV show: The Big Bang Theory

Places I love: New Zealand, Starbucks, my brother's house

Dear Readers,

I can still recall how my family reacted when I said I wanted to study communication. *You already know how to communicate,* I remember one relative saying. Communication seemed like common sense to my family members, so they weren't entirely sure why I needed a PhD just to understand it.

As it turns out, a lot of other people feel the way my relatives do. Because each of us communicates in some form nearly every day of our lives, it's hard not to think of communication as completely intuitive.

That is especially true for interpersonal communication, since forming and maintaining relationships with others is such a pervasive human activity. What can we learn from research and formal study that we don't already know from our lived experience? Aren't we all experts in interpersonal communication? Just for the sake of argument, let's say we were. Why, then, do we so often misunderstand each other? Why is our divorce rate as high as it is? How come it seems like conflict and deception are all around us? How do we explain the popularity of online support groups? If we're all experts at communicating interpersonally, why is it so challenging so often? Maybe communication isn't as intuitive as one might think.

My goal with *Interpersonal Communication* is to help students see how communication not only affects their relationships but also influences their health, happiness, and quality of life. I want to encourage students to go beyond commonsense notions about communication and help them see the value of investigating interpersonal processes—both face-to-face and online—in a systematic way. Importantly, I strive to meet those priorities while speaking to students in a way that interests them and helps them to use both the content and the cognitive tools to relate theories and concepts to their own experiences.

And those experiences—along with the ways we communicate—are changing quickly these days. With electronically mediated communication, what used to be unprecedented is now commonplace. Deployed servicemen watch the birth of their children live via Skype. College students organize rallies with less than a day's notice on Twitter. Adults given up for adoption as infants use Facebook to find their biological parents. Each new technology expands our world just a little more, making interpersonal communication skills increasingly valuable. With a focus on well-being, everyday applications, and adaptability to situations and channels, *Interpersonal Communication* helps students build the interpersonal skills they'll need to communicate effectively in today's quickly changing environments.

Just as our communication adapts to new communication channels, so do the ways we study and teach. *Interpersonal Communication* now provides students and teachers with a holistic course solution through Connect. An all-inclusive learning tool, Connect offers students a personalized reading experience with SmartBook, an adaptive ebook that targets areas for improvement and serves up interactive learning resources as needed. Connect also helps instructors gauge students' skills and comprehension through online quizzes and homework assignments. Meanwhile, the Instructor's Manual, Test Bank, and PowerPoint slides provide additional tips and activities—adding to the robust support found in the Annotated Instructor's Edition. By seamlessly integrating all the resources for *Interpersonal Communication* in one place, Connect helps teachers get the most out of their class time and helps students study smarter.

I hope you will find the result of these efforts to be a well-integrated package of engaging and contemporary materials for the study of interpersonal communication.

brief contents

contents

"With SmartBook, I remember more of what I read."

4 Interpersonal Perception 106

"I like applying what I've read by answering the questions in SmartBook."

PART 2 INTERPERSONAL COMMUNICATION SKILLS IN ACTION

5 Language 140

"SmartBook lets me know I am retaining the information."

"SmartBook helps me identify what we are going to be covering in class."

PART 3 DYNAMICS OF INTERPERSONAL RELATIONSHIPS

9 Forming and Maintaining Personal Relationships 274

10 Interpersonal Communication in Close Relationships 308

"SmartBook helps me feel more prepared for class."

boxes

McGraw-Hill Connect: An Overview

McGraw-Hill Connect offers full-semester access to comprehensive, reliable content and learning resources for the Interpersonal Communication course. Connect's deep integration with most Learning Management Systems (LMS), including Blackboard and Desire2Learn (D2L), offers single sign-on and deep gradebook synchronization. Data from Assignment Results reports synchronize directly with many LMS, allowing scores to flow automatically from Connect into school-specific grade books, if required.

The following tools and services are available as part of Connect for the Interpersonal Communication course:

Tool	Instructional Context	Description
SmartBook	• SmartBook is an engaging and interactive reading experience for mastering fundamental Interpersonal Communication content. • The metacognitive component confirms learners' understanding of the material. • Instructors can actively connect SmartBook assignments and results to higher-order classroom work and one-on-one student conferences. • Learners can track their own understanding and mastery of course concepts, and identify gaps in their knowledge.	• SmartBook is an adaptive reading experience designed to change the way learners read and learn. It creates a personalized reading experience by highlighting the most impactful concepts a student needs to learn at that moment in time. • SmartBook creates personalized learning plans based on student responses to content question probes and confidence scales, identifying the topics a learner is struggling with and providing learning resources to create personalized learning moments. • SmartBook includes a variety of learning resources tied directly to key content areas to provide students with additional instruction and context. This includes video and media clips, interactive slide content, and mini-lectures and image analyses. • SmartBook Reports provide instructors with data to quantify success and identify problem areas that require addressing in and out of the classroom. • Learners can access their own progress and concept mastery reports.

(Continued)

Connect Insight for *Instructors*	• Connect Insight for *Instructors* is an analytics resource that produces quick feedback related to learner performance and learner engagement.
	• Designed as a dashboard for both quick check-ins and detailed performance and engagement views.
		• Connect Insight for *Instructors* offers a series of visual data displays that provide analysis on five key insights:
		  • How are my students doing?
		  • How is this one student doing?
		  • How is my section doing?
		  • How is this assignment doing?
		  • How are my assignments doing?

Connect Insight for *Students*	• Connect Insight for *Students* is a powerful data analytics tool that provides at-a-glance visualizations to help a learner understand his or her performance on Connect assignments.	• Connect Insight for *Students* offers the learner details on each Connect assignment. When possible, it offers suggestions for the learner on how he or she can improve scores. These data can help guide the learner to behaviors that will lead to better scores in the future.
Instructor Reports	• Instructor Reports provide data that may be useful for assessing programs or courses as part of the accreditation process.	• Connect generates a number of powerful reports and charts that allow instructors to quickly review the performance of a given learner or an entire section. • Instructors can run reports that span multiple sections and instructors, making it an ideal solution for individual professors, course coordinators, and department chairs.
Student Reports	• Student Reports allow learners to review their performance for specific assignments or for the course.	• Learners can keep track of their performance and identify areas they are struggling with.
Simple LMS Integration	• Seamlessly integrates with every learning management system.	• Learners have automatic single sign-on. • Connect assignment results sync to the LMS's gradebook.
Pre- and Post-Tests	• Instructors can generate their own pre- and post-tests from the Test Bank. • Pre- and post-tests demonstrate what learners already know before class begins and what they have learned by the end.	• Instructors have access to two sets of pre- and post-tests (at two levels). Instructors can use these tests to create a diagnostic and post-diagnostic exam via Connect.

(Continued)

Tegrity	• Tegrity allows instructors to capture course material or lectures on video. • Students can watch videos recorded by their instructor and learn course material at their own pace.	• Instructors can keep track of which learners have watched the videos they post. • Learners can watch and review lectures by their instructor. • Learners can search each lecture for specific bites of information.
Speech Capture	• Speech Capture provides instructors with a comprehensive and efficient way of managing in-class and online speech assignments, including student self-reviews, peer reviews, and instructor grading.	• The Speech Capture tool allows instructors to easily and efficiently set up speech assignments for their course that can easily be shared and repurposed, as needed, throughout their use of Connect. • Customizable rubrics and settings can be saved and shared, saving time and streamlining the speech assignment process from creation to assessment. • Speech Capture allows users, both students and instructors, to view videos during the assessment process. Feedback can be left within a customized rubric or as time-stamped comments within the video-playback itself.
Speech Preparation Tools	• Speech Preparation Tools provide learners with additional support, such as Topic Helper, Outline Tool, and access to third-party Internet sites like EasyBib (for formatting citations) and SurveyMonkey (to create audience-analysis questionnaires and surveys).	• Speech Preparation Tools provide learners with additional resources to help with the preparation and outlining of speeches, as well as with audience-analysis surveys. • Instructors have the ability to make tools either available or unavailable to learners.

Instructor's Guide to Connect for *Interpersonal Communication*

When you assign Connect, you can be confident—and have data to demonstrate—that the learners in your courses, however diverse, are acquiring the skills, principles, and critical processes that constitute effective communication. This leaves you to focus on your highest course expectations.

Tailored to you.

Connect offers on-demand, single sign-on access to learners—wherever they are and whenever they have time. With a single, one-time registration, learners receive access to McGraw-Hill's trusted content. **Learners also have *a courtesy trial period* during registration.**

Easy to use.

Connect seamlessly supports all major learning management systems with content, assignments, performance data, and SmartBook, the leading adaptive learning system. With these tools, you can quickly make assignments, produce reports, focus discussions, intervene on problem topics, and help at-risk learners—as needed and when needed.

Interpersonal Communication SmartBook

A personalized and adaptive learning experience with SmartBook.

Boost learner success with McGraw-Hill's adaptive reading and study experience. The *Interpersonal Communication* SmartBook highlights the most impactful interpersonal communication concepts the learner needs to study at that moment in time. The learning path continuously adapts based on what the individual learner knows and does not know and provides focused help through targeted question probes and learning resources.

Enhanced for the new edition!

With a suite of new Learning Resources and question probes, as well as highlights of key chapter concepts, SmartBook's intuitive technology optimizes learner study time by creating a personalized learning path for improved course performance and overall learner success.

SmartBook highlights the key concepts of every chapter, offering learners a high-impact learning experience. Here, highlighted text and an illustration together explain a communication model. Highlights change color (right) when a learner has demonstrated his or her understanding of the concept.

Over 100 interactive Learning Resources.

Presented in a range of interactive styles, the Learning Resources in *Interpersonal Communication* support learners who may be struggling to master, or simply wish to review, the most important communication concepts. Designed to reinforce essential theories and skills—from competent online self-disclosure and nonverbal communication channels to detecting deceptive communication and managing relationships—every Learning Resource is presented at the precise moment of need. Whether a video, audio clip, or interactive mini-lesson, each Learning Resource is new and is designed to give learners a lifelong foundation in strong interpersonal communication skills.

More than 1,000 targeted question probes.

Class-tested at colleges and universities nationwide, a treasury of engaging question probes— new and revised—assess learners at every stage of the learning process, helping them to thrive in the course. Designed to gauge learners' comprehension of the most important concepts in *Interpersonal Communication,* and presented in a variety of interactive styles to facilitate learner engagement, targeted question probes give learners immediate feedback on their understanding of the content, identifying a learner's familiarity with the instruction and pointing him or her to areas where additional review is needed.

> You are at lunch with some colleagues and share your feelings about the upcoming election, assuming incorrectly that they share the same feelings. What are you guilty of?
>
> **Click the answer you think is right.**
>
> multicultural error
>
> shared knowledge error
>
> shared opinion error
>
> monopolization error
>
> **Do you know the answer?**   Read about this
>
> I know it   Think so   Unsure   No idea

Interpersonal Communication bridges theory and practice

New! Over 70 percent new scholarly references.

A thorough update of the entire text, including new theories and research on electronically mediated communication, immerses learners and instructors alike in the latest and best knowledge about interpersonal communication available today.

Seamless integration of scholarship, theory, and skills.

By combining the latest research with the everyday scenarios learners face, author Kory Floyd presents a systematic and modern approach to the study of interpersonal communication that helps learners build vital interpersonal skills and make sound choices—academically, personally, and professionally.

Emphasis on critical thinking and self-reflection.

Learners have numerous opportunities to make connections between the text and their own lives as well as consider how their communication choices influence the outcomes they experience.

- *Learn It/Apply It/Reflect on It.* This section-ending feature encourages learners to assess their comprehension, practice theory in their own lives, and reflect on their experiences to improve self-awareness.
- *Fact or Fiction?* This feature allows learners to challenge their assumptions about interpersonal communication.

Examples with real-world relevance relate content to real life.

New chapter-opening vignettes, refreshed examples in every chapter, and a current photo program enliven the content and allow learners to study interpersonal communication in an engaging way that directly relates to them.

Interpersonal Communication emphasizes critical contexts: technology, gender, culture, and relationships

New! Online and electronically mediated communication integrated in every chapter.

Every chapter includes comprehensive coverage of technology and digital devices' influence on interpersonal communication. Covering everything from online deception and relational maintenance via texts to improving listening and emotional expression when online, these sections provide learners with the latest research on electronically mediated communication, including practical skills they can immediately use in their own lives.

Competent Online Communication

These days, much of our interpersonal communication takes place in electronically mediated contexts. These include e-mail, instant messaging, and text messaging; social networking (such as on Facebook and LinkedIn); tweeting; image sharing (such as on YouTube and Flickr); and videoconferencing (such as on Skype and Facetime), among others. As you'll see in this section, communicating competently in these venues requires paying attention to their unique capabilities and pitfalls.

BEWARE OF THE POTENTIAL FOR MISUNDERSTANDING. Face-to-face conversations allow you to pay attention to behaviors that help to clarify the meaning of a speaker's words. People's facial expressions, gestures, and tone of voice, for example, generally provide clues about what they are trying to say. Are they speaking seriously or sarcastically? Are they upset or calm, tentative or self-assured? We can usually tell a lot about people's meaning by considering not only *what they say* but *how they say it*.

We saw earlier that some channel-lean forms of communication—such as tweeting and instant messaging—rely heavily on text, restricting our access to facial expressions and other clues. As a result, these forms of communication increase the potential for misunderstanding. Many of us have had the experience of teasing or joking with someone in a text message, for instance, only to discover that the person took our words seriously and felt offended or hurt.

To communicate competently when using channel-lean media, follow these guidelines:

Culture, gender, and diversity are integrated throughout the text.

In addition to a full chapter on culture and gender, every chapter includes essential information about how culture, gender, and sexual identity affect communication. Discussions include the priorities and challenges of socially marginalized groups such as the elderly, immigrants, sexual minorities, people with physical disabilities, people with psychological disorders, and economically disadvantaged individuals.

New organization for relationship chapters.

For many learners, coverage of close relationships is the heart of the interpersonal communication course. To promote a more straightforward approach to teaching and learning this material, these chapters have a new structure:

- Chapter 9 focuses on the theories and processes of relationship attraction, formation, maintenance, and dissolution.
- Chapter 10 focuses on communication in friendships, romantic relationships, families, and workplace relationships.

Interpersonal Communication promotes competence

Whether online or face-to-face, learners will understand how to be an effective communicator and learn the skills needed to make competent choices in their own lives.

Skills self-assessment.

The Assess Your Skills feature in the text and the Skills Assessment feature in Connect ask learners to evaluate their tendencies and competence in specific interpersonal skills.

Communication dark side/light side.

These boxes examine the common positive and negative communication issues that people face. In this practical feature, learners gain insight into how to best navigate these challenges and choices.

Got Skills? activities.

These innovative boxes tell learners why a specific interpersonal skill matters, while instructing them on how to practice the skill and reflect on the practice for a holistic understanding of the skill.

Data Analytics

Connect Insight provides at-a-glance analysis on five key insights, available at a moment's notice from your tablet device. You can see, in real time, how individual learners or sections are doing (or how well your assignments have been received) so you can take action early and keep struggling learners from falling behind.

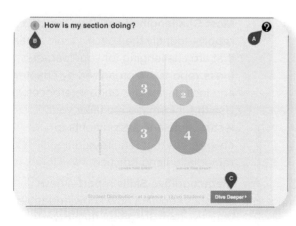

Instructors can see, at a glance, individual learner performance: analytics showing learner investment in assignments, and success at completing them, help instructors identify, and aid, those who are at risk.

Instructors can see how many learners have completed an assignment, how long they spent on the task, and how they scored.

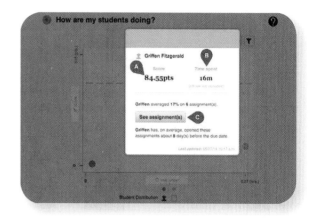

Connect Reports

Instructor Reports allow instructors to quickly monitor learner activity, making it easy to identify which learners are struggling and to provide immediate help to ensure those learners stay enrolled in the course and improve their performance. The Instructor Reports also highlight the concepts and learning objectives that the class as a whole is having difficulty grasping. This essential information lets you know exactly which areas to target for review during your limited class time.

Some key reports include:

Progress Overview report—View learner progress for all modules, including how long learners have spent working in the module, which modules they have used outside of any that were assigned, and individual learner progress.

Missed Questions report—Identify specific probes, organized by chapter, that are problematic for learners.

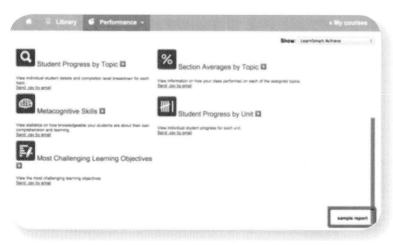

Most Challenging Learning Objectives report—Identify the specific topic areas that are challenging for your learners; these reports are organized by chapter and include specific page references. Use this information to tailor your lecture time and assignments to cover areas that require additional remediation and practice.

Metacognitive Skills report—View statistics showing how knowledgeable your learners are about their own comprehension and learning.

Speech Capture

Designed for use in face-to-face, real-time classrooms, as well as online courses, Speech Capture allows you to evaluate your learners' speeches using fully customizable rubrics. You can also create and manage peer review assignments and upload videos on behalf of learners for optimal flexibility.

Learners can access rubrics and leave comments when preparing self-reviews and peer reviews. They can easily upload a video of their speech from their hard drive or use Connect's built-in video recorder. Learners can even attach and upload additional files or documents, such as a works-cited page or a PowerPoint presentation.

PEER REVIEW
Peer review assignments are easier than ever. Create and manage peer review assignments and customize privacy settings.

SPEECH ASSESSMENT
Connect Speech Capture lets you customize the assignments, including self-reviews and peer reviews. It also saves your frequently used comments, simplifying your efforts to provide feedback.

SELF-REFLECTION
The self-review feature allows learners to revisit their own presentations and compare their progress over time.

Classroom Preparation Tools

Whether before, during, or after class, there is a suite of products designed to help instructors plan their lessons and keep learners building upon the foundations of the course.

ANNOTATED INSTRUCTOR'S EDITION
The Annotated Instructor's Edition features a plethora of marginal notes to help instructors make use of the full range of the coverage, activities, and resources in the text and online.

INSTRUCTOR'S MANUAL
The IM provides outlines, discussion questions, key terms and their definitions, a research library, and examples of in-class and out-of-class assignments for every chapter.

TEST BANK

Test Bank offers multiple-choice questions, true/false questions, short-answer questions, and essay questions for each chapter.

POWERPOINT SLIDES

The PowerPoint presentations provide chapter highlights that help instructors create focused yet individualized lesson plans.

Support to Ensure Success

- **Digital Success Academy**—The Digital Success Academy on Connect offers a wealth of training and course creation guidance for instructors and learners alike. Instructor support is presented in easy-to-navigate, easy-to-complete sections. It includes the popular **Connect** how-to videos, step-by-step **Click-through Guides,** and **First Day of Class** materials that explain how to use both the Connect platform and its course-specific tools and features. http://createwp.customer.mheducation.com/wordpress-mu/success-academy/

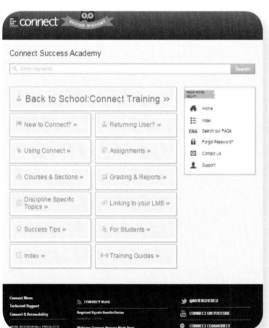

- **Digital Success Team**—The Digital Success Team is a group of specialists dedicated to working online with instructors—one-on-one—to demonstrate how the Connect platform works and to help incorporate Connect into a customer's specific course design and syllabus. Contact your digital learning consultant to learn more.

- **Digital Learning Consultants**—Digital Learning Consultants are local resources who work closely with your McGraw-Hill learning technology consultants. They can provide face-to-face faculty support and training. http://shop.mheducation.com/store/paris/user/findltr.html

- **Digital Faculty Consultants**—Digital Faculty Consultants are experienced instructors who use Connect in their classroom. These instructors are available to offer suggestions, advice, and training about how best to use Connect in your class. To request a Digital Faculty Consultant to speak with, please e-mail your McGraw-Hill learning technology consultant. http://connect.customer.mheducation.com/dfc/

- **National Training Webinars**—McGraw-Hill offers an ongoing series of webinars for instructors to learn and master the Connect platform, as well as its course-specific tools and features. We hope you will refer to our online schedule of national training webinars and sign up to learn more about Connect! http://webinars.mhhe.com/

CONTACT OUR CUSTOMER SUPPORT TEAM

McGraw-Hill is dedicated to supporting instructors and learners. To contact our customer support team, please call us at 800-331-5094 or visit us online at http://mpss.mhhe.com/contact.php

Changes for the Third Edition
Chapter-by-Chapter Changes

CHAPTER 1: ABOUT COMMUNICATION

- New opening vignette on *Portlandia*'s Carrie Brownstein and Fred Armisen.
- New "Communication: Dark Side" feature discusses the challenges of managing face-to-face communication when distracted by smartphones.
- New "Got Skills?" box on empathic communication.
- New "Assess Your Skills" box: "Are You a High Self-Monitor?"
- New section "Competent Online Communication" explores electronically mediated communication (EMC).
- Updated "Fact or Fiction?" box on same-sex relationships with new research.
- New "Got Skills?" box on using powerful language, specifically for EMC.

CHAPTER 2: CULTURE AND GENDER

- New opening vignette about cross-cultural friendships in diverse neighborhoods.
- New "Communication: Dark Side" box discusses cultural stereotyping during times of stress.
- New section "Social Media as a Co-Culture" explores the emerging culture of online communities across different social media platforms.
- Expanded discussion of similarity assumption and the role it plays in EMC.

CHAPTER 3: COMMUNICATION AND THE SELF

- New opening vignette on managing multiple identities on the TV show *Black-ish.*
- New discussions on expressions of self-esteem and identity in social media.
- New section "Challenges and Risks of Disclosing Online" provides advice on managing self needs when using social media.

CHAPTER 4: INTERPERSONAL PERCEPTION

- Updated discussion of challenges facing female professionals, including Sheryl Sandberg's *Lean In.*
- New section "Forming Perceptions Online" explores the way avatars and photos influence perception in EMC.
- Revised discussion of recency effect including comparisons between face-to-face and online impressions.
- New discussion of egocentrism and online communication.
- Revised "Fact or Fiction?" box on making accurate perceptions.

CHAPTER 5: LANGUAGE

- New "Fact or Fiction?" box explores the impact of texting on our ability to use language.
- Updated discussion of loaded language examines language choices by proponents and critics of the Patient Protection and Affordable Care Act.
- New section on criticism of the Sapir-Whorf hypothesis.

- New "Got Skills?" box on using ethical appeals to persuade others.
- New "Communication: Light Side" box on Facebook tribute pages.
- Revised coverage of communication climates (previously in Chapter 10) moved to a new section on the influence of language in relationships.
- New section "Create Positive Climates in Electronically Mediated Communication."
- New "Got Skills?" box on how to spot confirming messages.

CHAPTER 6: NONVERBAL COMMUNICATION

- New opening vignette discusses John Travolta's embrace of Scarlett Johansson at 2015 Oscars.
- New "Got Skills?" box on communicating emotion nonverbally.
- New "Communication: Light Side" box on affection at cuddling parties.
- New figure of Hall's Four Spatial Zones.
- New section "Managing Nonverbal Behavior in Electronically Mediated Communication" includes tips for videoconferencing and texting.

CHAPTER 7: LISTENING

- New opening vignette about veterans with PTSD.
- New "Assess Your Skills" box on identifying listening styles.
- Revised section on the effect of culture and sex on listening.
- New section "Effective Listening Online."
- New "Communication: Light Side" box on online listening groups.
- New "Fact or Fiction?" box on whether technology impairs listening abilities.
- New section on managing information overload during EMC.

CHAPTER 8: EMOTION

- New opening vignette examines emotions and communication on TV's *The Walking Dead*.
- New "Got Skills?" box on expressing anger constructively.
- New "Communication: Light Side" box about the life benefits of experiencing joy.
- New section explores relationship between emotion and EMC.
- Revised discussion of emotional contagion now covers online communication.

CHAPTER 9: FORMING AND MAINTAINING PERSONAL RELATIONSHIPS

- New opening vignette discusses the relationship types in the film *This is Where I Leave You*.
- New chapter structure focuses on relational theory—how personal relationships form and develop.
- New section "Relationship Development and Maintenance via Online Social Networking" examines the ways in which EMC affects and is affected by relationships.
- New "Fact or Fiction?" box on how opposites attract.
- New "Assess Your Skills" box about how to communicate positivity.
- New "Got Skills?" box on expressing affection online.

CHAPTER 10: INTERPERSONAL COMMUNICATION IN CLOSE RELATIONSHIPS

- New opening vignette details relationship of two real-life friends and co-workers.
- New chapter structure examines different types of relationships in detail—romantic, friendships, family, and workplace.
- New section "Online Communication in Workplace Relationships" examines the challenges of EMC in the workplace.
- New "Fact or Fiction?" box about the percent of marriages that end in divorce.
- New "Got Skills?" box on using upward, downward, and lateral communication.

CHAPTER 11: INTERPERSONAL CONFLICT

- New opening vignette highlights restorative justice programs used to manage conflict.
- New sections on cultural dimensions and conflict and cross-cultural conflict.
- New section "Managing Computer-Mediated Conflict".
- Revised section on how power influences communication.
- New "Communication: Dark Side" box on alcohol and conflict.

CHAPTER 12: DECEPTIVE COMMUNICATION

- New opening vignette explores the deception between a married couple in the film *Gone Girl*.
- Revised section "Defining Deception" including high-stakes, low-stakes, and middle-stakes lies.
- New section on how deception is common when communicating online.
- New Communication: Dark Side" box on lying to loved ones.

Contributors

I am most grateful to have had exceptional, astute groups of instructors across the country who served as reviewers and offered insights and suggestions that improved *Interpersonal Communication,* Third Edition, immeasurably:

Shae Adkins, *Lone Star College*
Julie Allee, *Ivy Tech Community College of Indiana*
Courtney Allen, *University of Florida*
Jacob Arndt, *Kalamazoo Valley Community College*
Cameron Basquiat, *College of Southern Nevada*
Isabelle Bauman, *Missouri State University*
Carol Benton, *University of Central Missouri*
Angela Blais, *University of Minnesota*
Gary Edward Brown, *Ivy Tech Community College of Indiana*
Leah Bryant, Lead Subject Matter Expert, *DePaul University*
Stefne Broz, *Wittenberg University*
Paul Cero, *Inver Hills Community College*
Thomas Chester, *Ivy Tech East Central*
Michelle Coleman, *Clark State Community College*
Janet Colvin, *Utah Valley University*
Angela Cordova, *Oregon State University*
Karen Coyle, *Pikes Peak Community College*
Tasha Davis, *Austin Community College*
Douglas Deiss, *Glendale Community College*
Melanie Finney, *DePauw University*
Edie Gaythwaite, *Valencia College*
Michelle Givertz, *California State University*
Donna Goodwin, *Tulsa Community College*
Maya Greene, *Columbia Greene Community College*
Trey Guinn, *University of the Incarnate Word*
Karen Hamburg, *Camden County College*
Annette Hamel, *Western Michigan University*
Heidi Hamilton, *Emporia State University*
April Hebert, *College of Southern Nevada*
Cheryl Hebert, *Estrella Mountain Community College*
Colin Hesse, *Oregon State University*
Dawn Hines, *Clark State Community College*
Gary Iman, *Missouri State University*
Jacob Isaacs, *Ivy Tech Community College of Indiana*
Deborah Johnson, *Metropolitan State University*
Melissa Hernandez Katz, *The University of Texas at Dallas*
Cynthia King, *California State University*
David Kosloski, *Clark College*

Rise Lara, *Austin Community College*
Lee Lavery, *Ivy Tech Community College of Indiana*
Sheryl Lidzy, *Emporia State University*
Kim Long, *Valencia College, East Campus*
Ron Mace, *Somerset Community College*
Sujanet Mason, *Luzerne County Community College*
Julie Mayberry, *North Carolina State University; Meredith College*
Katherine Maynard, *Community College of Vermont*
Nathan Miczo, *Western Illinois University*
Kristi Mingus, *North Dakota State University*
Mark Morman, *Baylor University*
Simone Mullinax, *Jamestown Community College*
Jan Muto, *Norco College*
Sorin Nastasia, *Southern Illinois University*
Laura Nunn, *South Texas College*
Steve Ott, *Kalamazoo Valley Community College*
Melanie Parrish, *Luzerne County Community College*
Fiona Patin, *Ivy Tech Community College of Indiana*
Carol Paulnock, *Saint Paul College*
Kaitlin Phillips, *University of Nebraska*
Leighann Rechtin, *Ivy Tech Community College of Indiana*
Amber Reinhart, *University of Missouri*
Loretta Rivers, *New Orleans Baptist Theological Seminary*
Stephanie Rolain-Jacobs, *University of Wisconsin*
Sudeshna Roy, *Stephen F. Austin State University*
Kelly Schutz, *Ivy Tech Community College of Indiana*
Toni Shields, *Ivy Tech Community College of Indiana*
Julie Simanski, *Des Moines Area Community College*
Carolyn Sledge, *Delta State University*
Lynn Stewart, *Cochise College*
Kelly Stockstad, *Austin Community College*
Charee Thompson, *Ohio University*
Mary Tripp, *Wisconsin Indianhead Technical College*
Stephanie Van Stee, *University of Missouri*
Shawn Wahl, *Missouri State University*
Julie Williams, *San Jacinto College*
Stacie Williams, *Clark College*
Lori Wisdom-Whitley, *Everett Community College*
Joansandy Wong, *Austin Community College*
Alesia Woszidlo, *University of Kansas*
Christina Yoshimura, *The University of Montana*
Kent Zimmerman, *Sinclair Community College*

Acknowledgments

One of my favorite parts about writing books is that so many people play key roles in helping a new book come together. This one was no exception, and it's my pleasure to thank those whose contributions and support are responsible for the book you are now reading.

First and foremost, my sincere gratitude goes to everyone at McGraw-Hill Higher Education. They are a true joy to work with and to know. David Patterson, Lisa Pinto, Nancy Huebner, Sally Constable, Laura Kennedy, Kim Taylo, Noel Hohnstine, and Linda Su have been a constant source of inspiration, energy, humor, and warmth, and I value immensely my relationship with each of them. Special thanks also to project managers Lisa Bruflodt and Sam Donisi-Hamm and the design team led by Matt Diamond, as well as to lead digital product analyst Janet Byrne Smith.

Ann Kirby-Payne was a truly excellent development editor. She has devoted countless hours to making this book as fresh and interesting as possible, and she has done so with an extraordinary measure of grace. Every page of this book is better because of her involvement, and I cannot thank her enough.

I also want to express enthusiastic thanks to the entire sales team at McGraw-Hill Higher Education. These are the professionals who visit your campus and make sure students and instructors have everything they need to succeed in the classroom. It's a demanding and sometimes thankless job, but the McGraw-Hill representatives are truly dedicated to your success, and I appreciate all they do.

Finally, I will always be grateful for the support of my family and friends. The more I learn about interpersonal communication, the more appreciative I become of the people who accept, value, challenge, and love me. You know who you are, and I thank you.

1

About Communication

© Minneapolis Star Tribune/ZUMA Press, Inc/Alamy

FROM FANS TO FRIENDS TO COLLABORATORS

Fred Armisen and Carrie Brownstein have been friends for more than a decade. The pair met at a *Saturday Night Live* after-party in 2003, and quickly bonded over their shared love of comedy (Armisen was a cast member) and indie rock (Brownstein was touring with her band, Sleater-Kinney). Despite living on opposite coasts, the two became fast friends, and eventually decided that they needed to work on something together, because as Brownstein explains, when two people are not romantically involved, "it begins to seem kind of weird if you're flying around the country" to spend time together.

This friendship yielded hilarious results: Their sketch comedy show, *Portlandia,* became a hit, first on the Internet and eventually as a regular series on IFC. Playing a rotating series of characters, the two get to explore different sorts of relationships and communication styles: "I get to play at connecting with people," Brownstein says, "because in every scene we're in a different relationship."[1] Their real relationship is more consistent: They text each other each night before bed, and look forward to working together each day.

I t is nearly impossible to overestimate the importance of close relationships. Our families can make us laugh, keep us sane, and pick us up when we're feeling down. Our romantic partners can make us feel as though we're the only person in the world who matters. And, on occasion, we meet people who become close working partners as well as valuable friends.

At the same time, relationships can be profoundly challenging. Even our closest friends can get under our skin. Sometimes our romantic partners aren't completely honest with us. And from time to time, we don't quite know how to support those who need our help. It's pretty remarkable that human relationships can be the source of such joy *and* such heartache. What makes the difference between a relationship that's going well and one that's going poorly? One of the biggest factors is how we communicate. To understand why that's true, let's look first at the critical role of communication in our lives.

CONNECT: Connect helps students build confidence in their skills and helps you track their progress. Look for hints on using and assigning Connect throughout the book.

 # 1 Why We Communicate

Asking why we communicate may seem about as useful as asking why we breathe. After all, could you imagine your life without communication? We all have times, of course, when we prefer to be alone. Nevertheless, most of us would find it nearly impossible—and very unsatisfying—to go through life without the chance to interact with others. Perhaps that's why we spend so much of our time communicating, whether face-to-face or electronically (see Table 1).

In the IM: The "Letters Home" activity will help students interpret and contextualize course material in this and subsequent chapters.

You might think that communicating as much as we do would make us all communication experts. In truth, however, we often don't recognize how many communication challenges we face. Learning to overcome those challenges starts with appreciating why we communicate in the first place. As we'll discover in this section, communication touches many aspects of our lives, from our physical and other everyday needs to our experiences with relationships, spirituality, and identity.

TABLE 1

Life Online: Communicating in Cyberspace

23	Number of hours per week the average American spends on the Internet
81	Percentage of American teenagers who sleep with, or next to, their cell phone
678	Number of text messages the average American sends per month
143,199	Number of messages received daily on Snapchat
400,000,000	Number of active blogs online
196,400,000,000	Average number of e-mail messages sent per day

Sources: The Mobile Youth Report; Business News Daily; Computerworld; Business Insider; Nielsen; Radicati Group. Statistics are from 2011–2015.

The need for social contact has fueled debates in cities such as New York over the use of solitary confinement for juvenile offenders. © Tinnapong/Getty Images, RF

 stigma A characteristic that discredits a person, making him or her be seen as abnormal or undesirable.

Communication Meets Physical Needs

Communication keeps us healthy. Human beings are such inherently social beings that when we are denied the opportunity for interaction, our mental and physical health can suffer. That is a major reason why solitary confinement is such a harsh punishment. Several studies have shown that when people are cut off from others for an extended period, their health can quickly deteriorate.[2] A recent study even showed that feeling rejected reduces the rate at which a person's heart beats.[3] Similarly, individuals who feel socially isolated because of poverty, homelessness, mental illness, or obesity can also suffer from a lack of quality interaction with others.[4]

It may sound like an exaggeration to say that we can't survive without human contact, but that statement isn't far from the truth, as a bizarre experiment in the thirteenth century helps to show. German emperor Frederick II wanted to know what language humans would speak naturally if they weren't taught any particular language. To find out, he placed 50 newborns in the care of nurses who were instructed only to feed and bathe them but not to speak to or hold them. The emperor never discovered the answer to his question because all the infants died.[5] That experiment was clearly unethical, meaning that it did not follow established principles that guide people in judging whether something is morally right or wrong. Such an experiment fortunately wouldn't be repeated today. But as touch expert Tiffany Field reports, more recent studies conducted in orphanages and adoption centers have convincingly shown that human interaction, especially touch, is critical for infants' survival and healthy development.[6]

Social interaction keeps adults healthy too. Research shows that people without strong social ties, such as close friendships and family relationships, are more likely to suffer from major ailments, including heart disease and high blood pressure, and to die prematurely than people who have close, satisfying relationships.[7] They are also more likely to suffer from lesser ailments, such as colds, and they often take longer to recover from illnesses or injuries.[8] Communication researchers Chris Segrin and Stacey Passalacqua have even found that loneliness is related to sleep disturbances and stress.[9]

The importance of social interaction is often particularly evident to people who are stigmatized. A **stigma** is a characteristic that discredits a person, causing him or her to be seen as abnormal or undesirable.[10] It isn't the attribute itself that stigmatizes a person, however, but the way that attribute is viewed by others in that person's society. In the United States, for instance, being HIV-positive has been widely stigmatized because of its association with two marginalized populations—gay men and intravenous drug users—even though many individuals with HIV do not belong to either group.[11] U.S. Americans don't tend to stigmatize people with asthma or diabetes or even cancer to the same extent as they do people with HIV, even though those other illnesses can also be serious and even life-threatening.

Stigmatized people might frequently feel like outsiders who "don't fit in" with others. As a result, they may be more likely to suffer the negative physical effects of limited social interaction. Going further, the less social interaction they have, the more they are likely to continue feeling stigmatized. Although not everyone needs the same degree of interaction to stay healthy, communication plays an important role in maintaining human health and well-being.

Communication Meets Relational Needs

Besides our physical needs, we have several relational needs, such as needs for companionship and affection, relaxation and escape.[12] We don't necessarily have the same needs in all our relationships—you probably value your friends for somewhat different reasons than you value your co-workers, for instance. The bottom line, though, is that we need relationships, and communication is a large part of how we build and keep those relationships.[13]

Imagine how challenging it would be to communicate if you couldn't speak the language everyone else was using. That is a common experience for many immigrants. © Erik Freeland/Corbis saba/Corbis News/Corbis

Think about how many structures in our lives are designed to promote social interaction. Neighborhoods, schools, workplaces, malls, theaters, and restaurants are all social settings in which we interact with people. In addition, the Internet offers innumerable ways of connecting with others, and many people have made new friends—or even met romantic partners—online.[14] Imagine how challenging it would be to form and maintain strong social relationships if you lacked the ability to communicate with people. This is a common experience for many immigrants, who often struggle to learn the cultural values, as well as the language, of their new environments and may feel lonely or ignored by others in the process.[15]

Some scholars believe our need for relationships is so fundamental that we can hardly get by without them.[16] For example, research has shown that having a rich social life is one of the most powerful predictors of a person's overall happiness.[17] Mere interaction isn't enough, though: Studies show that having *meaningful* conversations leads to happiness, whereas "small talk" can be associated with reduced well-being.[18] Casual conversation online *can* spark a new relationship, but deeper, more meaningful conversation helps it grow.

Studies have shown that the most important predictor of happiness in life—by far—is marital happiness.[19] Being happily married is more important than income, job status, education, leisure time, or anything else in accounting for how content people are. On the negative side, people in distressed marriages are much more likely to suffer from major depression, and they report being in worse physical health than their happily married counterparts.[20]

The cause-and-effect relationship between marriage and happiness isn't a simple one. It may be that strong marriages promote happiness and well-being, or it may be that happy, healthy people are more likely than others to be married. Whatever the association, personal relationships clearly play an important role in our lives, and communication helps us form and maintain them.

Communication Fills Identity Needs

Are you energetic? Trustworthy? Intelligent? Withdrawn? Each of us can probably come up with a long list of adjectives to describe ourselves, but here's the critical question: How do you *know* you are these things? In other words, how do you form an identity?

Writing Note: Have each student make a list of 10 friends and record the three or four things they most value about each. Use this exercise to generate conversation about relational needs and how we turn to a variety of people to meet them. This exercise will illustrate that no one person, not even a spouse, can meet our every relational need.

Talking Point: Ask students how many of them have met people online whom they consider genuine friends. In what ways has the Internet helped them form relationships? In what ways, if any, has it hurt their ability to relate to others?

Outside of Class: Have students informally interview significant people in their lives: a parent, a roommate, a romantic partner, a longtime friend. They should ask each person, "What are five terms you would use to describe my personality?" Have students write up a brief report in which they compare and contrast the five answers each person gives.

How we communicate with others, and how others communicate with us, play a big role in shaping how we see ourselves—whether it's as intelligent, as popular, or as altruistic. © *Digital Vision/Getty Images, RF,* © *McGraw-Hill Education, Lars A. Niki photographer,* © *McGraw-Hill Education, Christopher Kerrigan photographer*

The ways we communicate with others—and the ways others communicate with us—play a major role in shaping how we see ourselves.[21] As you'll learn in the Communication and the Self chapter, people form their identities partly by comparing themselves with others. If you consider yourself intelligent, for instance, what that really means is that you see yourself as more intelligent than most other people. If you think you're shy, you see most other people as more outgoing than you are. If you think of yourself as attractive, that translates into viewing yourself as better looking than most others.

One way we learn how we compare with others is through our communication with those around us. If people treat you as intelligent, shy, or attractive, you may begin to believe you have those characteristics. In other words, those qualities will become part of how you view yourself. Communication plays a critical role in driving that process, and good communicators have the ability to emphasize different aspects of their identities in different situations. During a job interview it might be most important for you to portray your organized, efficient side; when you're hanging out with friends, you might emphasize your fun-loving nature and sense of humor.

Besides expressing personal identity, communication also helps us express our cultural identity. As you'll discover in the Culture and Gender chapter, culture includes the symbols, beliefs, practices, and languages that distinguish groups of people. The ways you speak, dress, gesture, and entertain yourself all reflect the cultural values you hold dear.

Communication Meets Spiritual Needs

An important aspect of identity for many people in many cultures is their spirituality. Spirituality includes the principles valued in life ("I value loyalty" or "I value equal treatment for all people"). It also encompasses people's morals, or their notions about right and wrong ("It's never okay to steal, regardless of the circumstances" or "I would lie to save a life, because life is more important than honesty"). Finally, spirituality involves people's beliefs about the meaning of life, which often include personal philosophies, an awe of nature, a belief in a higher purpose, and religious faith and practices ("I believe in God" or "I believe I will reap what I sow in life").

A 2010 survey of more than 112,000 U.S. college students found that many students consider some form of spirituality to be an important part of their identity.[22] Almost half of those surveyed said they consider integrating spirituality into their lives to be very important or essential. For those in the study, spirituality didn't necessarily include

Communication lets people express their faith and spirituality. © Don Hammond/ Design Pics, RF

formal religion; over 68 percent believed that people can grow spiritually without being religious. For people who include spirituality as a part of their identity, communication provides a means of expressing and sharing spiritual ideas and practices with one another.

Communication Serves Instrumental Needs

Finally, people communicate to meet their practical, everyday needs. Researchers refer to those needs as **instrumental needs.** Instrumental needs include short-term tasks such as ordering a drink in a restaurant, scheduling a haircut on the telephone, filling out a rebate card, and raising one's hand to speak in class. They also include longer-term career goals such as getting a new job, earning a promotion, and getting one's work noticed and appreciated by supervisors and customers. Those communicative behaviors may not always contribute much to our health, our relationships, our identity, or our spirituality. Each behavior is valuable, however, because it serves a need that helps us get through our personal and professional lives.

instrumental needs
Practical, everyday needs.

Writing Note: Have students list the last five instrumental communication behaviors they took part in.

AT A GLANCE

Five Needs Served by Communication

Physical Needs	Communication helps us maintain physical and mental well-being.
Relational Needs	Communication helps us form social and personal relationships.
Identity Needs	Communication helps us decide who we are and who we want to be.
Spiritual Needs	Communication lets us share our beliefs and values with others.
Instrumental Needs	Communication helps us accomplish personal and professional tasks.

Meeting instrumental needs is important for two reasons. The first reason is simply that we have many instrumental needs. In fact, most of the communication you engage in on a day-to-day basis is probably mundane and routine—not heavy, emotionally charged conversation but instrumental interaction such as talking to professors about assignments or taking orders from customers at work. The second reason satisfying instrumental needs is so important is that many of them—such as buying groceries at the store and ordering clothes online—have to be met before other needs—such as maintaining quality relationships and finding career fulfillment—become relevant.[23]

LEARN IT How is communication related to our physical well-being? What relational needs does communication help us fill? In what ways do communication behaviors meet our identity needs? How does communication help us express spirituality? What are some of the instrumental needs served by communication?

APPLY IT Describe in a short paragraph how, in a recent conversation or online interaction, your communication behavior contributed to your physical, relational, identity, spiritual, and instrumental needs. Which need or needs took precedence? Why?

REFLECT ON IT Can you identify ways in which your own communication meets your relational or spiritual needs? Do you communicate for any reasons that are not discussed in this section?

2 The Nature of Communication

In the television comedy *The Big Bang Theory,* Sheldon Cooper is a theoretical physicist at Caltech. With two doctoral degrees and an IQ of 187, Cooper qualifies as a genius. Yet despite his intellect and professional accomplishments, Cooper is socially inept. He is childish and self-centered, and he rarely realizes how his lack of communication skills affects other people. How could someone so smart—and someone who has communicated practically every day he has been alive—be such a poor communicator?

In one way or another, you, too, have communicated daily since birth, so you may be wondering what you could possibly have left to learn about communication. In fact, researchers still have many questions about how we communicate, how we make sense of one another's behaviors, and what effects communication has on our lives and our relationships.

We begin this section by looking at different ways to understand the communication process. Next, we'll examine some important characteristics of communication, and we'll consider various ways to think about communication in social interaction. Finally, we'll tackle some common communication myths.

Three Models of Human Communication

model A formal description of a process.

How would you describe the process of communicating? It's not as easy as it might seem, and even researchers have answered that question in different ways. A formal description of a process such as communication is called a **model.** In this section, we'll look at three models developed by communication scholars: the action, interaction, and transaction models. These models represent the evolution of how communication researchers have defined and described communication over the years.

COMMUNICATION AS ACTION.   In the action model, we think of communication as a one-way process. Let's say you want to leave work early one day to attend a parent–teacher conference at your daughter's school, and you're getting ready to ask your supervisor for permission. As illustrated in Figure 1, the action model starts with a **source**—you—who comes up with a thought or an idea you wish to communicate.

To convey the idea that you'd like to leave early, you must **encode** it; that is, you must put your idea into the form of language or a gesture that your supervisor can understand. Through that process, you create a **message,** which consists of the verbal and/or nonverbal elements of communication to which people give meaning. In this example, your message might be the question "Would it be all right if I leave work a little early today?"

According to the action model, you then send your message through a communication **channel,** a type of pathway. You might pose your question to your supervisor face-to-face. Alternatively, you might send your question by e-mail, through a text message, or by leaving a voice mail message for your supervisor. Those are all channels of communication. Your supervisor acts as the **receiver** of the message—the person who will **decode** or interpret it.

During the communication process, there is also likely to be some **noise,** which is anything that interferes with a receiver's ability to attend to your message. The major types of noise are physical noise (such as background conversation in the room or static on the telephone line), psychological noise (such as other concerns your supervisor is dealing with that day), and physiological noise (such as fatigue or hunger). Experiencing any of those forms of noise could prevent your supervisor from paying full attention to your question.

Noise also interferes with the ability to interpret a message accurately. Decoding a message doesn't necessarily mean we have understood what the speaker is trying to say. Physical, psychological, and physiological noise can all cause us to misunderstand someone's words, which may prompt the person to say "That's not what I meant."

You can see that the action model is very linear: A source sends a message through some channel to a receiver, and noise interferes with the message somehow. Many people talk and think about the communication process in this linear manner. For example, when you ask someone "Did you get my message?" you are implying that communication is a one-way process. The problem is that human communication is rarely that simple. It is usually more of a back-and-forth exchange than a one-way process—more similar to tennis than to bowling. Over time, this criticism of the action model of communication gave rise to an updated model known as the interaction model.

COMMUNICATION AS INTERACTION. The interaction model, depicted in Figure 2, takes up where the action model leaves off. It includes all the same elements: source, message, channel, receiver, noise, encoding, and decoding. However, it differs from the action model in two basic ways. First, it recognizes that communication is a two-way process. Second, it adds two elements to the mix: feedback and context.

If you've studied physics, you know that every action has a reaction. That rule also

source The originator of a thought or an idea.

encode To put an idea into language or gesture.

message Verbal and nonverbal elements of communication to which people give meaning.

channel A pathway through which messages are conveyed.

receiver The party who interprets a message.

decode To interpret or give meaning to a message.

noise Anything that interferes with the encoding or decoding of a message.

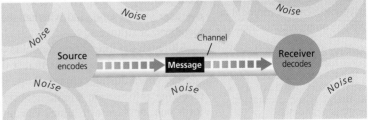

FIGURE 1 The Action Model In the action model of communication, a sender encodes a message and conveys it through a communication channel for a receiver to decode. Leaving someone a voice mail message illustrates the one-way process of the action model. © *Caiaimage/ Sam Edwards/Getty Images, RF*

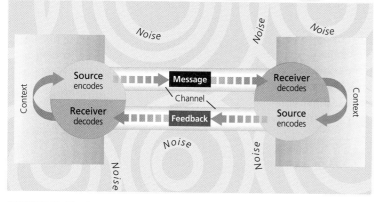

FIGURE 2 The Interaction Model The interaction model of communication explains that our messages are shaped by the feedback we receive from others and by the context in which we are interacting. Here we see speakers paying attention to their friends' feedback and communicating in a way that is appropriate for a public restaurant.
© *Flying Colours Ltd/Getty Images, RF*

feedback Verbal and nonverbal responses to a message.

context The physical or psychological environment in which communication occurs.

applies to communication. Let's say you're texting back and forth with your friend Julio about a problem you're having with your landlord. As you relate your story, Julio sends replies and emoticons to show you he's paying attention. He may also text you questions about your landlord's behavior. In other words, Julio reacts to your story by giving you **feedback,** or various verbal and nonverbal responses to your message. In that way, Julio is not just a passive receiver of your message. Instead, he is actively involved in creating your conversation.

Now let's imagine you're sharing your story with Julio while you're sitting together at a coffee shop. Would you tell your story any differently than you did by text messaging? What if your landlord were at the coffee shop with you?

Those questions concern the **context,** or the environment that you're in. That environment includes both the physical and the psychological context. The physical context is where you are physically interacting with each other. In contrast, the psychological context involves factors that influence your state of mind, such as how formal the situation is, how much privacy you have, and how emotionally charged the situation is. According to the interaction model, we take context into account when we engage in conversation. That is, we realize that what is appropriate in some contexts may be inappropriate in others, so we adapt our behaviors accordingly.

By taking account of feedback and context, the interaction model presents the communication process more realistically than the action model does. In the case of your telling Julio about the problems with your landlord, for instance, your story and Julio's feedback may be affected by where you were speaking, how many other people could overhear you (if any), and whether those people were co-workers, classmates, family members, or strangers.

Although the interaction model is more realistic than the action model, it still has limitations. One drawback is that it doesn't represent how complex communication can be. Often during conversations, it seems as though two people are sending and receiving information simultaneously rather than simply communicating back and forth one message at a time. The interaction model doesn't quite account for that process, however. To understand that aspect of communication, we turn to the transaction model, currently the most complete and widely used of the three models we examine in this chapter.

COMMUNICATION AS TRANSACTION. Unlike the action and interaction models, the transaction model of communication, illustrated in Figure 3, doesn't distinguish between the roles of source and receiver. Nor does it represent communication as a series of messages going back and forth. Rather, it maintains that both people in a conversation are simultaneously sources and receivers. In addition, it argues that the conversation flows in both directions at the same time.

To understand the transaction model, imagine you're a medical technician at a community clinic and you're explaining to an elderly patient how to apply a prescription cream to his skin. You notice a confused—perhaps even worried—look on his face. According to the interaction model, those facial expressions constitute feedback to your message. In contrast, the transaction model recognizes that you will interpret those expressions as messages in and of themselves, making the patient a source and you a receiver. Note that this process occurs while you are giving the patient instructions. In other words, you are both sending messages to and receiving messages from the other at the same time.

Not only does the transaction model better reflect the complex nature of communication, but it also leads us to think about context a little more broadly. It suggests that our communication is affected not only by the physical or psychological environment but also by our culture, experience, gender, and social class—and even by the history of our relationship with the person to whom we're talking.

Let's go back to our previous example. If you have a history with the elderly patient, you might help him understand your directions by referring to products you have prescribed for him in the past. If he isn't a native English speaker, you might have to demonstrate the use of the cream rather than just describing it verbally. If he comes from a very different socioeconomic class from yours, you might be taking it for granted that he can afford the medication. Sometimes it is hard to consider all the ways these aspects of context might affect how we communicate. According to the transaction model, however, they are always with us.

ASSESSING THE MODELS. Clearly, researchers have many different ways of understanding the communication process. Instead of debating which model is right, it is more helpful to look at the useful ideas each model offers. When we do so, we find that each model fits certain situations better than others.

For instance, sending an e-mail message to your professor is a good example of the action model. You're the source, and you convey your message through a written channel to a receiver (your professor). Noise includes any difficulty your professor experiences in opening up the message or in understanding its intent because of the language you have used.

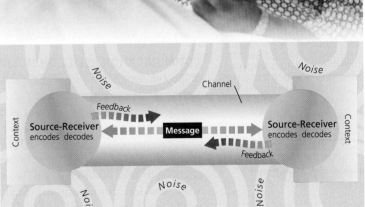

FIGURE 3 The Transaction Model The transaction model recognizes that both people in a conversation are simultaneously senders and receivers. The doctor encodes messages that her patient decodes, but the patient also encodes messages for the doctor to decode. © Image100/PunchStock, RF

A good example of the interaction model occurs when you are writing a group paper for a class and you distribute a draft to your group members for their comments. You (the source) have conveyed your message through your report, and your classmates (the receivers) provide their feedback, either in person or online. Noise in this example includes any difficulties either you or your group members experience in understanding what the other has said.

We have seen that most conversations are good examples of the transaction model because both parties are sending and receiving messages simultaneously. That process occurs, for instance, when you strike up a conversation with someone while standing in an airport security line. You might make small talk about where each of you is traveling that day or how annoying but necessary the screening process is. As you do so, each of you is sending verbal and nonverbal messages to the other and is simultaneously receiving and interpreting such messages from the other. Your conversation is affected by the context, in that you may be communicating only to pass the time until one of you goes through screening. It is also affected by noise, including the sound of the screeners' instructions.

Each model, then, is useful in some situations but not in others. The action model is too simplistic to describe a face-to-face conversation, but when you're just leaving a note for someone, it describes the situation quite well. As you come across examples of different communication situations in this book, you might ask yourself how well each model reflects them.

Keep in mind that these communication models were developed over time. As scholars came to appreciate the limitations of the action model, they developed the interaction model to take its place. Likewise, the shortcomings of the interaction model gave rise to the transaction model, which many researchers consider the most comprehensive description of communication. As our understanding of communication continues to grow, researchers will likely develop new models that will represent the communication process even more accurately.

Now that we've looked at different ways of modeling the communication process, let's consider some of communication's most important characteristics.

Six Characteristics of Communication

Describing the communication process requires more than just mapping out how it takes place. We also need to catalog its important features.

COMMUNICATION RELIES ON MULTIPLE CHANNELS.   In how many different ways do people communicate with one another? Facial expressions convey how a person is feeling. Someone's gestures and tone of voice help others interpret his or her messages. Touch can signal feelings such as affection and aggression. Even a person's clothing and physical appearance communicate messages about that individual to others.

Some situations are **channel-rich contexts,** meaning that they involve many different communication channels at once. In face-to-face conversations, for instance, you can pay attention to your partners' words, see their expressions and gestures, hear their tone of voice, and feel them touch you. Similarly, Skype and FaceTime conversations depict words, facial cues, gestures, and vocal tones. Because you experience multiple communication channels at once, you can evaluate the information you receive from all the channels simultaneously. Other situations are **channel-lean contexts,** with a smaller number of channels.[24] Text messaging and instant messaging, for example, rely much more heavily on text, so we don't experience a person's voice or gestures. As a consequence, we may pay more attention to that person's words.

channel-rich context
A communication context involving many channels at once.

channel-lean context
A communication context involving few channels at once.

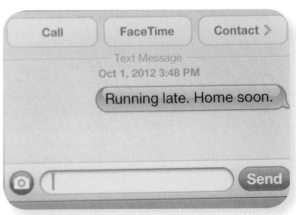

COMMUNICATION PASSES THROUGH PERCEPTUAL FILTERS. Anything you put through a filter—such as air, water, or light—comes out a little different from how it went in. The same thing happens when we communicate: What one person says is not always exactly what the other person hears. We all "filter" incoming communication through our perceptions, experiences, biases, and beliefs.[25]

Let's say you're listening to a senator speak on television. The way you process and make sense of the speech probably depends on how much you agree with the senator's ideas or whether you belong to the same political party. Two people with contrasting political viewpoints may listen to the same speech but hear something very different. I may hear a set of logical, well-thought-out ideas, whereas you may hear nothing but lies and empty promises.

Perceptual filters can also influence how people understand their own words. In the classic *Friends* episode "The One Where Ross and Rachel Take a Break," Rachel (played by Jennifer Aniston) and her boyfriend Ross (played by David Schwimmer) have a big fight and decide to go "on a break" from their relationship. They quickly learn that they perceive the meaning of that term quite differently. To Rachel, it simply means not seeing each other for a while but keeping their relationship intact. To Ross, being on a break means his relationship with Rachel is over. Thus, in the wake of their conflict, Ross has sex with someone else. Rachel feels completely betrayed

Some interpersonal communication contexts are channel-rich, such as a face-to-face conversation between friends. Other interpersonal communication contexts are channel-lean, such as sending and receiving text messages. © Brand X Pictures/PunchStock, RF, McGraw-Hill Education, © Mark Dierker photographer

In the IM: The "Perceptual Filters" activity is an out-of-class exercise that encourages students to think about their own perceptual filters.

Perceptual filters affect how we make sense of communication. In an episode of *Modern Family*, Claire encourages Haley not to marry someone who's immature. Claire is implying that Haley should be less serious with her boyfriend, but Haley thinks that Claire is referencing her own marriage and signaling an intention to divorce. © Michael Desmond/ABC/Disney ABC Television Group/Getty Images

when she finds out. As a result, she and Ross end their relationship officially. It is important to note that Ross and Rachel agreed that they were "on a break" when Ross slept with someone else, but they had very different perceptions of what the expression meant.

Many aspects of our lives can influence our perception of communication. Whether we're aware of it or not, our ethnic and cultural background, gender, religious beliefs, socioeconomic status, intelligence and education, level of physical attractiveness, and experiences with illness, disease, and death can all act as filters, coloring the way we see the world and the way we make sense of communication. You might listen sympathetically to someone describing her experiences of homelessness based on those and other characteristics. In contrast, other people might blame that person for her homelessness because they have different perceptual filters than you do.

PEOPLE GIVE COMMUNICATION ITS MEANING.

When we write or speak, we choose our words deliberately so we can say what we mean. Where does that meaning come from? By itself, a word has no meaning; it's just a sound or a set of marks on a piece of paper or a monitor. A word is a **symbol,** or a representation of an idea, but the word itself isn't the idea or the meaning. The meaning of words—and many other forms of communication—comes from the people and groups who use them.

symbol A representation of an idea.

© APCortizasJr/Getty Images, RF

Almost all language is arbitrary in the sense that words mean whatever groups of people decide they mean. As a result, we can't assume that other people understand the meanings we intend to communicate just because we ourselves understand what we mean. For instance, what is a mouse? If you had asked that question 40 years ago, the obvious answer would have been a small rodent that likes cheese and is chased by cats. Today, however, many people know a mouse as a pointing device for navigating on a computer screen. As another example, what is a robot? In the United States, it can be a humanlike machine that performs mechanical tasks or a software that generates online spam. In South Africa, it's a traffic light.

Those are just three examples of how the meaning of a word depends on who is using it and how meanings can vary over time and across cultures. How do you define each of the following words? What other meanings might they have, depending on who is using them?

pot	book
flat	gay
cell	biscuit

You might know that in some countries a flat is an apartment and a biscuit is a cookie. Is a book only a printed volume, or do e-books count as books? How have the meanings of words such as *pot, cell,* and *gay* changed in U.S. society over time?

COMMUNICATION HAS LITERAL MEANINGS AND RELATIONAL IMPLICATIONS.

content dimension
Literal information that is communicated by a message. See also *denotative meaning.*

Nearly every verbal statement has a **content dimension,** which consists of the literal information being communicated about the subject of the message.[26] When you say to your friend, "I'm kind of down today," the content dimension of your message is that you're feeling unhappy, bored, or depressed. When your roommate says, "We're out of detergent again," the content dimension of the message is that you have no detergent left.

got skills?

RELATIONAL DIMENSION OF COMMUNICATION

The relational dimension of messages is important—learn how to recognize it.

WHAT?
Identify the relational dimension of a statement.

WHY?
To understand the unspoken message(s) that a person may be trying to convey to you—that is, the relationship-based signals beyond statements, such as "I feel like a failure" and "The landlord called to remind us that our rent is late."

HOW?
1. Consider the statement from the sender's point of view.
2. Formulate a guess as to what the speaker is trying to convey to you about your relationship.
3. Check your interpretation.

TRY!
Your roommate wakes you to say, "It's snowing, and the driveway isn't shoveled." Based on your relationship with the roommate, what different messages might he or she be sending you?

CONSIDER: *What role do tone and manner play in your roommate's message?*

There's more to messages than their literal content, though. Many messages also carry signals about the nature of the relationship in which they're shared. Those signals make up the **relational dimension** of the message. For example, by telling your friend you're feeling down, you may also be sending the message "I feel comfortable enough with you to share my feelings," or you may be signaling "I want you to help me feel better." Likewise, you might interpret your roommate's statement that you're out of detergent as also saying "I'm sure you're aware of this, but I'm just reminding you," or you might take it as meaning "I'm irritated that you never replace household items when they are empty." Even though these messages were never spoken, we often infer meanings about our relationships from the tone and manner in which the statements are made.

Check out the "Got Skills?" box for suggestions on how to identify the relational dimension of interpersonal messages. As you come across the "Got Skills?" features in this book, you'll find practical advice for applying the principles of interpersonal communication in your own life.

One way in which people distinguish between content and relational dimensions is through **metacommunication,** which is communication about communication. Let's say that Ethan asks his stepdad Daniel to read over his senior thesis before Ethan submits it to his undergraduate advisor. Daniel reads the manuscript and marks it up with critical comments such as "this argument isn't convincing," "awkward wording," and "I can't tell what you're trying to say." After reading Daniel's comments, Ethan is crushed.

relational dimension
Signals about the relationship in which a message is being communicated.

metacommunication
Communication about communication.

> **Daniel:** I thought you wanted my feedback. I was just trying to help you make your thesis better; that's what you asked for. Why are you taking my comments so personally?
>
> **Ethan:** It's not so much what you said, it's how you said it.

By focusing his attention on Ethan's request for feedback, Daniel is attending to the content dimension of their conversation. He can't understand why Ethan is upset, because Ethan had asked him for his feedback. To Ethan, however, Daniel's comments were overly harsh and insensitive, and they made him think that Daniel didn't care about his feelings. Therefore, Ethan's focus is on the relational dimension of their

Your behavior sends messages, whether intentional or not. What message is this person's behavior sending? © *Belinda Images/Belinda Images/SuperStock*

conversation. To highlight that distinction, Ethan metacommunicates with Daniel by explaining that his hurt feelings were not caused by what Daniel said but by the way in which he said it. That phrase conveys Ethan's thoughts about his communication with Daniel; thus, it is metacommunicative.

COMMUNICATION SENDS A MESSAGE, WHETHER INTENTIONAL OR UNINTENTIONAL. Much of what we communicate to others is deliberate. When you set up a job interview, for instance, you do so intentionally, having thought about why you want the job and how you will respond to the interviewer's questions. Very rarely do you schedule an interview by accident.

You might, however, communicate a number of other things without meaning to. For example, have you ever tried hard to stay awake in an important meeting? Despite your efforts to look engaged and interested, you might not have been aware that your slouched posture and droopy eyelids were signaling the fatigue you were feeling, perhaps after a long day of working at a part-time job and attending several classes. In that instance, your behavior was sending unintentional messages.

Communication scholars have debated for many years whether unintentional messages should qualify as communication. Some researchers believe that only deliberate, intentional messages are a part of communication and that if you don't intend to communicate, then you aren't communicating.[27] Others subscribe to the belief that "you cannot not communicate," meaning absolutely everything you do has communicative value.[28]

My own position lies somewhere in between. Although I don't believe every possible behavior is a form of communication, neither do I think behaviors must be intentional to have communicative value.[29] I would suggest that even unintended messages—such as the ones you might have expressed while trying to stay awake during a meeting—are forms of communication because they still convey meaning.[30] Many aspects of appearance illustrate that effect. For instance, seeing someone in a wheelchair probably leads you to different conclusions than seeing someone in a white lab coat or an orange prison jumpsuit, yet those messages might not be intentional on that person's part.

COMMUNICATION IS GOVERNED BY RULES. Rules tell us what behaviors are required, preferred, or prohibited in various social contexts.[31] Some rules for communication are **explicit rules,** meaning that someone has clearly articulated them. Perhaps your parents used to say, "Don't talk with your mouth full." Your college or university

explicit rule A rule about behavior that has been clearly articulated.

may have explicit rules banning hate speech at campus events or in school publications. These are examples of explicit communication rules because they express direct expectations for communicative behavior.

It's easy to make mistakes when you don't know the explicit communication rules you are expected to follow. Suppose you're researching women's experiences with date rape for a class project. To learn more, you find an online support group for date rape survivors, and you begin posting questions to the group and contacting members directly to learn about their experiences. In response, the group's moderator informs you that only registered users of the support group are allowed to submit posts. She also mentions that e-mailing members directly is strictly forbidden. As a consequence, the moderator blocks you from any further contact with the support group. By not learning the group's explicit rules beforehand, you made communication mistakes that you could easily have avoided.

However, many communication rules are **implicit rules**—rules that almost everyone in a certain social group knows and follows, even though no one has formally articulated and expressed them. In North American cultures, for instance, there are implicit rules about riding in an elevator, such as "Don't get on if it's already full" and "Don't make eye contact with others while you're riding." There are also implicit rules about lining up while you're waiting for something, including "Maintain an orderly line" and "Don't cut ahead of someone else." Most people seem to know and accept those rules, even though they usually aren't posted anywhere—they're just part of everyone's cultural knowledge. Because they're implicit, though, they are likely to vary more from person to person than explicit rules do. For example, some people believe it's an implicit rule that you shouldn't talk on your cell phone while in a crowded environment, whereas other people don't see that behavior as inappropriate.

Now that we know more about the basic characteristics of communication, let's take a look at some common beliefs about communication that are not as valid as they might seem.

implicit rule A rule about behavior that has not been clearly articulated but is nonetheless understood.

Outside of Class: Have students, working in pairs, intentionally violate some implicit social rules and observe and document the reactions of those around them.

Dispelling Some Communication Myths

Perhaps because communication is such an essential part of life, people have many different ideas about it. Some of these notions are not very accurate. In this section, we'll probe five common communication myths—in the process, honing our ability to separate fact from fiction.

MYTH #1: EVERYONE IS AN EXPERT IN COMMUNICATION. People communicate constantly, so it's easy to believe that just about everyone is an expert in communication. Indeed, in a nationwide survey of U.S. American adults conducted by the National Communication Association, fully 91 percent of participants rated their communication skills as above average.[32] It's important to remember, though, that having *experience* with something is not the same as having *expertise* in it. Many people drive, but that doesn't make them expert drivers. Many people have children, but that doesn't make them experts at parenting. Experience can be invaluable, but expertise requires the development of knowledge and ability that goes beyond personal experience. Thus, experts in driving, parenting, or communication have training in those areas and a level of understanding that most people who drive, parent, or communicate do not have.

Focus on Scholarship: A 1997 study found that 91 percent of personnel interviewers in established businesses said that applicants had inadequate communication skills. This study illustrates the pragmatic value of studying communication.

MYTH #2: COMMUNICATION WILL SOLVE ANY PROBLEM.   The classic Paul New-man movie *Cool Hand Luke* (1967) features a prison warden who has his own special way of dealing with inmates. Whenever things go wrong, he says, "What we've got here is a failure to communicate," after which he beats a particular inmate unconscious and sends him to solitary confinement. Sometimes it seems as though we could solve almost any problem, especially in our relationships, if only we could communicate better. It's easy to blame a lack of communication when things go wrong. The fact is, however, that poor communication isn't the cause of every problem.[33]

Talking Point: Ask students why they think the notion that communication can solve any problem is so widespread.

On his television talk show *Dr. Phil,* psychologist Phil McGraw often counsels couples encountering difficulties in their relationships. Suppose that Matt and Belinda appear on *Dr. Phil* complaining that they have been drifting apart for some time. Belinda feels they need to communicate better to save their relationship. However, Matt states very clearly that his feelings have changed and that he is no longer in love with Belinda. Will communication solve this couple's marital problems? No—but it will probably cause Belinda to realize that their relationship is already over. We must be careful not to assume that better communication can resolve any problem we might face in our relationships.

MYTH #3: COMMUNICATION CAN BREAK DOWN.   Just as we sometimes blame our problems on a lack of communication, many of us also point to a "breakdown in communication" as the root of problems. When a married couple divorces, the spouses may say it was a breakdown in communication that led to their relational difficulties.

The metaphor of a communication breakdown makes intuitive sense. After all, our progress on a trip is halted if our car breaks down, so it's easy to think that our progress in other endeavors is halted because our communication has broken down. The fact is that communication isn't a mechanical object like a car, a computer, or an iPad. Instead, it's a process that unfolds between and among people over time.

It may be easy to blame a breakdown in communication for problems we face in personal relationships. What's really happening in these situations is that we are no longer communicating *effectively.* In other words, the problem lies not with communication itself but with the way we're using it. That is one reason why learning about communication—as you are doing in this class—can be so beneficial.

© Ephraim Ben-Shimon/Spirit/Corbis, RF

MYTH #4: COMMUNICATION IS INHER-ENTLY GOOD.   Watch or listen to almost any talk show and you'll hear people say they no longer communicate with their romantic partners, parents, or others who are important to them. "Sure, we talk all the time," someone might say, "but we don't really communicate anymore." Reflected in that statement is the idea that *talking* means just producing words, but *communicating* means sharing meaning with another person in an open, supportive, and inherently positive manner.[34]

Thinking that communication is inherently good is similar to thinking that money is inherently good. Sometimes money can be put to a positive use, such as providing a home for your family or donating to a worthy charity. At other times it can be used

communication | *DARK SIDE*

SMARTPHONES VS. FACE-TO-FACE COMMUNICATION

Interpersonal communication has many positive aspects, but it isn't all rosy. At times, we also have to deal with negative feelings and events. We can therefore say that communication has both a "light side" and a "dark side," and it's to our advantage to understand both. In the "Communication: Light Side" and "Communication: Dark Side" boxes in this book, we will examine interpersonal communication issues that people commonly experience, respectively, as positive or negative. In this instance, we'll talk about distraction, a dark side matter.

Cell phones are so common these days that some people can't imagine life without them. Like other communication technologies, cell phones have certainly made it easier for people to keep in touch. You can get in touch with people by cell phone—and they can reach you—from just about anywhere.

For example, many of us have had the frustrating experience of being in the middle of a conversation with someone, only to have that person answer a phone call or glance down at a text. It can be discouraging to feel like you're competing with a device for someone's attention . . . and losing. In fact, recent research has found that your phone doesn't even have to be ringing to ruin your conversation: the mere presence of a cell phone makes you feel less close and connected to the people you're actually with, according to psychologists Andrew Przybylski and Netta Weinstein.

Even if you never touch the device, having it visible during a conversation reminds those we're with that they could lose our attention at any moment. If we do pause a conversation to take a call, it's easy for our face-to-face companions to feel neglected. Not surprisingly, nearly 90 percent of us report feeling hurt by friends or relatives who ignored us for technology, according to social scientist Joseph Grenny.

These findings don't necessarily mean that technology is bad for relationships. Instead, they suggest that we can improve our relationships by using technology more mindfully.

In some of the text boxes in this book, I will include a personal hint about improving your interpersonal communication. These additions will be called "From Me to You," and here's the first:

FROM ME TO YOU

Don't allow communication technology to determine how you spend your energy and attention. When spending time with people you care about, put your cell phone away. Unless you are expecting a specific and urgent phone call, turn down the ringer, or even shut it off entirely. Let callers leave you a message. Let texts and e-mails wait until you have time to tend to them. Ignore all those push notifications. Instead, give your energy and attention to the person you're with, and show that person that he or she is more important to you than the messages coming in on your phone.

© Westend61/Getty Images, RF

Sources: Przybylski, A. K., & Weinstein, N. (2013). Can you connect with me now? How the presence of mobile communication technology influences face-to-face conversation quality. *Journal of Social and Personal Relationships, 30,* 237–246; Grenny, J. (2014). *Digital divisiveness: Electronic displays of insensitivity take toll on relationships* [online]. Retrieved February 2, 2015, from: http://vitalsmarts .com/digitaldivisivenessstudy

negatively, such as in providing funding for a terrorist group or squandering a hard-earned paycheck on online gambling. In either case, it isn't the money itself that's good or bad—it's how it is used.

We can make the same observation regarding communication. We can use communication for positive purposes, such as expressing love for our parents and providing comfort to a grieving friend. We can also use it for negative purposes, such as

Talking Point: *Dark side* is the term used in interpersonal communication research to describe aspects of interpersonal interaction that are experienced as negative. The principal researchers in this area are Bill Cupach and Brian Spitzberg.

intimidating and deceiving people. In fact, one common communication behavior—talking on cell phones—has been linked to stress in relationships, as "Communication: Dark Side" explains.

MYTH #5: MORE COMMUNICATION IS ALWAYS BETTER.   Lorenzo has strong political views that he shares constantly on Facebook. He believes that when others don't agree with his opinions, the problem is that they simply don't understand him. In those situations, he expresses himself more frequently and forcefully, figuring that others will eventually see things his way if he just gives them enough information. Perhaps you know someone like Lorenzo. Is it really the case that more communication always produces a better outcome?

When people have genuine disagreements, more talk doesn't always help. In some cases, increasing communication can just lead to frustration and anger. A 2007 study of consultations between doctors and patients found that the more doctors talked, the more likely they were to get off-track and forget about the patients' problems, a pattern that can translate into worse care for the patient.[35]

Sometimes it seems that the less said, the better. The *effectiveness* of our communication—rather than the *amount* of communication—is often what matters. That fact explains why learning to be a competent communicator is so advantageous.

LEARN IT   What are the primary differences among the action, interaction, and transaction models of communication? What does it mean to say that communication has literal and relational implications? What is the difference between having experience and having expertise?

APPLY IT   Talk with a friend or a classmate about a topic that is very important to you. Experiment with talking less and caring less about getting your point across than you usually would. What happens when you talk less than you normally would? How do the transactional features of the conversation change? Document your findings in a one-page report.

REFLECT ON IT   What are some implicit communication rules that you can recall? Why do you suppose we so often think communication can solve any problem?

3 How We Communicate Interpersonally

Communication takes place in many contexts. Sometimes it involves one person talking to a large audience, as when the president gives a speech on TV or a journalist writes an article for a magazine. At other times it involves a small group of people communicating with one another, as in a college seminar, a team of surgeons in an operating room, or a football huddle. It also includes people communicating by text and tweet, Skype and Snapchat. Communication occurs in families, in business organizations, in political institutions, in schools, and through the media. And, as you are probably aware, it often differs from one context to another. For example, few of us would talk to a grandparent in the same way we would address a TV reporter or a group of customers.

We communicate in many ways, so how do we know whether we're communicating interpersonally? In this section, we'll look at what makes communication interpersonal, and we'll consider how interpersonal communication—relative to other forms of communication—is unique in terms of its effects on people and their relationships.

Characteristics of Interpersonal Communication

On the Netflix series *Orange Is the New Black,* inmates Tasha "Taystee" Jefferson (played by Danielle Brooks) and Poussey Washington (played by Samira Wiley) come from very different backgrounds. The former is an orphan, raised in the inner city by a drug-running "adoptive mother," the latter a military brat raised abroad by a loving family. But the two nonetheless find themselves thrown together by circumstance when they are incarcerated in federal prison. As African American women, they are drawn to support each other in a prison environment that is harshly divided along racial and ethnic lines. But their friendship runs deeper, resting largely on their shared sense of humor and similarly quick intellect. Their relationship faces challenges at times, but they are able to work through difficulties by talking to each other openly and honestly. Although they've probably never really thought about it, Taystee and Poussey clearly understand the value of interpersonal communication.

Interpersonal communication consists of communication that occurs between two people within the context of their relationship and that, as it evolves, helps them to negotiate and define their relationship. The content of an interpersonal conversation is sometimes highly intimate, as when two romantic partners discuss the details of a sensitive health issue that one of them is experiencing. Interpersonal conversations can also focus on more mundane, impersonal content, as when the same romantic partners talk about what they need to buy at the grocery store. The content of yet other interpersonal conversations falls somewhere along the continuum between intimate and mundane topics. Each of those conversations is interpersonal, however, to the extent that it helps two people negotiate and define their relationships.

Talking Point: Definitions of interpersonal communication vary among communication scholars, sometimes substantially. Not all scholars agree, for instance, that interpersonal communication occurs between only two people.

interpersonal communication Communication that occurs between two people within the context of their relationship and that, as it evolves, helps them to negotiate and define their relationship.

Interpersonal communication is the foundation of Taystee and Poussey's friendship on *Orange Is the New Black.* © Netflix/ Courtesy Everett Collection

Interpersonal communication is different from many other forms of communication. To understand how, let's survey some of its most important characteristics.

INTERPERSONAL COMMUNICATION OCCURS BETWEEN TWO PEOPLE. The word *interpersonal* means "between people," and interpersonal communication involves interaction between two people at once. If only one person is involved—as when you talk to yourself—that is **intrapersonal communication.** Intrapersonal communication is important because it often affects how we relate to others; how often, for instance, do you rehearse a conversation in your mind before talking with someone?

There are other forms of communication, too. Communication that is being transmitted to large numbers of people is known as **mass communication.** Communication that occurs in small groups of three or more people, as in a family, in an online seminar, or in a support group, is called **small group communication.**

Most research on interpersonal communication, however, focuses on interaction within a **dyad,** a pair of people. Two people can communicate face-to-face, over the telephone, by text message, on FaceTime, or in many other ways.

INTERPERSONAL COMMUNICATION OCCURS WITHIN A RELATIONSHIP. People who communicate interpersonally share some sort of relationship. To some people, the word *relationship* implies an intimate bond, such as the union between spouses or romantic partners. However, the truth is that we have relationships with many different people. Some relationships, such as those with relatives or close friends, tend to be close significant relationships that may last for many years. Others, such as those with classmates, acquaintances, and co-workers, may not be as close and may last only as long as people live or work near one another.

In general, we communicate with each person on the basis of the expectations we have for that relationship. For instance, we might reveal private information, such as news about a family member's marital problems or serious health issues, to a friend but not to a co-worker, because we expect a friendship to be a closer relationship.

Much of our day-to-day communication is *impersonal,* meaning that it focuses on a task rather than on a relationship. Ordering coffee, calling a tech support line, and e-mailing a public official with a complaint are all examples of communication that helps you accomplish a task but does not necessarily help you build or maintain a relationship with others.

INTERPERSONAL COMMUNICATION EVOLVES WITHIN RELATIONSHIPS. Long-distance friends sometimes say that when they see each other, they pick up their conversation right where they left off, as if no time had passed. Interpersonal communication in those friendships—and in all relationships—unfolds over time as people get to know one another better and have new experiences. In fact, people in long-term relationships can often recall how their communication has changed over the course of their relationship.[36]

In the early stages of a romantic relationship, for instance, individuals may spend hours at a time talking and disclosing facts about their life, such as where they grew up and what their career goals are. As they get to know each other better, their communication might become more instrumental, focusing on tasks such as where they're going to spend the holidays and who's going to make a dinner reservation, instead of sharing deep disclosures. They might even start to experience conflict. In any case, interpersonal communication is something that occurs over time. It's not a one-shot deal but something that is continually evolving within relationships.

---

intrapersonal communication Communication with oneself.

mass communication Communication from one source to a large audience.

small group communication Communication occurring within small groups of three or more people.

dyad A pair of people.

Talking Point: Ask students to raise their hands if they talk to themselves. If any do not, you can point out the inner monolog they went through while deciding: "Do I talk to myself? No, I don't talk to myself!"

Talking Point: Small groups and mass audiences differ by size. Researchers generally consider small groups to comprise at least 3 people, but no more than 20.

INTERPERSONAL COMMUNICATION NEGOTIATES AND DEFINES RELATIONSHIPS.
Every relationship has its own identity. When you think about all your friends, for example, you can probably group them into friendship types, such as very close friends, casual friends, work friends, and school friends. Within every group, each friendship is probably a little different from the others.

How does each relationship get its own personality? The answer is that you negotiate the relationship over time using interpersonal communication. The way you talk to people you know, the topics you talk (or don't talk) about, and the kinds of nonverbal behaviors you use all help to define the kind of relationship you have with each person. You can also use interpersonal communication to change the nature of a relationship, as when friends disclose feelings of romantic interest in each other.

So, what makes communication interpersonal? Interpersonal communication evolves over time between people in some type of dyadic relationship and helps to define the nature of their relationship. You might notice we haven't said anything about how intimate the communication is. Some people think interpersonal communication means only sharing secrets and other private information, but that isn't the case. It includes *all* communication behaviors, verbal as well as nonverbal, that unfold over time to form and maintain relationships, whether those relationships are casual or intimate.

Let's turn to some of the reasons why interpersonal communication can be so important.

Why Interpersonal Communication Matters

You can probably think of many reasons why interpersonal communication is important to you. For example, you practice it almost every day, you use it to maintain your current relationships and form new relationships, and you find it engaging and enjoyable. The many reasons why interpersonal communication matters to people fall in three general categories: pervasiveness, relational benefits, and health benefits.

INTERPERSONAL COMMUNICATION IS PERVASIVE.   We all have relationships, so we all engage in interpersonal communication. For most of us, interpersonal communication is as much a part of everyday life as sleeping or eating or putting on clothes. Sometimes we take part in face-to-face interpersonal communication with the people with whom we live or work. At other times interpersonal communication takes place over the telephone, such as when we talk to relatives or friends we don't see regularly. At still other times we communicate interpersonally via electronically mediated channels, as when we share text messages or tweets with people in our social circles. No matter how we do it, nearly everyone engages in some form of interpersonal communication almost every day.

INTERPERSONAL COMMUNICATION CAN IMPROVE OUR RELATIONSHIPS.   We've seen that not every problem in relationships can be traced back to communication. Nevertheless, many relationship problems do stem from poor communication. In fact, in a nationwide survey conducted by the National Communication Association, respondents indicated that a "lack of effective communication" is the number one reason why relationships, including marriages, end.[37] Therefore, improving our interpersonal communication skills will also help us to improve our relationships. Significantly, this

In Everyday Life: When a friend tells us something too intimate for that friendship, we reevaluate the identity of that relationship. Either the relationship changes to accommodate a higher degree of intimacy or the receiver will react negatively to the violation.

Talking Point: Some students may also assume that interpersonal communication must be positive. In fact, even very negative forms of communication can be interpersonal, because they often help to negotiate and define the nature of a relationship.

In the IM: To help students identify common relationship challenges and consider the extent to which communication might play a role in such challenges, have them complete the out-of-class activity titled "The Role of Communication in Relationship Challenges."

fact **OR** *fiction?* THE INTERNET MAKES US HAPPIER

You're likely to encounter a number of intuitive findings as you study interpersonal communication, and your own intuition is probably right most of the time. The occasional failure of intuition is one reason why the systematic study of communication is so useful. In the "Fact or Fiction?" box in each chapter, we'll take a look at some common ideas about communication to determine whether they're as true as we might think they are.

For instance, the Internet is such an important means of communication that you might think your well-being would suffer if you didn't have access. Is that notion fact or fiction? Research indicates that it's a fact.

A British research team recently examined data from a survey of over 35,000 adults from around the world. The researchers asked participants about their ability to access the Internet to communicate with others. They also measured participants' life satisfaction, which encompasses their happiness and mental well-being. The team's analyses found a direct relationship between life satisfaction and the

ability to communicate online. Participants' age didn't matter—older adults benefited as much as younger adults did. Notably, however, the benefits of Internet communication were greater for people with lower incomes and less education. They were also greater for women than men, particularly in developing nations. Those findings led the researchers to speculate that access to online communication empowers people to form relationships, share ideas, and get information that their life circumstances might otherwise inhibit.

ASK YOURSELF

- Why do you think women might benefit more than men from access to online communication?
- Besides life satisfaction, what other physical and/or mental health benefits might computer-mediated communication enhance?

Source: Trajectory Partnership. (2010, May). *The information dividend: Can IT make you "happier"?* London, England: Author.

observation is true for far more than intimate relationships. Indeed, research shows that effective interpersonal communication can improve a wide range of relationships, including those between and among friends, physicians and patients, parents and children, and businesspeople and customers.[38]

"But, sweety, why don't you just read my blog like everyone else?"
© www.CartoonStock.com

INTERPERSONAL COMMUNICATION CAN IMPROVE OUR HEALTH. As we saw earlier in this chapter, we communicate partly to meet our physical needs for social contact. Close personal relationships are very important to our health. Several studies have shown, for example, that married people live longer, healthier, and more satisfying lives than individuals who are single, divorced, or widowed.[39] Even having close friendships and other supportive relationships helps us manage stress and stay healthy.[40]

Interpersonal communication doesn't have to be face-to-face to benefit us. As the "Fact or Fiction?" box explains, a 2010 study of over 35,000 people from around the world found that the ability to interact with others online was significantly related to mental health, happiness, and well-being. Importantly, access to interpersonal interaction via computer-mediated communication benefited people regardless of their age and was particularly positive for women, for individuals with little education, and for those without financial means.

LEARN IT What are the features of communication that determine whether it is interpersonal? How and why is interpersonal communication important for health?

APPLY IT Using the Internet to help you, look up a friend you've lost touch with and make contact with that person again. Even if you don't communicate with long-term friends often, they are worth holding onto because of the history and the good times you have shared with them.

REFLECT ON IT In what ways do your close relationships improve your life? What are some of the challenges involved in maintaining those relationships?

4 Building Your Communication Competence

No one is born a competent communicator. Rather, as with driving a car, playing a musical instrument, or writing a computer program, communicating competently requires skills that we have to learn and practice. That doesn't mean nature doesn't give some people a head start. Research shows that some of our communication traits—for example, how sociable, aggressive, or shy we are—are partly determined by our genes.[41] No matter which traits we're born with, though, we still have to learn how to communicate competently.

What Communicating Competently Involves

Think about five people you consider to be really good communicators. Who's on your list? Any of your friends or relatives? Teachers? Co-workers? Politicians or celebrities? Yourself? You probably recognize that identifying good communicators means first asking yourself what a good communicator is. Most scholars seem to agree that **communication competence** means communicating in ways that are effective and appropriate in a given situation.[42]

COMMUNICATING EFFECTIVELY. Effectiveness describes how well your communication achieves its goals.[43] Suppose that you want to persuade your neighbor to donate money to a shelter for abused animals. There are many ways to achieve that goal. You could explain how much the shelter needs the money and identify how many services it provides to animals in need. You could offer to do yard work in exchange for your neighbor's donation. You could even recite the times when you have donated to causes that were important to your neighbor. No single communication strategy will be effective in all situations. Being an effective communicator means choosing the messages that will best meet your goals.

COMMUNICATING APPROPRIATELY. Besides being effective, competent communication should also be appropriate. That means attending to the rules and expectations that apply in a social situation. Recall that communication is governed by rules. A competent communicator takes those rules into account when deciding how to act.

Talking Point: Several researchers have found that married people are in better health than unmarried people, but they don't always agree on why. Some think married people are healthier because they have more resources at their disposal. Others say married people are less likely to engage in risky behaviors.

communication competence Communicating in ways that are effective and appropriate for a given situation.

Focus on Ethics: The more students learn about persuasion strategies, the better able they will become at persuading and manipulating others. What are the ethical implications of learning those skills?

When communicating in an online class, for instance, it is polite to show sensitivity to other students' postings and to avoid letting disagreements escalate. You may also be expected to post a certain number of comments each week. If you violate those rules, therefore, others are likely to find your communication inappropriate.

Communicating appropriately can be especially challenging when you're interacting with people from other cultures. Because many communication rules are culture-specific, what might be perfectly appropriate in one culture could be seen as inappropriate or even offensive in another.[44] For example, if you're visiting a Canadian household and your hosts offer you food, it's appropriate to accept the food if you're hungry. In many Japanese households, however, it is inappropriate to accept the food even if you're hungry, until you decline it twice and your hosts offer it a third time.

Communication competence, then, implies both effectiveness and appropriateness. Note that those are aspects of communication, not aspects of people. Thus, the next question we need to consider is whether competent communicators share common characteristics.

Characteristics of Competent Communicators

Look again at your list of five competent communicators. What do they have in common? Competence itself is situation-specific, so what works in one context may not work in another. However, good communicators tend to have certain characteristics that help them behave competently in most situations.

self-monitoring Awareness of one's behavior and how it affects others.

SELF-AWARENESS.   Good communicators are aware of their own behavior and its effects on others.[45] Researchers call this awareness **self-monitoring.** People who are high self-monitors pay close attention to the way they look, sound, and act in social situations. In contrast, people who are low self-monitors often seem oblivious to both their own behaviors and other people's reactions to them. Self-monitoring usually makes people more competent communicators because it enables them to see how their behavior fits or doesn't fit in a given social setting. What's your level of self-monitoring? Check out the "Assess Your Skills" box to find out.

ADAPTABILITY.   It's one thing to be aware of your own behavior; it's quite another to be able to adapt it to different situations. Competent communicators are able to assess what is going to be appropriate and effective in a given context and then modify their behaviors accordingly.[46] That ability is important because what works in one situation might be ineffective in another. Using abbreviations such as LOL (laughing out loud) and BRB (be right back) are fine in a text message, for instance, because they help you conserve space and communicate efficiently. Competent communicators would generally not use such abbreviations in a face-to-face conversation, however.

empathy The ability to think and feel as others do.

EMPATHY.   Good communicators practice **empathy,** the ability to be "other-oriented" and understand other people's thoughts and feelings.[47] When people say "Put yourself in my shoes," they are asking you to consider a situation from their perspective rather than your own. Empathy is an important skill because people often think and feel differently than you do about the same situation.

For example, suppose you want to ask your boss for a one-week extension on an assignment. You might think, "What's the big deal? It's only a week." To your boss, though, the extension might mean that she would be unable to complete her work in time for her family vacation. If the situation were reversed, how would you feel? An

assess your skills | ARE YOU A HIGH SELF-MONITOR?

One of the ways to improve your communication ability is to think about how you communicate now. Each "Assess Your Skills" box will help you do so by presenting a self-assessment of a communication skill or tendency. For instance, we have seen that self-monitoring is one of the characteristics of competent communicators. How high a self-monitor are you? Read each of the following statements, and indicate how much it describes you by assigning a number between 1 ("not at all") and 7 ("very much").

1. _____ I tend to show different sides of myself to different people.
2. _____ I would probably make a good actor.
3. _____ I can usually tell when I've said something inappropriate by reading it in the listener's eyes.
4. _____ I pay attention to how other people react to my behavior.
5. _____ I can adjust my behavior to meet the requirements of any situation I'm in.
6. _____ I am often able to read people's true emotions through their eyes.
7. _____ I can usually tell when others are lying to me.
8. _____ I am not always the person I appear to be.

When you're finished, add up your scores and write the total on this line: _____. The ranges below will help you see how high your self-monitoring is.

- 7–22: Self-monitoring is a skill you can work on, as you are doing in this class.
- 23–38: You are a moderate self-monitor, with a good sense of self-awareness. Continued practice will strengthen that skill.
- 39–56: You are a high self-monitor, which usually makes your interpersonal communication more effective.

Your score on this quiz—and on all of the quizzes in this book—reflects only how you see yourself at this time. If your score surprises you, take the quiz again later in the course to see how studying interpersonal communication may have changed your assessment of your communication abilities.

Source: Lennox, R. D., & Wolfe, R. N. (1984). Revision of the self-monitoring scale. *Journal of Personality and Social Psychology, 46,* 1349–1364.

empathic person would consider the situation from the boss's perspective and then choose his or her behaviors accordingly.

People who don't practice empathy tend to assume everyone thinks and feels the same way they do, and they risk creating problems when that assumption isn't accurate. How can you improve your empathy skills? Check out the "Got Skills?" box for guidance on developing your empathic abilities.

COGNITIVE COMPLEXITY. Let's say you see your friend Tony coming toward you in the hallway. You smile and get ready to say hi, but he walks right by as if you're not even there. Several possibilities for Tony's behavior might come to mind. Maybe he's mad at you. Maybe he was concentrating on something and didn't notice you. Maybe he did smile at you and you didn't see it. The ability to consider a variety of explanations and to understand a given situation in multiple ways is called **cognitive complexity.** Cognitive complexity is a valuable skill because it keeps you from jumping to the wrong conclusion and responding inappropriately.[48]

In Everyday Life: Empathy is a particular challenge for individuals with disorders such as autism and Asperger's syndrome. Both conditions impair a person's ability to interpret other people's nonverbal behaviors.

cognitive complexity The ability to understand a given situation in multiple ways.

Do you believe this woman is practicing appropriate communication behavior? Why or why not? © Ariel Skelley/Blend Images/Getty Images, RF

Someone with little cognitive complexity might feel slighted by Tony's behavior and might therefore ignore him the next time they meet. In contrast, someone with more cognitive complexity would remember that behaviors do not always mean what we think they mean. That person would be more open-minded, considering several possible interpretations of Tony's actions.

ethics A code of morality or a set of ideas about what is right.

ETHICS. Finally, competent communicators are ethical communicators. **Ethics** guides us in judging whether something is morally right or wrong. Ethical communication, then, generally dictates treating people fairly, communicating honestly, and avoiding immoral or unethical behavior. That can be easier said than done, because people often have very different ideas about right and wrong. What may be morally justified to one person or one culture may be considered unethical to another. Competent communicators are

AT A GLANCE

Five Characteristics of Competent Communicators

Self-Awareness	Awareness of how your behavior is affecting others
Adaptability	Ability to modify your behaviors as the situation demands
Empathy	Skill at identifying and feeling what others around you are feeling
Cognitive Complexity	Ability to understand a given situation in multiple ways
Ethics	Guidelines in judging whether something is morally right or morally wrong

got skills?

EMPATHY

Learn to be more empathic in the way you communicate.

WHAT?

Think and feel the way others do.

WHY?

To communicate in constructive ways with people, by considering how you would feel and what you would think if you were in their situation.

HOW?

1. Recognize your own thoughts and feelings in a given situation, and ask yourself what would make someone think or feel differently in that situation.

2. Listen to what others say and pay attention to what they do. Notice how they react to the situation in ways that are different from your own.

3. Acknowledge different perspectives. Making statements such as "I can understand why you would feel that way" shows people that you recognize their viewpoints.

4. Once you have identified another person's thoughts or feelings, imagine yourself thinking or feeling the same way they do. Notice how this changes your perspective on the situation, if at all.

TRY!

1. Think of someone who constantly tries your patience. It might be a co-worker, a relative, or a roommate with whom you frequently have conflict.

2. Now, consider your relationship with that person from his or her point of view. What would he or she say about you, and why? Write a paragraph about your relationship *as if you were the other person.* Express the thoughts and feelings you think he or she has.

3. If you feel comfortable, show the other person your paragraph and ask for his or her reaction. Even if you don't take this last step, challenging yourself to think and feel the way this person does can improve your ability to empathize.

CONSIDER: *Empathizing with someone can be especially difficult when you have conflict with that person. It's hard to see things from another's point of view if you already disagree with that person's perspective. This is where empathy can be particularly valuable, however.*

aware that people's ideas about ethics vary. However, they are also aware of their own ethical beliefs, and they communicate in ways that are consistent with those beliefs.

When it comes to communication competence, the mode of communication matters. People who grew up before the invention of the Internet may feel comfortable talking to others face to face or by telephone, for instance, but they may be less competent at using Instagram, sending tweets, or posting to Facebook. For some others, it's just the opposite. Because social media have greatly expanded our options for interpersonal communication, it pays to consider specifically what makes people competent online communicators.

Self-awareness was turned on its head in the 2010 movie *Inception*, which featured characters affecting one another's dreams. © *Warner Bros/ Photofest*

Competent Online Communication

These days, much of our interpersonal communication takes place in electronically mediated contexts. These include e-mail, instant messaging, and text messaging; social networking (such as on Facebook and LinkedIn); tweeting; image sharing (such as on YouTube and Flickr); and videoconferencing (such as on Skype and FaceTime), among others. As you'll see in this section, communicating competently in these venues requires paying attention to their unique capabilities and pitfalls.

BEWARE OF THE POTENTIAL FOR MISUNDERSTANDING. Face-to-face conversations allow you to pay attention to behaviors that help to clarify the meaning of a speaker's words. People's facial expressions, gestures, and tone of voice, for example, generally provide clues about what they are trying to say. Are they speaking seriously or sarcastically? Are they upset or calm, tentative or self-assured? We can usually tell a lot about people's meaning by considering not only *what they say* but *how they say it.*

We saw earlier that some channel-lean forms of communication—such as tweeting and instant messaging—rely heavily on text, restricting our access to facial expressions and other clues. As a result, these forms of communication increase the potential for misunderstanding. Many of us have had the experience of teasing or joking with someone in a text message, for instance, only to discover that the person took our words seriously and felt offended or hurt.

To communicate competently when using channel-lean media, follow these guidelines:

- *Review your message before you share it.* Although the meaning of your words is clear to you, think about the ways in which it may be unclear to your recipient. In particular, identify words or phrases in your message that could have more than one meaning.

- *Clarify your meaning wherever possible.* When you find parts of your message that could be misinterpreted, consider whether using a different word or phrase would be clearer.

- *Use emoticons and emoji to convey emotion.* Adding symbols to express your emotional state—such as a smiling face, a winking face, or a crying face—can help receivers understand how to interpret your message.

PRESUME THAT EVERYTHING IS PERMANENT AND NOTHING IS SECRET.   Perhaps you've had the embarrassing experience of sending a text message to the wrong person. Words you intended for one recipient are therefore read by someone else, who may choose either to delete them or to save them. That situation illustrates an important characteristic of electronically mediated communication: Everything you say and do leaves behind a record. That creates the possibility that your messages can be seen or heard by virtually anyone. Sometimes this occurs by accident, as when you send your text message to the wrong person. On other occasions, however, people can copy or forward your messages to others without your knowledge or permission.

It is best, therefore, to remember that anything you communicate via electronically mediated channels could reach people other than your intended receivers, and to modify your messages accordingly. Here are some specific tips:

- *Write as though others will read your words.* Psychologist Ken Siegel, who advises companies on workplace efficiency, offers this advice: "send e-mail with the assumption that the person you really don't want to read it *will* read it."[49]

- *Double-check your recipients before hitting "Send."* When drafting a text message, make sure you have chosen the proper receiver. Before you send an e-mail message, ensure that you haven't hit "Reply All" when you intended to reply only to one person.

- *Take sensitive messages offline.* When your message includes sensitive information, communicate it face to face whenever possible. Never send private financial information, personal evaluations of others, or similarly sensitive details in an e-mail or instant message that could easily be saved and shared with others.

AVOID COMMUNICATING IN ANGER.   When someone else's words or actions upset us, it can be easy to lash out by sending a nasty text message or posting words of anger on Facebook. Doing so may soothe our feelings in the short run, but our words can continue to wound and upset others long after our anger is gone. That's important to remember, because anger can cloud our ability to think clearly and make us less likely to care about the repercussions of our words. Because electronically mediated messages can be read—and misunderstood—by broad audiences, however, competent online communicators recognize this danger and avoid communicating in anger.

To do the same, consider these suggestions:

- *Consider whether your anger springs from misunderstanding.* We have seen that electronically mediated messages—especially channel-lean forms such as e-mails and texts—are easy to misinterpret. If your anger was sparked by a message you received from someone else, consider the possibility that you misunderstood what he or she was saying. Before lashing out at the person, think about whether you might have misinterpreted his or her meaning.

- *Write a draft, then set it aside.* There's nothing wrong with *composing* messages while you're in an emotional state. You just want to be cautious about sending them. A good option is to write a draft of your message and then set it aside, without sending it. Later, after you feel less angry, read your draft carefully and consider how you want to modify it, if at all.

Considering the potential for misunderstanding, remembering the scope of your audience, and avoiding communication while angry can be helpful in most any interpersonal context. They are particularly important while communicating in electronically mediated ways, however. Although they aren't the only components of online communication competence, these suggestions can help you interact interpersonally in effective and appropriate ways across a range of contexts.

In the IM: You can now access the Master the Chapter Discussion Questions and the Research Library in the Instructor's Manual for each chapter.

LEARN IT What is the difference between effectiveness and appropriateness? How is cognitive complexity defined?

APPLY IT Choose your favorite reality TV show and think about the characters and their communication behaviors. On the basis of what you've learned in this section, how would you rate each character in terms of communication competence? What makes some characters more competent than others? Try to identify specific skills, such as empathy and cognitive complexity, that differentiate the characters from one another. Consider how each person might improve his or her communication competencies.

REFLECT ON IT How would you describe your own level of self-monitoring? What challenges do you face when trying to communicate effectively online?

MASTER the chapter

1 Why We Communicate (p. 3)

- Communication meets physical needs, such as helping us to stay healthy.
- Communication meets relational needs by helping us form and maintain important relationships.
- Communication fills identity needs by helping us see how others think of us.
- Communication meets spiritual needs by letting us express our beliefs and values.
- Communication serves instrumental needs, such as helping us to schedule a meeting and order a meal.

2 The Nature of Communication (p. 8)

- Through various models, communication scholars have viewed communication as action, as interaction, and most recently as transaction.

- Communication relies on multiple channels, passes through perceptual filters, is given its meaning by the people who use it, has literal and relational implications, sends intentional and unintentional messages, and is governed by rules.

- Five myths about communication are (1) everyone is an expert in communication, (2) communication can solve any problem, (3) communication can break down, (4) communication is inherently good, and (5) more communication is always better.

3 How We Communicate Interpersonally (p. 20)

- Interpersonal communication occurs between two people, evolves over time within their relationship, and helps them to negotiate and define their relationship.
- Interpersonal communication is pervasive, has benefits for our relationships, and has benefits for our health.

4 Building Your Communication Competence (p. 25)

- Communicating competently means communicating effectively and appropriately.
- Competent communicators typically have high self-awareness, adaptability, empathy, cognitive complexity, and ethics.

- Competent online communicators consider the potential for misunderstanding, remember the breadth of their potential audience, and avoid communicating while angry.

KEY TERMS

channel (p. 9)
channel-lean context (p. 12)
channel-rich context (p. 12)
cognitive complexity (p. 28)
communication competence (p. 25)
content dimension (p. 14)
context (p. 10)
decode (p. 9)
dyad (p. 22)
empathy (p. 26)

encode (p. 9)
ethics (p. 28)
explicit rule (p. 16)
feedback (p. 10)
implicit rule (p. 17)
instrumental needs (p. 7)
interpersonal communication (p. 21)
intrapersonal communication (p. 22)
mass communication (p. 22)
message (p. 9)

metacommunication (p. 15)
model (p. 8)
noise (p. 9)
receiver (p. 9)
relational dimension (p. 15)
self-monitoring (p. 26)
small group communication (p. 22)
source (p. 9)
stigma (p. 4)
symbol (p. 14)

connect

To maximize your study time, check out CONNECT to access the SmartBook study module for this chapter, watch videos, and explore other resources.

Culture and Gender

© Image Source/Alamy, RF

COMMUNICATION IN THE WORLD'S BOROUGH

High school students Cameron and Eduardo are teammates, but Cameron calls the sport they play "soccer," whereas Eduardo has known it for most of his life as "football." Between school, practice, and epic video game battles, the two spend much of their time together, despite the fact that Cameron was born in the United States and Eduardo was born in Trinidad. Their friendship might seem unlikely to some, but among residents of Queens, in New York City, it's not unusual at all.

Known as "The World's Borough," Queens is the most diverse county in the already quite diverse United States, and possibly on the planet: more than 45 percent of the population is foreign born,[1] and more than half the residents speak a language besides English.[2] The borough is dotted with ethnic enclaves and integrated neighborhoods where Old World traditions endure alongside contemporary American ones. For residents, the rich diversity of Queens presents frequent opportunities to communicate interpersonally—and form friendships—across cultures in ways that those who live in many other places may never experience.

No matter where we live, nearly all of us will communicate with people from different cultures at some point in our lives. Culture is a powerful influence on communication behavior. It can affect not only how we express ourselves but also how we interpret and react to the interpersonal behaviors of others. Another powerful influence on interpersonal communication—one that is always with us—is gender. Indeed, many people feel that communicating across genders can be nearly as confusing as communicating across cultures, if not more so. Other lenses, such as ethnicity, age, and socioeconomic status, also can influence communication. However, gender and culture shape our behaviors and interpretations in so many ways that it's worth taking an in-depth look at each.

1 Understanding Culture and Communication

Our cultural traditions and beliefs can influence how we make sense of communication behavior even without our realizing it. Each of us is affected by the culture in which we were raised, and we tend to notice other cultures only when they differ from ours. In many people's minds, culture—like an accent—is something that only *other* people have. Let's begin by understanding in what sense we all have cultural traits and biases.

Defining Culture

We use the term *culture* to mean all sorts of things. Sometimes we connect it to a place, as in "French culture" and "New York culture." Other times we use it to refer to an ethnic or a religious group, as in "African American culture" and "Jewish culture." We also speak of "deaf culture" and "the culture of the rich."

For our purposes, we will define **culture** as the system of learned and shared symbols, language, values, and norms that distinguish one group of people from another. That definition tells us that culture isn't a property of countries or ethnicities or economic classes; rather, it's a property of people. Each of us identifies with one or more groups that have a common culture comprising a shared language, values, beliefs, traditions, and customs. We'll refer to a group of people who share a given culture as a **society.**

DISTINGUISHING BETWEEN IN-GROUPS AND OUT-GROUPS.   Researchers use the term **in-group** to refer to a group with whom we identify, and **out-group** to describe a group we see as different from ourselves.[3] If you grew up in the U.S. Midwest, for example, you would probably view other Midwesterners as part of your in-group, whereas someone from the Pacific Northwest would not. Similarly, when you are traveling in foreign countries, the residents may perceive you as being from an out-group if you look or sound different from them or behave differently.

Talking Point: When introducing culture and gender, note that *influencing* behavior is not the same thing as *determining* behavior. This point is raised at the end of the chapter, but it may be useful to foreshadow that distinction up front.

Writing Note: Ask students to list five ways they think their own cultural upbringing influences their behavior.

culture The system of learned and shared symbols, language, values, and norms that distinguish one group of people from another.

society A group of people who share symbols, language, values, and norms.

in-group A group of people with whom one identifies.

out-group A group of people with whom one does not identify.

ethnocentrism Systematic preference for characteristics of one's own culture.

For some people, being perceived as different can be an exciting or intriguing experience. For others, however, that experience can be stress inducing. For example, research shows that immigrants often experience abnormally high stress during their first year in their new homeland.[4] We often refer to that stress as *culture shock,* or the jarring reaction we have when we find ourselves in highly unfamiliar situations. That's a common experience for students who come to the United States from other countries to attend college, for instance, as they often struggle to adapt to an entirely new cultural environment. Research shows that the stress of culture shock can contribute to illnesses such as high blood pressure, depression, and heart disease.[5]

Some researchers point out that our ability to distinguish between those who are similar to us and those who are different probably helped our ancestors survive by encouraging them to associate with people whose goals and priorities were similar to their own.[6] That tendency endures today, and research shows that many people exhibit strong preferences for individuals and groups they perceive to be like themselves. In other words, people are often more suspicious and less trusting of others whose ethnic, national, and/or cultural backgrounds are different from their own.[7] Researchers use the term **ethnocentrism** to describe the systematic preference for characteristics of one's own culture. That tendency can make it particularly discomforting to live or work someplace where you are considered a minority. In its account of Muslim students studying in the United States, the "Communication: Dark Side" box illustrates that point.

The in-group/out-group distinction is a major reason why so many nations struggle with the issue of immigration. Some countries, including Sweden and the United States, have relatively lenient policies that allow many immigration applicants to move to those countries and eventually to become citizens. Other nations have much stricter immigration policies. Denmark, for instance, significantly toughened its immigration policies in 2001, making it harder for foreign-born people to immigrate or become citizens.[8]

In the sitcom *Fresh Off The Boat*, young Eddie sees hip-hop as a way to fit in to American culture, and to differentiate himself from his immigrant parents. © Nicole Wilder/ABC/Getty Images

communication | *DARK SIDE*

CULTURAL STEREOTYPING IN STRESSFUL TIMES

Distinguishing between in-groups and out-groups may be a natural tendency among humans, but it can lead to erroneous judgments. During times of stress or uncertainty, it may be especially easy to make broad generalizations about groups of people. In the wake of terror attacks committed in the United States and abroad by a very small number of radical Islamic groups, this kind of stereotyping presents a particular burden for Muslim Americans. Already a minority in the United States (where they make up less than 1 percent of the population), Muslim Americans are frequently treated with suspicion or outright contempt by those who fail to recognize that the vast majority of Muslims have nothing to do with these attacks, and do not support or condone terrorism in any way.

In fact, most major Islamic organizations have explicitly condemned these terrorist acts. But many non-Muslim Americans remain distrustful of Islam, and continue to treat those who adhere to the faith with suspicion, or even contempt. In 2014, for example, as atrocities committed by the group calling itself "Islamic State" unfolded in the Middle East, many Muslim students reported being on the receiving end of behaviors ranging from subtle exclusion to outright abuse by others who blame all Muslims for the terrorist actions of a few. For competent communicators, however, it is vitally important not to condemn an entire group based on the actions of a few individuals. In fact, some communicators actively work to avoid such stereotyping. In the days after the tragic attack on the French satire magazine *Charlie Hebdo,* for example, when the hashtag #JeSuisAhmed (I am Ahmed) began trending, Twitter users paid tribute to Ahmed Merabet, one of those killed in the tragedy. Merabet was a Muslim police officer, murdered while protecting the free speech of writers who regularly ridiculed his faith.

ASK YOURSELF

- What can be done to prevent hostile behaviors toward Muslims in the United States?
- Why is it so easy to stereotype people, especially during times of stress or uncertainty?

Sources: Pew Research Religion & Public Life Project, Religious landscape survey, http://religions.pewforum.org/reports. Accessed 3/1/2015; Howell, B. (2014, December 22); "Muslim students cope with discrimination in wartime America." Retrieved February 6, 2015, from http://bgsujournalism.com/j3200/?p=1185

Although Danish authorities have recently worked to ease the country's immigration policies, they remain among the strictest in Europe.

How best to manage immigration—and the population of immigrants living in the country illegally—is a controversial issue in the United States. It illustrates the complex and sometimes contentious relationship between in-groups, such as the country's current citizens and residents, and out-groups, such as those who have immigrated or who wish to move to the country.

ACQUIRING A CULTURE.   Because cultures and societies vary so much around the world, it might seem that we inherit our culture genetically, the same way we inherit our eye color; but that isn't the case. Rather, culture is learned. Researchers call that learning process *enculturation.* Moreover, culture is not necessarily related to or based on our **ethnicity,** which is our perception of our ancestry or heritage. Nor is culture necessarily tied to our **nationality,** our status as a citizen of a particular country. Culture is determined by who raised us, by where we were raised, and by the symbols, language, values, and norms of that place. For instance, a Cambodian citizen raised in the United States will likely adopt the language and practices common to where she was brought up. Her ethnicity and citizenship are Cambodian, but her culture is American.

Outside of Class: One powerful tool for enculturation is the mass media. Outside class, have students analyze TV shows and/or printed advertisements for their cultural messages. For example, how do portrayals of families on TV reflect cultural understandings of families?

ethnicity An individual's perception of his or her ancestry or heritage.

nationality An individual's status as a citizen of a particular country.

Your culture depends not on where you were born but rather on where and by whom you were raised. Although their adopted son Maddox was born in Cambodia, adopted son Pax was born in Vietnam, and adopted daughter Zahara was born in Ethiopia, each child will acquire Angelina Jolie and Brad Pitt's cultural norms, values, symbols, and language. © Gonzalo/Bauer-Griffin/Getty Images

Focus on Ethics: Encountering unfamiliar cultural norms can challenge us to think about our own cultural beliefs. An American visiting the Middle East might be appalled, for example, at seeing a man hit a woman in public. What is the ethical response? Is it more ethical to respect another culture's values or to stand up for gender equality, even if that imposes one's own cultural values on another?

© Brand X Pictures/PunchStock, RF

Talking Point: Encourage students to identify other cultural symbols, both positive and negative.

The Components of Culture

Cultures and societies vary enormously. Imagine a group consisting of people raised in Saudi Arabia, Vietnam, Iceland, Namibia, Paraguay, Israel, and the U.S. Southwest. Not only would the group's members differ in their native languages, but they most likely would also have different religious beliefs and political views, enjoy different sports, prefer different foods, wear different clothing styles, and have varying ideas about education, marriage, money, and sexuality. In fact, it might be harder to identify their similarities than their differences. Yet even people from vastly different societies can share experiences online. Social media such as YouTube, Instagram, and Twitter link people from around the world—creating what is, in a sense, a new mass culture.

Values, beliefs, and preferences often vary even among different regions of the same country. For example, native Hawaiians, native Texans, and native New Yorkers might differ considerably in their customs and values, even though they were all raised in the United States. No matter what their differences, though, cultures have some common components, as our definition of culture made clear. Those components include symbols, language, values, and norms.

SYMBOLS. A symbol is something that represents an idea. Words are symbols, and every culture has its own symbols that represent ideas that are vital to that culture. For example, people use the U.S. flag, the bald eagle, and "The Star-Spangled Banner" as symbols of the United States. Many people also associate particular foods with their culture. Whereas hot dogs and apple pie have come to symbolize the culture of the United States, for instance, a Hungarian might consider goulash—a stew of beef and vegetables—as the national dish. Similarly, the fermented cabbage dish kimchi is considered the national dish of Korea, and a variety of curries are associated with Indian culture.

LANGUAGE. Researchers believe there are about 7,100 languages used in the world today.[9] (And, according to the New York State Comptroller's Office, more languages are spoken in Queens, New York, than in any other city in the world: 138 at last count, prompting Queens to call itself "The World's Borough.")[10] Language allows for written and spoken communication, and it also ensures that cultures and cultural ideas are passed from one generation to the next. Today, Chinese, Spanish, and English—in that order—are the three most commonly spoken languages in the world.[11] Unfortunately, many other languages are in danger of extinction. In fact, researchers believe that at least 10 percent of the world's languages are spoken

U.S. culture values freedom, opportunity, choice, and material comfort. Those values are epitomized in the media by scenes such as this—where two people are driving a sports car on a spacious open road with the sun on their face and the wind in their hair. © *Corbis, RF*

by fewer than 100 people each.[12] We'll cover written and spoken communication extensively in the Language chapter.

VALUES.   A culture's values are its standards for judging how good, desirable, or beautiful something is. In short, they're cultural ideas about what ought to be. Sociological research indicates that U.S. culture values ideals such as equal opportunity, material comfort, practicality and efficiency, achievement, democracy, free enterprise, and individual choice.[13] When you travel to other countries, you might find that their cultural values are dramatically different from yours.

NORMS.   Finally, norms are rules or expectations that guide people's behavior in a culture. As an example, consider the norms for greeting people. In North American countries, people shake hands and say "Nice to meet you." In other cultures, it's normal to hug, kiss on both cheeks, or even kiss on the lips. Cultures also vary in their norms for politeness: A behavior that would be considered very polite in one culture may be frowned upon in another. Check out the "Got Skills?" box to learn more about cultural norms.

Cultures and Co-Cultures

When you think about culture as shared language, beliefs, and customs, it may seem as though you belong to many different cultures at once. If you grew up in the United States, for example, then you likely feel a part of the U.S. culture. At the same time, if you're really into computers, music, or skateboarding, you may notice that the people who share those interests appear to have their own ways of speaking and acting. You may notice, too, that people in your generation have different values and customs than older people—or that different ethnic or religious groups at your school have their own traditions and beliefs. Does each of those groups have a culture of its own? In a manner of speaking, the answer is yes.

Writing Note: Ask students to list and describe the various co-cultures to which they belong.

In the IM: The out-of-class activity "Learning About Different Co-Cultures" will encourage students to expand their familiarity with co-cultures other than their own.

got skills?

Discover the politeness norms of another culture.

WHAT?

Learn about a cultural norm for politeness in a society that is different from your own.

WHY?

To avoid giving offense when communicating with people from that culture, such as during a cultural pride event or in classroom or on-the-job interactions.

HOW?

1. Think about a friend or an acquaintance who comes from a different society than yours.

2. Use the Internet to research the behavioral norms for politeness that characterize the culture of that person's society.

Focus in particular on the communication behaviors—verbal and nonverbal—that are considered polite or impolite in that culture. The website www.executiveplanet.com provides many such examples.

TRY!

1. In a short report, document what you have learned about the cultural norms of politeness in that society.

2. In your next couple of conversations with your friend or acquaintance, practice those cultural norms of politeness.

CONSIDER: *How has your intercultural communication improved with this exercise?*

---

co-cultures Groups of people who share values, customs, and norms related to mutual interests or characteristics beyond their national citizenship.

Eye contact serves some indispensable functions in the deaf co-culture.
© Don Ryan/AP Images

DEFINING CO-CULTURES. Within most large cultures, such as those of Italian, Vietnamese, or U.S. societies, are a host of smaller cultural entities that researchers call co-cultures. **Co-cultures** are groups of people who share values, customs, and norms related to mutual interests or characteristics besides their national citizenship. A co-culture isn't based on the country where we were born or the national society in which we were raised. Instead, it is composed of smaller groups of people with whom we identify.

THE BASES OF CO-CULTURES. Some co-cultures are based on shared activities or beliefs. If you're into fly fishing, organic gardening, or political activism, for example, then there are co-cultures for those interests. Similarly, Buddhists have beliefs and traditions that distinguish them from Baptists, regardless of where they grew up.

Some co-cultures reflect differences in mental or physical abilities. For instance, many deaf populations have certain values and customs that differ from those of hearing populations.[14] Even if they don't share the same language, political positions, or religious beliefs, deaf people often share distinctive social customs. For example, whereas many people would be uncomfortable having constant eye contact with another person while talking, deaf people frequently maintain a steady mutual gaze while communicating through sign language. As well, they often make it a point to notify others in the group if they are leaving the room, even if just for a few moments. Because they cannot hear one another call out from another room, that practice helps prevent frantic searches for the person who has left. (Among hearing people, it would be considered annoying at the very least to announce one's every departure.) Sharing those and other customs, then, helps deaf people interact with one another as members of a shared co-culture.[15]

BELONGING TO MULTIPLE CO-CULTURES. Most people identify with several co-cultures at once. You can probably relate to co-cultures for your age group, ethnicity, religion, sexual orientation, musical tastes, athletic interests, and even your college major. Every one of those groups probably has its own values, beliefs, traditions, customs, and even ways of using language that distinguish it from other groups. Going further, some co-cultures have smaller co-cultures within them. For example, the deaf co-culture comprises people who advocate using only sign language, as well as individuals who support the use of cochlear implants, devices that may help a person hear.

Social Media as a Co-Culture

When thinking about cultures and co-cultures, it can be easy to focus only on groups of people who are similar in geography (such as "the culture of the South") or in their personal characteristics (such as "the culture of the elderly"). To the extent that users of social media have symbols, language, values, or norms in common, however, it makes sense also to think of the culture of social media. Various social media platforms—such as Twitter, Facebook, Instagram, Snapchat, Pinterest, and Google Plus—are a primary means of communicating interpersonally for a great many people. That's especially true for adolescents and young adults, who have grown up with online communication technologies fully integrated into their communication lives. Has social media become so dominant that it deserves to be considered its own co-culture? Consider the following:

- Approximately 400 million snaps are sent every day on Snapchat.
- One out of every six people on the planet has a Facebook account.
- Roughly 500 million tweets are sent every day.
- Six billion hours of video are watched on YouTube every month.
- Twenty-three percent of adolescents name Instagram as their favorite social network.[16]

As we have discussed in this chapter, cultures and co-cultures are characterized by symbols, language, values, and norms. Consider the ways that social media has, in just a few years, evolved to create a unique co-culture, and how that culture is reflected interpersonally when we communicate online. Within that culture, we can recognize "the co-culture of Instagram," for instance, and "the co-culture of Twitter." In these and other co-cultures, words and symbols emerge—for example, hashtags, memes, and jargon—that become cultural norms among users of each platform.

Focus on Scholarship: People often *prefer* similarity, judging similar others more favorably than dissimilar others. In one study, African American, Hispanic, and Caucasian applicants were interviewed for a job by someone of either their own or a different ethnic group. The applicants then rated the interviewers. African American and Hispanic applicants scored interviewers of their same ethnic group significantly more favorably than interviewers of a different ethnic group. The differences for Caucasian applicants were not significant.[ii]

[ii]Lin, T.-R., Dobbins, G. H., & Farh, J.-L. (1992). A field study of race and age similarity effects on interview ratings in conventional and situational interviews. *Journal of Applied Psychology, 77*, 363–371.

similarity assumption
One's tendency to presume that others think the same way he or she does.

Communicating with Cultural Awareness

People with different cultural backgrounds don't just communicate differently; in many cases, they also *think* differently. Those differences can present real challenges when people from different cultures interact.

The same thing can happen even when people from different co-cultures communicate. For instance, teenagers and senior citizens may have difficulty getting along because their customs and values are so different. Adolescents often enjoy the most contemporary music and fashions, whereas seniors frequently prefer songs and clothing that they enjoyed as younger adults. Teenagers may value independence and individuality; older people may value loyalty, family, and community.

Young and elderly people might speak the same language, but they don't necessarily use language in the same ways. Young adults may have no problem understanding one another when they talk about blogging and texting, for example, but their grandparents may have no idea what these terms mean. Maybe you've experienced that kind of situation, or perhaps you've seen other co-cultures have difficulty understanding each other, such as Democrats and Republicans, or gay and straight people.

To complicate that problem, people from different cultures (and co-cultures) not only differ in how they think and behave, they're also often unaware of how they differ. For instance, a U.S. college professor might think a Japanese student is being dishonest because the student doesn't look her in the eyes. In the United States that behavior can suggest dishonesty. Within Japanese society, however, it signals respect. If neither the professor nor the student is aware of how the other is likely to interpret the behavior, it's easy to see how a misunderstanding could arise.

Communicating effectively with people from other cultures and co-cultures requires us to be aware of how their behaviors and ways of thinking are likely to differ from our own. Unfortunately, that is easier said than done. Many of us operate on what researchers call a **similarity assumption**—that is, we presume that most people think the same way we do, without asking ourselves whether that's true.[17] In the preceding example, the professor thought the student was being dishonest because she assumed the lack of eye contact had the same meaning for the student that it had for her. The student assumed the professor would interpret his lack of eye contact as a sign of respect, because that's how he understood and intended it.

The similarity assumption is also reflected in people's communications online. When posting a tweet or commenting on a news item, for instance, many communicators express strong opinions on issues without considering whether others might disagree. As an example, Justin believes strongly in same-sex marriage rights, so he makes statements online that leave no room for debate, such as his Facebook posting that "no one in his or her right mind could be against marriage equality for same-sex partners." Justin expresses himself this way because he assumes that anyone who reads his post would agree. A more competent approach would be for Justin to recognize that his opinion reflects his own perspective and to acknowledge that others may think differently. A better way for Justin to make his statement might be to post something like "I believe in marriage equality for everyone. If you agree, now is the time to pressure the legislature to lift the ban on same-sex marriage in our state."

Questioning your cultural assumptions can be a challenge, because you're probably often unaware that you hold them in the first place. However, it's worth the effort to try, since checking your assumptions when interacting with people of other cultures can make you a more effective communicator.

LEARN IT What is a culture, and how is it different from a society? How do societies use symbols, language, values, and norms to reflect their cultures? What are some examples of co-cultures? What is the similarity assumption, and how does it affect how you communicate with others, both in person and online?

APPLY IT Choose two of your close friends, and make a list of the co-cultures to which each friend belongs. Include co-cultures for age, ethnicity, disability, religion, and activities or interests if they are relevant. Next to each co-culture that you list, write down one statement about how you think it affects your friend's personality or communication style. What did you learn about each friend by going through this exercise?

REFLECT ON IT With which in-groups do you identify the most strongly? When have you noticed your own cultural awareness being challenged? How did you respond?

2 How Culture Affects Communication

If you've ever had difficulty communicating with someone from a different cultural background, you've experienced the challenge of overcoming cultural differences in communication. Dutch social psychologist Geert Hofstede and American anthropologist Edward T. Hall have pioneered the study of cultures and cultural differences. Their work and that of others suggest that seven cultural differences, in particular, influence how people interact with one another.

In the IM: Try the in-class activity "Culture/Gender Challenges in a Hat" to illustrate some challenges inherent in communicating across cultures or across the sexes.

Individualism and Collectivism

One way cultures differ is in how much they emphasize individuals rather than groups. In an **individualistic culture,** people believe that their primary responsibility is to themselves. Children in individualistic cultures are raised hearing messages such as "Be yourself," "You're special," and "There's no one else in the world who's just like you." Those messages emphasize the importance of knowing oneself, being self-sufficient, and being true to what one wants in life.[18] Indeed, the motto in an individualistic culture might be "I gotta be me!" People in individualistic societies also value self-reliance and the idea that people should "pull themselves up by their own bootstraps"—help themselves when they need it—instead of waiting for others to help them. Research shows that the United States, Canada, Great Britain, and Australia are among the world's most individualistic societies.[19]

individualistic culture
A culture that emphasizes individuality and responsibility to oneself.

In contrast, people in a **collectivistic culture** are taught that their primary responsibility is to their families, communities, and employers. Instead of emphasizing the importance of being an individual, collectivistic cultures focus on taking care of the needs of the group. People in collectivistic cultures place a high value on duty and loyalty, and they see themselves not as unique or special but as a part of the groups to which they belong. Among the Kabre of Togo, for instance, people try to give away many of their material possessions to build relationships and benefit their social groups.[20] The motto in a collectivistic culture might be "I am my family and my family is me." Collectivistic cultures include Korea, Japan, and many countries in Africa and Latin America.[21]

collectivistic culture
A culture that places greater emphasis on loyalty to the family, workplace, or community than on the needs of the individual.

Cultural values are often expressed through personal appearance. Among the Maori of New Zealand, tattoos are commonly used to reflect collectivism, their shared sense of heritage and community. When people in the United States sport similar, tribal-style tattoos, it's often to express their individuality rather than their connection to a group or community. © *Topham/The Image Works,* © *Lisa Anne Auer Bach/Corbis, RF*

Focus on Ethics: Ask students to suppose they're starting their junior year of college when an elderly family member falls ill and needs care. Should they put their education on hold to tend to their relative's needs, or determine that taking care of this relative isn't their responsibility? The former response is more collectivistic, the latter more individualistic. What are the ethical implications of each?

low-context culture A culture in which verbal communication is expected to be explicit and is often interpreted literally.

high-context culture A culture in which verbal communication is often ambiguous, and meaning is drawn from contextual cues, such as facial expressions and tone of voice.

How individualistic or collectivistic a culture is can affect communication behavior in several ways. When people in individualistic cultures experience conflict with one another, for instance, they are expected to express it and work toward resolving it. In contrast, as communication scholars Deborah Cai and Edward Fink explain, people in collectivistic cultures are taught to handle disagreements much less directly, to preserve social harmony.[22] Instead of confronting the person with whom they have disagreements, for instance, they may avoid the conflict entirely or try to find a compromise that meets everyone's needs.

Low- and High-Context Cultures

If you've traveled much, you may have noticed that people's language in various parts of the world differs in how direct and explicit it is. In a **low-context culture,** people are expected to be direct, say what they mean, and not "beat around the bush." Low-context cultures value expressing oneself, sharing personal opinions, and trying to persuade others to see things one's way.[23] The United States is an example of a low-context society, as are Canada, Israel, and most northern European countries.

In contrast, people in a **high-context culture,** such as Korea, the Maori of New Zealand, and Native Americans, are taught to speak much less directly. In those societies, maintaining harmony and avoiding offending people are more important than expressing one's true feelings.[24] As a result, people speak in a less direct, more ambiguous manner and convey much more of their meaning through subtle behaviors and contextual cues such as facial expressions and tone of voice.

As an example of how this cultural difference affects communication, consider a conversation between Hae-Won, an accountant who grew up in South Korea, and Terrance, her American colleague. Because she has been raised in a high-context culture, Hae-Won is uncomfortable being direct about what she wants, preferring instead to communicate indirectly. As the lunch hour approaches in their office, she tells Terrance that she is hungry but cannot leave her desk to get lunch. She hopes Terrance will "read between the lines" of her message and offer to pick up some lunch for her. Having grown up in a low-context culture, however, Terrance interprets her words literally.

He assumes that if she wanted him to bring her lunch, she would ask for that. On the basis of her words, he instead concludes that Hae-Won is choosing to skip lunch and keep working.

When people from low- and high-context cultures communicate with one another, the potential for misunderstanding is great. Imagine that you have asked two of your friends if they'd like to meet you tomorrow evening for a coffee tasting at a popular bookstore café. Your friend Tina, who's from a low-context culture, says, "No, I've got a lot of studying to do, but thanks anyway." Lee, who grew up in a high-context culture, nods his head and says, "That sounds like fun." Thus, you're surprised later when Lee doesn't show up.

How can you account for those different behaviors? The answer is that people raised in high-context cultures are often reluctant to say no—even when they mean no—for fear of causing offense. Another person from Lee's culture might have understood from Lee's facial expression or tone of voice that he didn't intend to go to the coffee tasting with you. Because you grew up in a low-context society, however, you interpreted his answer and head nods to mean he was accepting your invitation.

When people from low- and high-context cultures communicate with one another, the potential for misunderstanding is great. © Sam Edwards/ Getty Images, RF

Low- and High-Power-Distance Cultures

A third way cultures differ from one another is in the degree to which power is evenly distributed. Several characteristics can give someone power, including money or other valuable resources, education, expertise, age, popularity, talent, intelligence, and experience. In democratic societies, people believe in the value of equality—that all men and women are created equal and that no one person or group should have excessive power. That belief is characteristic of **low-power-distance cultures.** The United States and Canada fall in this category, as do Israel, New Zealand, Denmark, and Austria.[25] People in low-power-distance cultures are raised to believe that even though some individuals are born with more advantages (such as wealth or fame), no one is inherently better than anyone else. That doesn't necessarily mean that people in such cultures *are* treated equally, only that they value the idea that they should be.

In **high-power-distance cultures,** power is distributed less evenly. Certain groups, such as the royal family or the ruling political party, have great power, and the average citizen has much less. People in such cultures are taught that certain people or groups deserve to have more power than others and that respecting power is more important than respecting equality. Mexico, Brazil, India, Singapore, and the Philippines are examples of high-power-distance cultures.[26]

Power distance affects many aspects of interpersonal communication. For example, people in low-power-distance cultures usually expect friendships and romantic relationships to be based on love rather than social status. In contrast, people in high-power-distance cultures are expected to choose friends or mates from within their social class.[27]

Another difference involves the way people think about authority. In low-power-distance cultures such as the United States and Canada, individuals are often taught

Cultural norms about power distance can change over time. A few generations ago, Britons would have been shocked by Prince William's marriage to Kate Middleton, a commoner. © *Mark Cuthbert/Getty Images*

that it is their right—even their responsibility—to question authority. For example, it is not uncommon for an American child to ask "Why?" when he or she is told to do something by a parent or teacher. In contrast, children raised in India or Japan would be unlikely to question their parents or supervisors, because high-power-distance cultures place great emphasis on obedience and respect for those in power. In high-power-distance cultures, people are taught to obey parents and teachers without question.[28]

That difference is also seen in the relationships and communication patterns people have with their employers. Workers in low-power-distance cultures value autonomy, the right to make choices about the way they do their jobs, and the ability to have input into decisions that affect them. Such workers might provide their input through union spokespersons or employee satisfaction surveys. In contrast, employees in high-power-distance cultures are used to having little or no say about how to do their jobs. They expect their employers to make the decisions and are more likely to follow those decisions without question.

Masculine and Feminine Cultures

We usually use the terms *masculine* and *feminine* when referring to people. Hofstede has suggested that we can also apply those terms to cultures.[29] In a highly masculine culture, people tend to cherish traditionally masculine values, such as ambition, achievement, and the acquisition of material goods. They also value sex-specific roles for women and men, preferring that men hold the wage-earning and decision-making positions (such as corporate executive) while women occupy the nurturing positions (such as homemaker). Examples of masculine cultures are Austria, Japan, and Mexico.

In contrast, in a highly feminine culture, people tend to value nurturance, quality of life, and service to others, all of which are stereotypically feminine qualities. They also tend to believe that men's and women's roles should not be strongly differentiated. Compared with masculine cultures, therefore, it would not be as unusual for a man to care for children or a woman to be her family's primary wage earner. Examples of feminine cultures are Sweden, Chile, and the Netherlands.

According to Hofstede's research, the United States has a moderately masculine culture. U.S. Americans tend to value sex-differentiated roles—although not as strongly as Austrians, Japanese, or Mexicans do—and they place a fairly high value on stereotypically masculine qualities such as achievement and the acquisition of resources.[30]

Monochronic and Polychronic Cultures

Cultures also vary with respect to their norms and expectations concerning the use of time. Societies that have a **monochronic** concept of time, such as Swiss, Germans, and most Americans, view time as a commodity. We save time, spend time, fill time, invest time, and waste time as though time were tangible. We treat time as valuable, believe that "time is money," and talk about making time and losing time.[31]

A monochronic orientation toward time influences several social behaviors. Because people in monochronic cultures think of time as valuable, they hate to waste it. Therefore, they expect meetings and classes to start on time (within a minute or so), and when that doesn't happen, they are willing to wait only so long before leaving. They also expect others to show up when they say they will.

⋮ **monochronic** A concept that treats time as a finite commodity that can be earned, saved, spent, and wasted.

In comparison, societies with a **polychronic** orientation—which include Latin America, the Arab part of the Middle East, and much of sub-Saharan Africa—conceive of time as more holistic and fluid and less structured. Instead of treating time as a finite commodity that must be managed properly to avoid being wasted, people in polychronic cultures perceive it more like a never-ending river, flowing infinitely into the future.[32]

Schedules are more fluid and flexible in polychronic than in monochronic cultures. In the polychronic culture of Pakistan, for instance, if you're invited to a wedding that begins at 4:30 P.M. and you arrive at that hour, you will most likely be the first one there. A bank may not open at a specified time—as would be expected in a monochronic society—but whenever the manager decides. People in a polychronic culture do not prioritize efficiency and punctuality. Instead, they attach greater value to the quality of their lives and their relationships with others.

Uncertainty Avoidance

People have a natural tendency to avoid unfamiliar and uncomfortable situations. In other words, we dislike uncertainty, and in fact uncertainty causes many of us a good deal of stress.[33] Not all cultures find uncertainty to be equally problematic, however. Cultures vary in what Hofstede called **uncertainty avoidance,** or the extent to which people try to avoid situations that are unstructured, unclear, or unpredictable.[34] Individuals from cultures that are highly uncertainty avoidant are drawn to people and situations that are familiar, and they are relatively unlikely to take risks, for fear of failure. They are also uncomfortable with differences of opinion, and they tend to favor rules and laws that maximize security and reduce ambiguity wherever possible. Argentina, Portugal, and Uruguay are among the most uncertainty avoidant societies.

In contrast, people in uncertainty-accepting cultures are more open to new situations, and they are more accommodating of people and ideas that are different from their own. They take a "live and let live" approach, preferring as few rules as possible that would restrict their behaviors. Societies with cultures that are highly accepting of uncertainty include Hong Kong, Jamaica, and New Zealand. Hofstede has determined that U.S. society is more accepting than avoidant of uncertainty, but it is closer to the midpoint of the scale than many countries are.

Cultural Communication Codes

Finally, cultures differ from one another in their use of **communication codes,** which are verbal and nonverbal behaviors whose meanings are often understood only by people from the same culture. Three kinds of communication codes—idioms, jargon, and gestures—differ greatly from society to society and can make intercultural communication especially challenging.

IDIOMS.   An idiom is a phrase whose meaning is purely figurative; that is, we cannot understand the meaning by interpreting the words literally. For example, most U.S. adults know the phrase "kicking the bucket" has nothing to do with kicking a bucket. In U.S. society, that is an idiom that means "to die." Similarly, "shaking a leg" means hurrying, "breaking a leg" means having a great performance, and to "re-boot" means to start over.

polychronic A concept that treats time as an infinite resource rather than a finite commodity.

uncertainty avoidance The degree to which people try to avoid situations that are unstructured, unclear, or unpredictable.

communication codes Verbal and nonverbal behaviors, such as idioms and gestures, that characterize a culture and distinguish it from other cultures.

Every society has its own idioms whose meanings are not necessarily obvious to people from other cultures. In Portugal, for instance, a person who "doesn't give one for the box" is someone who can't say or do anything right. In Finland, if something "becomes gingerbread," that means it goes completely wrong. Likewise, if an Australian is "as flash as a rat with a gold tooth," he's very pleased with himself. When we interact with people from other societies, we need to be aware that they may use unfamiliar phrases.[35]

Cultural differences in language use can also make it hard to translate phrases or slogans from one society to the next. The challenge is evident in the following humorous examples of mistranslated signs and advertisements:

- Sign in a Bangkok dry cleaner: "Drop your trousers here for best results!"
- Sign in a Copenhagen airline ticket office: "We take your bags and send them in all directions."
- Sign in a Hong Kong tailor shop: "Ladies may have a fit upstairs."
- Sign in an Acapulco restaurant: "The manager has personally passed all the water served here."
- Sign in a Moscow hotel room: "If this is your first visit to the USSR, you are welcome to it."

JARGON. A specific form of idiomatic communication that often separates co-cultures is jargon, or language whose technical meaning is understood by people within that co-culture but not necessarily by those outside it. Physicians, for instance, use precise medical terminology to communicate among themselves about medical conditions and treatments. In most cases, that technical jargon is used only with people in the same co-culture. Therefore, although your doctor might tell her nurse that you have "ecchymosis on a distal phalange," she'd probably just tell you that you have a bruise on your fingertip. Similarly, if your dentist orders a "periapical radiograph," he wants an X-ray of the roots of one of your teeth.

Not understanding co-cultural jargon can make you feel like an outsider. You might even get the impression that co-cultures such as doctors and dentists talk the way they do to reinforce their in-group status. However, jargon can serve an important function by allowing people to communicate specifically, efficiently, and accurately.

GESTURES.   Societies also differ a great deal in their use of gestures, which are movements, usually of the hand or the arm, that express ideas. The same gesture can have different meanings from society to society. For instance, U.S. parents sometimes play the game "I've got your nose!" with infants by putting a thumb between the index and middle finger. That gesture means good luck in Brazil, but it is an obscene gesture in Russia and Indonesia. Similarly, holding up the index and pinky finger while holding down the middle and ring finger is a common gesture for fans of the University of Texas Longhorns. In Italy, however, that gesture is used to suggest that a man's wife has been unfaithful.[36]

The "At a Glance" box summarizes the seven aspects of culture we have surveyed. Keep these dimensions in mind as you communicate cross-culturally, to hone your skill in such interactions.

How sensitive are you to other cultures? Fill out the Intercultural Sensitivity Scale in the "Assess Your Skills" box to find out. If your score is lower than you'd like,

© Kelly-Mooney Photography/ Documentary Value/Corbis

Seven Aspects of Culture

Individualism and Collectivism	Whether a culture emphasizes the needs of the individual or the group
Low and High Context	Whether language is expected to be explicit or subtle
Low- and High-Power Distance	Whether power is widely or narrowly distributed among people
Masculine and Feminine	Whether traditionally masculine or feminine values are promoted
Monochronic and Polychronic	Whether time is seen as a finite commodity or an infinite resource
Uncertainty Avoidance	Whether people welcome or shy away from uncertainty
Communication Codes	How idioms, jargon, and gestures reflect cultural values

(web site)

remember that the first step to becoming more culturally sensitive is learning as much as you can about what culture is and how cultures vary.

Do you ever feel that men and women don't speak quite the same language? In the next section, we examine several reasons why that may sometimes be the case.

LEARN IT In what ways do people from individualistic and collectivistic cultures differ in their communication behaviors? Do people use more explicit language in high- or low-context cultures? Is power more evenly distributed in a high- or a low-power-distance culture? What makes a culture feminine as opposed to masculine? How do people from monochronic and polychronic cultures differ in their use of time? In what ways does a culture's uncertainty avoidance affect the communication behaviors of its members? Why are idioms and gestures examples of cultural communication codes?

APPLY IT Select a gesture that is commonly used in U.S. society, such as the thumbs-up or OK sign. Using the Internet, research and document the many different interpretations that gesture has in cultures around the world. This exercise will sharpen your skill as an intercultural communicator by helping you avoid awkwardly misusing that gesture.

REFLECT ON IT How are culture's effects on communication learned and reinforced? What challenges have you experienced when communicating with people from other cultures?

3 Understanding Gender and Communication

What do you look like online? Avatars are graphic representations that communicators construct to represent themselves in online environments. In the world of online gaming, some players choose avatars that resemble their true identities, but others construct personas far different from themselves. A common example is the practice

Talking Point: Students might be interested to know that even though there are slightly more females than males in the world, more males are actually born. Males are more likely than females to die as infants.

assess your skills | HOW CULTURALLY SENSITIVE ARE YOU?

On the line before each of the following statements, record your level of agreement on a 1–5 scale. Higher numbers mean you agree more, and lower numbers mean you agree less.

1. _____ I enjoy interacting with people from different cultures.
2. _____ I am pretty sure of myself when interacting with people from different cultures.
3. _____ I rarely find it very hard to talk in front of people from different cultures.
4. _____ I like to be with people from different cultures.
5. _____ I respect the values of people from different cultures.
6. _____ I tend to wait before forming an impression of people from different cultures.
7. _____ I am open-minded to people from different cultures.
8. _____ I am very observant when interacting with people from different cultures.
9. _____ I respect the ways people from different cultures behave.
10. _____ I try to obtain as much information as I can when interacting with people from different cultures.

When you're finished, add your scores and write the total on this line: _____. The ranges below will help you assess how culturally sensitive you are.

- 10–25: Cultural sensitivity is a skill you can improve, and the material in this chapter may help.

- 26–35: You are sometimes comfortable in intercultural conversations, but they make you uncomfortable from time to time. Continued practice may improve your ease in communicating interculturally.

- 36–50: You find it relatively easy to interact with people from other cultures.

Source: Chen, G. M., & Starosta, W. J. (2000). The development and validation of the Intercultural Sensitivity Scale. *Human Communication, 3*, 1–14.

of gender-switching, wherein players play as characters of the opposite sex. In a 2014 project, for instance, researchers recruited 375 gamers to complete a quest in *World of Warcraft* while their movements and chats were recorded. They found that nearly a quarter of the men chose female avatars, and played the game as though they were female (compared to only 7 percent of women whose avatars were male). Importantly, though, the men who gender-switched didn't play their female parts very convincingly: They communicated in more expressive and emotional ways than the men who didn't gender-switch, but their movement through the quest remained stereotypically male. Compared to women, men stayed farther away from groups, jumped more often, and moved backward more frequently—whether they were pretending to be female or not.[37]

The experiences of online gamers reflect a very real truth: In both overt and subtle ways, gender influences who we are and how we act. It is a defining feature of our identity, shaping the way we think, look, and communicate. After all, what's the first question you ask about a new baby? "Is it a boy or a girl?"

Although gender is powerful, it is far from simple or straightforward. The concept of gender includes many influences, such as psychological gender roles, biological sex,

Online gamers often create and play as characters that do not conform to their own gender. Research suggests that their style of play may be related to their choice of avatar.
© McGraw-Hill Education/Aaron Roeth, photographer

and sexual orientation. Some interpersonal behaviors are strongly influenced by psychological gender roles, and others are more strongly influenced by biological sex or sexual orientation. In this section, we'll take a look at these components of gender, and we'll critique one of the most common explanations for why communicating across gender lines can be so challenging.

I will use the word *gender* as a broad term encompassing the influences of gender roles, biological sex, and sexual orientation in places where I'm not drawing specific distinctions among those terms. Otherwise, I will use *gender roles* in reference to masculinity, femininity, and androgyny. When addressing the differences between females and males, I'll apply the term *biological sex* (or simply *sex*), and I'll use *sexual orientation* when discussing how one's sexuality influences behavior. See Figure 1 for an illustration of how I'm using these various terms.

Talking Point: The challenge in communicating across gender lines is a common theme for movies and television shows, especially comedies. Ask students what examples they can think of.

In the IM: The in-class activity "Sex Stereotypes" will encourage students to articulate, and perhaps to evaluate, their stereotypes about women and men.

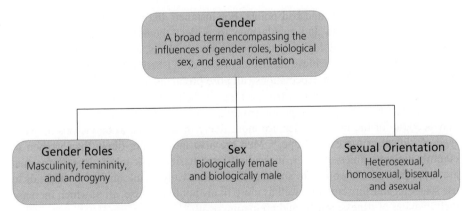

Gender
A broad term encompassing the influences of gender roles, biological sex, and sexual orientation

Gender Roles
Masculinity, femininity, and androgyny

Sex
Biologically female and biologically male

Sexual Orientation
Heterosexual, homosexual, bisexual, and asexual

FIGURE 1 Diagram Explaining Gender, Biological Sex, and Sexual Orientation
Communication research has examined effects of gender roles, biological sex, and sexual orientation on interpersonal communication behavior.

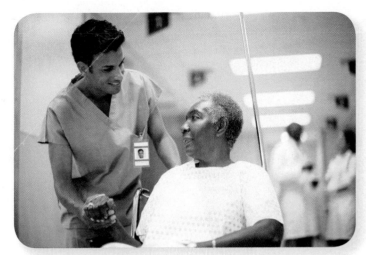
Caregiving has stereotypically been considered a feminine behavior, yet many skilled caregivers are men. © Brooklyn Production/Corbis, RF

Gender Roles and Communication

A role is a set of behaviors expected of someone in a particular social position. Expectations for male and female behavior make up a culture's **gender roles,** or norms for how women and men are supposed to act. In the United States, for instance, by tradition men are the breadwinners, and women are the homemakers. Men are supposed to be interested in cars, sports, and guns; women, to like shopping, cooking, and childrearing.[38] That doesn't mean men and women always *have* those interests, only that traditional gender roles suggest that they ought to. Similarly, in many cultures, men are expected to make the decisions and occupy the positions of power, although that is not always the reality.[39]

Such expectations reflect culturally influenced ideas about what it means to be a woman or a man. We can think of gender roles as falling into three specific categories: masculinity, femininity, and androgyny.

THE MASCULINE GENDER ROLE. When used in reference to people rather than cultures, the term **masculinity** refers to the set of gender role expectations a society typically assigns to men, although anyone can have masculine characteristics and communication behavior patterns. Specific masculine qualities might differ from one culture to the next, but the masculine role usually emphasizes strength, competition, independence, sexual aggressiveness, risk taking, logical thinking, and the acquisition of resources. Traditional masculinity also tends to reject weakness, emotional expressiveness, and characteristics or behaviors that resemble those of women.[40] In childhood, masculine behavior includes playing with toy guns and cars and competing in sports, since those activities emphasize strength, dominance, and winning. Masculine behavior in adulthood includes being a leader, being a breadwinner, and focusing more on action than on talk.

Masculinity has good and bad points. For instance, the emphasis on strength and dominance can motivate and enable men to protect themselves and their families against threats. Thinking logically can help solve problems, and being willing to take risks can help someone achieve things he or she didn't believe were possible. At the same time, masculine role expectations can pose problems. For example, the emphasis on independence may keep men from asking for help—such as medical care—when they need it.[41] Focusing on competition and aggression can put men in harm's way and may account for the fact that men are more likely than women to be victims in every type of violent crime except rape.[42] Men are also much more likely than women to commit violent crimes. Further, masculinity emphasizes risk taking; therefore, men are more likely than women to smoke, drink excessively, drink and drive, and fail to use seatbelts and sunscreen, as well as more likely not to exercise, all of which increase their chances of illness, injury, and premature death.[43]

THE FEMININE GENDER ROLE. The set of role expectations a society typically assigns to women is called **femininity,** although this term can characterize either sex.[44]

gender role A set of expectations for appropriate behavior that a culture typically assigns to an individual based on his or her biological sex.

masculinity A gender role, typically assigned to men, that emphasizes strength, dominance, competition, and logical thinking.

Focus on Scholarship: Scholars disagree as to why, generally speaking, men and women have such different interests. Some suggest that it's because parents encourage different interests in their male and female children (e.g., by encouraging boys to play football and girls to play house). Others argue that girls and boys are inherently interested in different activities and that parents are simply reinforcing a difference that already exists, not creating it.

femininity A gender role, typically assigned to women, that emphasizes expressive, nurturing behavior.

In general, the feminine gender role typically emphasizes empathy and emotional expressiveness; a focus on relationships and on maintaining them; an interest in bearing and raising children; and attentiveness to appearance. Traditional femininity also emphasizes cooperation and submissiveness and tends to downplay intellectual achievement and career ambition.

Like masculinity, femininity has pros and cons. The focus on caregiving has helped to ensure the survival of countless generations of children and families. The emphasis on empathy and relationships has allowed women to build strong, intimate friendships with one another and to excel at careers that require interpersonal sensitivity, such as teaching and counseling. Emphasizing cooperation instead of competition has probably also helped women to solve interpersonal problems in mutually beneficial ways. However, traditional femininity can also impose limits on the choices and options available to women. In the past, tradition discouraged many women from pursuing their education and achieving their career goals out of the belief that a woman's proper place is in the home. In addition, the emphasis on appearance puts tremendous pressure on women to achieve certain body types. As a result, women are far more likely than men to develop depression and eating disorders.[45] The focus on submissiveness has also made it difficult for some women to leave abusive relationships.[46]

THE ANDROGYNOUS GENDER ROLE. Masculinity and femininity are separate concepts, but they are not mutually exclusive, meaning that it is possible for people to identify strongly with both masculinity and femininity. For instance, Carole identifies with the feminine gender role in many ways—she loves raising her children, she enjoys caring for cancer patients as an oncology nurse, and she takes great pride in her appearance. In many other ways, though, she also identifies with the masculine gender role: she is the primary breadwinner for her family, an assertive leader in her union at work, and a fiercely competitive athlete on the basketball court. **Androgyny** is the term used to describe such a combination of masculine and feminine characteristics. When a person strongly identifies with both gender roles, we say that he or she is psychologically androgynous.[47]

Being androgynous does not mean that a person tries to look, act, or sound like the other sex, and it is not necessarily related to sexuality. Androgynous individuals are in touch with both masculine and feminine traits, able to behave in either masculine or feminine ways, depending on what the situation calls for. In her role as a cancer nurse, for example, Carole shows great compassion for her patients and tends to their needs in a comforting and understanding way. In her job as a union leader, however, she communicates assertively, logically, and unemotionally with hospital management.

HOW GENDER VARIES BY TIME AND CULTURE. Gender roles are never set in stone. Like most roles, they change over time, and they vary from culture to culture. In the United States, for example, images of women and men in the media—including movies, television shows, and advertisements—have changed dramatically within the last several decades. In the 1950s, TV shows such as *Leave It to Beaver* and *Father Knows Best* depicted men, women, and children in gender-specific ways. Fathers were strong, authoritative, and the sole family breadwinners. Mothers were homemakers whose concerns centered on their husbands, children, and housework. Boys were interested in masculine activities, such as fishing and playing with cars, and girls pursued feminine activities, such as playing with dolls and baking cakes. More recent television shows, including *Law & Order, Madam Secretary,* and *Modern Family,* have portrayed

Outside of Class: Contemporary adults may have difficulty identifying educational or career limitations associated with femininity. Have your students informally interview older women they know (mothers, grandmothers, and so on) to see if these individuals felt at all constrained in their educational or career choices as younger women.

androgyny A gender role distinguished by a combination of masculine and feminine characteristics.

a more flexible femininity and masculinity. Women work outside the home, sometimes in traditionally masculine professions such as law enforcement and politics, and men express their feelings, even with other men. And in fact, television shows such as *The Good Wife* and *Hawaii Five-O* offer uncharacteristically strong portrayals of female characters.

Gender roles also differ by culture. For example, in nomadic societies, in which people move from place to place to hunt and forage, there is little difference in girls' and boys' upbringing. Everyone's daily tasks are similar—to find food and water—so there is little need to differentiate the roles of girls and boys. In contrast, agricultural societies that rely on farming and herding for their food usually socialize boys and girls very differently, raising girls to care for the children and home and boys to tend to the livestock and crops.[48]

As discussed earlier, culture's influence on gender roles is so strong that researchers label cultures themselves as masculine or feminine. In masculine cultures, roles for women and men are clearly defined and differentiated, and there is little overlap. It would be highly unusual in a masculine culture for a man to be a stay-at-home dad, for instance, because childcare is considered part of the feminine role. Gender roles in feminine cultures are far less differentiated, however, so there is less of an expectation that women and men will behave differently.

There's no question that gender role expectations influence our lives, but being masculine or feminine is not the same thing as being physically male or female. Next, we'll explore the meaning of biological sex, along with its effects on communication behavior.

Biological Sex and Communication

The term *biological sex* refers to being female or male rather than feminine or masculine. Before we examine how biological sex influences communication behavior, let's take a closer look at what biological sex is and how it differs from gender roles.

When you were conceived, you were neither male nor female. About seven weeks later, though, your genes activated your biological sex. Each of us has 23 pairs of chromosomes, which are strands of DNA, in our cells. The 23rd pair is made up of the sex chromosomes that determine whether we're female or male. Human sex chromosomes are called X and Y, and we inherit one from each parent. Mothers supply us with one X chromosome. Fathers give us either a second X or a Y, depending on which one their sperm is carrying. If we get another X, we grow up female. If we get a Y, we become male.

We tend to think of "male" and "female" as the only categories of biological sex, but some people have difficulty fitting into one or the other group. Understanding the diversity in forms of biological sex helps us appreciate why studying sex differences in communication behavior is often more complex than it may first seem. Consider the following:

- Some people experience conflict between the sex they were born into and the sex they feel they should be. For instance, a person may see herself as male even though she was born female. The term *transgender* describes individuals who experience such conflict.[49] Transgender people may use hormone therapy or sex-reassignment surgery to bring their physical body in line with their self-image. We often refer to those who have undergone such procedures as *transsexual* individuals.[50]

- Not everyone is born with either XX (female) or XY (male) chromosomes. Women with Turner syndrome, for example, have an X chromosome only (XO), and men with Klinefelter syndrome have an extra X chromosome (XXY). Researchers estimate that about 1 in 1,700 people is born with some type of chromosomal disorder.[51]

- Finally, some people have internal sex organs that do not match their external appearance. For instance, a child might be born with a penis but have ovaries instead of testicles. Doctors call that condition *inter-sex,* and it can be caused by delayed physical develop-ment or by hormonal problems.[52] People with this condition are often able to lead normal, healthy lives, although questions about their correct biological sex may make it difficult for others in their social envi-ronments to accept them.[53]

Many individuals struggle with gender identity well into adulthood. On the Amazon.com drama *Transparent,* Jeffrey Tambor's character fully embraces her true, female identity as Maura later in life, when she is already a grandparent. © *Beth Dubber/Amazon Studios/Everett Collection*

Like gender roles, biological sex is a fundamental part of a person's identity. No matter the person's bio-logical sex and gender roles, however, interpersonal behavior can also be influenced by a third aspect of gen-der: sexual orientation.

Sexual Orientation and Communication

Sexual orientation describes the sex or sexes to which an individual is sexually attracted. Scientists disagree over the extent to which sexual orientation is determined genetically (the way biological sex is) versus socially (the way gender roles are). Sexual orientation isn't always considered an aspect of gender, but a growing body of research suggests that it influences communication behavior just as gender roles and biological sex do. We'll look briefly at four patterns of sexual orientation: heterosexuality, homo-sexuality, bisexuality, and asexuality.

HETEROSEXUALITY.   **Heterosexuality** refers to being physically and romantically attracted to people of the other sex. Several studies have confirmed that the major-ity of adults in most societies have experienced mostly heterosexual attraction and have engaged in primarily heterosexual behavior.[54] One possible reason for this tendency is that heterosexual interaction has the potential to support reproduction, whereas other forms of sexual interaction do not. Another reason is that in most cultures, heterosexuality is the most socially approved form of sexuality. Therefore, heterosexual people in those cultures enjoy a level of social support that others often do not.[55]

HOMOSEXUALITY.   **Homosexuality** refers to romantic and sexual attraction to mem-bers of one's own sex. Homosexual males are commonly referred to as "gay," and female homosexuals are typically called "lesbian." Although sexual contact between members of the same sex has been common across cultures and time periods, homo-sexuality did not become a recognized part of a person's identity until the 1800s.[56] Before that point, it was not uncommon for adults of the same sex to sleep in the same bed or to write love letters to each other, but such behaviors were interpreted as expres-sions of affection rather than markers of sexual orientation.[57]

Researchers have developed many different theories to explain homosexuality. Some studies have focused on the social influences of parents and other role models, whereas others have emphasized physiological or genetic differences.[58] According to a national

sexual orientation A characteristic determin-ing the sex or sexes to which someone is sexually attracted.

heterosexuality A sexual orientation characterized by sexual interest in members of the other sex.

homosexuality A sexual orientation characterized by sexual interest in members of one's own sex.

fact OR fiction?   SAME-SEX RELATIONSHIPS ARE LESS STABLE THAN HETEROSEXUAL RELATIONSHIPS

There's a great deal of disagreement these days about whether homosexual adults should be allowed to marry. A 2015 U.S. Supreme Court decision made same-sex marriage legal throughout the United States, yet many people fiercely disapprove. Opponents of same-sex marriage have long claimed that gay and lesbian relationships are less stable and more dysfunctional than heterosexual relationships. Is that true?

At this point the answer appears to be no. In fact, several studies have shown that same-sex romantic relationships are just as stable and satisfying, on average, as opposite-sex relationships. For example, one study compared heterosexual married couples with same-sex couples who had legal civil unions. After ruling out any differences in the participants' age, education level, and income, the researchers found that people in same-sex couples actually reported higher relationship quality, intimacy, and compatibility than those in heterosexual

© Creatas Images/2009 Jupiterimages Corporation/Jupiter Images, RF

couples. Same-sex pairs also experienced less conflict in their relationships.

Those findings do not suggest that all gay and lesbian couples are happy and problem-free. They do indicate, however, that same-sex relationships can be just as stable and satisfying as heterosexual relationships. Whatever your individual beliefs about the morality of homosexual relationships, the argument that they are prone to dysfunction does not stand up to the evidence.

ASK YOURSELF

- Where do you stand on this issue? What type of evidence is the most persuasive to you?

- What do you think contributes to relationship stability and satisfaction?

Source: Balsam, K. F., Beauchaine, T. P., Rothblum, E. D., & Solomon, S. E. (2008). Three-year follow-up of same-sex couples who had civil unions in Vermont, same-sex couples not in civil unions, and heterosexual married couples. *Developmental Psychology, 44,* 102–116.

Focus on Ethics: In 2007, the online dating service eHarmony was sued for refusing to offer its services to gays, lesbians, and bisexuals. As a private business, is eHarmony ethically obligated to make its services available to people seeking any kind of romantic relationship? Would it be ethical for an online dating service to cater only to gays, lesbians, and bisexuals and exclude heterosexuals?

bisexuality A sexual orientation characterized by sexual interest in both women and men.

survey conducted by the Centers for Disease Control and Prevention (CDC), 1.7 percent of American men aged 18–44 identified themselves as homosexual, although 5.8 percent reported having had sexual interaction with another man. Similarly, 1.1 percent of American women identified themselves as homosexual, although 12 percent reported having had sexual interaction with another woman.[59]

The question of whether homosexual adults should be allowed to marry or form legal domestic partnerships has been contentious in the United States for some time. The argument against formalizing homosexual romantic relationships often implies that such relationships are inherently less stable than heterosexual marriages. Is that true? Check out the "Fact or Fiction?" box to find out.

BISEXUALITY.   Bisexuality refers to having romantic and/or sexual attraction to both women and men. Although bisexuals have some level of attraction to both sexes, they are not necessarily attracted to both sexes equally.[60] Moreover, bisexual people don't usually maintain long-term romantic relationships with members of both sexes. Rather, they often have a romantic relationship with a partner of one sex while engaging in or thinking about sexual interaction with people of the other sex.[61] According to the CDC survey mentioned earlier, 1.1 percent of men and 3.5 percent of women in the United States identify themselves as bisexual.[62]

Three Components of Gender

Gender Roles	Psychological orientation toward masculinity, femininity, or androgyny
Biological Sex	Genetic characteristics that distinguish females from males
Sexual Orientation	Sexual attraction toward members of the other sex, the same sex, both sexes, or neither sex

ASEXUALITY.   **Asexuality** is used to describe people who have very little interest in sex. This orientation is fairly uncommon. In one U.S. study, for example, fewer than 1 percent of respondents indicated they had never been sexually attracted to anyone.[63] Researchers aren't sure whether asexuality is a disorder or whether it represents another sexual orientation. Asexuality is not the same as *celibacy,* which is the practice of abstaining from sex. In fact, some asexual people do have sex, and most celibate people are not asexual.

A summary of the three primary components of gender appears in the "At a Glance" box.

Some Explanations for Gendered Communication

From time to time, you may feel as though talking with a person of the other sex is like talking to an extraterrestrial. Popular author John Gray captured that sentiment in his book *Men Are from Mars, Women Are from Venus.*[64] According to Gray, "Men and women differ in all areas of their lives. Not only do men and women communicate differently but they think, feel, perceive, react, respond, love, need, and appreciate differently. They almost seem to be from different planets, speaking different languages and needing different nourishment."[65]

Communication experts do not go as far as Gray and claim that men and women might as well be from different planets. Nevertheless, some researchers, including communication scholar Julia Wood and linguist Deborah Tannen, do argue that women and men constitute different *gender cultures,* with each sex being a distinctive culture with its own rules and values.[66] The fundamental difference between the two cultures is that each sex values different components of relationships. Specifically, women are taught to value the communicating of intimacy and emotional support, whereas men are taught to value the sharing of activities.

When Zach and his friend Sergio get together, for instance, their time is likely to revolve around a mutual activity, such as going for a hike or watching car racing on TV, because for them sharing activities is a means of bonding. Sometimes they talk about personal topics, but their conversation is of lesser importance than the shared activity. For Zach's wife Aisha and her friend Thérèse, however, time together is more likely to revolve around conversation. Whatever shared activity they may be doing is often of lesser importance than the conversation itself.

The concept of gender cultures further maintains that when women and men communicate with each other, they each bring their own rules and values to the table. Because these rules and values differ, the result is often *gender clash,* or the experience of each sex not understanding the other.[67] For instance, when Sergio's daughter was undergoing treatment for leukemia, Aisha couldn't understand why Zach didn't invite him over "just to talk" but instead invited him to a baseball game. That action seemed insensitive to Aisha, who

asexuality A sexual orientation characterized by a general lack of interest in sex.

From time to time, you may feel as though talking with a person of the other sex is like talking to an extraterrestrial. © *John Burke/ Polka Dot Images/Jupiter Images, RF*

Focus on Scholarship: Studies on U.S. American adults show that men and women don't differ on how affectionate they are. Rather, they differ in how they communicate affection. Women are more likely to show affection directly, such as through hugs and kisses, whereas men are more likely to express it through supportive behaviors, such as favors.[iii]

[iii]Floyd, K. (2006). *Communicating affection: Interpersonal behavior and social context.* Cambridge, England: Cambridge University Press.

thought Zach should be a better friend to Sergio by getting him to open up about his feelings. As Zach explained, however, going to a ball game and just hanging out with no expectation of a deep conversation was his way of letting Sergio know he cared. He also assured Aisha that Sergio would interpret it that way.

There's little question that communicating across genders can be challenging and that several communicative behaviors appear to be affected by sex, gender roles, and/or sexual orientation. However, some scholars disagree that the sexes constitute different cultures. For example, communication scientists Brant Burleson and Adrianne Kunkel have pointed out that the "different cultures" idea has not been well supported by the data.[68] Several studies have demonstrated that women and men are more similar than different in the forms of communication they value.[69] Indeed, the lack of scientific evidence for the gender cultures idea has led communication researcher Kathryn Dindia to suggest a more modest metaphor for gendered communication: "Men are from North Dakota, women are from South Dakota."[70]

Each of those perspectives—the sexes come from different planets, the sexes represent different cultures, and the sexes are more similar than different—is intuitively appealing in its own way. In fact, it's easy for many of us to see sex differences in communication behavior almost anywhere we look. The fact that many societies make sex differences the focus of jokes, comedic movies, and television shows probably adds to our tendency to see sex differences as large and pervasive.

However, just because an idea is intuitive or seems to reflect our personal experience doesn't mean the idea is accurate. That is one reason why scientific research is so important: It allows us to subject our ideas to rigorous scrutiny. The best scientific evidence tells us that sex, gender roles, and sexual orientation all play a part in how people communicate, but not as large a part as we might think. Women and men differ from each other in many ways—as do masculine, feminine, and androgynous people, and heterosexual, homosexual, bisexual, and asexual people. When it comes to communication behavior, however, we are more alike than different. The research tells us that Gray's claim that women and men "differ in all areas of their lives" may be an exaggeration. It is true that our differences are often more apparent to us than our similarities, but the scientific evidence suggests that as communicators, we are not as different as we often think we are.

LEARN IT How do masculinity, femininity, and androgyny compare with one another? In what ways do psychological, genetic, and anatomical differences influence one's biological sex? What is a sexual orientation? What are the principal ways of explaining gendered communication, and how well are those explanations supported by scientific evidence?

APPLY IT In small groups or with your class as a whole, create a discussion board or blog to identify the ways in which masculine and feminine communication behaviors are taught and reinforced in your society. Consider not only the family, the school system, religion, and the media, but other aspects of social life that teach people how to communicate in gender-specific ways.

REFLECT ON IT How do you feel about people whose sexual orientation is different from yours? How do you think those feelings affect your communication with them? What are the biggest challenges you have noticed in male–female communication?

4 How Gender Affects Communication

Clearly, then, our gender roles, biological sex, and sexual orientation all play a part in how we communicate. In this section, we'll look at differences in language (the use of spoken and written words) and nonverbal behavior (the ways we communicate without words) to gain specific insight into how these various aspects of gender affect our interactions with others.

Before we go on, we need to consider two important points. First, even though gender includes the influences of biological sex, gender roles, and sexual orientation, most of the research we'll examine has simply compared the communication behaviors of men and women. As a result, we know quite a bit about sex differences but comparatively little about the effects of gender roles and sexual orientation on communication. Second, although some behaviors differ between the sexes, other behaviors do not. In addition, some sex differences are large, but many others are fairly small. In fact, several scholars have called for caution when we are looking at sex differences in behavior so that we don't exaggerate them beyond what the evidence supports.[71]

In U.S. culture, women often practice expressive talk, treating communication as a way to establish closeness. © BananaStock/ Alamy, RF

Gender and Verbal Communication

Research shows that gender influences both the content and the style of our speech. Let's take a close look at three gender effects:

- Expressive and instrumental talk
- Language and power
- Gendered linguistic styles

EXPRESSIVE AND INSTRUMENTAL TALK. Some communication scholars have argued that women and men grow up in different "speech communities," meaning they have different norms and beliefs concerning the purpose of communication.[72] That idea is similar to the gender cultures theory, but it focuses more specifically on differences in speech and communication behaviors. In particular, those researchers believe that women are socialized to practice **expressive talk,** which means they are taught to view communication as the primary way to establish closeness and intimacy in relationships. In contrast, men are taught to practice **instrumental talk,** or to see communication as a means to solve problems and accomplish tasks.[73]

To understand these sex-related differences in communication, consider the following scenario. Shannon has noticed that whenever she talks to her co-worker Max about a problem, he always responds by telling her what she should do to fix it. The following exchange illustrates that point.

Shannon: My boss is totally blaming me for losing one of our biggest accounts—but it's completely his fault! He's the one who never returns the customer's calls and wouldn't let me help last year when one of their shipments was delayed.

In the IM: Gender may also influence self-presentation. Students can do the out-of-class activity "Sex Differences in Self-Presentation" to see how.

expressive talk Verbal communication whose purpose is to express emotions and build relationships.

instrumental talk Verbal communication whose purpose is to solve problems and accomplish tasks.

Max: You should call your regional manager and tell her what's going on. Show her the paperwork from the order that got delayed so she'll see that you tried to help.

Max's response is a good example of instrumental talk. When Shannon explains her problem, Max views it as a request for help, and he suggests how to make the situation better. Contrast Max's comments with the response Shannon gets when she shares the same problem with her sister Sabrina:

Sabrina: That's so unfair! I'm sorry he's blaming you—you must be so frustrated, especially since it's his fault in the first place.

In Everyday Life: Understanding the difference between expressive and instrumental talk can help women and men communicate better. Men should remember that when women share problems, they aren't necessarily looking for solutions. Likewise, women should remember that when men offer solutions, they see that as a way of being supportive.

Sabrina's response is an example of expressive talk. Instead of suggesting how Shannon might solve the problem, Sabrina acknowledges Shannon's feelings and expresses her own unhappiness at Shannon's frustration. According to communication scholars such as Julia Wood, that is a common difference between women and men. That is, for women the purpose of sharing problems is to express one's feelings. From that perspective, a good friend should listen and empathize. For men, though, the purpose of sharing problems is to get advice on how to solve them. From that perspective, a good friend should offer his opinions about what to do.[74]

How do men and women become socialized into different speech communities? One of the earliest influences seems to be the childhood games they play. If you think back to your own childhood, you probably remember that at an early age most children played only with other children of their same sex and that boys and girls played very different games.[75] Boys' games, such as football and model building, emphasize structure, rules, and competition. Girls' games, such as playing house and jumping rope, emphasize cooperation, sensitivity, and flexibility. One possible result of those patterns is that boys learn to use language to give instructions and share information, and girls learn to use language to express their feelings and to build camaraderie.[76]

With respect to sexual orientation, the common stereotypes of gay men as feminine and lesbians as masculine would suggest that gay men engage in more expressive and less instrumental talk than heterosexual men, whereas lesbians engage in more instrumental and less expressive talk than heterosexual women. Research indicates that both of those predictions are accurate, although the differences are not large.[77] Importantly, that observation does not mean that gay men talk like women or that lesbian women talk like men. Rather, it suggests only that gay men's speech patterns are more expressive and less instrumental than those of heterosexual men and that lesbian women's speech is more instrumental and less expressive than that of heterosexual women.

LANGUAGE AND POWER.   For years, researchers have noticed that men and women talk to each other in a style that reflects how superiors and subordinates talk to each other.[78] Powerful speech behaviors, such as those used by superiors, include talking more, interrupting more frequently, giving more directions, and expressing more opinions. Less powerful speech behaviors, such as those used by subordinates, include asking more questions, using more hedges ("sort of," "might be") and disclaimers or qualifying statements ("I could be wrong, but . . ."), and speaking less overall.

In an extensive review of the current research, communication scholars Pam Kalbfleisch and Anita Herold found that, on average, American men use more powerful forms of speech than American women.[79] For instance, research indicates that contrary to the stereotype, men are often as talkative as women, as the "Fact or Fiction?" box

Language is described as more powerful or less powerful based on communication behaviors such as interrupting, giving directions, expressing opinions, asking questions, using disclaimers, and speaking more or speaking less. From the perspective of language and power, how would you characterize the speaking styles of the judges on The Voice?
© Trae Patton/NBC/NBCU Photo Bank/Getty Images

explains. In fact, men often talk *more* than women do, particularly about impersonal topics such as money and work.[80] Men also interrupt more frequently, give more directions, and express more opinions—all characteristics of powerful speech.[81] In contrast, women's language use is more attentive to others.[82] Compared with men, women ask more questions and use more disclaimers and hedges in their speech.[83]

The following exchange between two colleagues at an advertising firm illustrates more powerful and less powerful forms of communication.

> **Emelie:** I don't know if this is a good idea, but I sort of think we should keep the new ad slogans secret until we launch the marketing campaign, don't you?
>
> **Stefan:** Find out what the client wants and then we'll decide. The slogans aren't that great anyway. We need to bring some new account reps in on this project and get some fresh ideas in here.

In this exchange, Emelie starts off with a disclaimer ("I don't know if this is a good idea"); she then hedges her opinion ("I sort of think"); and she concludes with a question that seeks validation from others ("don't you?"). In contrast, Stefan's words are directive ("Find out what the client wants") and opinionated ("The slogans aren't that great"). Also, unlike Emelie, Stefan doesn't end his statement by asking if others agree with him. Their conversation exemplifies less powerful (Emelie) and more powerful (Stefan) forms of speech.

Although the research findings are important, keep in mind two critical points. First, the findings don't apply equally to every woman and man. There are women who use very powerful styles of speaking and men whose language styles are less powerful. Whenever we compare groups (such as women and men), we're focusing specifically on average differences. Clearly, there can be many individual exceptions to whatever differences we discover. Second, even if a man uses more powerful speech patterns than a woman does, that doesn't necessarily mean that he *is* more

fact **OR** *fiction?* | WOMEN ARE MORE TALKATIVE THAN MEN

When it comes to sex differences in communication, perhaps the most common stereotype is that women are more talkative than men. Is that idea fact or fiction?

Carefully conducted research tells us that it's fiction. The truth is that women and men speak approximately the same number of words per day: roughly 16,000 on average. The study that identified that finding took place between 1998 and 2005 and involved almost 400 students from universities in the United States and Mexico. Each participant wore a device called an electronically activated recorder, or EAR. The EAR is a digital voice recorder that unobtrusively tracks a person's real-world interactions with others by recording 30-second snippets of sound every 12.5 minutes while the person is awake. The researchers then transcribed each recording and counted the number of words spoken, analyzing them as a function of the percentage of waking time the EAR recorded.

When the researchers compared the results by sex, they found that women and men spoke, on average, 16,215 and 15,669 words per day, respectively. Those totals were not significantly different and thus suggested that the stereotype that women are more talkative than men is more fiction than fact.

ASK YOURSELF

- Why does the stereotype of talkative women persist?
- What other stereotypes about sex and communication do you think may be inaccurate?

Source: Mehl, M. R., Vazire, S., Ramírez-Esparza, N., Slatcher, R. B., & Pennebaker, J. W. (2007). Are women really more talkative than men? *Science, 317,* 82.

---

powerful. Rather, he is simply using the speech patterns that are typical for men in our society. The "Got Skills" box offers suggestions for improving your ability to use powerful language.

A particularly troubling example of the difference between powerful and powerless speech is the use of *linguistic violence,* language that degrades and dehumanizes a group of people.[84] One way the more powerful nature of men's speech is expressed, for instance, is through terms that objectify and degrade women.[85] Using language to put down other people can constitute a type of emotional violence in the same way that hitting can constitute a type of physical violence. Linguistic violence is also frequently directed against homosexual, bisexual, and/or transgender people. Those communities are frequently *marginalized,* meaning they are subjected to unfair discrimination and prejudice on the basis of their sexual orientation or gender identity.[86]

GENDERED LINGUISTIC STYLES. In addition to gender differences in the purpose (expressive versus instrumental) and power of speech, research suggests that men and women differ in other aspects of their speech patterns, or *linguistic styles.* For example, women are more likely than men to use second- and third-person pronouns ("we," "they") and to make references to emotions ("hurt," "scared") when they talk. They also use more intensive adverbs, such as describing someone as "really" tall or "so" smart. As well, women speak in longer sentences than men do, on average.[87] Carmen, for example, might describe her new house in this way:

> We love our new home! It has a really big yard where the neighborhood children can play, and two very large guestrooms on the ground floor for when we have company. We also have a really nice kitchen, and the master suite is so spacious!

Talking Point: Some students will find this result difficult to believe because they will immediately think of counterexamples. Emphasize that this finding, like most research findings, doesn't apply to every woman and man but only to the average difference between the sexes. Also, this study simply recorded the number of words spoken per day as the measure of talkativeness. It may still be the case that one sex is more talkative than the other in certain social situations.

got skills?

POWERFUL LANGUAGE

Learn to use powerful language when it is appropriate.

WHAT?

Practice speaking to others using powerful language.

WHY?

To communicate with people—such as close friends and co-workers—in active and assertive ways.

HOW?

1. In a particular situation, consider the message you want to get across to another person. Before conveying your message—such as via e-mail or in a face-to-face conversation—write out the words you intend to use.

2. Examine your words carefully for hedges ("maybe," "kind of") and disclaimers ("I'm not sure, but. . ."). When you find them, re-word those phrases to make your words more assertive. Instead of saying "I wonder if maybe we should call a plumber," for instance, say "We should consider calling a plumber."

3. Remember that using powerful language doesn't mean being aggressive, domineering, or bossy. It simply means expressing your message in a confident manner.

TRY!

1. Find an e-mail message you have written or received that uses less-powerful language.

2. Rewrite the e-mail message to eliminate hedges and disclaimers and to reframe questions as statements. For instance, instead of asking "Do you think the deadline for our paper is going to get changed?" say "I wonder if the deadline for our paper is going to get changed." The second phrase still acknowledges the question of whether the deadline will be changed, but it does so in the form of an active statement.

3. Mask the names in the e-mail messages and change any details that would reveal the sender's and receiver's identities. Then, in a small group, show the original message and your revised message to your classmates and ask for their feedback on which message is more effective.

CONSIDER: *Using powerful language is often advantageous. Be sensitive to the communication context, however, and consider what your goals are. In some situations, it's better to use less-powerful language.*

Men's linguistic style makes greater use of self-references ("I" statements) and judgmental adjectives such as "good" or "worthless." Compared with women, men also use more references to quantity, such as informing other people that something "costs $400" or someone "is 6 feet, 8 inches tall." Men are also more likely than women to use location statements ("It's in the back") and incomplete sentences

Talking Point: In comparison, women would be more likely to say that something "costs a lot" or that a person "is really tall." The sex difference is in the tendency to use numbers as references to quantity.

("Nice job.").[88] For example, Carmen's husband Diego might describe their new home in this way:

> The house is great. It's got 2,200 square feet, plus a three-car detached garage. There's about an acre and a half of land. I got a good deal on the mortgage, too. 4.1 percent for 30 years.

In these examples, Carmen uses the pronoun "we" whereas Diego uses the pronoun "I." Carmen also uses intensive adverbs ("really big yard," "very large guestrooms"), whereas Diego makes specific references to quantity ("2,200 square feet," "acre and a half of land"). Carmen's sentences are also longer than Diego's on average, and Diego uses an incomplete sentence ("4.1 percent for 30 years"), whereas Carmen does not. Only a few studies have examined whether those patterns are influenced by sexual orientation, and most of the results indicate that they are not.[89] Whether gender role affects the use of these linguistic styles is still unclear.

Gender and Nonverbal Communication

Talking Point: Students may have a tendency to think of touch as including only nurturing, affectionate touch (such as hugging). Point out that any person-to-person contact qualifies as touch, including ritualistic touch (such as a handshake) and aggressive touch.

We use several behaviors that are *nonverbal*—carried out without words—to communicate. Nonverbal behaviors include gestures, facial expressions, tone of voice, and conventions about personal space. To understand how gender affects nonverbal communication, let's look at three specific areas:

- Touch and body movement
- Emotional communication
- Affectionate behavior

© Digital Vision, RF

TOUCH AND BODY MOVEMENT.   Touch is an important form of nonverbal communication because it can express warmth and intimacy as well as power and dominance (as we'll see in the Nonverbal Communication chapter). Many studies have shown that women and men exhibit different patterns of touch behavior. In an analysis of several of these studies, one research team discovered that sex differences in touch depend on whether the touch involves two adults or an adult and a child.[90]

When only adults are interacting, the researchers found that

- Men are more likely to touch women than women are to touch men, unless the touch is occurring as part of a greeting (such as a handshake).
- Other-sex touch is more common than same-sex touch.
- In same-sex pairs, women touch each other more than men do, but that difference is smaller in close friendships than among acquaintances.

In general, these results show that men do more touching than women in other-sex relationships, whereas women do more touching than men in same-sex relationships.

The patterns are quite different when one of the parties is a child:

- Same-sex touch is more common than other-sex touch.
- Women are more likely than men to initiate touch.
- Boys and girls are about equally likely to be touched.

These patterns may also be affected by culture. In feminine cultures, for instance, women and men may behave more similarly than in masculine cultures.

In addition to touch, sex appears to affect other forms of body movement. Compared with women, men use more body movement, prefer a greater amount of personal space around them, and try harder to preserve their personal space when it is violated.[91] Men also use more relaxed body movements. Both men and women appear to be more relaxed in their posture and gesturing when talking to men than to women.[92]

With respect to personal space, however, some evidence suggests that gender role rather than biological sex (or sexual orientation) is the most influential factor. For instance, one experiment found that masculine people (whether male or female) maintained a greater amount of personal distance from others than did feminine people (whether male or female).[93]

EMOTIONAL COMMUNICATION.   Common stereotypes would have us believe that women are more emotional than men. We often expect women to cry more than men at sad movies, for instance, and to be more expressive of their feelings for one another than men are. Indeed, a 2001 Gallup poll found that adults in the United States are significantly more likely to use the term *emotional* to describe women than men.[94]

Even if women are more emotional than men, what does that mean, exactly? Does it mean that women experience more emotion than men or just that they're more willing to express the emotions they feel? Going further, if women are more expressive than men, does that difference apply to every kind of emotion or just to certain ones? Let's look at what research tells us about the effects of sex on emotional communication.

To begin with, women generally express more positive emotions—such as happiness and joy—than men do.[95] The most basic behavior we use to communicate positive emotions is smiling, and several studies have found that women smile more than

Focus on Scholarship: Children's preference for same-sex touch is a function of their overall preference to interact with others of their same sex (as in play, etc.).[iv]

[iv]See, e.g., Maccoby, E. E. (1988). Gender as a social category. *Developmental Psychology, 24,* 755–765.

men.[96] Women also use more *affiliation behaviors* than men do. Affiliation behaviors demonstrate feelings of closeness or attachment to someone else. Common affiliation behaviors include eye contact, head nods, pleasant facial expressions, and warm vocal tones.[97] Research even suggests that women are more likely than men to express positive emotions in text messages through the use of emoticons.[98]

When it comes to negative emotions, though, sex differences appear to vary according to which emotion we consider. Some studies have found that men are more likely than women to express anger, but other studies haven't found a difference.[99] Men appear to express jealousy in more intense forms than women do, by engaging in dangerous, aggressive behaviors such as getting drunk, confronting a romantic rival, and becoming sexually involved with someone else.[100] Women are more likely than men to express the emotions of sadness and depression, however.[101]

Do women actually experience more emotion than men, or are they just more likely to express it? In a pair of studies, researchers Ann Kring and Albert Gordon found that although women were more expressive than men, they didn't report actually experiencing any more emotion than men did. Rather, men and women reported experiencing the same amount of emotion. Women simply expressed their emotions more frequently and openly, whereas men were more likely to mask their feelings.[102]

Although most research on gender and emotion has focused on biological sex, some studies have examined the influence of gender roles or sexual orientation. In one study, participants reported on their psychological gender roles. Afterward, they watched film clips that were emotionally arousing while researchers videotaped and subsequently coded their facial expressions. The researchers found that both women and men were more emotionally expressive if they were androgynous than if they were primarily masculine or feminine.[103]

In another experiment, lesbian and gay romantic couples took part in conflict discussions in a laboratory while their facial expressions were video-recorded. The researchers found that compared with gay men, lesbians were more expressive of both positive and negative emotion. This finding suggests that the biological sex difference in expression—meaning that women are more expressive than men—is not really affected by sexual orientation.[104]

AFFECTIONATE BEHAVIOR. *Affectionate communication* includes those behaviors we use to express our love and appreciation for people we care about. Several studies have shown that women use more nonverbal affection behaviors—such as hugging, kissing, and handholding—than men do.[105] This observation appears to be especially true in same-sex relationships. That is, the sex differences in nonverbal affection behaviors are even greater when women and men are interacting with same-sex friends or relatives than when they are interacting with members of the other sex.[106]

Why are women more affectionate than men? Researchers have offered several explanations. One theory is that because girls receive more affection than boys do, they are more likely to grow up perceiving interpersonal interactions as opportunities for communicating affection.[107] Another explanation is that men are more likely than women to see affectionate communication as a feminine behavior, so they avoid expressing affection out of a fear of appearing feminine.[108] A third possible reason is that the different balances of hormones typically found in men and women make women more likely to behave affectionately.[109] Any or all of these factors may play a part in making women more affectionate than men.

People sometimes interpret the same behavior differently depending on the sex of those enacting it. What interpretations would you make of each of these behaviors? © *Michael Blann/Digital Vision/Getty Images, RF,* © *Sebastian Pfuetze/Getty Images, RF*

Masculinity and femininity are also related to affectionate behavior, although not in the way you might guess. Because affection is often thought of as a "feminine" way of behaving—at least in North American cultures—you might expect that the more feminine people are, the more affectionate they are. Several studies have found this to be the case. The same studies have shown, however, that the more masculine people are, the more affectionate they are.[110] So, it appears that people who score high on both femininity and masculinity are particularly affectionate.

Only a small number of studies have examined the influence of sexual orientation on affectionate communication. One large national U.S. survey reported that both gay men and lesbian women were more expressive of affection and positive emotion within their romantic relationships than were heterosexual spouses with children. They were not more expressive than heterosexual spouses without children or heterosexual unmarried partners, however.[111]

Two other studies looked specifically at affectionate behavior between adult men and their fathers. The results indicated that fathers are most affectionate with heterosexual sons, less affectionate if they are unsure of their sons' sexual orientation, and least affectionate with sons who are homosexual or bisexual.[112]

Considered together, the studies we've reviewed in this section present a complex picture of how gender roles, biological sex, and sexual orientation influence verbal and nonverbal communication behaviors. Sometimes these factors make a difference, other times they don't, and in some cases they matter in unexpected ways, as when masculinity is positively related to affectionate communication. In addition, as we saw earlier, even when we do find differences—for example, women use longer sentences than men, or lesbian women use more instrumental speech than heterosexual women—we must keep in mind that these are *average* differences. Thus, not every woman speaks in longer sentences than every man. Rather, women use longer sentences than men do on average.

We should take care not to exaggerate or oversimplify the influence of gender roles, sex, or sexual orientation on communication behavior. These features often influence how we behave, but they do not affect every aspect of our lives at all times. In addition, our interpersonal interaction is affected by many influences besides the gender role, biological sex, or sexual orientation with which we identify.

In the IM: You can now access the end-of-chapter Discussion Questions and the Research Library in the Instructor's Manual for each chapter.

LEARN IT What is the difference between expressive and instrumental talk? How do gender roles, biological sex, and sexual orientation influence the experience and expression of emotion?

APPLY IT The next time you talk to an adult of the other sex, pay attention to your language style. Is your speech more instrumental or more expressive? Are you using powerful or powerless speech? Think about the ways your language style influences how effectively you are communicating. Write a paragraph or two documenting your observations.

REFLECT ON IT How would you characterize your verbal and nonverbal behavior? What role do you think your biological sex, gender role, and sexual orientation play in how you communicate with others?

MASTER the chapter

1 Understanding Culture and Communication (p. 35)

- Culture is the system of learned and shared symbols, language, values, and norms that distinguish one group of people from another.

- Cultures vary in their symbols, language, values, and norms.

- Co-cultures are groups of people who share values, customs, and norms related to a mutual interest or characteristic.

- Communicating with cultural awareness means paying attention to one's own cultural values and biases and remembering that others don't always share them.

2 How Culture Affects Communication (p. 43)

- Individualistic cultures emphasize the importance of individuality and personal achievement, whereas collectivistic cultures emphasize the needs of the family and community.

- People in low-context cultures expect language to be direct and explicit; those in high-context cultures rely more on contextual cues to interpret verbal statements.

- In a low-power-distance culture, power is more equitably distributed among people; in a high-power-distance culture, most of the power is held by relatively few people.

- Masculine cultures value competition and achievement and maintain largely different expectations for women and men. Feminine cultures value nurturing behavior and do not enforce rigidly different expectations for women and men.

- Time is considered to be a finite commodity in a monochronic culture; it is considered to be more infinite in a polychronic culture.

- Cultures vary in their uncertainty avoidance, or their aversion to novelty and uncertainty.

- Cultures differ in their use of communication codes, such as idioms and gestures, which often have meaning only to people in a given culture.

3 Understanding Gender and Communication (p. 49)

- Gender roles include masculinity, femininity, and androgyny, the meanings of which evolve over time.
- Biological sex differentiates men and women but is influenced by psychological, genetic, and anatomical factors.
- Sexual orientations include heterosexuality, homosexuality, bisexuality, and asexuality.

- Some writers have argued that women and men communicate as though they come from different planets or at least different cultures. Others have asserted that those metaphors are exaggerations.

4 How Gender Affects Communication (p. 59)

- Gender influences verbal communication, such as expressive and instrumental talk, power, and linguistic styles.
- Gender influences nonverbal communication, including touch and body movement, emotional communication, and nonverbal affection.

KEY TERMS

androgyny (p. 53)
asexuality (p. 57)
bisexuality (p. 56)
co-cultures (p. 40)
collectivistic culture (p. 43)
communication codes (p. 47)
culture (p. 35)
ethnicity (p. 37)
ethnocentrism (p. 36)
expressive talk (p. 59)

femininity (p. 52)
gender role (p. 52)
heterosexuality (p. 55)
high-context culture (p. 44)
high-power-distance culture (p. 45)
homosexuality (p. 55)
individualistic culture (p. 43)
in-group (p. 35)
instrumental talk (p. 59)
low-context culture (p. 44)

low-power-distance culture (p. 45)
masculinity (p. 52)
monochronic (p. 46)
nationality (p. 37)
out-group (p. 35)
polychronic (p. 47)
sexual orientation (p. 55)
similarity assumption (p. 42)
society (p. 35)
uncertainty avoidance (p. 47)

connect

To maximize your study time, check out CONNECT to access the SmartBook study module for this chapter, watch videos, and explore other resources.

Communication and the Self

© Adam Taylor/ABC/Getty Images

LIVING MULTIPLE LIVES

The ABC television sitcom *Black-ish* is a story of identity clash. The plot centers on an upper-middle-class African American family struggling to maintain their cultural identity in an affluent suburban co-culture. At the heart of the show is Dre Johnson (played by Anthony Anderson), a successful advertising executive anticipating a promotion that would make him the first African American senior vice president in his firm. But Dre worries that his success, and all the trappings of wealth that come with it, will lead his children to abandon—or at least have less of an appreciation for—their unique cultural heritage. Dre's wife, Rainbow (played by Tracee Ellis Ross), has a different experience and different ideas. A successful doctor and a woman of mixed race, Rainbow feels that cultural and racial identity are more fluid, and embraces the idea that her children can grow up in a "colorless" society. And while Dre worries that their children's posh lives have made them soft, Rainbow is comfortable providing their children with the advantages of their hard earned prosperity. Throughout the series, the Johnson family's experiences illustrate the complexity of negotiating multiple identities at once.

chapter preview

1 **Understanding the Self: Self-Concept**

2 **Valuing the Self: Self-Esteem**

3 **Presenting the Self: Image Management**

4 **Communicating the Self: Self-Disclosure**

F rom time to time, many of us experience situations in which two or more of our selves clash, and we are left feeling uncomfortable and unsure. In their case, the Johnsons find themselves caught between the traditions and values of their urban, African American heritage and the rituals and expectations of the upper-middle-class suburban lifestyle that they've worked very hard to achieve. As you negotiate your own life—particularly during the transition into young adulthood—you'll likely experience the need to reevaluate your childhood self and figure out who you want to be as an adult. In that process, it's not at all uncommon to find various parts of your identity at odds with each other, just as the Johnsons do.

1 Understanding the Self: Self-Concept

Interpersonal communication begins with you and your understanding of yourself. Who are you? How do you relate to others? What is the *self* in *myself*? Answering those questions allows you to communicate and form relationships with a solid understanding of who you are and what you have to offer.

In this section, we examine the self-concept and consider various influences on its development. We probe how individuals manage their identities in day-to-day life and how communication with others reflects one's self-concept.

What Is a Self-Concept?

Think about the ways you would answer the question "Who am I?" What words would you choose? Which answers would be most important? Each of us has a set of ideas about who we are that isn't influenced by moment-to-moment events (such as "I'm happy right now") but is fairly stable over the course of life (such as "I'm a happy person"). Your **self-concept,** also called your **identity,** is composed of your stable ideas about who you are. Self-concepts have three fundamental characteristics: They are multifaceted, partly subjective, and enduring but changeable.

SELF-CONCEPTS ARE MULTIFACETED. We define ourselves in many ways. Some ways rely on our name: "I'm Michaela"; "I am Bill." Some rely on physical or social categories: "I am a woman"; "I'm Australian." Others speak to our skills or interests: "I'm artistic"; "I'm a good cook." Still others are based on our relationships to other people: "I am an uncle"; "I do volunteer work with homeless children." Finally, some rely on our evaluations of ourselves: "I am an honest person"; "I am an impatient person."

Each of those descriptions taps into one or more parts of a person's self-concept, and in this sense the self-concept is *multifaceted*. Put another way, what we call the self is actually a collection of smaller selves, as Figure 1 depicts. If you're female, that's a part of who you are, but it isn't everything you are. If you're Asian, athletic,

> **self-concept** The set of stable ideas a person has about who he or she is; also known as *identity*.

> **identity** See *self-concept*.

FIGURE 1 Multiple Selves
What we call "the self" is actually a collection of smaller "selves," each representing only one aspect of who a person is.
© Jose Luis Pelaez Inc/Blend Images LLC, RF; © Rob Melnychuk/Photodisc/ PunchStock, RF; © Design Pics/Ron Nickel/Getty Images, RF; © Jose Luis Pelaez Inc/Blend Images LLC; © National Multiple Sclerosis Society; © Fuse/Getty Images, RF, RF; © Jeff Greenberg/Alamy; © Comstock/Getty Images, RF

Talking Point: Another way to understand self-concept is to examine what psychologists call the Big Five personality traits—**openness** (imagination and appreciation for varied experiences), **conscientiousness** (self-discipline and motivation for achievement), **extroversion** (the tendency to seek others' company), **agreeableness** (the tendency to be cooperative and compassionate), and **neuroticism** (emotional instability). A large body of research has used those dimensions to describe people's temperaments and personalities.[1]

[1]Soto, C. J. (2015). Is happiness good for your personality? Concurrent and prospective relations of the Big Five with subjective well-being. *Journal of Personality, 83,* 45–55.

Talking Point: The term *Johari* is a combination of the first names of the psychologists who created the Johari window: Joe and Harry.

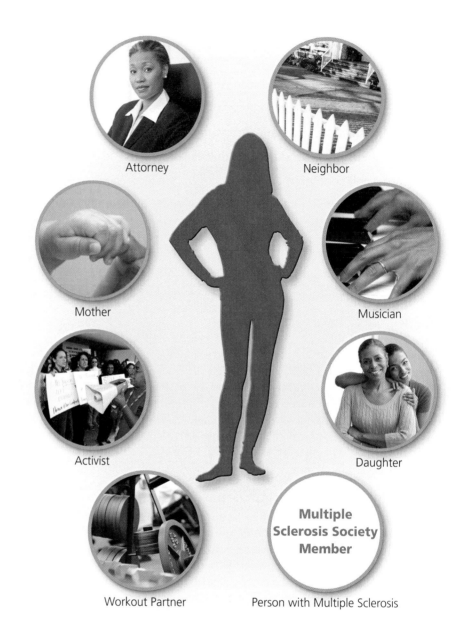

Attorney   Neighbor

Mother   Musician

Activist   Daughter

Multiple Sclerosis Society Member

Workout Partner   Person with Multiple Sclerosis

Johari window A visual representation of components of the self that are known or unknown to the self and to others.

agnostic, or asthmatic, these may all be parts of your self-concept, but none of these terms defines you completely. All the different ways you would describe yourself are pieces of your overall self-concept.

One way to think about your self-concept is to distinguish between aspects of yourself that are known to others and aspects that are known only to you. In 1955, American psychologists Joseph Luft and Harry Ingham created the **Johari window,** a visual representation of the self as composed of four parts.[1] According to the model (Figure 2), the *open area* consists of characteristics that are known both to the self and to others.

That probably includes your name, sex, hobbies, and academic major, and other aspects of your self-concept that you are aware of and freely share with others. In contrast, the *hidden area* consists of characteristics that you know about yourself but choose not to reveal to others, such as emotional insecurities or past traumas that you elect to keep hidden.

An innovative aspect of the Johari window is that it recognizes dimensions of an individual's self-concept of which he or she may be unaware. For instance, others might see you as impatient or volatile though you don't recognize those traits in yourself. Those characteristics make up the third part of the model, the *blind area*. Finally, the *unknown area* comprises aspects of your self-concept that are not known either to you or to others. For example, no one—including you—can know what kind of parent you will be until you actually become a parent. Likewise, no one can know how you would handle sudden wealth unless you unexpectedly become wealthy.

	Known to Self	Unknown to Self
Known to Others	**OPEN** What you know, and choose to reveal to others, about yourself.	**BLIND** What others know about you, but you don't recognize in yourself.
Unknown to Others	**HIDDEN** What you know about yourself, but choose not to reveal.	**UNKNOWN** The dimensions of yourself that no one knows.

FIGURE 2 The Johari Window

These four parts of the Johari window—open, hidden, blind, and unknown—are not necessarily of equal importance for each individual. For example, Raisa keeps many aspects of her self-concept to herself, so her hidden area is much larger than the other parts of her Johari window. In contrast, people describe Aaron as an "open book," meaning that he keeps little about his self-concept private. Thus, for Aaron, the open area is the largest area. The areas of the Johari window can also change in importance as a person's experiences change. For instance, when Denae was diagnosed with terminal cancer, she discovered emotional strength, compassion, and a sense of humor that she and others never knew she had. That experience moved those aspects of her self-concept from her unknown area to her open area.

On the USA Network series *White Collar,* Neal Caffrey is a forger and thief who agrees to help FBI agent Peter Burke catch white-collar criminals in exchange for an early release from prison. Given Caffrey's background, Burke is frequently unsure if Caffrey will keep his word—or if he will lie to the FBI. Applying the principles of the Johari window, we could say that Burke is uncertain about how much of Caffrey's open area—as opposed to his hidden area—he is actually seeing.

Your own open, hidden, and blind areas of the Johari window are also relevant to your image online. When you create a Facebook page, for instance, you choose to share particular information about yourself with others (part of your open area), but you decide to keep some details private (part of your hidden area). Other people's Facebook pages may also contain information about you that you aren't aware of but that others can see (part of your blind area). Because the Internet is so vast, managing your online image can seem like a never-ending task. It's an important skill, though, as the "Assess Your Skills" box emphasizes.

SELF-CONCEPTS ARE PARTLY SUBJECTIVE. Some of the details we know about ourselves are based on objective facts. For instance, I'm 5 feet, 8 inches tall and have brown hair, I was born in Washington but now live in Arizona, and I teach at a college for a living. Those aspects of my self-concept are *objective*—they're based on fact and

Writing Note: Asking students to answer the question "Who am I?" in 10 different ways is a good in-class writing activity before your discussion of the self-concept. Have students refer to their lists as you illustrate different points.

assess your skills | GOOGLE YOURSELF: MANAGING YOUR ONLINE IMAGE

Creditors, potential employers, and even prospective romantic partners use the Internet to learn about you. Will you like what they find? To assess your online image, type your name into google.com and explore the first dozen websites that the search identifies that are relevant to you (rather than to someone else with your name). Then respond with "true" or "false" to each of the following statements.

1. _____ Nearly everything I saw about myself online was positive.
2. _____ I came across information I wouldn't necessarily want others to have about me.
3. _____ I would be fine knowing that a prospective romantic partner was looking at these websites.
4. _____ I found pictures of myself that I wouldn't be comfortable letting my employer see.
5. _____ Most people would have a positive impression of me after seeing the websites I found.
6. _____ Some of the information I found might make me look irresponsible.
7. _____ I'd feel comfortable letting my parents read the websites I came across.
8. _____ I wouldn't want someone coming across these websites before going out with me.
9. _____ All in all, I feel good about the information and photographs of myself that I found.
10. _____ At least some of what I found online about myself was troubling.

It's best if you answered "true" to the odd-numbered statements and "false" to the even-numbered statements. If any of your answers were otherwise, consider taking steps to alter the online content. If the information or photos that concern you appear on websites over which you have some control—such as your Facebook page and a friend's personal web page—remove the material or make it viewable only by close acquaintances. This may be a particularly important consideration before you go on a job interview or set up a date.

not on someone's opinion. That doesn't mean I have no choice about them. I chose to move to Arizona and get a teaching job, and although I was born with brown hair, I could change my hair color if I wanted to. Referring to those personal characteristics as objective simply means that they are factually true.

Many aspects of our self-concept are *subjective* rather than objective. "Subjective" means that they're based on our impressions of ourselves rather than objective facts. Importantly, it's often difficult for us to judge ourselves accurately or objectively.

Sometimes our self-assessments are unreasonably positive. For instance, you might know people who have unrealistic ideas about their intelligence, special talents, or understanding of the world or other people. In one study, the College Board (the company that administers the SAT college entrance examination) asked almost a million U.S. high school seniors to rate their ability to get along with others. *Every single student* in the study responded that he or she was "above average," which is mathematically impossible! Moreover, 60 percent claimed their ability to get along with others was in the top 10 percent, and a whopping 25 percent rated themselves in the top 1 percent, both of which are highly improbable.[2]

In contrast, sometimes our judgments of ourselves are unreasonably negative. That is especially true for people with low self-esteem. Several studies have shown that such people tend to magnify the importance of their failures.[3] They often underestimate their abilities, and when they get negative feedback, such as a bad evaluation at work or a disrespectful remark from someone they know, they are likely to believe that it accurately reflects their self-worth. Multiple studies have also suggested that people with low self-esteem have a higher-than-average risk of being clinically depressed, a condition that impairs not only an individual's mental and emotional well-being but also physical health and the quality of social relationships.[4]

People with high self-esteem tend to minimize the importance of negative feedback, treating it as a fluke or a random event. We'll look more closely at how self-esteem influences our interpersonal communication behaviors later in the chapter.

CONNECT: Students who use SmartBook can track their own progress and identify areas for improvement through student reports.

SELF-CONCEPTS ARE ENDURING BUT CHANGEABLE.   For the most part, the self-concept develops slowly, over a lifetime. As we'll see, many factors affect how our self-concept comes together, including biological makeup, how and where we were raised, and the kinds of people with whom we spend our time.

Those and other influences create an understanding of the self that is not easily changed. In fact, several studies have shown that once we develop a self-concept, we tend to seek out others who will confirm it by treating us as we see ourselves.[5] If you're someone with a positive self-concept, for instance, you'll likely associate with friends, co-workers, classmates, and relatives who also have a positive impression of you. In contrast, if your self-concept is negative, you may be more likely to surround yourself with people whose impression of you is also negative.[6] When you associate with people who see you as you see yourself, your self-concept is continually reinforced, and it becomes even more resistant to change.

Talking Point: You might ask students if they can think of people they know who have gone through substantial changes in their self-concepts, and what event(s) precipitated those changes.

Self-concepts do change, however, in response to developmental changes and significant life events. As we go through developmental changes in life, for instance, many of us grow to feel more positive or less positive about ourselves. One study reported that between the ages of 14 and 23—a period when changes in self-concept are often the most pronounced—both men and women go through shifts in their level of confidence and self-esteem. Child psychologists Jack Block and Richard Robins found that approximately 80 percent of people experienced either an increase or a decrease in their self-esteem during this period.[7]

People can also undergo changes in their self-concept as a result of a significant life event, such as undergoing a religious conversion or battling a serious illness.[8] After being widowed and losing her job, for instance, Sherry found herself homeless and living in her car. The more she adapted to the routines of homelessness, the more she came to think of herself as homeless and shunned by society—and the more distrustful she became of people she was once close to. Friends and relatives offered their help, but Sherry felt too ashamed to accept it.

Battling cancer or another serious illness can significantly affect a person's self-concept, as it did for both Hazel Grace and August in *The Fault in Our Stars*. © Photos 12 / Alamy

Over time, she began to prefer the company of other homeless people because she felt she could relate to them more easily.

A healthy self-concept is flexible and can change as life circumstances evolve. That doesn't mean that every significant event changes a person's self-concept, but it does suggest that shifts in a person's self-concept are frequently associated with noteworthy events in his or her developmental stage. Undergoing extensive therapy can also help a person change his or her self-concept, usually for the better. Overall, however, an individual's self-concept generally does not change dramatically over adult life, at least in Western cultures.[9]

How a Self-Concept Develops

None of us is born with a self-concept.[10] In this section, we explore how factors such as personality and biology, culture and gender roles, reflected appraisal, and social comparison help determine who we are.

PERSONALITY AND BIOLOGY.   An important part of your self-concept is your **personality,** the pattern of distinctive ways you tend to think and act across most situations. Are you usually talkative and outgoing, or shy and reserved? Are you a worrier, or happy-go-lucky? Do you tend to be suspicious or trusting of others? Each of those questions relates to a different personality *trait,* a characteristic that describes you in most circumstances. If you have an outgoing personality, for instance, that means you're friendly and talkative most of the time.

Some aspects of our personality are undoubtedly affected by where we grow up or how we are raised. Research suggests, however, that biology also plays a role in shaping personality.[11] For instance, several studies have shown that identical twins, who share 100 percent of their genes, are much more similar in their personality than fraternal twins, who share only 50 percent of their genes, the same as regular siblings.[12]

Other research shows that children start displaying certain personality traits early in life, before the effects of culture or upbringing are likely to be influential, and that those traits often remain as the children grow up. Toddlers who act shy around strangers, for example, are likely to continue being shy as adolescents and adults. Although personality is strongly affected by biology, however, with concerted effort many people can change their personality traits if they choose.[13]

CULTURE AND GENDER ROLES.   The way we see ourselves is also strongly affected by the culture in which we grow up and the gender roles we enact. As we saw in the Culture and Gender chapter, cultures differ from one another in how individualistic they are: Some are highly individualistic, some are highly collectivistic, and some are in the middle. People in highly collectivistic cultures tend to think of their identities as embedded within their families and communities. In other words, they define the self in terms of the groups to which they belong, and they place more emphasis on the group than on the individual. In comparison, people in highly individualistic cultures think of themselves as independent and unique and not as strongly defined by family or community.[14]

Gender also matters when it comes to the self-concept. Recall that gender roles are socially constructed ideas about how women and men should think and behave. Most cultures expect men to exhibit more stereotypically masculine traits, such as assertiveness and self-sufficiency, than women. Conversely, they expect women to exhibit more traits that are stereotypically feminine, such as empathy and emotional expressiveness.

personality The pattern of behaviors and ways of thinking that characterize a person.

Focus on Scholarship: Studies of personality characteristics show substantial similarity between identical twins, even if they haven't been raised together, and minimal similarity between nongenetic siblings (such as stepsiblings and adopted siblings), even if they have been raised together. Those findings raise the intriguing possibility that much of our personality is more strongly related to our genes than our upbringing. How do students react to that possibility? How does it relate to the idea that we create our self-concepts rather than discover them?[ii]

[ii]See, e.g., Kandler, C., Riemann, R., Spinath, F. M., Bleidorn, W., Thiel, W., & Angleitner, A. (2013). The Bielefeld Longitudinal Study of Adult Twins (BiLSAT). *Twin Research and Human Genetics, 16,* 167–172.

Talking Point: Hillary Clinton's bid for the U.S. presidency in the 2016 election stands as one example of a high-profile individual challenging gender role expectations.

Those observations don't imply that all men are assertive or that all women are emotionally expressive. Rather, they acknowledge general tendencies that can significantly affect the self-concepts that women and men develop. For instance, competition and achievement may be more important to the self-concept of a masculine person, whereas a feminine person may place a greater emphasis on having strong, equitable relationships.

REFLECTED APPRAISAL.   As we grow up, one of the ways we figure out who we are is by considering who other people think we are. Perhaps you can recall someone important from your childhood who made you feel especially loved and appreciated. That individual may have been a favorite teacher who encouraged you to pursue your interests or an aunt or uncle who always listened to you talk about your favorite music. It's also possible that you were influenced in negative ways by people who were important to you, such as a callous older sibling who teased you in front of your friends.

Those types of positive or negative messages help us form a mental picture of what others think of us. In turn, that mental picture often affects the image we form of ourselves. The process whereby our self-concept is influenced by how we think other people see us is called **reflected appraisal.**[15] When other people treat us with love and appreciation, we may come to think of ourselves as lovable and worthy. In the same way, when other people tease, ignore, or physically or verbally abuse us, we may perceive ourselves as inadequate or unimportant. In these ways, reflected appraisal can move aspects of our personality from the blind section of the Johari Window to the open section.

In the early 1900s, sociologist Charles Horton Cooley conceived of what he called the "looking-glass self" to explain how reflected appraisal works. In his model, each of us imagines how we appear to others. For instance, you might believe that others see you as caring and compassionate. Next, we imagine how others evaluate their image of us. For example, if people see care and compassion as positive traits, you would likely imagine they would evaluate you positively. Finally, we develop our self-concept based on those evaluations. For instance, if people seem to think positively of you, then you would think positively of yourself.[16]

In general, the more important someone is to us, the more his or her judgments will affect the way we see ourselves. Parents, friends, teachers, coaches, and others who play a significant role in our lives are usually the ones whose opinions matter the most.[17] As a result, their appraisals often exert more influence on the development of our self-concept than other people's appraisals.

The effects of reflected appraisal aren't confined to childhood. For example, after years of being told by his father that he's "no good," Jerome lacks confidence in his abilities, even though he is highly intelligent. That problem has made it difficult for him to hold down a job for more than a couple of years at a time. He also finds it hard to develop a lasting romantic relationship. Because his father's behavior led him

reflected appraisal The process whereby a person's self-concept is influenced by his or her beliefs concerning what other people think of the person.

In *The Blind Side,* football star Michael Oher's self-concept is influenced by the way his adoptive mother saw him. That process is called reflected appraisal. © Ralph Nelson/©Warner Bros./Courtesy Everett Collection

to feel unworthy of love, Jerome has a tough time believing that any romantic partner will ever want to stay with him. As a result, his relationships are fleeting.[18] In Jerome's case, the reflected appraisal he received from his father while growing up shapes his self-concept as a "no good" adult.

SOCIAL COMPARISON.   Besides taking note of what other people think of us, we also notice how we compare with the people around us. Maybe you're the least athletic of all your friends. Perhaps you find that you're funnier, better looking, or more musically talented than most of the people with whom you interact. A large part of the way we form a self-concept is through this type of **social comparison,** or observation of how we compare with others. Thus, if you're more attractive than most of the people you know, attractiveness is likely to be a part of your self-concept.

With social comparison, as with reflected appraisal, some people influence our self-concept more than others. For that reason, a key element in social comparison is the individuals or groups with whom we compare ourselves. The people we use to evaluate our characteristics are called **reference groups.** In most cases, our reference groups are our peers. You're more likely to consider yourself a smart person, for instance, if your reference group consists of your classmates than a group of Nobel Prize winners. Similarly, you'll probably feel wealthier if you compare yourself with your friends than with Facebook's founder Mark Zuckerberg, one of the world's youngest billionaires.

Those are extreme examples, but research shows that people sometimes pick unreasonable reference groups when they evaluate themselves. Unfortunately, comparing oneself with unreasonable reference groups can be frustrating—and even dangerous. For example, both men and women are likely to develop negative images of their bodies when they compare themselves with movie stars or models. In response, they often put pressure on themselves to achieve an unrealistic body. In some cases, this pressure leads to eating disorders, which can be very serious or even life-threatening.[19]

The influences we've just reviewed—personality and biology, culture and gender roles, reflected appraisal, and social comparison—can significantly affect self-concept. Importantly, none of those factors operates on self-concept by itself. Rather, *all* come into play in shaping self-identity.

Awareness and Management of the Self-Concept

Part of being a competent, skilled communicator is being aware of your self-concept and managing its influences on your behavior. Two pathways through which self-concept can shape communicative behavior are self-monitoring and the self-fulfilling prophecy.

SELF-MONITORING.   In the About Communication chapter, we defined self-monitoring as an individual's awareness of how he or she looks and sounds and of how that person's behavior is affecting others. Recall that people on the high end of the self-monitoring scale pay attention to how others are reacting to them, and they have the ability to adjust their communication as needed. Conversely, people on the low end express whatever they are thinking or feeling without paying attention to the impression they're creating.

To understand how self-monitoring operates, imagine that you've fixed up your friends Jin and Katie to go out. As a high self-monitor, Jin pays a great deal of attention to his clothes and grooming to make sure he looks and smells good. As a low self-monitor, Katie doesn't spend much time thinking about those things. During their date, Jin is aware of what he's saying, so he comes across as nice, easygoing, and funny. Katie,

social comparison The process of comparing oneself with others.

reference groups The groups of people with whom one compares oneself in the process of social comparison.

however, says whatever is on her mind without considering what Jin might think. Jin notices if his behavior seems to make Katie uncomfortable, and he adjusts his actions accordingly, whereas Katie doesn't particularly pay attention to what she's doing and how she's affecting Jin.

Self-monitoring certainly has its advantages. High self-monitors tend to be better at making whatever kind of impression they want to make, because they are aware of their behaviors and of others' responses to them. They often find it easier than low self-monitors to put other people at ease in social situations. High self-monitors also tend to be good at figuring out what others are thinking and feeling, an ability that gives them a clear advantage in many social settings. However, being a high self-monitor also has its drawbacks. Because high self-monitors are constantly aware of themselves and others, they may have a hard time relaxing and "living in the moment."

Temple Grandin, who was diagnosed with autism at an early age, learned to deal successfully with the communication challenges posed by the disorder. Today an animal scientist at Colorado State University, she is also an inspiring world-renowned speaker on the topic of autism. © *Rosalie Winard*

Also, the fact that they can adjust their behaviors to create a certain impression can make it difficult to tell what they are genuinely thinking or feeling. Their motto might be "What you see is what I want you to see."[20]*

Being a low self-monitor also has advantages and disadvantages. On the positive side, low self-monitors spend less time and energy thinking about their appearance and behavior, so they are probably more relaxed than high self-monitors in many situations. Indeed, their motto might be "What you see is what you get." In addition, because they are less aware of, or concerned with, the impressions they make, they are often more straightforward communicators—and may even be seen as more genuine and trustworthy. At the same time, however, because low self-monitors are less skilled than high self-monitors in adjusting their behaviors to the demands of the situation, they frequently appear unsophisticated or socially awkward. As a result, they are more likely to make a poor first impression, both in person and online.[21]

Some medical conditions can inhibit self-monitoring ability, including autism, a developmental disorder that impairs a person's capability for social interaction. A 2012 report from the Centers for Disease Control and Prevention found that approximately 1 in 88 U.S. American children has some form of autism.[22] Individuals with autism are often unresponsive to others. They frequently avoid eye contact and have difficulty understanding other people's thoughts and feelings. That obstacle limits their ability to notice how others are reacting to them and to adjust their behaviors accordingly, two hallmarks of self-monitoring. Despite these challenges, however, it is possible for many people with autism to lead relatively independent, productive lives.

SELF-FULFILLING PROPHECY. Imagine meeting a new co-worker whom you've heard other people describe as painfully shy. Because you don't want to make her uncomfortable, you spend little time talking to her when you meet her, and you don't

Focus on Ethics: Because their motto might be "What you see is what I want you to see," high self-monitors might occasionally be accused of being dishonest (by not being upfront about their thoughts or feelings). Is it unethical to be a high self-monitor?

Focus on Scholarship: Researchers are prone to a type of self-fulfilling prophecy called the *experimenter expectancy effect*. This effect occurs when a researcher's expectations about a study's outcome cause him or her to behave in ways that make those outcomes more likely. This is why research assistants are often kept "blind" to the predictions or specifics of a study while they are involved in it.[iii]

[iii]Klein, O., Doyen, S., Leys, C., Magalhaes de Saldanha da Gama, P. A., Miller, S., Questienne, L., & Cleeremans, A. (2012). Low hopes, high expectations: Expectancy effects and the replicability of behavioral experiments. *Perspectives on Psychological Science, 7,* 572–584.

*Emanuel, L., Neil, G. J., Bevan, C., Fraser, D. S., Stevenage, S. V., Whitty, M. T., & Jamison-Powell, S. (2014). Who am I? Representing the self online and in different online contexts. Computers in Human Behavior, 41,146-152.

got skills?

SELF-FULFILLING PROPHECY

Influence others' communication behaviors in positive ways.

WHAT?
Learn to use the self-fulfilling prophecy to your advantage in interpersonal communication.

WHY?
To help make potentially contentious interactions—such as asking an instructor to reconsider the grade he or she gave you on an assignment—more positive.

HOW?
1. Let's say you make an appointment to ask your instructor to reconsider your grade. Before the conversation, repeat to yourself positive messages such as "This instructor will deal with me kindly and fairly" and "He will recognize my intelligence and integrity."
2. Mentally remind yourself of those messages as you engage in the conversation. In every way possible, behave as though those statements are already true.

TRY!
1. With a classmate, friend, or co-worker, role-play a conversation about a *different* difficult interaction. Do not tell the person beforehand of your expectations.
2. Afterward, discuss what went well during the conversation and what would have made it even more positive. Ask the person to identify the behaviors you enacted that contributed to positivity. Identify the ways in which you believe your expectations influenced your partner's behavior.

CONSIDER: *How did having positive expectations about the conversation help to produce positive results?*

---

self-fulfilling prophecy
An expectation that gives rise to behaviors that cause the expectation to come true.

invite her to join you and your friends for lunch. Consequently, she says little to you all day and eats lunch alone at her desk. You think to yourself, "I guess everyone was right about her; she *is* really shy." Why did your expectation about a shy co-worker come true? Most likely, it's due to a phenomenon called **self-fulfilling prophecy**—a situation in which a prediction causes people to act and communicate in ways that make that prediction come true.

As another example, let's say you volunteer at an afterschool literacy program, and everyone is talking about how much they like the new program director. Because everyone else seems to like him, you expect that you will too. You therefore communicate in a positive, outgoing way when you meet him. You introduce yourself to him in the hallway, and you listen with interest when he tells you about his background. In return, he treats you in a friendly manner. As a result, you do like him! What has happened here is that your expectation ("I will like this person") led you to behave in a certain way (talking in a friendly way toward him; not interrupting him as he talked about himself) that caused your expectation to be fulfilled (he acted friendly toward you, and therefore you liked him).

How do self-fulfilling prophecies affect how we communicate? Sometimes our expectations influence our communication behavior, as when we think it's going to be a bad day and we then have a bad day. Similarly, when we expect our relationships to fail, we behave in ways that sabotage them, and when we expect to be socially rejected, we perceive and react to rejection even when it isn't really there.[23]

Just as our expectations can influence our behavior, so can other people's expectations. In one study, some college men were informed that a certain woman was attracted to them, and other men were told she wasn't. After each man had a conversation with the woman, the researchers found a self-fulfilling prophecy: When the man believed the woman was attracted to him, she was more likely to behave as if she were.[24] The most likely explanation for that outcome is that the men who thought the woman was attracted to them communicated in a friendly, outgoing way toward her, causing her to reciprocate those communication behaviors and thus behave as though she were attracted to them.

Research has shown that other people's expectations cause us to behave in expectancy-confirming ways across a range of situations, including the management of our relationships, our ability to heal from illness, and even our productivity on the job.[25] You can use that information to help generate positive encounters with others, as the "Got Skills?" box illustrates.

There is one very important clarification about self-fulfilling prophecies. For a prophecy to be self-fulfilling, it's not enough that you expect something to happen and then it does. Rather, it has to be your expectation that *causes* it to happen. To illustrate the point, let's say you expected it to rain yesterday, and it did. That isn't a self-fulfilling prophecy, because your expectation didn't cause the rain—it would have rained whether you thought it would rain or not. In other words, your expectation was fulfilled, but it was not *self*-fulfilled. A self-fulfilling prophecy is one in which the expectation itself causes the behaviors that make it come true.

LEARN IT   What does it mean to say that self-concepts are partly subjective? Compare and contrast reflected appraisal and social comparison as influences on the development of a self-concept. What are the advantages and disadvantages of being a low self-monitor?

APPLY IT   Create a version of Figure 1 for yourself. Around the figure in the middle, draw six to eight small images that represent your different selves. Then draw three or four new selves that represent not the person you are but the person you would like to become. Next to each of those ideal selves, write one statement describing something you can do to become more like that ideal self.

REFLECT ON IT   How do your friends and relatives affirm and reinforce your perceptions of yourself? If you had to create a time capsule to describe yourself to future generations and could include only five things, what things would you choose? Why?

2 Valuing the Self: Self-Esteem

The 2012 comedy *Pitch Perfect* features actress Rebel Wilson as Amy, a member of Barden University's all-female a cappella singing group. Overweight but confident, she introduces herself as "Fat Amy" in order to prevent others from calling her "fat" behind her back. By doing so, Amy clearly communicates that her high self-confidence is not impaired by her appearance or by the expectations that others may associate with it.

In *Pitch Perfect,* Rebel Wilson's character Fat Amy does not let other people's opinions about her appearance affect her self esteem. © *AF Archive/Alamy*

 self-esteem One's sub- jective evaluation of one's value and worth as a person.

How do *you* feel about *yourself*? Are you satisfied with your looks? Your accomplishments? Your person- ality? Your relationships? Do you feel confident and proud of who you are? Those questions ask you to think about your **self-esteem,** your subjective evaluation of your value and worth as a person.

Many people have speculated about the value of having high self-esteem, but the research results have been mixed. As we'll see, some behaviors and charac- teristics do appear to be enhanced by high self-esteem. Others seem as though they would be, but they really aren't. In this section, we'll look at what it means to have high or low self-esteem, and we'll investigate how characteristics such as sex and culture affect our self-esteem. We'll conclude by focusing on three inter- personal needs that interact with self-esteem to influence the way we communicate with others.

Benefits and Drawbacks of Self-Esteem

Turn on any talk show or browse the self-help aisle of any bookstore and you'll find plenty of discussion about the importance of self-esteem. High self-esteem is often believed to boost academic performance and shield people from stress, whereas low self-esteem is frequently blamed as the underlying cause of juvenile delinquency and antisocial behavior. Such beliefs have led many parents, educators, and government agencies to pay more attention to improving children's self-esteem as a way to help them grow into more successful adults.

Those ideas make good sense in part because they're intuitively appealing. It's easy to believe that if you feel good about yourself, you'll be more successful in school, work, and relationships. Although research shows that high self-esteem does have some important benefits, it also suggests that we might be giving self-esteem more credit than it's due.

SELF-ESTEEM AND SOCIAL BEHAVIOR. Maintaining a positive image of ourselves does appear to have its advantages when it comes to behavior. Compared with people with lower self-esteem, those with higher self-esteem are generally more outgoing and more willing to communicate.[26] After trying and failing at a difficult task, they try harder to accomplish it a second time.[27] They are more comfortable initiating relation- ships, and they're more likely to believe that their partners' expressions of love and support are genuine.[28] They don't necessarily have more friends than people with lower self-esteem, however. Moreover, when their self-worth is threatened, they are less lik- able than people with low self-esteem.[29]

Several researchers have speculated that lower self-esteem is related to antisocial behavior, especially among adolescents and young adults. They suggest that people who view themselves negatively are more likely to act aggressively toward others, to abuse drugs or alcohol, and to become sexually active at a young age than people with a more positive self-image. The research hasn't supported those ideas, however. In fact, aggressive people tend to have higher self-esteem, not lower.[30] In addition, the evi- dence suggests that self-esteem is not related to drinking or drug use, at least among teenagers.[31]

A similar scenario occurs with teenage sexuality: Adolescents with higher self-esteem are more prone to be sexually active and to engage in risky sexual behaviors than teens with lower self-esteem.[32] One explanation for those conclusions is that high self-esteem gives some adolescents confidence in their ability to win a fight, attract a sexual partner, or escape the problems of risky sexual behaviors, making them more prone to engage in those types of interactions. In contrast, low self-esteem might lead other adolescents to avoid those situations.

Some research indicates that problems associated with low self-esteem—which include social anxiety, loneliness, and depression—can lead people to use the Internet as a way to escape those troubles. Although it provides a wealth of information, entertainment, and social-networking opportunity, excessive reliance on the Internet as a substitute for interpersonal relationships can be problematic. Internet use can even become addictive for those who turn to it as a means of escaping their social difficulties.[33]

SELF-ESTEEM AND HOW WE SEE OURSELVES AND OTHERS. Research indicates that people who have high self-esteem are happier with their lives than are people with low self-esteem.[34] That finding is true around the world, although there is a stronger relationship between happiness and self-esteem in countries with individualistic cultures—which emphasize the importance of the self—than in others with collectivistic cultures—which emphasize the needs of the group or community (Table 1).[35] In addition, people with high self-esteem have a lower risk of depression[36] and an enhanced ability to recognize and manage emotions, a skill researchers call *emotional intelligence*.[37]

In contrast, people who have a poorer image of themselves adopt more negative emotions and ways of looking at and handling situations. They tend to be more judgmental of others than people with higher self-esteem.[38] They're also more likely to speak poorly of others and to express racial prejudices.[39] When others put them down, they often respond by being excessively critical of others, so as to appear more impressive.[40] Some research has also shown that having low self-esteem in childhood is a predictor of having thoughts of suicide[41] and of making suicide attempts[42] in adolescence or young adulthood.

Self-esteem affects our communication online as well. Those with negative views of themselves post more negative status updates on Facebook, for instance.[43] Their negative updates then draw discouraging feedback from others, which only reinforces their low self-esteem. People with poor self-images can also be dismayed by the fun and exciting activities they see depicted in their friends' tweets, posts, and photos—a reaction that one reporter dubbed "Instagram envy."[44] In fact, research shows that even people with positive self-images can be envious when they read on Facebook about how satisfying and fulfilling their friends' lives are.[45]

SELF-ESTEEM AND PERFORMANCE. Much emphasis has been placed on self-esteem in schools and its effects on students' academic performance. Many people have argued that high self-esteem gives students the confidence to work hard in school and achieve academic success. They have also maintained that low self-esteem is often the root cause of poor grades.

Those beliefs have led parents and educators to implement policies to boost students' self-esteem. One fairly common approach has been to reduce or eliminate opportunities for competition among students, particularly competition based on academic achievement. For instance, many schools refuse to publish an honor roll, fearing that recognizing high achievers will diminish the self-esteem of students who didn't

Talking Point: Why are people with low self-esteem more likely to speak poorly of others or to express racial prejudices?

Talking Point: The motivation to protect the self-esteem of students has led some universities to eliminate grades. What do students think about these policies?

In the IM: The in-class activity "Self-Esteem and Performance" examines how temporarily enhancing or diminishing self-esteem affects performance on a cognitive task.

TABLE 1

The Relationship between Self-Esteem and Happiness in Various Parts of the World

The higher the number, the more strongly self-esteem is related to happiness in that country.

Country	Self-Esteem/Happiness Relationship
United States	.58
New Zealand	.59
Germany	.50
Spain	.39
Brazil	.36
Jordan	.34
Bangladesh	.16

Note: The countries shown are listed from most individualistic to most collectivistic. As you can see, self-esteem generally has a stronger relationship to happiness in individualistic societies than in collectivistic ones. This relationship is not perfect; for instance, the United States is more individualistic than New Zealand, but the New Zealand correlation is slightly stronger. Rather, the relationship is general. These correlations are averaged for women and men.

Source: Diener, E., & Diener, M. (2009). Cross-cultural correlates of life satisfaction and self-esteem. In E. Diener (Ed.), *Culture and well-being* (pp. 71–91). Dordrecht, The Netherlands: Springer.

earn the grades to qualify. Some schools have gone so far as to eliminate grades.[46] Some U.S. school districts have even stopped participating in the National Spelling Bee—a national student spelling competition—because only one child in each grade can win in any given year, a tradition that, concerned observers say, might harm other children's self-esteem.[47] Those and similar school policies are based on the notion that competition is problematic because students who don't win will suffer a loss of self-esteem that in turn will impair their academic performance.

The research shows, however, that efforts to protect students' self-esteem have had little effect. In fact, several studies suggest that students' self-esteem has very little association with their academic performance.[48] For instance, some studies have found no correlation between students' self-esteem and their scores on standardized tests.[49] At least one study has shown that attempting to boost students' self-esteem can backfire and cause the students to perform more poorly.[50] That may be because inflating students' self-esteem causes the students to have such a degree of confidence in their natural abilities that they study less than they otherwise would.

Importantly, those conclusions are not true just for students. The evidence suggests that self-esteem is also largely unrelated to performance on the job.[51]

Some school districts have stopped participating in the National Spelling Bee out of concern for students' self-esteem. © *Stefan Zaklin/Corbis Wire/Corbis*

Research has shown, for instance, that high self-esteem provides no advantage when performing arithmetic tasks[52] or tasks that require sensitivity to nonverbal behaviors,[53] two common components of many jobs.

In summary, having high self-esteem is a real benefit in some ways, such as in making us happier. In other regards, such as preventing delinquency or improving our academic performance, it isn't a particular benefit. Those mixed results don't mean we shouldn't care about the self-esteem of those around us. Rather, they suggest that the benefits of high self-esteem are largely limited to social and emotional areas and may not be as broad as people once thought.

Many people have suggested that self-esteem differs according to a person's sex and cultural background. Let's examine the extent to which that variation is true.

Culture, Sex, and Self-Esteem

Sex and culture are such powerful influences in our lives that it's easy to assume they affect almost everything about who we are and how we communicate. The effects are not always what we might guess, however.

CULTURE AND SELF-ESTEEM.   Many people might assume that ethnic minorities in the United States would have lower self-esteem than non-Hispanic Caucasians—who form the majority ethnic group—because of the social stigmas that minorities often face.[54] In fact, the research tells a slightly different story. According to psychologists Jean Twenge and Jennifer Crocker, Hispanic Americans, Native Americans, and Asian Americans do tend to rate themselves lower than non-Hispanic Caucasians in self-esteem.[55] Beginning in the 1980s, however, African Americans have reported the highest self-esteem of all U.S. ethnic groups, including non-Hispanic Caucasians.[56] The differences among these groups aren't substantial, but they have been relatively consistent over the past few decades.

If ethnic minorities experience discrimination and social stigma, how do they maintain their self-esteem? Researchers believe that socially marginalized groups—a category that can also include sexual minorities and people with disabilities—use three general strategies. First, they value the things at which they excel. To the extent that one group excels academically, athletically, or artistically, for instance, that group will emphasize those activities more heavily than activities in which they perform less impressively. Second, they tend to attribute their problems to prejudices in society rather than to their own behaviors or decisions. Third, like most people, they compare themselves with others in their own group more than with people from other groups.[57]

SEX AND SELF-ESTEEM.   Unlike culture, sex does not by itself appear to affect self-esteem. Despite alarming reports that girls suffer from a shortage of self-esteem,[58] there is no scientific evidence, either among children or among

Talking Point: Some educators believe that putting children into sex-segregated schools will enhance the self-esteem of both girls and boys. Ask your students what they think of that policy and why they suspect it would or would not work.

Since the 1980s, African Americans have reported the highest self-esteem of all ethnic groups in the United States. © *Alex Wong/Getty Images News/Getty Images*

adults, to support that belief. In fact, among ethnic minorities, self-esteem is higher for U.S. females than for U.S. males. There is no sex difference among non-Hispanic Caucasians, however.[59] Some experts have suggested that for ethnic minorities, experiences of racial discrimination are more damaging to the self-esteem of males than of females. That theory might explain why males have lower self-esteem than females among ethnic minorities but not among non-Hispanic Caucasians, at least in the United States.[60]

We've seen that self-esteem benefits us in some ways and not in others, and that it varies by culture and sex, but not always in the ways we might expect. In the following discussion, we'll tie self-esteem more directly to interpersonal communication by examining three fundamental interpersonal needs that appear to be facilitated by self-esteem.

The Self and Interpersonal Needs

In his *interpersonal needs theory,* social psychologist Will Schutz proposed that self-esteem interacts with three important interpersonal needs to affect our communication with others: the need for control, the need for inclusion, and the need for affection. As we'll see, each of these needs motivates us to interact with other people in particular ways.

need for control One's need to maintain a degree of influence in one's relationships.

NEED FOR CONTROL.   We all have a **need for control,** which is our motivation to maintain some degree of influence in our relationships. As infants, we relied almost completely on our caregivers to make decisions for us. As we grew up, however, we needed to play a more decisive role in determining the course of our relationships. In many relationships, people share control, so that each person has some say in what happens. We're often less satisfied in relationships when we feel we have no control.[61]

Research shows that the higher a person's self-esteem, the more that individual feels in control of the events in her or his life.[62] By the same token, many of us also have a need to relinquish control from time to time. Just as we're dissatisfied with having too little control, we can also feel overwhelmed by the responsibility of having too much control. Allowing others to exert influence over us is an important part of the interdependent nature of personal relationships. We're often most satisfied, therefore, with a moderate amount of control.

need for inclusion One's need to belong to a social group and be included in the activities of others.

NEED FOR INCLUSION.   Our **need for inclusion** is our need to belong, to be included in the activities of others, and to have positive human contact. Some of us have a stronger need for inclusion than others, but even people whom we would describe as loners need some interaction with others. Studies have shown that people can experience mental and physical distress when their need for inclusion is not met.[63] For individuals with a high need for inclusion, then, the opportunities to form and maintain interpersonal relationships contribute to their self-esteem.

AT A GLANCE

Schutz's Interpersonal Needs

Need for Control	Our need to maintain some degree of control in a relationship
Need for Inclusion	Our need to belong to a social group and to have positive contact with others
Need for Affection	Our need to feel loved and appreciated by others

From a different perspective, people with higher self-esteem tend to be more outgoing and extroverted than people with lower self-esteem. For that reason they might be more motivated to seek out relationships that will meet their need for inclusion.[64] For example, they may be more likely to join social groups, religious organizations, or sports teams to meet others. Nevertheless, even people with a high need for inclusion also enjoy periods of solitude.

Affection and a sense of belonging are two fundamental human needs. In *The Perks of Being a Wallflower,* Sam and Patrick provide shy, unpopular Charlie with both. © *Photos 12 / Alamy*

NEED FOR AFFECTION. Finally, each of us also has a **need for affection.** We need to have people in our lives who love and appreciate us and who communicate their affection to us. We also need to give love and intimacy to others. Some researchers believe that people are born with the capacity for affection, and studies have shown that the more affection people give and receive, the healthier and happier they are.[65] People with higher self-esteem also tend to be more expressive of their affectionate feelings than people with lower self-esteem.[66]

The "At a Glance" box summarizes Schutz's proposed three interpersonal needs. Schutz believed that all three needs are fundamental, meaning that everyone has them to some degree. Furthermore, the greater these needs are, he argued, the more motivated we are to seek and form relationships with people who can help us meet them. People with high self-esteem don't necessarily have stronger needs for inclusion, affection, and control than others do, but they appear to be more successful at meeting those needs through their communication with other people.

> **need for affection** One's need to give and receive expressions of love and appreciation.

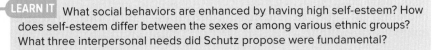

LEARN IT What social behaviors are enhanced by having high self-esteem? How does self-esteem differ between the sexes or among various ethnic groups? What three interpersonal needs did Schutz propose were fundamental?

APPLY IT This week, make a point of expressing affection—in whatever ways feel natural—to close family members, co-workers, and/or friends. Then, in a short report, briefly describe two or three instances of this expression of affection and explain how your efforts have supported both your own and others' need for affection.

REFLECT ON IT When do you feel better or worse about yourself? What factors, besides sex and culture, do you think influence self-esteem?

CONNECT: The Assignment Statistics Report shows you a section's highest, lowest, and average scores on each assignment attempt. You can even compare multiple sections' scores.

3 Presenting the Self: Image Management

As we've considered, your self-concept is related to *the way you see yourself.* When you communicate interpersonally, however, you are also concerned with *the way you want others to see you.* In some situations, you might want others to regard you as friendly, outgoing, and fun. In different situations, you might want people to look at

The Social Network portrays a fictionalized version of Mark Zuckerberg as having little concern for image management. In contrast, most people consider how they want others to perceive them. © Columbia Pictures/Photofest

image The way one wishes to be seen or perceived by others.

image management The process of projecting one's desired public image.

you as reliable, competent, and serious. Perhaps there are circumstances when you'd like others to think of you as independent and open-minded.

When you consider how you want others to perceive you, you're considering the kind of **image** you want to project. In this section, we'll see that managing your image is a collaborative, multidimensional, and complex process. We'll also consider the contributions of communication researcher Myra Goldschmidt, sociologist Erving Goffman, and other scholars whose work has helped us understand the process of image management.

Principles of Image Management

In its depiction of the development of Facebook, the film *The Social Network* (2010) visits the question of whether founder Mark Zuckerberg (played by Jesse Eisenberg) generated the idea for the networking site himself or pirated it from three classmates. When Zuckerberg's classmates sue him for intellectual property theft, he comes across in legal depositions as aggressive, impatient, and condescending. Partly as a result of the way Zuckerberg has presented himself, one of his lawyers indicates that they will be settling a second lawsuit out of court. The impression Zuckerberg would make in a trial, she believes, would lead to a highly unsympathetic jury.

When your goal is to make a positive first impression, you've probably heard that it's best to "just be yourself." Indeed, many people try to project an image that accurately reflects their self-concept. Yet there are many times when the way you act reflects a specific image you wish to project, and you adjust your behavior accordingly. That projection might be "you just being yourself," or it might be an image that suits the occasion or the outcome you desire. This is the process of **image management.** Let's explore three fundamental principles of this process:

- Image management is collaborative.
- We manage multiple identities.
- Image management is complex.

IMAGE MANAGEMENT IS COLLABORATIVE. To some extent, managing your image is an individual process. After all, your image is yours. You also get a lot of help managing your image, however, from the people around you. As psychologist Dan McAdams has suggested, each of us develops a *life story,* or a way of presenting ourselves to others that is based on our self-concept but also influenced by other people.[67]

If others accept the image you portray, they'll tend to behave in ways that encourage that image. Let's say you see yourself as a confident person, and you project that image to others. If other people regard you as confident, they'll treat you as though you are—and their response to you will strengthen that part of your identity in your own mind. If others don't accept the image of yourself that you portray, however, they may see you as less credible or as untrustworthy. Trying to be someone you aren't, or portraying an image of yourself that isn't genuine, might mean that people don't take you seriously.

WE MANAGE MULTIPLE IDENTITIES.   Consider that all the people who interact with you know you only in a certain context. You have your circle of friends, who know you as a friend. You have your family members, who know you as a mother, a son, an aunt, a brother, a cousin, or a grandchild. Your boss and co-workers know you as an employee. Your doctor and your dentist know you as a patient, your professors know you as a student, and your landlord knows you as a tenant.

Significantly, each of these contexts carries its own distinctive role expectations, so you probably enact a somewhat different identity in each one. You likely communicate differently at work than at home, and your friends probably know you differently than your professors do. You may also communicate differently in various online venues, such as Facebook, Snapchat, and Twitter. The point is that we all manage multiple identities; that is, we show different parts of ourselves to different people in our lives.

On occasion, people enact images of themselves that are inaccurate or dishonest. For instance, some people post photos and stories to Facebook, Instagram, or YouTube that portray their lives as far more exciting and glamorous than they actually are. Others present inaccurate information about themselves, such as a job applicant who exaggerates her work experience on her résumé or a man who describes himself in an online personal ad as younger than he is.

The challenge of managing multiple identities is especially pronounced for people with "invisible" medical conditions, which are illnesses or disorders that are not necessarily apparent to others. Conditions such as Down syndrome, stuttering, developmental disabilities, and confinement to a wheelchair are relatively "visible" because many people will notice those conditions after seeing or listening to someone who has them. In contrast, people can, to varying degrees, hide the fact that they have conditions such as cancer, diabetes, asthma, and depression if they don't want others to know. Most people can't identify a person with diabetes or asthma, for example, simply by looking at him or her.

For that reason, people with those and other invisible conditions have both the ability and the responsibility to determine how to incorporate their conditions into the image they project. For instance, many people must continually decide whom to tell about their conditions, when to make those disclosures, and how to do so. That decision can be particularly agonizing for individuals suffering from invisible conditions that are also socially stigmatized, such as mental health disorders and HIV-positive status, because of the fear of how others will react to their disclosures. The "Communication: Dark Side" box addresses that issue as it pertains to HIV-positive individuals.

Image management is similarly challenging for many sexual minorities. Like an invisible medical condition, a person's sexual orientation is not always evident in the way he or she looks, sounds, or communicates. That gives lesbian, gay, and bisexual people the ability to choose to whom to reveal their sexual orientation. Many find this to be a consequential decision, because sexual minorities are often discriminated against throughout the world, including much of the United States.[68] To avoid prejudice, sexual minorities may choose to "stay in the closet" and keep their sexual orientation a secret, even from their closest friends and relatives.

Writing Note: Ask students to pick three or four people who know them in very different contexts, such as an uncle, a customer, a roommate, and a doctor. Have students write one short paragraph describing them—the students—as though from the perspective of each of those people. Ask students to comment on which aspects of their identities they think are consistent and which are different across the descriptions.

In Everyday Life: What are some everyday situations in which we feel conflict between various aspects of our identity?

Focus on Ethics: What are the ethical implications of hiding an invisible illness in, say, a job interview? U.S. federal law largely prohibits employers from asking a potential employee about mental and physical health conditions unless they are directly relevant to the job being sought. The law aside, is it ethical to fail to disclose conditions that, even if they aren't directly relevant to the job, could impair a person's ability to be a good, reliable employee?

When we select images to share on social media—such as travel or fine dining "selfies," rather than lunch at our desk—we are engaging in image management. © *Coloroftime/Getty Images, RF*

communication · DARK SIDE

RISKS OF DISCLOSING HIV-POSITIVE STATUS

t is traumatic for people to learn that they are infected with HIV. Being HIV-positive puts individuals at risk for developing AIDS, a terminal disease with no known cure. It also requires that people decide with whom they're going to share the news of their infection.

Many people with HIV may feel in a bind when deciding whether to disclose their condition to others. On the one hand, disclosing the illness may help them acquire both medical and emotional support, and it may encourage others to adopt healthier sexual or drug-use behaviors themselves. On the other hand, disclosure can be risky. Psychologists Valerian Derlega and Barbara Winstead and their colleagues explain that HIV-positive people may have several reasons for choosing not to disclose their illness:

- *Privacy:* It's no one else's business but their own.
- *Self-blame:* They feel guilty for being HIV-positive.
- *Communication difficulties:* They don't know how to tell others about it.
- *Fear of rejection:* They worry that others will reject or even hurt them.
- *Fear of discrimination:* They fear that employers, landlords, or others will discriminate against them.
- *Protection of others:* They don't want others to worry about them.
- *Superficial relationships:* They don't feel close enough to others to trust them with this information.

Despite these risks, disclosing HIV status can be useful in many ways. Not only can it help secure needed medical attention and emotional support, but it can also help to strengthen relationships, particularly with others who are also HIV-positive. It is also extremely important for the health and safety of a romantic or sexual partner. In fact, to protect potential partners, several U.S. states have enacted laws making it a felony to expose someone else knowingly to HIV without that person's consent, as would happen if an HIV-positive individual engaged in sexual behavior with a partner without informing that partner of his or her HIV status.

FROM ME TO YOU

Many of us are uncomfortable discussing HIV. In the United States, being HIV-positive is widely stigmatized because of its association with two marginalized groups: gay men and intravenous drug users. The stigma makes it easier to believe that if you don't belong to either of those groups, you can't or won't develop HIV. The truth, however, is that HIV infects people from all walks of life—homosexual and heterosexual, rich and poor, female and male, adult and child.

Source: Derlega, V. J., Winstead, B. A., Mathews, A., & Braitman, A. L. (2008). Why does someone reveal highly personal information? Attributions for and against self-disclosure in close relationships. *Communication Research Reports, 25,* 115–130.

A person's decision to disclose his or her sexual orientation has some important health consequences. To begin with, long-term concealment of such a fundamental aspect of an individual's identity is stressful.[69] Over time, such stress can elevate the risks for cardiovascular diseases,[70] rapid progression of HIV,[71] and suicide.[72] There is some evidence that those problems are magnified for lesbian, gay, and bisexual adolescents, who, in contrast to adults, may lack the social support and emotional maturity to manage the stress of concealing their sexual orientation.[73]

Although concealing one's sexual orientation can be problematic for health, so can disclosing it. For instance, a study of gay and bisexual men found that those who had disclosed their sexual orientation in their workplace experienced more daily stress and negative moods than did those who kept their orientation secret.[74] Other research has found that lesbians and gay men are at elevated risk for depression and stress even if they are open about their sexual orientation.[75]

IMAGE MANAGEMENT IS COMPLEX. If image management sounds complicated, that's because it often is. For instance, we may have competing goals in our interactions with others. Let's say you've been offered a prestigious internship at a startup company in California's Silicon Valley, and you ask your older sister and her husband, who live close to that area, if you can move in with them for the semester. You probably want your sister to think of you as a mature, responsible adult rather than as the carefree teenager you were when she moved out of your parents' house. As a result, you will have to present your request in a way that preserves your image as a responsible person. At the same time, you want to persuade your sister and brother-in-law that you really need a place to stay and that you can't afford to rent one on your own because the internship pays poorly. This reality may cause you to project the image that you need help. Thus, you may find your image needs in conflict: You want to appear responsible but also in need of assistance. How to manage these competing image needs—while still persuading your sister to let you move in—can be complex.

In the IM: The out-of-class activity "Identity Collage" encourages students to consider the complexity of their self-images by creating a visual depiction of them.

Communication researcher Myra Goldschmidt found that when people ask others for favors, they often create narratives that help to maintain their images while still being persuasive.[76] To your sister, you might say things like "I need a place to stay for just a couple of months while I do this internship," and "I promise to help around the house." Such strategies can help preserve your image as a responsible individual even in a situation where that image might be threatened.

We've seen that image management is a collaborative process that often requires negotiating several identities in a complex way. How do we determine what our image needs are in the first place?

Managing Face Needs

In a recurring segment on the nightly comedy *Jimmy Kimmel Live!*, the host invites guests to read some of the disparaging remarks made about them on Twitter, aloud, on camera. Part of the appeal of the "Mean Tweets" segment is the way that the actors,

When celebrities like Pharrell Williams read mean tweets people write about them on *Jimmy Kimmel Live,* they are managing their face needs.
© *AP Images/Alex J. Berliner / ABImages*

got skills?

FACEWORK

Practice offering complaints in a nonthreatening manner.

WHAT?
Learn to protect the face needs of another person.

WHY?
Receiving complaints, such as grievances about poor service in a restaurant or car dealership, can threaten a person's competence face. When you are dissatisfied with something, you can express your complaints constructively—and, by so doing, perhaps even improve your chances of getting satisfactory resolution of the issue—if you know how to preserve the face needs of the individual to whom you are complaining.

HOW?
1. Imagine a specific situation in which you feel you must complain about poor service. List two or three ways in which your complaint might threaten the competence face of the person receiving it.
2. Write out sentences and phrases that would minimize those face threats. For instance, focus on describing the problem rather than assigning blame: "When I got my car back, I noticed that the 'check engine' light was on. Can you tell me why?"

TRY!
1. Role-play a conversation about poor service with another person. Try to minimize threats to your communication partner's competence face.
2. Ask the person for feedback on how well you communicated your complaint in a nonthreatening manner.

Consider: *What skills did you learn? How will you apply them when you next need to express a complaint or problem?*

> **face** A person's desired public image.

> **facework** The behaviors one uses to project one's desired public image to others.

> **face needs** Components of one's desired public image.

> **fellowship face** The need to feel liked and accepted by others.

> **autonomy face** The need to avoid being imposed upon by others.

> **competence face** The need to be respected and viewed as competent and intelligent.

musical artists, and sports figures who take part react to the attacks, often dismissing the comments with laughter, countering with comments of their own, or even showing how the comments hurt their feelings. Researchers might say that these celebrities are making an attempt to "save face," by taking action to avoid embarrassment and maintain dignity in a situation that threatens it. Although we sometimes associate losing or saving face with collectivistic cultures such as Korea and Japan, the ability to save face is important to people in many cultures.[77] Let's take a look at what happens when our desired public image is threatened.

FACE AND FACE NEEDS. Each of us has a desired public image—a certain way that we want others to see and think of us—and we work to maintain that image. For instance, if you want others to see you as intelligent and competent, you will likely behave in ways that give that impression, and you will try to avoid situations that will make you look incompetent or uninformed. Sociologist Erving Goffman coined the term **face** to describe our desired public image and the term **facework** to describe the behaviors we use to project that image to others.[78] The "Got Skills?" box offers suggestions for improving your own facework abilities.

Researchers believe that our face is made up of three **face needs,** or important components of our desired public image. **Fellowship face** refers to the need to have others like and accept us. That is the part of our identity that motivates us to make friends, join clubs or social groups, and behave pleasantly around others. **Autonomy face** refers to our need to avoid being imposed upon by others. It's our autonomy face that motivates us to be in control of our time and resources and to avoid having other people make decisions for us. Finally, **competence face** is our need to have others respect us and to acknowledge our abilities and intelligence. That need drives us to seek careers and hobbies that we're good at and to avoid situations in which we will embarrass

AT A GLANCE

Three Types of Face

Fellowship Face	Our need to have others like and accept us
Autonomy Face	Our need not to be imposed upon by others
Competence Face	Our need to be respected for our intelligence and abilities

ourselves.[79] You might find it easy to remember those face needs by noting that the first letters of their names—fellowship, autonomy, and competence—constitute the first three letters in the word *face*. The "At a Glance" box summarizes the three face needs.

FACE THREATS. Each of us has a different desired public image, and so our face needs vary. Fellowship, autonomy, and competence are largely independent face needs, so having a high level of one need does not necessarily affect a person's levels of the other two needs. For instance, some people have a very strong fellowship face need, meaning it is extremely important that others like them. Other people much prefer to be respected than liked. Similarly, one person may have a very high need for autonomy, whereas another person may not mind having decisions made for him or her. Those differences are part of what makes everyone's identity unique.

Although we all have our own face needs, we often become consciously aware of them only when they're threatened. Let's say you applied to join an honor society but were not accepted. The decision not to include you could threaten your fellowship face. It could also threaten your competence face by making you feel you weren't smart enough to get into the group. The rejection of your application, therefore, is a **face-threatening act** because it fails to fulfill one or more of your face needs.

Face-threatening acts often lead people to behave in ways that help restore their face. In the case of the honor society, you could say "I didn't really want to be in that society anyway."[80*] Making such a statement doesn't mean you actually believe it. Indeed, you probably did want to be in the honor society, or you wouldn't have bothered applying. Rather, you would likely say this to manage your image with others by making it appear as though your face needs weren't threatened. This response is therefore a type of *defense mechanism* that helps minimize the effects of a face-threatening act.

Face threats are common experiences within many marginalized populations. For example, threats to autonomy face may arise among marginalized people who have to rely on others to meet their material needs or who feel they don't have a voice in decisions that affect them. Elderly people, for instance, frequently experience losses of autonomy as a result of various physical and cognitive limitations associated with aging.[81] Individuals with certain disabilities may also

Talking Point: Ask students to relate autonomy face with individualistic and collectivistic cultural values.

Talking Point: How do people whose disabilities force them to rely on others for help with dressing or using the restroom maintain their autonomy face? When you are at the doctor's office or in a hospital, how do you maintain your autonomy face?

face-threatening act Any behavior that threatens one or more face needs.

Authorities in Ferguson, Missouri, worked to manage their competence face needs in the wake of outrage surrounding the death of Michael Brown. © AP Images/Jeff Roberson

See Kim, W., Guan, Z., & Park, H. S. (2012). Face and facework: A crosscultural comparison of managing politeness norms in U.S. and Korea. International Journal of Communication, 6, 19.

Focus on Scholarship: The self-serving bias in attribution making indicates that people tend to attribute their successes to internal causes (such as their talent) and their failures to external causes (such as another person's incompetence). This pattern helps to maintain competence face by suggesting that when we succeed, we deserve to succeed, but when we fail, it isn't our fault. Of course, sometimes our failures *are* our fault; the self-serving bias merely encourages us to tell ourselves and others that they aren't. The self-serving bias differs from the fundamental attribution error, which relates to attributions made for other people's behaviors and says we are more likely to attribute others' behaviors to internal rather than external causes, regardless of whether the behaviors are positive or negative.[iv]

[iv]Mezulis, A. H., Abramson, L. Y., Hyde, J. S., & Hankin, B. L. (2004). Is there a universal positivity bias in attributions? A meta-analytic review of individual, developmental, and cultural differences in the self-serving attributional bias. *Psychological Bulletin, 130,* 711–747.

perceive threats to their autonomy if they are unable to do things that others can do, such as driving a car and going for a walk. Still other groups may feel their autonomy is threatened when they don't have the ability to make certain decisions for themselves, as in the case of lesbian and gay adults who may be prevented from adopting children.

Being marginalized also leads many people to feel disrespected and shamed. Such feelings can threaten both their fellowship face and their competence face. U.S. society has stigmas associated with being homeless, poor, old, disabled, lesbian, gay, mentally ill, and (in some circles) even divorced, even though a person may have no choice about belonging to any such groups.[82] Stigmatized people might feel like outsiders who don't fit in with those around them, and those perceptions threaten their fellowship face by leading them to feel unaccepted. They may also perceive that others judge them not on the basis of their intelligence or abilities but simply because of their stigmatized condition—a perception that threatens their competence face by making them feel disrespected.

LEARN IT What does it mean to say that image management is collaborative? How are fellowship face, autonomy face, and competence face similar? How are they different?

APPLY IT Imagine you're asking someone in your family for a favor. Think about the types of images you would want to project to that person. With those images in mind, write out the words you would use to make your request.

REFLECT ON IT When do you notice that you have to manage multiple identities? What strategies do you use to do so? How do you usually react when your face needs are threatened?

4 Communicating the Self: Self-Disclosure

Now that we have explored how we form a self-concept and how we manage our image, let's complete our analysis by looking at how we communicate about ourselves, or *self-disclose*. **Self-disclosure** is the act of intentionally giving others information about ourselves that we believe to be true but that we think they don't already have. From a highly intimate conversation with a romantic partner about our hopes and dreams to a mundane chat with a co-worker about where we dined last evening, self-disclosure involves sharing a part of ourselves with someone else.

In this section, we're going to look at several principles of self-disclosure and examine various benefits that self-disclosure can bring to us and to our relationships. Finally, we'll take stock of some of the risks of self-disclosing.

self-disclosure The act of giving others information about oneself that one believes they do not already have.

Principles of Self-Disclosure

Most of us engage in self-disclosure, in one form or another, on a fairly ongoing basis. Self-disclosure has several important attributes.

SELF-DISCLOSURE IS INTENTIONAL AND TRUTHFUL.   For an act of communication to qualify as self-disclosure, it must meet two conditions: (1) We must deliberately share information about ourselves, and (2) we must believe that information is true. Let's say that you accidentally overhear your friend Dean telling someone about his financial problems over the telephone. That wouldn't constitute an act of self-disclosure according to the definition just given, because Dean didn't share the information with you deliberately.

Similarly, self-disclosing means sharing information that we believe is true. If you tell a co-worker that you've never traveled outside your home country, for instance, that qualifies as self-disclosure if you believe it to be true. It's your belief in the truth of the information that matters, not the absolute truth of the information. Perhaps you traveled outside the country when you were an infant and were too young to remember. If you believe the information you're providing is true, however, then it qualifies as self-disclosure. Intentionally giving people information about ourselves that we believe to be false is an act of deception, as we'll see in the Deceptive Communication chapter.

SELF-DISCLOSURE VARIES IN BREADTH AND DEPTH.   Social penetration theory, developed by social psychologists Irwin Altman and Dalmas Taylor and depicted in Figure 3, illustrates how self-disclosure over time is like peeling away the layers of an onion: Each self-disclosure helps us learn more and more about a person we're getting to know.

According to social penetration theory, peeling away the layers to get to know someone requires sharing disclosures that have both breadth and depth. **Breadth** describes the range of topics you discuss with various people. With some people, you might disclose about only certain aspects of your life. For instance, you might tell your doctor all about your health but not about other aspects of your life. You might disclose only about your professional life with a co-worker, or only about your academic life with a professor. In those relationships, your self-disclosure has little breadth, because you disclose only about a limited range of topics. In contrast, with your relatives, close friends, and romantic partner you probably talk about several different aspects of your life, such as your work and school experiences, your financial concerns, your professional ambitions, your health, your spiritual or religious beliefs, your political opinions, and your desires for the future. Your disclosure in these relationships is characterized by greater breadth, because you disclose about a wider range of topics.

The second dimension, **depth,** measures how personal or intimate your disclosures are. The depth of our self-disclosures is largely a function of how carefully we feel we must guard the information in the disclosures. Let's say Maya and her romantic partner are having problems. Maya might describe her problems in detail to her mother, not only because she values her opinion, but also because she trusts her mother to keep the information private. Because she doesn't feel the need to guard this information from her mother, Maya can engage in disclosure that has great depth. With her secretary, by contrast, Maya discloses that she is having difficulty, but she doesn't go into detail because she doesn't feel comfortable entrusting her secretary with the specifics. In this instance, Maya engages in self-disclosure of lesser depth.

SELF-DISCLOSURE VARIES AMONG RELATIONSHIPS.   Not every relationship is characterized by the same breadth and depth of self-disclosure. Some relationships involve depth of disclosure but very little breadth. With your accountant, for instance,

social penetration theory A theory that predicts that as relationships develop, communication increases in breadth and depth.

breadth The range of topics about which one person self-discloses to another.

depth The intimacy of the topics about which one person self-discloses to another.

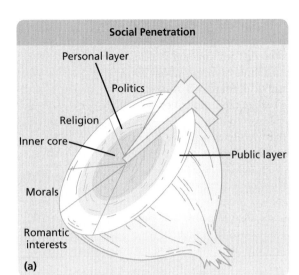

Social Penetration

Personal layer

Politics

Religion

Inner core

Public layer

Morals

Romantic interests

(a)

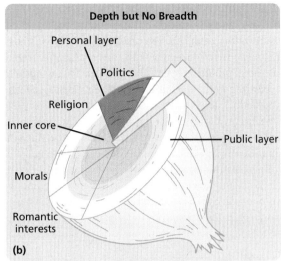

Depth but No Breadth

Personal layer

Politics

Religion

Inner core

Public layer

Morals

Romantic interests

(b)

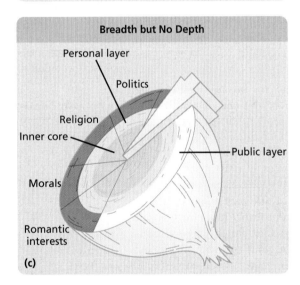

Breadth but No Depth

Personal layer

Politics

Religion

Inner core

Public layer

Morals

Romantic interests

(c)

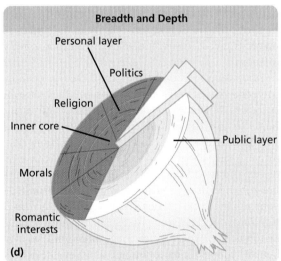

Breadth and Depth

Personal layer

Politics

Religion

Inner core

Public layer

Morals

Romantic interests

(d)

FIGURE 3 Social Penetration Theory Researchers use the image of a multilayered onion to represent the process of social penetration in a relationship. The outer layer of the onion represents breadth of self-disclosure. That layer is referred to as the "public layer" because it reflects details you would share with most people. The inner layers of the onion reflect depth of self-disclosure. We call those the "personal layers" because they represent details you would share only with people you know quite well. If you share personal details about your political ideas with someone, but nothing else, then your relationship has depth but not breadth. If you tell someone only superficial information about your political, religious, moral, and romantic experiences but do not provide more personal details on any of those topics, then your relationship has breadth but not depth. In our closest relationships, we usually disclose both superficial and private information about many issues, so those relationships have both breadth and depth.

you might disclose in-depth information about your financial matters but not about anything else. Likewise, you might tell your doctor intimate details about your health but very little about other issues in your life. In Figure 3b, this type of relationship is depicted by coloring one wedge of the circle from the outermost ring to the innermost but leaving the other circles untouched.

Other relationships are characterized by breadth of disclosure but very little depth. With casual friends at school or work, for example, you might disclose a little about several areas of your life—family, hobbies, political ideas, career ambitions—but not provide intimate details about any of them. As Figure 3c indicates, you would depict this type of relationship by coloring in several of the wedges on the circle, but only on the outermost ring, leaving the smaller internal rings untouched.

Still other relationships, such as romantic partnerships and close friendships, thrive only with high degrees of both breadth and depth. In such relationships, people typically share both public and private information about multiple aspects of their lives. Figure 3d, by coloring in several of the wedges around the circle—some of which extend all the way to the center—illustrates both the breadth and the depth of self-disclosure in those kinds of relationships.

SELF-DISCLOSURE IS A GRADUAL PROCESS.   Even our closest relationships usually aren't close right away. Closeness develops over time as two people get to know each other and reveal more and more information about themselves. In new relationships, people often disclose slowly, sharing just a few details at first and offering more personal information only if they like and trust each other.[83]

When they started becoming friends, Deepak and Prasad shared mostly routine information, such as their hometowns, favorite sport teams, and occupations. As they got to know and trust each other more, they shared their opinions on politics, relationships, and religion. Only after they had known each other for quite a while did they feel comfortable talking about more personal things, such as Prasad's health problems and the challenges in Deepak's marriage. Although people in some relationships begin sharing intimate information quickly, self-disclosure usually moves in small increments.

ONLINE SELF-DISCLOSURE FOLLOWS A DIFFERENT PATTERN.   One exception to the general pattern of gradual self-disclosure occurs in relationships formed online, such as through e-mail, chat rooms, or blogs.[84] You might predict that people would be less disclosive in computer-mediated contexts than in face-to-face settings, on the reasoning that they might not feel as engaged with online conversational partners or as comfortable sharing personal information. Just the opposite appears to be true, however. Research shows that the lack of face-to-face interaction in computer-mediated contexts encourages self-disclosure, so that people are often more disclosive at the start of an online relationship than in a face-to-face one.[85] For example, a study of new romantic relationships discovered that couples disclose personal information earlier in their relationship via computer-mediated communication than in person.[86]

How do researchers account for that behavior? Communication scholar Joseph Walther explains that the computer-mediated environment encourages not just personal communication but also communication that is "hyperpersonal," meaning that it contains more private information than people would typically share face-to-face.[87] Walther believes that hyperpersonal communication occurs partly because we see communication partners in a more positive light online than face-to-face, so we feel less inhibited about disclosing highly personal information. This hyperpersonal nature of online disclosure can accelerate feelings of closeness between people. As we will see, however, it also involves certain risks, and this reality suggests that people may benefit from disclosing less personal information online.

Focus on Scholarship: Research suggests that self-disclosure also varies within relationships; many long-term relationships go through self-disclosure "cycles" wherein relational partners disclose more to each other during some periods and less during others. That is normal and is not necessarily a sign of relationship distress.[v]

[v]Sprecher, S., & Hendrick, S. S. (2004). Self-disclosure in intimate relationships: Associations with individual and relationship characteristics over time. *Journal of Social and Clinical Psychology, 23,* 857–877.

Talking Point: What are some other exceptions to the rule that self-disclosure usually proceeds slowly? Is it that way with a counselor or a therapist? How about a stranger on an airplane?

© Hans Neleman/Getty Images

SELF-DISCLOSURE IS USUALLY RECIPROCAL.

You may have heard the expression "One good turn deserves another." This saying suggests that when someone gives you some type of gift or resource, you are expected to return the favor. Sociologist Alvin Gouldner called that expectation the **norm of reciprocity**.[88] In North American cultures, at least, the norm of reciprocity usually extends to self-disclosure; that is, when we disclose things to other people, we typically expect them to disclose things to us in return.[89]

There are some exceptions to this rule. For example, when we disclose to a physician or a counselor, we don't expect her or him to disclose back to us. In our friendships and other personal relationships, however, we generally expect that others will share information with us as we share it with them.

norm of reciprocity A social expectation that resources and favors provided to one person in a relationship should be reciprocated by that person.

Talking Point: What happens when the norm of reciprocity is violated—when one person in a relationship doesn't reciprocate the breadth and depth of the other's disclosures?

In Everyday Life: When you go to the doctor and disclose personal information about yourself, how does it feel when you can't ask your doctor to disclose the same information to you? How do you trust your doctor with this information, when your disclosures aren't reciprocated?

SELF-DISCLOSURE CAN SERVE MANY PURPOSES. People self-disclose to one another for many reasons. Let's say you have been laid off from your job, and you're debating whether to tell your roommates. Disclosing this information to them might serve several purposes. One purpose is simply to share the information. Another might be to signal to your roommates that you could use their support or that you might be late with your share of the rent that month. Your disclosure might also remind your roommates that you trust them, and this act of trust may strengthen your friendships with them.

Although self-disclosure can serve multiple functions, it isn't appropriate in every case. There are times when it is more important to be discreet and to keep information to yourself. It's often important to maintain professional relationships with colleagues or customers, for instance, because of the business you transact with them. In such relationships, you may find it best to keep personal information to yourself and to focus your communication on the business you're conducting.

One reason discretion is often advisable in professional relationships is that information a person self-discloses can later be used against him or her. Suppose you work for a construction company, and your job is to provide cost estimates for projects. Gena calls you and asks for a bid on a large demolition job. In the course of your many conversations with Gena, she discloses to you that her family is having severe financial problems. Because of the norm of reciprocity, you feel as though you ought to disclose something equally personal to her. As a result, you tell her you have been having financial problems, too, and are considering looking for a new job to improve your situation—something you have not yet shared with your current employer.

After Gena receives your company's bid, she calls you to ask if you can lower the price. When you reply that you have offered the lowest estimate you can reasonably provide, Gena asks you to reconsider, saying, "I'm sure you wouldn't want your boss to know you're thinking of looking for a new job." At that point, you realize that Gena self-disclosed to you only to elicit a disclosure back from you that she could later use as leverage when negotiating the demolition bid. This example doesn't suggest you shouldn't trust others, but it illustrates the fact that some people use self-disclosure only to serve their own needs.

SELF-DISCLOSURE IS INFLUENCED BY CULTURAL AND GENDER ROLES. Self-disclosure is affected by norms for sex and culture.[90] Regarding gender, many people probably believe that women self-disclose more than men because disclosure and emotional expressiveness are a bigger part of the feminine gender role than of the masculine gender role, especially in North America.[91] Is that generalization true? In fact, the evidence suggests that women, on average, do self-disclose more than men, although the difference isn't as large as many people believe it is. In an analysis of more than 250 studies about sex differences in self-disclosure, communication researchers Kathryn Dindia and Mike Allen also found that the sex of the person receiving the disclosure makes a difference.[92] Specifically, women are more likely than men to disclose to females, but women and men are equally likely to disclose to males.

In formal settings, such as a business dinner, discretion is often more appropriate than self-disclosure. © *Commercial Eye/Stone/Getty Images*

Self-disclosure is also affected by cultural norms. In some cultures, such as those of North America and northern Europe, people are often encouraged to express themselves and self-disclose to their friends and family. Other cultures, such as most Asian and Middle Eastern cultures, value discretion and encourage people to disclose only under more limited circumstances. Consequently, people in those cultures may be inclined to disclose personal information exclusively within their families or romantic relationships rather than sharing it with social and professional acquaintances.[93]

Benefits of Self-Disclosure

There are many ways that self-disclosure can be good for us and for our relationships. In brief, four key benefits of self-disclosure are

- *Enhancement of relationships and trust:* Self-disclosure often helps us maintain high-quality relationships. We tend to disclose the most to people we like, and we also tend to like people who disclose to us.[94] Sharing appropriate self-disclosure with friends, relatives, and romantic partners helps us to maintain those relationships and reinforces the trust we share with those individuals.[95] Conversely, a lack of self-disclosure in a long-term relationship such as a marriage or a close friendship can be a sign of distress in the relationship.[96]

In the IM: The in-class activity "Self-Disclosure and Closeness" helps students consider both the benefits and the risks of self-disclosure in close relationships.

CONNECT: Learning Resources in SmartBook help students practice their skills by evaluating conversations and analyzing situations for communication competence.

fact OR fiction? | LET IT OUT: DISCLOSURE DOES A BODY GOOD

When you've gone through troubling times, have you ever noticed that you feel better after putting your feelings into words? Some people say they benefit from talking with supportive friends or counselors about their experiences. Others say that even writing about their feelings in a private journal makes them feel better, both mentally and physically. Is that idea fact or fiction?

A large body of research suggests that it's a fact. Multiple experiments by psychologist James Pennebaker and his colleagues have demonstrated that disclosing feelings in writing—particularly feelings related to experiences of trauma—produces measurable benefits in physical and mental health. In a typical study, participants write once a week for 20 minutes at a time over a three-week period about a traumatic event. People in a control group write on the

© Stockbyte/PunchStock/
Getty Images, RF

same schedule about emotionally neutral topics, such as what they did over the weekend. Pennebaker and his team have found that compared to the control group, participants who disclose about traumatic events experience significant improvements in their mental and physical health, some of which last several months after the experiment has ended. Pennebaker believes that suppressing emotions requires effort that can also impair a person's health. Expressing emotions in words—even in writing—may relieve people of the effort required to suppress their emotions and cause their health to improve as a result.

ASK YOURSELF

- How do you notice that you feel better, if at all, after disclosing your emotions?

- Are you generally more comfortable self-disclosing to members of one sex than to members of the other, or do you feel equally comfortable disclosing to both women and men?

Source: Pennebaker, J. W., & Chung, C. K. (2011). Expressive writing: Connections to physical and mental health. In H. S. Friedman (Ed.), *The Oxford handbook of health psychology* (pp. 417–437). Oxford, England: Oxford University Press.

Outside of Class: An interesting out-of-class exercise is to have students talk to people about their experiences with self-help groups (either in person groups or online groups). Students might ask people what they found most useful about the ways that group members assisted one another through their own stories and disclosures.

- *Reciprocity:* Many of us follow a norm of reciprocity when it comes to self-disclosure: When we disclose to others, they tend to disclose back to us.[97] Thus, one way to get to know other people is to tell them things about ourselves. When we share personal information with others, they may feel more comfortable doing the same in return.

- *Emotional release:* Sometimes the best part of self-disclosing is the feeling of getting something "off your chest." Let's say that Caryn borrowed her sister Amy's car and accidentally put a small dent in the fender. Instead of telling Amy about the dent, Caryn hoped she wouldn't notice. Pretty soon, Caryn felt so guilty that she had trouble sleeping. When she finally disclosed the accident to Amy and apologized, she felt relief. Appropriate self-disclosures like Caryn's can often provide emotional release.[98] Several studies have also shown that they can reduce the stress of holding on to a secret. That is an important benefit, because reducing stress can improve both mental and physical health.[99] You can read more about the connection between disclosure and health in "Fact or Fiction?"

Students benefit when they feel comfortable talking to their teachers about personal issues that affect school performance.
© *Fuse/Getty Images, RF*

- *Helping others:* You can self-disclose in ways that help other people, particularly when you're consoling people who are going through hard times. If your friend is having difficulty handling his parents' divorce, for instance, you might disclose how you managed traumatic situations in your own family. Your disclosure can provide comfort and signal to your friend that he's not alone. Many self-help programs, such as Alcoholics Anonymous, use this principle to help their members realize they are all going through a similar struggle.[100] Some disclosures even have the effect of protecting others against threats to their health—as in the situation when a person who is HIV-positive discloses that status to health care providers and potential sexual partners.[101]

Enhancement of relationships, reciprocity, emotional release, and assistance to others are not the only benefits provided by self-disclosure, but they're among the most important for interpersonal communication. Before we conclude that self-disclosure is always a positive behavior, however, let's take a look at some of its most notable risks.

Risks of Self-Disclosure

Some scholars believe we spend so much time thinking about the benefits of disclosure that we tend to ignore the risks it entails for both the people who make the disclosures and those who receive them.[102] Here we'll look at four potential risks:

Media Note: In the instructor resources available on the Online Learning Center, the video clip "Should She Tell?" asks students to consider some risks of self-disclosure.

- *Rejection:* When we self-disclose, we allow others to know information about us that they didn't know before. Although such information sharing can lead to very good outcomes, such as emotional release and enhancing trust, it also involves some serious risks.[103] For instance, what if the people to whom we're disclosing don't like what we tell them? On the television series *Glee,* for instance, Santana confides in her grandmother that she is gay and in love with a woman. Far from bringing them closer together, her disclosure leads Santana's grandmother to reject her and her relationship. Often, the way a person reacts to a disclosure will determine whether its outcome is positive or negative.

- *Chance of obligating others:* Have you ever had someone confide in you, and then felt obligated to disclose something about yourself? If so, you have felt the burden of disclosure—the feeling that you are expected to reciprocate or respond to someone's disclosure with a disclosure of your own. Likewise, when you self-disclose, you risk the other person feeling obligated to disclose something back to you when he or she might not be comfortable doing so. Beyond the potential for creating awkward silences and feelings of discomfort, such feelings could encourage the person to avoid you.

- *Hurt to others:* Beyond making someone uncomfortable, it's possible to hurt others with disclosures that are too critical or too personal. Despite the maxim that "honesty is the best policy," uncensored honesty can lead to wounded feelings and even resentment. Imagine that your wife has asked you what you think of a childhood friend with whom she recently reunited over the Internet. You have never been a big fan of Sonya, but you find yourself torn between wanting to be honest and wanting to be nice, because their renewed friendship seems to be lifting your wife's spirits. Indeed, you may have been taught that if you can't say something nice, you shouldn't say anything at all. This rule for politeness is meant to reduce the chances that someone will be hurt by a self-disclosure that's too critical.

- *Violation of other people's privacy:* Inappropriate disclosures can even hurt people who aren't participating in the conversation. In December 2014, for instance, 12-year-old Ronin Shimizu of Folsom, California, committed suicide after allegedly being taunted due to rumors about his sexuality. His death focused increased media attention on the problems that can ensue when people's privacy is violated through inappropriate disclosures.

People in many relationships, including families, friendships, and workplace relationships, share private information with one another that is not meant to be shared with others. When we disclose that information to third parties without permission—a behavior we call **gossip**—we risk hurting people and damaging their trust in us.

Challenges and Risks of Disclosing Online

Earlier in this chapter, we considered how disclosures made in online environments—such as in chat rooms or on Facebook—are often hyperpersonal, or of a more personal nature than they would be if they were shared face-to-face. The same can be true of messages sent by text or tweet. The tendency to be hyperpersonal makes disclosing in electronically mediated channels vulnerable to many risks.

As we'll discover in the Interpersonal Conflict chapter, researchers believe that online communication venues have a "disinhibition effect," encouraging people to say or do things that they wouldn't if they were in face-to-face settings.[104] For instance, you might not feel comfortable sharing the intimate details of your health while sitting with a friend in a coffee shop, but you might describe them in explicit detail to members of an online support group. The disinhibition effect associated with online communication can be liberating, because it helps us feel free to express ourselves in ways we normally wouldn't.

Focus on Ethics: People sometimes think that sharing private information about others is all right if they trust the person they're sharing it with to keep it secret. Even if the receiver does keep the secret, does this still constitute an unethical act?

gossip The sharing of an individual's personal information with a third party without the individual's consent.

We have to be careful, however, that we don't disclose inappropriate information about ourselves or others, which is easier to do when we feel disinhibited. Because so much electronically mediated communication is written, recipients can save disclosures made online and use them against you, even sharing them with others without your knowledge or consent. Here are some specific tips for protecting yourself when communicating in electronically mediated ways:

Social media offer the ability to manage our identities online. In fact, they prompt some people to disclose more information than they would face-to-face. © CJG - Technology/Alamy

- *Be careful what you say.* In 2013, a teenage girl was murdered while home alone in Tulsa, Oklahoma. Shortly before she died, she had tweeted, "Have the house to myself, everybody gone."[105]* Whether her killer had seen her Twitter feed before coming to her house is unknown—nonetheless, announcing to the general public that you're alone is unwise. In the same vein, checking in on Facebook or Foursquare wherever you go can alert would-be burglars that you aren't at home.

- *Protect your personal information.* Giving out your address, date of birth, Social Security number, passwords, or credit card details through an e-mail, text, or Facebook post is an invitation to trouble. Similarly, avoid posting photos of your new driver's license or the huge bill you've just paid off. You may feel safe in doing so if you trust the intended recipient of your message, but electronic forms of communication are vulnerable to being intercepted. If your personal details end up in the wrong hands, you can easily become the victim of identity theft.

- *Think twice before posting photos.* Many people are careful about the information they write in a text or tweet, but give little thought to posting photos of themselves. These days, however, many photographic devices—especially those on smartphones—embed details about one's location in the photos they produce. You might think it harmless to snap a picture of yourself and post it with the caption "Just relaxing at home," for instance, but viewers may be able to use the photo's properties to determine where you are. To protect yourself, consider disabling location-tracking features on your tablet or smartphone.

- *Don't say or show something you wouldn't want shared.* Because they are in electronic format, your text messages, tweets, e-mail messages, and Facebook postings can all be saved and potentially shared with others you wouldn't want to see them. Even if you trust the recipient of your message not to show it to others, he or she may do so accidentally or mindlessly. In that situation, your information or opinions can reach people you didn't intend, causing you embarrassment or harm.

*IKeepSafe blog. (2013, April 30). Real danger in sharing too much info online. Retrieved February 13, 2015, from http://www.ikeepsafe.org/cybersafety/real-danger-in-sharingtoo-much-info-online/

There's no question that electronically mediated communication can help you build and maintain important personal and professional relationships. When it comes to self-disclosure, however, communicating online poses special risks. Because people often feel uninhibited about disclosing online, it's wise to be especially careful about what you say or post in electronically mediated environments.

LEARN IT What is meant by breadth and depth of self-disclosure? In what ways can self-disclosure enhance relationships? What are the primary risks of self-disclosure? What aspects of online communication make a person particularly vulnerable to the risks of self-disclosure?

APPLY IT Choose one friend, one family member, and one school or work relationship. For each one, re-create the drawing in Figure 3, specifying both the depth and the breadth of disclosure that you typically share with that person. Notice the similarities and differences in breadth and depth across those three relationships.

In the IM: You can now access the end-of-chapter Discussion Questions and the Research Library in the Instructor's Manual for each chapter.

REFLECT ON IT In what ways do you benefit from disclosing to other people? How do you feel when people share inappropriate disclosures with you? Do you think you communicate differently when disclosing online?

MASTER the chapter

1 Understanding the Self: Self-Concept (p. 71)

- Your self-concept consists of your perceptions about who you are. Self-concept is multifaceted, partly subjective, and enduring but changeable.
- Personality, cultural and gender roles, reflected appraisal, and social comparison all influence the development of self-concept.
- Self-monitoring and the self-fulfilling prophecy are two pathways through which self-concept can shape communicative behavior.

2 Valuing the Self: Self-Esteem (p. 81)

- Your self-esteem is your subjective evaluation of your value and worth as a person. Having high self-esteem is a benefit in some ways and a liability in others.
- Ethnic groups appear to differ somewhat in their self-esteem. In the United States, women report higher self-esteem than men among ethnic minorities but not among non-Hispanic Caucasians.

- Humans have fundamental needs for control, inclusion, and affection; self-esteem is affected by the extent to which those needs are met.

3 Presenting the Self: Image Management (p. 87)

- Your image consists of the way you want others to perceive you. Most people manage multiple images in collaborative and complex ways.
- Humans have three kinds of face needs: fellowship face, autonomy face, and competence face. Behaviors that impinge on face needs are called face-threatening acts.

4 Communicating the Self: Self-Disclosure (p. 94)

- Self-disclosure is the deliberate act of giving others information about ourselves that we believe to be true and think they don't already have. It is intentional and involves true information, varies in breadth and depth, varies among relationships, usually follows a process, is usually reciprocal, serves many purposes, and is influenced by sex and culture.

- Benefits of self-disclosure include the enhancement of relationships and trust, the probability of reciprocity, emotional release, and the provision of assistance to others.

- Risks of self-disclosure include rejection, the chance of obligating others, the potential to hurt others, and the violation of another person's privacy.

- Some of the risks of self-disclosure are made more likely when self-disclosure takes place online.

KEY TERMS

autonomy face (p. 92)
breadth (p. 95)
competence face (p. 92)
depth (p. 95)
face (p. 92)
face needs (p. 92)
face-threatening act (p. 93)
facework (p. 92)
fellowship face (p. 92)

gossip (p. 102)
identity (p. 71)
image (p. 88)
image management (p. 88)
Johari window (p. 72)
need for affection (p. 87)
need for control (p. 86)
need for inclusion (p. 86)
norm of reciprocity (p. 98)

personality (p. 76)
reference groups (p. 78)
reflected appraisal (p. 77)
self-concept (p. 71)
self-disclosure (p. 94)
self-esteem (p. 82)
self-fulfilling prophecy (p. 80)
social comparison (p. 78)
social penetration theory (p. 95)

McGraw Hill Education connect®

To maximize your study time, check out CONNECT to access the SmartBook study module for this chapter, watch videos, and explore other resources.

CHAPTER

4

Interpersonal Perception

© Gary Hershorn/Reuters/Corbis

MAKING SENSE OF OUR SOCIAL WORLD

He was already infamous for interrupting Taylor Swift's acceptance speech in 2009 for the MTV Video Music Award for best female video, when he grabbed the microphone from her hand and uttered the now immortal words, "I'm gonna let you finish..."* and suggested that pop singer Beyoncé should have won the award instead. Six years later, at the 2015 Grammy Awards, rapper Kanye West appeared poised for an encore when he stormed the stage moments after singer-songwriter Beck received the award for Album of the Year. In the audience, jaws dropped as the impulsive West once again leapt from his seat and headed toward the stage, only to stop before reaching it and turn back toward his seat. Some viewers thought he was merely spoofing his 2009 stunt. In an interview shortly after the ceremony, however, West opined that "Beck needs to respect artistry and he should have given his award to Beyoncé."[1][†] West's tendency to disrupt awards ceremonies naturally leads many people to wonder about his motives.

chapter preview

1 **The Process of Perception**

2 **Fundamental Forces in Interpersonal Perception**

3 **Explaining What We Perceive**

4 **Improving Your Perceptual Abilities**

*Kanye West Quoted in "Kanye West Steals Taylor Swift's Thunder...but Not for Long" by Breanne L. Heldman E! Entertainment Television, LLC.
†Stern, Marlow. (February 9, 2015). "Kanye West Blasts Beck's Album of the Year Grammys Win." The Daily Beast. http://www.thedailybeast.com/articles/2015/02/09/kanye-west-blasts-beck-s-album-ofthe- year-grammys-win-beck-needs-to-respect-artistry.html

When we encounter social behavior, especially behavior we find surprising, our nearly automatic reaction is to try to make sense of it. We need to understand what is happening if we are to know how to react to it properly. Therefore, getting along in our social world depends a great deal on our ability to make meaning out of other people's behaviors. When we talk about making meaning, we're talking about the process of perception. Our minds and senses help us understand the world, but they can also lead us to make mistakes, such as misinterpreting other people's behaviors. The more we learn about our perception-making abilities, the better we know ourselves, one another, and our world. We can all learn to perceive behavior more accurately, and this chapter focuses on how.

 ## 1 The Process of Perception

Despite being one of the most productive marketing managers at her publishing company, Gisele has a hard time earning favor from her supervisor Dale. Gisele enthusiastically presents new products and innovative marketing plans at her weekly meetings with Dale, but he seems interested only in the bottom line. Instead of sharing Gisele's excitement about fresh ideas, his concerns always center on how much a new product will cost and how much profit it will generate. Gisele has come to perceive Dale as an uninspired manager who is simply biding his time until retirement. Dale concedes that Gisele is energetic and smart, but he perceives her as naïve concerning the way business works.

Part of what makes Gisele and Dale's relationship so challenging is the differences in their interpersonal perceptions. In this section, we will examine the process of perception by defining interpersonal perception, identifying the stages of perception making, and probing factors that influence the accuracy of our perceptions of others.

Interpersonal Perception Defined

Gisele and Dale clearly have quite different perceptions of each other, but what does that mean, exactly? **Perception** is the process of making meaning from the things we experience in our environment, and when we apply this process to people and relationships, we engage in **interpersonal perception.**[2] We are involved in interpersonal perception constantly. Gisele experiences Dale's repeated references to costs and profits, for instance, and she makes meaning from them ("he has no enthusiasm for anything except the bottom line"). You notice what your friends, colleagues, relatives, and co-workers do and say, and their words and actions have meaning to you based on the way you interpret them.

Writing Note: Have students write about a situation in which they misinterpreted another person's behaviors. Ask them to describe the situation, the behavior they misinterpreted, and their discovery that they had misinterpreted it. How did their emotions, their perceptions, and other events surrounding the situation lead to their misinterpretation?

In Everyday Life: It's tempting to treat perceptions—because of their subjective nature—as being above reproach. In other words, some people treat perceptions as though they are never right or wrong; they just are what they are. However, perceptions can be inaccurate. Perception making is a skill that can be improved with practice.

perception The process of making meaning from the things we experience in the environment.

interpersonal perception The process of making meaning from the people in our environment and our relationships with them.

Three Stages of the Perception Process

Your mind usually selects, organizes, and interprets information so quickly and so subconsciously that you may think your perceptions are objective, factual reflections of the world. You might say you perceived that Kanye West is rude, because he behaves rudely at awards ceremonies. In fact, you created that perception on the basis of the information you selected for attention (his behavior at the 2009 VMAs and 2015 Grammys), the way you organized that information (what he did is viewed as inconsiderate behavior), and the way you interpreted it ("he's being rude").[3]

Selection, organization, and interpretation are the three basic stages of the perception process. Let's examine each one.

SELECTION.   The process of perception begins when one or more of your senses are stimulated. You pass a construction site and hear two workers talking about the foundation they're pouring. You see one of your classmates smile at you. A co-worker bumps you on the shoulder as he walks past. If you notice these sensory experiences of hearing, seeing, and being bumped, then they can initiate your process of forming perceptions.

In truth, your senses are constantly stimulated by objects and events in your environment. It's simply impossible, though, to pay attention to everything you're seeing, hearing, smelling, tasting, and feeling at any given moment.[4] When you're walking past the construction site, for instance, you're probably no longer hearing the sounds of traffic going by.

selection The process of attending to a stimulus.

Rather than paying attention to all the stimuli in your environment, you engage in **selection,** the process in which your mind and body help you choose certain stimuli to attend to. For example, you notice your classmate smiling at you without paying attention to what others in the classroom are saying or doing. You notice that your friend failed to wish you a happy birthday on Facebook, but you ignore the text message she sent you. Clearly, the information you attend to influences the perceptions you form.

Importantly, we don't necessarily make conscious decisions about which stimuli to notice and which to ignore. Rather, as research indicates, three characteristics especially make a particular stimulus more likely to be selected for attention.

First, being unusual or unexpected makes a stimulus stand out.[5] For instance, you might not pay attention to people talking loudly while walking across campus, but hearing the same conversation in the library would probably spark your attention, because it would be unusual in that environment. Or perhaps you're walking back to your car after a night class and you don't take particular notice of other students walking along the same sidewalk, but you do notice an older, poorly dressed man pushing a shopping cart. His presence stands out to you because you aren't used to seeing people on campus who look like him.

We are constantly making decisions about which stimuli to attend to and which to ignore.
© Red Poppy / Alamy

Second, repetition, or how frequently you're exposed to a stimulus, makes it stand out.[6] For example, you're more likely to remember radio ads you've heard repeatedly than ones you've heard only once. Similarly, you tend to notice more characteristics about the people you see frequently than about those you seldom see, such as their physical appearance and behavior patterns.

Third, the intensity of a stimulus affects how much you take notice of it. You notice strong odors more than weak ones, for instance, and bright and flashy colors more than dull and muted ones.[7]

ORGANIZATION.   Once you've noticed a particular stimulus, the next step in the perception process is to classify it. This task, called **organization,** helps you make sense of the information by revealing how it is similar to, and different from, other things you know about. To classify a stimulus, your mind applies a *perceptual schema* to it, or a mental framework for organizing information.

According to communication researcher Peter Andersen, we use four types of schema to classify information we notice about other people: physical constructs, role constructs, interaction constructs, and psychological constructs.[8]

- *Physical constructs* emphasize people's appearance, causing us to notice *objective* characteristics such as height, age, ethnicity, and body shape, as well as *subjective* characteristics such as physical attractiveness.

- *Role constructs* emphasize people's social or professional position, so we notice that a person is a teacher, an accountant, a father, a community leader, and so on.[9]

- *Interaction constructs* emphasize people's behavior, so we notice that a person is outgoing, aggressive, shy, sarcastic, or considerate.

- *Psychological constructs* emphasize people's thoughts and feelings, causing us to perceive that a person is angry, self-assured, insecure, envious, or worried.

Think about the first time you met your interpersonal communication instructor. What sensory information did you notice about him or her, and which schema did you apply to it? Perhaps you paid attention to your instructor's age, ethnicity, and clothing. If so, you probably organized those pieces of information as physical constructs, meaning you recognized that they all dealt with your instructor as a physical being. If you paid attention to how friendly or how demanding your instructor is, you probably organized those pieces of information as interaction constructs, recognizing that they all dealt with how your instructor behaves or communicates. If your focus was on how well your instructor taught, you were emphasizing role constructs by attending to your instructor's professional function in the classroom. Finally, if you took note of how happy or self-confident your instructor seemed, you focused on psychological constructs by paying attention to his or her disposition or mood.

Whichever schema we use to organize information about people—and we may use more than one at a time—the process of organization helps us determine the ways in which various pieces of information that we select for attention are related.[10] If, for example, you notice that your neighbor is a Little League softball coach and the father of three children, those two pieces of information go together because they both relate to the roles he plays. If you notice that he seems irritated and angry, those pieces of information go together as examples of his psychological state. In addition, you recognize them as being different from information about his roles, physical characteristics, or behaviors.

Perceptual schemas can also help us determine how other people are similar to and different from us. If your dentist is female, that's one way in which she is similar to (or different from) you. If she is friendly and outgoing, that's another similarity (or difference). Perceptual schemas help us organize sensory information in some meaningful way so that we can move forward with the process of perception.[11]

INTERPRETATION.   After noticing and classifying a stimulus, you have to assign it an **interpretation** to figure out what it means for you. Let's say one of your co-workers has been acting especially friendly toward you for the last week. She smiles at you all the time, sends you encouraging text messages, and offers to run errands for you during

organization The process of categorizing information that has been selected for attention.

CONNECT: Reports from SmartBook assignments show you where students are struggling and excelling. You can view reports for an entire class or an individual student.

interpretation The process of assigning meaning to information that has been selected for attention and organized.

How would you describe Hillary Clinton according to Andersen's four perceptual schemas?
© Trevor Collens/Getty Images

her lunch break. Her behavior is definitely noticeable, and you've probably classified it as a psychological construct because it relates to her thoughts and feelings about you. What does her behavior *mean*, though? How should you interpret it? Is she being nice because she's getting ready to ask you for a big favor? Does she want to look good in front of her boss? Or does she like you? If she does like you, does she like you as a friend—or as a potential romantic partner?

To address those questions, you likely will pay attention to three factors to interpret her behavior: your personal *experience,* your *knowledge* of her, and the *closeness* of your relationship with her. Your personal experience helps you assign meaning to behavior. If co-workers have been nice to you in the past just to get favors from you later, then you might be suspicious of this co-worker's behavior.[12] Your knowledge of the person helps you interpret her actions. If you know she's friendly and nice to everyone, you might interpret her behavior differently than if you notice that she's being nice only to you.[13] Finally, the closeness of your relationship influences how you interpret a person's behavior. When your best friend does you an unexpected favor, you probably interpret it as a sincere sign of friendship. In contrast, when a co-worker does you a favor, you are more likely to wonder whether he or she has an ulterior motive.[14]

We've seen that perception is a process, which means it happens in stages. That doesn't necessarily mean the process is always linear, however. The three stages of perception—selecting, organizing, and interpreting information—overlap.[15] How we interpret a behavior depends on what we notice about it, for example, but what we notice can also depend on the way we interpret it.

Let's assume, for example, that you're listening to a politician's speech. If you find her ideas and proposals favorable, then you might interpret her demeanor and speaking style as examples of her intelligence and confidence. In contrast, if you oppose her ideas, then you might interpret her demeanor and speaking style as examples of

Stages of the Perception Process

Selection	We select certain sensory information for attention.
Organization	We categorize each piece of information to determine how it is similar to, and different from, other pieces of information.
Interpretation	We assign meaning to each piece of information.

arrogance or incompetence. Either interpretation, in turn, might lead you to select for attention only those behaviors or characteristics that support your interpretation and to ignore those that don't. Therefore, even though perception happens in stages, the stages don't always take place in the same order. The "At a Glance" box summarizes the three stages of perception.

We're constantly noticing, organizing, and interpreting things around us, including other people's behaviors. Like other skills, perception takes practice, and our perceptions are more accurate on some occasions than others.

Influences on Perceptual Accuracy

Because we constantly make perceptions, you might think we'd all be experts at it by now. In truth, perceptual mistakes are often easy to make. For example, perhaps your sister calls to check on you out of concern when you're feeling ill. Because your illness makes you short-tempered and grumpy, however, you perceive that she is calling only because she feels obligated. As another example, on your overseas trip you perceive that two adults you see in a restaurant are having a heated argument. In fact, as you later find out, they are engaging in behaviors that signify interest and involvement in that culture.

Why do we continue to make perceptual errors despite our accumulated experience? Three factors in particular influence the accuracy of our perceptions and can lead to errors: our physiology, our cultural and co-cultural backgrounds, and our social roles.

PHYSIOLOGICAL STATES AND TRAITS. *Physiology* is the study of the mechanical and biochemical ways in which our bodies work. Many aspects of our physiology influence the way we perceive the world.[16] Here we focus specifically on physiological states and traits.

Physiological states are conditions that are temporary. We enter and leave various physiological states, meaning that their influence comes and goes over time. For instance, the physiological state of feeling tired alters our perception of time and can make us anxious. Therefore, the five minutes we're waiting in line at the grocery store might seem much longer.[17] Similarly, being hungry or sick seems to sap our energy and make us grumpy and impatient, reducing our ability to get along with others.[18]

In contrast, our *physiological traits* are conditions that affect us on an ongoing basis. Compared with states, which are continually changing, traits are more

In Everyday Life: It's easy for us to be short-tempered with people when we are sick, hungry, tired, or rushed. How can we guard against such behavior?

Talking Point: Differences in sensory abilities are important to remember when interacting with people who have certain disabilities, among them impaired hearing or sight. Imagine how the inability to hear, for instance, might affect a person's perceptions, even if that person could read lips. He or she would likely miss clues such as volume, intensity, and tone of voice that would help a hearing person in the perception-making process.

Your physiological traits influence how you react to various foods as well as how you perceive various behaviors.
© *BananaStock/PunchStock, RF*

enduring. For example, perception relies a great deal on our senses—our abilities to see, hear, touch, taste, and smell. A voice that sounds just right to a hearing-impaired person may seem too loud to others. A food you find too spicy might seem bland to someone else.[19] You might think a room is too hot, another person might think it's too cold, and a third person might think it's just right. Our senses help us perceive and understand the world. So, when our sensory abilities differ, our perceptions often do as well.

Another physiological trait is our biological rhythm, or the cycle of daily changes we go through in body temperature, alertness, and mood.[20] As levels of various hormones rise and fall throughout the day, our energy level and susceptibility to stress change as well. Consequently, there are times during the day when we interact positively with people, and other times when we feel cranky and are more easily annoyed.

Everyone's biological rhythm is a little different. You might be most refreshed and alert first thing in the morning, whereas your roommate might be a night owl who doesn't get going until late in the day. Most of the time, these differences aren't a huge problem. Research shows, however, that when romantic partners have very different biological rhythms, they report more conflict and less intimacy than partners whose rhythms are more closely matched.[21]

CULTURE AND CO-CULTURE.   Another powerful influence on the accuracy of our perceptions is the culture and co-cultures with which we identify. Cultural values and norms have many different effects on the way we communicate interpersonally. In addition to affecting our behavior, culture influences our perceptions and interpretations of other people's behaviors.[22]

Let's say that Jason, an American, meets Rosella, an Italian, at their company's international sales meeting. Jason notices that Rosella stands very close to him and touches him frequently, and these behaviors make him uncomfortable. He might perceive that Rosella is being dominant and aggressive, because in the United States people usually maintain more personal space and touch new acquaintances less often than do Italians. Noticing Jason's discomfort, Rosella might perceive that he's shy or socially awkward, because Italians are used to closer interpersonal distances and more frequent touch.[23] In this situation, Rosella and Jason's cultural norms affect not only their own behavior but also their perceptions of each other's behaviors.

Co-cultural differences can also influence perceptions. Teenagers might perceive their parents' advice as outdated or irrelevant, for instance, whereas parents might perceive their teenagers' indifference to their advice as naïve.[24] Some middle-class people might perceive that wealthy people are constantly taking advantage of them, whereas wealthy people may see lower-class people as lazy or ungrateful.[25] Liberals and conservatives might each perceive the others' behaviors as rooted in ignorance.[26]

Each of us has multiple "lenses" through which we perceive the world. Some of those lenses are products of our cultural background. Many others are influenced by our age, social class, political orientation, education, religion, and hobbies, and by other elements of our co-cultures.

SOCIAL ROLES.   A *social role* is a set of behaviors that are expected of someone in a particular social situation. Each of us plays several social roles, and those roles can also influence the accuracy of our perceptions. One example is gender roles. Gender and biological sex affect a range of communication behaviors, so it's not surprising that they influence the perceptions we form of others.

In her 2013 bestseller *Lean In,* for instance, Facebook chief operating officer Sheryl Sandberg vividly describes the challenges facing female managers in the workplace, because they are perceived very differently from their male counterparts, even when they are exhibiting the same behaviors.[27] As she explains, experienced, motivated, and confident women may be perceived by other women as powerful, assertive, and excellent role models. Men, however, may perceive such women as pushy, aggressive, and "bossy" for behaving in stereotypically unfeminine ways. The same behaviors can therefore elicit different perceptions based on the gender role of the person enacting them.

In the workplace, male and female managers are often perceived differently, even when their behavior is similar. © *Image Source / Alamy, RF*

Our experience and occupational roles can also influence our perceptions of others' behaviors.[28] As a first-time mother, for instance, Charlotte was terrified when her infant son began jerking and convulsing while she was holding him one day. She was certain he was having a seizure, so she rushed him to the emergency room. Derek, an experienced pediatric nurse, recognized the problem immediately: The baby simply had the hiccups. He explained to Charlotte that newborns often don't make the "hiccup" sound, so it's easy to mistake the baby's jerking motion for something more serious. Because of the differences in their training and experience with babies, Derek and Charlotte perceived the same behavior quite differently.

In Everyday Life: Unfortunately, this example can also occur in reverse: An inexperienced parent or caregiver might perceive something to be inconsequential when in fact it is threatening to a baby's health. This illustrates the point that our perceptions often have consequences for others.

Forming Perceptions Online

Physiological states and traits, culture and co-culture, and social roles all affect how people perceive one another. When they interact online, however, additional cues become relevant. Consider online dating sites, such as Match.com and eHarmony.com, for instance. How do people form perceptions of users' personal profiles? In one study, psychologists asked one group of women to rate the physical attractiveness of photographs posed in men's profiles.[29] A separate group of women rated the men's descriptions of themselves from their headlines, introductions, and "About Me" sections.

The researchers found that physically attractive men were perceived to communicate in kinder, more intelligent, more confident, and more humorous ways, compared to their less-attractive counterparts. This finding illustrates how visual cues can affect people's perceptions of what they read, which is important on the online dating context. Because users do not always describe themselves accurately in their profiles, it is useful to be aware of how readers' perceptions can be swayed by users' attractiveness.[30]

A second example concerns the use of an *avatar,* which is a graphic representation of a user that online communicators construct. Although avatars are not "real" people, they represent real people, so we become accustomed to perceiving them in many of the same ways we perceive people around us. Including an avatar alongside an e-mail message or chat room posting can make our words seem more personal to others—but how is our avatar *really* being perceived? To find out, communication researchers Kristine Nowak and Christian Rauh had college students evaluate a series of avatars and report on their perceptions.[31] They learned that

If you create an avatar to use in computer-mediated communication, remember that others will perceive it as a representation of you.
© AP Images/Itsuo Inouye

- *Avatars should look as human as possible.* Some people create avatars that are based on images of animals or inanimate objects. Nowak and Rauh found, however, that human-looking avatars were perceived to be more credible and more attractive.

- *Avatars should have a defined gender.* Many avatars appear androgynous, meaning that it is difficult to tell whether the avatar is intended to be female or male. According to the research, people prefer interacting with avatars that they perceive as clearly male or female rather than androgynous.

- *Communicators prefer avatars that match themselves.* When asked to select the avatar they would most prefer to use as their own, the research participants showed a strong preference for human-looking avatars that matched their own gender.

Photographs and avatars are only two out of many possible examples of online characteristics that can affect people's perceptions of you. When communicating in electronically mediated environments, remember that perception can be more a matter of *what people see* than *what you say.*

LEARN IT What does it mean to engage in interpersonal perception? How are selection, organization, and interpretation similar to and different from one another? How do physiological states or traits, culture, co-culture, and social roles affect our perception-making ability?

APPLY IT Think of a perception you recently made of someone else's behavior. In writing, describe what the person did and what your perception was. Given what you now know about the effects of physiology, culture, and social roles on perception making, formulate at least two alternative perceptions that you might have made about the same behavior.

REFLECT ON IT What sensory information are you attending to right now? How do your co-cultures influence the perceptions you make of others?

2 Fundamental Forces in Interpersonal Perception

Most of the time we believe we're seeing the world as it really is. For instance, you may perceive Kanye West's awards ceremony antics as inconsiderate or rude, but others may see it in quite different ways. Even though we rely a great deal on our perceptions, research shows that those perceptions are vulnerable to a number of biases, many of which operate outside our conscious awareness. In this section, we examine six fundamental forces that affect our perceptions.

Stereotyping Relies on Generalizations

You're probably familiar with **stereotypes,** which are generalizations about a group or category of people that can have powerful influences on how we perceive those people.[32] Stereotyping is a three-part process:

- First, we identify a group we believe another person belongs to ("you are a blonde").
- Second, we recall some generalization others often make about the people in that group ("blondes have more fun").
- Finally, we apply that generalization to the person ("therefore, you must have more fun").

You can probably think of stereotypes for many groups.[33] What stereotypes come to mind when you think about elderly people, for instance? How about people with physical or mental disabilities? Wealthy people? Homeless people? Gays and lesbians? Science fiction fans? Immigrants? Athletes? What stereotypes come to mind when you think about yourself?

Many people find stereotyping distasteful or unethical, particularly when stereotypes have to do with characteristics such as sex, race, and sexual orientation.[34] There's no question that stereotyping can lead to some inaccurate, even offensive, evaluations of other people. The reason is that stereotypes underestimate the differences among individuals in a group. It may be true, for instance, that elderly people are more conservative than other age groups, but that doesn't mean that every elderly person is conservative or that all elderly people are conservative to the same extent. Similarly, people of Asian descent are sometimes stereotyped as being more studious than those in other ethnic groups, but that doesn't mean every Asian person is a good student or that all Asians do equally well in school.[35]

Importantly, there is variation in almost every group. However, stereotypes focus our attention only on the generalizations. In fact, we have a tendency to engage in *selective memory bias,* remembering information that supports our stereotypes but forgetting information that doesn't.[36] During interpersonal conflicts, for instance, both women and men tend to remember only their partners' stereotypical behaviors.[37] Let's take a look at a conflict between Carmen and her boyfriend, Nick, regarding their division of household labor:

Carmen: You were supposed to vacuum and put in a load of laundry when you got home; instead you're just sitting there watching TV. Why am I the one who has to do everything around here?

Nick: Look, I'm sorry. I've had a long day, and all I want to do is sit here for a while and de-stress.

Carmen: I understand that, Nick, but I've also had a long day; I'd like to just sit around doing nothing too, but this stuff has to get done, and it shouldn't be my responsibility to do it all.

Nick: Whatever. Can't we talk about this later?

What do you think Carmen and Nick will remember most about this conflict after it's over?

Stereotyping often leads us to make inaccurate judgments about others. On the situation comedy *Brooklyn Nine-Nine,* Captain Ray Holt does not necessarily conform to the stereotypes people may have of him as a black man, a gay man, and as a police officer. © Eddy Chen/NBC/NBCU Photo Bank/Getty Images

To deal productively with stereotypes, we must first be aware of how they influence our perceptions and behavior. What stereotypes would you apply to this person? © BananaStock/ JupiterImages/PictureQuest, RF

Focus on Ethics: What are the ethical implications of behaving toward a person on the basis of a stereotypical assessment? How much does it matter if the assessment is accurate? Is it unethical to perpetuate stereotypes even if they are accurate?

primacy effect The tendency to emphasize the first impression over later impressions when forming a perception.

Nick may recall that Carmen nagged and criticized him, but he may forget that she also listened to what he was saying. Likewise, Carmen may report that Nick "tuned her out," but she may overlook that he also apologized. In other words, both may remember only the other person's behaviors that conformed to stereotypes for female and male behavior.

That is one reason why it's so important to check our perceptions before we act on them. After an argument like Nick and Carmen's, for instance, ask yourself what communication behaviors the other person engaged in that were not necessarily stereotypical. That may help you form a more accurate memory of the conflict; it may also help you to treat the other person as an individual and not simply as a representative of his or her sex.[38]

Note, however, that perceptions about an individual made on the basis of a stereotype are not always inaccurate.[39] Consider the stereotype that women love being around children. If you met a woman and assumed (on the basis of this stereotype) that she enjoyed being around children, you might be wrong—however, you also might be right. Not every woman enjoys spending time with children, but some do. By the same token, not every elderly person is conservative, but some are. Not every male florist is gay, but some are. The point is that just because your perception of someone is consistent with a stereotype, it isn't necessarily inaccurate. Just as we shouldn't assume a stereotypical judgment is true, we also shouldn't assume it is false.

At this point, you might be wondering whether you should abandon stereotyping altogether—but in fact doing so would be unrealistic. A more productive way of dealing with stereotypes involves two elements: awareness and communication. First, be aware of the stereotypical perceptions you make. What assumptions do you make, for instance, when you meet an elderly Asian woman, an African American teenage boy, or an adult in a wheelchair? It's natural to form perceptions of such individuals based on what you believe to be true about the groups to which they belong. Try to be aware of situations when you do so, however, and also try to remember that your perceptions may not be accurate. Second, instead of assuming that your perceptions of other people are correct, get to know them and let your perceptions be guided by what you learn about them as individuals. By communicating interpersonally, you can begin to discover how well other people fit or don't fit the stereotypical perceptions you formed of them.

The Primacy Effect Governs First Impressions

As the saying goes, you get only one chance to make a good first impression. There's no shortage of advice on how to accomplish this, from picking the right clothes to polishing your conversational skills. Have you ever noticed that no one talks about the importance of making a good *second* impression? What is so special about first impressions?

According to a principle called the **primacy effect,** first impressions are critical because they set the tone for all future interactions.[40] Our first impressions of someone seem to stick in our mind more than our second, third, or fourth impressions do. In an early study of the primacy effect, psychologist Solomon Asch found that a person described as "intelligent, industrious, impulsive, critical, stubborn, and envious" was evaluated more favorably than one described as "envious, stubborn, critical, impulsive, industrious, and intelligent."[41]* Notice that most of those adjectives are negative, but when the description begins with a positive one (intelligent), the effects of the more negative ones that follow it are diminished.

Asch's study illustrates that the first information we learn about someone tends to have a stronger effect on how we perceive that person than information we receive later on.[42] That's why we work so hard to make a good first impression in a job interview, on a date, or in other important social situations. When people evaluate us favorably at first, they're more likely to perceive us in a positive light from then on.[43]

Although first impressions are powerful, they aren't necessarily permanent.[44] For instance, when Traci first met her suite-mate Bradley while traveling on her study abroad program, she didn't like him at all. He had just arrived after experiencing a series of airport delays, so he was in a bad mood when Traci introduced herself at a get-acquainted meeting. Because he seemed irritable and short-tempered, he made a poor impression on Traci, who tried to avoid him whenever possible. Once they started taking classes together, however, Bradley was always friendly, upbeat, and humorous. He even friended her on Facebook so he could share his photos from their travels. Over time, Traci began to realize that her initial negative impression of Bradley was inaccurate and that he was actually a warm, caring person.

To reiterate, the primacy effect means that first impressions are powerful, not that they are unchangeable. When subsequent communication is more positive than initial interactions, as in the case of Traci and Bradley, negative first impressions can sometimes be overcome.

Talking Point: Students have probably heard that hiring decisions are often made within the first few minutes of a job interview. That is a perfect example of the primacy effect—the first information the interviewer receives (which is largely visual, based on the candidate's appearance and behavior) becomes the basis for the hiring decision.

Barney Stinson, a character on *How I Met Your Mother*, is constantly looking for ways to impress women. For Halloween parties, Barney always brings a spare costume. That way, if he strikes out with the most desirable women, he has a second chance to make a first impression. © *CBS / Landov*

The Recency Effect Influences Impressions

We've considered the importance of making a good first impression. As standup comedians and most other entertainers know, it's equally important to make a good final impression, because that's what the audience will remember after leaving. The principle in play is the **recency effect,** which says that the most recent impression we have of someone is more powerful than our earlier impressions.[45]

Suppose you have recently started following your political science professor, Dr. Williams, on Twitter. She frequently tweets about current political events, usually offering some insight or perspective that you find intriguing. In particular, you have been fascinated by her comments regarding the persecution of ethnic and religious minorities around the world. Although you don't know her particularly well, you have always had a positive impression of Dr. Williams as a thoughtful and well-informed commentator.

A series of recent tweets from Dr. Williams, however, prompted you to question your impression of her. Even though you generally agree with Dr. Williams politically, her

recency effect The tendency to emphasize the most recent impression over earlier impressions when forming a perception.

*Allen, M., & Valde, K. S. (2006). The intersection of method- ological and ethical concerns when researching a gendered world. In D. J. Canary & K. Dindia (Eds.), Handbook of sex differences and similarities in communication (2nd ed., pp. 97–110). Mahwah, NJ: Lawrence Erlbaum Associates.

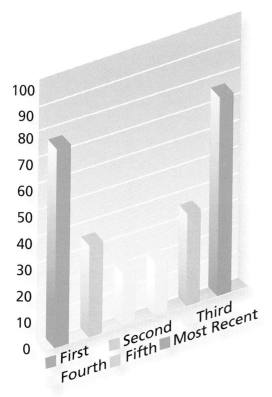

FIGURE 1 Our first impressions and our most recent impressions are more important than those that come in between.

perceptual set A predisposition to perceive only what we want or expect to perceive.

In the IM: In the activity "Priming to Create a Perceptual Set," you can use a psychological technique called priming to generate a perceptual set among students, illustrating its effects.

most recent comments strike you as extremely biased and short-sighted. You had been planning to take her class over the summer, because you've always had a positive opinion of her, but your most recent impressions of her have been negative—and according to the recency effect, you will give these impressions greater weight than previous ones.

At first glance, it might seem as though the recency effect and the primacy effect contradict each other. Which is the more important impression—the first or the most recent? The answer is that *both* appear to be more important than any impressions that we form in between.[46] To grasp this point fully, consider the last movie you saw. You probably have a better recollection of how the movie started and how it ended than you do of everything in between.

The same observation applies to our perceptions of other people. In the example above, your view of Dr. Williams was most heavily affected by the first impressions she made on you (which were positive) and by the most recent impressions (which were negative). Figure 1 illustrates the relationship between the primacy effect and the recency effect.

Our Perceptual Set Limits What We Perceive

"I'll believe it when I see it," people often say. Our perception of reality is influenced not only by what we see, however, but also by our biases, our expectations, and our desires. These elements can create what psychologists call a **perceptual set,** or a predisposition to perceive only what we want or expect to perceive.[47] An equally valid motto, therefore, might be "I'll see it when I believe it."

For example, our perceptual set regarding gender guides the way we perceive and interact with newborns. Without the help of contextual cues such as blue or pink baby clothes, we sometimes have a hard time telling whether an infant is male or female. However, if we're told the infant's name is David, we perceive that child to be stronger and bigger than if the same infant is called Diana.[48] Our perceptual set tells us that male infants are usually bigger and stronger than female ones, so we "see" a bigger, stronger baby when we're told it's a boy.

A dramatic example of perceptual set occurred after the publication of a photo taken of the surface of Mars. In 1976, while surveying the Martian topography, *Viking Orbiter 1* captured what many observers believed to be the unmistakable image of a human face; see Figure 2, photograph (a). That perception fueled the public's imagination about the existence of intelligent life on our neighbor planet. A quarter century later, the *Mars Global Surveyor* captured a higher-resolution photo of the same site—see Figure 2, photograph (b)—proving that the "face" in the 1976 picture was an optical illusion created by light and shadow.

It was people's perceptual set that led them to see the face to begin with. Indeed, the face is such a fundamental tool for interpersonal recognition and communication that we are led to recognize it in nearly any pattern that resembles it. Research has shown that even newborns stare longer at figures that resemble faces than at similar figures that do not (Figure 3).[49]

FIGURE 2 These two photos are of the same place on the Martian landscape. Picture (a), taken in 1976, shows what to most people looks like a human face. Picture (b), taken in 2001, revealed that the "face" was an optical illusion created by light and shadow. The reason we "see" a face in the first place is that our perceptual set leads us to recognize faces in anything that resembles them—including rocks on Mars! © *Viking 1/Historical/Corbis; JPL/MSSS/Nasa*

Our perceptual set also influences how we make sense of people and circumstances. Deeply religious people may perceive a medical healing as a miracle or the answer to a prayer, whereas others may see it as a natural response to medication.[50] Highly homophobic people are more likely than others to perceive affectionate behavior between men as sexual in nature.[51]

Perceptual set is relevant for interpersonal communication because it can shape the way we interpret social situations. Suppose, for instance, that Ryan, Emilio, and Penny are sitting around a café table eating ice cream when a married couple enters the café and walks up to the cash register to place an order. The man seems irritated, the woman looks as if she has recently been crying, and neither spouse talks to—or even looks at—the other. They order two coffees and walk to an outdoor patio behind the café, leaving Ryan, Emilio, and Penny to form their own perceptions of the situation.

Having grown up with an abusive alcoholic father, Penny perceives that the spouses had recently been fighting and that the woman was probably crying because of something her husband had said or done. Penny's perceptual set, therefore, causes her to "see" the aftermath of a

FIGURE 3 Research suggests that humans are attuned to recognizing faces at a remarkably early age. Studies show that newborns—some less than an hour old—stare significantly longer at drawings that loosely resemble faces (such as the picture on the left) than at similar drawings that do not (the picture on the right).

Adapted Sources: Monloch, C. J., Lewis, T. L., Budreau, D. R., Maurer, D., Dannemiller, J. L., Stephens, B. R., & Kleiner-Gathercoal, K. A. (1991). Face perception during early infancy. *Psychological Science, 10,* 419–422; Morton, J., & Johnson, M. H. (1991). CONSPEC and CONLERN: A two-process theory of infant face recognition. *Psychological Review, 98,* 164–181.

conflict that was the man's fault. In contrast, Emilio, who has lost several relatives to chronic illness in the past few years, isn't primed to perceive conflict the way Penny is. Instead, his perceptual set leads him to perceive that the couple might well be worried about the failing health of a family member. Finally, Ryan is madly in love with his new romantic partner, and his budding relationship puts him in such an elated mood that he doesn't notice there is anything at all wrong with the spouses.

All three friends witness the same couple walk into the café, place an order, and then leave. Their distinctive perceptual sets, however, lead them to form quite different perceptions about the situation.

Egocentrism Narrows Our Perspective

If you've spent any time around preschoolers, you've probably noticed that they often behave in ways that, to adults, seem selfish or inconsiderate. Timmy stands right in front of the TV, blocking your view. Susie asks you questions while you're on the phone. Such behaviors can be frustrating for parents, but in reality, the children aren't being selfish or inconsiderate. Instead, they are **egocentric,** meaning they lack the ability to take another person's perspective.[52]

According to developmental psychologist Jean Piaget, egocentrism is a normal part of development for children ages 2 to 6.[53] Timmy doesn't understand that he is blocking your view because he assumes you can see what he sees. Susie assumes you can hear only what she hears, so she doesn't know she is interrupting your phone conversation.

Although most people grow out of the egocentric stage by mid-childhood, even adults can behave egocentrically from time to time.[54] More important, our egocentrism can influence our perceptions of others. That happens when we assume that other people experience the world the same way we do.

Let's say that, while watching Barack Obama's State of the Union speech in early 2015, your friend Marty heard the President describe his plans to offer two years of free community college tuition to students making steady progress toward a degree. Because he had just completed his own community college degree the month before, Marty wishes Obama would have proposed this plan a couple years earlier. In mock frustration, he immediately posts on Facebook: "Wonder if this means I can get a refund for the last two years." He thinks his posting is clever, even humorous, so he's surprised when he later finds that only a couple people have "liked" it and no one has left any comments.

In this instance, Marty is presuming that others will understand the meaning of his statement, because it makes sense to him. Specifically, he assumes other people know about Obama's plan to cover community college tuition, and also about the money he has spent to put himself through school. Marty is perplexed that others don't find his comment funny because he doesn't consider the possibility that they don't have the context to understand it. In other words, Marty is being egocentric.

The opposite of being egocentric is being *altercentric,* or focused on the perspective of another person instead of your own. To what extent do you communicate in altercentric ways? See the "Assess Your Skills" box to find out.

Positivity and Negativity Biases Affect Perception

Sometimes our perceptions are influenced more by positive or negative information than by neutral information. When we pay the most attention to positive information, we are exhibiting what researchers call a **positivity bias.**[55]

egocentric Unable to take another person's perspective.

In Everyday Life: When we get frustrated with children for behaving egocentrically, we ourselves are demonstrating egocentrism through the implicit expectation that children ought to think and behave as *we* would. We must keep in mind that the ability to take another's perspective is a developmental stage and that children who have not yet reached that stage simply lack that ability.

CONNECT: Visual and interactive, Insight reports allow you to see at a glance how students are doing and easily dig deeper to learn more about individual students' performance.

positivity bias The tendency to focus heavily on a person's positive attributes when forming a perception.

assess your skills | BEING ALTERCENTRIC

How much do you agree with each of the following statements? On the line before each, record your level of agreement on a 1–5 scale. Higher numbers mean you agree more; lower numbers mean you agree less.

In conversations with other people, I usually:

1. _____ Try to see things from their point of view.
2. _____ Don't assume they think the same way I do.
3. _____ Focus mostly on their ideas or opinions.
4. _____ Pay attention to their facial expressions and body language to figure out how they feel.
5. _____ Try to "put myself in their shoes."
6. _____ Attempt to avoid making assumptions about what they think or feel.
7. _____ Don't assume they're thinking whatever I'm thinking.
8. _____ Try to focus more on them than on myself.

Add up your scores and write the total on this line: _____. That total score represents the extent to which you try to be altercentric rather than egocentric when communicating with others.

- Between 8 and 18: Your conversation style is primarily egocentric.
- Between 19 and 29: You strike a balance between egocentrism and altercentrism.
- 30 or higher: You're fairly altercentric.

Shortly before the 2015 Super Bowl, for instance, controversy erupted in the National Football League (NFL) over allegations that the New England Patriots had intentionally used underinflated footballs when they defeated the Indiana Colts in the American Football Conference Championship Game. The scandal, which became known as *Deflate-gate,* centered on whether Patriots' quarterback Tom Brady and head coach Bill Belichick knew the game balls being used by the Patriots during offensive plays were less inflated than NFL rules require, providing a decided advantage over their opponents, who were using regulation balls when on offense. Many Patriots' fans around the United States were quick to come to the team's defense, however, declaring the allegations to be false even in the absence of evidence. The positivity that many fans felt for Brady and his team, therefore, led them to presume the team's innocence.

One form of the positivity bias is the tendency of people in love to look at each other "through rose-colored glasses," overestimating the partner's positive qualities while underestimating or ignoring his or her faults or shortcomings.[56] Perhaps you've been around people who have seen their love interests in that way. Research suggests that this is a normal stage of relationship development and that a certain amount of "idealizing" is healthy for new relationships.[57] Most relationships grow out of that stage, however. People who cling to an idealized view of their romantic partners may experience disappointment when they realize the person is not as perfect as they thought.

Talking Point: Ask students what it is like to be around two people who are madly in love. Their answer will likely include the observation that lovebirds think their significant other is perfect. Some researchers believe this tendency to see a new romantic partner through rose-colored glasses is adaptive in that it motivates two people to stay together long enough to get to know each other rather than to see each other's faults at the very beginning.

negativity bias The tendency to focus heavily on a person's negative attributes when forming a perception.

In Everyday Life: A similar point might be made about how people choose political candidates. Often, one piece of negative information is enough to overshadow a host of positive qualities.

The opposite of the positivity bias is the **negativity bias,** or the tendency to weigh negative information more heavily than positive.[58] According to the negativity bias, even one piece of negative information can taint your perception of someone you would otherwise like. The negativity bias is particularly strong in competitive situations, such as job interviews and graduate school admissions.[59] When many people are competing for a limited number of opportunities, even seemingly minor pieces of negative information can ruin an otherwise positive impression.

Let's say you're calling references to check up on a person you have just interviewed for a key position on your work team. If the candidate is described as "innovative," you'll probably form a positive impression of her. If she's described as "rigid," your impression will probably be negative. What happens, however, if the candidate is described as both "innovative" and "rigid"? The answer is that you are likely to form a negative impression. In other words, the negative information will override the positive.[60]

Positivity biases and negativity biases are particularly influential for communication and satisfaction in long-term relationships, such as marriages. People in almost any significant relationship will encounter positive events, such as the birth of a new child and a long-anticipated vacation. They will also encounter negative events, such as a prolonged conflict and an unexpected job loss. When they consider their relationship as a whole, however, satisfied couples tend to emphasize its positive characteristics; in other words, they are biased toward the positive. In contrast, dissatisfied couples tend to emphasize the negative characteristics.[61]

Stereotyping, primacy, recency, perceptual set, egocentrism, positivity, and negativity are all powerful influences, and simply knowing about them doesn't shield us from their effects. The more we know about perceptual errors, however, the better we can think critically and question our judgments to form more accurate perceptions of the people around us.

Patriot fans' positivity bias may influence the way they perceive news about their favorite team. © Boston Globe/Getty Images

LEARN IT   What are the three stages of stereotyping? How are the primacy and recency effects related? How does a perceptual set influence interpersonal perception? What does it mean to be egocentric? What are the effects of the positivity biases and negativity biases?

APPLY IT   Watch the movie *Crash* (2004), which highlights numerous cultural stereotypes. In a written report, identify as many stereotyped beliefs as you can from the movie, and briefly describe the ways in which each character's stereotyped beliefs influenced his or her behaviors toward other characters. Also, list examples of other perceptual influences, particularly egocentrism or negativity bias, that affected the characters' behaviors.

REFLECT ON IT   What is one inaccurate stereotype that someone might have of you? When are you most likely to make egocentric perceptions of others?

3 Explaining What We Perceive

People have an almost constant need to make sense of the world. It's not enough just to notice someone's behavior, for instance—we are also driven to figure out *why* it happened. Why did no one comment on Marty's Facebook posting? Why did Kanye interrupt Taylor's speech? We want to know.

Explaining Behavior through Attributions

During a trip to Johannesburg in 2013, President Barack Obama made headlines when he snapped a selfie with the prime ministers of Denmark and Great Britain while attending the memorial service for former South African president Nelson Mandela. Obama's behavior, which seemed disrespectful to some, left many wondering "Why did he do that?"

When we experience behavior we don't immediately understand, we usually try to make sense of it. We do so by formulating an attribution. An **attribution** is simply an explanation, the answer to a "why" question.[62] You notice your brother ignoring text messages from his girlfriend, for instance, and you wonder to what you should attribute his behavior. Your advisor asks you why you failed your history midterm, and you consider to what you should attribute that outcome. Attributions for behavior vary along three important dimensions—locus, stability, and controllability.[63]

attribution An explanation for an observed behavior.

LOCUS. Locus refers to where the cause of a behavior is "located," whether within ourselves or outside ourselves.[64] Some of our behaviors have internal causes, which means they're caused by a characteristic of ourselves. Other behaviors have external causes, meaning they're caused by something outside ourselves.

Let's say your boss is late to a lunch meeting, and you're trying to figure out why. Some internal attributions are that he has lost track of time, he's rarely punctual, and he's making you wait on purpose. Those attributions are all different, but they all identify some internal characteristic of your boss as the cause of his lateness. External attributions are that traffic is really heavy, that your boss has a long way to walk, and that his employees always have numerous questions for him in the morning. Again, those are all different attributions, but each one points to something in your boss's external environment—not within him personally—as the cause of his behavior.

Many observers wondered why President Obama would pose for a selfie during a memorial service, as he did at South African president Nelson Mandela's service in 2013. © *Roberto Schmidt/Getty Images*

STABILITY. A second dimension of attributions is whether the cause of a behavior is stable or unstable.[65] A stable cause is one that is permanent, semipermanent, or at least not easily changed. Why was your boss late for lunch? Rush-hour traffic would be a stable cause for lateness, because it's a permanent feature of many people's morning commutes. In contrast, a traffic accident would be an unstable cause for lateness, because accidents occur only from time to time in unpredictable places with unpredictable effects.

Notice that these are both external attributions. Internal causes for behavior also can be either stable or unstable, however. Imagine that you are trying to understand why your roommate snapped at you this morning. If you claim the reason is that she's a mean person, that would be a stable attribution, because most people's personalities don't change dramatically over the course of their lives. If you conclude that she snapped at you because she has the flu and is feeling tired, however, that's an unstable attribution, because having the flu is a temporary condition.

CONTROLLABILITY. Finally, causes for behavior also vary in how controllable they are.[66] If you make a controllable attribution for someone's behavior, then you believe that the cause of that behavior was under the person's control. In contrast, an uncontrollable attribution identifies a cause outside the person's control.

Let's say your brother is supposed to pick you up from the airport, but he isn't there when you arrive. You might assume he has failed to show because he spent too much time hanging out with his friends beforehand and is running late. That is a controllable attribution, because the cause of his lateness (spending time with friends) is within his control. Alternatively, you might assume he got into a car accident. That is an uncontrollable attribution, because he couldn't help but be late if he wrecked his car.

Locus, stability, and controllability are all related to one another. However, different attributions can reflect different combinations of these dimensions. In fact, any combination of locus, stability, and controllability is possible.

For example, just because an attribution is internal doesn't necessarily mean it's also stable or uncontrollable. Referring back to an earlier example, one attribution for why your roommate snapped at you this morning is that she's not a "morning person." That is an internal attribution (she's not a morning person) that is stable (she's probably never been a morning person) and relatively uncontrollable (it probably has to do with her biological rhythms). A different attribution is that she was grumpy because she got only two hours of sleep, having been out partying most of the night before. That attribution is also internal (she's grumpy), but it is probably unstable (she isn't grumpy every morning) and controllable (she chose to stay up late the night before). Table 1 provides eight different attributions for a single behavior that represent all the possible combinations of locus, stability, and controllability.

Although most of us probably try to come up with accurate attributions for other people's behaviors, we are still vulnerable to making attribution mistakes.[67] Such errors can create problems for us because our response to other people's behaviors is often based on the attributions we make for those behaviors.

Let's say that Adina and her 14-year-old son Craig get into an argument one night about whether Craig can go on a school-sponsored overseas trip. After their argument, they both go to bed angry. When Adina gets up the following morning, she finds that Craig hasn't done the dishes or taken out the trash, two chores he is responsible for doing every night before bed. It turns out that Craig was so flustered by the previous night's conflict that doing his chores slipped his mind. Adina makes a different attribution, however: She perceives that Craig didn't do the chores because he was deliberately disobeying her. On the basis of that attribution, she tells Craig he is grounded for a week and is not going on the school trip. Her actions only prolong and intensify the conflict between them.

TABLE 1

Eight Attributions for Rudeness

We generally expect social interaction to be pleasant, so when someone is rude to us, we usually wonder why. Let's say your classmate Ricardo posted sarcastic comments to the online discussion board this morning about the presentation you gave in class yesterday, and you're forming an attribution for his behavior. Below are eight attributions representing every possible combination of locus, stability, and controllability.

Internal, Stable, and Controllable	*He's a jerk.*	Personality traits (such as being a jerk) are internal and usually stable, but he should be able to control whether he acts like a jerk.
Internal, Stable, and Uncontrollable	*He's mentally challenged, and he doesn't always understand politeness.*	Although being mentally challenged is internal and stable, he can't help being mentally challenged.
Internal, Unstable, and Controllable	*He's hung over.*	Physical states such as being hung over are internal, but they aren't stable (because they will go away), and they are controllable (he didn't have to drink).
Internal, Unstable, and Uncontrollable	*He's got the flu.*	Illness is internal but unstable (because he'll get better). Presumably he didn't choose to get sick, so it's also uncontrollable.
External, Stable, and Controllable	*He's got a girlfriend who picks a fight with him every single morning; he needs to get out of that relationship.*	The source is external (a girlfriend); her influence is stable (they interact every day) but controllable (he can end the relationship if he wants).
External, Stable, and Uncontrollable	*The medication he takes to control his heart condition makes him irritable.*	Medication is an external source; it's stable (because it's for an ongoing condition) and uncontrollable (because he has to take it).
External, Unstable, and Controllable	*He's cranky because the air conditioning in his apartment isn't working; he should get it fixed.*	The air conditioning is an external cause; it's unstable (because it will eventually get fixed) and controllable (because he can get it fixed).
External, Unstable, and Uncontrollable	*Someone rear-ended his truck this morning, so he's upset.*	The source is external (another driver); it's unstable (it was a one-time incident) and uncontrollable (it was an accident).

If, instead, Adina attributed Craig's behavior to an honest oversight, she might have been able to overlook it instead of making it the basis for additional conflict. As we'll see in the next section, learning how to recognize common attribution errors will best equip us to avoid making mistakes that, as in the case of Adina and Craig, transform a bad situation into a worse one.

Recognizing Common Attribution Errors

We might think we always explain behavior in an objective, rational way, but the truth is that we're all prone to taking mental shortcuts when coming up with attributions. As a result, our attributions are often less accurate than they ideally should be. Three of the most common attribution errors are the self-serving bias, the fundamental attribution error, and overattribution.

Talking Point: It's difficult, if not impossible, to be objective about one's own performance, so it might not surprise your students to learn that the self-serving bias is common.

self-serving bias The tendency to attribute one's successes to internal causes and one's failures to external causes.

We often extend the self-serving bias to our relationships. Why did your partner remember your birthday? Was it because your partner is a thoughtful person or because you reminded him or her repeatedly? © C Squared Studios/Photodisc/Getty Images, RF

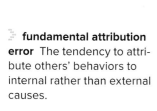

fundamental attribution error The tendency to attribute others' behaviors to internal rather than external causes.

SELF-SERVING BIAS.   The **self-serving bias** refers to our tendency to attribute our successes to stable, internal causes while attributing our failures to unstable, external causes.[68] For example, if you got an *A* on your test, you did so because you're smart, but if you got an *F,* the reason is that the test was unfair or because you work so much to keep up with tuition payments that you didn't have time to study. Those attributions are called self-serving because they suggest that our successes are deserved but our failures are not our fault.

The self-serving bias deals primarily with attributions that we make for our own behaviors. However, research shows that we often extend that tendency to other important people in our lives.[69] In a happy marriage, for instance, people tend to attribute their spouse's positive behaviors to internal causes ("She remembered my birthday because she's thoughtful") and negative behaviors to external causes ("He forgot my birthday because he's been very distracted at work"). That tendency is especially pronounced among people who are currently in love and are seeing each other through rose-colored glasses, as the "Communication: Light Side" box explains. In distressed relationships, the reverse is often true: People attribute negative behavior to internal causes ("She forgot my birthday because she's completely self-absorbed") and positive behavior to external causes ("He remembered my birthday only because I reminded him five times").

The self-serving bias is a natural, self-protective tendency, although it is a form of self-delusion.[70] Virtually none of us is responsible for all our successes and none of our failures. If we're being honest, most of us would agree that our failures are sometimes our fault (you got an *F* because you didn't keep up with your coursework). Similarly, most of us would admit that our successes sometimes result from factors outside our control (you got an *A* because of the curve, not because of your performance).

Those observations also apply to communication in relationships. We might like to think, for instance, that we are responsible for everything that is going well in our relationships but are not responsible for anything that is going poorly. Again, that attitude is unrealistic. As you've probably learned from your own experience, both people in an interpersonal relationship contribute to its positive and negative aspects. When you commit the self-serving bias and act as though you're responsible only for successes but not for failures, your actions are likely to cause resentment from others. For those reasons, it's important to be aware of our self-serving biases and to be honest about the attributions we make for our behavior and the behavior of others. Check out the "Got Skills?" box on p. 128 for hints on doing so.

FUNDAMENTAL ATTRIBUTION ERROR.   Think about how you reacted the last time someone cut you off in traffic. Specifically, what attribution did you make for the driver's behavior? You might have said to yourself, "She must be late for something important" or "He must have a car full of noisy children," but you probably didn't. "What a jerk!" is likely to be closer to your reaction.

The reason for that response is that we commit the **fundamental attribution error,** in which we attribute other people's behaviors to internal rather than external causes.[71] The high school student ran the pledge drive because she's a caring, giving person, not because she earned extra credit for doing so. The cashier gave you the wrong change because he doesn't know how to count, not because he was distracted by an announcement being made over the loudspeaker. That driver cut you off because he or she is a

communication *LIGHT SIDE*

SEEING THE WORLD DIFFERENTLY: LOVERS AND THEIR ROSE-COLORED GLASSES

Perhaps you've noticed that people in love perceive each other more positively than others do. Although they have little difficulty pointing out each other's good qualities, they seem unable even to notice each other's flaws and shortcomings. Indeed, it is as though being in love allows people to see past their partners' exteriors to appreciate the "real person" underneath. Colloquially, we call that ability "seeing through rose-colored glasses," to suggest that being in love makes one's partner—and perhaps everyone else as well—look rosier than usual.

Research has confirmed that people in love perceive and communicate with each other differently than people who are not in love. In one study, psychologists followed newlywed couples over their first three years of marriage. As the researchers expected, most of the spouses reported decreases in their relationship satisfaction during that three-year period. Importantly, however, those who idealized their partner—seeing him or her in unrealistically positive ways—experienced no declines in satisfaction. It seems that seeing each other through rose-colored glasses protected the spouses from noticing each other's limitations and becoming less enchanted with

their marriage as a result. Other research has found that people who are madly in love engage in less self-monitoring behavior (perhaps because they feel more unqualified acceptance from their romantic partners) and less thrill-seeking behavior (maybe because they find their romantic relationships more thrilling). These studies suggest that seeing through rose-colored glasses is a normal, and even beneficial, phase for new lovers to experience, as it encourages them to ignore each other's faults while their feelings for each other deepen.

ASK YOURSELF

- Besides being in love with that person, what else might cause you to see someone through rose-colored glasses?

- Are there people you tend to see through rose-colored glasses? If so, how does that influence the attributions you make for their behavior?

Source: Murray, S. L., Griffin, D. W., Derrick, J. L., Harris, B., Aloni, M., & Leder, S. (2011). Tempting fate or inviting happiness? Unrealistic idealization prevents the decline of marital satisfaction. *Psychological Science, 22,* 619–626.

---

jerk, not because of noisy children or any other external factor that might have motivated that behavior.

The fundamental attribution error is so strong, in fact, that we commit it even when we know better. For instance, you can probably think of at least one actor you dislike simply because you don't like the characters he plays. Most of us understand that acting involves playing a role and pretending to be a character that someone else has created; an actor's words and behaviors clearly aren't his own. However, we often commit the fundamental attribution error by assuming (even subconsciously) that an actor's behavior reflects who he is as a person.

Just how strong is the fundamental attribution error? Consider that in one classic study people explained a person's behavior in terms of internal factors even after they were specifically told that it was caused by external factors.[72] In the study, college students talked with a young woman whose behavior was either friendly or unfriendly. Before their conversations, half the students were told the woman's behavior would be spontaneous, but the other half were told she had been instructed to act either friendly or unfriendly.

How did this information influence the students' attributions for the woman's behavior? The answer is that it had no effect at all. When the woman acted friendly, the students maintained it was because she is a friendly person, and when she acted

Talking Point: Why do people tend to attribute others' behaviors to internal causes? One explanation is that of the cognitive miser: We do it because it requires less mental energy than searching for external causes.

got skills?   SELF-SERVING BIAS

Recognize the self-serving bias—and learn to avoid it.

WHAT?

Learn to avoid the self-serving bias when making attributions about your interpersonal behavior.

WHY?

To recognize and acknowledge that you share responsibility for both the positive and the negative aspects of your personal relationships.

HOW?

1. Choose a relationship that matters to you, and list its five most positive and five most negative characteristics.

2. Write out the ways in which (a) you contribute to the positive aspects of your relationship, and (b) the other person contributes to the negative aspects.

3. Next write out the ways in which (a) you contribute to the negative aspects of the relationship, and (b) the other person contributes to the positive aspects. If you find this task difficult, consider what the other person might say.

TRY!

1. The next time you encounter a problem in this relationship, stop yourself before you assign blame. Carefully consider the role that each of you played in creating that problem.

2. Let your relationship partner hear you sharing the credit with him or her for the positive aspects of your relationship.

3. Over the course of a week, in a short journal entry, document the times when you successfully avoid the self-serving bias. At the week's end, write a paragraph reflecting on what you have learned.

CONSIDER: *How does your interpersonal communication improve when you keep the self-serving bias in check?*

In the IM: The activity "Fundamental Attribution Error" allows students to investigate whether they make more internal attributions about others than about themselves.

unfriendly, they maintained it was because she is an unfriendly person. In both cases, students attributed the woman's behavior to her personality, even when they were specifically told that she was only behaving as instructed.

As interpersonal communicators, we should bear in mind that people's behaviors—including our own—are often responses to external forces. For instance, when the new doctor you're seeing spends only three minutes diagnosing your condition and prescribing a treatment before moving on to the next patient, you might conclude that she's not a very caring person. This would be an internal attribution for her behavior, which the fundamental attribution error increases your likelihood of making. If you think your doctor rushed through your consultation because she's uncaring, that attribution might lead you to give her a poor evaluation to your friends and co-workers or to switch to another doctor altogether.

Was your attribution correct, however? Ask yourself what external forces might have motivated the doctor's behavior. For example, she might have rushed through your consultation simply because another doctor's absence that day forced her to see twice as many patients as usual, not because she's an uncaring person. If that's the case, then you might have switched to another doctor for no reason, forgoing your opportunity to form a positive professional relationship with her. To the extent that we base our decisions on inaccurate attributions, we run the risk of needlessly damaging our relationships in the process.

OVERATTRIBUTION.   A third common attribution error is **overattribution,** in which we single out one or two obvious characteristics of a person and then attribute everything he or she does to those characteristics.[73] Let's use the example of Fatima, who is an only child. When you see her being impatient or acting selfishly, you might say to yourself, "That's typical of an only child." Maybe you notice that she pushes herself to make good grades, she is very conservative with her money, or she doesn't seem to enjoy the holidays. "Well, she *is* an only child!" you might say to yourself, as if that one characteristic is the underlying cause of everything she does.[74]

Overattribution is a form of mental laziness. Instead of trying to understand why Fatima might push herself so hard in school, we pick something obvious about her (she's an only child) and conclude that it must have something to do with that.

Although that example might seem inconsequential, overattribution can contribute to problematic behavior in some contexts. For instance, psychologists William Schweinle, William Ickes, and Ira Bernstein have studied overattribution in the context of marital aggression. On the basis of the principle of overattribution, the researchers predicted that when women communicate in a certain way, such as by being critical, men sometimes explain the behavior as being typical of women in general. In other words, they focus on one aspect of a person ("she's a woman") as the cause of her behavior ("because she's a woman, she's being critical").

Schweinle and his colleagues found that the more men engage in this form of overattribution with women in general, the more likely they are to be verbally abusive with their own wives.[75] The researchers noted that engaging in this form of overattribution causes men to perceive their wives as being critical even when they aren't, simply because they are women. As one result, men form defensive thoughts that provoke their verbal aggression.[76]

Overattribution is particularly easy to do with marginalized groups such as sexual minorities, homeless people, and people with disabilities.[77] Because members of these groups are marginalized, some people don't have much experience interacting with them. This lack of communication might make it easier to believe that the group a person belongs to is the primary cause of his or her behaviors. For that reason, it's important to remember that being homeless or gay might be one characteristic of a person, but it doesn't define the person completely, and it's not the cause of everything that person says or does.[78]

Humans are complex social beings. So, if we want to understand the reasons behind another person's behaviors, we need to look past his or her outward characteristics and consider what aspects of the individual's physical and/or social environment might be motivating his or her behavior.

Like other forms of perception, attributions are important but prone to error. That observation doesn't imply that we never make accurate attributions for other people's behavior. It simply acknowledges that the self-serving bias, the fundamental attribution error, and overattribution are easy mistakes to commit. The more we know about those processes, the better able we'll be to examine the attributions we make. The "At a Glance" box summarizes the three common attribution errors.

overattribution The tendency to attribute a range of behaviors to a single characteristic of a person.

Talking Point: Ask students for examples of when they have committed overattribution with others—or when others have committed it with them.

Overattribution can be easy to do with people in socially marginalized groups, such as individuals with an intellectual disability—especially when interaction with them is limited. Humans are complex social beings, though. We cannot understand people simply by characterizing their most obvious qualities. © *Digital Vision/Punchstock, RF*

AT A GLANCE

Three Common Attribution Errors

Self-Serving Bias	We attribute our successes to internal causes and our failures to external causes.
Fundamental Attribution Error	We attribute other people's behaviors to internal causes more often than to external causes.
Overattribution	We focus on one characteristic of a person and attribute a wide variety of behaviors to that characteristic.

LEARN IT What does it mean to say that attributions vary according to locus, stability, and controllability? How are the self-serving bias, the fundamental attribution error, and overattribution examples of attribution errors?

APPLY IT For one week, keep a list of all the attributions you give to someone else about something you have done. At the end of the week, go back through your list, and evaluate each attribution for accuracy. How many attributions fit the self-serving bias? How many were accurate? Were any of your attributions overly negative?

REFLECT ON IT When do you commit the fundamental attribution error? With which group(s) of people would you be most likely to make overattributions?

4 Improving Your Perceptual Abilities

We've examined how easy it is to make perceptual mistakes. We stereotype people. We assume they think the same ways we do. We attribute all their behaviors to one or two characteristics. Clearly, perception making is hard work. On the positive side, despite all those limitations, we can do a better job of it if we know how. Improving our perceptual ability starts with being mindful of what our perceptions are and what influences them. Next, it involves checking the accuracy of our perceptions. Before we examine those steps, though, imagine yourself in the following situation.

You have just started working at a store that sells and services swimming pools. You've noticed that the social atmosphere at the store seems playful and fun, but you sense tension between Dmitri, the store manager, and Min, one of the salespeople. Dmitri grew up in Greece, went to college in Canada, and has been living in the United States since he graduated. Min's parents emigrated from South Korea when she was an infant and raised Min and her older brother in the Pacific Northwest.

From what you've observed, Dmitri is friendly and informal with almost everyone, including his employees. Min is also friendly, but she communicates with others in a more formal, reserved manner than Dmitri. On a couple of occasions, you have seen Dmitri put his arm around Min and flirt with her. You have observed him doing the same with several other people as well; Dmitri is a very gregarious person. You've also heard from another employee, however, that Min has asked Dmitri not to behave that way toward her at work, although you are not certain whether that is true.

Then, one morning while you're working in the swimming pool showroom, you overhear what sounds like an argument in Dmitri's office. You recognize the voices as Dmitri's and Min's, and although you can't hear everything they're saying, you hear enough to figure out that Min is upset because Dmitri promoted another employee instead of her to the position of lead salesperson. Eventually you see Min walk out of Dmitri's office looking visibly upset. By that afternoon, you start hearing a rumor that Min has filed a harassment complaint against Dmitri.

We'll use this scenario throughout this section to illustrate how you can improve your perception-making abilities. As you imagine yourself in this scenario, consider what perceptions you would form. Has Dmitri harassed Min by denying her a promotion because she expressed discomfort at his flirtatious behavior? Alternatively, is Min falsely accusing Dmitri of harassment because she is angry at not getting the promotion? Or are both parties at fault? Arriving at an accurate perception of the situation will be difficult given the limited information you have. Nevertheless, with effort, you can improve your perceptual ability.

Being Mindful of Your Perceptions

We form perceptions of people and situations constantly—so often, in fact, that we're sometimes unaware that we're doing it. We can improve our perceptual abilities, however, only when we're mindful of our perceptions. In other words, we must first be aware of what our perceptions are; then we must consider how they might be affected by our own characteristics, by the characteristics of the people we're perceiving, and by the context in which we're perceiving them.

KNOW YOURSELF. How can several people observe the same event and form different—even contradictory—perceptions of it? As we've seen, the reason is that our individual characteristics often shape the way we perceive people and situations. One part of being mindful of your perceptions, therefore, is to ask yourself how they are influenced by your personal attributes.

For instance, how might your perception of Dmitri and Min's situation be affected by your sex? Perhaps you identify more with Min if you're female because you are projecting how you would feel in the same situation. Likewise, you might identify more with Dmitri if you're male. In the same vein, your cultural values and expectations might also influence your perception of the situation. If you grew up in a low-power-distance culture that values equality and workers' rights, you might be predisposed to perceive that Dmitri is abusing his power and victimizing Min. Conversely, if you were raised in a high-power-distance culture that values hierarchy and discourages the questioning of authority, you might be more likely to perceive that Min is overreacting and needlessly causing problems.

Remember that your physiological states and traits can also shape your perceptions. If you were tired or hungry when you overheard Dmitri and Min's exchange, for example, you might have felt short-tempered and been more likely than usual to rush to judgment one way or the other. That could have led you to select, organize, and interpret only those clues that supported your initial perception and to ignore any information that did not.

Your experiences with previous jobs could also bias your perceptions of Dmitri and Min by creating a perceptual set. Let's say that one of your closest friends at your last

Talking Point: Point out that being mindful starts by recognizing that people's perceptions are in fact perceptions, not unmediated reflections of reality. Only when we are aware of this can we examine how aspects of ourselves, others, and the context influenced the perceptions we have formed.

In Everyday Life: One reason we often rush to judgment when we're tired, hungry, or ill is that we are less likely than usual to expend the energy necessary to consider our perceptions more fully. Rather, we conserve our energies (including mental energies) in such states.

job was the victim of harassment. Noticing the pain and frustration she went through may have sensitized you to instances of harassment, leading you to "see" a situation as an example of harassment because that's what you expect to see.

Suppose instead that your friend was wrongfully accused of harassment by a disgruntled employee. That experience might sensitize you to "see" even legitimate victims of harassment as simply vindictive and dishonest, because that's what you expect to see. In either case, your experiences would have created a perceptual set that shaped your perceptions.

We can't always change these influences on our perception-making ability. Try as we might, for example, we can't just choose to think like someone of a different gender or cultural background. But what we *can* do is ask ourselves how factors such as our experiences, sex, cultural background, and physiological states and traits might affect the perceptions we make. Acknowledging those influences is one of the first steps in improving our perceptual ability.

FOCUS ON OTHERS' CHARACTERISTICS: THE INFLUENCE OF GENDER AND CULTURE.
Being mindful of our perceptions also means acknowledging how they are influenced by characteristics of the people we're perceiving. For instance, are you more inclined to believe Dmitri and Min's situation is an example of harassment because the supervisor is male and the employee is female? What if the situation involved a male employee accusing a female supervisor of harassment? Might that detail change your perception of the accusation's merit? You might think the sex of the people involved wouldn't matter—legally and ethically, it shouldn't—but several studies have shown that people are more likely to perceive harassment when the supervisor is male as opposed to female.[79]

How does what you know about Dmitri and Min influence the way you perceive their behavior? © Aaron Farley/The Image Bank/Getty Images, © Image Source/Getty Images, RF

Another characteristic of Min and Dmitri that may affect your perceptions of their situation is their cultural backgrounds. Culture has a strong influence on how we behave and communicate, so it should come as no surprise that it also influences the way we perceive behavior. When we observe interactions between people from our own culture, our shared knowledge about cultural norms enables us to perceive and interpret their behaviors with relative ease. However, when we observe interactions between people from other cultures, we are more likely to misinterpret their behaviors. One reason why this is true is that people's cultural backgrounds can activate stereotypes that can influence our perceptions.

For example, perhaps you stereotype Greek men as being naturally gregarious, so you see Dmitri's friendly behavior toward his employees merely as an expression of his nature, not as harassment. Or perhaps you stereotype Asian women (even those raised in the United States) as being accommodating and respectful of authority. If so, then you would likely perceive that Min wouldn't have argued with her supervisor unless she truly felt victimized. Neither of those stereotypes may actually be valid. Nevertheless, to the extent that you hold stereotyped beliefs that are relevant to Dmitri or Min, those beliefs can color the way you perceive the situation.

CONSIDER THE CONTEXT. The last step in being mindful of your perceptions is to consider how the context itself influenced them. In the example of Dmitri and Min, the context includes not only the argument you overheard but also the observations you made of Dmitri's and Min's communication behaviors before the argument. Let's say that when you started working at the store, your first impression of Dmitri was that he was inappropriately affectionate toward his employees. Because of the primacy effect, that first impression might encourage you to perceive his behavior toward Min as harassment. Conversely, let's say that you recently observed Min communicating in an unprofessional manner with two customers. Because of the recency effect, that recent negative impression might encourage you to perceive that she is accusing Dmitri unfairly.

Positivity biases and negativity biases can also shape your perceptions. If you really like Min and have always gotten along well with her, then you might be inclined to believe only positive things about her. That inclination could bias you toward believing her side of the story and concluding that Dmitri had in fact harassed her. However, if you and Min don't get along, then you might be inclined to believe the worst about her, and this inclination could bias you against believing her accusations.

Don't forget, too, that you heard only bits and pieces of Dmitri and Min's argument. It's possible, then, that your limited ability to hear the conversation caused you to miss parts of the argument that would have changed your perception of the situation. In other words, the context itself limited the information that you could select for attention. An important part of being mindful of your perceptions, therefore, is to ask whether there are pieces of information to which you didn't have access.

These three clues—knowing yourself, focusing on the characteristics of others, and considering the context—can all help you think critically about your perceptions by acknowledging the range of factors that can influence them.

Checking Your Perceptions

Being mindful of your perceptions is an important step toward improving your perceptual abilities, but it is only the first step. After you have considered which factors led you to form a particular perception, the next step is to check the accuracy of that perception. To do so, let's continue with the example of Dmitri and Min.

SEPARATE INTERPRETATIONS FROM FACTS. *Dragnet* was a radio and television police drama that debuted in the early 1950s. Its main character, Sgt. Joe Friday, was a detective best known for requesting "just the facts, ma'am." That phrase implies that objective facts are different from interpretations of those facts.

Let's say you saw Dmitri put his arm around a customer and kiss her on the cheek. If you were asked to describe the scene, you might say that "Dmitri was acting friendly with that woman" or "he was flirting with her" or even "he was coming on to her."

Talking Point: Remind students that the context includes the social, psychological, and emotional context as well as the physical context. It also includes the temporal context, which takes into account the order in which events occurred.

In Everyday Life: It is particularly important in relationships to remember that interpretations and facts are not the same. People tend to interpret what they see and hear in ways that are consistent with their mental and emotional state—so, we make more positive interpretations of a partner's behaviors when we are feeling positive than when we are feeling negative. However, we should also take stock of the facts of our partner's behaviors, and not just our interpretations of them.

Sgt. Joe Friday
© Everett Collection

Which of those reports is factual? Technically, none of them is. Rather, they are all interpretations, because they all assign *meaning* to what you observed. You witnessed Dmitri's behavior and interpreted it as friendliness, as flirtation, or as a sign of sexual interest, so you described it in those ways. In fact, if you and two co-workers had witnessed the behavior, you could easily have interpreted it in three different ways.

If all three of your perceptions were subjective interpretations, then what are the facts here? The essential fact is that you saw Dmitri put his arm around the woman and kiss her on the cheek. That's what you objectively observed. Perhaps you also noticed other clues that helped you arrive at your interpretation, such as what occurred right before or how the customer reacted. The point is that *describing* what you actually saw or heard is not the same thing as *interpreting* it. If we are to check the accuracy of our perceptions, we must start by separating what we heard or saw from the interpretation we assigned it.

GENERATE ALTERNATIVE PERCEPTIONS. Once you have assigned meaning to an event, ask yourself what other meanings or interpretations you might have come up with. As we considered earlier, most people arrive at a perception and then pay attention only to information that supports their perception, ignoring any information that doesn't. A better approach is to look for alternative ways of perceiving the situation, even if they contradict your initial perception.

Your observations of Dmitri and Min, for example, might lead you to perceive that Min is accusing Dmitri of harassment only out of anger at not getting the promotion. What are alternative ways of perceiving the situation? One alternative we have already identified is that Dmitri has actually harassed Min. Are there others? Perhaps Dmitri feels threatened by Min and worries that he might put his own job in jeopardy by promoting her. Perhaps Min and Dmitri have had a contentious relationship for a long time. In that case, the conflict you witnessed wasn't about Min's promotion at all but instead reflected long-standing grudges on the part of both individuals.

The practice of generating alternative perceptions is important for two reasons. First, it requires you to look at information about the situation that doesn't match your original perception. For example, if you initially perceived that Min accused Dmitri of harassment only out of anger at not getting the promotion, then it would be easy for you to ignore your observations of Min's discomfort with Dmitri's overly friendly behavior because those observations don't support your perception. In contrast, to generate an alternative perception, you would have to take those observations into account.

By checking our own perceptions, we increase their accuracy.
© *Kathrin Ziegler/Getty Images*

Second, generating alternative perceptions encourages you to ask yourself what information you don't have that might be relevant. How much do you know about Dmitri and Min's history with each other, for instance? If you knew they used to be a romantic couple but had an emotional breakup just a few months before you started working at the store, that information might give you a more accurate context for interpreting their behaviors toward each other.

Keep in mind, however, that even if you are able to generate alternative perceptions, that doesn't necessarily mean your initial perception was inaccurate or should be discarded. In fact, looking at alternatives will sometimes make you even more convinced that your first perception was accurate. The purpose of considering alternative perceptions is to make certain you aren't ignoring or discounting clues from the situation simply because they are inconsistent with the perception you formed.

Once you have separated interpretations from facts and have considered alternative ways of perceiving the situation, you can engage in direct and indirect forms of perception checking.

ENGAGE IN PERCEPTION-CHECKING BEHAVIORS. Perception checking is the process of testing your perceptions for accuracy. This is an important step toward improving your perceptual abilities because when you act on the basis of inaccurate perceptions, you run the risk of turning a situation from bad to worse, as you saw Adina do with her son Craig earlier in this chapter. You can engage in either direct or indirect means of perception checking.

Direct perception checking involves simply asking other people if your perception of a situation is accurate. If you perceive that Min is angry at Dmitri, for instance, one way to find out if you're right is to ask her. Direct perception checking involves three elements:

1. Acknowledging the behavior you witnessed

2. Interpreting that behavior

3. Asking whether your interpretation was correct

Here's an example of how you might directly check your perception that Min is angry with Dmitri:

> "I heard you talking to Dmitri in his office [*acknowledging behavior*]. It sounded like you were pretty mad at Dmitri [*offering an interpretation*]. Is that true?" [*asking about your interpretation*]

Depending on your relationship with Min, she may feel comfortable telling you how she feels: "Yeah, I'm furious with him!" Or she might downplay her feelings if she doesn't feel comfortable disclosing them to you: "I'm just a little upset about not getting the promotion, that's all." If your perception is wrong, she might tell you that: "No, I'm not mad at Dmitri at all; why would you think that?" She might even choose not to respond to your question: "I'd appreciate it if you could just leave me alone for a little while." Direct perception checking will be the most useful, therefore, when you approach people who are willing either to confirm your perceptions or to correct them. You can learn more about direct perception checking in the "Got Skills?" box.

In contrast, *indirect perception checking* involves listening and observing in order to seek additional information about the situation. Instead of asking Min if she is angry, for example, you might observe her facial expressions, listen to how she talks to others, and watch her body language when she's around Dmitri. If you notice that Min looks and sounds angry, that observation gives you additional confidence in the accuracy of your perception. If she seems to interact with Dmitri in a calm, pleasant manner, that observation might suggest that your perception was off base.

Neither direct nor indirect perception checking will provide foolproof results every time. As we saw, asking people if your perceptions are correct is useful only if they are willing to tell you. Indirect perception checking can fail, too, because your initial perception ("Min is angry") might lead you to pay attention only to clues that reinforce that perception. For instance, you might notice Min's distressed tone of voice without also noticing that her facial expression appears calm. Another danger of indirect perception checking is that you might pay attention to information that isn't relevant. To determine

In Everyday Life: Direct perception checking may not be considered appropriate in high-context cultures. In a high-context culture, one would be expected to ascertain the meaning of a situation from contextual cues rather than through direct inquiry.

got skills?

DIRECT PERCEPTION CHECKING

Learn to check your perceptions directly.

WHAT?
Learn to use direct perception checking.

WHY?
To verify the accuracy of your interpersonal perceptions so that you can correct them when they are wrong.

HOW?
1. After formulating an interpretation of someone's behavior, describe the behavior to the person and then indicate how you interpreted it. For example, "You're shaking; you seem really nervous."

2. Ask the individual if your interpretation is correct. If it is, the other person will typically confirm it. If it isn't, the correct interpretation will usually follow ("No, I'm just cold right now").

TRY!
1. When you encounter an ambiguous behavior, formulate your interpretation but remember that it may be inaccurate.

2. If you feel it's appropriate, ask the other person whether your interpretation of his or her behavior is accurate.

3. Over a few weeks, take note of when your interpretations have been accurate and when they have not. Write a short journal entry reflecting on the differences between your successful and unsuccessful interpretations.

CONSIDER: *In cases when you interpreted the behavior incorrectly, what relevant information did you disregard when formulating your interpretation?*

whether Min is angry, for example, you might take careful note of the way she's sitting at her desk and how she's looking at others, even though those behaviors might not be affected by her emotion.

Although you might think that gathering more information will always lead you to make more accurate perceptions, there are instances when having more information makes your perceptions *less* accurate, as the "Fact or Fiction?" box details. For those reasons, it's often in your best interest to engage in both direct and indirect perception checking, so that each strategy can compensate for the shortcomings of the other.

The process of perception checking will increase your confidence in the accuracy of your perceptions in some cases and will give you reason to question them in other cases. The last step in improving your perceptual ability is to make use of this information by revisiting your perceptions and revising them, if necessary.

REVISE YOUR PERCEPTIONS AS NECESSARY.   Good communicators use what they learn from perception checking to modify their perceptions of a situation. Sometimes you'll find that your perceptions were accurate from the start. At other times, you'll realize that they were not accurate, for any of the reasons we've considered: (1) They

Talking Point: Stress the idea that having more information about a situation does not necessarily improve the accuracy of one's perceptions. Students are likely to find this idea strongly counterintuitive.

fact OR fiction? WHEN MAKING PERCEPTIONS, MORE INFORMATION IS ALWAYS BETTER

People sometimes criticize others for making snap judgments—that is, arriving at their perceptions on the basis of limited information. After listening to one speech, for example, you decide to vote for a political candidate without learning anything else about her. Or a customer comes into your store, and after taking one look at him, you perceive that he's trouble. It's easy to see how those on-the-spot judgments can be misleading and how your perceptions might have been more accurate if you'd had additional information.

In many cases, this observation is true: When forming perceptions of others, we should remember that first impressions can be misleading. That political candidate might *sound* good, but you may have a different perception of her when you learn that she has no experience. That customer might *look* suspicious, but you might think differently when you find out he's a youth minister just home from a long and tiring retreat. In many situations, the more information we can gather to check our perceptions, the more accurate our perceptions will be.

Research shows, however, that in certain cases our snap judgments are surprisingly accurate. Going further—gathering additional information about someone, such as through indirect perception checking—*can* make our perceptions more accurate, but it doesn't *always* make them more accurate.

You might think, for instance, that you could get to know someone better by meeting them face-to-face rather than by simply chatting online. An interesting experiment in 2013 proved otherwise, though. In the study, pairs of strangers communicated in one of three ways. Some conversed by Internet chat, where they had access only to each other's words. Others talked on the telephone, giving them access to their partners' words and voice. The rest met face-to-face, where they could hear and see each other in person. After short interactions, the participants reported their perceptions of each other's personalities, and the researchers compared those perceptions to the partners' reports of their own personalities.

The results showed some differences based on the "richness" of the communication channel. Participants' judgments of their partners' friendliness and moodiness were most accurate after face-to-face conversations and least accurate after Internet chats. In other words, the more information they had about each other, the more accurate their perceptions were. The opposite pattern was observed for perceptions of the partners' conscientiousness and openness, however. Those perceptions were most accurate after Internet chats and least accurate after face-to-face meetings. This experiment illustrates that having more information about a person—as you would if you had talked face-to-face instead of online—does not always make your perceptions of him or her more accurate. More information is sometimes better, but not always.

FROM ME TO YOU

The observation that more information is not always better might leave you feeling a little torn. On the one hand, it's useful to check your perceptions by gathering additional information; on the other hand, additional information can sometimes make your perceptions less rather than more accurate.

The trick to solving this paradox is to learn which pieces of information to pay attention to and which to ignore. That's a difficult skill to be taught, and in fact most of us learn it by our experience at forming and checking perceptions. Just knowing that more information isn't always better gives you an advantage. When you engage in indirect perception checking, you can ask yourself whether each new clue you gather about a situation is relevant to your perception. Over time, that practice should improve your perceptual accuracy.

Source: Wall, H. J., Taylor, P. J., Dixon, J., Conchie, S. M., & Ellis, D. A. (2013). Rich contexts do not always enrich the accuracy of personality judgments. *Journal of Experimental Social Psychology, 49*, 1190–1195.

were limited by characteristics of yourself, of the people involved, or of the situation; (2) you were confusing facts and interpretations; or (3) you didn't consider any alternative perceptions. As one example, perhaps you initially perceived that Min was being dishonest and vindictive by accusing Dmitri of harassment, but after you dug deeper into the situation, you discovered that Dmitri did in fact harass Min. When the results

FIGURE 4 Improving Your Perceptual Ability Improving your perceptual ability involves two stages. First you need to identify your initial perception by exploring characteristics about yourself, the other person, and the context of the situation that may be influencing your perception. Then you need to check your perception by considering what is factual and interpretive, and whether there may be alternative perceptions.
© iStockphoto.com/Izabela Habur, RF

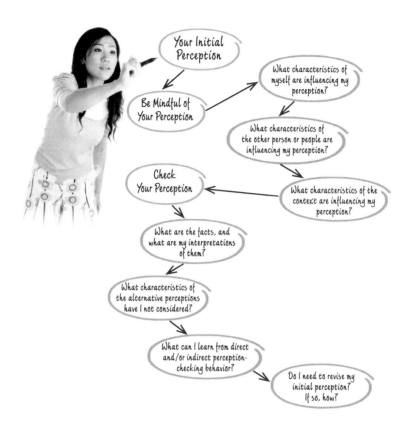

of perception checking give you reason to believe your perceptions are inaccurate, it's your responsibility as a communicator to revise them.

Improving your perceptual ability therefore involves two major strategies. First, you have to be mindful of the factors that influence what perception you form of a situation. Second, you have to check that perception by separating facts from interpretations, considering alternative perceptions, engaging in direct and indirect perception checking, and revising your perception if necessary. With practice, these skills, which are represented in Figure 4, will help you improve your perceptions of people in interpersonal contexts.

LEARN IT What aspects of ourselves, the people we are perceiving, and the context can influence our perceptions? How do direct and indirect perception checking differ?

APPLY IT Distorted or inaccurate perceptions often provide the basis for comedy story lines. Spend a few days watching your favorite sitcoms, and pay attention to how the characters' perceptions are limited, how they might be affected by culture, and how they might confuse interpretation with fact. Document your findings in class or in a brief written report. Noticing these behaviors in others—even television characters—can help us to notice them in ourselves.

REFLECT ON IT How do you notice that your own perceptions are limited? When do you mistake interpretations for facts?

MASTER the chapter

1 The Process of Perception (p. 107)

- Interpersonal perception is the process of making meaning from the people and the relationships we encounter.
- The process of perception includes selecting stimuli for attention, organizing them into relevant categories, and interpreting their meaning.
- Physiological states and traits, cultures, co-cultures, and social roles all influence the accuracy of our perceptions.

2 Fundamental Forces in Interpersonal Perception (p. 114)

- Stereotyping is the process of applying generalizations about a group to a person we perceive to belong to that group.
- According to the primacy effect, our first impressions are more powerful than any of our later impressions.
- The recency effect maintains that the most recent impression we have formed will overshadow the impressions that came before it.
- Our perceptual set causes us to perceive only what we want or expect to perceive.

- When we are egocentric, we lack the ability to adopt another person's perspective.
- The positivity bias encourages us to focus on a person's positive aspects; the negativity bias encourages us to focus on his or her negative aspects.

3 Explaining What We Perceive (p. 123)

- Attributions, or explanations for behavior, vary according to their locus, stability, and controllability.
- The self-serving bias, the fundamental attribution error, and overattribution are common attribution mistakes.

4 Improving Your Perceptual Abilities (p. 130)

- Being mindful of your perceptions involves focusing on the aspects of yourself, others, and the context that are influencing what you perceive.
- Checking the accuracy of your perceptions involves separating interpretation from fact, generating alternative perceptions, engaging in direct and indirect perception checking, and revising your perceptions as necessary.

KEY TERMS

attribution (p. 123)
egocentric (p. 120)
fundamental attribution error (p. 126)
interpersonal perception (p. 107)
interpretation (p. 109)
negativity bias (p. 122)

organization (p. 109)
overattribution (p. 129)
perception (p. 107)
perceptual set (p. 118)
positivity bias (p. 120)
primacy effect (p. 116)

recency effect (p. 117)
selection (p. 108)
self-serving bias (p. 126)
stereotypes (p. 115)

McGraw Hill Education connect

To maximize your study time, check out CONNECT to access the SmartBook study module for this chapter, watch videos, and explore other resources.

5

Language

© Search For Common Ground

WORDS CAN HEAL OLD WOUNDS

Heartfelt words of apology can mend emotional wounds, restore relationships, and inspire change, even when those words come half a century after the fact. Such was the case when Elwin Wilson—a white southern man—apologized in 2009 for having attacked John Lewis—an African American—in the "whites only" waiting room of a Greyhound bus station in 1961. Lewis was a member of the U.S. House of Representatives in 2009, but at that earlier time he was a freedom rider in the racial equality movement of Martin Luther King Jr., while Wilson was a young man aggressively opposed to racial integration.

After the election of Barack Obama to the presidency in 2008, Wilson began a personal crusade to make amends to those he had wronged. When Wilson was reunited with Representative Lewis, the congressman said, "For you to come here today, it's amazing to me. It's unreal. It's unbelievable. Maybe, just maybe, others will come forward because there needs to be this healing. Good to see you, my friend."[1]*

*Shipman, Claire, Cindy Smith, and Lee Ferran (February 6, 2009). "Man asks entire town for forgiveness for racism." ABC News/ Good Morning America. http://abcnews.go.com/GMA/story?id=6813984

inding the right words can be challenging under the most ordinary circumstances, let alone extraordinary ones. We may not always know what to say to make someone feel comforted, informed, entertained, motivated, or persuaded. If we know how to use language effectively, however, we can employ it to accomplish those goals in our personal relationships—and in many others.

1 The Nature of Language

Many species communicate in one form or another, but we humans are the only creatures on the planet who use language. Although most of us are born with verbal ability, we have to learn the specific languages we use; and, like most learned skills, our language abilities improve as we practice and learn about them.

In this chapter's opening story, Elwin Wilson communicated his sincere apologies to Representative John Lewis in words. Like Wilson, we use language as a way to represent or symbolize our thoughts and feelings.

We can understand **language** as a structured system of symbols used for communicating meaning. Many scientists believe that language evolved from early humans' use of gestures to communicate.[2] For instance, many of us hold out our hands when we ask for something. We share this gesture with other primates, such as chimpanzees. The human brain, however, appears to have a specific capacity for learning and using language that is not shared by other species. Researchers in the field of biolinguistics have proposed that our advanced cognitive capacity has allowed humans to develop the symbolic system we know as language.[3]

You can probably think of many behaviors and items that represent or symbolize some type of meaning. A smile often symbolizes happiness, for instance; a red traffic light symbolizes the need to stop. Many gestures also have symbolic meaning, in that they represent a particular concept or idea. For example, you probably wave to say "hello" or shrug your shoulders to say "I don't know." Significantly, although traffic lights, gestures, and facial expressions all symbolize meaning, none of those behaviors or items qualifies as a language. Instead, a language is characterized by the use of a specific type of symbol: words.

Talking Point: The observation that humans are the only species to use language may cause confusion, because many species use noises to communicate, and it's easy to mistake those noises for language. Animal noises and calls are certainly communicative, but they are not technically language because they lack the structure and rules that characterize language.

language A structured system of symbols used for communicating meaning.

The human brain seems to have a specific capacity for learning and using language that is not shared by other species. These images identify brain regions associated with the ability to hear words, see words, and speak words.
© Gwen Shockey/Science Source

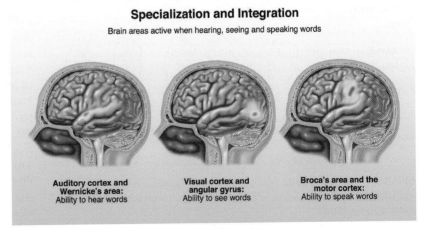

Specialization and Integration
Brain areas active when hearing, seeing and speaking words

Auditory cortex and Wernicke's area: Ability to hear words

Visual cortex and angular gyrus: Ability to see words

Broca's area and the motor cortex: Ability to speak words

Words are the building blocks of verbal communication. As we'll see in this chapter, we use words to represent ideas, observations, feelings, and thoughts. Words have a profound influence on how we relate to others. One key point here is that the power of verbal communication isn't limited to the words we speak; it also includes the words we write. When we hear the term *verbal,* we sometimes think only of spoken language. In fact, written messages are also verbal, because they also use words. Keep that in mind as we take a look at some of the most important features of language.

Language Is Symbolic

Language is symbolic. That statement means that each word represents a particular object or idea, but it does not constitute the object or idea itself. For example, the word *barn* represents a structure often used for storing hay, grain, or livestock. The word itself is not the structure; rather, it merely symbolizes it. Similarly, the word *five* represents a specific quantity of something (one more than four and one fewer than six), but the word itself is not the quantity; it simply represents it.

One way to understand the symbolic nature of language is to remember that different languages have different words for the same thing. The English word *barn,* for instance, is *schuur* in Dutch, *celeiro* in Portuguese, 축사 in Korean, and σιταποθήκη in Greek. Those are completely different symbols, but they all represent the same object or idea. If you were to invent your own language, you could create any term you wanted to represent the concept of a barn.

As an illustration of the use of different symbols to represent the same idea, Figure 1 displays the word *speak* as represented in five different alphabets. These include (1) the Roman alphabet, with which you are already familiar; (2) Braille, an alphabet consisting of raised dots, used by people who are blind to read and write; (3) Morse code, a system of long and short sounds used to communicate by means of a telegraph machine; (4) American Sign Language, a system of gestures and body language used to communicate with people who have hearing impairments; and (5) Gregg shorthand, a symbolic alphabet used for rapid note taking. Notice how different those symbols look, even though they are all symbolizing the same idea.

We saw in the About Communication chapter that the meaning of words—that is, what they symbolize—can change over time. For instance, *awful* used to mean "full of awe," and *neck* used to mean "a parcel of land" (as in "my neck of the woods"). Those terms now symbolize something different, and it is entirely possible that they will represent something different in the future. This example illustrates the important point that the symbolic nature of language is never static. Rather, it changes and evolves as words take on new meanings.

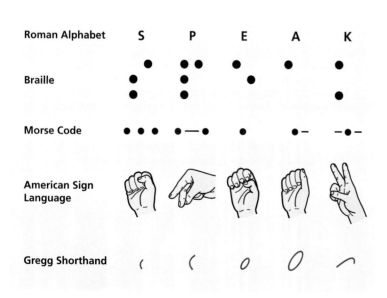

FIGURE 1 Alphabet Soup Many forms of language have their own alphabets. Here is the word SPEAK according to several different language systems.

Language Is Arbitrary (Mostly)

Why do words symbolize the particular things they do? For the most part, words have only an arbitrary connection to their meanings.[4] Think of the word *car*. The actual word doesn't look like a car or sound like a car, so why does it make us think of one? The only reason is that speakers of English have agreed to give the word *car* that particular meaning. We could just as easily call cars "whickles" or "geps" or "mumqualls." Those words don't mean anything, but they would if we assigned them a meaning. The point is that the meaning of almost all words is arbitrary: Words literally mean whatever we, as users of a language, choose for them to mean.

© Hannu Liivaar/Alamy, RF

Language can be arbitrary precisely because it is symbolic. As we saw earlier, words only symbolize their meanings; they don't constitute their meanings themselves. For that reason, we can assign almost any word to symbolize a particular meaning, making the connection between language and meaning arbitrary.

Art by Harris, S © CartoonStock.com

One major exception to that rule is **onomatopoeia,** a word formed by imitating the sound associated with its meaning. Words such as *buzz, meow, splash,* and *click* are all onomatopoetic words because their sounds reflect their meanings. For that reason, we can say that those types of words have an *iconic* connection to their meanings—that is, they serve as an icon or a representation of the meaning they symbolize—rather than an arbitrary one.

It's worth noting, however, that even onomatopoeia varies by language. To a U.S. American speaker of English, a dog goes "bowwow," but to an Indonesian, it says "gong gong." A sheep says "baa" to an English speaker, but "me'e'e" to the Navajo. The sound of a gunshot is "bang" in the United States but "pum" to the Spanish, "peng" to the Germans, and "pan" to the French.[5]

> **onomatopoeia** A word formed by imitating the sound associated with its meaning.

Writing Note: Have students write out 10–12 onomatopoetic words before discussing this section so that they have a point of reference for learning about onomatopoeia.

Language Is Governed by Rules

We have said that language is symbolic and that the meaning of most words is arbitrary. That assertion leads to an obvious question: How is it that we all understand one another? The answer is that every language is governed by rules.

Even if you can't state all the rules of your native language, you generally notice them when they're violated. To a native speaker of English, for instance, the statement "I filled the tub with water" sounds correct, but the phrase "I filled water into the tub" does not. Even if you aren't quite sure why the second sentence sounds wrong, you probably still recognize that it does. Along these same lines, when you learn a new language, you don't learn just the words; you also learn the rules for how the words work together to convey meaning.

Researchers distinguish among four types of language rules:

- *Phonological rules* deal with the correct pronunciation of a word, and they vary from language to language. If you speak French, for example, you know that the proper way to pronounce *travail* is "trah-VYE." In contrast, according to English phonological rules, the word looks as though it should be pronounced "trah-VALE."

- *Syntactic rules* govern the way we put together words and phrases to create well-formed sentences. Syntactic rules vary by language. An English speaker might

In Everyday Life: Language acquisition in early life illustrates the arbitrary nature of language. Before speaking words, children make many vocal sounds, most of which have no prescribed meaning. Often a child's first "word" is simply one of those sounds that happens to correspond to a particular meaning in the parents' language. A child might say "mama," and the parents regard it as a word. Yet when the child says "gaga," they don't. That is only because *mama* has a prescribed meaning, whereas *gaga* does not, but these may be completely indistinguishable to the child.

AT A GLANCE

Rules of Language

Phonological Rules	Deal with the correct pronunciation of words
Syntactic Rules	Dictate the proper order of words for the intended meaning
Semantic Rules	Govern the meanings of individual words
Pragmatic Rules	Apply social and cultural information to the interpretations of statements

refer to a *red card,* for example, because in English, most modifiers ("red") come before nouns ("card"). In Spanish, though, most modifiers come after nouns, so you would say *la tarjeta roja* (literally, "the card red").

- *Semantic rules* govern the meanings of individual words. These meanings may be arbitrary, as we have seen, but they are agreed upon by speakers of a language. When you hear the word *car,* for instance, you think of an automobile, not a washing machine, a rock concert, or an iPad. It is a semantic rule that connects *car* with "automobile" and not with one of the other meanings.

- *Pragmatic rules* address how we use social and cultural information to determine the meaning of statements. They direct us to pay attention to context, tone of voice, and other clues to make sense of what someone is saying. Think of the phrase "Nice to meet you," a common greeting among speakers of English. Depending on the context and the speaker's tone of voice, you might think the speaker really is happy to meet you, or you might infer that he or she is just saying so to be polite. If the speaker's tone is sarcastic, you might even infer that he or she is actually unhappy to meet you. In each instance, it is pragmatic rules that lead you to your conclusion.

The "At a Glance" box summarizes the four types of language rules.

As children acquire a language, they gain an almost intuitive sense of its phonological, syntactic, semantic, and pragmatic rules. That knowledge allows native speakers of a language to speak and write fluently. In contrast, people who are less familiar with the language are more prone to violate these rules.[6]

The widespread use of electronically mediated forms of communication, such as texts and tweets, has led some to worry that students are no longer learning to use language properly. Is that concern valid? Check out the "Fact or Fiction?" box to see.

Language Has Layers of Meaning

denotative meaning
A word's literal meaning or dictionary definition.

connotative meaning
A word's implied or secondary meaning, in addition to its literal meaning.

Many words imply certain ideas that differ from their literal meanings. The literal meaning of a word—that is, its dictionary definition—is called its **denotative meaning.** Think of the word *home.* Its denotative meaning is "a shelter used as a residence." When you hear the word *home,* however, you probably also think of a concept such as "a place where I feel safe, accepted, and loved" or "a space where I am free to do whatever I want." Those are examples of the word's **connotative meaning,** the implications that a word suggests in addition to its literal meaning.

Many people have worried aloud that sending text messages impairs a person's ability to use grammatically correct language. One reason why is that texting makes heavy use of abbreviations, such as *u* for *you* and *ppl* for *people*. Young Americans send and receive more than 3,300 texts per month, on average, raising concerns that they are losing their capacity for language in the process. Is that concern fact or fiction?

A 2014 study reports that there is no cause for alarm: Text messaging does not have a negative effect on people's ability to use language properly. The study followed a group of students ranging in age from 8 to 30 years. The researchers collected all of the text messages participants wrote in a two-day period and coded them for improper uses of grammar and punctuation. They then compared participants' scores with their performance in standardized measures of grammatical performance and intelligence.

The researchers reported that grammatical violations in text messages had no negative effects on the students' abilities to use language properly. In fact, omitting words and using ungrammatical word forms while texting were actually related to better spelling ability, especially for younger texters. If texting has any effect on language use, then, the effect appears to be a positive one.

Sources: Wood, C., Kemp, N., & Waldron, S. (2014). Exploring the longitudinal relationships between the use of grammar in text messaging and performance on grammatical tasks. *British Journal of Developmental Psychology, 32*, 415–429; Nielsen Co. (2010, October 14). U.S. teen mobile report calling yesterday, texting today, using apps tomorrow. Retrieved March 4, 2015 from www.nielsen.com/us/en/insights/news/2010/u-s-teen-mobile-report-calling-yesterday-texting-today-using-apps-tomorrow.html

THE SEMANTIC TRIANGLE.   To illustrate the relationship between words and their denotative and connotative meanings, psychologist Charles Ogden and English professor Ivor Richards developed the *semantic triangle* (Figure 2).[7] In its three corners, the semantic triangle portrays three necessary elements for identifying the meaning in language. The first element is the *symbol,* which is the word being communicated. In the second corner is the *referent,* which is the word's denotative meaning. Finally, there's the *reference,* or the connotative meaning.

As the semantic triangle illustrates, if several listeners hear the same word, they might attribute the same denotative meaning to it but different connotative meanings. For instance, if I say "euthanasia," the word itself is the symbol, and its referent is a medically assisted death. To one listener, the word represents a merciful way to end a person's pain and suffering. To another person, it represents a form of homicide. To still other listeners, it represents an unfortunate—but sometimes justified—component of the death experience. These are all differences in the word's reference, or connotative meaning, rather than in its denotative meaning.

This example illustrates the essential point that the meanings of words are situated in the people who use them and not in the words themselves. Consequently, people may use a word such as *euthanasia* to connote a range of different meanings. As the transaction model of communication, discussed in the About Communication chapter, suggests, most words don't have meanings of their own but receive their meanings through the social interaction of the people who use them.

LOADED LANGUAGE.   In March 2010, President Obama signed into law the Patient Protection and Affordable Care Act, intended to reform existing health care laws, increase access to health insurance, and reduce health care costs for individuals and the government. The law was highly controversial among members of the U.S. public, and

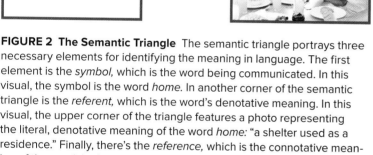

the controversy was reflected in the language people used to describe it. Those who wrote the law, and those who favored it, called it the "Affordable Care Act." Those who opposed it—and who also tended to be very critical of the president—called it "Obamacare." Both of those terms are examples of **loaded language,** words with strongly positive or negative connotations. Notice that "Affordable Care Act" sounds positive because it implies providing less expensive health care to more citizens. "Obamacare," however, seems to focus more on the desires of the president than on the health care needs of the country.

Loaded language reflects the observation that denotations and connotations represent different layers of meaning. At a denotative level, for instance, the word *cancer* refers to a malignant growth or tumor in the body. For many people, however, the term connotes any evil condition that spreads destructively. For example, you might hear someone describe a condition such as poverty or bigotry as a "cancer on society." That example illustrates that people can use the word *cancer* as a loaded term when they wish to evoke feelings of fear, disgust, or anger on the part of listeners. People can also use loaded words to evoke positive emotions. Terms such as *peace, family,* and *freedom* have emotionally positive connotations, even though their denotative meanings are emotionally neutral.[8]

Language Varies in Clarity

Josh is driving his brother Jeremy to an appointment with a new physician, and Jeremy has the directions. As they approach an intersection, they have the following conversation:

> **Josh:** I need to turn left at this next light, don't I?
>
> **Jeremy:** Right.

Which way should Josh turn? When Jeremy responded to Josh's question by answering "right," was he saying that Josh was correct in thinking he should turn left, or was he correcting Josh by instructing him to turn right? We don't really know, because Jeremy has used **ambiguous language** by making a statement that we can interpret to have more than one meaning. Jeremy's reply was ambiguous because the word *right* could mean either "correct" or "turn right" in this situation.

A certain amount of ambiguity is inherent in our language. In fact, according to the *Oxford English Dictionary (OED)*, the 500 most frequently used words in the English language have an average of 23 meanings each. The word *set* has so many meanings—nearly 200, more than any other English word—that it takes the *OED* 60,000 words to define it![9]

FIGURE 2 The Semantic Triangle The semantic triangle portrays three necessary elements for identifying the meaning in language. The first element is the *symbol,* which is the word being communicated. In this visual, the symbol is the word *home.* In another corner of the semantic triangle is the *referent,* which is the word's denotative meaning. In this visual, the upper corner of the triangle features a photo representing the literal, denotative meaning of the word *home:* "a shelter used as a residence." Finally, there's the *reference,* which is the connotative meaning of the word. In the right corner of this visual, the connotative meaning of the word is depicted by family members sharing breakfast in their kitchen. *©Phillip Spears /Photodisc / PunchStock, RF, © BananaStock/PunchStock, RF*

loaded language Terms that carry strongly positive or strongly negative connotations.

ambiguous language Language having more than one possible meaning.

Outside of Class: Have students collect examples of loaded language from opinion editorials, print advertisements, or other media and bring them to class as illustrators. Loaded language is particularly common in political speeches and advertisements.

Words such as *mother* and *marriage* have emotionally positive connotations, even though their denotative meanings are neutral. A term such as *marriage* generates controversy among some groups of people when it is applied to same-sex couples. © *American Images Inc/The Image Bank/Getty Images,* © *(c) Esbin-Anderson Photog /Brand X Pictures/PunchStock, RF,* © *AP Images/Steven Senne*

One reason language varies in clarity is that some words are more concrete than others. A word that is *concrete* refers to a specific object in the physical world, such as a particular laptop computer, a specific restaurant, or an individual person. In contrast, a word that is *abstract* refers to a broader category or organizing concept of objects. According to English professor Samuel Hayakawa, words can be arrayed along a "ladder of abstraction" that shows their progression from more abstract to more concrete.[10]

An example of Hayakawa's ladder of abstraction appears in Figure 3. At the bottom of the ladder is a reference to all living beings, which is a broad, abstract category. Moving upward, the concepts become more and more concrete, referring to all animals, then all mammals, all primates, all *Homo sapiens,* and all males, before reaching the most concrete reference to a specific individual.

Language Is Bound by Context and Culture

Finally, the meaning in language is affected by the social and cultural context in which it is used. Societies and cultures differ in many ways, including their degree of individualism and their use of communication codes. Many of those differences are reflected in people's verbal messages. For instance, when you hear someone say, "I'm looking out for number one," you're hearing a very self-focused message that would be less common in a collectivistic than an individualistic society. In fact, a common Japanese adage is "It is the nail that sticks out that gets hammered down," which reflects the collectivistic culture of that nation.[11]

Studies have shown that for individuals who speak more than one language, the choice of language can affect their perceptions.[12] While

Talking Point: The *Oxford English Dictionary* added hundreds of new terms in 2014. They include *man crush,* representing one man's nonromantic admiration for another; *headcam,* a small video camera strapped to the head or attached to a helmet; and *amazeballs,* for something that is extremely impressive.

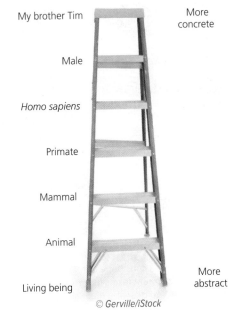

My brother Tim — More concrete

Male

Homo sapiens

Primate

Mammal

Animal

Living being — More abstract

© *Gerville/iStock*

FIGURE 3 Ladder of Abstraction According to English professor Samuel Hayakawa, words can be arrayed along a "ladder of abstraction" that shows their progression from more abstract to more concrete. In this figure, the bottom of the ladder refers to a living being, a broad, abstract category.

completing a values test, for instance, students in Hong Kong expressed more traditional Chinese values while speaking Cantonese than while speaking English. Jewish and Arab students in Israel both described themselves as more distinct from outsiders when speaking their native languages than when speaking English. Just as each language is distinctive, the language we use leads us to see the world in a particular way.

In fact, the idea that language shapes our views of reality was proposed by anthropologist Edward Sapir and linguist Benjamin Whorf in what became known as the **Sapir-Whorf hypothesis.** Their notion was that language influences the ways that members of a culture see the world—and that the attitudes and behaviors of a culture's people are reflected in its language.[13]

Sapir-Whorf hypothesis The idea that language influences the ways that members of a culture see and think about the world.

The Sapir-Whorf hypothesis embodies two specific principles. The first, called *linguistic determinism,* suggests that the structure of language determines how we think. In other words, we can conceive of something only if we have a term for it in our vocabulary.[14] Imagine a language, for instance, that includes no word describing the emotion of envy. According to the principle of linguistic determinism, people who speak that language would not experience envy because their experiences of the world would be limited to what their language allowed them to communicate about.

The second principle, called *linguistic relativity,* suggests that because language determines our perceptions of reality, people who speak different languages will see the world differently. In his research, for instance, Whorf discovered that the language of the Hopi Indians makes no distinction between nouns and verbs. Whereas English uses nouns to refer to things and verbs to refer to actions, the Hopi language describes just about everything as an action or a process. Compared with English speakers, then, the Hopi tend to see the world as being constantly in motion.[15]

The Sapir-Whorf hypothesis is provocative, but researchers have offered three criticisms that call it into question. The first criticism centers on the cause-and-effect relationship between language and thought. The hypothesis proposes that language shapes and constrains how we think. It is equally possible, though, that our thoughts shape and constrain our language. For instance, an experienced fashion designer might look at four jackets and label their colors "scarlet," "ruby," "crimson," and "vermilion." You might look at the same jackets and call them all "red." Does the designer think of the four colors as different because she has more terms for them than you do, or does she have more terms because she has more experience thinking about differences among colors? It's difficult to know for sure, but either idea is possible.

Second, even if people don't have a word for a particular experience, that doesn't necessarily mean they don't have that experience. Perhaps you can recall a situation when you were embarrassed for someone else, for instance. That experience is called *fremdschämen* in German—and although there is no equivalent term in English, you may have had the experience nonetheless.

Our experiences can shape our use of language. A veteran fashion designer might have different terms for various shades of red, whereas you might use the term "red" to describe them all. © Datacraft Co Ltd/Imagenavi/Getty Images, RF

Finally, even people who don't acquire language, perhaps because of mental or cognitive deficiencies, are able to think, count, and interact with others. They wouldn't be able to do those things if language determined thought.

These criticisms don't necessarily mean that the Sapir-Whorf hypothesis is entirely wrong. They suggest, however, that language may not shape and constrain our ways of thinking quite to the extent that Sapir and Whorf believed.

LEARN IT What does it mean to say that language is symbolic? How is onomatopoeia an exception to the rule that language is arbitrary? How do syntactic rules differ from semantic rules? Describe the difference between a word's denotative meaning and its connotative meaning. When is a word or phrase ambiguous? What is the Sapir-Whorf hypothesis?

APPLY IT To observe how language evolves, invent a new word or expression. Write out a definition for it, and begin using it in everyday conversation with your friends. Take note of how well your word or expression catches on and whether your friends begin using it in their own conversations.

REFLECT ON IT In what ways is your language use affected by your culture? Where did you learn all the rules associated with your native language?

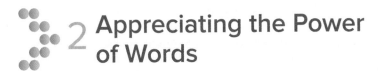

2 Appreciating the Power of Words

English writer Rudyard Kipling, author of *The Jungle Book,* once called words "the most powerful drug used by mankind." To understand his point, think about how you feel when someone you love expresses affection to you, or when you listen to a speech by a politician you can't stand, or when you have to comfort a grieving friend. Words can literally change a person's day—or a person's life—in positive or negative ways.

Whole books have been written about the power of language. Here we'll focus on five important contexts in which words have special power: naming, persuasion, credibility and power, affection, and comfort.

Naming Defines and Differentiates Us

What's something that belongs to you yet is constantly used by others? The answer is *your name.*

A name is simply a linguistic device that identifies something or someone. Your name does more, however, than just differentiate you from others—it's also an important component of your sense of self. From the perspective of interpersonal communication, naming is one way we represent ourselves to others and one way we gain information about other people. Let's examine how names relate to identity and look at some common ways that names come about.

In Everyday Life: We associate people's names with their identities so strongly that it's hard to adjust when someone we know changes his or her name. A last name might change because of marriage, divorce, adoption, or for professional reasons. People might also change their first name legally or in practice (e.g., "I would like to be called Thomas instead of Tommy").

Talking Point: Ask how many of your students were named after someone (with either a first or a middle name). Of those, how many were named after a relative? Of those, how many were named after a parent? A grandparent? An uncle or an aunt? Naming a child after someone else is a common practice worldwide.

NAMING AND IDENTITY. As we considered in an earlier chapter, first impressions are often critical to the perception we form of someone. Although impressions are influenced by factors such as a person's appearance or behaviors, they can also be shaped by his or her name. A person's first name, for instance, frequently suggests information about the person's demographic characteristics. One such characteristic is the person's sex. In Western societies, for instance, we usually assign names such as Jacob, Michael, and Caleb only to males and names such as Emma, Savannah, and Nicole to females.

Names can also provide clues about a person's ethnicity. For example, you might infer that LaKeisha is African American, Huong is Asian, and Santiago is Latino. Some names even suggest a person's age group, so you might assume that Jennifer, Emily, and Hannah are younger than Edna, Mildred, and Bertha.

In addition to demographic information, names can suggest information about our disposition and sense of self. For instance, we might perceive an adult man who goes by the name William differently than one who goes by Billy, even though those are two forms of the same name. Indeed, research shows that we do make assumptions about people—accurately or not—on the basis of their names.[16]

Talking Point: Ask your students how many of them use different screen names or e-mail addresses for different purposes.

In one classic study, for instance, people made more positive evaluations of men named David, Jon, Joshua, and Gregory than they did of men named Oswald, Myron, Reginald, and Edmund, even though they were given no information about the men other than their names.[17] Other studies have shown that people whose first names strongly suggest a nonwhite ethnicity sometimes experience discrimination based only on their names.[18]

TABLE 1

Popular Names over the Last Century

Year	Top Three Boys' Names	Top Three Girls' Names
2013	Noah	Sophia
	Liam	Emma
	Jacob	Olivia
1975	Michael	Jennifer
	Jason	Amy
	Christopher	Heather
1950	James	Linda
	Robert	Mary
	John	Patricia
1925	Robert	Mary
	John	Dorothy
	William	Betty
1900	John	Mary
	William	Helen
	James	Anna

NAMING PRACTICES. In the United States, the Social Security Administration keeps track of the most popular first names given to newborns throughout the country. Certain names have remained fashionable for quite some time. Beginning in 1880, for example, Mary and John were the most popular female and male first names nearly every year until 1925, when Robert took over the top spot for boys. Mary dominated the list for girls until 1947, when it was replaced with Linda. As times change, though, so do naming preferences. By 1985, Jessica and Michael were the most popular first names. Sophia and Noah topped the list in 2013.[19] Table 1 lists the most popular first names since 1900.

Practices of naming also vary according to culture and religion. In predominantly Catholic communities around the world, for instance, males are often given a feminine middle name, such as Marie or Maria. (In French Catholic families, men often have a compound first name, such as Paul-Marie, to accommodate the same tradition.) These naming practices appear to reflect cultural traditions rather than specific church doctrine. Among the Sikh of India, boys are given the surname Singh and girls the surname Kaur, although adults of both sexes often take these as middle names instead. The Sikh practice of giving common surnames to all boys and girls is meant to symbolize the abolition of class inequalities. In Mexico, children often receive two last names, including their father's last name and their mother's maiden name. This practice is intended to honor both the maternal and the paternal lineages.

In many parts of the world, it is also traditional for women to adopt their husband's last name when they marry, or at least to add his name to hers. So, when marrying George Rogers, Jean Levitt might become Jean Rogers, or Jean Levitt Rogers, or Jean Levitt-Rogers. Alternatively, she might choose to remain Jean Levitt. What factors influence that decision?

In a study by communication researchers Karen Foss and Belle Edson, married women who kept their birth names gave more importance to their personal concerns than to their relationships. In contrast, women who took their husband's names rated their relationships as more important than issues of self. Women who hyphenated their last names were in the middle, rating their relationships and personal concerns about equally.[20]

In early 2015, readers of *Entertainment Weekly* complained that the magazine had incorrectly listed the name of Oscar-winning movie director Alejandro González Iñárritu, believing that editors didn't understand Mexican naming practices. In fact, the magazine had printed the name exactly as the director himself wished: Alejandro G. Iñárritu. © *C Flanigan/Getty Images*

Other research has confirmed that women who retain their birth names at marriage score higher than other women on self-reports of masculinity and feminist attitudes.[21] However, name changers and name keepers don't appear to differ from each other in their self-esteem, autonomy, or reports about the balance of control in their marriages.[22]

Many people also prefer to be addressed using courtesy titles. For instance, some women prefer to be called "Miss" (if they are unmarried) or "Mrs" (if they are married), whereas others prefer "Ms," which is unrelated to marital status. Similarly, you might use "doctor" or "professor" when speaking with your communication instructor, although only an instructor who holds a Ph.D. or other doctoral degree is technically a doctor. In either case, it can be easy to feel uncomfortable if you're not sure what someone prefers to be addressed. When you encounter that situation, the easiest solution is simply to ask the person how he or she wishes to be addressed.

To a large extent, your name tells your story. Like your clothes or your hairstyle, it is a part of how you present yourself to others and how others relate to you.

We Use Words to Persuade

Persuasion is the process of moving people to think or act in a certain way. Every time we watch a TV commercial, read a billboard, or listen to a political speech, someone is trying to influence our beliefs or behavior. Much of our ability to persuade others comes from the language we use. Greek philosopher Aristotle (384–322 B.C.) described three forms of *rhetorical proof,* which are ways to support a persuasive argument. He explained that persuasive messages could be supported by appeals to ethos, pathos, and logos.

Let's say you're trying to persuade your neighbor to support a proposition that would raise his property taxes but increase the security of area schools. What are some ways of asking for his support that would encourage him to agree?

APPEALING TO ETHOS. Aristotle recognized that, to be persuaded, people needed to have positive regard for the person whose message they were considering. Consequently, a speaker who appears respectable and trustworthy is generally more persuasive than one who does not.[23] Aristotle used the term **ethos** to refer to a speaker's respectability, trustworthiness, and moral character.[24]

ethos A speaker's respectability, trustworthiness, and moral character.

One strategy for persuading your neighbor, therefore, is to appeal to your level of knowledge and expertise with respect to the topic. Your neighbor may be inclined to defer to your opinion about the proposition if your opinion seems more trustworthy and better informed than his own. In contrast, if your description of the proposition comes across as ill informed, your neighbor may not respect it enough to find it persuasive.

Note that judgments about ethos always belong to the people with whom you're speaking. Listeners decide for themselves how much integrity, respectability, and trustworthiness a speaker has. Good persuasive speakers therefore establish and reinforce their ethos, knowing that it will enhance their persuasive abilities.[25] You can test your ability to appeal to ethos by checking out the "Got Skills?" box.

APPEALING TO PATHOS. A second persuasive strategy is to appeal to people's emotions. When people are emotionally aroused, their receptivity to new ideas is enhanced. Aristotle used the term **pathos** to refer to listeners' emotions, and he understood that emotion can be a significant persuasive tool.

pathos Listeners' emotions.

Although stirring virtually any emotion can be persuasive, people's interpersonal emotional appeals often focus on generating negative emotions—such as fear, guilt, disgust, anger, and sadness—particularly when a change in behavior is the desired outcome.[26] The reason is that we generally dislike experiencing such emotions, so we are motivated to respond to the persuasive appeal as a way of reducing those feelings. Some research has shown, however, that appealing to positive emotions—such as joy or gratitude—can be more effective when the goal is to change someone's opinions rather than his or her behaviors.

You might use an emotional appeal when asking your neighbor to support the school safety proposition. Because your goal is to affect his behavior (specifically, his voting behavior), you could employ a fear appeal by asking him to imagine how scared he would be if one of his own children were abducted from the school grounds. That fear might then motivate him to vote for the proposition increasing school security. Some additional examples of emotional appeals appear in Table 2.

APPEALING TO LOGOS. A third way to persuade people is to appeal to their sense of reason. If a particular belief, opinion, or behavior makes good sense,

TABLE 2

Some Examples of Emotional Appeals

Suppose you were trying to persuade your aunt to stop smoking. Here are examples of appeals to pathos that you might use.

Type of Appeal	Example Statement
Appeal to fear	Thousands of people die from lung cancer every year; you could be next.
Appeal to guilt	Think about how many innocent children you're hurting every day with secondhand smoke.
Appeal to joy	Imagine how happy you'd be if you were free of your nicotine addiction.
Appeal to disgust	See this charred skin tissue? That's what your lungs look like right now.
Appeal to shame	You're an embarrassment to your family when you smoke.
Appeal to anger	Aren't you sick and tired of nicotine controlling every day of your life?
Appeal to sadness	Imagine saying goodbye to your kids because smoking claimed your life.

got skills?   APPEALING TO ETHOS

Highlight your credibility to persuade others.

WHAT?

Learn to persuade by appealing to your respectability, trustworthiness, and character.

WHY?

To encourage individuals to think or act in a particular way by highlighting your credibility, as when you are trying to persuade someone to contribute to a cause you support.

HOW?

1. Select someone you want to persuade and an issue on which you want to persuade that person. For example, suppose you want a tech company manager to create a summer communication internship for you.

2. In a letter, lay out two specific reasons why the person should do as you suggest. Remember, your goal is to show that the person should follow your advice because of your respectability, trustworthiness, and good character.

3. For each reason, give evidence for your claims. As an example of your trustworthiness, for instance, you might describe a situation when a former supervisor entrusted you with important information. To illustrate your character, you could quote a letter of recommendation written by one of your teachers.

TRY!

1. Write your persuasive letter, but don't send it to the addressee. Rather, share it with a small group in your class or with your instructor, while asking for feedback on ways to make your appeal to ethos more effective.

2. Once you have received feedback on your letter, you may either keep it or send it to see if it is persuasive.

CONSIDER: *In what instances is it more persuasive to appeal to emotion or reason than to your personal credibility?*

---

then people will be inclined to adopt it if they have the capacity to do so. Logical appeals aren't always effective, particularly if some other force—such as an addiction—influences a person's behavior. When people are free to choose their beliefs, opinions, and behaviors, however, they are frequently persuaded by a solidly logical argument. Aristotle used the term **logos** to refer to listeners' ability to reason.

To **reason** means to make judgments about the world based on evidence rather than emotion or intuition. When we appeal to logos, we formulate logical arguments that support our position, and we provide specific information or evidence to bolster those arguments. To maximize our effectiveness, we attempt to select the arguments and evidence we believe will be most relevant to our listeners.

Perhaps you've heard your neighbor complain in the past about the high tax burden of living in your municipal area. That dissatisfaction suggests to you that he will not be excited about the prospect of a tax increase. To persuade him to support the school safety proposition, you might therefore explain to him how the increase in property

logos Listeners' ability to reason.

reason To make judgments about the world based on evidence rather than emotion or intuition.

In the IM: The in-class activity "Persuasion and Loaded Language" will teach students to listen critically for the use of loaded language in verbal persuasion attempts.

taxes will be offset by a decrease in the city's emergency services fees, given that school security will be enhanced. To support your argument, you could show him the relevant figures from the county auditor's report, as published in your local newspaper. Rather than arousing his emotions or enhancing his personal respect for you, such a tactic appeals to your neighbor's sense of logic and reason.

Credibility Empowers Us

credibility The extent to which others find someone's words and actions trustworthy.

Our **credibility** is the extent to which others perceive us to be competent and trustworthy. Some speakers have credibility on certain topics because of their training and expertise. You'll probably have more confidence in medical advice if you hear it from a doctor or a nurse, for instance, than if you hear it from the barista at your local coffee shop. If the advice is about making a great latte, however, you'll probably trust your barista more than your doctor or nurse. In either case, you are assigning credibility on the basis of the speaker's specific expertise.

Language is intimately tied to issues of credibility. Irrespective of our training or credentials, our words can portray us as confident, trustworthy communicators, or they can make us appear unsure of ourselves. In either situation, our ability to get what we want out of our interpersonal interactions is affected by the credibility that our use of language gives us.

A speaker's credibility is often based on his or her training and expertise, and is reflected in language he or she uses. © Blend Images/Ariel Skelley/Getty Images, RF

CLICHÉS. Several forms of language have the potential either to enhance or to damage perceptions of a person's credibility. One language practice that can diminish credibility is the use of *clichés,* or phrases that were novel at one time but have lost their effect because of overuse. When politicians talk about "making a difference" or businesspeople refer to "thinking outside the box," they may lose credibility with their audiences because those phrases are clichés that may make speakers sound uninformed or out-of-touch.

CONNECT: The Student Performance Report allows you to see an individual student's scores, status of assignments, and time spent on each assignment.

DIALECTS. People can also affect perceptions of their credibility by using certain *dialects,* which are variations on a language that are shared by people of a certain region or social class. Many U.S. Americans, for example, can tell the difference between a speaker from the South and one from New England on the basis of the words these speakers use. The southern speaker might use words characteristic of a southern dialect, such as saying "y'all" to mean "you all," whereas the speech of the New Englander might reflect the dialect of that region, perhaps calling something "wicked good" rather than "very good."

According to *communication accommodation theory,* we may be able to enhance our credibility by speaking in a dialect that is familiar to our audience.[27] In contrast, when we use a dialect that is different from that of our listeners, we can cause them to see us as an outsider, and such a perception might lead them to question our credibility.

EQUIVOCATION. Another form of language that sometimes influences a speaker's credibility is *equivocation,* or strategically vague language that disguises the speaker's true intentions. We often criticize politicians for failing to provide clear answers to controversial questions, but in fact many people use equivocal language when faced with a communication dilemma in which no good options exist.

Suppose, for example, that you're asked to provide a reference for your friend Dylan, who is applying for a job on the town police force. You are asked how well Dylan handles pressure. Though Dylan is your friend, you can immediately think of several occasions when he hasn't handled pressure well. Now you're in a bind. On the one hand, you want Dylan to get the job because he's your friend. On the other hand, you don't want to lie to the police lieutenant who's phoning you for the reference.

Several studies have shown that when we're faced with two unappealing choices such as those, we often use equivocal language to get ourselves out of the bind.[28] In response to the lieutenant's question about how well Dylan handles pressure, for instance, you might say: "Well, that depends; there are lots of different kinds of pressure." Note that such a statement doesn't give the lieutenant much information. Instead, it might imply that you don't know how well Dylan handles pressure but you don't want to admit that you don't know. It might also imply that you do know how well Dylan handles pressure but don't want to say. In either case, you are likely to come across as less credible than if you had answered the question directly.[29]

Researchers John Daly, Carol Diesel, and David Weber have suggested that those sorts of conversational dilemmas are common and that we frequently use equivocal language in such situations.[30] Other theorists, including the linguist Robin Lakoff, suggest that women use more equivocal language than men because equivocation reflects a lack of assertiveness that corresponds to feminine gender expectations.[31]

WEASEL WORDS. A form of language related to equivocation is the use of *weasel words:* terms and phrases that are intended to mislead listeners by implying something that they don't actually say. Advertisers commonly use weasel words when making claims about their products. For instance, when you hear that "four out of five dentists prefer" a certain chewing gum, the implication is that 80 percent of all dentists prefer that brand. That would indeed be impressive—but that isn't what the statement actually said. For all we know, only five dentists were surveyed to begin with, making the support of "four out of five" appear much less impressive.

One way people use weasel words in interpersonal communication is by making broad, unsupported generalizations. To make herself sound intelligent and informed, for instance, Eva is fond of starting statements with "People say that . . ." or "It's widely known that . . ." These phrases are weasel words because they imply a broad level of agreement with whatever Eva is saying, but they provide no evidence of that agreement. That is, Eva never specifies which people say or know whatever she is claiming, or how many people say or know it, or why we should trust their beliefs or knowledge in the first place.

ALLNESS STATEMENTS. One specific form of weasel words is an *allness statement,* or a declaration implying that a claim is true without exception. For instance, when you hear somebody claim that "experts agree that corporal punishment is emotionally damaging to children," the implication is that all experts agree. Note, however, that the speaker provides no evidence to back up that claim. Likewise, when someone says "There's no known cure for depression," the implication is that no cure exists. All the statement actually means, however, is that no cure is known to the speaker.

CHOOSING CREDIBLE LANGUAGE. The various forms of speech we've examined can cause listeners to conclude that the speaker's words are imprecise, untrustworthy, and lacking in credibility. That perception can have negative effects on how other people respond to the speaker. Several studies have shown, for instance, that people perceive speakers who use such forms of language as less competent, less dynamic, and even less attractive than speakers whose language is free of those characteristics.[32] In fact, using even *one* of those forms is enough to taint someone else's perceptions of the speaker.[33]

More credible forms of speech avoid using weasel words and allness statements. Try this: Instead of claiming, for example, that what you're saying "is widely believed," simply state that *you* believe it, unless you do have evidence to support it. Instead of saying something like "experts agree" with what you're claiming, say that "some experts agree," and be prepared to give examples of those who do.

Language Expresses Affection and Intimacy

Language has a profound ability to communicate affection and create or enhance intimacy in our personal relationships. Affection and intimacy are closely related but not the same. *Affection* is an emotional experience that includes feelings of love and appreciation that one person has for another. In contrast, *intimacy* is a characteristic of close, supportive relationships. We humans use language both to convey our affectionate feelings for one another and to strengthen our intimate bonds with those who are most important to us.

Verbal statements can communicate affection or intimacy in many ways. Some statements express our feelings for another person, such as "I like you" and "I'm in love with you." Others reinforce the importance of our relationship with another person, such as "You're my best friend" and "I could never love anyone as much as I love you." Still others convey hopes or dreams for the future of the relationship, including "I can't wait to be married to you" and "I want us to be together forever." Finally, some statements express the value of a relationship by noting how we would feel without it, such as "I can't stand the thought of losing you" and "My life would be empty if I hadn't met you."

Statements like those are characteristic of our closest personal relationships. In fact, evidence suggests that communicating intimacy and affection is good both for relationships and for the people in them. For example, family studies researcher Ted Huston and his colleagues found that the more affection spouses communicated to each other during their first 2 years of marriage, the more likely they were still to be married 13 years later.[34] Other research has found that the more affection people receive from their parents during childhood, the lower their chances of developing depression, anxiety, and physical health problems later in life.[35]

Although verbal statements of affection and intimacy are probably more precise than nonverbal gestures (such as hugging), they can still be ambiguous. Consider, for instance, how many different meanings you can have when you say "I love you" to someone. Do you love that person romantically? As a platonic friend? As a family member? Research shows it's not uncommon for people to

We use language to convey affectionate feelings for others and to strengthen our intimate bonds. © *Paul Burns/Fancy Photography/Veer, RF*

misinterpret verbal displays of affection—to think someone is expressing romantic love when he or she means to express platonic love, for instance.[36] That kind of situation can be very uncomfortable for both the sender and the receiver.

In many cases, nonverbal behaviors (such as tone of voice and facial expression) and contextual information help to clarify the meaning of an affectionate message. Nevertheless, there's still a risk of misinterpretation, especially when we use affectionate language with new friends or with people we don't know well.[37]

Words Provide Comfort and Healing

Finally, we use words to comfort people in distress. Exchanges of comfort can be mundane, as when a mother soothes a child with a stubbed toe. They can also occur in extraordinary circumstances, as when someone gives comfort and support to a young man who has lost his romantic partner to cancer.

© AP Images/VICTOR R. CAIVANO

Recall that verbal communication includes both written and spoken words. To convey support, we often use written messages. Consider that the greeting card industry is an $8 billion-a-year business. People send greeting cards not only to acknowledge birthdays and celebrate holidays but also to express verbal messages of comfort, such as through get-well and sympathy cards.[38] There are also cards that express gratitude and ones that convey hope. When someone has passed away, we may also comfort his or her loved ones by creating a tribute page on Facebook, where people can post fond memories of the deceased and words of support for his or her survivors.[39] For information on this phenomenon, check out the "Communication: Light Side" box.

USING LANGUAGE TO COMFORT OTHER PEOPLE.   Perhaps you've tried to help someone who was grieving a significant loss but felt unsure about what to say. Professional counselors provide several specific tips for using language to comfort other people in times of loss:[40]

- *Acknowledge the loss:* "I'm so sorry to hear about your sister's accident. I know that everyone who knew her will miss her greatly."

- *Express sympathy:* "Words can't express how sorry I feel. Please know that my heartfelt sympathies are with you."

- *Offer a positive reflection:* "I will always remember your sister's wonderful sense of humor and her great compassion for others."

- *Offer assistance:* "Please remember I'm here for you, whatever you need. I'll give you a call this weekend to see if there's anything I can do for you."

In addition, many other situations call for words of comfort, such as a divorce, a job loss, or a serious illness. The words we use may be different in each case, but the underlying goals are the same: to acknowledge the person's feelings and to offer support.

communication LIGHT SIDE

CELEBRATING LIFE: FACEBOOK TRIBUTE PAGES

Memorializing people who have passed away has traditionally been a private activity for those who were closest to the deceased. The popularity of Facebook, however, has created opportunities for people to honor their loved ones through *tribute pages,* Facebook sites devoted to the life and memory of someone who has died. Although tribute pages are common for celebrities and other public figures, many individuals now create them to memorialize their own loved ones. In some cases, the Facebook wall of the deceased becomes an informal memorial, with the person's posts and photos preserved, where friends and family turn to express their grief.

Tribute pages on Facebook typically include photos and stories of the deceased, as well as information about his or her memorial services. Importantly, they also allow people to post words of condolence to the person's family, as well as their own stories and memories of the person who has passed. In one study, researchers examined nearly 400 Facebook tribute pages and found that they served a variety of functions for people. For instance, some pages functioned to represent the identity of the deceased by referencing his or her accomplishments and influence. Others tried to influence viewers to take specific actions, such as participating in a candlelight vigil honoring the deceased. Many pages also promoted a sense of community by allowing posters to communicate and comfort each other. On some pages, posters even left messages directed at the deceased, such as "watch over us from Heaven."

One of the most beneficial aspects of Facebook tribute pages is that they can remain active for months or even years after the person's death. This allows relatives and friends to return to the page whenever they choose, to re-read words of comfort and revisit stories about the person's life. As a result, they offer an ongoing stream of support for those who are mourning the loss of a loved one.

FROM ME TO YOU

When someone close to you loses a loved one, offering to manage a Facebook tribute page can be a thoughtful gesture of support. On the page, encourage people to share their photos and memories of the deceased and to post words of comfort for the survivors. Especially if the survivors are not regular Facebook users, make sure they know how to gain access to the page and its content. This is one way you can communicate comfort and encourage healing for those hardest hit by the loss.

Source: Forman, A. E., Kern, R., & Gil-Egui, G. (2012). Death and mourning as sources of community participation in online social networks: R.I.P. pages in Facebook. *First Monday: Peer-Reviewed Journal on the Internet, 17*(9). Retrieved March 6, 2015, from http:firstmonday.org/ojs/index.php/fm/article/view/3935/3288

Focus on Scholarship: In a typical Pennebaker study, participants write about traumatic events on two to four separate occasions for 20 minutes at a time. The writing activities are usually done on either consecutive days or recurrent days (e.g., every Monday for four weeks). Meta-analyses show that the benefits of this expressive writing are greater when there are more writing sessions (e.g., four instead of two) and when they are spread out over time (e.g., on recurrent days rather than consecutive days).

USING LANGUAGE TO COMFORT OURSELVES.   Just as we can use our words to comfort other people, we can also use them to comfort ourselves. Many people find that "journaling," or keeping a diary of their feelings, helps them find comfort and meaning even in traumatic events. In fact, some evidence indicates that writing about our thoughts and feelings can improve our health. Psychologist James Pennebaker has conducted many studies showing that when people write about a trauma they've gone through—such as physical abuse or the death of a loved one—they often experience reduced levels of stress hormones, strengthened immune systems, and a decrease in doctor visits.[41]

Pennebaker's theory is that holding in negative emotions requires effort that we might otherwise use to support our health. For that reason, expressing those emotions (even on paper) allows us to put that energy to better use. The healing effects of expressive writing can be so strong, in fact, that participants in Pennebaker's studies have seen improvements after only two or three writing sessions of 20 minutes each.

In a similar vein, communication scholars have shown that when people are in distress, writing about their positive feelings for a loved one can accelerate their recovery. In one experiment, for instance, participants were put through a series of stressful tasks, such as mentally solving complicated math problems under time constraints and watching video clips of married couples fighting.[42] Those tasks elevated their levels of the hormone cortisol, which the body produces under conditions of stress.

Research by psychologist James Pennebaker demonstrates the health benefits of expressing one's thoughts and feelings in a journal. © Carey Kirkella/Digital Vision /Getty Images, RF

The participants were then assigned to one of three conditions. Participants in the first group were instructed to write a letter expressing their affection to someone they loved. The second group merely thought about a loved one but didn't put their feelings into words. Finally, the third group did nothing for 20 minutes. The researchers found that when people wrote about their affectionate feelings, their cortisol level returned to normal the most quickly. Putting their affectionate feelings into words accelerated their recovery from stress.

Just thinking about a loved one didn't provide any more benefit than doing nothing. Only those participants who translated their feelings into language recovered quickly from their elevated stress. As with Pennebaker's work, this study demonstrated the health benefits of using words to express one's feelings.

In summary, people use language to accomplish a number of important tasks. They assign people names and grant identities to others. They persuade others to adopt certain ideas or behaviors. They gain credibility and power. They convey affection and build intimacy with others. They provide comfort and support, both to others and to themselves. Many interpersonal situations require us to perform one or more of these tasks. Therefore, our understanding of how language serves those functions will help us communicate effectively in those contexts.

In the IM: In the in-class activity "Language and Health," students take part in a Pennebaker writing exercise.

LEARN IT Which characteristics about a person are often implied by his or her name? How can you use an appeal to pathos to persuade someone? How is equivocation related to credibility? In what ways do we express affection to others verbally? What types of statements should messages of comfort contain?

APPLY IT When you're feeling stressed, try a version of Pennebaker's emotional writing activity. Sit quietly in a room with a pen and paper, and begin to write about your feelings. Why are you feeling stressed? What else are you feeling? Don't worry about punctuation and grammar; just write nonstop for at least 20 minutes. Even if you feel a little worse immediately afterward (because you've been thinking so hard about what's bothering you), notice how you feel later in the day. Does putting your feelings into words help your frame of mind?

REFLECT ON IT If you had to choose a different name for yourself, what would it be? Why? What makes one speaker more credible than another to you?

3 The Use and Abuse of Language

We've seen that language helps us achieve a wide variety of purposes. Now let's look at the ways in which language can vary in its form. Some forms, such as humor, are generally positive and can produce all sorts of good outcomes, such as entertaining others, strengthening relationships, and even contributing to healing. Others, such as hate speech, are known for the devastating hurt they can cause.

In this section, we explore several forms of language: humor, euphemism, slang, libel and slander, profanity, and hate speech. Many of these forms are neither entirely good nor entirely bad. Like many human inventions, language can be used well, and it can also be abused. We will look at examples of both.

Humor: What's so Funny?

A few years ago, psychologist Richard Wiseman designed a study with an ambitious goal: to discover the world's funniest joke. More than 2 million people from around the world visited his website and rated some 40,000 jokes for their level of humor. Here was the winning entry—the funniest joke in the world:

> Two hunters are out in the woods when one of them collapses. He doesn't seem to be breathing, and his eyes are glazed. The other guy takes out his phone and calls the emergency services. He gasps: "My friend is dead! What can I do?" The operator says: "Calm down, I can help. First, let's make sure he's dead." There is a silence, then a gunshot is heard. Back on the phone, the guy says: "Okay, now what?"[43]

Talking Point: The violation of expectations is usually made clear in the joke's punch line. Most students can probably recall hearing jokes that don't seem to have a punch line—such jokes might be thought provoking, but they won't be funny.

You may or may not find that joke funny, and you might even find it offensive. Nonetheless, you can probably recognize the humor in it. The joke contains what researchers believe to be the most important aspect of humor: a violation of our expectations. Most of us would interpret the operator's statement ("Let's make sure he's dead") as a suggestion to check the hunter's vital signs, not as a recommendation to shoot him. It's that twist on our expectations that makes the joke funny. In fact, researchers have discovered that specific parts of the brain process humor, and that without the violation of expectations—without the punch line—those neurological structures don't "light up" or provide the mental reward we associate with a good joke.[44]

Humor can enhance our interpersonal interactions in many ways. It can bring us closer to others and make social interaction more pleasant and enjoyable.[45] It can defuse stress, such as when people are in conflict with one another.[46] Within relationships, "inside jokes" can reinforce people's feelings of intimacy. Humor can provide so many personal and social benefits, in fact, that a good sense of humor is something both women and men strongly seek in a romantic partner.[47] Research shows that self-deprecating humor—jokes in which people poke fun at themselves—are seen as especially attractive in others.[48]

Not all effects of humor are positive, however. Humor can also be used to demean social or cultural groups, as in the case of racial jokes or jokes about elderly people or persons with

© Nicolas McComber/Getty Images, RF

disabilities. Moreover, even when they are made without the intention to offend, jokes told at another's expense can cause embarrassment or distress and might even qualify as harassment.[49] When using humor, it's therefore important to take stock of your audience to make certain that your jokes will amuse rather than offend.

Euphemisms: Soft Talk

Some topics are difficult or impolite to talk about directly. In such cases, we might use a **euphemism,** a vague, mild expression that symbolizes something more blunt or harsh. Instead of saying that someone has died, for instance, we might say that he has "passed away." Rather than mentioning that she is pregnant, a woman might say she's "expecting." You can probably think of many euphemisms, such as "let go" (instead of "fired"), "sleep together" (instead of "have sex"), and "praying at the porcelain altar" (instead of "vomiting in the toilet").

In almost every case, the euphemistic term sounds less harsh or less explicit than the term it stands for, and that's the point. We use euphemisms when we want to talk about sensitive topics without making others feel embarrassed or offended.[50] Importantly, euphemisms require more than just a technical understanding of the language in which they're made; they also require an understanding of cultural idioms. The reason why such understanding is necessary is that euphemisms often have a literal meaning that differs from their euphemistic meaning. For example, at a literal level, the phrase "sleep together" means just that: to engage in sleep while together. If you didn't realize that the phrase is a cultural euphemism for "have sex," then you wouldn't understand the meaning when it is used in that way.

Many euphemisms change over time. What we today call "posttraumatic stress disorder" was called "shell shock" during World War I, "battle fatigue" during World War II, and "operational exhaustion" during the Korean War. Sometimes societies change euphemisms in order to treat the groups of people they refer to with greater dignity. The euphemism "differently abled," for instance, began as "lame," then became "crippled," then "handicapped," and then "disabled" before evolving into its present form. Those and other euphemisms may continue to evolve as our culture and cultural ideas develop over time.

Like humor, the use of euphemisms has good and bad points. As we've seen, euphemisms provide people a way to talk about sensitive topics—such as sexuality, disability, and death—without having to use uncomfortable language. That aspect is beneficial, particularly to the extent that people otherwise would avoid communicating about those important topics. Some researchers have warned, however, that the excessive use of euphemisms can desensitize people, causing them to accept situations they would otherwise find unacceptable.[51]

In line with that idea, communication researchers Matthew McGlone, Gary Beck, and Abigail Pfiester found that when a euphemism becomes conventional or commonplace, people may use it without thinking about what it really means.[52] Euphemisms that are common during times of war, for instance, include "friendly fire" (for firing on one's own troops) and "collateral damage" (for civilians killed inadvertently).[53] The practice of using euphemisms specifically to distort meaning or to make offensive or upsetting news seem more acceptable is referred to as *doublespeak*.[54] Some language experts believe that using doublespeak for horrendous

> **euphemism** A vague, mild expression that symbolizes something more blunt or harsh.

Talking Point: "Sick jokes" make humor out of morbid situations. Although such jokes are often considered tasteless and in poor form, some scholars have argued that they may help a society cope with an otherwise horrific experience.

Euphemisms are common during times of war. Do you think euphemistic language lessens our sensitivity to the harshness of combat? © *Joe Raedle/Photonica World/Getty Images*

slang Informal, unconventional words that are often understood only by others in a particular group.

Whether you're into gardening, political activism, or surfing, slang allows you to connect and identify with others who share your interests. © Adie Bush/ Getty Images, RF

situations of military combat can lead people to feel emotionally detached from—or even accepting of—the horrors of war.[55] Using euphemisms competently therefore requires us to consider whether "softening" the topic of discussion will facilitate open communication—or encourage us to tolerate what we might otherwise find intolerable.[56]

Slang: The Language of Co-Cultures

Closely related to euphemism is **slang,** the use of informal and unconventional words that often are understood only by others in a particular group. If you grew up in Boston, for instance, you probably know that "rhodie" is a slang term for people from nearby Rhode Island. In Australia, "snag" is slang for "sausage." A "grom" is a young surfer, and a "goofy-foot" is a surfer who rides with his or her right foot leading.

People have slang terms for all sorts of things. "Taking a selfie" means shooting a photograph of yourself (usually with a cell phone camera), and "photobombing" means inserting yourself without permission into the field of view of someone else's photograph. To "chill out" means to relax, and to "rip off" means to steal something of value from someone else. On the Internet, "flaming" is an insulting and hostile interaction between people, and "lurking" is the practice of reading posts on a message board or group but not participating in the discussion.

Slang can serve an important social function by helping people distinguish between those who do and don't belong to their particular social networks. Many social, cultural, and religious groups have their own terminology for certain ideas, and a person's ability to use a group's slang appropriately can "mark" him or her as belonging to that group. For instance, if you don't know that "bubbly-jock" means "turkey," you're probably not from Scotland, and if you don't know whether you're in "T Town" (Texarkana) or "Big T" (Tucson), chances are you're not a trucker.

A form of informal speech closely related to slang is *jargon.* As we saw in the Culture and Gender chapter, jargon is the technical vocabulary of a certain occupation or profession. The purpose of jargon is to allow members of that occupation or profession to communicate with one another precisely and efficiently. For example, many law enforcement officers in North America talk to one another using "10-code," or number combinations that represent common phrases. In that jargon, "10-4" means you've received another person's message; "10-24" means your assignment is completed. Health care providers also use jargon specific to their profession. For instance, they refer to a heart attack as a "myocardial infarction," a headache as a "cephalalgia," and athlete's foot as "tinea pedis." Attorneys, engineers, dancers, airplane pilots, television producers, and military personnel are among many other occupations and professions that have their own jargon.

Like humor and euphemisms, slang and jargon are neither inherently good nor inherently bad. They can be used for positive purposes, such as to reaffirm one's membership within a particular social community. Whether you're into surfing, wine tasting, calligraphy, or restoring old cars, learning and using the slang appropriate to those interests serves as a type of membership badge, allowing you to connect with others like you. By the same token, however, the use of slang and jargon can also make people feel like outsiders.

If you're a police officer, for instance, saying that you're "10-7" instead of "done for the day" might make those around you who are not in law enforcement feel excluded from the conversation. For that reason, you should consider how your use of slang and jargon might come across to those around you.

Defamation: Harmful Words

In March 2009, singer Courtney Love tweeted to her 40,000 followers that fashion designer Dawn Simorangkir was a drug-pushing prostitute with a history of assault and battery. Simorangkir subsequently filed suit against Love, claiming that the Twitter comments had ruined her reputation and destroyed her fashion career.

The designer's claim was that Love had engaged in **defamation,** language that harms a person's reputation or gives that person a negative image. Defamation comes in two forms. The first, **libel,** refers to defamatory statements made in print or some other fixed medium, such as a photograph or a motion picture. The second, **slander,** is a defamatory statement that is made aloud, within earshot of others.

For instance, let's say that Aliyah wants to open a day care center in a town where Toni also operates one. To discourage parents from using Aliyah's center, Toni circulates rumors that Aliyah has been charged with child molestation. That statement is defamatory because it would harm Aliyah's reputation and cause her financial damage in the form of lost business.

Does it matter whether Toni's accusation is true? Usually the answer is yes: Under most legal systems, a statement must be false to be considered libel or slander. There are situations, however, when even a true accusation can qualify as slander or libel. Such cases often involve public figures, like politicians and celebrities, and hinge on the importance of the information for the public. Disclosing in print that a senator has tested positive for HIV, for example, might qualify as libel even if it were true, if disclosing it serves no prevailing public interest.

Slander is more common than libel in interpersonal interaction. Although slander is a legal term, behaviors we would call gossiping or spreading rumors often amount to the same thing. If you've ever had someone spread rumors about you, you know how painful that can be. Although gossip can serve some positive functions, such as reinforcing bonds of intimacy among people, the targets of gossip or rumors can experience profound distress.[57]

Profanity: Offensive Language

Profanity is a form of language that is considered vulgar, rude, or obscene in the context in which it is used. We sometimes call profane terms "swear words" or "curse words," and they come in many forms. Some profane terms are meant to put down certain groups of people, such as calling a woman a "bitch" or a homosexual man a "fag." (Many of those also qualify as hate speech, which we examine next.) Other profane terms are attacks on religious beliefs or figures considered sacred by followers of a particular religion. Others describe sexual acts or refer to people's sex organs or bodily functions. Still others are general expressions of anger or disappointment, such as "Damn!"

Profanity is context-specific: What makes a word profane is that it is considered rude or obscene in the language and context in which it is used. For instance, calling a woman a "bitch" might be profane, but using the same term to describe a female dog is

defamation Language that harms a person's reputation or image.

libel A defamatory statement made in print or in some other fixed medium.

slander A defamatory statement made aloud.

profanity A form of language considered vulgar, rude, or obscene in the context in which it is used.

In Everyday Life: The U.S. Federal Communications Commission (FCC) regulates the use of profanity on radio and television. Rules for TV vary according to the time a program is broadcast and whether it appears on a network or a cable channel. Many people believe that even prime-time network television has become too profane; others disagree. Poll your students for their views.

"But it's not a four-letter word if I used *texting!*"

Art by Roy Delgado © CartoonStock.com

not. In the United States, "fag" is a derogatory term for gay men, but to the British, it refers to a cigarette.

Every language ever studied has included swear words. Some swear words translate among languages; for example, the expression "Damn!" in English is "Zut!" in French and "Verflucht!" in German and can be profane in all of them. Other expressions appear to be unique to certain languages; for instance, a Dutch speaker might say "Krijg de pest!" which translates to "Go get infected with the plague!"

Profanity has many different effects on social interaction. Often, it makes people feel uncomfortable or insulted. In recent years, some social groups have recognized that they can reduce the negative effects of certain profane terms themselves by making the terms more commonplace, thus lowering or eliminating their shock value. That practice is called *reclaiming the term.* For instance, when homosexuals call one another "queers," their intent is not to cause insult but rather to remove the power to insult from the word. In recent years, even the "n-word" has become a term of inclusion and friendship within some groups of African Americans.

Not all effects of profanity are negative. In certain contexts, the use of profanity can act as a *social lubricant* by establishing and maintaining an informal social atmosphere. Profanity is a common element in comedy, for instance, partly because it creates an expectation that nothing is taboo in that context and that ideas can flow freely. In addition, using profanity within one's own social network can actually reinforce interpersonal bonds by sending the metamessage that "I feel comfortable enough with you to use profanity in your presence." Research has even shown that people have an increased tolerance for physical pain when they swear, perhaps because swearing activates the body's "fight-or-flight" system."[58]

hate speech A form of profanity meant to degrade, intimidate, or dehumanize groups of people.

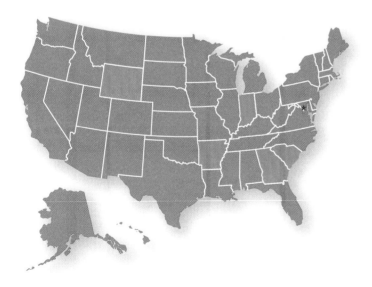

FIGURE 4 U.S. States with Hate Crime Laws As of 2015, all U.S. states except Wyoming, Arkansas, Indiana, South Carolina, and Georgia have laws prohibiting hate crimes such as the use of hate speech.

Hate Speech: Profanity with a Hurtful Purpose

Hate speech is a specific form of profanity meant to degrade, intimidate, or dehumanize people on the basis of their gender, national origin, sexual orientation, religion, race, disability status, or political or moral views.[59] Calling people derogatory names, intimidating them, and advocating violence against groups of individuals might all qualify as forms of hate speech. For instance, the terms "bitch" and "fag" can be used not only as profanity but also as hate speech if they're directed at women or homosexuals with the intent to degrade or intimidate them.

Several laws and regulations exist in North America to restrict hate speech or other acts of intimidation against minority groups and to punish people who engage in them (Figure 4). Many of those restrictions are found in campus speech codes, which dictate the types of statements that students, staff, and faculty can and cannot make on a college campus. There is little question that most, if not all, of the effects of hate speech are negative, a fact justifying laws and regulations to restrict it.

Still, hate laws and regulations are controversial. Supporters argue that the regulations are necessary to promote civility and to protect people—especially minority-group members—from the discrimination and even violence that hate speech can incite. Opponents counter that it is difficult to determine what qualifies as hate speech and what does not. They also maintain that restricting speech is a form of censorship and a violation of the First Amendment of the U.S. Constitution.[60] Given the complexities of defining hate speech and determining how best to respond to it, those points of contention are likely to be debated for some time.

As we've seen in this section, language comes in many forms, including humor, euphemism, slang, libel and slander, profanity, and hate speech. Some of those forms, such as humor, generally have positive effects but can also produce unwanted negative outcomes. Other forms, such as profanity, are generally negative even though they can have positive effects on the people using them. Understanding the positive and negative aspects of those diverse forms of language helps us to appreciate the power and complexity of verbal communication.

Talking Point: Where do your students' opinions fall on this issue?

Outside of Class: A relevant out-of-class assignment would be to have students research the speech codes enforced at your school. Have them pay particular attention to how hate speech is defined (if it is defined at all) and to how speech codes are enforced.

CONNECT: Insight reports are built around common questions (like "How are my students doing?") so you can easily get the insights you are looking for.

LEARN IT   What makes a joke funny? What are the purposes of using euphemisms? In what ways does the use of slang reflect a person's subcultures? How is libel different from slander? What makes a word or a phrase profane? What is hate speech?

APPLY IT   Many groups have their own slang. Talk to some people who have hobbies, interests, or jobs very different from yours, and learn some of the slang common to those groups. Document what you've learned in a short report.

REFLECT ON IT   What euphemisms do you tend to use? Do you feel that prohibiting hate speech is a good idea or a bad one? Why?

4 Creating a Positive Communication Climate

Perhaps you've noticed that each of your close relationships has its own "personality." You might call on different family members depending on whether you need social support, require a critical ear, or just feel like kicking back. Maybe you feel comfortable teasing and being teased by your romantic partner, or maybe you take his or her teasing personally. Researchers refer to the emotional tone of a relationship as its **communication climate.**

Communication climate reflects how you feel about the relationships you're in. Studies show that having a positive communication climate is beneficial for a broad range of relationships such as those in marriages,[61] in families,[62] in friendships,[63] in the workplace,[64] and in educational settings.[65] Communication climate is even important for the quality of computer-mediated interactions, such as ones you might have with online friends or virtual work partners.[66] How can you contribute to positive communication climates in your own relationships? We'll examine six important skills in this section.

communication climate The emotional tone of a relationship.

Writing Note: To generate discussion, have students write a paragraph or two describing the emotional tone of one of their important relationships and identifying the factors that most heavily influence it.

Listening intently to others—even if you do not agree with what they are saying—sends a confirming message.
© Robin Skjoldborg/Getty Images

confirming messages
Behaviors that indicate how much we value another person.

In Everyday Life: Reflecting the idea of communication "climates," people often describe relationships using climatic language: a warm relationship, a chilly reception from a friend, etc.

disconfirming messages
Behaviors that imply a lack of regard for another person.

Focus on Scholarship: Suicide expert Thomas Joiner theorizes that repeatedly feeling disconfirmed is one of three necessary and sufficient conditions for suicide (the others are a lack of belonging and a lack of fear about self-harm).

Use Confirming Messages and Minimize Disconfirming Messages

One way to contribute to positive communication climates is to practice using **confirming messages,** which are statements that convey value for other people. Communication researchers have identified three types of confirming messages, which are described here in order from least to most confirming.

- *Recognition.* The most basic act of confirmation is to recognize that another person exists and is worthy of your attention. Replying to a text message from a sibling, calling to ask about a friend's day, and making eye contact with a new acquaintance you see in class are all ways of sending the message "I recognize that you matter."

- *Acknowledgment.* A more positive form of confirmation is to acknowledge another person's feelings and thoughts. You engage in acts of acknowledgment when you ask someone's opinion, solicit someone's ideas, or inquire about someone's feelings. Just as important as *asking* for that information is *listening actively* to what the person says.

- *Endorsement.* The most positive form of confirmation is to provide endorsement, which is the signal that you agree with what another person has said. On some occasions, you may endorse another's message fully, as when expressing complete agreement with an opinion. On other occasions, you may provide partial endorsement, as when you tell a friend that you agree with her feelings but not necessarily with her actions.

If some statements qualify as confirming messages, then others constitute **disconfirming messages,** or statements that imply a lack of regard for other people. Research indicates that minimizing the use of disconfirming messages in our intimate relationships is important for the satisfaction and stability of those relationships.[67] Communication researchers have identified several types of disconfirming messages, described here in order from most to least disconfirming.

- *Impervious response.* As you read, the most fundamental act of confirmation is recognition. In contrast, we disconfirm others when we enact an impervious response, which means ignoring those people altogether. Adopting an impervious response sends the message that "I don't care enough about you even to recognize your existence," which can make people feel neglected and unimportant.[68]

- *Verbal abuse.* Verbal abuse is an overt form of disconfirming message that involves using words to hurt people emotionally and psychologically, such as calling someone derogatory names, offering insults or put-downs, or threatening physical harm. Such abuse can cause many significant problems in close relationships, particularly when directed at children.[69]

- *Generalized complaining.* Particularly in a conflict situation, offering specific complaints often helps by focusing the conversation on particular problems. In contrast, offering generalized complaints—complaints that simply indict the other person's value or character—is unhelpful and disconfirming. Messages such as "Why can't you be more like your brother?" and "You never think of anyone but yourself" usually do little beyond making the recipient feel unvalued.

- *Irrelevant response.* Offering an irrelevant response means replying to someone's message with a completely unrelated statement. Suppose your spouse says, "We really need to work out a schedule for the kids' soccer practices next week" and you reply by saying "Don't forget it's my mom's birthday on Saturday." Your reply isn't only off-topic, it also conveys the message that you don't care enough about your spouse to pay attention to his or her words.

- *Impersonal response.* You enact an impersonal response when you reply to someone's words with a cliché that conveys no real empathy. After your sister confides in you about her recent battles with depression, for instance, you shrug your shoulders and say, "Well, life's a struggle." Whereas an irrelevant response implies that you aren't paying attention to another's message, an impersonal response implies that you are indifferent to that message.

Complaints can be useful if they are specific and relevant. Generalized complaining sends a disconfirming message, however. © Ocean/Corbis, RF

Using confirming messages in your own relationships is an effective way to create positive communication climates. To do so, however, you must be able to distinguish between confirming and disconfirming statements. Check out the "Assess Your Skills" box to see how well you can make the distinction now.

Avoid Making Others Defensive

Several years ago, communication researcher Jack Gibb determined that communication climates alternate between defensiveness and supportiveness. **Defensiveness** is a feeling of excessive concern with guarding ourselves against the threat of criticism or

> **defensiveness** Excessive concern with guarding oneself against the threat of criticism.

---

assess your skills | HOW WELL CAN YOU SPOT A CONFIRMING MESSAGE?

Can you tell confirming and disconfirming messages apart? Suppose your mother e-mails you to say she is concerned about a lump she recently found under her arm. On the line following each reply below, write a "C" if you believe it is a confirming statement or a "D" if you believe it is a disconfirming statement.

C or D?

1. _____ "Maybe if you stopped smoking a pack a day, you'd be in better health."
2. _____ "What do you think it might be?"
3. _____ "I doubt it's a tumor, but I do agree that you should see your doctor."
4. _____ "Someone at my office got fired yesterday."
5. _____ "You always think you're sick. Stop trying to get attention."
6. _____ "So you're saying it's just under your left arm?"
7. _____ "I have enough to worry about already without this."
8. _____ "You're in the best position to know if something is wrong in your body."

Statements 2, 3, 6, and 8 are confirming messages. Statements 1 and 7 are generalized complaints; statement 4 is an irrelevant response, and statement 5 is verbally abusive.

We feel defensive when others communicate in ways that attack our ego and self-worth. © Berc/Getty Images, RF

 supportiveness
A person's feeling of assurance that others care about and will protect him or her.

Talking Point: People sometimes use strategic language—such as "Are you busy next weekend?"—to avoid putting others on the spot. Despite the intention behind them, however, strategic statements such as that may elicit defensiveness because they withhold information.

attacks to our ego. People often feel defensive, for instance, when others make fun of something they're sensitive about, such as their weight, income, or physical attractiveness. In contrast, **supportiveness** is a feeling of assurance that others care about us and will protect us. People feel supported when others encourage them and express concern for their well-being.

According to Gibb, communication plays a central role in creating both defensive and supportive communication climates. When we use defensive messages in our personal relationships, we create emotional and psychological distance between others and us, increasing the likelihood that others will react defensively. In contrast, supportive messages focus on the content of the conversation without making others feel attacked.

Gibb identified six types of messages that promote defensiveness in interpersonal communication, and six contrasting types of messages that promote supportiveness. For each pair, we'll examine the defensive message type first, then the supportive message type that we should use instead.

- *Evaluation versus description:* An evaluation expresses an opinion on the value or worth of another person's behaviors. A description provides detail about the person's behaviors without passing judgment.

    Evaluative: "This is the worst article you've ever written."

    Descriptive: "There are some opportunities for improvement in this article."

- *Control versus problem orientation:* Control-oriented messages manipulate others to act only a specific way. Problem-oriented messages encourage collaboration and creative thinking.

    Control-oriented: "You can't watch TV right now; my show is on."

    Problem-oriented: "Let's figure out a way we can both watch what we want."

- *Strategy versus spontaneity:* Strategic messages withhold information in an attempt to control the listener. Spontaneous messages express thoughts and desires openly and honestly, without a "hidden agenda."

    Strategic: "Are you busy next weekend?"

    Spontaneous: "I'm planning a hike for next Saturday; want to come?"

- *Neutrality versus empathy:* Neutral statements imply a lack of concern for the well-being of others. Empathic statements convey concern for what others are feeling and experiencing.

    Neutral: "Not everything goes the way you want. That's life."

    Empathic: "I'm sorry your plans fell through. You must be disappointed."

- *Superiority versus equality:* Messages of superiority encourage division and an "us vs. them" mentality. Messages of equality emphasize inclusiveness and minimize status differences between people.

    Superior: "You don't know what you're doing."

    Equal: "That's an interesting approach. I've never thought about this situation in that way before."

- *Certainty versus provisionalism:* Messages of certainty offer inflexible conclusions with no room for debate. Provisional messages offer ideas flexibly, in the hope of generating dialogue.

    Certain: "You're wrong."

    Provisional: "What leads you to believe that? Is it possible that the source of your information is mistaken?"

Provide Effective Feedback

A third way to contribute to a positive communication climate in your intimate relationships is to provide effective feedback during conversations. Feedback includes the verbal and nonverbal behaviors through which you convey your attention to a person's message. It is effective only when it matches what the speaker wants or needs—so providing effective feedback requires you to assess the situation and determine what type of reply is called for, whether non-evaluative or evaluative.

When people describe their problems, they aren't always looking for suggestions. Often, they simply want to be heard. Non-evaluative responses allow you to engage in the conversation without making assessments. © *Ariel Skelley/Blend Images, RF*

NON-EVALUATIVE FEEDBACK.   When someone describes a problem to you, you may tend to respond by offering your suggestions for fixing it. Many people ask their loved ones for advice—but often, what they want instead is simply to be heard and understood. In those cases, you want to provide **non-evaluative feedback,** which is a reply that withholds assessment of what the speaker has said or done. People usually use non-evaluative feedback to gain information about a situation and to help others work through their feelings. As an example, suppose your sister Sara has described her frustrations about being unable to conceive a child with her husband, Kris. Let's look at three techniques of non-evaluative feedback you could use.

> **non-evaluative feedback**
> A reply that withholds assessment of what the speaker has said or done.

- *Probe.* Probing means asking questions to gain more information. In Sara's case, you might ask whether she has explored the option of fertility treatments or considered the possibility of adoption. You might also ask how she and Kris are handling the situation emotionally. When probing, it is useful to ask questions that are specific rather than general.

    Example: "What have your doctors told you about in vitro fertilization as an option?"

- *Paraphrase.* Paraphrasing—or repeating what someone has said in your own words—assures the person that you are paying attention to his or her words. It also lets the other person correct any misunderstandings you may have about what he or she said.

    Example: "It sounds like you're really interested in pursuing in vitro fertilization but Kris is worried about how effective it would be."

- *Offer support.* Offering support includes sharing your perceptions of the situation and confirming the validity of the problem. Even if you disagree with Sara's perspective, you can say so without implying that her feelings are invalid. Convey the message that you respect her decisions even though yours might differ.

    Example: "I can certainly understand how hard this must be for you and Kris. I'm not sure what I would do in your situation—but you have my support whatever you decide to do."

Probing, paraphrasing, and offering support are all ways of conveying interest in what Sara has said without expressing your assessment or judgment. Unless someone asks for your opinion on how to address a problem, you may create a more positive communication climate simply by providing non-evaluative feedback.

EVALUATIVE FEEDBACK. There are situations, of course, when others want or need your input. In those circumstances, you can use **evaluative feedback,** which is a reply that offers assessment of what the speaker has said or done. Offering effective evaluative feedback can involve one or both of two steps: providing praise and criticizing constructively. For instance, imagine that your nephew Luke has asked you to read and provide feedback on his term paper for his high school literature class.

> **evaluative feedback** A reply that offers an assessment of what the speaker has said or done.

- *Provide praise.* Remember that evaluating something isn't just about identifying its shortcomings; it's also about noting its strengths. Therefore, start by praising what Luke has done well. Even if you find only one aspect of his paper to praise, doing so will likely make Luke more open to your suggestions for change.

    Example: "I really like your introduction. You do a good job of getting people's attention and previewing what you plan to cover. Great job with that!"

- *Criticize constructively.* If your evaluation is entirely positive, then praise is all that is required. If you have negative assessments, then you want to criticize constructively. Criticizing constructively doesn't mean pointing out *what's wrong;* it means pointing out *what can be made better* and offering ideas for improvement.

    Example: "Let's make the body of your paper as good as your introduction is. If you discuss your third main point first, I think that will help your points flow more smoothly."

> **Talking Point:** Evaluative feedback doesn't *have to* include criticism. If an evaluation is entirely positive, it should include only praise.

Notice that you are focusing specifically on the merits of your nephew's paper when providing both praise and constructive criticism. Offering praise helps Luke appreciate what he has already done well, providing a point of comparison that is helpful when he is trying to improve other parts. Constructive criticism identifies specific parts of the paper that can benefit from his additional attention. By focusing on what he can improve—instead of what he has done wrong—you send the implicit message that improvement is possible. That's important because it is never constructive to criticize something that a person cannot change.

Own Your Thoughts and Feelings

A fourth way to contribute to positive communication climates is to take ownership of your thoughts and feelings. People often use language that shifts responsibility for their thoughts and feelings to others. Perhaps you dread meeting with your boss because whenever she doesn't understand you, she says, "You're not being clear," but when you don't understand her, she says, "You're not paying attention." By using that pattern of language, she blames you for misunderstandings but takes no responsibility for her own role in the communication process.

> **I-statement** A statement that claims ownership of one's thoughts or feelings.

> **you-statement** A statement that shifts responsibility for one's own thoughts or feelings to the listener.

Good communicators take responsibility for their thoughts and feelings by using I-statements rather than you-statements. An **I-statement** claims ownership of what a person is feeling or thinking, whereas a **you-statement** shifts that responsibility to the other person. Instead of saying, "You're not being clear," your boss might say, "I'm having a hard time understanding you." Rather than saying, "You make me mad," I might say "I'm angry right now."

I-statements don't ignore the problem; they simply allow us to acknowledge that we control how we think and feel. Constructive I-statements include four parts that clearly express our ownership of our thoughts and feelings:

- "I feel _____" (expresses responsibility for your own feelings)
- "when you _____" (identifies the behavior that is prompting your feelings)
- "because _____" (points to the characteristic of the behavior that is prompting your feelings)
- "and I would appreciate it if you would _____" (offers an alternative to the behavior)

Let's say, for instance, that Colin is frustrated with Ji, his officemate, because she often leaves the door to their office open when neither of them is inside. Here's one way he might express his feelings:

> "You need to stop leaving our door open, because anyone can come in here and take whatever they want. You're really starting to make me mad."

That statement rightfully points out that the problematic behavior is Ji's. After all, she is the one who leaves the door open. What it doesn't do, however, is acknowledge that Colin's feelings of frustration belong to him. Now let's take a look at a more constructive way of communicating his feelings:

> "I get angry when you leave our door open, because anyone could come in here and steal my briefcase or your purse. I would really appreciate it if you would close the door whenever you step out of the office."

Notice how that statement doesn't ignore or downplay the problem. Rather, it allows Colin to take responsibility for his feelings of frustration and to identify clearly how he would like Ji to change her behavior.

The major benefit of using I-statements is that they are less likely than you-statements to cause a listener to become defensive.[70] By saying "You're really starting to make me mad," Colin sounds as though he is accusing Ji, a situation that would likely cause her to respond defensively. In contrast, by saying "I feel angry when you leave the door open," Colin acknowledges that he is responsible for his own feelings, and that he is only suggesting a change in Ji's behavior. Ji may still disagree with his assessment, but she may be less likely to feel that he is attacking or accusing her. To practice the ability to use I-statements constructively, check out the "Got Skills?" box.

Separate Opinions from Factual Claims

Recall from the Interpersonal Perception chapter that factual claims ("she hit him") are different from interpretations ("she assaulted him"). Factual claims are also different from opinions. A factual claim makes a statement that we can verify with evidence and show to be true or false in an absolute sense ("I've taken piano lessons for 10 years"). An opinion expresses a personal judgment or preference that we could agree or disagree with but that is not true or false in an absolute sense ("I'm a great piano player"). A fifth way of contributing to a positive communication climate is knowing how to keep opinions and factual claims separate in verbal communication.

Distinguishing factual claims from opinions is often easier said than done, especially when we're dealing with strong opinions on emotionally heated issues. Let's say that you and several friends are discussing an upcoming election in which you're choosing between two candidates. Half of you prefer Candidate C, the conservative, and the other

got skills?   I-STATEMENTS

Using I-statements helps you own your thoughts and feelings.

WHAT?	WHY?	HOW?	TRY!
Learn to use I-statements.	To acknowledge ownership and responsibility for your thoughts and feelings, as when you are dealing with an interpersonal issue such as a problem with something a friend or relative is doing—or not doing.	**1.** Start by saying "I feel _____," which identifies your feelings. **2.** Then say "when you _____," which identifies the behavior prompting your feelings. **3.** Next say "because _____," which identifies what you find problematic about the behavior. **4.** Finally, say "and I would appreciate it if you would _____," which suggests a solution to the problem.	**1.** The next time you find someone's behavior problematic, don't say "You're making me angry" or "You're worrying me." Instead, express your message in the form of an I-statement. **2.** Practice by imagining that your roommate has been leaving your house a mess, not paying you for groceries, and playing music while you're trying to sleep. In writing, craft two different I-statements you might use to address the situation with your roommate. **CONSIDER:** *Why is it beneficial to acknowledge ownership of your thoughts and feelings?*

half prefers Candidate L, the liberal. Consider the following statements you might make about the candidates, and indicate which are factual claims and which are opinions:

- *"Candidate C has more experience in government."* Because we can show this statement to be true or false by looking at the candidates' records, this is a factual claim.

- *"Candidate L is the better choice for our future."* This is an opinion, because it expresses a value judgment (this candidate is better), which we cannot objectively validate.

- *"Candidate C is immoral."* This is an opinion, because the truth of this claim depends on what morals you subscribe to. Morals are subjective; therefore, the statement can't be proved true or false in an absolute sense.

- *"Candidate L accepted illegal bribes."* This is a factual claim, because you can examine the evidence to discover whether or not it's true.

Opinions and factual claims require different types of responses. Suppose you tell me that "Candidate C has never held an elective office," and I reply by saying "I disagree." That isn't a competent response. You have made a factual claim, so by definition it is either true or false. Therefore, whether I agree with it is irrelevant. Instead, if I had responded by saying "I think you're incorrect," that would be a competent reply because we would now be discussing the truth of your statement rather than my agreement with it.

As you develop the skill of distinguishing opinions from facts, keep two principles in mind. First, *opinions are opinions whether you agree with them or not.* If you believe abortion should be legal in the United States, for instance, you might be inclined to call that statement a fact. It isn't, though. It is still an opinion because it expresses an evaluation about what "should be." Second, *factual claims are factual claims whether they are true or not.* If you think it's untrue that men talk as much as women do, for example, you might be inclined to call that statement an opinion. It isn't, though. Even if the statement isn't true, it is still a factual claim because it expresses something that could be verified by evidence.

Although it is probably more difficult to separate opinions from facts when you feel strongly about an issue, that's often when it is most important to do so. Instead of telling others that their positions on sensitive issues are right or wrong, you can contribute to a more positive communication climate simply by saying that you agree or disagree. That way, you express your own position but acknowledge that different—even contradictory—opinions may still exist.

Create Positive Climates in Electronically Mediated Communication

The benefits of a positive communication climate aren't limited to face-to-face inter-actions. Much of our interpersonal communication occurs in electronically mediated contexts, from e-mails and text messages to Facebook posts and tweets—and positive mediated interaction contributes to higher-quality relationships as well.[71] When interacting with others in mediated ways, competent communicators adapt their behavior to the affordances and limitations of each channel. Following these tips can help you contribute to a positive climate in your own communication:

- *Don't expect feedback to be immediate.* When you send someone an e-mail or text message, it is easy to expect that recipients will read and respond to your words immediately. You may therefore feel impatient if you don't receive a response right away. However, receivers may not see your message the moment you send it, particularly if they are driving, or away from their cell phones or computers when you write. Even when they do find your message, they may be engaged in other tasks at the time and unable to respond until later. When using these forms of mediated communication, therefore, try not to feel hurt or offended if the other person's response doesn't come immediately.

- *Be careful not to use mediated communication as a shield.* Especially when you feel vulnerable, it can be tempting to "hide" behind e-mail or other forms of mediated communication instead of dealing with people directly. For instance, Jessica was afraid of her parents' reactions when she came out as gay, so she told them in a text message. That may have saved her from discomfort in the moment, but it sent her parents the message that she didn't care enough about them to have the conversation in person. She could have fostered a more positive communication climate by not using a text message to share such important information.

© Ariel Skelley/Blend Images, RF

- *Get permission before sharing others' photos.* Your friends and loved ones may feel comfortable showing you pictures of themselves and their activities. That doesn't necessarily mean they want you sharing those images with others. Respect their privacy by getting permission before you forward or repost their photos. The same advice applies to any sensitive information others have shared with you.

- *Pay attention to auto-correct.* Many cell phones and tablets make use of an auto-correct function that replaces improperly spelled words ("umblelal") with the term it thinks you meant to write ("umbrella"). On occasion, the auto-correct function makes the wrong guess, generating a word you didn't intend ("umbilical"). Without paying attention, you might miss one of these inaccurate substitutions and end up sending a message you didn't intend. Thus, a good rule of thumb is always to read your text messages before sending them.

- *Reflect instead of reacting.* Messages that rely heavily on written words, such as texts and tweets, can be easy to misinterpret because they don't let us see the sender's facial expressions or hear the person's tone of voice. When you receive such messages, you may *think* you understand their meaning and then reply to them immediately, only to find out later that your interpretation was inaccurate. Especially when a message makes you angry or upset, a better approach is to ask yourself how you might be misunderstanding it before you respond to it.

Electronically mediated forms of communication offer us many ways of staying in touch with the people who matter to us. Even as we use language to foster positive communication climates in face-to-face interaction, we can do the same to make mediated communication positive and fulfilling.

In the IM: You can now access the end-of-chapter Discussion Questions and the Research Library in the Instructor's Manual for each chapter.

LEARN IT What are examples of disconfirming messages? How are opinions and factual statements different? Why is using I-statements helpful for developing positive communication climates?

APPLY IT With a classmate, role-play a conversation in which you are roommates in conflict over your "house rules" regarding chores, visitors, and use of each other's personal property. Afterward, identify as many examples as you can of defensive statements made by you or your partner. For each, note which type of defensive statement it is (according to Gibb's list) and then craft a supportive version of the same statement.

REFLECT ON IT In what ways do you contribute to positive climates in your mediated communication? Why is it important to separate opinions from claims of fact?

MASTER the chapter

1 The Nature of Language (p. 141)

- Language consists of words that represent, or symbolize, objects or concepts.

- The connection between most words and the objects or concepts they symbolize is arbitrary.

- Languages are governed by phonological, syntactic, semantic, and pragmatic rules.

- Words have both denotative and connotative meanings.

- Verbal statements vary in how ambiguous they are.

- The meaning of language is affected by the social and cultural contexts in which it is used.

2 Appreciating the Power of Words (p. 149)

- Naming is a fundamental way of giving identity to someone or something.
- Language can be used to persuade others to think or act in a particular way.
- Some forms of language are perceived as more credible than others.
- People use verbal behavior in personal relationships to convey affection and create intimacy.
- We can use words to provide comfort to others and also to ourselves.

3 The Use and Abuse of Language (p. 160)

- Humor relies on a violation of expectations.
- Euphemisms allow us to discuss sensitive topics in a minimally discomforting way.
- Many subcultures have their own slang, which serves to mark membership in those groups.

- Libel is defamatory language that appears in print; slander is defamatory language that is spoken.
- Profanity is a form of language that is generally considered offensive.
- Hate speech is a form of profanity aimed at degrading or intimidating a specific group of people.

4 Creating a Positive Communication Climate (p. 165)

- Send confirming messages as a way to emphasize positivity.
- Use supportive communication to prevent making others defensive.
- Give constructive feedback, whether evaluative or non-evaluative.
- Take ownership of your thoughts and feelings by using I-statements.
- Learn to separate opinions from statements of fact and respond appropriately to each.
- Adapt to the features of electronically mediated messages to foster positive communication climates.

KEY TERMS

ambiguous language (p. 146)
communication climate (p. 165)
confirming message (p. 166)
connotative meaning (p. 144)
credibility (p. 154)
defamation (p. 163)
defensiveness (p. 167)
denotative meaning (p. 144)
disconfirming message (p. 166)
ethos (p. 152)

euphemism (p. 161)
evaluative feedback (p. 170)
hate speech (p. 164)
I-statement (p. 170)
language (p. 141)
libel (p. 163)
loaded language (p. 146)
logos (p. 153)
non-evaluative feedback (p. 169)
onomatopoeia (p. 143)

pathos (p. 152)
profanity (p. 163)
reason (p. 153)
Sapir-Whorf hypothesis (p. 148)
slander (p. 163)
slang (p. 162)
supportiveness (p. 168)
you-statement (p. 170)

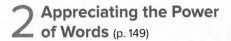 connect

To maximize your study time, check out CONNECT to access the SmartBook study module for this chapter, watch videos, and explore other resources.

6 Nonverbal Communication

© Kevin Mazur/Getty Images

THE EMBRACE VIEWED 'ROUND THE WORLD

Actor John Travolta has turned a few heads during his 40-year show business career. In February 2015, he did so yet again at the Academy Awards ceremony when he approached actress Scarlett Johansson on the red carpet, wrapped his arm around her waist, and kissed her on the cheek. The gesture, captured in a photo that quickly went viral, struck many people as more intimate than would normally be expected for two people who are not romantically involved with each other. Johansson's facial expression during the encounter also seemed to suggest that she was annoyed by the behavior. Media commentators and bloggers immediately started speculating about the meaning of Travolta's hug. Many labeled his behavior as awkward, creepy, and an invasion of Johansson's personal space. But Johansson disagreed, calling the image "an unfortunate still-frame" from "an encounter that was very sweet and totally welcome,"* and clarifying that she hadn't seen Travolta in several years and was happy to be greeted by him.[1]

*Miller, Judy. (February 26, 2015). "Scarlett Johansson Defends John Travolta." VanityFair.com, http://www.vanityfair.com/hollywood/2015/02/john-travoltascarlett- johansson-oscars

Nonverbal communication is powerful. Sometimes the smallest gesture—a glance; a warm vocal tone; a brief, affectionate touch with a fellow celebrity—can send unmistakable messages about ourselves to others. Moreover, so much of what we learn about other people's thoughts and feelings comes not through listening to their words but through observing their body language—watching their facial expressions, seeing how they move and gesture, and taking note of their eye contact. Those and other behaviors often convey enormous amounts of information about people in efficient and sometimes subtle ways.

1 The Nature of Nonverbal Communication

On the animated television show *The Simpsons,* Marge Simpson is seldom shy about expressing disapproval when her husband or her children misbehave. She frequently communicates her feelings through her facial expressions, posture, and the stressful grunting sound she makes when she's annoyed. Those and other nonverbal communication behaviors clearly convey Marge's state of mind to anyone who happens to be around her. What makes nonverbal behavior such an effective form of communication? We will find out in this section, first by differentiating nonverbal communication from verbal communication and then by examining five of its most important characteristics.

What Is Nonverbal Communication?

Nonverbal means just what it sounds like—not verbal. Nonverbal communication requires neither words nor language. How, exactly, do we communicate with others, if not with words and language?

The answer is, in many ways. We can tell a great deal about people by watching their facial expressions and listening to their tone of voice. When you listen to your doctor tell you the results of your recent blood tests, for instance, you might hear the tension in her voice and determine that something is wrong, or you might see the pleasant look on her face and conclude that everything is fine. We also interpret people's gestures and notice the way they carry themselves. Perhaps you see two people punching each other but you determine from their behaviors that they are playing rather than genuinely fighting.

In addition, we frequently make judgments about people on the basis of their appearance. While scanning personal ads online, for example, you might be more drawn to some people than to others based on their photographs. Sometimes we even perceive others according to the way they use their time and the space around them. Perhaps you tried talking to your boss about your recent evaluation, but you felt ignored because

Writing Note: Students often think of "body language" when they think of nonverbal communication. In class, have students list as many features of body language as they can within five minutes. As you progress through your discussion of the various channels of nonverbal communication, see if all their examples are accounted for, and discuss any that are not.

he kept looking at his new iPhone. People routinely communicate more information through their appearance and nonverbal behaviors than they do through language. When it comes to interpersonal communication, looks and actions often do speak louder than words.

 nonverbal communication Behaviors and characteristics that convey meaning without the use of words.

We can define **nonverbal communication,** then, as behaviors and characteristics that convey meaning without the use of words. Nonverbal communication behaviors frequently accompany verbal messages to clarify or reinforce them. For instance, if someone asks you for directions to the bookstore and you point and say "It's that way," your nonverbal behavior (pointing) clarifies the meaning of your verbal message. In contrast, if you just say "It's that way" without pointing, then your verbal message is ambiguous—and not very helpful. At other times, however, nonverbal communication behaviors convey meaning on their own. For example, if you ask me where the bookstore is and I shrug my shoulders, you will probably infer from my behavior that I don't know the answer to your question, even though I never actually said so.

Talking Point: Pointing is a good example of how efficient nonverbal communication can be. Gestures and facial expressions often convey information more quickly than verbal expressions do.

Nonverbal behavior is a powerful way of communicating, and it comes naturally to many of us. Yet there's a lot more to interpreting nonverbal behavior than you might think. The more you learn about nonverbal communication, the better you will be able to understand it.

Five Characteristics of Nonverbal Communication

It's difficult to imagine life without nonverbal communication. Communicating nonverbally is particularly critical for people who lack language skills, such as infants, who can only vocalize without words, and for individuals with certain types of neurological problems, such as a stroke, that limit their language use. But even people with language ability depend immensely on nonverbal communication. For example, because she had only a limited knowledge of Spanish, Bergitta depended on nonverbal behaviors while traveling through Bolivia, Uruguay, and Argentina. She was frequently amazed at how well she could understand others simply by observing their gestures and facial expressions. Her communication was more challenging than it would have been if she had known the language, but she was still able to understand—and be understood by— others through nonverbal behaviors. Let's look at five key characteristics of such nonverbal communication.

Talking Point: Traveling in areas where one doesn't speak or understand the language can truly be an experience of illiteracy, even for literate adults.

NONVERBAL COMMUNICATION IS PRESENT IN MOST INTERPERSONAL CONVERSATIONS. Whether you talk to people one-on-one or in a group, you have access not only to the words they speak but also to several dimensions of nonverbal communication. In many situations, you can watch people's facial expressions for signs of how they're feeling. For instance, you might tell from his facial expression that your supervisor is bored at his business lunch and eager to leave. Voice also conveys data about a person's state of mind. At a party, you can determine from the tone of her voice when your host is being serious and when she's kidding. Even the way people dress and smell can send you information. Glancing around the room at a large business event, you might be able to guess which people are managers and which are staff members by the formality of their clothing. We are flooded with nonverbal signals in many kinds of social situations.

© stockerteam/Getty Images, RF

In other communication contexts, such as talking on the telephone and sending e-mail, we don't have access to as many nonverbal cues as we do in face-to-face conversation. We still make use of what's available, however. Even if we haven't met those to whom we're speaking on the telephone, for instance, we can make judgments about their voices—noticing, for example, how fast they're talking, how loudly, with what tone, and with what type of accent. In electronically mediated communication—such as e-mail, tweeting, and text messaging—we can introduce nonverbal cues through the use of **emoticons,** textual representations of facial expressions often used in e-mail messages, and **emoji,** cartoon depictions of faces and other objects that first became popular on Japanese cell phone services. There are also other cues to help us make judgments in electronic media, such as pauses and the use of all capital letters.

emoticons Textual representations of facial expressions.

emoji Cartoon depictions of faces and other objects.

Most of our interpersonal communication includes at least some form of nonverbal communication. Going further, when we only have a few nonverbal signals to go on, we pay them extra attention. For example, vocal characteristics such as pitch and tone are important nonverbal cues in face-to-face conversation, but they are even more important on the telephone because so many other nonverbal signals, such as facial expressions and gestures, are unavailable to us. By the same token, when people lose the ability to use one of their senses to communicate, they typically compensate by relying more heavily on their remaining senses. Deaf people, for example, pay extra attention to visual cues when communicating with others because they are unable to interpret vocal characteristics. Similarly, blind people often rely more heavily on hearing and touch to help them communicate, because they are unable to see gestures or facial expressions.

NONVERBAL COMMUNICATION OFTEN CONVEYS MORE INFORMATION THAN VERBAL COMMUNICATION. Go to the self-help section of almost any bookstore, and open up titles such as *How to Read a Person Like a Book*[2] and *How You Act Is*

Nonverbal communication often involves multiple channels at once. During a face-to-face conversation, speakers can attend to facial expressions, eye behaviors, tone of voice, gestures, posture, and touch as sources of information. © *Photodisc/Getty Images, RF*

 nonverbal channels The various behavioral forms that nonverbal communication takes.

More Important Than What You Say.[3] You'll probably get the impression that nearly all the information people get by communicating with others comes through nonverbal behavior. In fact, some unreliable but frequently cited studies have estimated that as much as 93 percent of meaning is transmitted nonverbally.[4] Nonverbal communication isn't quite that powerful, however. More realistic estimates from nonverbal communication scholar Judee Burgoon suggest that 65 to 70 percent of meaning comes from nonverbal clues.[5] Importantly, even Burgoon's more conservative statistics suggest that people communicate more through nonverbal behaviors than words.

The most likely reason why nonverbal communication adds up to such a significant percentage is that it makes use of many **nonverbal channels,** which are the various behavioral forms that nonverbal communication takes. Some of those channels rely on our sense of vision, such as facial expressions, gestures, and personal appearance. Vocal characteristics, such as loudness, pitch, and tone of voice, engage our sense of hearing. We also use our senses of touch and smell to communicate. We often express different messages with a handshake and a hug, and we convey subtle messages about attraction to others through our use of smell.

NONVERBAL COMMUNICATION IS USUALLY BELIEVED OVER VERBAL COMMUNICATION.
It's not uncommon to get conflicting messages between what a person says and does. Most of the time, we believe the nonverbal clues.[6]

Let's say you're waiting for your friend Dante at your favorite bookstore café. When he walks in, Dante slumps down on the seat next to you, rolls his eyes, and sighs heavily. You ask him how he's doing, and he says, "It's been a *great* day." Dante's verbal behavior is sending you one message ("I'm having a great day"), but his nonverbal behavior is suggesting something quite different ("I'm having a terrible day"). Which of those contradictory messages do you believe? Most of us would put more stock in what Dante is *doing* than in what he is *saying*. In other words, as multiple studies have shown, we would believe his nonverbal message.

Experts think we put more trust in nonverbal communication because we believe people have a harder time controlling nonverbal signals than verbal ones. Thus, we assume that nonverbal behaviors more accurately reflect what a person is really thinking or feeling. It's easy for Dante to *say* he's having a great day, but if he feels frustrated or depressed, it's probably tougher for him to *act* as though his day is going well. Therefore, when he slumps, rolls his eyes, and sighs, you probably would conclude that his day is going poorly, despite what he says.

The human preference for believing nonverbal signals even when they conflict with words is especially critical for detecting deception, because people often display inconsistent verbal and nonverbal behaviors when they're lying. Imagine that Tawny fails to show up for her work shift on time because she overslept, yet she tells her manager that she was in the emergency room with a severe migraine. Tawny might feel nervous telling such a lie, especially because she knows she could lose her job were she to get caught. Her nervousness may affect her nonverbal behavior. She might perspire, get dry in the mouth, sound unusually tense, and assume an especially rigid posture. In contrast, if she really had been in the hospital, there's probably no reason she would be nervous telling her manager about it. She would be able to explain her medical emergency calmly and apologize for her absence. So, if she looks or sounds nervous, those nonverbal messages will contradict her verbal message and may convince her manager that she's not telling the truth.

NONVERBAL COMMUNICATION IS THE PRIMARY MEANS OF COMMUNICATING EMOTION.   We have a large verbal vocabulary for describing our emotions, but our nonverbal behaviors do it much more efficiently. How many times have you been able to tell how someone is feeling just by looking at the person? We may not always be right about the emotions we sense—and some of us are better than others at interpreting people's emotions—but research shows that humans are acutely sensitive to nonverbal emotion cues.[7]

Emotion is a powerful influence on our behavior, and our primary way of communicating how we feel is through our nonverbal behaviors. Two channels of nonverbal behavior that are particularly important in communicating emotion are facial expressions and vocal behaviors.

Humans are highly visually oriented beings, meaning that we tend to pay a great deal of attention to people's facial expressions when we want to figure out their emotional state. We take close note of those expressions whether we're talking to people face-to-face, listening to them speak to a group, or even watching them on television. On reality TV shows such as *The Voice, The Amazing Race,* and *Chopped,* for instance, producers often shoot close-ups of people's faces during critical moments to capture

One aspect of reality television shows that makes them so compelling is the spontaneous expression of emotion. © *ZUMA Press, Inc/Alamy*

emotions in their expressions. Most of us can easily think of the type of facial expression that connotes happiness: The eyes tend to be wide and bright, and the person tends to be smiling. That expression differs notably from the facial expressions we associate with anger, sadness, surprise, and other emotional states. The distinctive patterns we perceive for each are keys to helping us interpret other people's emotions.

Several studies suggest that facial expressions of these basic emotions are interpreted very similarly across cultures.[8] In a classic study, psychologist Paul Ekman took photographs of people communicating six basic emotions through their facial expressions: happiness, fear, disgust, anger, sadness, and surprise. He then showed the photos to participants in Chile, Brazil, Argentina, Japan, and the United States. He asked the participants to match each photograph with what they believed was the emotion being displayed. Ekman then compared the participants from different countries and found that they were equally accurate at describing which emotion was displayed in each photograph.[9]

Similar studies have repeated those results using groups from a range of cultures, including Greek, Chinese, Turkish, Malaysian, Ethiopian, Swedish, Italian, Sumatran, Estonian, and Scottish.[10] The degree of similarity in interpretations of emotion displays does differ from culture to culture. It also differs from emotion to emotion, with facial displays of some emotions, such as happiness, being interpreted more consistently than others, such as fear.[11] Overall, however, it appears that facial expressions of our most basic emotions are interpreted similarly around the world.

We also pay attention to vocal cues to understand a person's emotional state. When someone is screaming and using harsh vocal tones, we usually infer that he or she is angry, whereas laughter and lots of pitch variation suggest happiness or excitement. It turns out that we may be more accurate at interpreting emotions through vocal cues than through facial expressions.[12] That appears to be particularly true when the vocal channel is the only channel we have access to, such as when we're speaking with someone on the telephone. We don't necessarily get *more* information about their emotional state from their voice than from their facial expressions, but we might get *more accurate* information.

In Everyday Life: Why would facial displays of happiness be easier to interpret than facial displays of fear? Do people vary more in how they express fear than happiness?

Talking Point: When making judgments about people's emotions, we rely on the channels that are most available to us. Thus, although vocal cues are an important source of emotional information in face-to-face conversation, they become even more influential when visual cues are filtered out, as when we're talking on the telephone.

Nonverbal behaviors can be metacommunicative. When a friend or relative whispers and covers her mouth with her hand, those behaviors convey that what she's telling you is meant to be a secret.

NONVERBAL COMMUNICATION METACOMMUNICATES.
Recall from the About Communication chapter that metacommunication is communication *about* communication and that we often metacommunicate verbally. When we use phrases such as "Let me tell you what I think" and "Don't take this the wrong way," we are sending messages related to our other messages—that is, we're communicating about our communication. Usually, we do so to avoid misunderstanding and to provide listeners with greater clarity about our meaning. Several *nonverbal* behaviors also help us achieve the goal of communicating clearly.

Suppose, for example, that you're sitting at the dinner table with your sister and she leans over to you, lowers her voice to a whisper, and cups her mouth with her hand, as though she's about to tell you a secret. That combination of nonverbal behaviors sends you the message "What I'm about to say is meant for only you to hear." In other words, her nonverbal behavior metacommunicates her intentions to you.

We often use nonverbal behaviors such as facial expressions and gestures to indicate how someone else should

© Nacivet/Photographer's Choice/Getty Images

interpret our messages. For instance, we might smile and wink to indicate that we're being sarcastic or raise our eyebrows to signal that what we're saying is very serious. All those are examples of how we can use nonverbal cues to metacommunicate with others.

Functions of Nonverbal Communication

Later we will see that nonverbal behaviors come in a number of forms, or channels. People use those channels for many reasons. Here, let's look at six common functions of nonverbal communication in personal relationships.

MANAGING CONVERSATIONS. Even though conversations involve the exchange of verbal communication, we use several nonverbal behaviors to help our conversations with others go smoothly. In particular, nonverbal cues assist us in inviting, maintaining, and ending conversations.

- *Inviting conversations:* Three nonverbal cues are especially relevant for inviting conversations: personal space, physical appearance, and eye contact. First, you're most likely to initiate conversations with people who are physically closest to you rather than with people who are farther away.[13] Therefore, whom you happen to be standing by partly determines whom you'll talk to. Second, you'll be more inclined to initiate conversations with people you find physically attractive.[14] Because attractive people are often sought out as conversational partners, you may not always succeed in striking up conversations with them. Their physical attractiveness, though, will often motivate you to try. Finally, you'll be more likely to talk with people who make eye contact with you.[15] Conversely, when people avoid making eye contact with you, they're often signaling that they're unavailable for conversation.

- *Maintaining conversations:* During a conversation, you'll probably use gestures, eye contact, and tone of voice as **turn-taking signals**—nonverbal signs that indicate when each person's speaking turns begin and end. For example, you might raise a finger, a gesture that indicates you have something to say or that signals that you're not yet finished with your speaking turn. Eye contact can serve similar turn-taking functions. Research shows that most of us maintain more eye contact with a conversational partner when we're listening than when we're speaking.[16] You can therefore withhold eye contact while you're speaking as a way of signaling that you're not yet done with your turn.

- *Ending conversations:* Changes in eye behavior and posture are particularly common strategies for ending a conversation. When communication scholar Mark Knapp and his colleagues induced experimental participants to try to end conversations, the most frequent nonverbal leave-taking behavior was breaking eye contact.[17] Because we tend to look at people when we're listening to them, one way we can signal that we're ready for a conversation to end is to break eye contact with the other person. A second strategy is to angle our posture away from the person and toward the direction in which we wish to go. That behavior, called *left-positioning*, signals that we are preparing to leave the site of the conversation.[18]

EXPRESSING EMOTIONS. The fact that many nonverbal human behaviors communicate information about emotional state means that interpreting another person's

immediacy behavior Nonverbal behavior that conveys attraction or affiliation.

emotions can give us important clues about how best to interact with that person. The two most expressive nonverbal channels for emotion are facial expressions and vocal behaviors.

- *Facial expressions of emotion:* Many of us "wear" our emotions on our face.[19] Facial expression is such a central part of our experience as social beings that we begin signaling our emotions through facial displays very early in life. For instance, studies have shown that infants begin smiling in response to external stimuli, such as a pleasant voice and a gentle touch, around the end of the first month of life.[20] By two months of age, most infants smile more in the presence of a parent than a stranger, suggesting they are happier when the parent is present.[21]

- *Vocal expressions of emotion:* The voice is also remarkably emotionally expressive.[22] We sometimes can tell how a person is feeling not by what he or she says but by the way his or her voice sounds. Experimental research on vocal displays of emotion has shown that emotion affects the voice in many ways. Specifically, intense emotional experiences increase the pitch and loudness of the voice, while decreasing the rate of speech.[23] Less-intense emotions cause fewer changes in the voice.[24]

Facial and vocal behaviors are powerful ways of expressing emotion, but they are not the only options. People can also convey their feelings through eye behaviors, movement, and touch. To practice doing so yourself, check out the "Got Skills?" box.

MAINTAINING RELATIONSHIPS. Communication plays a central role in how most of us maintain our close relationships, and nonverbal behaviors are especially important for several key features of those relationships. Those behaviors include attraction and affiliation, power and dominance, and arousal and relaxation.

- *Attraction and affiliation:* Many nonverbal behaviors send messages of attraction or affiliation. Researchers call those **immediacy behaviors.** When two people flirt, for example, they use their eye contact to signal attraction; they stand or sit close to each other; they touch each other playfully; and they use expressive tones of voice to convey the message that they are interested in each other.[25] People in many cultures use the same types of behaviors in initial interactions to signal that they are attracted to each other and wish to explore the possibility of future interaction.[26]

In more established relationships, nonverbal behavior is a common means of expressing affection and love. We hug, kiss, and hold hands with the people we love, and we speak to them in softer and higher-pitched tones of voice. Those kinds of behaviors help to reinforce feelings of affiliation, intimacy, and love, whether with our romantic partners, our family members, or our friends.[27]

- *Power and dominance: Power* is the potential to affect another person's behavior, and *dominance* is the actual exercise of that potential. Adults

Many nonverbal behaviors convey affiliation and affection in close relationships. © *Jose Luis Pelaez Inc/Blend Images, RF*

got skills?   **COMMUNICATING EMOTION NONVERBALLY**

Use nonverbal communication to express how you feel.

WHAT?

Learn to convey emotion through the use of eye behaviors, movement, and touch.

WHY?

To communicate your emotions in a more expressive manner.

HOW?

1. Form a small group and ask each member to think of one emotion without sharing his or her selection with others.

2. One at a time, ask each member to try expressing his or her chosen emotion to the rest of the group using eye behaviors only. Ask others in the group to try to guess which emotion is being displayed.

3. Have each member select a different emotion and repeat the procedure, this time asking members to express their emotion only through their movement.

4. Repeat the process once more, asking members to convey their chosen emotion through the use of touch.

TRY!

1. As the exercise progresses from eye behavior to movement to touch, take note of how accurate group members are at interpreting the emotions being displayed. Pay additional attention to which behaviors (eye behavior, movement, or touch) members find it easiest to use for emotional expression.

2. After the exercise, write a short paragraph or blog post in which you describe how people used eye behaviors, movement, and touch to convey various emotions.

CONSIDER: *How can emotion be expressed through personal appearance? How about the use of time or the use of space?*

---

often convey messages about their power and status nonverbally. For example, supervisors touch subordinates more than subordinates touch superiors, and a powerful person is more likely to keep a less-powerful person waiting than vice versa.[28]

Many of us also use *artifacts*—objects or visual features in an environment, to be examined further below—as status symbols. For instance, we might hang college diplomas on our office walls to signal our level of education or leave our expensive cars parked conspicuously in the driveway to signal our wealth. People also use nonverbal behaviors to assert dominance and control over others. Teachers do that, for example, when they use a certain look to convey disapproval about a child's behavior. Police officers control drivers' behaviors when they hold up a hand to signal "stop." Finally, some of us use silence to stop others from continuing to speak when we're in an uncomfortable conversation.

- *Arousal and relaxation: Arousal* refers to an increase in energy. We experience arousal in two fundamentally different ways depending on whether it is accompanied by positive or negative emotions. When it is accompanied by positive emotions, we experience arousal as excitement. Most of us express excitement through nonverbal cues such as an increase in eye contact with others, more laughter, faster rate of speech, higher vocal pitch and volume, and closer proximity to others.[29]

When arousal is accompanied by negative emotions, however, we experience it as anxiety. Feeling anxious tends to cause fidgeting and random movement, nervous smiling or laughter, the use of more gestures and self-adaptors, higher vocal pitch and rate of speech, and the use of more filler words.[30]

The opposite of arousal is *relaxation,* which we feel in situations of decreased energy. As with arousal, we experience relaxation in two different ways depending on the emotion involved. When relaxation is accompanied by positive emotion, we experience it as contentment. Feeling content leads most of us to smile more than usual, have a more relaxed posture, and increase our eye contact with and proximity to those around us.[31]

In contrast, when relaxation is accompanied by negative emotion, we experience it as depression. Some people suffer from clinical depression, a psychiatric disorder thought to be caused by problems with chemicals called neurotransmitters, which relay signals between neurons and other cells in the brain.[32] Others just feel down from time to time, experiencing some of the symptoms of depression without the underlying psychiatric problems. In either case, feeling depressed often leads people to smile less, make less frequent eye contact, and use fewer gestures and more self-adaptors.[33]

FORMING IMPRESSIONS.   Many of us enjoy people watching while, say, sitting in a coffee shop or waiting at the airport. We pay attention to what individuals look and sound like and how they behave, and we use that information to form impressions about them. Those impressions are also strongly affected by people's nonverbal behaviors. In particular, nonverbal cues influence two general types of impressions: those related to a person's demographic characteristics and those related to a person's sociocultural characteristics.

- *Demographic impressions:* A person's *demographic characteristics* include his or her age, ethnic background, and sex. Research indicates that on the basis of visual cues, most of us can accurately classify a person into broad categories for age—such as infant, teenager, or elderly adult—and ethnicity—such as Asian, Hispanic, or non-Hispanic white.[34] Making a finer distinction, such as whether a woman is 50 or 60 years old or whether a man is Cambodian or Vietnamese, is more challenging. Similarly, most people can correctly identify an individual's biological sex by attending to visual cues such as the shape of the face and the body, hairstyle, clothing, jewelry, and cosmetics.[35]

    The voice is another nonverbal channel that helps us form demographic impressions of others. Vocal behaviors tend to be particularly good clues as to a person's age, sex, and sexual orientation. As people age, for instance, their vocal pitch and rate of speech typically decrease.[36] Consequently, many of us can determine a person's age with relative accuracy by listening to the sound of his or her voice.[37] By the same token, women's and men's voices differ from each other in average pitch and vocal quality.[38] As a result, listeners can distinguish between male and female adult voices with nearly perfect accuracy.[39]

- *Sociocultural impressions:* People's *sociocultural characteristics* include their socioeconomic status, which is an index of how much money and education a person has and how prestigious his or her career is. They also include the cultural and co-cultural groups with which people identify.

    Personal appearance is usually the most informative nonverbal channel for forming sociocultural impressions. When you see a woman in an expensive, tailored

When it comes to forming sociocultural impressions about someone, personal appearance is highly influential. What impressions would this person's appearance suggest to you?
© *Tanya Constantine/Brand X Pictures/ PunchStock, RF*

business suit, for instance, you're likely to infer that she is of higher socioeconomic status than a woman wearing torn jeans and a sweatshirt.[40] You may not be accurate in your impression of those particular women, but the quality of a person's clothing is a relatively reliable visual cue to his or her socioeconomic status.[41]

Many organized co-cultural groups, such as those associated with particular sports interests or music preferences, adopt fashions that identify their members. You might infer, therefore, that a young man in a football jersey and tennis shoes is a sports fan, whereas a young woman in black pants and a black shirt featuring a skull and crossbones is into alternative rock.

INFLUENCING OTHERS.   You probably find yourself in many social situations in which you wish to influence others' behaviors. Perhaps you're trying to persuade your friends to sponsor you in a marathon for cancer research—or you might be trying to get a good tip from the diners you've been serving. In those and many other contexts, you can use nonverbal behaviors to influence others. Nonverbal communication can be persuasive when it is applied as part of several strategies, including creating credibility and promoting affiliation.

- *Creating credibility:* One of the most effective strategies for influencing other people's behaviors is to project an image of credibility. We often do that by adopting a personal appearance that conveys expertise and authority. Consider uniforms. A judge's black robes, a doctor's white lab coat, and a police officer's badge and uniform all symbolize particular forms of experience and authority.[42] Other nonverbal cues are also influential. Speaking loudly, quickly, and expressively, with a good deal of pitch variation, makes a person sound more credible.[43] The use of eye contact and gestures that clarify the verbal message also enhances a person's credibility.[44] In particular, maintaining eye contact with someone while one is speaking powerfully influences persuasiveness.[45]

- *Promoting affiliation:* We are more persuaded by people we like than by people we don't.[46] Nonverbal behaviors that promote a sense of affiliation, closeness, and liking can therefore enhance our persuasive ability.

One behavior that often contributes to a sense of affiliation is touch.[47] Because we share more touch within close relationships than casual ones, being touched in appropriate, familiar ways can make us feel close to others. Several experiments have demonstrated that casual touches—such as a brief touch to the hand, forearm, or shoulder—make people more likely to comply with our requests.[48]

Affiliation is also enhanced by *interactional synchrony,* which is the convergence of two people's behaviors. When you mirror another person's posture, gestures, facial expressions, or vocal behaviors, you may cause that person subconsciously to perceive you as similar to him or

Your personal appearance, clothing, and demeanor can give you the credibility to influence others. © *Comstock Images/Getty Images, RF*

her.[49] That perception is consequential for persuasion, because people like people who are similar to themselves.[50]

CONCEALING INFORMATION. A final function of nonverbal communication is to help people conceal information. Despite the cultural adage that "honesty is the best policy," people frequently decide not to be entirely truthful in their conversations with others. As we'll see in the Deceptive Communication chapter, individuals have many reasons for choosing to conceal information. Sometimes people lie to benefit themselves, such as faking an illness to get out of work. Sometimes they lie to avoid hurting themselves, such as concealing marital infidelity. Often, however, people choose to be deceptive to avoid hurting others—for example, by saying they're happy to receive a gift that they actually dislike.

One of the most commonly studied facial behaviors that can indicate deception is smiling. Most research studies have found that people don't differ in how much they smile when they're being honest as opposed to being deceptive. Rather, they differ in *how* they smile.[51]

When we're telling the truth, we're more likely to use a genuine smile that reflects actual positive emotion. That is the kind of smile we display when we hear good news or smell a delicious dinner cooking. When we're being dishonest, we're more likely to use a false smile, one that makes it appear as though we're happy even though we aren't. That is the smile we display when we run into a co-worker we don't like and are trying to appear glad to see him. Both types of smile draw the edges of the mouth upward, but a genuine smile also causes the skin around the eyes to wrinkle, whereas a false smile does not.

Attempting to conceal information can also influence certain vocal behaviors, particularly the pitch of the voice. Several studies have demonstrated that people speak with a higher pitch when they are deceiving than when they're telling the truth.[52] In a classic study, for instance, student nurses were asked to watch either a pleasant nature film or a grotesque film depicting amputations and burns. After viewing each film, the student nurses were told to convince an interviewer that the film they had just watched was pleasant and enjoyable. In one condition, therefore, the students were to be truthful, and in the other they were to be deceptive. By recording the participants' voices and analyzing them later, the researchers determined that the students' vocal pitch was significantly higher when they were attempting to deceive the interviewer than when they were telling the truth.[53]

Managing conversations, expressing emotions, maintaining relationships, forming impressions, influencing others, and concealing information are not the only functions of nonverbal behavior, but they are among the most valuable. In its own way, each of these functions helps us to communicate with others in efficient, productive ways.

LEARN IT What determines whether a form of communication is verbal or non-verbal? Why are we more likely to believe nonverbal behaviors than words when the two conflict? In what ways can nonverbal behavior help manage conversations or improve persuasion?

APPLY IT Consider how the tone of one's voice can influence meaning. Take a simple phrase such as "She made me do that." Say it first as though you're angry, then surprised, and, finally, sarcastic. Describe in a journal entry how your voice changes each time, even though the words are the same.

REFLECT ON IT How accurate do you think you are at interpreting other people's nonverbal behaviors? Why do you suppose that some people are better at "reading" nonverbal behavior than others?

2 Ten Channels of Nonverbal Communication

Nonverbal communication engages nearly all our senses, so it's probably no surprise that we experience it in so many different forms, or channels. In this section, we consider ten channels: facial displays, eye behaviors, movement and gestures, touch behaviors, vocal behaviors, the use of smell, the use of space, physical appearance, the use of time, and the use of artifacts.

Facial Displays

It's hard to overstate the importance of **facial displays,** or facial expressions, in nonverbal communication. Indeed, according to the *principle of facial primacy,* the face communicates more information than any other channel of nonverbal behavior.[54] That principle is especially true for three important functions of facial displays: identity, attractiveness, and emotion.

IDENTITY. The face is the most important visual clue that humans use to identify one another.[55] You usually don't hang pictures of people's hands or feet on the wall; rather, you hang pictures of their faces, because the appearance of the face is the most reliable clue to identity. It's your face that appears on your driver's license and in your passport to help authorities identify you. Likewise, it's your face that appears in your high school yearbook to help your classmates remember you.

ATTRACTIVENESS. The face also plays a major role in attractiveness. Even though we like to think that "beauty is in the eye of the beholder," there is remarkable consistency in what people find attractive in faces, both within and across cultures. Two properties that appear to be especially important in assessing attractiveness are symmetry and proportionality.

Symmetry refers to the similarity between the left and right sides of the face. For most of us, the two sides of our face look similar, but they aren't exactly alike. For both women and men, however, attractive faces have greater symmetry than unattractive faces.[56] Look at the photos in Figure 1 for an example of symmetric and asymmetric faces.

Proportionality refers to the relative size of one's facial features. Is your nose too big for your face? Are your ears too small? On a proportional face, all the features are of the proper size, not in an absolute sense but relative to one another.

Just as with symmetry, attractive faces have greater proportionality than unattractive ones. Unlike symmetry, which can be measured objectively, proportionality is a subjective judgment we make about a person's face. It makes a difference for the attractiveness of a face, however. Our tendency to find proportional faces attractive is a major reason why *rhinoplasty,* a surgical procedure to alter the size and shape of the nose, is one of the most commonly performed cosmetic surgeries in the United States.[57] Because the nose occupies such a prominent position, making its size more proportional to that of other facial features often enhances a person's facial attractiveness.

It may seem odd to identify symmetry and proportionality as primary contributors to facial attractiveness, because we so often think of attractiveness as a highly individual

facial display The use of facial expression for communication.

Talking Point: Why do people pay so much attention to facial expressions?

symmetry The similarity between the left and right sides of the face or body.

proportionality The size of facial features relative to one another.

Talking Point: Other common cosmetic surgery procedures performed on the face include blepharoplasty, which reshapes the eyelids; otoplasty, which reshapes the ears; collagen injection, which creates fuller lips; and administration of botulinum toxin, or Botox, to reduce the appearance of facial wrinkles and lines.

In Everyday Life: The image of the face is commonly used as a form of identification, such as in a passport and on a driver's license, even though the appearance of the face is easy to manipulate and changes over time. Fingerprints are more reliable but are not as frequently used, further attesting to the importance of the face in social interaction.

Focus on Scholarship: Many scholars believe that people are attracted to symmetry and proportionality because those properties signal good health, which is important for mating. As evidence, studies have shown that having an attractive face predicts both longevity and number of sexual partners.[ii]

[ii]Henderson, J. J. A., & Anglin, J. M. (2003). Facial attractiveness predicts longevity. *Evolution and Human Behavior, 23,* 351–356; Rhodes, G., Simmons, L. W., & Peters, M. (2005). Attractiveness and sexual behavior: Does attractiveness enhance mating success? *Evolution and Human Behavior, 26,* 186–201.

In the IM: The in-class activity "Consistency in Judging Attractiveness" invites students to see how consistently they evaluate attractiveness on the basis of facial appearance.

FIGURE 1 Facial Symmetry All else being equal, symmetrical faces are more attractive than asymmetrical faces. Researchers often study facial symmetry by taking a photograph of a face and modifying it with computer software to make it appear more symmetrical. For instance, the image on the left is an original, unretouched photo of an adult man's face. The image on the right has been modified by taking the right side of the face and mirroring it on the left. Research indicates that most people would find the face on the right more attractive. Which face do you find more attractive? Why?
© SensorSpot/Getty Images, RF

assessment. As the "Fact or Fiction?" box explores, however, we're much more similar than dissimilar when it comes to judging a person's attractiveness.

EMOTION. Recall from our earlier discussion that nonverbal behaviors communicate emotions more effectively than verbal communication. Because the face is the major channel of nonverbal behavior, we should not be surprised to learn that facial behavior is our primary means of communicating emotion. Our face enables us to make hundreds of different expressions, which we use to convey a host of emotions, from happiness, surprise, and determination to anger, fear, sadness, and contempt.

How accurately we decode those emotions from other people's facial expressions depends on several factors. The first factor is the emotion itself. As we saw in the earlier discussion of facial expressions, certain emotions are easier to decode than others. Happiness seems to be the easiest to decode. In one study, for instance, people accurately interpreted facial expressions of happiness more often than expressions of sadness or surprise.[58]

Another factor that affects our ability to decode messages is sex. In general, women tend to be better than men at decoding facial displays of emotion.[59] That observation is true across different cultures. It might reflect the fact that in many societies, women are taught to be more friendly, supportive, and nurturing than men, so they learn better decoding skills as a result.[60] Finally, people who are very outgoing and extroverted tend to be better at interpreting facial emotion displays than people who are shy or introverted.[61]

fact OR fiction? IN THE EYE OF WHICH BEHOLDER? CULTURES VARY WIDELY IN PERCEPTIONS OF BEAUTY

Most of us have heard the cliché that "beauty is in the eye of the beholder," meaning that what one person finds attractive may not be appealing to another. This idea dates back at least to the third century B.C., a fact indicating that humans have long considered beauty to be subjective. If that were the case, we would expect to find little agreement from person to person, and from culture to culture, about what is physically attractive. How true is it that beauty is a matter of individual taste?

Not very true, according to research. In fact, a host of studies has shown just the opposite: When evaluating faces, people are remarkably consistent in their judgments of attractiveness. In 2000, developmental psychologist Judith Langlois and her colleagues reviewed 130 of these studies and found that within cultures, people showed 90 percent agreement with one another when judging how attractive someone's face is. Moreover, people from different cultures agreed in their judgments of attractiveness 94 percent of the time. Thus, although we sometimes think of beauty as being culturally specific, Langlois and her team found

that there was more agreement *across* cultures than *within* cultures in assessing attractiveness. Other studies have shown a similar level of cultural consistency when evaluating the attractiveness of body shape.

The researchers' findings indicate that people are much more similar than different when it comes to judging looks. Therefore, people who are considered attractive by one social group are much more likely than not to be considered attractive by other groups.

ASK YOURSELF

- Why does the idea that "beauty is in the eye of the beholder" persist?
- What do you find most physically attractive in members of the other sex? In members of your own sex?

Sources: Singh, D., Dixson, B. J., Jessop, T. S., Morgan, B., & Dixson, A. F. (2010). Cross-cultural consensus for waist-to-hip ratio and women's attractiveness. *Evolution and Human Behavior, 31,* 176–181; Langlois, J. H., Kalakanis, L. E., Rubenstein, A. J., Larson, A. D., Hallam, M. J., & Smoot, M. T. (2000). Maxims or myths of beauty: A meta-analytic and theoretical review. *Psychological Bulletin, 126,* 380–423.

As a way to convey meaning, facial expressions are also extremely important to people who communicate through sign language. In sign language, facial expressions are sometimes called *nonmanual signals* because they work alongside hand signs to help express a particular meaning. For instance, when someone asks a yes-or-no question using sign language, his or her eyes are wide open, the eyebrows are raised, and the head and shoulders are pushed forward. Sometimes a person can change the entire meaning of a sign just by changing the facial expression that goes with it (Figure 2).[62]

oculesics The study of eye behavior.

© Masterfile, RF

Eye Behaviors

Because the eyes are part of the face, it may strike you as odd that researchers study eye behavior separately from facial behavior. However, just as facial behavior communicates more than any other nonverbal channel, the eyes communicate more than any other part of the face—thus, specialists treat **oculesics,** the study of eye behavior, as a separate nonverbal channel.

When people think about eye behavior, eye contact first comes to mind, for good reason. Eye contact plays a role in several important types of relational interaction. We use eye contact to signal attraction to someone and to infer that someone is attracted to us. We use it to gain credibility and to come across as sincere or trustworthy. We use it to persuade others and to signal

FIGURE 2 Facial Expressions in American Sign Language Facial expression plays a vital role in communicating ideas in American Sign Language (ASL). In some instances, the same hand sign is associated with different meanings if it is accompanied by different facial expressions. Both photographs feature the hand sign for "you," for example, but they involve different facial displays. The photo on the left would be interpreted as a question, such as "Are you?" or "Did you?" The photo on the right, however, would be interpreted as an exclamation, such as "It's you!" Although the hand sign is the same in the two photographs, the meaning differs because of the accompanying facial expression. © *Courtesy of Kory Floyd*

Talking Point: Researchers use the term *gaze avoidance* to refer to an intentional lack of eye contact, and *gaze omission* to refer to the unintentional lack of eye contact. What different messages might gaze avoidance and gaze omission send?

Focus on Scholarship: Pupil dilation often occurs when people are lying. Researchers use a technique called *pupillometry* to track very small changes in pupil dilation that can indicate how truthful a person is being.[iii] A camera is used to magnify the image of the eye, and a computer records fluctuations in pupil size.

[iii]Franklin, M. S., Broadway, J. M., Mrazek, M. D., Smallwood, J., & Schooler, J. W. (2013). Window to the wandering mind: Pupillometry of spontaneous thought while reading. *Quarterly Journal of Experimental Psychology, 66,* 2289–2294.

kinesics The study of movement.

that we are paying attention and understanding what others are saying. We can even use eye contact when we want to intimidate someone or take a dominant or authoritative position in a conversation or a group discussion. Indeed, there are few times when we feel as connected to other people—in either positive or negative ways—as when we are looking each other in the eyes. As we'll see later in the chapter, however, those functions of eye contact often vary by culture.

Another eye behavior that has communicative value is pupil size. The pupil is the dark spot right in the center of each eye, which you can see in a mirror. Your pupils control how much light enters your eyes; as a result, they continually change in size. In darker environments, they dilate, or open wider, to take in all available light. In brighter environments, they contract, or become smaller, to avoid taking in too much light at once. What communication researchers find interesting, however, is that your pupils also dilate when you look at someone you find physically attractive and when you feel any kind of arousal, whether it is a positive response, such as excitement or sexual arousal, or a negative response, such as anxiety or fear. Watching how a person's pupils react to different social situations or conversational partners can therefore tell us something about his or her interest and arousal.

Movement and Gestures

Think about the different ways you can walk. When you're feeling confident, you hold your head high and walk with smooth, consistent strides. When you're nervous, you probably walk more timidly, stealing frequent glances at the people around you. Your *gait,* or the way you walk, is one example of how your body movement can communicate a particular message about you to others, such as "I feel proud" or "I feel scared." The study of movement is called **kinesics.**

Now consider how you use your arms and hands to communicate. Perhaps it's to wave at your neighbor when you see her at the grocery store. Maybe it's to hold up two

Gestures comprise body movements that have communicative meaning, and we begin to use them when we are young children. How would you interpret the gestures used by each of these people? © McGraw-Hill Education, Christopher Kerrigan photographer, © Courtesy of the United States Army, © Bloomimage/Collage/Corbis, RF

fingers to signal that you want two hot dogs at the football game concession stand. The use of arm and hand movements to communicate is called **gesticulation.** Research indicates that most people—even people who are born blind—use gestures even before they begin speaking.[63] Communication scholars divide gestures into several forms:

- **Emblems** are any gestures that have a direct verbal translation. Whenever you see an emblematic gesture, you should be able to translate it into words. Examples include the wave for "hello" or "goodbye" and the upright extended palm for "stop."
- **Illustrators** are gestures that go along with a verbal message to clarify it. If you hold up your hands a certain distance apart when you say that fish you caught was "this big," your gesture serves as an illustrator to clarify what you mean by "this big."
- **Affect displays** are gestures that communicate emotion, or *affect*. Some people wring their hands when they're nervous, and some cover their mouth with their hands when they're surprised. Those are both affect displays because they coincide with particular emotions.
- **Regulators** are gestures that control the flow of conversation. One regulator with which you're probably very familiar is raising your hand when you're in a group and wish to speak. Gestures such as that help regulate who is speaking, and when, so that communication can flow smoothly.
- **Adaptors** are gestures that are used to satisfy some personal need, such as scratching an itch or picking lint off one's shirt. When we do those behaviors to ourselves, we call them *self-adaptors*. When adaptors are directed at others (say, picking lint off someone else's shirt), they're called *other-adaptors*.

Touch Behaviors

Touch is the first of our five senses to develop. Even before an infant can see, hear, taste, or smell, his or her skin can respond to stimuli in the environment. Touch is the only sense without which we cannot survive. No matter how much we may cherish our other senses, it's entirely possible to survive without being able to see, hear, taste, or smell. Without our sense of touch, however, we would constantly be susceptible to burn, frostbite, and other potentially life-threatening injuries.

gesticulation The use of arm and hand movements to communicate.

emblem A gesture with a direct verbal translation.

illustrator A gesture that enhances or clarifies a verbal message.

affect display A gesture that communicates emotion.

regulator A gesture that controls the flow of conversation.

adaptor A gesture used to satisfy a personal need.

Talking Point: Cultural variation in emblems comes in two forms. First, some cultures assign different meanings to the same gesture. Second, some cultures use different gestures to convey the same meaning.

Talking Point: Unlike emblems, which can be used in place of words, illustrators must go along with a verbal message to have any meaning.

No matter how much we cherish our other senses, touch is the only sense we cannot survive without. © *Science Photo Library/Alamy, RF*

> **haptics** The study of how people use touch to communicate.

Haptics is the study of how we use touch to communicate. In terms of human communication, there are five major areas in which touch plays a critical role in conveying meaning: affection, caregiving, power and control, aggression, and ritual.

AFFECTIONATE TOUCH. Sharing affection is one of the most important functions of touch. Behaviors such as hugging, kissing, and handholding communicate love, intimacy, commitment, and safety; they are commonplace in many romantic relationships, parent–child relationships, and friendships.[64] One reason affectionate touch is so important is that it contributes to our physical and mental well-being. Infants who are regularly cuddled experience faster physical development than those who are not, and people who are touched during stressful events experience less stress than those who are not.[65] Psychologist Harry Harlow is credited with many groundbreaking discoveries regarding the importance of touch for children.[66]

In recent years, concerns over sexual abuse of children have caused many public school districts to adopt strict "no touch" policies that prevent teachers, counselors, and other school staff from touching students in any way unless it is a medical emergency. As educator Tony Del Prete explains, "In an effort to keep one step ahead of sexual offenders, more and more schools are sending the message to adults—hands off! Touching children in schools has become virtually taboo."[67]*

Although such zero-tolerance policies are designed to protect children, many experts have wondered whether preventing children from being touched actually does more harm than good. For example, researcher Tiffany Field, an internationally recognized expert on touch, believes that no-touch policies are "not a good idea, because children need touch for survival. Their growth and development thrive on touch. And how will they learn about love and affection if not through touch?"[68]†

Affectionate touch is so important that people suffer when they don't receive enough. To explore one solution to that problem that is gaining in popularity, check out the "Communication: Light Side" box.

CAREGIVING TOUCH. You're often touched by others while receiving some form of care or service. When you get your hair cut, have your teeth cleaned, receive a massage, or work with a personal trainer, you're touched in ways that correspond to those activities. Babysitters touch young children while cleaning or dressing them, and nursing home employees touch elderly residents while changing a bandage or helping them take a medication. Each of those actions is an example of caregiving touch because it is done in the course of providing a specific type of care or service.

Caregiving touch is distinguished from affectionate touch because it doesn't necessarily reflect any affection or positive emotion for the person being touched. When a physician touches you as part of a physical exam, for example, you don't infer from

---

Del Prete, T. (1997). Hands off? A touchy subject. The Education Digest, 62, 59–61. Quote is from p. 59.

†*See Blum, D. (2002). Love at Goon Park: Harry Harlow and the science of affection. New York, NY: Basic Books.*

communication *LIGHT SIDE*

BATTLING AFFECTION DEPRIVATION AT CUDDLE PARTIES

Affectionate touch is so important for maintaining physical and mental well-being that many interpersonal scholars consider it to be a fundamental human need. According to research, however, a growing number of Americans now experience *affection deprivation*—that is, a significant deficit in the amount of affectionate touch they receive. Studies have found that affection deprivation is associated with a wide range of problems, from chronic pain and sleep difficulties to depression and disorders of the immune system. Unfortunately, many people who feel deprived of affection are unsure about how to address the problem.

One resource beginning to gather steam is the *cuddle party*, a group of individuals coming together under the guidance of a trained facilitator to share affectionate, nonsexual contact with each other. Most cuddle parties begin with a brief orientation in which participants introduce themselves, learn about the rules, and practice communicating about what they want and don't want from the experience. That orientation is followed by two hours of self-directed socializing and snuggling. Participants are encouraged to explore both emotional and physical connections with each other, while respecting each person's individual boundaries and not letting the interaction become romantic.

Cuddle parties started in New York in 2004 and now take place regularly across the United States and Canada. Facilitators aim to create a safe, structured environment where people can gain the benefits of affectionate touch, especially if they don't receive adequate touch in their personal lives.

FROM ME TO YOU

If the idea of cuddling with strangers at a party strikes you as odd, you're not alone. Facilitators note that many first-time attendees are nervous and unsure of what to expect. Remember that a cuddle party is only one way to experience more affectionate touch. When you find yourself feeling deprived of affection, consider spending time in contexts that offer opportunities for contact, such as at social gatherings or at your church or synagogue. Even visiting a pet shelter and sharing affection with four-legged friends can provide a much-needed boost of connection.

Sources: Floyd, K. (2014). Relational and health correlates of affection deprivation. *Western Journal of Communication, 78,* 383–403; Fortenbury, J. (2014, July 15). Fighting loneliness with cuddle parties: As Americans report feeling more isolated, some people turn to snuggling with strangers. *The Atlantic.* Retrieved March 10, 2015, from www.theatlantic.com/health/archive/2014/07/fighting-loneliness-with-cuddle-parties/373335/

her touch that she has personal feelings for you. Rather, you interpret her touch as task-oriented. Your general expectation is that caregiving touch should be limited to caregiving contexts. Although you allow a dentist to touch your teeth and gums as part of a dental exam, for example, you probably wouldn't be comfortable allowing the same kind of touch if you ran into him at an art fair.

The fact that caregiving touch is task-oriented doesn't mean it isn't beneficial. Indeed, several forms of caregiving touch have important health benefits. For instance, adolescents and adults who receive therapeutic massage show improvement in a host of medical conditions, ranging from depression and stress to asthma, diabetes, cancer, multiple sclerosis, and HIV.[69] Caregiving touch can also induce calm and relieve stress for nursing home residents, as well as patients in a hospital or clinic.[70]

POWER AND CONTROL TOUCH. Touch is sometimes used to exert power over other people's behavior. We occasionally touch people merely to suggest a certain course of behavior, as when the host of a party puts his hand on a guest's back to lead her in a certain direction. In other instances, we touch people to protect them by restricting their movement, such as when a nursing aide holds the arm of an elderly patient to help him walk without falling.

Talking Point: The acknowledgment that caregiving touch doesn't necessarily reflect positive affect for the recipient doesn't mean it *never* does. Indeed, caregiving touch is often enacted by people who have positive feelings for the targets of that touch, as in the case of adults taking care of their children or tending to the needs of their elderly parents. Caregiving touch is done in the service of a caregiving task, however, whereas affectionate touch is not.

Talking Point: Terms such as *power* and *control* are not necessarily meant to have negative connotations in this discussion. There are many legitimate reasons why we exert control over other people's behavior.

Although those behaviors involve some degree of control, they are intended to be friendly and helpful. In other cases, however, we touch people to control their behavior against their wishes. That type of touch can constitute a legitimate exercise of power, such as when police officers hold a suspect on the ground while applying handcuffs. It can also embody an illegitimate or unlawful exercise of power, such as when bullies hold an adolescent immobile to steal from him.

The use of control touch became controversial in the United States in 2010 when the Transportation Security Administration (TSA) adopted new airport passenger screening procedures requiring agents to pat down travelers in very invasive ways while searching for weapons. Some believed the searches violated passengers' privacy rights, whereas others considered them to be justified in the service of national security.

AGGRESSIVE TOUCH.   Behaviors done to inflict physical harm—such as punching, pushing, kicking, slapping, and stabbing—are forms of aggressive touch. Using touch behaviors to inflict physical harm on others almost always constitutes a criminal act. In fact, in some U.S. states, even acting as though you are going to touch someone to inflict harm, such as raising your hand as if you're about to strike, is a crime whether you actually touch the person or not. In those states, threatening to hit somebody is called "assault," and hitting the person is called "battery."

Despite such laws, incidents of violence and abuse using aggressive touch are still common, both in North America and in many societies around the world. Research indicates that although men are more likely than women to be the victims of violence at the hands of a stranger, women are more likely than men to be victimized by a close relational partner, such as a spouse.[71]

In Everyday Life: Laws in many countries, including the United States, dictate that police officers can use reasonable force to stop a crime or detain a suspect. When officers inflict unnecessary violence in the course of controlling a suspect, however, they can be prosecuted for the use of excessive force.[iv] In one notorious incident in 2014, Eric Garner died in New York City after a police officer put him in a "chokehold," a form of strangulation. Using a chokehold is prohibited by New York City Police Department policies, and the incident spurred public outrage and charges of police brutality.

[iv]For discussion of excessive force in one U.S. city, see Johnson, M. S. (2004). *Street justice: A history of police violence in New York City.* Boston, MA: Beacon Press.

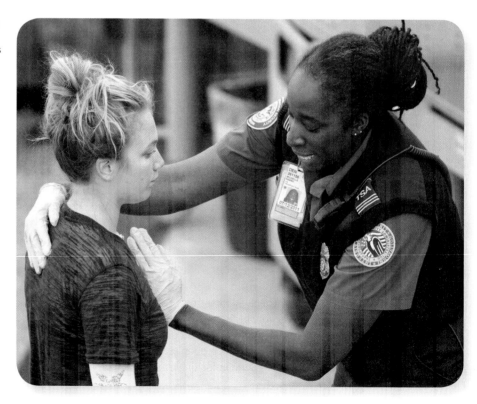

Pat downs by the Transportation Security Administration have stirred controversy. In what ways do the pat downs represent power and control touch?
© Gary C. Caskey/UPI /Landov

RITUALISTIC TOUCH. Some touches are ritualistic, meaning that we do them as part of a custom or a tradition. In North America, shaking hands is one such example: When we shake hands with people as part of a greeting ritual, we understand that the handshake does not convey any particular meaning about the relationship (the way that, say, holding hands would). In contrast, the greeting ritual in many cultures involves kissing on the lips or on the cheeks; people in those cultures would also understand those touches to be part of a ritual, not necessarily expressions of love or affection. Other ritualistic touches take place in the context of athletics. For example, basketball, wrestling, soccer, water polo, and many other sports involve body-to-body contact between players.[72] One study even found that professional basketball teams are more successful the more their players touch each other during games.[73]

Vocal Behaviors

Perhaps you have a high, breathy voice or a deep, booming voice. Maybe you usually talk very fast or quite loudly. Perhaps you have an accent that indicates where you grew up. And there may be times when you speak with a particular tone of voice to suggest that you are irritated, amused, or bored. We refer to those and other characteristics of the voice collectively as **vocalics.** We also refer to them as *paralanguage* (meaning "beside language") to indicate that they go along with the words we speak to convey meaning.

Some people are surprised to learn that the voice is a channel of nonverbal communication. After all, we speak with our voices, and spoken communication is verbal, right? That's true, but the only aspect of spoken communication that is verbal is *what we say*—the words themselves. Everything else about our voices, including the following characteristics, is nonverbal.

- *Pitch:* The pitch of the voice is an index of how high or deep it sounds. Every person's voice has an average *fundamental frequency,* which is the pitch one's voice hits the most often. On average, women's voices have a higher pitch than men's voices, and adults have deeper voices than children.

- *Inflection:* The inflection in the voice refers to the variation in its pitch. Voices that have a great deal of inflection are usually described as very expressive; those with little inflection are said to be monotone.[74]

- *Volume:* Volume is an index of how loud or quiet one's voice is. Most of us alter our vocal volume as the social context demands, such as by speaking quietly in a library and more loudly at a crowded reception. Everyone's voice also has an *average volume,* meaning that some people generally speak more loudly than others.

- *Rate:* The average adult speaks at a rate of approximately 150 words per minute,[75] but an individual might speak faster when excited or slower when unsure of himself or herself.

- *Filler words:* Filler words are nonword sounds such as "umm" or "er" that many people use to fill the silence during pauses while they're speaking. If we have to pause while speaking—say, to remember the word we want to use or the fact we want to describe—we can use filler words during the pause to indicate that we intend to continue speaking.

- *Pronunciation:* Pronunciation reflects how correctly a person combines vowel and consonant sounds to say a word. For example, how would you pronounce the word

In Everyday Life: When speaking to others who don't understand their language, some people tend to speak more loudly than usual. That occurs out of frustration at not being understood, but of course it doesn't enhance comprehension.

vocalics Characteristics of the voice that convey meaning in communication; also referred to as *paralanguage.*

Talking Point: In 1995, Canadian Sean Shannon set the record as World's Fastest Talker by reciting a 260-word soliloquy in 23.8 seconds, which translates to over 10.92 words per second, or over 655 words per minute. This is more than four times the speaking rate of the average adult.

Focus on Scholarship: Research suggests that children acquire their accents from their friends and classmates more than from their parents.[v] Suppose that a couple lives in Brooklyn but moves to Dallas and then has children. You might think the children would speak with a Brooklyn accent, because they would hear their parents' accent in the home while they were acquiring language. Instead, the children are more likely to acquire the accent of their peers—a southern U.S. accent.

[v]Vandell, D. L. (2000). Parents, peer groups, and other socializing influences. *Developmental Psychology, 36,* 699–710.

Focus on Scholarship: Certain odors, particularly food odors, also evoke sexual arousal. Studies by the Smell and Taste Treatment and Research Foundation found that men had the greatest sexual arousal when smelling a combination of lavender and pumpkin pie, whereas the greatest sexual arousal for women was caused by a combination of cucumber and Good & Plenty candy.[vi]

[vi]Hirsch, A. R. (1998). Scent and sexual arousal: Could fragrance help relieve sexual dysfunction? *Medical Aspects of Human Sexuality, 1,* 9–12.

Focus on Scholarship: Sexual orientation also plays a role in the bodily scents we find attractive. A study in which participants rated the pleasantness of underarm perspiration found that gay men strongly preferred the odor of other gay men. In contrast, lesbians preferred the scent of heterosexual men and women or other lesbians. These judgments were based only on smell; participants did not know the identity of the person whose scents they were smelling.[vii]

[vii]Martins, Y., Preti, G., Crabtree, C. R., Runyan, T., Vainius, A. A., & Wysocki, C. J. (2005). Preference for human body odors is influenced by gender and sexual orientation. *Psychological Science, 16,* 694–701.

olfactics The study of the sense of smell.

© Reg Charity /Corbis Photography/Veer, RF

victuals? Although it looks as though it should be pronounced VIK-TULES, its correct pronunciation is VITTLES.

- *Articulation:* Articulation, or *enunciation,* refers to how clearly one speaks. People who mumble or who speak with their mouth full demonstrate poor articulation. In contrast, people whose words are clear and easily understandable are good articulators.

- *Accent:* An accent is a pattern of pronouncing vowel and consonant sounds that is representative of a particular language or geographic area. Everyone speaks with an accent—even you—although individuals typically notice only those accents that are different from theirs.

- *Silence:* Silence is the absence of sound. We frequently use silence to convey meaning in conversations.[76] For instance, we often become silent when we are unsure how to respond to a question or when we have said as much as we wish to about a topic. We might also give someone the "silent treatment," ignoring him or her to convey defiance or disdain.[77] Finally, we can use silence to indicate that we do not wish to answer a question, perhaps to avoid embarrassment or offense.[78]

The Use of Smell

Of all the channels of nonverbal behavior, you might have the hardest time figuring out what smell has to do with human communication. It turns out that your sense of smell, called **olfactics,** operates subtly but powerfully to influence your reactions to others. In fact, two phenomena that are central to the human experience and to communication—memory and sexual attraction—are profoundly affected and regulated by smell.

MEMORIES. Smells can affect our communication behavior by influencing our memories and moods. Have you ever smelled a particular scent—maybe a certain food or cologne—and instantly remembered a specific person, event, or place? Maybe the aroma of banana bread makes you think of your grandmother's kitchen, or the odor of motor oil reminds you of your uncle who used to work on cars. Those connections are examples of *olfactic association,* the tendency of odors to bring to mind specific memories. Why do olfactic associations matter for communication? It happens that memories often come with specific emotions, so when a smell reminds us of a particular person or place, it has the potential to affect our mood and behavior.

SEXUAL ATTRACTION. Smell also affects our communication by playing a role in determining to whom we are sexually attracted. Although you may think of sexual attraction as being driven mostly by visual cues—whether you think an individual *looks* attractive—in fact, your judgments about a person's sexual attractiveness are strongly affected by the way he or she smells to you. More specifically, research tells us that when we are looking for opposite-sex romantic partners, we are drawn to people whose natural body scent is the most different from our own. Why?

If two people have very similar scents, scientists have determined that their genes are also very similar, and that similarity can increase the probability of their producing genetically abnormal children. People produce much healthier children when they mate with partners who are genetically dissimilar to them. It happens that a person's natural body scent sends a signal to your brain that tells you how similar his or her genes are to yours. The more dissimilar a person's body odor is to yours, therefore, the more sexually attractive you will instinctively judge that individual to be.

Of course, not all instances of sexual attraction coincide with the desire to reproduce. Nonetheless, nature has connected smell to sexual attraction to help motivate healthy mate choices when procreation is our goal. We don't sniff out a person's scent profile consciously, however.

The Use of Space

When we interact socially, we constantly negotiate our use of space. That behavior becomes particularly apparent when our personal space is limited. Think of being in a crowded elevator or on a full airplane. Why do so many of us find such situations to be uncomfortable? The scientific study of spatial use, known as **proxemics,** explains that we each have a preferred amount of personal space that we carry like an invisible bubble around us. How much personal space each of us prefers depends on our temperament, the type of situation we're in, and how well we know the people around us.

Anthropologist Edward T. Hall discovered that in Western cultures, people use four *spatial zones,* or levels of personal distance, when interacting with one another.[79] **Intimate distance,** which ranges from 0 to approximately 1½ feet, is the zone we willingly occupy with only our closest and most intimate friends, family members, and romantic partners. With other friends and relatives, we typically maintain a **personal distance,** which Hall defined as extending from 1½ to about 4 feet. With customers, casual acquaintances, and others whom we don't know very well, we occupy a **social distance.** That ranges from about 4 to 12 feet and conveys more formal, impersonal interaction. Finally, **public distance** typically applies when someone is giving a speech

proxemics The study of spatial use.

intimate distance The distance most people in Western cultures maintain with intimate partners; ranges from 0 to 1½ feet.

personal distance The distance most people in Western cultures maintain with friends and relatives; ranges from 1½ to 4 feet.

social distance The distance most people in Western cultures maintain with casual acquaintances; ranges from 4 to 12 feet.

public distance The distance most people in Western cultures maintain with public figures during a performance; ranges from 12 to 25 feet or more.

Intimate zone	Personal zone	Social zone	Public zone
0–18 inches	18 inches to 4 feet	4–12 feet	More than 12 feet

FIGURE 3 Hall's Four Spatial Zones: Edward T. Hall suggested that people observe four zones of space with each other: an intimate zone, a personal zone, a social zone, and a public zone. © Andres Rodriguez/Alamy, RF, © Sam Edwards/AGE Fotostock, RF, © Image Source/ Punchstock, RF, © Brzozowska/Getty Images, RF, © SuperStock, RF

or performing in front of a large audience. Public distances are usually 12 to 25 feet or greater, depending on the circumstance.

In interpersonal interaction, one factor that influences physical proximity is a person's disability status. Many people who do not have physical disabilities stand or sit farther away from individuals with physical disabilities than they do from others. In fact, communication scholars Dawn and Charles Braithwaite have suggested that people often shy away from interacting with persons with disabilities in the same way they tend to avoid people from other cultures.[80] Some researchers think that happens because people are inherently cautious around anyone they think of as different from themselves.[81]

Physical Appearance

Whether we intend to or not, we make all sorts of judgments about people on the basis of how they look. In particular, we have a strong predisposition to attribute positive qualities to physically attractive people, a tendency researchers refer to as the **halo effect.** In other words, when a person *looks* good, most of us subconsciously assume that he or she *is* good. Indeed, research has shown that we think attractive people are friendlier, more competent, and more socially skilled than less attractive people.[82]

Those perceptions translate into some real advantages for attractiveness. For instance, attractive people have higher self-esteem and date more frequently than less attractive people.[83] We are also nicer and more cooperative toward attractive people and more lenient toward attractive criminal defendants.[84] So if it seems at times that good-looking people get all the breaks, research tells us that is often the case. Much as we may like to claim otherwise, most of us are strongly influenced by physical appearance when making assessments about other people.

That preference for beauty has a dark side, however. Because physical attractiveness is so highly valued, some people go to dangerous extremes to achieve it. In particular, an alarming number of people suffer from eating disorders. Those with *anorexia nervosa* pursue thinness relentlessly, through excessive dieting and exercise, self-induced vomiting, and the abuse of laxatives or diuretics. *Bulimia nervosa* is characterized by bingeing on large quantities of food and then compensating for overeating by vomiting or abusing laxatives. Finally, *binge eating disorder* causes people to experience episodes of excessive eating in which they feel a lack of self-control. All three disorders are associated with substantial health risks.[85]

The Use of Time

Chronemics is the way people use time. You might not immediately think of time usage as nonverbal behavior, but the way we give (or refuse to give) our time to others can send them important messages about the way we feel about them. Because most of us spend our time on the people and activities that matter to us, for instance, the way we use time communicates messages about what we value. When we give our time to others, we imply that we value those people.

Our use of time also sends messages about power. When you go to see someone who is in a position of power over you, such as your supervisor, it is not uncommon to be kept waiting. However, you would probably consider it bad form to make a more powerful person wait for you. Indeed, the rule seems to be that the time of powerful people is more valuable than the time of less powerful people.

halo effect The tendency to attribute positive qualities to physically attractive people.

[viii]Snyder, M., Tanke, E. D., & Berscheid, E. (1977). Social perception and interpersonal behavior: On the self-fulfilling nature of social stereotypes. *Journal of Experimental Social Psychology, 35*, 656–666.

chronemics The use of time.

The Use of Artifacts

Each of us has certain physical environments that we inhabit and control, such as a house or an apartment, a residence-hall room, and an office. **Artifacts** are the objects and visual features within an environment that reflect who we are and what we like. One office you routinely visit, for instance, may be plush and opulent, with an oak desk, leather furniture, soft lighting, and expensive paintings on the walls. Another office may be plain and basic, featuring metal desks and chairs, fluorescent lighting, and bare walls. What messages might those different artifacts convey about the occupants of those two offices?

The way we place artifacts such as furniture within an environment can facilitate or inhibit interpersonal interaction. For example, teachers at Phillips Exeter Academy, a private preparatory school in New Hampshire, practice the "Harkness method" of teaching, which involves arranging up to 12 students and a teacher around an oval table. That arrangement is meant to diminish the separation between students and teachers, encouraging everyone to interact in an open, engaging way. In contrast, people who wish to discourage conversation in their offices or work environments might place their desks so that their back is to others.

The color of our environments can also influence nonverbal behavior by affecting our mood and disposition.[86] Specifically, "warm" colors such as red, orange, and yellow tend to be arousing, whereas "cool" colors such as blues and greens have calming effects.[87] Some researchers have suggested that those associations may have been formed early in human history, when individuals associated blues and greens with nature and nighttime—and therefore with being passive—and bright colors with sunshine and daytime—and therefore with being active.[88]

> **artifact** An object or a visual feature of an environment with communicative value.

Artifacts reflect who we are and what we like. What messages would you infer about the person who resides in this room? © *Tribune Content Agency LLC / Alamy*

> **Talking Point:** One reason why the use of time carries messages of value is that, at least in some cultures, we consider time to be a tangible and finite commodity similar to money. That is why we talk about "spending time," "saving time," "making time," "investing time," and "wasting time." In the same way we spend money on what we value, we spend time on what we value.

AT A GLANCE

Ten Channels of Nonverbal Communication

Facial Displays	Important for identity, attraction, and emotion
Eye Behaviors	Communicative value of eye contact and pupil size
Movement and Gestures	Serve as emblems, illustrators, affect displays, regulators, and adaptors
Touch Behaviors	Used for conveying affection, caregiving, power and control, aggression, and ritual
Vocal Behaviors	Voice variations in pitch, inflection, volume, rate, use of filler words, pronunciation, articulation, accent, and silence
Use of Smell	Important for memory and sexual attraction
Use of Space	Four spatial distances: intimate, personal, social, and public
Physical Appearance	Assumption that attractive people have other positive qualities (halo effect)
Use of Time	Sends messages of value and power
Use of Artifacts	Includes selection and placement of objects, use of light, and use of color

Talking Point: People's color preferences are remarkably consistent. According to a meta-analysis of studies involving more than 21,000 participants, the preferred color is blue, followed (in order) by red, green, purple, orange, and yellow. This rank-ordering of color preferences is independent of ethnicity or sex.[ix] Some researchers have suggested that we prefer blue because of the calmness we associate with it.[x]

[ix]Eysenck, H. J. (1981). Aesthetic preferences and individual differences. In D. O'Hare (Ed.), *Psychology and the arts* (pp. 76–101). Atlantic Highlands, NJ: Humanities Press.

[x]Crozier, W. R. (1999). The meanings of colour: Preferences among hues. *Pigment and Resin Technology, 28,* 6–14.

Because the ten channels by which we communicate with others nonverbally encompass almost all our senses, nonverbal communication is a truly engaging experience. The "At a Glance" box summarizes those nonverbal channels. However, not everyone enacts nonverbal behavior in the same ways. As we'll see in the next section, culture and sex are both powerful influences on nonverbal communication styles.

LEARN IT What are three primary communicative functions of the face? How is eye behavior affected by culture? When is a gesture an emblem? Why is touch the most important sense for survival? Which aspects of the voice are verbal and which are nonverbal? How does smell affect memory and sexual attraction? What are Hall's four spatial zones? What is the halo effect? How does the use of time communicate messages about value? What is an artifact?

APPLY IT Dress in conservative business attire, and visit a restaurant, a department store, a bank, or some other business. Take note of how quickly you are helped by the employees and how friendly and eager they are to serve you. Now repeat the experiment in casual or shabby clothing. What differences do you notice in other people's behaviors toward you? What differences do you notice in your own behavior?

REFLECT ON IT What olfactic associations do you have? Why do you think the halo effect is so powerful?

3 Culture, Sex, and Nonverbal Communication

Suppose you've won an Olympic gold medal. As you stand atop the podium listening to your national anthem, with your friends and family beaming with pride from the stands, imagine the immense joy you would feel. In which nonverbal behaviors would you likely be engaged? How would you stand? What expression would be on your face? What gestures might you make?

It's easy to imagine that everyone would behave the same way you would in that situation. Research tells us, however, that our ways of communicating nonverbally are affected not only by our individual emotions and the demands of the situation but also by two major influences on nonverbal communication: culture and sex.

Culture Influences Nonverbal Communication

Talking Point: Another example of an emblem gesture whose meaning varies by culture is the head nod. Although it signifies yes in the United States, it signifies no in Bulgaria and Greece.

Many Americans who tune in to the Olympic Games on TV are surprised by certain of the nonverbal behaviors of athletes from different cultures. With regard to greeting behaviors, for example, foreign athletes may stand closer to—or farther from—one another than is typical in U.S. culture. The reason is that those and many other nonverbal behaviors are shaped by the cultural practices with which people are raised.

Consider these many ways in which culture influences nonverbal communication:

- *Emblems:* The specific messages that an emblem symbolizes often vary by culture. The "come here" gesture commonly used in the United States means "goodbye" in China, Italy, and Colombia.[89] Gestures such as A-OK, thumbs up, and crossed fingers have sexual or obscene meanings in many parts of the world.[90]

- *Affect displays:* Some displays of affect (emotion) are specific to certain cultures. In China, for example, women express emotional satisfaction by holding their fingertips over their closed mouths. Similarly, a man in Uruguay will hold his fists together and turn them in opposite directions, as if wringing out a wet cloth, to express anger.

- *Personal distance:* People from Arab countries generally converse with each other at closer distances than do U.S. Americans.[91] One study found that because of differences in their preferred conversational distance, Arab college students regarded those from the United States as aloof, whereas the American students regarded the Arab students as overbearing.[92]

- *Eye contact:* In many Western cultures, direct eye contact signifies that someone is sincere, trustworthy, and authoritative, whereas the lack of eye contact elicits negative evaluations from others.[93] In comparison, some Asian, Latin American, and Middle Eastern cultures emphasize the lack of eye contact as a sign of deference or respect for authority.[94]

- *Facial displays of emotion:* Decades of research indicate that people around the world express emotions—particularly primary emotions such as happiness, sadness, fear, anger, surprise, and disgust—in highly similar ways.[95] What tends to differ across cultures is how expressive people are of emotion, with those in individualistic cultures routinely being more emotionally expressive than those in collectivistic cultures.[96]

- *Greeting behavior:* People in Western countries typically greet social acquaintances with a handshake, whereas people in Mediterranean countries usually kiss each other on both cheeks. In Asian countries, it is common to greet others by bowing, with the longest and lowest bows reserved for the most respected individuals.[97]

- *Time orientations:* As you'll recall from the Culture and Gender chapter, the uses of time vary from culture to culture. Some cultures—including the United States, Canada, Finland, Great Britain, and Germany—are *monochronic,* meaning that they see time as a tangible commodity, expect events to begin "on time," and dislike having their time wasted.[98] Other cultures—such as France, Brazil, Mexico, and Saudi Arabia—are *polychronic,* meaning they see time as flexible and diffused and don't necessarily expect punctuality.[99]

- *Haptics:* People in **high-contact cultures,** which include France, Mexico, and Greece, touch each other significantly more often than do people in **low-contact cultures,** such as Japan, Sweden, and Finland.[100] High-contact cultures are also characterized by less personal space than low-contact cultures. Research indicates that the United States is most accurately classified as a *medium-contact culture.*[101]

- *Vocalics:* Besides their readily noticeable differences in accents, cultures also differ in their use of filler words.[102] Although "umm" and "er" are common filler words for English speakers, Chinese speakers often say "zhege zhege zhege"—which translates to "this this this"—as filler words.

In Everyday Life: It's helpful to remember that not all societies are equally expressive of emotion. It would be easy to mistake another's relative lack of emotional expression as indifference when none was intended.

high-contact culture
A culture in which people touch frequently and maintain little personal distance with one another.

low-contact culture
A culture in which people touch infrequently and maintain relatively high levels of personal distance with one another.

Parents around the world speak babytalk to their infants.
© commerceandculturestock/ Moment/Getty Images, RF

Importantly, not *every* nonverbal behavior differs by culture. People around the world interpret a laugh as an expression of joy.[103] Parents in every known culture speak *babytalk*—soft, high-pitched vocal tones and highly simplified language—to their infants.[104] The fact that two people come from different cultures doesn't mean they can't communicate with each other nonverbally. It simply means they should be aware of the many ways in which their cultural background is influencing how they do so.

Sex Influences Nonverbal Communication

A second major influence on nonverbal communication is a person's sex. Women and men sometimes react with different nonverbal behaviors—or react to different degrees—to the same situation.

One research explanation for why sex affects nonverbal behavior is that beginning in early childhood, boys and girls are socialized to communicate in gender-specific ways (masculine for boys, feminine for girls).[105] Another explanation is that anatomical and physiological differences between the sexes cause them to behave in different ways.[106] Both possibilities have received extensive support from research, but not always for the same behaviors. In other words, sex differences in some nonverbal behaviors appear to be more influenced by socialization than biology, whereas others are more affected by biology than socialization.

No matter the reason, sex influences several forms of nonverbal communication, including

- *Emotional expressiveness:* Several studies document that women are more expressive than men with respect to a variety of emotional states, including joy,[107] affection,[108] fear,[109] and shame.[110] Some research indicates that men are more expressive than women of anger,[111] although other studies have found that women and men simply express anger in different ways.[112]

- *Eye contact:* When communicating with others of their same sex, women engage in more eye contact than do men,[113] a difference that has been demonstrated in both the United States and Japan.[114] In fact, female pairs use higher amounts of gaze than do male pairs when speaking, while listening, and even during silence.[115] Research indicates that male–female pairs are similar to female–female pairs in terms of eye contact.[116]

- *Personal space:* In comparison to men, women are approached more closely, give way more readily to others, stand and sit closer to each other, and tolerate more violations of their personal space.[117] In opposite-sex interactions, men are also more likely to violate women's personal space than women are to violate men's.[118]

- *Vocalics:* On average, men's voices have a lower average pitch than do women's. The primary reason why is that men have a larger voice box and longer vocal cords—which produce the sound of the voice—than women do, as a result of physiological changes that occur during puberty.[119] Research indicates that men also use more filler words and pauses while speaking than do women.[120]

 **got skills?**   **ADAPTING TO SEX DIFFERENCES**

Adapt to the nonverbal style of the opposite sex.

WHAT?
Learn to adapt to the nonverbal communication style of the other sex.

WHY?
To communicate more effectively and empathically with members of the other sex.

HOW?
1. With a same-sex friend, role-play an interaction in which the two of you behave verbally like your own sex but act nonverbally as though you are of the other sex.
2. After the interaction, discuss between yourselves what you found challenging—even uncomfortable—about the task. Was it easy to adapt your behaviors?

TRY!
1. Afterward, in a small mixed-sex group of friends or classmates, practice adapting your nonverbal behaviors as best you can to those of the other sex. Having spent time trying to behave nonverbally like the other sex may make that task easier to do.
2. In two paragraphs, explain how you dealt with the challenges of adapting to the nonverbal behavior of the other sex. Indicate what would make that experience easier in the future.

CONSIDER: *Why is nonverbal adaptation advantageous?*

- *Touch:* Among adults, men are more likely to touch women than women are to touch men, unless the touch is occurring as part of a greeting (such as a handshake).[121] In same-sex pairs, however, women touch each other more than men do, although that sex difference is smaller in close friendships than among acquaintances.[122]
- *Appearance:* Sex differences in appearance are also influenced by culture. Moreover, women and men typically adorn themselves in notably different ways. In Western cultures, for example, cosmetic use is significantly more common for women than for men.[123] Also, women and men usually wear different styles of clothing and jewelry and adopt different hairstyles, and those conventions further accentuate the differences in their appearance.

One of the most effective ways to bridge the gap when communicating with people of the other sex is to learn to adapt to their nonverbal behavior. Adapting means altering our own behavior to be more in line with theirs. Adaptation can be a highly effective tactic for communicating across the gender divide, but it is a skill that requires practice. Check out "Got Skills?" to learn more.

Just as not every nonverbal behavior varies with culture, not every nonverbal behavior differs by sex. Perhaps more important is that, as communication scientist Kathryn Dindia has suggested, sex differences, even when present, aren't always substantial—not nearly as significant as popular writer John Gray proposed (see the Culture and Gender chapter).

LEARN IT What are the differences between high-contact and low-contact cultures? Why do men's voices have a lower average pitch than women's voices?

APPLY IT Identify an opportunity at your school or in your community to interact with a group of people whose cultural background is markedly different from yours. Beforehand, learn what you can about the nonverbal behaviors that are common in that culture, and practice those behaviors when you interact with those people. Afterward, write a short journal entry describing what you learned about nonverbal communication within that cultural community.

REFLECT ON IT When do you feel uncomfortable communicating with people from other cultures? Why do you think sex differences in communication are so commonly discussed in popular culture?

4 Improving Your Nonverbal Communication Skills

In the television comedy series *The Office,* actor Steve Carell played Michael Scott, a socially awkward regional manager of a paper distribution company. In conversations with employees and customers, Scott often had difficulty expressing his emotions, using inappropriate humor to mask feelings of insecurity or inadequacy. At the same time, he frequently failed to notice when other people react negatively to his communication style. Although he tried to get others to like him and even came across as likable, he was not a particularly skilled nonverbal communicator. Michael Scott would be well advised to read this section, in which we explore ways of improving three fundamental communication skills: interpreting nonverbal communication, expressing messages nonverbally, and managing nonverbal communication in electronically mediated contexts.

Interpreting Nonverbal Communication

We've seen that people use nonverbal communication to express many types of messages, including messages related to emotions and attitudes, power and dominance, persuasion, and deception. An important skill for communicators, therefore, is the ability to decode, or interpret, other people's nonverbal behaviors. That ability requires two separate but interrelated skills: being sensitive to nonverbal messages and deciphering their meaning.

BE SENSITIVE TO NONVERBAL MESSAGES.   When your daughter grimaces after learning you're having broccoli for dinner or your son has an excited tone in his voice when he describes his last fencing bout, do you notice those nonverbal emotion cues? When a competitor at work intentionally keeps you waiting for an appointment or seems unusually tense during your conversation, do you pick up on those potential signs of dominance or deception?

Sensitivity to such nonverbal behaviors is important because we can't interpret messages unless we first take note of them. Although research indicates that some people are more nonverbally sensitive by nature than others, you may be able to increase your

Focus on Scholarship: The specific ability to decipher another person's messages of emotion is called *empathic accuracy.* Research indicates that women are, on average, better at empathic accuracy than are men.[xii]

[xii]Hodges, S. D., Lewis, K. L., & Ickes, W. (2015). The matter of other minds: Empathic accuracy and the factors that influence it. In M. Mikulincer, P. R. Shaver, J. A. Simpson, & J. F. Dovidio (Eds.), *APA handbook of personality and social psychology* (vol. 3, pp. 319–348). Washington, DC: American Psychological Association.

nonverbal sensitivity through mindful awareness.[124] When you're interacting with someone, even online, try these approaches:

- Remind yourself that as much as two-thirds of the person's communication is being conveyed through nonverbal behaviors. It's useful to interpret his or her words, but remember that nonverbal communication is often more important.

- Pay particular attention to facial expressions for signs of what he or she is feeling. Remember that the face communicates more emotion than other nonverbal channels do.

- Take note of his or her tone of voice and body movements, because those behaviors are particularly relevant for signaling dominance and deception.

To the extent that you can remind yourself of these principles when you are interacting with others, you may be able to increase your nonverbal sensitivity.

DECIPHER THE MEANING OF NONVERBAL MESSAGES.   Nonverbal messages sometimes carry multiple meanings. If you notice a young man smiling, for instance, it might mean he's happy. However, it might also mean that he's persuading a customer to make a purchase or flirting with his attractive new neighbor.[125] If you hear him speaking loudly, it might mean he's excited, or it might mean he's talking with someone who's hard of hearing.

An essential part of interpretation, therefore, is deciphering the meaning of the nonverbal behaviors exhibited by others. Accurately deciphering a nonverbal behavior means taking it to mean what the sender intended it to mean.[126] Suppose that while you are describing your grandmother's failing health to your friend Vanessa, she squeezes your hand to convey her support. If you take her behavior as a gesture of support, then you have accurately deciphered her nonverbal message. If you interpret it to mean she's interested in you romantically, however, then you have deciphered her message inaccurately.

To improve your skill at deciphering nonverbal messages, try the following strategies:

- *Be aware of the situation.* Consider both the social situation a person is in and what other nonverbal behaviors he or she is enacting. If you notice a man crying, for instance, your first instinct might be to conclude that he's sad. Perhaps you also notice, however, that he is surrounded by smiling friends and relatives who are hugging him and patting him on the back. You even hear him laugh, although tears are running down his face. When you take these additional pieces of information into consideration, you might take his crying to mean that he is happy or relieved rather than sad.

Talking Point: In a different social context, Vanessa's behavior might have the romantic connotation. This illustrates the importance of taking the context into consideration when assigning meaning to a nonverbal behavior.

Keep cultural differences in mind when you interpret nonverbal behavior. Although kissing often conveys romantic feelings in Western cultures, it is a common component of routine social greetings in many parts of the world. © *Robert Harding Library*

got skills?

GENERATING INTERPRETATIONS FOR NONVERBAL BEHAVIORS

Consider how you make sense of other people's nonverbal communication.

WHAT?
Learn to take broad account of the possible interpretations of a nonverbal behavior.

WHY?
To interpret nonverbal communication more accurately.

HOW?
1. When you encounter a nonverbal behavior— say, a gesture or a facial expression—take note of your initial interpretation of it. What do you think it means?
2. Generate at least three other interpretations of the behavior that are different from your initial interpretation. Notice what is occurring in the environment and social context. Take note of other nonverbal behaviors the person is enacting and any verbal statements he or she makes. Consider the person's background, culture, and gender. Look for relevant cues that can help you interpret the behavior differently than you originally did.

TRY!
1. Spend time people watching in a public place. When you notice a nonverbal behavior, write down your initial interpretation of it. Then examine the situation and generate at least three additional interpretations.
2. For each interpretation, write down the clues that supported that interpretation. At the end, write a detailed paragraph describing the behavior and all the pieces of evidence you took into account when forming your interpretations of it.

CONSIDER: *How challenging is it to question your initial interpretation of someone's behavior?*

- *Keep culture in mind.* Remember that cultural differences sometimes influence the meaning of a nonverbal message. That observation appears to be particularly true for gestures and eye behaviors. We've seen, for instance, that using the thumbs-up gesture or maintaining eye contact while talking with someone can have different meanings in different cultures. The more you learn about cultural variation in nonverbal behaviors, the more accurately you'll be able to decipher those behaviors.

- *Ask for clarification.* When you're unsure of how accurately you've deciphered a person's nonverbal message, consider asking the person. Let's say you're describing a new product to a client, and her facial expression suggests confusion. Instead of assuming you've deciphered her expression accurately, you might ask her, "Did my description make sense?" If she replies that she found it confusing, then you can explain the product again using simpler language.

Generating and considering more than one possible interpretation of a nonverbal behavior is a skill you can practice. For starters, try out the "Got Skills?" exercise. Practicing your sensitivity and deciphering skills should help you to improve your ability to interpret the meaning of nonverbal behaviors.[127]

Expressing Nonverbal Messages

Some of us are good at interpreting nonverbal behaviors but not particularly good at expressing ourselves nonverbally. Skill in expressing nonverbal messages is valuable for the same reason that interpretation skill is: because people communicate more information nonverbally than verbally. If you're skilled at expressing nonverbal messages, you'll therefore be able to communicate with other people more effectively and more efficiently than someone who is less skilled.

Just as with interpretation skills, some people are naturally more expressive, charismatic, and outgoing than others.[128] To improve your own skill at expressing nonverbal messages, try the following:

- *Learn from others.* Spend time with highly expressive people. Some researchers have suggested that we can learn how to become more nonverbally expressive by being around individuals who are extroverted and charismatic.[129] Research also suggests that certain professions attract highly expressive people. These professions include teachers and lecturers, actors and singers, politicians, salespeople, diplomats, customer service representatives, counselors and therapists, and members of the clergy.[130] To perform effectively in any of those professions, an individual must be able to communicate clearly and competently with others. Being nonverbally expressive is a key component of competent communication.

- *Practice being expressive.* Take part in games and activities that exercise your nonverbal expression skills. A good example is charades, a popular game in which you act out a word or a phrase without speaking while members of your team try to guess the word based on your depiction. Because success in charades depends on your ability to depict your word or phrase nonverbally, this game can be a good exercise of your expression skill. Another activity that can improve your nonverbal expression skills is role playing, which involves acting out the roles of characters in a specific situation the way you would if you were actually in that situation.

To become skilled at conveying nonverbal messages, you need to do more than simply be expressive. You also must learn to express yourself using nonverbal behaviors that other people can interpret accurately. Spending time with people who are skilled at nonverbal expression may help you learn or improve this ability. Similarly, taking part in activities such as charades and role playing can provide you with an opportunity to exercise your skills.

Managing Nonverbal Behavior in Electronically Mediated Communication

As important as nonverbal communication is in face-to-face contexts, it can be even more critical when you are interacting with others in electronically mediated ways, such as by videoconferencing or by sharing texts and instant messages. That's because electronically mediated forms of communication restrict the number of nonverbal channels to which people have access. As a result, the channels that *are* accessible take on greater importance. To make positive impressions on others, it therefore pays to adapt your nonverbal behavior to electronically mediated contexts. Two ways to do so are to manage visual and vocal cues during video chats and to express emotions clearly in text.

CONNECT: Learning Resources in SmartBook provide additional hints and explanations to help break down complex topics and reach students with different learning styles.

Talking Point: Being expressive doesn't necessarily mean being ostentatious. People in professions such as counseling or the ministry may be fairly reserved in their personality but still very expressive nonverbally.

In Everyday Life: Role playing doesn't have to be formal; we can also role-play during conversations with others, when we enact imagined interactions or take on the perspective of others.

© Noel Hendrickson/Masterfile/Corbis

**ATTEND TO VISUAL AND VOCAL CUES WHILE VIDEOCON-
FERENCING** Videoconferencing applications such as Skype, WebEx, and FaceTime allow you to see and hear users in other locations while speaking with them online. Although many people use these technologies to keep in touch with relatives and friends, many businesses also use them to host virtual meetings or conduct job interviews. Because these programs allow the exchange of both visual and vocal cues, it helps to keep certain considerations in mind:

- When planning a conversation, find a location with as little background noise as possible so that your conversational partners can hear you clearly. Make sure you are using a computer or smartphone with a reliable Internet connection.

- Check out the other person's visual view of you before the conversation starts. That's especially important if the conversation is of a professional nature. You might use the camera feature on your computer or arrange a video chat with a friend beforehand so that you can see how you look and sound. Pay attention to how the light hits your face, so that you won't look washed out or have dark shadows cast on you.

- During a conversation, sit close enough to your computer or smartphone camera that your face and upper body will take up most of the screen. That helps the other party to focus on you, rather than on your surroundings.

- Be sure the other person won't see anything in your environment that you don't want seen. As you view yourself on screen, look at everything behind you, and make sure there are no inappropriate photos or other objects that would attract negative attention. In addition, make sure your background isn't especially cluttered or distracting.

- During your conversation, remind yourself to *look at your camera* most of the time, especially while listening. Try not to stare at the image of the other person or the image of yourself. Looking at your camera may feel unnatural to you. It will appear natural to the other party, however, because you will appear to be looking at him or her.

- When you are listening rather than speaking, pay attention to the other person's facial expressions, gestures, and body movement. These are often valuable clues as to what someone is thinking or feeling, so attending to these clues can help you make the most of your video chat experience.

Attending to how you look and sound during a video chat will help you make a positive impression on others. Take a look at the "Assess Your Skills" box to reflect on and evaluate your preparations for a successful video chat.

EXPRESS EMOTION IN TEXT-BASED COMMUNICATION Many forms of electronically mediated communication—such as text messaging, instant messaging, e-mailing, and tweeting—rely heavily on the use of text. That can limit your ability to convey emotion and increase the odds that others will misunderstand you. These tips can help you express yourself more clearly:

- Use emoticons and emoji to convey appropriate emotion. Text-based messages can be easy to misinterpret because the same words can have more than one meaning. That's especially true when you're sending a sarcastic message, as a New York

assess your skills | SHARPENING YOUR VIDEOCONFERENCING SKILLS

Successful video chats—especially for professional conversations such as a job interview—require attention to a variety of issues. Are you prepared for success? Indicate your level of agreement with each of the following statements on a scale of 1 to 7, where 1 means you strongly disagree and 7 means you strongly agree.

Before an important video chat, I...

1. _____ Make sure I'm in an environment where I won't be interrupted.
2. _____ Ensure that there is proper lighting on my face, without distracting glare or shadows.
3. _____ Make certain I'm in an environment where I can minimize background noise.
4. _____ Video chat with a friend to make sure my voice is heard clearly.
5. _____ Ensure that there is nothing visible behind me that I would not want the other party to see.
6. _____ Give the other party my e-mail address or telephone number in case our video chat gets disconnected.
7. _____ Practice looking at my web camera, instead of at my own image.

When you're finished, add up your scores. Your total should range from 7 to 49.

- Between 35 and 49: You are already quite skillful at preparing for successful video chats.
- Between 21 and 34: You have moderate skill in videoconferencing; with additional practice, you can improve your abilities.
- Between 7 and 20: You can especially benefit from the guidance provided in this chapter for improving your videoconferencing experience.

teacher discovered in 2014 when he texted his wife asking her to "call in a bomb threat" to the school so he could escape a boring meeting.[131] Missing the "haha" he sent later, she called police to report a bomb threat at the school. The teacher might have averted the misunderstanding by using an emoticon or emoji showing a wink to indicate that his statement was intended as sarcasm.

- Avoid addressing sensitive issues in a text-based message. In a study of young adults, family therapist Lori Schade and her colleagues discovered that using text messages to address a conflict or apologize for a transgression had a tendency to harm people's relationships.[132] The researchers found that expressing positive emotions via text was beneficial, but they recommend addressing emotionally negative issues face-to-face.

- Use punctuation to indicate your emotional state. The informality of texting can encourage people to forego punctuation marks—such as periods, question marks, and exclamation points—that can clarify a sender's meaning and mood. According to one study, receivers of text messages and instant messages make inferences about a sender's emotional state by his or her use of punctuation.[133] For instance, messages with a period at the end—such as "I am fine."—were perceived as assertive or aggressive, whereas those with ellipses—such as "I am fine. . ."—were seen as more passive and calm.

Many of us pay close attention to our nonverbal behavior while communicating with others face-to-face. When we shift to electronically mediated contexts, however, it can be easy to overlook the nonverbal channels that influence the quality of our messages. Competent interpersonal communicators remember that virtually all forms of communication have a nonverbal dimension, and they manage those dimensions strategically to create positive impressions.

In the IM: You can now access the end-of-chapter Discussion Questions and the Research Library in the Instructor's Manual for each chapter.

LEARN IT What is the difference between being sensitive to a nonverbal message and deciphering its meaning? How can you express emotion in a text message?

APPLY IT Record an episode of one of your favorite television shows and then watch a few minutes of it with the sound turned off. Pay attention to the characters' nonverbal behaviors and try to figure out what emotions they are experiencing. Once you have an idea of a character's emotion, ask yourself what other conclusions you might have come to with the information available to you. Then watch the same few minutes again with the sound turned on to determine how accurate you were.

REFLECT ON IT Which nonverbal behaviors are you the most sensitive to? Which are you least likely to notice in others? Why is your ability to express yourself nonverbally in electronically mediated contexts important?

MASTER the chapter

1 The Nature of Nonverbal Communication (p. 177)

- Nonverbal communication comprises behaviors and characteristics that convey meaning without the use of words.

- Nonverbal communication has the following characteristics: (a) It is present in most interpersonal conversations, (b) it usually conveys more information than verbal communication, (c) it is usually believed over verbal communication, (d) it is the primary means of communicating emotion, and (e) it is metacommunicative.

- Nonverbal communication serves the following functions: (a) managing conversations, (b) expressing emotions, (c) maintaining relationships, (d) forming impressions, (e) influencing others, and (f) concealing information.

2 Ten Channels of Nonverbal Communication (p. 189)

- Facial displays are important for identity, attractiveness, and emotion.

- Eye behaviors include eye contact and pupil dilation.

- Movement and gestures include emblems, illustrators, affect displays, regulators, and adaptors.

- Touch behaviors include affectionate, caregiving, controlling, aggressive, and ritualistic touch.

- Voices vary in pitch, inflection, volume, speaking rate, use of filler words, pronunciation, articulation, silence, and accent.

- Smell is particularly important for memories and sexual attraction.

- People maintain four levels of space: intimate, personal, social, and public.

- Physical appearance is important because we attribute positive qualities to attractive people, a phenomenon called the halo effect.

- The use of time sends messages of value and power.

- We use artifacts to communicate through the selection and placement of objects and the use of color.

3 Culture, Sex, and Nonverbal Communication (p. 202)

- Many nonverbal behaviors—but not all—differ from culture to culture.

- Sex influences the communication of several nonverbal behaviors.

4 Improving Your Nonverbal Communication Skills (p. 206)

- The ability to interpret nonverbal messages is a function of being sensitive to those messages and deciphering their meanings.

- The ability to express nonverbal messages can be enhanced by spending time with expressive people and taking part in activities that exercise your expressiveness.

- Being sensitive to your nonverbal behaviors during videoconferencing and in text-based messages can improve your effectiveness as a communicator.

KEY TERMS

adaptor (p. 193)
affect display (p. 193)
artifact (p. 201)
chronemics (p. 200)
emblem (p. 193)
emoji (p. 179)
emoticons (p. 179)
facial display (p. 189)
gesticulation (p. 193)
halo effect (p. 200)

haptics (p. 194)
high-contact culture (p. 203)
illustrator (p. 193)
immediacy behavior (p. 184)
intimate distance (p. 199)
kinesics (p. 192)
low-contact culture (p. 203)
nonverbal channels (p. 180)
nonverbal communication (p. 178)
oculesics (p. 191)

olfactics (p. 198)
personal distance (p. 199)
proportionality (p. 189)
proxemics (p. 199)
public distance (p. 199)
regulator (p. 193)
social distance (p. 199)
symmetry (p. 189)
turn-taking signal (p. 183)
vocalics (p. 197)

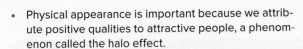

To maximize your study time, check out CONNECT to access the SmartBook study module for this chapter, watch videos, and explore other resources.

7

Listening

© Chris Hondros/Getty Images News/Getty Images

UNIQUELY QUALIFIED TO LISTEN

Shortly after returning home to Florida after his tours of duty in Kuwait and Iraq, Army Sergeant John Castro found himself in the grip of post-traumatic stress disorder, or PTSD. At any given time, roughly 8 million Americans are experiencing symptoms of post-traumatic stress, including sleeplessness, anxiety, and severe emotional or physical reactions to stimuli. Among combat veterans like Castro, the disorder is even more common. Although as many as 20 percent of military personnel returning from duty in the Middle East suffer symptoms of PTSD, Castro felt alone.[1] Fellow veteran Ray Nazareth understood the problem, having seen veterans as young as 18 develop PTSD after serving in combat zones overseas. Nazareth took action by starting a support group for young veterans in Florida's West Palm Beach County. The group provides a safe space for veterans to talk about the problems they face when returning home from military duty. Importantly, the people listening aren't counselors or psychologists, but other veterans who have been through the same experiences.

chapter preview

1 **The Nature of Listening**

2 **Ways of Listening**

3 **Common Barriers to Effective Listening**

4 **Becoming a Better Listener**

You've probably had the experience of feeling as though someone was hearing you but not really listening. If so, you most likely felt frustrated. As you might imagine, problems with listening are fairly common in interpersonal relationships.[2]

Those problems arise because listening effectively is more difficult than you might think. Like other aspects of communication, listening is a skill you have to learn and practice. When you listen properly, the activity adds a great deal to the quality of your relationships. When you don't, your communication and relationships both suffer.

1 The Nature of Listening

In 2008, the nonprofit group StoryCorps instituted the National Day of Listening to encourage Americans to listen to one another. The idea is that on the day after Thanksgiving, those who are interested spend one hour recording an interview with a loved one. Among the questions StoryCorps suggests posing are "What are some of the most important lessons you have learned in life?" and "How would you like to be remembered?" Participants* are encouraged to archive the recordings of their interviews and to share them with relatives and friends so that everyone can experience the joy of listening.

If you're like most people, you probably don't give much thought to how well you listen. You can take classes to become a better speaker or better writer, but few schools offer courses to improve your listening skills. Yet most people spend much more time listening than speaking, writing, or engaging in other communicative behaviors. That's one reason why listening effectively is such a valuable skill.

The National Day of Listening acknowledges the importance of effective listening behaviors. © *Susan tripp pollard/ Mct/Landov*

What Is Listening?

Many people find effective listening hard to define. When someone complains "You never listen!" what exactly does that mean?

We can define **listening** as the active process of making meaning out of another person's spoken message.[3] Two details about that definition are important to note. First, listening is an active process. That means it isn't automatic; rather, you have to *make* yourself listen to someone. Second, listening isn't just about hearing, or receiving input, but also about creating *meaning* from what you hear. Even if you and someone else are hearing the same message, you may construct different meanings for it, an indicator that the two of you are listening differently.

To understand that point, imagine you are listening to your brother's description of his new officemate, and you conclude that he finds her very competent and likable. After listening to the same description, however, your mother concludes that your brother feels threatened by his officemate's intelligence and self-confidence. The two of you heard the

listening The active process of making meaning out of another person's spoken message.

Do-It-Yourself Guide from StoryCorps.

assess your skills | PEOPLE, ACTION, CONTENT, TIME: WHAT'S YOUR LISTENING STYLE?

As you've discovered, researchers have identified four distinct styles of listening. Which one best describes you? After each of the following statements, indicate how much you agree or disagree by writing a number from 1 (*strongly disagree*) to 7 (*strongly agree*).

1. _____   I am concerned with the emotions of others.
2. _____   I prefer clear, to-the-point communication.
3. _____   I like to focus on details.
4. _____   I keep a tight schedule and carefully allocate my time.
5. _____   I tend to be very trusting of others.
6. _____   I take a "business-like" approach to communication.
7. _____   I prefer to have all necessary information before making a decision.
8. _____   I like it when others respect my time limitations.

When you're finished, add your scores in this manner:

- Add your scores for questions 1 and 5. This is your *people-oriented style* score.
- Add your scores for questions 2 and 6. This is your *action-oriented style* score.
- Add your scores for questions 3 and 7. This is your *content-oriented style* score.
- Add your scores for questions 4 and 8. This is your *time-oriented style* score.

Note which of your four scores is highest. This indicates which listening style describes you best. If two scores tie for highest, this suggests that you identify equally with two separate styles.

same description, but you listened to it differently. Each of us listens with a particular style, and that style influences what we hear and what meaning we make of it.

LISTENING STYLES.   People listen for various reasons—sometimes to learn, sometimes to evaluate, and sometimes to provide empathy. Researchers have identified four distinct styles, each consisting of a different set of attitudes and beliefs about listening. However, most of us have one primary style that we use the most often. Here is a brief overview of each style.

- *People-oriented style:* This style emphasizes concern for other people's emotions and interests. As the name suggests, someone with a people-oriented style tries to find common interests with others. For instance, when Palik listens to his middle school students, he tries to understand what they are thinking and feeling so that he can relate to them effectively.

- *Action-oriented style:* This style emphasizes organization and precision. An action-oriented listener likes neat, concise, error-free presentations. For example, Monica approves when her interns fill her in on the week's activities in a clear, straightforward way, and gets frustrated when she can't understand them.

- *Content-oriented style:* This style emphasizes intellectual challenges. Someone with a content-oriented style likes to attend to details and think things through. Emma really enjoys listening to political commentators, for instance, because they make her think about her own social and political views.

- *Time-oriented style:* This style emphasizes efficiency. Someone with a time-oriented style prefers conversations that are quick and to-the-point. As an emergency room physician, for example, Ben relies on short and fast reports of a patient's condition from paramedics and nurses, and he gets impatient when they take more of his time than is necessary.

Each style has its distinctive strengths and weaknesses, so none is inherently better than the others. If you're primarily a people-oriented listener, for example, you're likely to get to know other people well, but you might not be able to work as efficiently as a time-oriented listener. Action-oriented listeners might do best in majors that emphasize clarity and precision, such as engineering and computer science, whereas content-oriented listeners might prefer majors that involve greater ambiguity and room for debate, such as art and political science.

Regardless of your primary listening style, research demonstrates that we adopt different styles for different situations. For instance, you might prefer a time-oriented style when you're in a rush but a people-oriented style when you're visiting loved ones. Similarly, you might adopt a content-oriented style when listening to your professor give a lecture but an action-oriented style when listening to the evening news.[4] What's your listening style? Check out the "Assess Your Skills" box to find out.

© Jgi/Masterfile /Blend Images, RF

LISTENING EFFECTIVELY. Listening to someone doesn't necessarily mean you're listening *effectively*. Effective listening involves listening with the conscious and explicit goal of understanding what the speaker is attempting to communicate. You might never know for certain whether you have understood a speaker's meaning exactly as he or she intended. However, if you're listening with the goal of understanding the speaker's meaning as best you can, you're listening effectively.

There are several barriers that make effective listening difficult, and different situations call for different types of listening. Understanding those dimensions of listening can help you improve your ability to listen effectively. That's a worthwhile goal, as we'll consider next.

The Importance of Listening Effectively

One of the reasons it's important to understand listening is that we do it so much of the time. How much of your day do you think you spend listening? In one study, researchers Richard Emanuel and colleagues found that college students spent more time listening than engaging in any other communication activity. As shown in Figure 1, participants spent 54 percent of their waking hours listening.[5] In comparison, they spent only 17 percent of the time reading, 16 percent speaking, and 11 percent writing. Overall, then, they spent as much time listening as they did performing all other communication behaviors combined. Other studies have found similar results, at least with college students, suggesting that most of us spend a similar percentage of our communication time listening.[6]

© Fancy Photography/Veer, RF

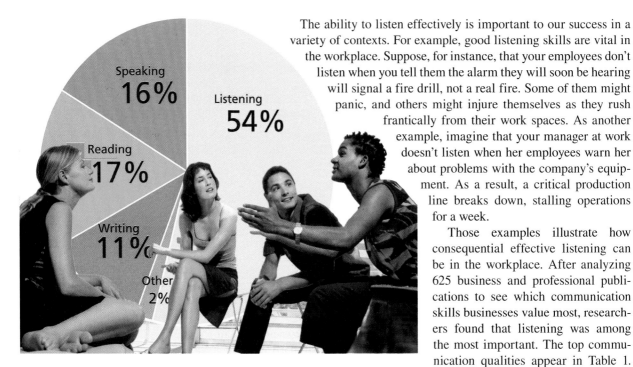

The ability to listen effectively is important to our success in a variety of contexts. For example, good listening skills are vital in the workplace. Suppose, for instance, that your employees don't listen when you tell them the alarm they will soon be hearing will signal a fire drill, not a real fire. Some of them might panic, and others might injure themselves as they rush frantically from their work spaces. As another example, imagine that your manager at work doesn't listen when her employees warn her about problems with the company's equipment. As a result, a critical production line breaks down, stalling operations for a week.

Those examples illustrate how consequential effective listening can be in the workplace. After analyzing 625 business and professional publications to see which communication skills businesses value most, researchers found that listening was among the most important. The top communication qualities appear in Table 1. In other research, listening topped the list of the most important communication skills in families and in

FIGURE 1 Percentages of Various Communication Activities
Source: Emanuel, R., Adams, J., Baker, K., Daufin, E. K., Ellington, C., Fitts, E., . . . Okeowo, D. (2008). How college students spend their time communicating. *International Journal of Listening, 22,* 13–28.
© Image 100/Corbis, RF

TABLE 1

Most Important Business Communication Competencies, According to 625 Business Publications

1. Interpersonal communication: Ability to manage conversations, build rapport, engage in small talk, and manage conflict
2. Mediated communication: Ability to manage social networking and engage in training and learning online
3. Intergroup communication: Ability to communicate within and across cultural and age groups
4. Communication of enthusiasm and creativity: Ability to communicate with a positive attitude and motivate others
5. Nonverbal communication: Ability to manage time, space, appearance, and other nonverbal cues in the workplace
6. Listening and speaking: Ability to listen to others' ideas, facilitate conversation, and engage in public speaking

Source: Waldeck, J., Durante, C., Helmuth, B., & Marcia, B. (2012). Communication in a changing world: Contemporary perspectives on business communication competence. *Journal of Education for Business, 87,* 230–240.

personal relationships.[7] Indeed, being a good listener is vital to just about every social and personal bond we have.[8]

Listening well doesn't affect just our relationships; it also has implications for our physical health. When a pharmacist gives us instructions about how to take a medication, for instance, we need to listen carefully, to avoid taking the medication improperly. When a doctor tells us what foods to avoid and when a nurse instructs us about caring for a wound, we need to be sure we've understood.

If listening skills are so valuable, why don't we work harder to improve them? One reason is that many of us overestimate our listening abilities. In one study, 94 percent of corporate managers rated themselves as good or very good at listening, whereas not a single one rated himself or herself as poor or very poor. Several of their employees told quite a different story, however: They rated their managers' listening skills as weak.[9] Studies like those indicate that there is little association between how good we think we are at listening and how good other people think we are.[10]

Some Misconceptions about Listening

Are you surprised to learn that people often overestimate their listening abilities? Here are some other misunderstandings about the listening process.

MYTH: HEARING IS THE SAME AS LISTENING.   Some people use the terms *hearing* and *listening* interchangeably, but they aren't the same activity. Hearing is merely the perception of sound. Most people hear sounds almost continuously—you hear the neighbor's dogs barking, the television playing in the background, the car alarm that wakes you in the middle of the night. Hearing is a passive process that occurs when sound waves cause the bones in your inner ear to vibrate and send signals to your brain.

Just because we're hearing something doesn't mean we're listening to it. Unlike hearing, listening is an active process of paying attention to a sound, assigning meaning to it, and responding to it. Hearing is a part of that process, but listening requires much more than just perceiving the sounds around you.

By the same token, we sometimes listen without hearing, and our understanding can be impaired as a result. That point is illustrated humorously in a series of television ads aired a few years ago by the Cingular/AT&T telephone company. Each ad depicted a cell phone call between two people in which they unknowingly lost their cellular connection halfway through the conversation. In every case, one speaker interpreted the other's silence as meaningful, when in fact it was simply the result of the dropped call. For instance, just after telling her husband that she was expecting a baby, one woman's call was dropped without her knowledge. Although her husband exclaimed his excitement about the pregnancy, all she heard was silence, which she incorrectly interpreted as indifference

Writing Note: Ask students to think of a person in their lives whom they feel is an excellent listener and to describe, in writing, a situation in which they witnessed the person's listening skills in action. What specific behaviors and mannerisms do they recall about the individual?

Talking Point: Point out that even though hearing and listening are not the same thing, hearing is *a part of* listening. This point receives greater attention below.

CONNECT: Learning Resources in SmartBook help students practice their skills by evaluating conversations and analyzing situations for communication competence.

Listening skills are particularly important in the workplace. However, one study found that many employees rated their employers' listening skills as weak.
© Andersen Ross/Digital Vision/Getty Images, RF

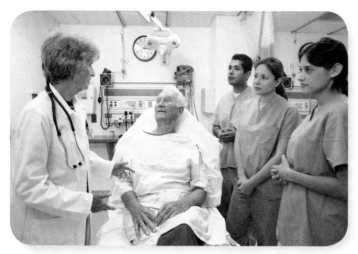

Recognizing the importance of good listening skills in the health care field, several medical schools in the United States have added coursework to teach young doctors how to listen effectively to their patients. © ERproductions Ltd./Blend Images/Masterfile, RF

Talking Point: Anyone who's been around young children will testify that children are often not good at listening. That is an example of the principle that listening must be learned.

or fear on his part. Even though she was trying to listen, then, she wasn't hearing.

MYTH: LISTENING IS NATURAL AND EFFORTLESS. It's easy to think of listening as a completely natural, mindless process, much like breathing. However, listening is a learned skill, not an innate ability like hearing. We have to acquire our listening abilities. Just as we are taught to speak, we have to be taught to listen—and to listen effectively.[11] Many of us are taught by our experiences. Perhaps you can recall instances when you didn't listen effectively to a supervisor's instructions about how to accomplish a work project, and you made poor decisions as a result. Maybe you have been in situations with a romantic partner when you didn't listen as effectively as you could have, and an unnecessary argument followed. Good communicators learn from their mistakes, so such experiences have probably taught you the importance of effective listening.

We also learn through instruction, such as the instruction you are receiving in your interpersonal communication course. The more you learn about what makes listening effective and what barriers to watch out for, the better equipped you'll be to listen effectively to other people.

The fact that listening is a skill also means that people vary in their listening abilities. Just as some people are better athletes, singers, or writers than others, some people are better listeners than others. Finally, as with most skills, you can improve your listening ability through education and training.[12] Counselors and social workers are trained to listen effectively to clients, a skill that improves the quality of services they provide. In recent years, medical schools around the United States have added coursework and role-play activities on effective listening and other interpersonal skills to their curricula for training physicians. People in many professions—from education and the ministry to customer service and politics—can benefit from training in effective listening.

MYTH: ALL LISTENERS HEAR THE SAME MESSAGE. We might assume that when several people are listening to the same message, they are all hearing and understanding the message in the same way. As we learned in the Interpersonal Perception chapter, however, our perceptions of what we see and hear are always limited. Our experiences, our biases, and even our gender and culture all influence how we create meaning from the information we take in.

The safer assumption is that all listeners are hearing something slightly different, because each of us is filtering the message through our own unique experiences and biases. As communication scholar Ben Broome points out, even the most skilled listener can't "step outside" himself or herself entirely.[13] Broome is not implying that no one can ever understand another person's meaning. Rather, he is encouraging us to learn to be aware of how different people might interpret and understand the same message differently.

Culture and Sex Affect Listening Behavior

Cultural messages shape many communication behaviors, and listening is no exception. In particular, listening behavior appears to be affected by how people in a given culture think about the importance of time. In some cultures, people think of time as a resource. For example, Americans commonly say that "time is money," and they often view time as a commodity that can be saved, spent, and wasted. As a result, they frequently place a premium on efficiency and become impatient with speakers who don't "get to the point."[14] In contrast, cultures such as Korea emphasize social harmony over efficiency. As part of their listening behaviors, people often pay close attention to nonverbal behavior and contextual cues to determine the meaning of a speaker's message.[15]

Research shows that women and men have different styles of listening. Women are more likely than men to say they use their listening skills to learn about people and make personal connections. Men are more likely to say they use their listening skills to solve intellectual challenges. © Randy Faris/Corbis RF/Photolibrary, RF

Fewer studies have focused on sex, but research has identified some differences between women and men in listening behavior. For one, men are more likely than women to interrupt someone they are listening to.[16] Women have also been shown to maintain eye contact while listening to their conversational partners more than men do.[17]

Some commentators have even gone so far as to suggest that women and men have completely different styles of listening, and there is evidence to support that claim. In a study of adults' listening styles, researchers Stephanie Sargent and James Weaver found that women scored themselves higher on people-oriented listening than men did.[18] That result suggests that women use their listening skills to learn about people and make connections with others. In contrast, men scored themselves higher on content-oriented listening than women did, suggesting that men use their listening skills to take in content and solve intellectual challenges. The study's findings don't mean that women don't engage in content-oriented listening and that men don't engage in people-oriented listening—they do. Rather, the research shows that women and men—overall—have different approaches to listening.

LEARN IT How is listening different from hearing? Approximately how much of a person's communication time is spent listening? Why isn't listening a natural, effortless process? How do people in individualistic and collectivistic cultures listen differently?

APPLY IT The next time you have a conversation with someone, focus your attention on what she or he is saying rather than on how you're going to respond. With practice, you can learn to listen more intently to others.

REFLECT ON IT In what situations do you find you have difficulty listening effectively? How do you think your own cultural values and experiences influence the way you listen?

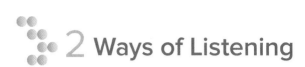

2 Ways of Listening

Until now, we've been viewing listening as though it were a single, unified activity. In truth, listening effectively consists of several stages, all of which are equally important.

Stages of Effective Listening

HURIER model A model of effective listening that involves hearing, understanding, remembering, interpreting, evaluating, and responding.

In Everyday Life: Hearing ability usually declines with age, so as people get older, they have a more difficult time listening effectively to others. Students might encounter this decline in their interactions with the elderly. Discuss how they might accommodate to the situation.

In the IM: The out-of-class activity "Listening Among the Hearing Impaired" encourages students to learn about the listening challenges of hearing impairments and about the ways hearing-impaired people accommodate them.

Judi Brownell, a professor of organizational communication, is an expert on listening who developed the **HURIER model** to describe the six stages of effective listening: hearing, understanding, remembering, interpreting, evaluating, and responding.[19] ("HURIER" is an acronym for those stages.) We don't necessarily have to enact the stages in order; sometimes listening effectively requires us to go back and forth among them. When we listen effectively, however, those are the behaviors we adopt. Let's take a closer look at each one.

HEARING.   Recall that hearing is the physical process of perceiving sound. That is where the listening process begins. As we've considered, we can hear someone without listening to what he or she is saying. We tend to do so when we're tired, uninterested in what the person is saying, or hearing multiple voices at once as in a crowded restaurant. Although we sometimes hear without listening, however, we can't really listen to people unless we can hear them, or at least have access to their words. In computer-mediated communication, we can also pay close attention to another person's words even if they are written rather than spoken. In face-to-face interaction, though, hearing is the first step in effective listening. People with hearing impairments find ways to overcome that challenge, such as reading lips and using sign language.

UNDERSTANDING.   It's not enough simply to hear what someone is saying—you also have to understand it. To understand means to comprehend the meanings of the words and phrases you're hearing.[20] If someone is speaking in a language you don't understand, you might be able to hear that person, but you won't be able to listen effectively. The same is true when you hear technical language or jargon that is unfamiliar to you: Even if the speaker is speaking your language, you can't effectively listen if you don't understand the words. If you're uncertain whether you understand what a speaker is saying, the most effective course of action is usually to ask the person questions to check your understanding.

REMEMBERING.   The third stage of the HURIER model is remembering, or being able to store something in your memory and retrieve it when needed.[21] Remembering what you hear is important for interpersonal communication because it can help you to avoid awkward situations. For instance, you might have had the embarrassing experience of running into someone whose name you couldn't remember, even though you had met the person on several prior occasions. In such interpersonal encounters, remembering what you heard previously can help you communicate with others more effectively.

Research shows that most people can recall only 25 percent of what they hear—and of that portion, they remember only about 20 percent of it accurately.[22] The average person is therefore not especially good at remembering.

Fortunately, remembering is a skill you can practice and improve. *Mnemonic devices* are tricks that can improve short- and long-term memory. Such devices come in several forms. If you've ever studied music, for instance, perhaps you learned to recall the lines of the treble staff—EGBDF—by treating the letters as an initialism for a phrase, such as "every good boy does fine." You might also develop rhymes to help you remember certain rules, such as when spelling in English "*i* before *e, except after c.*" Another mnemonic device is the *acronym,* a word formed from the first letters or parts of a compound term. If you remember the elements of Brownell's effective listening model by learning the word *HURIER,* you are employing that type of mnemonic device. Research suggests that using mnemonic devices can significantly enhance memory.[23]

INTERPRETING.   Besides hearing, understanding, and remembering, an effective listener must interpret the information he or she receives. The process of interpreting has two parts. The first part is paying attention to all the speaker's verbal and nonverbal behaviors so you can assign meaning to what the person has said. Suppose your friend Maya says, "It's a beautiful day outside." On the basis of her facial expressions and tone of voice, you might interpret this message either as sincere— meaning that Maya thinks today's weather is beautiful—or as sarcastic—meaning she thinks the weather is awful. Those are very different interpretations of Maya's message, even though her words are the same.

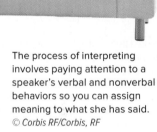

The second part of interpreting is signaling your interpretation of the message to the speaker. If you interpret Maya's statement as sincere, you might smile and say you're looking forward to getting outside to enjoy the great weather. However, if you interpret her statement as sarcastic, you might laugh or respond with a sarcastic remark of your own. Signaling not only lets the speaker know you're following along with what he or she is saying but also allows you to confirm your interpretations. Suppose Maya intended her comment about the weather to be sarcastic but you interpreted it as sincere. If you smiled and said you were looking forward to getting outside, that response would probably signal to Maya that you have misinterpreted the intent of her statement. She might then say, "I was just kidding" to correct your interpretation.

The process of interpreting involves paying attention to a speaker's verbal and nonverbal behaviors so you can assign meaning to what she has said.
© Corbis RF/Corbis, RF

Talking Point: Unlike hearing and remembering, the ability to interpret correctly relies on understanding not only the language but also the speaker's cultural norms for communication.

EVALUATING.   Several events happen at the evaluation stage. For one, you're judging whether the speaker's statements are accurate and true. You're also separating facts from opinions and trying to determine why the speaker is saying what he or she is saying. Finally, you're considering the speaker's words in the context of other information you have received from that speaker or other sources. All those activities help you to be an active, engaged listener rather than a passive recipient of information.

RESPONDING.   The last stage of effective listening is responding, or indicating to a speaker that you're listening. We sometimes call that process *giving feedback,* and we do it both verbally and nonverbally using a variety of strategies.[24] The following

Focus on Scholarship: John Gottman's research has determined that when romantic couples engage in stonewalling, particularly in the context of conflict conversations, that is a strong predictor of divorce or relational dissolution.[i]

[i]Gottman, J. M., & Driver, J. L. (2005). Dysfunctional marital conflict and everyday marital interaction. *Journal of Divorce & Remarriage, 43,* 63–77.

are seven types of listening responses, arranged in order from the most passive to the most active strategies:

- *Stonewalling:* Responding with silence and a lack of facial expression. Stonewalling often signals a lack of interest in what the speaker is saying.

- *Backchanneling:* Nodding your head or using facial expressions, vocalizations such as "uh-huh," and verbal statements such as "I understand" and "That's very interesting" to let the speaker know you're paying attention.

- *Paraphrasing:* Restating in your own words what the speaker has said, to show that you understand. Check out the "Got Skills?" box for tips on practicing that useful skill.

- *Empathizing:* Conveying to the speaker that you understand and share his or her feelings on the topic, such as by saying "I know how you feel."

- *Supporting:* Expressing your agreement with the speaker's opinion or point of view.

- *Analyzing:* Providing your own perspective on what the speaker has said, such as by explaining your opinion or describing your experience.

- *Advising:* Communicating advice to the speaker about what he or she should think, feel, or do.

In Everyday Life: For many students, informational listening is probably their most common form of listening, since they use it so much in the course of their education.

Depending on the situation, some of those responses may be more useful or appropriate than others. For instance, if you're listening to a friend who has just lost her favorite uncle to heart disease, empathizing and supporting are probably the most helpful responses. Stonewalling, backchanneling, or paraphrasing might make it seem as though you don't care about your friend, and analyzing or advising may seem insensitive. In comparison, if you're an accountant listening to a client who is wondering how she can make the most of her stock portfolio, then analysis and advice are probably called for.

In addition to the specific situation, our cultural expectations influence our ideas concerning appropriate listening responses, particularly with respect to appropriate nonverbal behavior. As we considered in the Nonverbal Communication chapter, for instance, most Americans expect listeners to maintain eye contact with them while they're speaking. For that reason, they often assume that listeners who look down or away aren't listening. In many Native American cultures, however, looking down or away while listening is a sign of respect.[25]

The "At a Glance" box recaps the HURIER model. According to Brownell, the model's six stages characterize effective listening no matter why we happen to be listening. Let's shift gears a bit and take a look at a closely related topic: the most common types of listening.

In the HBO series *The Sopranos,* Tony Soprano (played by James Gandolfini) was a powerful, dangerous man with a large ego and many dark secrets. Dr. Jennifer Melfi (played by Lorraine Bracco) had the daunting task of counseling him. During therapy sessions, Dr. Melfi used backchanneling, paraphrasing, and analyzing as effective ways of responding. Because of Tony Soprano's involvement in crime, she was often unable to empathize or support and was reluctant to advise. © *HBO/Photofest*

Types of Listening

When we talk about different types of listening, we're referring to the varying goals we have when we listen to other people. Sometimes we listen to learn. At other times, our goal is to evaluate. On still other occasions, our goal is to empathize.

 **got skills?**   **PARAPHRASING**

Paraphrasing is a handy listening skill.

WHAT?
Learn to restate a speaker's message in your own words.

WHY?
To indicate that you understand the message and to give the speaker a chance to correct your interpretation if necessary, as when someone is giving you driving directions or providing advice.

HOW?
1. When you encounter a statement whose meaning is potentially ambiguous, determine what you *think* the statement means.
2. Formulate a way of making the same statement using different words.
3. Respond to the speaker: "So what you're saying is . . ." and then make the statement in your own words.

TRY!
1. Role-play a conversation about politics with a classmate. When you're unclear about the meaning of one of your partner's statements, paraphrase it.
2. Your partner will likely either confirm your interpretation of the statement or correct it. Either way, your understanding of his or her meaning will be enhanced.

CONSIDER: *Why is it useful to check your understanding of a speaker's statements when you're listening?*

Those goals aren't necessarily distinct; sometimes we listen with more than one of them in mind. When we distinguish among types of listening, we therefore are considering what our primary listening goal is at a given time.

INFORMATIONAL LISTENING.   Much of the listening you engage in during class or at work is **informational listening,** or listening to learn. Whenever you watch the news or listen to driving directions or pay attention to a professor's lecture, you're engaged in informational listening.

Informational listening is both very common and extremely helpful. Indeed, it is one of the most important ways we learn. It is also the most passive type of listening. When

informational listening
Listening to learn something.

AT A GLANCE

HURIER Model of Effective Listening

Hearing	Physically perceiving sound
Understanding	Comprehending the words we have heard
Remembering	Storing ideas in memory
Interpreting	Assigning meaning to what we've heard
Evaluating	Judging the speaker's credibility and intention
Responding	Indicating that we are listening

In the IM: The in-class activity "Hearing What Isn't Said: The Effect of Priming" introduces students to one way their informational listening skills can be put to the test.

we're engaged in informational listening, we are simply taking in information. Even though we may be listening effectively and even taking notes, we are listening primarily to learn something new rather than to analyze or support the speaker's information.

© Alloy Photography/Veer, RF

CRITICAL LISTENING.   When your goal is to evaluate or analyze what you're hearing, you are engaged in **critical listening.** You listen carefully to a commercial to determine whether you want to buy the product it's advertising. You listen to a political speech and evaluate the merits of what you're hearing. You listen critically to your mother's description of her recent medical appointment to determine how worried she is about the results of her blood test.

A key point is that "critical" listening doesn't necessarily mean disapproving of or finding fault with what you're hearing. Instead, it means analyzing and evaluating the merits of what a speaker is saying. Compared with informational listening, therefore, critical listening is a more active, engaging process. It requires you not only to take in information but also to assess and judge it. As we will see at the end of this chapter, practicing critical listening is one of the best ways of becoming a better listener.

critical listening Listening with the goal of evaluating or analyzing what one hears.

empathic listening Listening in order to experience what another person is thinking or feeling.

EMPATHIC LISTENING.   Perhaps the most challenging form of listening is **empathic listening,** which occurs when you are trying to identify with the speaker by understanding and experiencing what he or she is thinking or feeling.[26] When you are talking to a friend who has just lost his job or listening to a family member describe the stress of her divorce, you can use empathic listening to give comfort and support.

Effective empathic listening requires two skills:

- The first skill is *perspective taking,* which is the ability to put yourself in another person's place and consider a situation from his or her point of view.[27] When you imagine yourself in another person's position—such as by thinking about what it must be like to be the only person in your residence hall with a physical disability—you are using this skill.

- The second skill is *empathic concern,* which is the ability to identify how someone else is feeling and then experience those feelings yourself.[28] When you listen to another person's story and it makes you cry, even though it doesn't involve you, you are expressing empathic concern.

Empathic listening is different from *sympathetic listening,* which means feeling sorry for another person. If your neighbors lost their grandson to leukemia, for instance, you might be able to sympathize with them even if you can't truly understand their feelings. In contrast, the goal of empathic listening is to understand a situation from the speaker's perspective and to feel what he or she is feeling. For example, you might be listening to a friend who didn't get into her first-choice graduate school and trying to convey that you share her disappointment. Listening empathically is a challenge, because your perceptions can cause you to focus on how *you* would be feeling in the same situation rather than how *the speaker* is feeling.

OTHER TYPES OF LISTENING.   We sometimes engage in *inspirational listening,* which is listening in order to be inspired. That type of listening is common when we're listening to a sermon or motivational speech. At other times, we engage in *appreciative* *listening,* which is listening for pure enjoyment. We listen appreciatively when someone tells a funny story or sings one of our favorite songs. Appreciative listening also comes into play when we watch a TV show or film we enjoy, or attend a performance featuring talent we admire. When it comes to interpersonal interaction, however, informational, critical, and empathic listening are often the most common and most important types.

Effective Listening Online

We may think of listening as being primarily a face-to-face activity, and it often is. But effective listening isn't limited to face-to-face interaction: Given how much of our communication takes place online, it pays to consider how people can listen effectively in that context as well. In this section, we'll examine some strategies for finding an effective listener online and how to be an effective listener yourself.

FINDING AN EFFECTIVE LISTENER ONLINE. Where do you turn when you need someone to listen to you? These days, many people go online, whether it's to communicate with existing friends and loved ones or to make new connections with people who understand what they're going through. In either case, it's possible to find good listeners in online venues.

One of the most common online sources for listening—especially empathic listening—is the online support group. At the beginning of this chapter, you read about a support group devoted to helping veterans deal with the trauma and stress of military deployments. Support groups give people a context for sharing their challenges and being heard by others who can empathize—usually because they have faced similar challenges themselves. Research shows that communicating with others who have endured the same situations can give people a sense of safety and community, reducing feelings of loneliness and isolation.[29]

Many support groups meet in face-to-face settings. Millions of others are hosted online, for issues ranging from eating disorders, Parkinson's disease, and infertility to child rearing, debt relief, and suicide prevention. One study found that Facebook alone hosted over 600 support groups, containing more than a million members total, devoted specifically to the topic of breast cancer.[30] Even Alcoholics Anonymous—which offers thousands of support groups for people struggling with alcoholism—hosts more than a hundred online meetings in a variety of languages.[31]

Online support groups are especially helpful for those who are bedridden or suffering from rare disorders, as they offer the opportunity to connect with others who are going through a similar experience, no matter where they live. © *KatarzynaBialasiewicz/Getty Images, RF*

For many participants, one of the biggest benefits of online support groups is the opportunity to have others listen actively and empathically to what they say. If you're grieving over the loss of a parent, for instance, it helps to be listened to by others who have endured the same experience. Research shows that when people in online support groups feel heard and understood, they experience improvements in their well-being as a result.[32]

A key characteristic of many online support groups is that they allow participants to talk and listen anonymously, by using fake user names instead of their real names. That anonymity can be therapeutic, especially when people are discussing sensitive topics. According to research, people are more likely to seek support online—rather than

communication *LIGHT SIDE*

NEED SOMEONE TO LISTEN? JUST CLICK

From time to time, we all need someone to listen to us. We often turn to close friends and relatives, but they aren't always available and they may not be particularly skilled at listening. Sometimes it's easier to talk to a stranger, but seeing a licensed counselor can be expensive and can make people feel stigmatized. As a solution to those problems, psychologist Glen Moriarty started the website 7cupsoftea.com. The site brings together hundreds of individuals from around the world who are trained to listen with compassion, empathy, and respect. Users are able to chat—anonymously and for free—with trained listeners about any topic they wish to discuss. Moriarty got the idea for the site while sitting at his kitchen table talking to his wife about a problem. He acknowledged that he was fortunate to have someone to listen to him, and he realized that many people don't.

Users of the site seek listeners for a wide variety of reasons, including feeling lonely, trying to get over a breakup, and simply wanting to "vent" to someone. Others look for listeners whom they can talk to about more serious issues, such as feeling depressed or having suicidal thoughts. All conversations are encrypted to maintain security, and users can evaluate listeners' abilities to be supportive, empathic, and kind.

Moriarty stresses the value of his listeners' nonjudgmental approach. As the website explains, "Unlike talking to family or friends, a 7 Cups of Tea listener doesn't judge or try to solve problems and say what to do. Our listeners just listen. They understand."*

FROM ME TO YOU

When you're dealing with a problem and just want someone to listen, it may not occur to you to turn to the Internet. There is certainly value in talking with your close friends, relatives, and peers. Their advice and perspective can be useful, especially because they know you and understand your priorities. Don't overlook the value of talking to a stranger who will do nothing but listen, however. When we share our problems with others, we don't always want or need advice on what to do—sometimes, simply having someone listen is enough.

Source: www.7cupsoftea.com

*www.7cupsoftea.com

in person—if they feel stigmatized by the issue for which they are seeking support.[33] Suffering from a mental illness, being significantly in debt, and dealing with suicide are examples of issues that can invite judgment from others, which may encourage people to look for support in environments where they can be heard anonymously.

Online support groups provide a venue for people who need someone to listen—but they aren't the only option. Check out the "Communication: Light Side" box for information on finding someone to listen one-on-one in a free and confidential manner.

BEING AN EFFECTIVE LISTENER ONLINE.   Having discussed ways to find a good listener online, let's now consider what it means to be an effective online listener yourself. Whether your listening is informational, critical, or empathic, you can benefit by remembering these tips.

- *Be attentive.* When you interact with someone online, it's sometimes easy to become distracted by other stimuli in your environment. Perhaps you're watching a television program or checking your e-mail at the same time, for instance, so you are dividing your attention between multiple tasks. Just as those behaviors would impair your ability to listen in a face-to-face conversation, they diminish your ability to listen effectively online. Instead, stay attuned to what the other person is saying. That's especially important when you're communicating with the person in real time—such as in an online chat or via instant messaging—because it will be more evident if you aren't responding to the person's words in a timely manner.

- *Remember that words can be misinterpreted.* When you listen to someone in a face-to-face conversation, you can use nonverbal behaviors—such as facial expressions and tone of voice—to help you interpret the meaning of his or her words. As we discussed in the Nonverbal Communication chapter, however, many computer-mediated messages rely heavily on words, and words can have more than one meaning. Without nonverbal cues to guide you, therefore, it can be easier to misinterpret what someone else is saying. Good online listeners remind themselves that words in an e-mail message, instant message, or text can have multiple meanings, and they ask for clarification when they're not sure how to interpret someone's statements.

- *Don't be a lurker.* In support groups and other online communities, a *lurker* is someone who regularly reads other people's words but rarely if ever contributes to the conversation. Because lurkers pay attention to the words of others, it may seem as though lurking is all about listening. Remember, however, that listening is an active process of making meaning out of another person's message. Lurking, on the other hand, is a passive process that requires no engagement in the conversation. According to research, 90 percent of users in most online communities are lurkers who never contribute to the discussion.[34] When people lurk, they simply benefit from others' contributions without adding anything to the interaction.[35] Moreover, if too many people in an online community are merely lurking, then the knowledge shared in that community may not be representative of everyone there.[36] Lurking isn't as big of a problem when you aren't particularly interested or invested in the topic of conversation. When you do care about what others are saying, however, take a more active role by interpreting, evaluating, and responding to other people's comments.

As you discover more about good listening behaviors in this course, practice what you learn in both your online and offline environments.

LEARN IT What are the differences between interpreting a message and responding to it? How are the goals of informational, critical, and empathic listening different? What can you do to be an effective listener online?

APPLY IT Develop a mnemonic device to help you remember the seven types of listening responses in order from most passive to most active (stonewalling, backchanneling, paraphrasing, empathizing, supporting, analyzing, advising). Record the device in a journal and then practice it, particularly as you review for quizzes or exams.

REFLECT ON IT When do you have a hard time understanding a speaker? Which type of listening are you the best at?

3 Common Barriers to Effective Listening

On the FX show *Louie,* comedian Louis C.K.'s semi-autobiographical character, Louie, often displays poor listening skills. When his love interest, Pamela (played by Pamela Aldon), tells him in no uncertain terms that she is not romantically interested in him, he refuses to accept what she says. Driving her to the airport for a trip on which she plans to reconnect with her former partner, she tells him, "Listen, here's the

deal . . . I'm going to Paris to make it work with my kid's dad. And I'm not coming back. You understand?" Louie shrugs, and replies, "Yeah, but you might come back." Later, watching Louie standing motionless, staring at her as she waves goodbye from the airport escalator, Pamela shouts "Wave to me!" Louie, hearing what he wants to hear, is quite certain she's told him "Wait for me!"*

This scene raises the question, Why are so few of us good listeners? One answer is that several problems get in our way, acting as barriers to our ability to listen well. In this section, we examine several obstacles to effective listening.

Noise

How many stimuli are competing for your attention right now? How many different stimuli demand your attention at work when your boss, customers, and co-workers all try to talk to you at once? In the context of listening, *noise* refers to anything that distracts you from listening to what you wish to listen to.

Most of us find it more difficult to listen to a conversational partner when there are other sounds in the environment, such as a TV or loud music.[37] It isn't just sound that can distract us, though. If we're hungry, tired, or in an environment that is especially cold or hot, those influences can also qualify as noise because they interfere with our ability to listen effectively.[38] Even the presence of a cell phone can impair our ability to listen in a face-to-face conversation, as the "Fact or Fiction?" box explains.

When you're faced with such distractions, try to focus your attention on your conversational partner and listen intently to what he or she is saying. To do so, you must be conscious of noise in your environment and identify those factors that are drawing your attention away from your conversation. Eliminating or ignoring those noise sources—for example, by turning off your car radio or ignoring your ringing cell phone—will help you focus on your partner. If you're being distracted by noise that you can't ignore or reduce at the time, you might reschedule your conversation for a time when fewer stimuli are competing for your attention.

Pseudolistening and Selective Attention

At one time or another, you've probably pretended to be paying attention to someone when you weren't really listening. That behavior is called **pseudolistening.** When you pseudolisten, you use feedback behaviors that make it seem as though you're paying attention, even though your mind is elsewhere. When she babysits, for instance, Josie maintains eye contact with four-year-old Charlie and nods as though she were hanging on his every word, but her attention is actually focused on the text messages she receives from her friends.

A variation of pseudolistening is **selective attention,** which means listening only to what you want to hear and ignoring the rest.[39] When you engage in selective attention, you are listening to some parts of a person's message and pseudolistening to other parts. In her job as an insurance adjuster, for instance, Sue-Ann receives an evaluation from her supervisor every January. Usually, most of her supervisor's comments are positive, but some of them suggest ways in which Sue-Ann could improve her performance. The problem is, Sue-Ann doesn't listen to those suggestions.

*Dilogue from the TV Series "Louie" by FX Networks, LLC

Talking Point: Hearing other sounds doesn't always limit one's listening ability. For instance, many people find background music conducive to conversation. In such cases, although the music constitutes a sound, it doesn't qualify as noise because it isn't distracting.

Focus on Ethics: Some would call pseudolistening a form of deception since it knowingly creates the false impression that we are listening. Others would call it a politeness behavior, like saying "Nice to meet you" even if it isn't sincere. What do your students think?

pseudolistening Using feedback behaviors to give the false impression that one is listening.

selective attention Listening only to what one wants to hear.

Instead, she listens selectively, paying close attention to her supervisor's praise and only pretending to listen to her critiques.

Engaging in pseudolistening and selective attention occurs for many reasons. Maybe you're bored with what the speaker is saying, but you don't want to seem rude. Maybe you don't understand what you're hearing, but you're too embarrassed to admit it. Maybe you're paying attention to something else while someone is talking to you, or maybe you simply don't like what the other person is saying. Whatever the reason, pseudolistening and selective attention not only are barriers to effective listening but also can be a source of frustration for the speakers you're pretending to listen to. This frustration arises because people are often aware when others aren't listening to what they're saying. How do you feel when you know someone is only pretending to listen to you or is paying only partial attention to what you're saying?

Media Note: In the instructor resources in the Online Learning Center, the video clip "Pat Goes On" portrays an instance of pseudolistening.

Information Overload

A third barrier to effective listening is **information overload,** the state of being overwhelmed by the huge amount of information one is required to take in every day. We talk to people, watch television, listen to the radio, search the Internet, and thumb through all sorts of printed matter. At times, the sheer volume of information we have to attend to can seem overwhelming. When it does, we find it harder to listen effectively to new information.

information overload
The state of being overwhelmed by the amount of information one takes in.

Information overload can be a particular challenge for children with attention deficit hyperactivity disorder (ADHD). © Westend61/ SuperStock, RF

SOURCES AND EFFECTS OF INFORMATION OVERLOAD.   As just one example of information overload, consider how many advertising messages you see or hear on a daily basis. These might include ads on television, in magazines and newspapers, on billboards, on people's clothing, in junk mail, and during movie previews. You might receive ads by fax, hear them on the radio, and find them in product inserts. You perhaps see them at gas pumps, at automated teller machines, on banners flying behind airplanes, and on the stickers you peel off fruit. You might also receive ads in the form of e-mail spam and pop-up announcements on the Internet. Researchers have estimated that the average U.S. American is exposed to between 600 and 625 advertising messages each day.[40]

You might conclude that information overload is a product of the digital age, which has made overwhelming amounts of information easily available. In fact, the term *information overload* was coined in 1970 by sociologist Alvin Toffler in a book titled *Future Shock,* which discussed the downside of rapid technological change.[41] Clearly, then, people were experiencing the distracting effects of information overload even before computer-mediated communication was widely used. The problem is simply amplified in the digital age, due to the volume of information available to us.

One of the biggest problems arising from information overload is that it can interrupt people's attention. If you're e-mailing with an important client, for instance, your ability to pay attention to her messages can be compromised repeatedly by each new radio advertisement you hear, each new faxed announcement you receive, and each new pop-up ad you see. Those interruptions may seem small and inconsequential, but when you consider their effects on the entire population over time, they become a significant distraction. In fact, a 2007 analysis by a New York–based management research firm estimated the annual cost to U.S. companies of unnecessary interruptions from information overload to be a staggering $650 billion.[42]

MANAGING INFORMATION OVERLOAD ONLINE.   Between Snapchat, Twitter, Facebook, and YouTube, keeping up with the people in your life can seem like a full-time job. Texting alone can overwhelm: Young adults in the United States send and receive an average of over 3,800 text messages every month.[43] You've learned in this chapter that information overload hampers your ability to listen effectively in face-to-face conversations. Scientists have discovered that the same effect occurs in electronically mediated communication.

When you're swamped with texts, tags, and tweets, you experience what researchers call *conversational overload,* which reduces your ability to attend to those messages adequately.[44] In particular, research has found that:

© Lifesize/Getty Images, RF

- *People are more likely to attend to—and respond to—simple messages than complex ones.* Paying attention to a message requires cognitive energy, and each person has only so much to spend. When their attention is already stretched thin, people attend to messages that are simple and direct.

- *When people feel overloaded, they end or reduce their communication.* People experience overload when the energy required to attend to their communication tasks exceeds what they are willing or able to invest. In those situations, a very common strategy is to reduce the number of incoming messages, such as by un-friending Facebook users or opting out of listservs.

Good listening skills are as important in electronically mediated communication as they are in face-to-face interaction. The better you can prevent barriers to effective listening—including information overload and conversational overload—the more effective an interpersonal communicator you'll be.

© Wavebreakmedia Ltd/Getty Images, RF

Glazing Over

A fourth reason why effective listening is challenging is that our minds think so much faster than most people talk. Most of us are capable of understanding up to 600 words per minute, but the average person speaks fewer than 150 words per minute.[45] That leaves quite a bit of spare time for the mind to wander. We frequently use that time to engage in what researchers call **glazing over,** or dividing our attention between listening and daydreaming. When glazing over, we go back and forth between listening to the other person and allowing our mind to wander with other thoughts.

For instance, Rochelle picks up her 6-year-old daughter and her 9-year-old son every afternoon, and they describe what they did in school during the drive home. Although she listens to what they say, Rochelle frequently allows her mind to wander during this time. She thinks about the novel she's reading, daydreams about taking a Caribbean vacation, and ponders next week's grocery list. Because her children speak more slowly than she can listen, and because their reports of their school activities are similar every day, Rochelle often glazes over when she's listening to them.

Glazing over is different from pseudolistening. When you pseudolisten, you're only *pretending* to listen, and you're giving false feedback that makes it seem as though you're paying attention. When you're glazing over, you actually *are* listening to what the speaker is saying—you're just allowing your mind to wander while doing so. Glazing over can lead to at least three problems. First, it can cause you to miss important details in what you're hearing. If you're glazing over while listening to a lecture in your communication theory course, for instance, you might fail to hear a critical piece of information about the term paper assignment. Second, glazing over might lead you to listen less critically than you normally would. For example, if your mind is wandering while you're listening to a salesperson describe the terms of a car loan, you might not realize that the deal isn't as good as it sounds. Finally, glazing over can make it appear to a speaker that you aren't listening to what he or she is saying, even though you are. Consequently, you can come across as inattentive or dismissive. An effective listener will work to keep his or her focus on what the speaker is saying instead of daydreaming or thinking about other topics.

glazing over Daydreaming during the time not spent listening.

Talking Point: Ask your students when they are most likely to glaze over. Many will probably say they glaze over when they're bored with or don't understand what a speaker is saying.

Rebuttal Tendency

Regan has recently started work as a customer service representative for an electronics retailer, but his first two weeks on the job have not gone well. He knows he should listen nonjudgmentally to customers as they describe their frustrations with the products they bought, and then offer them his assistance and advice. Instead, Regan begins arguing with customers in his mind, even while they're still speaking.

Rather than listening carefully to their concerns, Regan jumps to conclusions about what the customers have done wrong, and he formulates his response even before the customers have stopped talking.

Regan is enacting a **rebuttal tendency,** which is the propensity to disrupt our listening in order to debate a speaker's point in our mind and formulate one's reply while the person is still speaking.[46] According to research by business professor Steven Golen, thinking only of how one is going to respond to a speaker, arguing with the speaker in one's mind, and jumping to conclusions before the speaker has finished talking are all barriers to effective listening, for two basic reasons.[47] First, the rebuttal tendency uses mental energy that should be spent paying attention to the speaker. That is, it's difficult to listen effectively when all one is thinking about is how to respond. Second, by not paying close attention to the speaker, a listener can easily miss some of the details that might change how the listener responds in the first place.

To understand that second point, consider Regan's experience during his second shift. A customer returned a wireless Internet router she was having trouble installing. As usual, Regan was quick to conclude that she hadn't followed the instructions, and he was crafting his response as she continued talking. Consequently, he didn't hear her explain that she'd already had a technician guide her through the installation procedure and inform her that the router was defective. If he had heard that important detail, Regan could have exchanged the product quickly and sent the customer on her way. Instead, he spent 10 minutes telling her to do what she had already done, leaving her frustrated and dissatisfied.

Closed-Mindedness

Another barrier to effective listening is **closed-mindedness,** the tendency not to listen to anything with which one disagrees.[48] Closed-minded individuals refuse to consider the merits of a speaker's point if it conflicts with their own beliefs. They also tend to overreact to certain forms of language, such as slang and profanity, and to stop listening to speakers who use them.[49]

© Digital Stock/Corbis, RF

Many people are closed-minded only about particular issues, not about everything. For instance, Bella prides herself in being open to diverse opinions on a range of topics. When it comes to choosing a college to attend, however, she is thoroughly convinced that an out-of-state private school is the right choice. As a result, she refuses even to listen to her parents' suggestion to consider a local state university, even though it could provide her a similar education at a lower cost. For all practical purposes, Bella closes her mind to the possibility that another school—besides the one she has chosen—could have any appeal whatsoever. As a result, she doesn't listen to her parents when they point out the merits of colleges closer to home. Her parents find her closed-mindedness unfortunate because it prevents her from considering options that might be better for her in the long run.

Bella should remember that we can listen effectively to people even if we disagree with them. As the Greek philosopher Aristotle (384–322 B.C.) once wrote, "It is the mark of an educated mind to be able to entertain a thought without accepting it." When we refuse even to listen to ideas we disagree with, we limit our ability to learn from other people and their experiences. If you find yourself feeling closed-minded toward particular ideas, remind yourself that listening to an idea does not necessarily mean accepting it.

Competitive Interrupting

Normal conversation is a series of speaking "turns." You speak for a while, then you allow another person to have a turn, and the conversation goes back and forth. Occasionally, though, people talk when it isn't their turn. People interrupt for many reasons. Sometimes, the reason is to express support or enthusiasm for what the other person is saying ("Yeah, I agree!"); sometimes it's to stop the speaker to ask for clarification ("Wait, I'm not sure what you mean"); and sometimes it's even to warn the speaker of some impending danger ("Stop! You're spilling your coffee!").

For some people, however, interrupting is a way to dominate a conversation. Researchers use the term **competitive interrupting** to describe the practice of interjecting oneself when other people are speaking in order to take control of the conversation. For those who engage in competitive interrupting, the goal is to ensure that they get to speak more than the other person does and that their ideas and perspectives take priority. You can probably think of people who engage in such behavior—individuals with whom you feel you "can't get a word in edgewise."

Research shows that most interruptions aren't competitive. However, talking with a competitive interrupter can be frustrating.[50] Some people respond to constant interruptions by becoming competitive themselves, thereby turning the conversation into a battle of wits. Other people withdraw from the interaction.

The "At a Glance" box summarizes the barriers to effective listening. Each of those barriers can be overcome. With training and practice, most of us can improve our abilities to listen well.

competitive interrupting
Using interruptions to take control of a conversation.

Talking Point: People often accuse others of being closed-minded simply because they disagree with what is being said. Having a different opinion on something doesn't make a person closed-minded, however. Rather, being closed-minded means refusing even to listen to something about which one disagrees.

Outside of Class: Interruption is such a common conversational behavior that students probably encounter it daily. For two or three days, have students keep a journal describing the times when they themselves are interrupted while speaking. They might record who committed each interruption, what purpose they thought the interruption was serving, and how they felt about being interrupted. This exercise may make students more sensitive about interrupting others.

AT A GLANCE

Barriers to Effective Listening

Noise	Anything that distracts you from listening to what you wish to listen to
Pseudolistening	Using feedback behaviors to give the false impression that you are listening
Selective Attention	Listening only to points you want to hear and ignoring all other points
Information Overload	State of being overwhelmed by the huge amount of information you must take in every day
Glazing Over	Daydreaming when you aren't speaking or listening during a conversation
Rebuttal Tendency	Propensity to argue inwardly with a speaker and to formulate your conclusions and responses prematurely
Closed-Mindedness	Refusal even to listen to ideas or positions with which you disagree
Competitive Interrupting	Interrupting others to gain control of a conversation

LEARN IT What constitutes noise? What do people do when they pseudolisten? How does information overload affect listening ability? What does it mean to glaze over? When people have a rebuttal tendency, what do they tend to do while they're listening? What does it mean to be closed-minded? When are interruptions competitive?

APPLY IT For one week, keep a diary of times when you feel that other people haven't listened to you effectively. For each instance, try to identify the barriers to effective listening. After the week is over, read back through your notes and reflect on times when the same barriers have affected your own listening ability. Assess how you might avoid those barriers to effective listening in the future.

REFLECT ON IT In what ways do you notice information overload in your own life? What topics do you tend to be closed-minded about, if any?

4 Becoming a Better Listener

We've looked at several examples of ineffective listening in this chapter. Regan doesn't listen effectively to his customers' complaints, and Rochelle glazes over when listening to her children describe their school day. Clearly, listening effectively can be a challenge. Fortunately, effective listening is a skill that can be developed through education and practice. Author Mary Lou Casey once wrote that "what people really need is a good listening to," and her sentiment suggests that we can do much good in our interpersonal relationships if we sharpen our listening abilities. In this section, we'll look at strategies you can use to improve your skills in informational, critical, and empathic listening.

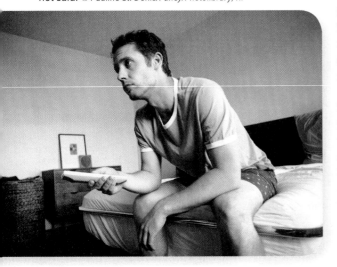

When watching the news on television—or listening to any informative source—it is important to separate what is and is not said. © Pauline St. Denis/Fancy/Photolibrary, RF

Becoming a Better Informational Listener

When you engage in informational listening, your goal is to understand and learn from the speaker's message. For instance, you might be attending a presentation about saving for retirement, or you might be listening to your CEO talk about a merger your firm has just completed. How can you make the most of such opportunities?

SEPARATE WHAT IS AND ISN'T SAID. One key strategy for improving your informational listening skills is to beware of the tendency to "hear" words or statements that aren't actually said. Think about the last time you saw a television commercial for a pain reliever, for instance. A common tactic for advertisers is to claim that "nothing is more effective" than their product. What do you learn from hearing that statement? In other words, how would you paraphrase it?

The advertisers are hoping you learn that their particular pain reliever is the strongest one available . . . but that's not really what they said, is it? All they said is that nothing is *more* effective, which means there may be several other products that are *just as* effective as theirs. It may also mean that all the products are equally ineffective! If you listened to this ad and concluded that this product is the most effective one available, you arrived at that conclusion on your own (although it was definitely the conclusion the advertiser wanted you to form). When you are engaged in informational listening, be careful to distinguish between what is actually being said and what you are simply inferring.

Perhaps the most effective way to determine whether you have understood a speaker's message is to paraphrase it—to restate the speaker's message in your own words to clarify the meaning of the message. If you paraphrase a statement in a way that accurately reflects its meaning, speakers tend to reply by confirming your understanding.

Let's suppose that while leaving a theater after watching a movie, your roommate Chad and you have the following exchange:

Chad: I think we should swing by that new barbecue place on the way home.

You: You want to pick up some dinner?

Chad: Yeah, I'm starving.

You think Chad is trying to imply that he's hungry and wants to get some food, but that isn't actually what he said. To check your understanding, you therefore paraphrase his statement by putting it into your own words. Because you understood Chad's statement correctly, he replied by confirming your interpretation.

Conversely, if you paraphrase a statement in a way that changes its meaning, a speaker generally will correct your misunderstanding. Let's say the exchange with Chad goes like this:

Chad: I think we should swing by that new barbecue place on the way home.

You: You want to pick up some dinner?

Chad: No, I want to see if my friend Blake is working tonight.

In this second instance, your interpretation of Chad's statement was inaccurate. By paraphrasing his statement, you invited him to correct your understanding—and he did. Paraphrasing is one of the most efficient ways to determine whether you have correctly distinguished between what a speaker has and has not said.

AVOID THE CONFIRMATION BIAS.   The **confirmation bias** is the tendency to pay attention only to information that supports one's values and beliefs while discounting or ignoring information that doesn't.[51] It becomes a problem for listening when it causes us to make up our minds about an issue without paying attention to all sides.

Let's say your close friend Tim is having a conflict with his girlfriend, Molly. Tim confides in you about the negative things Molly has been saying and doing, and because he's your friend, you're biased toward believing him. When Molly comes to talk to you about the situation, you therefore tune her out because you've already made up your mind that she's at fault.

In this case, you're falling victim to the confirmation bias. Because you've made up your mind that Tim is behaving fairly, you will pay attention only to information that confirms your belief and will tune out information that doesn't. Good informational listeners are aware that their beliefs are not necessarily accurate. Therefore, a strategy for improving your informational listening skills is to ask yourself whether you have listened to all sides of an issue before you form a conclusion, or whether you are simply avoiding information that would lead you to question your beliefs.

In the IM: The in-class activity "Paraphrasing" allows students an opportunity to practice their paraphrasing skills.

confirmation bias The tendency to pay attention only to information that supports one's values and beliefs while discounting or ignoring information that doesn't.

In the IM: The in-class activity "Pass It On: The Confirmation Bias in Listening" tests students' susceptibility to the confirmation bias.

vividness effect The tendency for dramatic, shocking events to distort one's perception of reality.

LISTEN FOR SUBSTANCE MORE THAN FOR STYLE. The psychological principle called the **vividness effect** refers to the tendency for dramatic, shocking events to distort one's perceptions of reality.[52] We watch news coverage of a deadly plane crash, for instance, and we become nervous about getting on a plane, even though the probability of dying in a plane crash is only about 1 in 8 million.[53] In a 2000 Gallup poll, 63 percent of Americans surveyed thought a shooting at their child's school was likely, even though only 3.3 percent of violent crimes occur in schools, according to the Federal Bureau of Investigation (FBI).[54]

The same effect can occur within interpersonal situations. If your parents went through a traumatic divorce when you were a child, for instance, that experience may have convinced you that a marriage is more likely to fail than is actually the case. Dramatic events are more vivid and memorable than everyday events, so we pay more attention to them.

You can experience much the same problem during informational listening if you focus only on what's most vivid. In class, for instance, you might be more entertained by a lecture with dramatic stories and flashy PowerPoint slides than by one that's dry. That doesn't mean that the flashy presentation contains better information than the dry one or that you'll learn more from it. Similarly, you might love being in classes with engaging, humorous teachers. That doesn't necessarily mean, however, that you'll learn more from them than from teachers who are disengaged and serious.

Being a good informational listener, then, means being able to look past what is dramatic and vivid to focus on the substance of what you're hearing. That process begins with being aware of the vividness effect and remembering that vivid experiences can distort your perceptions. The next time you go through a dramatic event or listen to a particularly entertaining speaker, ask yourself whether you are listening and paying attention to accurate information or are being swayed by the drama of the event or the charisma of the speaker.

Becoming a Better Critical Listener

Many interpersonal situations require you to assess the credibility of what you're hearing. Here are three ways to get better at it.

skepticism The practice of evaluating the evidence for a claim.

Talking Point: *Reiterate that skepticism is often confused with cynicism. Cynicism is about finding fault; skepticism is about evaluating the merits and the evidence of an argument.*

BE A SKEPTIC. Being a good critical listener starts with being skeptical of what you hear. Despite its reputation, **skepticism** isn't about being cynical or finding fault; rather, it's about evaluating the evidence for a claim. Recall from our discussion of the confirmation bias that people often pay attention only to evidence that supports their existing beliefs. Being skeptical means setting aside your biases and being willing to be persuaded by the merits of the argument and the quality of the evidence. A good critical listener doesn't accept claims blindly. Instead, he or she questions them to determine whether they're valid.[55]

Consider the following example. Your co-worker Fahid has come up with a business opportunity. He tells you about his plan and asks you to invest in it. If you're a poor critical listener, you may base your decision on how you feel about Fahid or how excited you are at the prospect of making money. In contrast, if you're a good critical listener, you'll set aside your feelings and focus on the merits of Fahid's idea. Does he have a sound business plan? Is there a market for his product? Has he budgeted sufficient funds for advertising? Did he explain in detail how he would use your investment? Being a critical listener doesn't mean that you automatically criticize his plans; it does mean that you carefully evaluate them to determine whether they make sense.

EVALUATE A SPEAKER'S CREDIBILITY. Besides analyzing the merits of an argument, a good critical listener pays attention to the speaker's credibility. Credibility is a measure of how reliable and trustworthy someone is. All other things being equal, you can generally presume that information you hear from a credible source is more believable than information you get from a noncredible source.

Several qualities make a speaker more or less credible. One is expertise. It makes more sense for us to trust a physician's medical advice than a professional athlete's, for instance, because the doctor is a medical expert and the athlete is not. At the same time, it doesn't make sense to trust a physician for legal or financial advice, because he or she isn't an expert on law or finance.

It's easy to confuse having *expertise* with having *experience.* Having experience with

Good critical listeners practice skepticism by evaluating the merits and the evidence for an argument. © Gallo Images/Age fotostock, RF

something may give a person credibility on that topic or area, but it doesn't necessarily make the individual an expert. After raising six children, for instance, Hannah is a very experienced parent and thus has credibility insofar as she can draw on her many experiences to give advice to other moms. However, Hannah isn't an expert on parenting, because her only source of credibility is her individual experience. For instance, she doesn't have a degree in child development, nor is she a recognized authority on parenting issues.

Yet individuals can be experts on topics with which they have no personal experience. As a board-certified obstetrician and gynecologist, Tyrell is an expert on pregnancy and women's health, even though, as a man, he has no direct experience with either. Similarly, Young Li is an outstanding marital therapist who has helped countless couples even though she has never been married herself. How can a man be a good obstetrician, and a single person be a good marital therapist? The answer is that they are drawing on their training and expertise to help others, not on their individual experiences.

Another characteristic that affects a speaker's credibility is bias. If the speaker has a special interest in making you believe some idea or claim, that fact tends to reduce his or her credibility. If a tobacco company executive claimed publicly that there were health benefits to smoking, for instance, a good critical listener would be highly skeptical, because the executive is a biased source.

Sometimes you have to dig below the surface to investigate the source behind a particular idea so you can meaningfully evaluate the idea's credibility. For example, you might be intrigued to hear about a research report claiming that using your cell phone while driving does not increase your risk of being in a collision. The study, you assume, may have been conducted by a reputable research team at a major university, a fact that would enhance its credibility. After you investigate, however, perhaps you discover that the study was funded by a group that lobbies on behalf of the telecommunications industry. Given its purpose, such a group would have a vested interest in the study's producing results that are favorable to cell phone use. The fact that a study is funded by a group with a vested interest in its results doesn't necessarily mean the study's conclusions are wrong. However, it does mean that you should be skeptical when you are exposed to them.

Talking Point: It's worth repeating that claims made by biased sources are not necessarily inaccurate. The fact that someone has a vested interest in a claim's being true doesn't mean the claim is false. Rather, it means that a good critical listener should be even more skeptical than usual when evaluating the claim.

© Jose Luis Pelaez Inc./Blend Images/Getty Images, RF

Media Note: In the instructor resources in the Online Learning Center, the video clips "Where There's Smoke" and "On the Air" give students a chance to practice their critical listening skills.

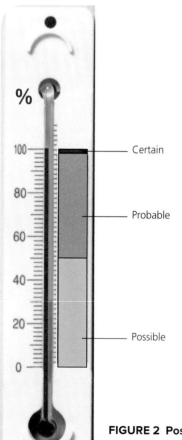

UNDERSTAND PROBABILITY. Evaluating the merits of a claim means speculating about the likelihood that the claim is true. That process can be tricky, because we sometimes confuse what's possible with what's probable, and what's probable with what's certain. An event or a fact is *possible* if there's even the slightest chance, however small, that it might be true. To be *probable,* a statement has to have greater than a 50 percent chance of being true. A statement is *certain* only if its likelihood of being true is 100 percent, nothing less. An illustration of the relationship among possibility, probability, and certainty appears in Figure 2.

Take a claim such as "I can survive without water for a month." There's a possibility that claim could be true, but the likelihood is very small. The claim certainly isn't probable, and a good critical listener wouldn't treat it as though it were. In contrast, the statement "I will get married someday" is not only possible, it's also probable, because a very large majority of people marry at least once. Does that fact mean that the claim is certain, therefore? The answer is no, because there's a chance, however small, that it may not happen. For a claim to be certain, there can be absolutely no chance that it isn't true. A claim such as "I will die someday" is certain, because every living creature eventually dies. People who are good at critical listening understand the differences among possibility, probability, and certainty. They bear in mind that just because a claim is possible, that doesn't mean it's worth believing.

Determining the probability of claims you hear isn't always easy. Suppose that Manuel visits his uncle Alfredo, who has been a vegetarian for most of his adult life. "If you eat red meat, you'll eventually die of heart disease," Alfredo constantly warns his nieces and nephews.

How should Manuel evaluate the probability of his uncle's claim? He should start by determining whether the claim is possible. In this case, it is, because there is a possibility that people who eat red meat will die of heart disease. He should then ask himself whether the claim is certain. In this case, it isn't, because many people who eat red meat do not die of heart disease. Manuel therefore knows that the chances that Alfredo's claim is true are between 1 percent and 99 percent. Thus, although he cannot accept the claim as a certainty, neither can he reject it as an impossibility. What he should do is to consider the probability that the claim is true. To determine probability, he needs to research the link between heart disease and the consumption of red meat. With that information, he can assess whether Alfredo's claim is probable—that is, true more often than it is false—or improbable—that is, false more often than it is true.

Becoming a Better Empathic Listener

Within our relationships, a common goal for listening is to provide empathy and support. Being a good empathic listener can be difficult at times, but it's not impossible.

FIGURE 2 Possibility, Probability, and Certainty A statement is *possible* if its likelihood of being true is between 1 percent and 50 percent. It is *probable* if its likelihood of being true is between 51 percent and 99 percent. It is *certain* only if its likelihood of being true is 100 percent.
© McGraw-Hill Education/Ken Cavanagh photographer

LISTEN NONJUDGMENTALLY.   When we listen to learn, and especially when we listen to evaluate, we often make judgments about the information we're taking in. Good empathic listening, however, is about being open-minded and nonjudgmental.

Two strategies are particularly helpful. The first is to listen without interrupting. Being supportive and empathic means letting the other person say what he or she needs to say without breaking in. Fight the urge to jump into the conversation, and simply listen. Second, don't offer advice unless asked. When you're hearing other people tell you their problems, your tendency is likely to be to respond with advice on how to solve those problems.[56] A good empathic listener will remember that people aren't always looking for advice—often, they just want someone to listen to them.

ACKNOWLEDGE FEELINGS.   Empathizing involves understanding how someone else is feeling and trying to relate to those feelings. It's not the same thing as sympathizing, which means feeling sorry for the other person. An important strategy for good empathic listening, therefore, is to acknowledge a speaker's feelings and allow him or her to continue expressing them.

We do so by responding to speakers with *continuer statements,* phrases that identify the emotions a person is experiencing and allow him or her to communicate them further. In contrast, it is important to avoid *terminator statements,* phrases that fail to acknowledge a speaker's emotions and thereby shut down the person's opportunity to express them. After listening to a patient describe her concerns about the progress of her illness, for instance, empathic physicians can use a continuer statement such as "That must make you feel very uncertain" or "I can imagine how scary this must be" to reassure the patient that they understand and appreciate her feelings. Physicians with less empathic ability are more likely to use terminator statements such as "We're doing everything we can" and "You just need to give this some time." Those types of responses imply to the patient that her feelings are unimportant.

In a 2007 study, researchers examined conversations between advanced cancer patients and their oncologists.[57] With permission, the researchers recorded nearly 400 conversations between patients and oncologists and listened for times when patients expressed negative emotions such as sadness, fear, and anxiety. When those moments arose, the researchers found that oncologists replied with continuer statements only 22 percent of the time. Younger physicians were more likely than older ones to use continuers, and female physicians were more likely than male physicians to do so. Those findings don't mean that oncologists lack empathy. Rather, the data suggest that they may have trouble communicating their empathy through emotionally supportive listening responses. Such responses are particularly important for individuals who are struggling with terminal illnesses.

There are times when it may be difficult to empathize with other people. If you have never lost a parent, for instance, it would be very difficult for you to understand that experience. When you find yourself in such a situation, resist the urge to tell the speaker "I know how you feel." Unless you really do understand the speaker's experience, he or she might find your statement disrespectful or insincere, even if you mean it as a show of support. Instead, use your listening skills to try to understand how the person is feeling. See the "Got Skills?" box to learn more about that skill.

COMMUNICATE SUPPORT NONVERBALLY.   One of the most important aspects of being a good empathic listener is to communicate your support nonverbally. When you're listening rather than speaking, your nonverbal behaviors convey your interest, understanding, and empathy to the speaker.

Media Note: The movie *Dead Man Walking* includes several scenes depicting empathic listening, which might be used to illustrate the advice to acknowledge feelings.

CONNECT: SmartBook is an adaptive reading and learning experience that highlights key concepts students need to know in the moment. SmartBook continuously adapts to students' learning needs as they engage with the content and even provides additional Learning Resources for an individualized and interactive study experience.

got skills?
LISTENING EMPATHICALLY DURING GRIEF

Offer an empathic ear when someone needs it.

WHAT?
Learn to listen empathically when another person is experiencing grief.

WHY?
To provide support to individuals at difficult times in their life, as when they lose a parent or other close relative, a dear friend, or a cherished pet.

HOW?
1. Tell the person that you are willing to listen and help however you can.
2. Let the person express his or her feelings without judgment. There is no right or wrong way to grieve.
3. Avoid telling the person "I know how you feel" unless you have experienced the same type of loss yourself.
4. Encourage the person to take care of his or her physical and other needs.
5. Listen patiently, and don't diminish the person's grief with a statement such as "You have to be strong," which can make the person feel ashamed of his or her feelings.

TRY!
1. When someone you know experiences a significant loss, tell the person you are available to listen if he or she wants to talk. Allow the person to decide when it is time to talk.
2. Find a quiet, comfortable place to listen, and minimize distractions. Do not answer text messages or cell phone calls. Give the person 100 percent of your attention.
3. If you're unsure of what to say, remember that you needn't say much at all. Your job is to allow the other person to speak.

CONSIDER: *During times of grief, why does it help to be listened to?*

Perhaps the most important nonverbal behavior in this situation is eye contact. Speakers often watch your eye behaviors to see whether you're paying attention to what they're saying. If you allow yourself to be distracted by your environment, you can convey the message that you aren't really listening. Other important behaviors are your use of facial expressions and touch. A reassuring smile and a warm touch can make people feel as though you understand, support, and empathize.[58]

LEARN IT What is the vividness effect? When should you question another person's credibility? Why is it important to listen nonjudgmentally?

APPLY IT Television commercials offer ample opportunity to sharpen your critical listening skills. Spend some time watching advertisements and thinking about the claims they're making. How credible are the sources? How probable are the claims? Do the commercials encourage you to make inferences that aren't supported by evidence? If so, how do they do this? Write up your findings in a brief report.

In the IM: You can now access the end-of-chapter Discussion Questions and the Research Library in the Instructor's Manual for each chapter.

REFLECT ON IT In what situations do you find it difficult to engage in informational listening? Whom do you know who is a particularly good empathic listener?

MASTER the chapter

1 The Nature of Listening (p. 215)

- Listening is the active process of making meaning out of another person's spoken message.
- The ability to listen effectively is important to success in a variety of communicative contexts.
- Listening is a learned skill that includes more than merely hearing.
- Cultural differences in the directness of verbal communication affect expectations for listening.

2 Ways of Listening (p. 222)

- Effective listening has six stages: hearing, understanding, remembering, interpreting, evaluating, and responding.
- People engage in informational listening, critical listening, and empathic listening in interpersonal contexts.

3 Common Barriers to Effective Listening (p. 229)

- Noise is anything that distracts you from listening to what you wish to listen to.
- Pseudolistening uses feedback behaviors that make it seem as if you're paying attention even when you aren't; selective attention means listening only to what you want to hear.
- Information overload refers to the state of being overwhelmed by the large amount of information each of us takes in daily.
- Glazing over is daydreaming during the time you aren't spending on listening.
- The rebuttal tendency is the tendency to debate a speaker's point and formulate your reply while the person is still speaking.
- Being closed-minded means failing to listen to anything with which you disagree.
- Some people engage in competitive interrupting, or interrupting to take control of a conversation.

4 Becoming a Better Listener (p. 236)

- Becoming a better informational listener means separating what is and isn't said, avoiding the confirmation bias, and listening for substance.
- Becoming a better critical listener means being skeptical, evaluating a speaker's credibility, and understanding probability.
- Becoming a better empathic listener means listening nonjudgmentally, acknowledging feelings, and communicating support nonverbally.

KEY TERMS

closed-mindedness (p. 234)
competitive interrupting (p. 235)
confirmation bias (p. 237)
critical listening (p. 226)
empathic listening (p. 226)

glazing over (p. 233)
HURIER model (p. 222)
information overload (p. 231)
informational listening (p. 225)
listening (p. 215)

pseudolistening (p. 230)
rebuttal tendency (p. 234)
selective attention (p. 230)
skepticism (p. 238)
vividness effect (p. 238)

connect

To maximize your study time, check out CONNECT to access the SmartBook study module for this chapter, watch videos, and explore other resources.

Emotion

© Photos 12/Alamy

A ROLLERCOASTER OF EMOTION

Fans of AMC's *The Walking Dead* know that every episode puts characters—and viewers—through the emotional wringer. Fear, anxiety, anger, and overwhelming sadness and grief hang in the air of this post-apocalyptic world. Glenn Rhee (played by Steven Yeun) and Maggie Greene (played by Lauren Cohan) met and fell in love as the world was falling apart, and their emotional connection is one of few glimmers of hope in an otherwise bleak existence.

Communication amid chaos has been the bedrock of Glenn and Maggie's relationship—and has made them both valuable assets in this violent world. But traumatic experiences threaten Glenn and Maggie's romance as well as their lives. Their relationship becomes strained after the pair is tortured for information by a character called "the Governor," but they are able to repair it by clearly expressing their feelings and verbalizing their commitment to each other. Glenn and Maggie manage to remain close, even after an extended separation (during which each is uncertain about the other's survival) and in the aftermath of seemingly unbearable personal losses, because they recognize and respect each other's emotions.

Emotion is a powerful force. When we experience an intense emotion, such as the profound sorrow of losing a loved one or the profound joy of reuniting with one, it can seem as though our emotions consume us. In some respects, that's exactly what happens: Our emotions are so connected to our body, mind, and behaviors that they practically overtake us. Understanding this powerful and often mysterious force can therefore help us appreciate the enormous role it plays in how we relate to others.

1 Emotion in Interpersonal Communication

So much of what we say, think, and do is affected by our emotions; yet we seldom stop to consider what emotions are. We realize that emotions cause us to feel and act in certain ways, but why? In this section, we'll define emotions and consider how they are related to moods. We'll then examine specific forms of emotions that are joyful and affectionate, hostile, or sad and anxious, considering their applications to interpersonal communication as we do.

What Is an Emotion?

Emotion might seem like the kind of phenomenon you can't really define, but when you feel it, you certainly recognize it. Emotions can be powerful, even life-changing, experiences, but what kind of experiences are they, exactly? According to researchers, an **emotion** is the body's multidimensional response to any event that enhances or inhibits a person's goals.[1] For example, you feel nervous before a final exam because the possibility of failing interferes with your goal of passing it. Doing well on the exam makes you happy because your goal has been met; doing poorly makes you angry or disappointed because your goal has been inhibited. You feel sad when a cherished pet dies because your goal of maintaining a relationship with that pet has been thwarted. Basically speaking, emotion is your mind and body's way of reacting so that meeting your goals feels good, and not meeting them feels bad.

EMOTION IS DIFFERENT FROM MOOD.   Many people refer to emotions as moods (and vice versa), but moods and emotions are different experiences. Whereas an emotion is a response to a specific event (such as passing an exam or losing a pet), a **mood** is a feeling that has no specific identifiable cause.[2] You might feel as though you're in a good or a bad mood for no obvious reason. If you can identify the reason you feel good or bad, then you're probably experiencing an emotion rather than a mood. Moods also are more persistent, often lasting for days or weeks at a time.[3] In contrast, most emotions are relatively short-lived.

Emotions come in many forms. Communication scientist and emotion expert Laura Guerrero has suggested that we can understand many emotions by placing them in one

emotion The body's multidimensional response to any event that enhances or inhibits one's goals.

mood A feeling, often prolonged, that has no identifiable cause.

Communication scientist Laura Guerrero suggests that most emotions fit one of three categories: those that are joyful or affectionate, those that are hostile, and those that are sad or anxious. © Stockbyte/Punchstock, RF; © Masterfile; © James Darell/ Digital Vision/ Getty Images, RF

of three categories: (1) joyful and affectionate, (2) hostile, or (3) sad and anxious.[4] Let's look at some of the specific emotions that constitute each category.

Joyful/Affectionate Emotions: Happiness, Love, Passion, and Liking

What makes you happy? If you're like most people, your personal relationships are high on the list.[5] Feeling connected to others is a source of profound joy for many people, and emotional experiences of joy and happiness play an important role in making those relationships rewarding. In this section, we will look at the emotions of happiness, love, passion, and liking to understand their functions in interpersonal communication.

HAPPINESS.   Of all human emotions, happiness is one of the most easily and universally recognized.[6] **Happiness** is a state of contentment, joy, pleasure, and cheer. People in all known cultures display happiness by smiling, laughing, and being energetic, and they all interpret those behaviors as indicating happiness.[7]

To some extent, happiness begins as an individual experience. When we feel happy, however, our tendency is to approach and reconnect with people.[8] In other words, happiness tends to make us share our joy with others by seeking contact and being emotionally expressive in our interactions.[9] Those behaviors, in turn, often make the other party happy, so that happiness becomes a truly social experience. Research indicates that happiness also contributes to our health and well-being by helping us recover from the harmful effects of stress.[10]

LOVE AND PASSION.   Love can be easier to recognize than to define. One reason is that we experience so many forms of love, including romantic love, love for friends, love for family members, love for God, and love for the self. Love is a remarkably powerful emotion that motivates people to behave in ways they otherwise would not. Love for a romantic partner, for instance, can cause people to quit their jobs, sell their homes, and even move thousands of miles to be together. Likewise, people make extraordinary sacrifices out of love for their children or love for God. **Love,** therefore, means caring for, feeling attached to, and feeling deeply committed to someone.[11]

Some forms of love are accompanied by **passion,** an emotion that mixes feelings of joy and surprise with experiences of excitement and attraction for the target of our passion.[12] People often feel passion in the early stages of a romantic or sexual

happiness A state of contentment, joy, pleasure, and cheer.

love The emotion of caring for, feeling attached to, and feeling deeply committed to someone.

passion A secondary emotion consisting of joy and surprise, plus experiences of excitement and attraction for another.

relationship, when behaviors such as kissing, handholding, saying "I love you," and interacting sexually are novel. Because passion is partially based on surprise, it is enhanced by the novelty of those behaviors.

For the same reason, however, passion also tends to fade as people get to know each other better.[13] In that way, passion acts to bring people together initially so they can discover and explore whatever feelings they have for each other. If they develop genuine love for each other, their relationship can develop and grow even after the experience of passion has faded away.[14] People can also feel passion in the absence of romantic love, as when they feel passionate about an activity or a cause.

When we like someone, we enjoy that person's company and want to spend time with him or her. © Cade Martin/CDC

Love and passion are examples of *social emotions,* which means they typically arise out of our social interactions. That is, social emotions are usually directed at specific people or other social entities (such as a pet or a deity). When you love, you love someone in particular. When you feel passion, it is for someone or something specific.

LIKING.   Another example of a social emotion is liking. You might consider liking simply to be a less intense form of love—but liking and loving actually are different emotions. Is there anyone you would say you love but don't really like? If so, then you already have an understanding of the difference between the two.

Whereas love means feeling attachment, caring, and commitment to someone, **liking** is a product of your overall evaluation of another person.[15] If you enjoy being around someone and generally view his or her personality and behavior positively, then you probably like that person even if you wouldn't say you love him or her. Likewise, if there are people you love and feel a sense of commitment to but don't enjoy spending time with, then you probably love those people even though you don't particularly like them.

When we feel liking for others, we often display that emotion using high immediacy behaviors such as smiling, touch, and standing or sitting close to them. We also tend to share activities, such as playing sports and shopping together, and we make an effort to spend time with them because we enjoy their company.[16]

Although happiness, love, passion, and liking are distinct emotions, they often have similar effects on interpersonal communication. Specifically, they all motivate us to seek the company of others.[17] When we feel happy, we often want to share our happiness with friends and family members by interacting with them. When we like, love, or feel passionate about someone, we enjoy being around that person, and we often feel dissatisfied when we're apart. In that way, joyful, affectionate emotions all act to enhance interpersonal communication by drawing us closer to the people we care about.

liking A positive overall evaluation of another person.

Joyful emotions enhance interpersonal communication by drawing individuals close to each other. © Rob Melnychuk/ Digital Vision/Getty Images, RF

Hostile Emotions: Anger, Contempt, Disgust, Jealousy, and Envy

Joyful, affectionate emotions produce positive sensations. However, there are occasions in our relationships when more unpleasant emotions become aroused. In this section, we'll look at five hostile emotions that are common in interpersonal relationships and that can be destructive if they aren't managed properly: anger, contempt, disgust, jealousy, and envy.

anger An emotional response to being wronged.

In Everyday Life: Many events in everyday life cause us some measure of anger. Ask your students to provide examples from their own lives of communication-oriented events that elicit anger.

Focus on Ethics: The frequent depiction of contemptuous behavior on television and in movies may partially desensitize people to its harmful effects on receivers. By definition, however, contemptuous behavior is done to hurt others. Is there any situation in which expressing contempt is ethical?

ANGER.   **Anger** is an emotional response to perceiving that you have been wronged in some way. If another driver cuts you off in traffic, if you get a lower final grade than you feel you deserve, or if your significant other forgets your anniversary, you'll likely feel some measure of anger, whether it be mild annoyance or outright rage. When you feel angry, your tendency is to attack or enact revenge on whomever you perceive has wronged you.[18] That's why the communication of anger involves behaviors such as yelling, throwing objects, making unpleasant facial expressions, and even physically attacking another person.[19]

Just as experiencing happiness can enhance well-being, research indicates that anger can be harmful to health. Several studies have shown that the stress of feeling and expressing anger puts people at elevated risk for coronary heart disease,[20] other heart problems,[21] circulatory disorders,[22] and stroke.[23] Other research has reported that individuals who are unable to control their anger have weakened immune systems[24] and take longer to heal from wounds[25] compared with people who manage their anger in more positive ways.

Anger may not feel good, but it can be a useful emotion if we express it constructively rather than destructively. For tips on doing so, check out the "Got Skills?" box.

contempt A feeling of superiority over, and disrespect for, others.

CONTEMPT.   **Contempt** leads you to feel that you're better than someone else. It is one of the most harmful emotions for personal relationships.[26] People express contempt by insulting or mocking others, putting others down, belittling or making fun of others, and signaling that others are stupid or incompetent.[27] Those actions send messages of judgment, disapproval, and disrespect. Research shows that they can trigger a cycle of negative behavior within relationships. Studies by psychologist John Gottman have found that expressions of contempt from one romantic partner often lead the other to withdraw and become distant—a reaction that can leave conflicts unresolved and put the couple at increased risk of breaking up.[28]

disgust A feeling of revulsion in reaction to something offensive.

Talking Point: Researchers have also found that people experience disgust when asked to eat chocolates molded into the shape of tarantulas or to drink orange juice from sterilized containers that would otherwise be used for collecting urine. Thus, disgust often overrides rational thought.

DISGUST.   **Disgust** is the feeling of revulsion you experience when confronted with something you find offensive or repellent.[29] Perhaps it's a foul odor that causes your stomach to churn or a message or image that profoundly offends you. In either case, disgust provokes a strong emotional and physical reaction that motivates you to avoid, reject, or expel whatever is disgusting you.[30]

Many researchers believe disgust developed as an instinctive reaction to prevent us from consuming food that is rancid or unclean.[31] If you feel disgusted at the thought of drinking sour milk or eating bacteria-ridden meat, for instance, that emotional response probably protects you from the physical harm that could result if you ate those foods.

How is disgust relevant to interpersonal communication? The answer is that people can feel the same type of repulsion when they are confronted with others whose values,

got skills?   EXPRESSING ANGER CONSTRUCTIVELY

When you feel angry, here's how to convey it in a healthy manner.

WHAT?

Learn to express anger in ways that are constructive, rather than destructive.

WHY?

To communicate about the *reasons behind your anger* while avoiding the problems that anger itself can cause.

HOW?

1. Recognize that all emotions, including anger, are temporary experiences. Give yourself time to *feel* your anger before you express it.

2. Don't bury your feelings. Suppressing your anger may be more comfortable than confronting it, but doing so can cause more anger to build up over time.

3. Separate people from their actions. Instead of saying "I'm angry with you," say "I'm angry about something you have done."

4. Focus on the present. When expressing anger, don't bring up past mistakes or conflicts. Instead, concentrate on what's going on now.

TRY!

1. Recall an event from your recent past in which someone's behavior caused you to feel angry.

2. Write a paragraph to the person in which you identify the problematic behavior and explain why you felt angry about it. Keep your anger focused on the behavior, not on the person.

3. After expressing your anger, indicate what you think should happen. If you feel the other person owes you an apology, say so. If there's something you think he or she should do, describe it. Tell the other person what would make the situation better.

CONSIDER: *How does your paragraph compare to the way you actually communicated with this person at the time?*

---

beliefs, or behaviors they abhor.[32] Their disgust often causes them to avoid interacting with such people and even to avoid artifacts they feel represent them. Researchers have found, for instance, that most Americans are unwilling to put on a sweater if they believe it was once worn by a convicted murderer.[33] The connection between people's disgust for the murderer and their rejection of his or her sweater is so strong, in fact, that most people remain unwilling to wear the sweater even if it has been completely unraveled and re-knit.[34]

JEALOUSY.   Many people use the term *jealousy* interchangeably with the term *envy,* or they say that they're jealous when they really mean they're envious. Jealousy and envy are two different emotions. We experience envy when we want what another person has. For instance, you might feel envious of a friend's new condo or your brother's new motorbike. **Jealousy** occurs when people feel that an important relationship is threatened by a third party.[35] You might feel jealous when you see your romantic partner flirting with someone else, for example.

The experience of jealousy mixes three emotions: fear (that your relationship is being threatened), anger (at the people who are threatening it), and sadness (at the

Media Note: On the student web page, the video clip "The Green Monster" illustrates the experience and expression of jealousy.

jealousy The perception that an important relationship is being threatened by a third party.

Emotions are personified in the film *Inside Out,* with Anger, Disgust, Joy, Fear, and Sadness all struggling to be expressed inside the mind of a young girl. © *Pictorial Press Ltd / Alamy*

envy The desire for something another person has.

Talking Point: Even though envy can motivate people toward self-improvement, many religions consider envy to be one of seven "deadly sins." Does the sinful part of envy depend more on how we react to our envy than on whether we experience it in the first place?

CONNECT: Reports from SmartBook assignments show you where students are struggling and excelling. You can view reports for an entire class or an individual student.

In Everyday Life: One of the most intense forms of sadness is the experience of having a "broken heart," which is often a reaction to love that is unrequited. Ask how many of your students have personally experienced this form of sadness.

thought of losing your relationship). Although we may associate jealousy primarily with romantic bonds, we can experience it within the context of other important relationships as well. For instance, we may feel jealous if a close friend begins spending time with a new friend, even though we don't usually think of friendship as an exclusive relationship.[36] What matters in that situation is that we consider our relationship with our friend to be important. We tend not to react with jealousy when unimportant relationships are threatened.

ENVY. As we just considered, **envy** occurs when we want what another person has.[37] For example, you may be envious of your co-worker's car or the attention your sibling gets from your family. We may envy one person's wealth, another person's intelligence, and another person's physical attractiveness because we want those attributes for ourselves. As those examples illustrate, envy involves comparing ourselves with others and perceiving that we come up short in the comparison.[38] We feel envious only when the object of our comparison is highly relevant to us. We envy another person's car, for instance, only if having a nice car is important to us.[39]

On its own, envy isn't always negative. In fact, it can be a good motivator. Envying another person's physique might motivate us to exercise more often. Envying someone else's income could motivate us to do well in school or start our own business.[40] The problem is that we sometimes harm or impede the people we envy. For instance, Collette's envy at her roommate's new promotion and higher salary leads her to try to get her roommate in trouble at work. She frequently calls and stops by the bank where her roommate works because she knows those actions annoy the bank manager and reflect poorly on her roommate. Instead of trying to improve her own work performance, Collette tries to sabotage her roommate's career. In short, envy can cause people to harm others, and in the process they can harm their relationships.

Like joyful emotions, hostile emotions influence the ways we communicate interpersonally. In contrast to joyful emotions, hostile emotions are often unpleasant and challenging for relationships. Anger leads us to attack or to seek revenge. Contempt leads us to put others down, and disgust motivates us to avoid them. Jealousy motivates us to attack a perceived rival, and envy can encourage us to harm those we envy.

Regardless of their negative outcomes for relationships, however, those emotions are normal aspects of the human experience. Just as it is normal to feel joy and love, it is also entirely normal to feel anger, contempt, disgust, jealousy, and envy from time to time. What matters for interpersonal communication is how we manage those emotions when we feel them. We will examine constructive ways of managing emotions in the fourth section of this chapter.

Sad/Anxious Emotions: Sadness, Depression, Grief, Fear, and Social Anxiety

Hostile emotions are unpleasant and often motivate us to hurt others in some way. Sad and anxious emotions are no less unpleasant than hostile emotions. In contrast to hostile emotions, however, they typically prompt us to withdraw instead of attack—that is, to shut ourselves off from others. In that sense, sad and anxious emotions can be just as problematic for relationships as hostile emotions. In this section, we will look at five types of sad/anxious emotions: sadness, depression, grief, fear, and social anxiety.

SADNESS AND DEPRESSION.   Sadness, which means feeling unhappy, sorrowful, and discouraged, is most often the result of some form of loss. Indeed, two of the most common causes of sadness are the loss of a person and the termination of a relationship.[41] For instance, we would feel sad about the death of a close friend and also about losing our relationship with a loved one because the person has Alzheimer's disease. Like our displays of happiness, expressions of sadness are highly similar across cultures. They tend to include frowning, crying, disengaging from routine activities, and speaking quietly, slowly, and without energy.[42]

Some people think of depression simply as extreme sadness, but the two are quite different. Sadness is a normal emotional response to loss, and although it is often painful, it is relatively short-lived. In contrast, clinical **depression** is a medically diagnosed physical illness that can linger for months or even years and is associated with symptoms such as excessive fatigue, insomnia, significant changes in weight, feelings of worthlessness, and recurring thoughts of suicide or death.[43] Whereas people are typically sad about specific events, they can be depressed for no apparent reason.

Suffering from clinical depression can be profoundly debilitating and can contribute to job loss, divorce, social isolation, and strained relationships with family and friends.[44] Fortunately, there are several ways of treating depression, including antidepressant medications and various forms of counseling and psychotherapy.[45] Exercising[46] and keeping a journal[47] also help individuals suffering from depression.

GRIEF. In the 2011 movie *Extremely Loud and Incredibly Close,* nine-year-old Oskar Schell (played by Thomas Horn) struggles to come to terms with the death of his father, who was killed in the World Trade Center during the terrorist attacks of September 11, 2001. When a loss is profound—such as the loss of a loved one—we experience sadness as **grief.** According to researchers, grief is not an isolated emotional experience so much as it is an emotional process of dealing with a terrible loss.[48]

Therapists have suggested that the grieving process comprises five steps. The first step, *denial,* means pretending the loss didn't occur and everything is fine. In the next step, *anger,* the grieving person is furious with whoever

sadness Emotion involving feeling unhappy, sorrowful, and discouraged, usually as a result of some form of loss.

depression A physical illness involving excessive fatigue, insomnia, changes in weight, feelings of worthlessness, and/or thoughts of suicide or death.

grief The emotional process of dealing with profound loss.

In *Extremely Loud and Incredibly Close* (2011), Oskar Schell experiences grief over the loss of his father. © AF archive / Alamy

fear The mind and body's reaction to perceived danger.

amygdala A cluster of neurons in the brain that largely controls the body's fear response.

social anxiety Fear of not making a good impression on others.

inflicted the loss, even if that person has passed away. The third step, *bargaining,* means offering deals with a higher power to restore what was lost (such as promising to live differently if God will take away the loss). The fourth step is called *depression,* and although it does not necessarily mean suffering from clinical depression, it entails feeling withdrawn or "numb." The final step, *acceptance,* occurs when the anger, sad-ness, and mourning have tapered off and the person accepts the reality of the loss.[49] Although each step is a normal part of grieving, not every grieving person experiences all five steps or goes through them in the same order.

FEAR.   **Fear** is the mind and body's reaction to perceived danger. Many people fear heights, enclosed spaces, snakes, or guns, for instance, because of the perceived dangers of falling, being trapped, being bitten, or being shot.[50] Fear causes immediate changes in our body that are largely controlled by a cluster of neurons in the brain called the **amygdala.**[51] When we experience fear, the amygdala causes our heart rate and breath-ing rate to go up, the pupils of our eyes to dilate, and our stress hormones to rise.[52]

Those physiological changes make us more aware of the potential threat and give us extra energy to respond to it.[53] The amygdala sometimes also causes us to become tense, or "freeze up." That response temporarily immobilizes the body, giving us a chance to assess the danger before reacting to it.[54] The purpose of fear, therefore, is to keep us safe from harm. When we experience fear, our tendency is usually to withdraw from the situation and protect ourselves, at least long enough to figure out what the danger is and how we can best deal with it.

SOCIAL ANXIETY.   From time to time, many people experience **social anxiety,** which is the fear of not making a good impression on others.[55] Perhaps you're meeting your romantic partner's family for the first time and you worry that they won't like you; or you fret about the impression you'll make on your first day at a new job. Maybe you're afraid you might mess up on a class presentation. Each situation is a form of social anxiety, which usually leads people to hide or avoid the situation.

Feeling social anxiety from time to time is normal. When social anxiety becomes chronic and starts to interfere with daily life, it may signify a mental health condi-tion known as *social anxiety disorder.*[56] Unlike routine social anxiety, social

Fear causes immediate changes in our body that are largely controlled by a cluster of neurons in the brain called the amygdala.

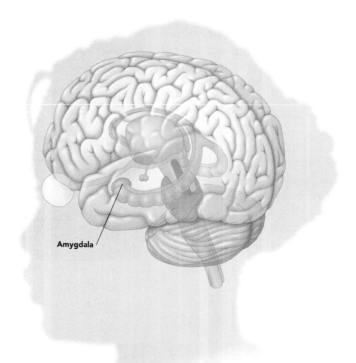

Amygdala

anxiety disorder often requires treatment with some combination of psychotherapy and medication.

Experiencing sadness, depression, grief, fear, or social anxiety often makes us want to withdraw from social interaction, for at least two reasons. In the cases of sadness, depression, and grief, we may avoid others—or, at least, limit our interactions with them—because we need time alone to deal with our emotion. In contrast, when we are fearful or socially anxious, withdrawing from others can help us feel protected and safe. When we perceive that others are experiencing sad or anxious emotions, however, we often want to interact with them more, to convey our care and concern. In such cases, it's important to remember that others may need time to themselves, just as we might if we were in the same situation.

LEARN IT What is an emotion, and how is it different from a mood? How are love and liking different? What's the difference between jealousy and envy? When do people experience grief?

APPLY IT Interview a faculty member in your school's psychology department to learn more about communicating effectively with people who are suffering from either depression or social anxiety disorder. Ask the professor for some specific tips about what to do—and what to avoid—in social interactions with depressed or socially anxious individuals. Write a detailed journal entry describing what you learn.

REFLECT ON IT When do you feel contempt or disgust? What experiences cause you fear?

2 The Nature of Emotion

We humans experience a broad range of emotions. Although every emotion is distinct, we can understand emotions better by examining their common characteristics.

Emotions Are Multidimensional

We call emotions multidimensional because every emotion has several components: physiological, cognitive, behavioral, social, and cultural. Let's briefly consider each.

EMOTIONS ARE PHYSIOLOGICAL. Suppose you're at home waiting for your friend Simone, whom you've invited for dinner, to arrive. When she's 15 minutes late, you start to wonder if she's okay—particularly because she's always punctual—but you figure that the rush-hour traffic is slowing her down. After an additional half hour passes, you begin to fidget and feel tense, so you try calling her on her cell phone. After the fifth time you've called and she hasn't answered, you get a sick feeling in your stomach, and you notice that you're breathing more heavily than normal. Then, when you finally see her pull into your driveway, you immediately begin to feel relaxed as your body returns to its normal state.

When you experience emotions, particularly intense ones, your body reacts in patterned, predictable ways. Fear, for instance, causes your heart to beat faster, your

© Latin Stock/Imagesource/ PictureQuest, RF

HAPPY PEOPLE LIVE LONGER: THE LIFE BENEFITS OF JOY

Happiness and other positive emotions—such as love, optimism, and gratitude—may feel good to us for a very important reason: because they are good *for* us. Multiple studies have now shown that people who are happy live longer and healthier lives than those who aren't. One study of nearly 5,000 university students found that their level of optimism when they started school predicted their longevity over the next 40 years. Another study of almost 90,000 adults found that happiness with life predicted a lower risk of cardiovascular disease, stroke, and death over a 12-year period. Importantly, the link between happiness and health is often independent of factors such as socioeconomic class, marital status, and religion, which can affect people's quality of life on their own.

Even though happiness is associated with a longer, healthier life, researchers recognize that happiness doesn't necessarily *cause* health. Being happy can cause us to be healthier, but having a long, healthy life can also lead us to be happier. In either case, the connection between positive emotion and longevity is well established, suggesting that positive emotions can be a boon to our quality of life.

Source: Diener, E., & Chan, M. Y. (2011). Happy people live longer: Subjective well-being contributes to health and longevity. *Applied Psychology: Health and Well-Being, 3,* 1–43.

breathing rate to increase, and your pupils to dilate. Your adrenal glands elevate the stress hormone cortisol, which increases your blood sugar and suppresses bodily systems (such as your digestive and reproductive systems) that aren't essential for fighting the source of your fear.[57] Those responses put you in a state of "high alert" so you can deal with whatever is causing you fear. Indeed, the main reason emotions such as fear, joy, sadness, and jealousy feel so distinct from one another is that they cause different physical changes in the body.[58]

The specific bodily changes that accompany each emotion serve a purpose. In particular, each emotion causes responses that help the body first to deal with that specific emotion and then to restore itself to a natural, balanced state. As the "Communication: Light Side" box describes, emotions can even have positive effects on our well-being and longevity.

EMOTIONS ARE COGNITIVE. Although each emotion feels distinct in some ways, different emotions can arouse some of the same physical sensations. For instance, both passion and fear cause increases in heart rate, breathing rate, and blood pressure. When we experience those reactions, how do we know whether we're feeling fear, passion, or some other emotion? We can identify the true emotion because our mind steps in and puts an emotional "label" on what we're feeling.[59] Emotions therefore also have a strong cognitive component.

You probably know that to be true if you've ever found yourself confused about which emotion you're feeling. Let's say you're sitting in class and find yourself unable to concentrate because you're perspiring, your heart is pounding, and you can barely sit still. There's no obvious reason why you should be feeling that way—you don't feel upset or nervous or especially excited. So your mind begins searching for an explanation. Perhaps you think about how you argued with your mother the day before and you say to yourself, "I must be more upset about that than I thought I was." Maybe you wonder if you're anxious about an upcoming exam and decide for yourself, "I'm obviously feeling stressed about that." Those are just two examples of how your mind makes inferences about your emotions. You notice how you're feeling physically, and your mind uses the available information to identify the emotion you must be feeling.

EMOTIONS ARE BEHAVIORAL. In addition to being physiological and cognitive events, emotions include a behavioral component. Specifically, they are associated with **action tendencies,** which are the kinds of actions a particular emotion prompts us to take.[60] For example, the action tendency associated with fear is self-protection. Therefore, feeling afraid causes us either to withdraw from a frightening situation or to defend ourselves against a threat.[61] If we successfully withdraw from or fight off the source of our fear, then we no longer feel afraid. When we feel angry, our action tendency is to attack or to enact revenge on the party that has wronged us.[62]

The action tendency for fear is self-protection. When we feel afraid, therefore, we take actions to protect ourselves from potential harm. © *Zuma Press, Inc / Alamy*

When we feel joyful, our action tendency is to interact with the people we care about.[63]

Action tendencies relate to the specific behavioral pattern that an emotion motivates us to engage in, but we don't necessarily always follow that pattern. If you feel frightened, for example, you aren't always able to fight the source of your fear or to withdraw from it, even though that's what you're motivated to do. As another example, regardless of how worried you are concerning your upcoming midyear review with your supervisor, you may not be able to avoid it even if you want to.

action tendencies Motivations to act in a particular way when experiencing an emotion.

EMOTIONS ARE SOCIAL AND CULTURAL. The emotions we feel in a given situation are shaped, in many ways, by our society's beliefs about that situation.[64] For instance, many Americans would feel disgust at the thought of eating dogs, cats, snails, snakes, camels, guinea pigs, or rats, even though those animals are routinely eaten in societies around the world.[65] People raised as Hindus would feel similar disgust at the thought of eating hamburger—a staple of the U.S. American diet—because cows are considered sacred in the Hindu religion.[66]

There's nothing inherently more disgusting about eating one type of animal rather than another. What causes some people to feel disgust and others to feel delight are the social practices and messages with which they are familiar. Social differences in emotions can translate into dramatically different behaviors.

Suppose you applied to several universities but didn't get into your top choice. If you grew up in a North American society, you'd probably experience disappointment at being turned down, or maybe even anger at yourself for not having prepared better for the admissions test. In response to those emotions, you might retake the test the following year (in hopes of reapplying to the college of your choice) or accept admission to a less desirable school. In contrast, if you grew up in Japan, your primary emotion in that situation would likely be shame at the dishonor or disgrace you have brought upon yourself and your family by failing to achieve admission. In fact, one way some people in Japan deal with severe shame is by committing suicide, because the action tendency for shame is to hide or disappear from others.[67] Japan has one of the world's

Talking Point: Besides influencing which emotions we feel in a given situation, our social and cultural norms also affect when and how we express our emotions, a point that will be examined later in this chapter.

AT A GLANCE

Components of Emotion

Physiological	Emotions cause changes in physiological outcomes, such as blood pressure, breathing rate, and hormone levels.
Cognitive	We cognitively label the physiological outcomes of emotion to identify a particular emotional state.
Behavioral	Emotions have action tendencies that urge us to behave in particular ways.
Social and Cultural	The emotions we experience and express are partially determined by the social and cultural messages and practices we have learned.

Talking Point: From a cognitive perspective, one might say "I feel good because I'm happy." From a physiological standpoint, however, a more accurate statement would be "I'm happy because I feel good." In other words, the physiological processes that accompany an emotion are largely responsible for the valence of the emotion.

valence The positivity or negativity of an emotion.

Look at this photograph for a moment and imagine yourself there. Do you feel calm? Relaxed? Happy? Positive emotions often have the same effect by promoting relaxation, reducing stress, and increasing the production of feel-good hormones. © *Guy Crittenden/ Photographer's Choice/Getty Images*

highest suicide rates, partly because shame is such a large part of Japan's emotional repertoire.[68]

See the "At a Glance" box for a summary of the four basic components of emotion.

Emotions Vary in Valence and Intensity

Although an emotional experience is simultaneously physiological, cognitive, behavioral, and sociocultural, emotions are not composed of the same exact combinations of those four dimensions. In this section, we will look at two variables that make each emotional experience distinctive: valence and intensity.

EMOTIONS VARY IN VALENCE.　Perhaps the most fundamental way to classify emotions is by their **valence,** which means whether they are positive or negative. Many emotions—such as joy, love, and gratitude—have a positive valence. As a result, we

generally enjoy experiencing them. Other emotions—such as anger, fear, and contempt—have a negative valence. We find those emotional experiences generally unpleasant.

In both cases, the physical processes that go along with those emotions are largely responsible for why they feel good or bad to us. For instance, a positive emotion such as love promotes relaxation, reduces stress, and increases the production of feel-good hormones such as oxytocin and dopamine.[69] In contrast, a negative emotion such as anger promotes anxiety, increases blood pressure, and elevates levels of stress hormones such as cortisol.[70]

We can classify *most* emotions as either positive or negative, but not all. An exception is the emotion of surprise, which is generally considered to have a neutral valence.[71] When we are happy about a surprise, such as a generous raise, we experience surprise positively. When we are unhappy about a surprise, such as a disappointing final grade, we experience it negatively. In either case, it is the *focus* of our surprise—the raise or the grade—and not the emotion of surprise itself that creates the positive or negative valence.

EMOTIONS VARY IN INTENSITY.   Emotions also vary in their intensity or strength. For instance, when Jerome received several voice mail messages from the loan officer at his bank, he felt anxious about what it might mean, because he had missed a couple of payments on his mortgage. When he called the loan officer and was asked to come in right away, Jerome felt worried about what the news would be. Finding out that the bank had decided to foreclose on his home made Jerome feel genuinely terrified about where he was going to live. Anxiety, worry, and terror are all forms of the same emotion—fear—but they differ from one another in their intensity. Anxiety is a mildly intense form of fear, worry is a moderately intense form, and terror is a very intense form. Similarly, some experiences might make you annoyed, others might make you mad, and still others might make you furious. Those are all forms of anger, but they differ in their intensity.

When emotional experiences become overly intense, they can be debilitating. That means they impair our ability to function. When you're terrified or furious, for instance, the intensity of those emotions can make it difficult to think or behave rationally. It can also inhibit your ability to communicate clearly with others, because your emotions may be overwhelming you. When you find yourself debilitated by the intensity of your emotions, it's important to recognize that you may not be in control of your thoughts or behaviors. In those cases, you should ask for help from someone you trust. The good news is that extreme emotional intensity rarely lasts for very long, so if you have someone who can help you through the emotional experience, you'll soon find that you are no longer debilitated.

Emotions Come in Primary and Secondary Forms

Perhaps you can think of times when you haven't been certain of which emotions you were feeling. One explanation may be that some emotional experiences are mixtures of other emotions. You might have learned about the primary colors—red, yellow, and blue—when you were a child. They're called *primary* because they are not derived from other colors. When you combine them, however, you get *secondary* colors: Red and blue make purple; blue and yellow make green; yellow and red make orange. In

In the IM: The out-of-class activity "Affect Graph" encourages students to document the valence of their emotions over the course of three days.

Talking Point: As a discussion point, ask your students to identify mild, moderately intense, and very intense forms of other emotions, such as joy, sorrow, or surprise.

In the IM: The in-class activity "The Primacy of Primary Emotions" tests students' abilities to encode and decode primary emotions.

primary emotions Distinct emotional experiences not consisting of combinations of other emotions.

some ways, emotions are the same. Researchers consider particular emotions to be **primary emotions,** meaning they are distinct emotional experiences, not combinations of other emotions.[72]

One important feature of primary emotions is that people experience and express them in fundamentally the same way across cultures. Psychologist Paul Ekman has proposed that six of the emotions we have surveyed thus far in this chapter are primary emotions: joy, sadness, anger, fear, surprise, and disgust.[73] How does he know? Because people in a wide range of cultures—including preliterate cultures minimally influenced by the Western world—encode and decode those emotions similarly.[74] In every known society, for instance, smiling means joy, frowning means sorrow, and scowling means anger. Researchers have also found that the primary emotions have fundamentally the same causes everywhere.[75] For example, people in all cultures feel surprised when unexpected events happen, joy when positive events happen, fear when they believe something bad is about to happen, and sorrow when bad events do occur.

People in every known culture experience joy in response to positive events, such as being reunited with a loved one. Cultural similarity in this and other emotional experiences suggests that emotion is not strongly influenced by culture; rather, it may be more innate. © *Image Source Pink/ Alamy, RF*

The fact that people experience and express primary emotions similarly across cultures suggests that primary emotions are not strongly influenced by culture. Rather, they may be more innate, which means we're born with the tendency to experience and express primary emotions in particular ways. If so, then primary emotions are likely to be directly affected by biological structures. The body's *limbic system* coordinates how the brain and nervous system regulate emotion and motivation. When you experience a primary emotion, the limbic system—and particularly the amygdala—is actively engaged.[76]

Focus on Scholarship:
Scholars disagree on how many primary emotions there are and on what they are. Nearly every list, however, contains fear, sadness, surprise, anger, and joy. Research has also found that cross-cultural similarity in emotion displays (at least, for facial displays of emotion) is higher for some emotions than others. One study found the highest rates of similarity for displays of joy and the lowest rates of similarity for displays of surprise and disgust.[ii]

[ii]Russell, J. A. (1994). Is there universal recognition of emotion from facial expression? *Psychological Bulletin, 115,* 102–141.

There is *some* cultural variation about which emotions are considered to be primary. Traditional Hindu beliefs propose nine primary emotions, including amusement, sorrow, fear, anger, wonder, perseverance, disgust, serenity, and sexual passion.[77] Traditional Chinese culture also recognizes shame and "sad love" (love for former partners) as primary. For the most part, however, the primary emotions are more similar than different across cultures.

Primary emotions can combine in various ways to produce **secondary emotions.** A good example is jealousy, which, as we've seen, is a combination of three primary emotions: anger, fear, and sadness.[78] Many other emotions are also combinations of primary emotions, including remorse (a mix of sadness and disgust), contempt (disgust and anger), and awe (surprise and fear).[79]

secondary emotions Emotions composed of combinations of primary emotions.

Referring to those and other emotions as secondary doesn't mean they are less important than the primary emotions. Later in the chapter, we'll explore how many secondary emotions play central roles in the ways people communicate within personal relationships. Calling an emotion secondary means only that it is made up of a combination of primary emotions.

Sometimes Emotions Are Meta-Emotions

Do you enjoy watching scary movies? Have you ever been embarrassed because you felt jealous of someone else? Have you felt excited about being in love, or guilty that you didn't feel sad enough when tragedy struck? If your answer to any of those questions is yes, then you can recall experiencing meta-emotions. You might recall from earlier chapters that metacommunication is communication about communication. Similarly, when researchers use the term **meta-emotion,** they are referring to emotion about emotion.[80] If you experience joy because of the controlled fear induced by a scary movie, for instance, you are feeling one emotion (joy) about another (fear). Your joy, therefore, is a meta-emotion. If you feel embarrassed about your jealousy, excited about your love, or guilty about your lack of sadness, then your embarrassment, excitement, and guilt are all meta-emotions.[81]

> **meta-emotion** An emotion about emotion.

Meta-emotion includes how we feel about other people's emotions as well as our own. Perhaps you've been surprised at a co-worker's anger, worried about a friend's depression, or happy about a child's joy. Your surprise, worry, and happiness are meta-emotions, too, even though they are feelings about someone else's emotions rather than your own.

Meta-emotions are important because they help us understand and reflect on the emotions that we or others are experiencing or not experiencing. If I feel guilty about not being sad when a tragic event occurs, then I evidently think I *should* feel sad even though I don't. My guilt can therefore cause me to reflect on what the tragedy means to me, why I'm not feeling sadder about it, and why I believe I should feel worse. In the process, I can come to understand my own emotions better.[82]

Many people enjoy feeling afraid when they watch a scary movie. In that instance, their joy is a meta-emotion. © Moodboard/Getty Images, RF

LEARN IT What are examples of the physiological, cognitive, behavioral, and sociocultural dimensions of emotion? What is the difference between an emotion's valence and its intensity? How do you know if an emotion is primary or secondary? What are some examples of meta-emotions?

APPLY IT The ability to interpret the valence and intensity of emotion displays is important when it comes to interacting with others. Go through some photos in magazines or newspapers that capture expressions of different emotions. For each, determine whether the emotion is positive or negative and whether it is mild, moderately intense, or very intense. Compare your assessments of valence and intensity with those made by others. This type of practice will help you to recognize emotion displays you encounter in other people.

REFLECT ON IT When do you have difficulty labeling an emotion you're feeling? What physical changes do you notice when you experience an intensely positive emotion?

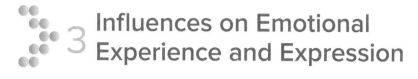

3 Influences on Emotional Experience and Expression

Several variables affect how we experience and express emotions. Those influences include cultural background, display rules, technology and computer-mediated communication, emotional contagion, sex and gender, personality, and emotional intelligence.

Culture

Even though people around the world experience the same range of emotions, cultural practices shape the expression of some emotions. For instance, collectivistic cultures such as India and Japan discourage people from expressing negative emotions toward members of their own culture, but they often condone negative emotions directed at people from other cultures.[83] That pattern is reversed in individualistic cultures such as the United States and Canada, which sometimes discourage the expression of negative emotion toward people from other cultures but often allow it when directed at "insiders."[84]

Even within the United States, cultural groups vary in their emotional expression. For example, Chinese Americans often reflect the traditional Chinese values of moderation and emotional control by being less demonstrative of their positive and negative emotions than Americans of European descent.[85] In contrast, traditional Mexican culture encourages people to express emotions openly, so Mexican Americans tend to be more demonstrative of emotion, on average, than European Americans.[86]

GEOGRAPHY. One factor that curiously appears to influence cultural differences in emotional expression is geography. In 1748, the French political thinker Charles de Secondat Montesquieu proposed that living in a warm climate would make people more expressive of their emotions than would living in a cold climate.[87] Contemporary

Montesquieu proposed that people are more emotionally expressive in warm climates than in cold climates, and contemporary research has supported that idea. © *Steve Vidler/Mauritius Images Gmbh/Alamy;* © *Jeff Schultz/Design Pics Inc / Alamy*

research has found that to be the case. In a survey of nearly 3,000 college students from 26 countries, psychologists James Pennebaker, Bernard Rimé, and Virginia Blankenship found that people from southern parts of countries are more emotionally expressive than those from northern regions.[88] Other research has found that, within the United States, people from the South touch each other more frequently than do people from the North.[89]

How do we account for that tendency? Montesquieu explained that warm weather causes the skin to relax, allowing nerve endings to become more exposed to pain, pleasure, and other sensations. He believed this heightened sensitivity made people more attentive to what they were feeling and therefore more likely to express it. In comparison, cold weather inhibits the sensitivity of nerves, causing people to be less attentive to various sensations and therefore less expressive of what they feel.

CO-CULTURES.   Co-cultures can also affect how we deal with emotions. Some co-cultures encourage people to examine their emotions directly and express them freely. For example, an artistic co-culture, such as a theater group or a community of sculptors, might encourage the ability to express and respond to emotions for its value in the creation and appreciation of those art forms.

Other co-cultures, however, discourage people from dealing openly with their emotions. As one example, many military personnel returning from active combat duty avoid seeking treatment for post-traumatic stress disorder (PTSD) because they perceive that the military co-culture stigmatizes such treatment. PTSD is an anxiety disorder that some people develop after experiencing a severely troubling event, such as combat or a natural disaster. You may recall reading in the Listening chapter about a support group for military personnel suffering from PTSD. In a study of soldiers returning to the United States from combat in Iraq and Afghanistan, medical researchers found that as many as 77 percent of individuals with signs of PTSD refused treatment, citing their fear of being stigmatized by the military as a primary concern.[90] Those results are significant because when PTSD is untreated, it frequently leads to other problems, including drug and alcohol abuse.

display rules Unwritten codes that govern the ways people manage and express emotions.

Display Rules

Another factor influencing the expression of emotion is what psychologists Paul Ekman and Wallace Friesen call display rules.[91] **Display rules** are a social group's norms for how emotions should be expressed. These unwritten codes govern the ways people manage and express their emotions, and they vary according to the individual's social situation. Display rules include:

- *Intensification:* Exaggerating your emotion to appear as though you are experiencing it more intensely than you are. For example, you may pretend to be overjoyed about seeing an old acquaintance at an event, when in fact you find it only mildly pleasant. In that case, you intensify your emotion to make your acquaintance feel good.

- *De-intensification:* The opposite of intensification—that is, downplaying an emotion to appear as though you are experiencing it less intensely than you are. You may be extremely angry with a co-worker for missing a deadline, but in the presence of your supervisor you

© Paul Bradbury/Getty Images, RF

AT A GLANCE

Emotion Display Rules

Intensification	Acting as though you're terrified when you're only mildly worried
De-intensification	Acting as though you're mildly worried when you're actually terrified
Simulation	Acting as though you're terrified when you are really indifferent
Inhibition	Acting as though you're indifferent when you are actually terrified
Masking	Acting as though you're terrified when you're actually sad

decide it's best to seem only mildly annoyed. In that situation, you de-intensify your emotion to be polite or to avoid damaging your colleague's reputation.

- *Simulation:* Acting as though you're feeling an emotion that you actually aren't experiencing. You may not really care about your neighbor's good news, but you act happy anyway when you hear about it because you want to appear supportive.

- *Inhibition:* The opposite of simulation—that is, acting as though you're indifferent or emotionless when you're actually experiencing an emotion. For example, it may make you jealous to see your romantic partner flirting with someone else, but you choose to act as though it doesn't bother you because you don't want to appear vulnerable in front of the other person.

- *Masking:* Expressing one emotion when you are actually experiencing a completely different one. You may be sad and nervous when your son or daughter leaves home for college, but you behave as though you're happy so that you don't spoil his or her excitement.

Additional examples of Ekman and Friesen's five display rules appear in the "At a Glance" box.

Communication technology impacts how we experience and express emotion. © *Diego Azubel/ Corbis Wire/Corbis*

Technology and Computer-Mediated Communication

People use technology so often that they may not realize how it affects their experience and expression of emotion. In fact, computer-mediated communication technologies can influence emotional behaviors in at least three ways.

First, as we recognized in the Nonverbal Communication chapter, many communication technologies rely heavily on text, preventing our conversation partners from seeing or hearing our nonverbal emotion cues. As a result, we can't use our facial expressions or tone of voice to convey what we're feeling, the way we would in a face-to-face talk. We have other means of representing emotion within the text, however. One approach is to use emoticons and emoji to convey facial expressions, such as a smiling face to represent happiness and a confused face to show when we're puzzled. These devices may seem contrived, but a 2014 study showed that the human brain reacts to emoticons in the same way it reacts to real faces.[92] Incorporating emoticons and emoji can therefore be an effective way of conveying emotion in a text-based format. Another approach is to embed statements about our emotions into the text. Sometimes we do so in abbreviated form, such as by writing "j/k," which stands for "just kidding," to convey that we are joking or being sarcastic. In such ways, we compensate for the limitations of channel-lean forms of communication on the expression of emotion.

A second way that communication technology affects our experience and expression of emotion is by increasing our opportunities for sharing emotion. For instance, social networking allows us to share stories, photographs, and other information about our life experiences with our friends and contacts. When we get good news, we can easily share it with a wide variety of people, and when we go through sad or stressful experiences, we can elicit support from others. In these ways, communication technology provides us with ongoing opportunities to disclose both positive and negative emotional experiences in our lives with others.

Relatedly, when we go through emotionally challenging experiences, the Internet provides multiple opportunities to discuss those situations with people who have also gone through them. We can find online chat rooms and support groups for a wide range of emotional experiences, including losing a loved one, dealing with a job loss or serious illness, and having to provide care for an elderly relative. In those sites, people express emotions about their situation to others whom they know can relate to them, and they listen to the experiences of other people. In such ways, the Internet creates many opportunities to share our emotions with others.

Finally, we experience and share emotions about technology itself. Perhaps you feel anxiety or frustration when your laptop crashes or your smartphone loses its signal. You may also remember feelings of excitement and joy the first time you encountered a new technology, such as Netflix or an iPad. Research confirms that many people experience intense and genuine emotions when they are interacting with technology.[93] Sometimes those emotions even affect our relationships with others. You may be able to recall times when you've felt closer to someone while watching television or playing a video game together, for instance. In all those ways, computer-mediated communication technology influences how we experience emotions—and also how we communicate them to others.

Emotional Contagion

The emotions we feel and express are influenced not only by our cultural heritage but also by the emotions that individuals around us feel and express in any given situation. That process, called **emotional contagion,** involves the tendency to mimic other people's experiences and expressions.[94] Maybe you've noticed, for instance, that when there's one unhappy person in your group, it's not long before everyone is unhappy. That's because emotions are "socially contagious." Therefore, being around a cheerful person can make you more cheerful, and being around an anxious person can lead you to feel nervous.[95]

Emotional contagion occurs even when people are communicating online. In one study, researchers induced sadness in a group of college students by having them watch a sad movie.[96] The students then took part in a 15-minute conversation via instant messaging. Compared to students who were *not* induced to be sad, the sad participants communicated in a more depressed manner, by using more terms connected to sadness and

Talking Point: It might be good advice to avoid text-based communication technologies when one is conveying strong emotions. Because these technologies are channel-lean, the potential for misinterpretation of emotion is great.

CONNECT: The Item Analysis Report provides a section's average score on each question within a single question bank assignment, or you can compare multiple sections' scores.

Focus on Scholarship: As one example of a contagion effect, people are highly likely to yawn when in the presence of others who are yawning. Although yawning is a behavior rather than an emotion, the "yawn contagion" effect is highest for those who score high on measures of empathy, suggesting that we mimic another's yawn as a way of empathizing with that person.[iii]

[iii]Platek, S. M., Mohamed, F. B., & Gallup, G. G., Jr. (2005). Contagious yawning and the brain. *Cognitive Brain Research, 23,* 448–452.

emotional contagion
The tendency to mimic the emotional experiences and expressions of others.

© Blend Images—JGI/Jamie Grill/Getty Images, RF

by exchanging their messages at a slower rate. Moreover, the partners of sad participants reported feeling sad themselves, indicating that the participants' emotions were contagious even in an IM chat.

In online communities, emotional contagion can occur on large scales. For instance, one study examined how rainfall in a city influences the emotion in Facebook status updates made by users in that city. Using data from millions of Facebook users, the researchers found that rainfall in a city affected emotions expressed by users in that city. More important, it also influenced the emotions conveyed by the users' Facebook friends, even in cities where no rain was falling. The researchers found that for every one user affected directly, rainfall influenced the emotion of another one to two users through emotional contagion.[97]

Sex and Gender

Biological sex and gender roles influence both the experience and the expression of emotions. Research shows, for instance, that men are more likely than women to report feeling hostile emotions such as anger across a range of cultures. Conversely, women are more likely than men to report feelings of fear, sadness, shame, and guilt.[98] The consistency of those findings across cultures suggests that such sex differences in emotional experience may have a biological cause.[99]

Women and men also differ in how likely they are to express the emotions they are feeling. People of both sexes feel positive emotions, such as joy and affection, but women are more likely than men to express those emotions when they feel them.[100]

Women are also more expressive of sadness and depression than men are.[101] Some studies have found that men feel freer to express anger when they feel it,[102] but other research has failed to find such a difference.[103]

Women and men often differ in their experiences of jealousy. According to several studies, women are more likely to feel jealous when their partners are emotionally unfaithful, but men are more likely to feel jealous when their partners are sexually unfaithful. © Izabela Habur/Getty Images, RF

SEX DIFFERENCE IN JEALOUSY? One emotion for which women and men may differ in both their experience and their expression is jealousy. Several studies have found that in personal relationships, men are more likely than women to experience *sexual jealousy* (stemming from a partner's sexual interaction with another person), whereas women are more likely than men to experience *emotional jealousy* (stemming from a partner's emotional connection with another person).[104] Research finds that sex difference across cultures[105] and also indicates that women and men have distinctly different patterns of brain activity when imagining sexual and emotional infidelity.[106]

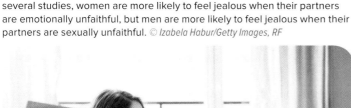

Other research has found that men are more likely than women to express their jealousy through behaviors such as confronting the rival, becoming sexually aggressive or promiscuous with others, wooing the partner back with gifts, or breaking off the relationship.[107] Women, in contrast, tend to express their jealousy through behaviors such as improving their own physical appearance, seeking support from others, demanding increased commitment from the partner, and trying to make the partner jealous himself.[108]

Not all research has supported those sex differences in jealousy, however. Some studies have suggested that the observed differences reflect flaws in the methodology of measuring jealousy.[109] Other studies have shown that both sexes experience more anger over sexual infidelity but more hurt over emotional infidelity.[110] Still other research has found that women and men differ from each other when they imagine how they *would feel* if a partner were unfaithful but not when they recall how they *did feel* during an actual experience of infidelity.[111] Researchers are likely to continue studying and debating sex differences in jealousy for some time.[112]

GENDER ROLES AND EMOTIONAL EXPRESSION.   Emotional expression is influenced by gender roles as well as by biological sex. Research indicates that individuals who classify themselves as *androgynous* (meaning they have both feminine and masculine traits) are more emotionally expressive than are individuals who classify themselves only as highly masculine. That finding appears to be true regardless of the type of emotion being displayed. Androgynous people have also been shown to be more expressive than people who are only highly feminine when it comes to certain emotions, such as happiness, sadness, and disgust.[113]

Why might gender role affect the expression of emotion? Some scholars believe that traditional femininity encourages women to express emotions that help them form relationships (such as happiness) and make them appear vulnerable (such as sadness) but to suppress emotions that make them appear dominant (such as anger). Conversely, traditional masculinity is thought to encourage men to express anger but discourage them from expressing most other emotions.[114] The scholars' observations don't mean that women and men always communicate in those ways. They do suggest, however, that traditional gender roles may encourage that type of differentiation.

There is evidence that gender roles affect not only the expression of emotion but the experience of it as well. In one study, for instance, highly feminine women were more likely than highly masculine women to experience negative emotions, including guilt, sadness, pessimism, and self-dislike. In comparison, highly masculine men were more likely than highly feminine men to report experiencing social withdrawal, dissatisfaction, and suicidal thoughts.[115] In both instances, that is, masculine women and feminine men reported more positive emotions.

The "Fact or Fiction?" box further explores the influence of gender on emotional expressiveness.

Personality

In the Communication and the Self chapter, we explored how personality profoundly influences many aspects of life. The experience of emotion is no exception. Research suggests that three particular aspects of personality affect the emotion experience: agreeableness, extroversion, and neuroticism.[116]

Agreeableness relates to how pleasant, accommodating, and cooperative you are. Compared with the average person, highly agreeable people are happier and are better

Focus on Scholarship: A counterintuitive finding regarding gender roles is that masculinity is positively associated with the expression of affection, meaning that more masculine people are more affectionate than less masculine people.[iv] Why might that be the case?

[iv]Floyd, K. (2006). *Communicating affection: Interpersonal behavior and social context.* Cambridge, England: Cambridge University Press.

Talking Point: Ask how many of your students would describe themselves as above average on agreeableness. A large percentage of your class is likely to respond affirmatively. By definition, agreeableness is a socially desirable trait, so social desirability biases likely cause people to overestimate this trait in themselves. Ask your students who might be a more accurate judge of their agreeableness.

Focus on Scholarship: Neuroticism is strongly associated with symptoms of clinical depression, according to research.[v]

[v]Boyle, L. L., Lyness, J. M., Duberstein, P. R., Karuza, J., King, D. A., Messing, S., & Tu, X. (2010). Trait neuroticism, depression, and cognitive function in older primary care patients. *American Journal of Geriatric Psychiatry, 18*, 305–312.

agreeableness One's tendency to be pleasant, accommodating, and cooperative.

fact **OR** *fiction?* WOMEN ARE MORE EMOTIONAL THAN MEN

A common stereotype, at least in North American cultures, is that women experience emotions more intensely than men do and that women are more likely to express their emotions than men are. Is that stereotype true?

The answer is yes and no. In a now-classic study, psychologists Ann Kring and Albert Gordon looked at whether women and men differ from each other on how emotionally expressive they are and what their physiological responses are to emotional situations. Participants in their studies watched movie clips designed to evoke strong emotional reactions.

Consistent with the stereotype, women in both studies expressed more emotion than men did. However,

women did *not* experience their emotions more intensely than men did, a finding that is contrary to the stereotype. In fact, men were more physiologically reactive than women, but only to the emotion of fear—reactions to other emotions did not differ between women and men.

It therefore appears that women *are* more emotional than men when it comes to expressing emotion, but *not* when it comes to how intensely they experience emotions.

FROM ME TO YOU

Because men usually aren't as emotionally expressive as women, the media often portray them as emotionally *deficient*. They aren't, though. There are certainly benefits to expressing your emotions, a skill at which many women excel.

There are also benefits to controlling your emotions, however, a point that is often lost in pop psychology books and talk-show discussions. Controlling emotions may give people an advantage in social situations. By not letting others know how they feel, those who control their expressions may avoid having their emotions exploited by others. Therefore, don't think of men's lesser expressiveness as a deficit but rather as a characteristic that can be advantageous in some circumstances.

Source: Kring, A. M., & Gordon, A. H. (1998). Sex differences in emotion: Expression, experience, and physiology. *Journal of Personality and Social Psychology, 74,* 686–703.

Rubberball/Mark Andersen/Getty Images, RF

at managing both stress and emotions in general.[117] They're also more likely than others to use constructive styles for managing conflict and are more willing to "lose" an argument to preserve a relationship with someone else.[118]

extroversion One's tendency to be sociable and outgoing.

Extroversion refers to how sociable and outgoing you are. Extroverted people enjoy social interaction and are often talkative, assertive, and enthusiastic. Extroverted people tend to focus on the positive aspects of other people or situations.[119] Perhaps as a result, extroverted people are happier, on average, than the typical person.[120]

neuroticism One's tendency to think negative thoughts about oneself.

Finally, **neuroticism** is the tendency to think negative thoughts about oneself. Unlike extroverted people, people who are highly neurotic tend to see the worst in situations and to focus much of their attention on negative events.[121] Thus, they are more likely than others to experience negative emotions such as anger, guilt, anxiety, and depression and are less likely to report being happy.[122] They also manage their emotions less successfully than do their less neurotic counterparts.[123]

assess your skills | HOW EMOTIONALLY INTELLIGENT ARE YOU?

Read the following statements, and indicate how much you agree or disagree with each by writing a number between 1 and 10. A response of 1 means you completely disagree, and 10 means you completely agree.

1. _____ I think about and reflect on my emotions.
2. _____ I can express my emotions to others.
3. _____ I understand the causes and effects of my emotions.
4. _____ I use my emotions to improve my relationships.
5. _____ I am able to experience both positive and negative feelings.
6. _____ I can accurately identify the emotions other people are feeling.
7. _____ I know the difference between emotions and moods.
8. _____ I can reorganize my thoughts on the basis of what I'm feeling.
9. _____ I understand how emotions change over time.
10. _____ I can manage my own emotions effectively.

When you're done, add up your responses. Here's how to interpret the results:

- If you scored between 10 and 40, then you probably can improve your emotional intelligence. Learning more about this topic may help you.

- If your score was 41–70, you are moderately emotionally intelligent, meaning you have the skills to express and perceive emotions accurately, but you can also improve that ability.

- If you scored between 71 and 100, you have high emotional intelligence, which probably benefits your interpersonal communication with others.

Source: Adapted from Mayer, J. D., & Salovey, P. (1997). What is emotional intelligence? In P. Salovey & J. D. Sluyter (Eds.), *Emotional development and emotional intelligence* (pp. 3–31). New York, NY: Basic Books.

Emotional Intelligence

Emotional intelligence refers to a person's ability to "perceive and accurately express emotions, to use emotion to facilitate thought, to understand emotions, and to manage emotions for emotional growth."*[124] People with high emotional intelligence are aware of their own emotions as well as the emotions of others and pay attention to their emotions when making decisions about how to act.[125]

Few studies have investigated the association between emotional intelligence and emotional expressiveness. Those that have tend to report that individuals with high emotional intelligence are more likely than those with lower levels to express warmth, affection, and other positive emotions.[126] Given what we know about sex differences in emotional expression, it may not surprise you to learn that women score higher than men on measures of emotional intelligence.[127]

How emotionally intelligent are you? Take the short quiz in the "Assess Your Skills" box to find out.

emotional intelligence
The ability to perceive and understand emotions, use emotions to facilitate thought, and manage emotions constructively.

*Brackett, M. A., Mayer, J. D., & Warner, R. M. (2004). Emotional intelligence and its relation to everyday behavior. Personality and Individual Differences, 36, 1387–1402. Quote is from p. 1389.

One condition that inhibits emotional intelligence is **alexithymia,** a personality trait characterized by a relative inability to understand, process, and describe emotions.[128] Studies indicate that the prevalence of alexithymia in the general population is approximately 5 to 9 percent and that it is equally common among women and men.[129] Those with alexithymia do not understand their own emotions and often seem stone-faced, distant, and unconcerned with others' feelings.[130] As a result, they may avoid developing emotionally close interpersonal relationships.[131] For people in established relationships, alexithymia can impair relationship satisfaction by making it difficult for partners to understand what each other is feeling.[132]

LEARN IT How do people from individualistic and collectivistic cultures differ in their expression of negative emotions? What are the five display rules for emotion? How does communication technology influence the expression of emotion? How do women and men differ in their emotional expression? Which aspects of personality influence emotion?

APPLY IT To identify how gender roles might influence the communication of emotion, spend five minutes with a few other classmates brainstorming about which emotions women are encouraged to express and discouraged from expressing. Then do the same for men's emotions. What patterns do you see?

REFLECT ON IT In what situations do you intensify or de-intensify your emotional expressions? In what ways does your gender role influence your experience and expression of emotion?

4 Sharpening Your Emotional Communication Skills

As is the case for many communicative behaviors, we can manage the expression of our emotions in either positive or negative ways. Denying and suppressing your emotions isn't healthy. In fact, medical research shows it can actually exacerbate a host of health problems, including asthma, heart disease, and cancer.[133] On the other hand, overreacting to your emotions isn't good for you, either.[134] The best strategy for dealing with emotions is to find a balance between those two extremes. This section will offer some suggestions for improving your ability to manage emotional expression in productive ways.

Identifying Emotions

Perhaps the most important emotional communication skill you can develop is the ability to recognize and identify the emotions you're experiencing.[135] Research shows that people who can accurately identify which emotion they're feeling—whether it's anger, nervousness, sadness, shame, or guilt, for instance—are best equipped to manage emotions in productive ways.[136]

To illustrate that point, let's say that a new co-worker has joined your team and is receiving a great deal of praise and attention from your supervisor. As a result, you begin to feel jealousy, which, as we have seen, is a combination of anger, sadness, and fear. What would happen, though, if you recognized that you were feeling only anger and not sadness and fear as well? In that situation, you'd respond only to your anger, perhaps by speaking harshly to your supervisor or co-worker. You wouldn't also deal with your fear of losing your supervisor's favor or your sadness that others might like or respect your co-worker more than you. As a result, your sadness and fear would go unaddressed, and your expressions of anger would likely be counterproductive.

If you find it difficult to identify your emotions in a given situation, there are at least three techniques that might help: Listen to your body, pay attention to your thoughts, and take stock of the situation.

LISTEN TO YOUR BODY. First, try paying attention to what your body is doing. Recall that emotions cause physiological changes. Although different emotions can have similar effects on the body, thinking about how your body is reacting to the situation may help you determine which emotion you're experiencing. On the basis of your experiences, for instance, you probably know that jealousy causes different sensations in your body than joy, disgust, and surprise do. Reflecting on how you feel physically can therefore help you determine which emotional experiences you are going through.

PAY ATTENTION TO YOUR THOUGHTS. Emotions affect the mind as well as the body, so paying attention to your thoughts can help you clarify your emotional experiences. Let's say you're questioning whether a particular situation is making you angry or sad. If you're feeling angry, your thoughts most likely are focused on hurting or punishing whoever is the source of your anger. For instance, if you notice that you're imagining yelling or speaking sternly to the person, those thoughts probably arise out of anger. In contrast, if you're feeling sad, your thoughts probably are focused on whatever you feel you're losing, whether it's a cherished friendship, an enjoyable time in your life, or a job you enjoy.

When you're uncertain about which emotion you're feeling, pay attention to how your body is reacting to the situation. © *Brand X Pictures/ PunchStock, RF*

TAKE STOCK OF THE SITUATION. Earlier in this chapter, you learned that emotions are reactions to events that you perceive to interfere with your goals. Unlike a mood, therefore, every emotion has a cause. A third strategy you can use to identify your emotions is to try to determine what is happening in your situation that you're reacting to.

Suppose, for example, you're upset but can't figure out whether you're anxious or envious. Take stock of what's occurring in your environment. Often, you can identify which emotion you're experiencing by considering what might be interfering with your goals. Has a recent illness caused you to fall behind in your schoolwork? If so, that situation might make you anxious because it's interfering with your goal of completing your work. From a different perspective, has a close friend recently become engaged? Although that situation might make you happy, it might also make you envious if you perceive that your friend has a better romantic relationship than you do—a perception that interferes with your goal of having the relationship you want.

Reappraising Negative Emotions

When you experience a negative emotion, emotional reappraisal is a productive strategy for dealing with it. **Emotional reappraisal** involves changing the way you think about the situation that gave rise to the negative emotion so that the effect of the emotion is reduced.[137]

emotional reappraisal The process of changing how one thinks about the situation that gave rise to a negative emotion so that the effect of the emotion is diminished.

got skills?

REFRAMING

Deal with negative situations by reframing.

WHAT?

Learn to reframe the meaning of a negative interpersonal situation.

WHY?

To make your emotional response to a negative event—such as an extended visit from your very loud young nephews—more constructive.

HOW?

1. Suppose you're babysitting your three nephews, and they are requiring every bit of your energy. Describe the situation.

EXAMPLE: *My nephews are hyperactive and they won't let me have one minute of peace.*

2. Identify the words with emotional connotations.

EXAMPLE: *hyperactive* = negative connotations, identified as something present in your situation; *peace* = positive connotations, identified as something lacking in your situation.

3. Rephrase in less negative terms.

EXAMPLE: *My nephews are very energetic and they definitely keep me busy.*

TRY!

1. Think about a recent negative or difficult interpersonal interaction you've had.

2. Describe the situation briefly in writing.

3. Identify any words you used in your description that have emotional connotations.

4. Now rephrase your description by changing only the emotion-laden words into words with positive connotations.

5. By changing the language you use to talk about your situation, you can often improve your own thoughts and emotions about it.

CONSIDER: *How does reframing force you to see your situation differently?*

Talking Point: The idea behind emotional reappraisal is that we can change our emotional experience by changing how we think about the situation that caused it. The fact that it can work is a reflection of the connection between emotions and cognitions.

Let's say you're upset with the grade you received on a research paper. Although you felt your work was highly original and well written, your instructor's evaluation didn't reflect that opinion. Going to your instructor's office while you're angry and distraught, however, may cause you to say or do something that will only make the situation worse. Instead, you could wait until you're less upset to reappraise the situation and then consider the best way to express your thoughts. You might think more analytically about your paper and what you might have done to make it better reflect the assignment. You might remind yourself that your grade isn't your instructor's evaluation of you as a person but rather of your performance on this one task. You might also remind yourself that your instructor was just doing his or her job by grading you or that this grade will have only a modest effect on your overall academic record. Such exercises help you to reappraise an emotional situation and to consider it from a broader perspective. Adopting a reappraisal strategy can also reduce your negative emotions and help you communicate more effectively.[138]

A technique that is closely related to emotional reappraisal, called *reframing,* involves changing not only the way you *think* about a negative situation but also the way you *talk* about it. Check out the "Got Skills?" box to learn more about this useful strategy.

Accepting Responsibility for Emotions

You learned in the Language chapter about the importance of *owning* your thoughts and feelings—that is, the importance of acknowledging that you determine your own thoughts and emotions by describing them with I-statements ("I feel angry") rather than you-statements ("You are making me angry"). Accepting responsibility for emotions is challenging because emotions are, after all, reactions to events that affect you. When someone teases or insults you, for instance, you probably feel hurt. You don't choose to feel hurt, however. Instead, you're simply reacting to that person's behavior.

The problem with describing your emotions with you-statements is that such statements fail to acknowledge the part you play in determining how you feel. Instead, they simply blame the other person for your emotions, without any prescription for change.[139] A more productive approach is to say "I feel hurt when you insult me." This statement acknowledges that your emotions are your own (I feel hurt . . .), but it also identifies the specific event that causes them (. . . when you insult me), making it clear to the receiver which behaviors you are asking him or her to change.

In Everyday Life: Using I-statements to describe emotions is easier said than done in everyday life. The reason is that we see our emotions as being reactions to things that are happening outside us (including other people's behaviors), so we perceive those as causing our emotions and naturally want to identify those causal relationships by using you-statements.

Separating Emotions from Actions

Emotion and behavior go hand in hand, and most emotions have specific action tendencies associated with them. Yet experiencing an emotion doesn't mean you have to act on it. Feeling angry with someone, for example, doesn't necessarily mean you must yell at that person. Likewise, feeling love for someone doesn't necessarily mean you must express it. Just as you "own" your emotions, you also "own" your behaviors. Part of being a competent interpersonal communicator is being able to determine the most appropriate and most effective way for you to act on your emotions.

Before you act on your emotions, it's generally best to stop and think about the possible effects of your actions. Let's say Gerard is worried about how much weight his brother-in-law Marcus has gained in the last year. Because of his fear, Gerard feels he should talk to Marcus about the health dangers of obesity and encourage him to exercise and adopt a low-calorie diet. Before Gerard does so, however, he weighs the pros and cons of acting on his fear in this way.

From a positive perspective, Marcus may appreciate knowing how much Gerard cares about him. He may also be motivated to reduce his weight, saving himself from potentially life-threatening health problems. From the opposite perspective, however, Marcus may resent Gerard's interference. He may tell Gerard to mind his own business and even more stubbornly refuse to change his behaviors, a stance that would put his health at even greater risk.

Although Gerard's primary concern is for Marcus's health, he also does not want to embarrass Marcus or jeopardize their relationship. In the end, Gerard decides to share his concerns with Marcus's wife in the hope that she might be able to persuade Marcus to lose weight.

Talking Point: Throughout history, various jurisdictions have recognized the *crime of passion* as a crime (usually murder) committed under extreme emotional duress. Such an extreme example aside, however, it is reasonable to expect most adults to control the effects of their emotions (both positive and negative) on their behaviors.

Most emotions motivate us to act in certain ways. However, experiencing an emotion doesn't necessarily mean you have to act on it. © *Glow Images/Getty Images, RF*

Identifying and reappraising emotions, accepting responsibility for emotions, and separating emotions from actions are all skills you can learn. The more you practice those skills, the more adept you'll become at managing your emotional communication.

In the IM: You can now access the end-of-chapter Discussion Questions and the Research Library in the Instructor's Manual for each chapter.

LEARN IT How can you identify emotions accurately? When is it helpful to reappraise an emotion? What does it mean to accept responsibility for your emotions? Why should you separate emotions from actions?

APPLY IT Emotional reappraisal is very useful, but it takes practice. The next time you experience a strong negative emotion, force yourself to stop and reappraise the situation before you act. This strategy will give your emotion time to cool down, and it will help you to understand the situation differently. You'll then be in a much better position to decide how best to act.

REFLECT ON IT When do you tend to blame other people for your emotions? For which emotions do you have the hardest time accepting responsibility?

MASTER the chapter

1 Emotion in Interpersonal Communication (p. 245)

- An emotion is your body's reaction to any event that enhances or inhibits your goals.
- Three classes of emotion are particularly relevant for interpersonal communication: joyful/affectionate emotions, hostile emotions, and sad/anxious emotions.
- Joyful/affectionate emotions include happiness, love, passion, and liking.
- Hostile emotions include anger, contempt, disgust, jealousy, and envy.
- Sad/anxious emotions include sadness, depression, grief, fear, and social anxiety.

2 The Nature of Emotion (p. 253)

- Emotions have physiological, cognitive, social, and behavioral components.
- Emotions vary in valence and intensity.
- Emotions come in primary and secondary forms.
- Emotions can be meta-emotions.

3 Influences on Emotional Experience and Expression (p. 260)

- People across cultures experience the same range of emotions, but cultural practices and messages affect how those emotions are communicated.
- Five display rules—intensification, de-intensification, simulation, inhibition, and masking—influence which emotions people express and how intensely they express them.

- Computer-mediated communication technologies affect how we experience emotions and how we communicate them to others.
- According to the emotional contagion effect, people have a tendency to mimic the emotional experiences and expressions of those around them.
- Women and men differ in their tendencies to experience emotion but not in the intensity of their experiences. Women are also more expressive than men. Androgynous adults are more emotionally expressive than masculine men or feminine women.
- Three characteristics of personality—agreeableness, extroversion, and neuroticism—influence the experience and expression of emotion.
- Emotionally intelligent people are attuned to which emotions they are experiencing, and they use their emotions to make decisions about behavior.

4 Sharpening Your Emotional Communication Skills (p. 268)

- Accurately identifying emotions in yourself and others is an important emotional communication skill.
- Reappraising negative emotions means changing the way you think about the situation that caused the emotions, which can lessen their negative effects.
- Competent communicators accept responsibility for their own emotions instead of blaming others for how they feel.
- Although emotions motivate you toward particular behaviors, you are not obligated to act on every emotion you experience.

KEY TERMS

action tendencies (p. 255)
agreeableness (p. 265)
alexithymia (p. 268)
amygdala (p. 252)
anger (p. 248)
contempt (p. 248)
depression (p. 251)
disgust (p. 248)
display rules (p. 261)
emotion (p. 245)

emotional contagion (p. 263)
emotional intelligence (p. 267)
emotional reappraisal (p. 269)
envy (p. 250)
extroversion (p. 266)
fear (p. 252)
grief (p. 251)
happiness (p. 246)
jealousy (p. 249)
liking (p. 247)

love (p. 246)
meta-emotion (p. 259)
mood (p. 245)
neuroticism (p. 266)
passion (p. 246)
primary emotions (p. 258)
sadness (p. 251)
secondary emotions (p. 258)
social anxiety (p. 252)
valence (p. 256)

To maximize your study time, check out CONNECT to access the SmartBook study module for this chapter, watch videos, and explore other resources.

9 Forming and Maintaining Personal Relationships

© Warner Bros./Album/Newscom

FAMILY MEMBERS BECOME FRIENDS

The movie *This Is Where I Leave You* (2014) features Jason Bateman as Judd Altman, a radio producer summoned to his parents' home after the death of his father. He reunites there with his sister and two brothers when their mother (played by Jane Fonda) insists that they stay for the week. During that time, the siblings contend with the complexities of their individual lives as well as the sorrow of losing their father. Judd, who has recently discovered his wife's ongoing affair with his own boss, confronts longstanding tensions in his relationships with his brothers and mother. In the process, he and his siblings come to redefine their relationships and discover ways to support and care for each other not only as family members but also as friends.

magine what life would be like if we could not form or maintain relationships with others. Even our casual relationships—a nodding acquaintance with a fellow congregant at our place of worship or our daily banter with our train conductor—can yield positive benefits. But it is our close relationships—the ones we have with friends, relatives, romantic partners, and even co-workers—that contribute most significantly to our well-being. Sometimes, it's by providing us with social and emotional support. Other times, it's by helping us make an important decision or deal with a problem. Relationships lift our spirits and remind us we're not alone in the world.

This chapter illustrates the importance of personal relationships and examines the processes we use to form and maintain them in our lives. Some material may seem more relevant to certain kinds of relationships than others. To a great extent, however, all relationships encounter similar communication issues. We will begin our discussion by acknowledging why relationships matter to us. Next, we'll explore a variety of ideas about how relationships come to be, and how some relationships grow closer than others. Finally, we'll turn our attention to the processes of maintaining close relationships, and we will examine how relationships are formed and ended.

Talking Point: You might point out that friendship is one of the most pervasive relationships we have. Not everyone has a spouse or siblings or children or even co-workers, but it's a rare person who would say that he or she has no friends.

It is in our nature to develop personal relationships.
© Amana productions inc./Getty Images, RF

1 Why Relationships Matter

Ann Atwater and C. P. Ellis were never destined to become friends. In the 1970s, Atwater—a poor African American mother—was a civil rights activist in Durham, North Carolina, where Ellis was a leader in the Ku Klux Klan, a violent white supremacist organization. During 10 days of community talks about school desegregation, Ellis came to believe that both whites and minorities would benefit from desegregation; he denounced the Klan, and he and Atwater became partners in the civil rights movement. They also became close personal friends. Together, they struggled against oppression and social stereotypes, and they leaned on each other heavily for support. When Ellis died of Alzheimer's disease in 2005, Atwater, having lost a dear—and most unlikely—friend, gave the eulogy at his funeral.

Having strong social ties with friends, neighbors, co-workers, and others improves the quality of our life in multiple ways. In this section, we'll see that we form social ties

In Everyday Life: In his influential book *Bowling Alone* (2000), Harvard professor Robert Putnam points out that Americans are less engaged in their social structures (such as neighborhood groups, churches, and political parties) than ever before. That change may mean that the circle from which we draw our friends has narrowed. Consequently, today we may gravitate more toward similar others as friends than we used to, a trend that could make our friendships less diverse. Putnam's subsequent book, *Better Together,* explores how contemporary social networks may be replacing earlier social structures.

© Goodshoot/Masterfile, RF

need to belong theory A theory that says each of us is born with a fundamental drive to seek, form, maintain, and protect strong relationships.

because we have a strong need to belong. We'll also examine some benefits of relationships, especially close relationships, as well as certain costs we incur by maintaining them.

We Form Relationships Because We Need to Belong

In his book *Personal Relationships and Personal Networks* (2007), communication scholar Mac Parks wrote: "We humans are social animals down to our very cells. Nature did not make us noble loners."[1]* He's right. One reason personal relationships matter is that it's in our nature to form them. In fact, evolutionary psychologists argue that our motivation toward relationships is innate rather than learned.[2] That fundamental human inclination to bond with others is the idea behind psychologist Roy Baumeister's **need to belong theory.**[3] The need-to-belong theory proposes that each of us is born with a drive to seek, form, maintain, and protect strong relationships. To fulfill that drive, we use interpersonal communication to form social bonds with others at work, at school, in our neighborhoods, in community and religious organizations, on sports teams, in online communities, and in other social contexts. According to Baumeister's theory, each of those relationships helps us feel as though we aren't alone because we belong to a social community.

The need-to-belong theory also suggests that for us to satisfy our drive for relationships, we need social bonds that are both interactive and emotionally close. For example, most of us wouldn't be satisfied if we had emotionally close relationships with people with whom we never got to communicate. Being cut off from social interaction can be physically and psychologically devastating. That's one of the reasons why solitary confinement is considered such a harsh punishment.[4] Women and men who are deployed for military service,[5] and many elderly individuals who live

*Parks, M. R. (2007). *Personal Relationships and Personal Networks*. Mahwah, NJ: Lawrence Erlbaum Associates. Quote is from p. 1.

Deployed military personnel and elderly individuals who live alone often experience intense loneliness when they don't see their relatives or friends for extended periods of time. *DoD photo by Staff Sgt. James L. Harper Jr., U.S. Air Force; © AP Images/Ted S. Warren*

alone,[6] also experience loneliness when they don't see their families or friends for extended periods.

By the same token, interacting only with people who have no real feelings for us would be largely unrewarding as well. Imagine that you moved to a large city where you didn't know anyone. Even though you'd have plenty of interactions with people— taxi drivers, grocery store clerks, an eye doctor—you may not encounter anyone you felt close to. Those task-oriented relationships would help you to fulfill various needs, such as getting from one place to another and having your vision checked, but they wouldn't fulfill your need to belong because they usually aren't emotionally close.

Many relationships do, however, fulfill our needs for both interaction and emotional closeness. You may feel especially close to your romantic partner or your longtime friends, for instance. Perhaps you maintain close relationships with your parents or siblings. You may even have formed some rewarding relationships online, which research shows can be just as emotionally close as your face-to-face bonds.[7] Each of those relationships can help us feel more connected than when we can't interact with people we care about or when we don't care about the people with whom we interact. Our need to belong is not the only reason relationships matter to us, but it's one of the most important ones.

Media Note: In *The Last Man on Earth*, Phil Miller populates an abandoned pub with "friends," each painted with a face and assigned a different name and personality, to serve as stand-ins for human contact. (This is a nod to the Tom Hanks film *Cast Away*, in which the protagonist befriends a volleyball he calls Wilson.) Phil continues to rely on these artificial relationships as a retreat from the more complicated ones he has with other survivors.

Media Note: In CONNECT, the video "We Need to Belong" illustrates how the need to belong can influence interpersonal behavior.

Relationships Bring Rewards

Besides fulfilling our need to belong, relationships— and close relationships in particular—bring us all sorts of rewards. In this section, we'll look briefly at three types of rewards that are often intertwined in our relationships: emotional, material, and health rewards.

EMOTIONAL REWARDS. Our relationships provide us with at least two types of emotional rewards. One is emotional support, or encouragement during times of emotional turmoil. Whether you're going through a serious crisis or just having a bad day, close relationships can provide comfort and empathy to help you make it through.[8] When Frank found out he had skin cancer,

In *The Last Man on Earth*, Phil Miller's "Alive in Tucson" messages draw survivors to Arizona in search of human connection after a virus wipes out most of the population. © *FOX/Getty Images*

for instance, his close friends and relatives made sure he knew they were there to listen to him and support him. Although the experience was difficult for Frank, the emotional support he received from his friends and family helped him to cope.

The second emotional reward of having close relationships is happiness. We enjoy interacting with people we care about because it's relaxing, entertaining, and fun. One of Angel's favorite ways to spend a Friday night, for example, is by inviting her co-workers over to cook dinner, watch movies, and talk about what's going on in their lives. Hanging out with her co-workers always makes Angel feel good. Indeed, many of our happiest times are spent in the company of our closest relationships.[9]

MATERIAL REWARDS.   A second way relationships benefit us is by helping us meet our material needs, such as our needs for money, food, shelter, and transportation. We tend to share those types of resources with people to whom we feel close. When you need someone to help you move, a place to stay for the weekend, or a few dollars to tide you over until payday, you're more likely to have those material needs met if you have strong relationships to draw on than if you don't. You're also more likely to offer those material rewards to your relatives and close friends than to strangers or to people you don't know well.

When we form relationships, we build networks of people who may help us in the future, which can bring us real material rewards.
© *Rawpixel Ltd/Getty Images, RF*

HEALTH REWARDS.   As we saw in the About Communication chapter, good relationships keep us healthy. For instance, one study found that people with a strong social network were twice as likely as those without strong relationships to survive after a heart attack.[10] In fact, after reviewing more than 60 published studies on the topic, sociologist James House and his colleagues concluded that a lack of strong, positive relationships is as big a risk factor for premature mortality as cigarette smoking, obesity, and elevated blood pressure.[11]

There are at least two reasons why having positive relationships may help keep us healthy. One reason is that the happiness and relaxation our relationships provide help us to ward off the negative effects of stress. We all face sources of stress in our daily lives, such as dealing with an illness or worrying if we'll have enough money to pay our rent. Stress can have many negative effects on the body, such as causing sleeping problems or unhealthy weight gain; increasing the risk for heart disease, stroke, and depression; and aggravating conditions such as intestinal disorders and acne.[12] Research shows, however, that having close, satisfying relationships acts as a buffer, protecting us from overreacting to stressful events.[13] That doesn't mean we don't experience stress when we have strong relationships. Rather, having close relationships helps us deal with stress in a more effective, optimistic way, so it doesn't threaten our health as much as it otherwise would.[14]

A second reason why people help us stay healthy is that they look out for our safety and well-being. Friends, relatives, and co-workers can encourage us to pursue healthy behaviors, such as wearing a seatbelt and not driving while intoxicated.[15] They can prompt us to seek medical attention when we need it, and they can encourage us to take preventive measures, such as eating properly and getting the car brakes inspected every six months.[16] They can exercise with us and hold us accountable for maintaining a healthy weight.[17] Finally, if we have a chronic health problem such as diabetes or cancer, they can help us with the daily tasks of managing those conditions.[18] Because they help us manage stress and look out for our welfare, social relations play an important role in keeping us healthy.

Relationships Carry Costs as Well as Rewards

It's easy to think of the rewards of relationships: They bring us emotional support, help us during times of need, and even make us healthier. Every relationship—in particular, our close relationships—carries costs as well as rewards, however. Think about what it "costs" you to be friends with someone. For example, you might have to spend time with your friend that you would prefer to spend doing something rewarding by yourself. In addition, you must make an emotional investment, particularly when your friend needs your support. There can also be material costs associated with doing things together, such as traveling or going out to dinner. Finally, friendships often require physical investments as well. You may not particularly want to help your friend move into his new apartment, but you do it anyway because he's your friend.

Having good friends helps to keep us healthy and happy. © FlairImages/Getty Images, RF

Much of the time, we decide that the rewards of strong relationships are worth the costs. We invest our energies and resources in others because they benefit us. We spend our time and money with people because we feel happy when we're around them. In some cases, however, the costs of staying in the relationship outweigh the rewards. As we'll see later in this chapter, a social exchange orientation suggests that being in that kind of "under-benefited" state can motivate people to end relationships—or at least to find them unsatisfying.

LEARN IT   What is the need to belong? In what ways do relationships reward us? What sorts of costs are associated with maintaining a close relationship?

APPLY IT   For a week, record the time, the energy, and other resources your friends, relatives, or co-workers give you, as well as those you give back. Write a journal entry comparing the resources you received to those you gave, and comment on whether you felt your exchanges of resources were fair.

REFLECT ON IT   How do your relationships benefit you emotionally, materially, and with respect to your health? In what ways do you provide those types of benefits in your relationships?

 2 **The Nature of Personal Relationships**

Close social bonds—whether between romantic partners, friends, family members, or even co-workers—have some common characteristics that distinguish them from other relationships we form. Specifically, close relationships require commitment, foster interdependence, require continuous investment, and spark dialectical tensions.

Even after Rachelle Friedman suffered a devastating injury, her fiancé Chris Chapman never wavered in his commitment to her. © *Peter Kramer/NBC/NBCU Photo Bank/Getty Images*

Close Relationships Require Commitment

At her bachelorette party in August 2010, Rachelle Friedman was pushed into a swimming pool by one of her bridesmaids as a joke. After hitting her head on the bottom of the pool, Friedman suffered a spinal cord injury that left her unable to walk or feel any sensation below her collarbone. Despite her devastating injury, her fiancé Chris Chapman never wavered in his devotion to her. Demonstrating his commitment, he says he never thought "What am I going to do?" but only "What are *we* going to do?" Public support for the couple was so overwhelming that donors fully covered the cost of their June 2011 wedding in Pittsboro, North Carolina.

Like Chapman, most of us are more committed to our close relationships than we are to our other relationships.

commitment A desire to stay in a relationship.

Commitment is our desire to stay in a relationship no matter what happens. When people are committed to each other, they assume they have a future together. That assumption is important because most close relationships—such as friendships, family relationships, and romantic pairs—experience conflict and distress from time to time. What allows us to deal with those difficult times is the belief that our relationship will survive them.

Our close relationships usually include some level of *emotional commitment,* a sense of responsibility for each other's feelings and emotional well-being. For example, it's your emotional commitment to your sister that leads you to listen to her problems, even if they seem trivial to you. Our close relationships also involve a level of *social commitment,* which motivates us to spend time together, to compromise, to be generous with praise, and to avoid petty conflict. In some romantic relationships, social commitment takes the form of spending time with a partner's friends or family members even if one doesn't enjoy their company. Finally, some close relationships are bound by *legal and financial commitments,* which are more formal expressions of people's obligations to each other. Parents have a legal responsibility to provide housing, food, clothing, health care, and education for their children who are minors, and family members often take on financial obligations to care for relatives who are aging or who have specific physical or mental needs. No matter what forms it takes, commitment is one of the foundations of close relationships.

Although commitment is important for many relationships, people can take commitment too far. At an extreme level, commitment can turn into obsession, a topic explored in "Communication: Dark Side."

Focus on Scholarship: One of the earliest studies of cyberstalking found that up to a third of respondents had experienced some form of computer-mediated relational intrusion.[i]

[i]Spitzberg, B. H., & Hoobler, G. (2002). Cyberstalking and the technologies of interpersonal terrorism. *New Media & Society, 4,* 71–92.

Close Relationships Foster Interdependence

interdependence A state in which each person's behaviors affect everyone else in the relationship.

Another hallmark of close relationships is that they include high degrees of **interdependence,** meaning that what happens to one person affects everyone else in the relationship. People in friendships, romantic partnerships, families, and professional relationships depend on one another, so one person's actions influence others. For instance, how parents use their time and money depends not only on themselves but also on their children's needs. Likewise, how children perform in school and how they treat their siblings also affects their parents. Parents and children are

communication | *DARK SIDE*

CROSSING THE LINE: WHEN COMMITMENT BECOMES OBSESSION

Although commitment is necessary in close relationships, excessive levels of commitment can turn into an unhealthy obsession with another person. According to communication scholars William Cupach and Brian Spitzberg, close relationships are healthy and satisfying only if both partners desire approximately the same level of connection and interaction with each other. When one person expresses a substantially higher level of interest in the relationship than the other, the result can be what Cupach and Spitzberg call *obsessive relational intrusion* (*ORI*). In some cases, ORI occurs between strangers, but it can also occur within the context of an established relationship in which one partner feels substantially more invested than the other.

The reason why ORI is so problematic is that it can lead someone to engage in upsetting or threatening behaviors aimed at increasing intimacy with the target of his or her affections. These behaviors can include spying on the target or invading his or her privacy, sending the target unwelcome expressions of attraction or love, and engaging in sexually harassing behaviors. They can also include demanding that the target curtail communication with others and commit to an exclusive relationship with the pursuer.

Although relational intrusion can occur in face-to-face contexts, it is also becoming increasingly common online. Using the Internet, e-mail, or other electronic devices to intrude on another person's life is called *cyberstalking*. Intrusive behaviors can have several negative effects on their recipients, including physical and psychological stress, disruptions in everyday routines, loss of sleep or appetite, potential physical violence, and impairment in the ability to trust others.

FROM ME TO YOU

When they find themselves the target of obsessive relational intrusion, many people are inclined to initiate conversation with the pursuer to persuade the individual to stop the intrusive behaviors. Because this approach involves open and direct communication, it might seem to be an effective strategy for dealing with this problem. Experts warn, however, that the pursuer might interpret such communication as positive attention. In such cases, it might encourage rather than discourage his or her pursuit.

Often, a more effective strategy is to make oneself as inaccessible to the pursuer as possible, cutting off all communication with the person and asking one's family and friends to serve as a shield against the pursuer. Many experts believe that, over time, that strategy is the most effective for eroding the pursuer's interest.

Sources: Cupach, W. R., & Spitzberg, B. H. (2004). *The dark side of relationship pursuit: From attraction to obsession and stalking.* Mahwah, NJ: Lawrence Erlbaum Associates; Dreßing, H., Bailer, J., Anders, A., Wagner, H., & Gallas, C. (2014). Cyberstalking in a large sample of social network users: Prevalence, characteristics, and impact upon victims. *Cyberpsychology, Behavior, and Social Networking, 17,* 61–67.

therefore interdependent. So are romantic partners: If a woman is offered a job promotion that requires her to relocate, for example, her decision will affect her romantic partner as much as it will affect her. The essence of interdependence is the idea that our actions influence other people's lives as much as they influence our own.

Almost all close relationships have some measure of interdependence. Our romantic and familial relationships usually have higher levels of interdependence than our friendships and work relationships, however. You may be willing to sell your house and relocate if your spouse is offered a new job, for instance, but you probably wouldn't do the same for a friend. Likewise, you may provide around-the-clock care for your hospitalized child, but perhaps not for your hospitalized boss.

Talking Point: You can distinguish *dependence* from *interdependence* by pointing out that the former involves one person's reliance on another (e.g., a child's dependence on her mother), whereas the latter involves two people's reliance on each other

Investing our time, attention, and affection in others helps us maintain our close relationships. © *Laurence Mouton/Getty Images, RF*

Close Relationships Require Continuous Investment

Close relationships usually have a high degree of **investment**—that is, the commitment of one's energies and other resources to those relationships. We invest a range of resources in our close relationships, including our time, money, and attention. Generally, we expect to benefit from our investments—similar to the way we benefit from financial investments—but know we cannot retrieve the resources we've dedicated to the relationship if it comes to an end. For example, if we drift apart from our siblings during adulthood, we may retain memories of our relationships, but we cannot retrieve the time, attention, and material resources we invested in them.

People in close relationships are often especially aware of how much—and how equitably—they are each investing. For instance, research shows that spouses are happiest when they feel they are both investing in their relationship to the same degree.[19] If you think you're putting more time or resources into your relationship than the other person is, it's easy to feel resentful. The most satisfying close relationships appear to be those in which both parties are investing equally.

investment The commitment of resources in our relationships.

In the IM: The in-class activity "Dealing with Dialectical Tensions" encourages students to brainstorm and role-play options for managing dialectical tensions.

dialectical tensions Conflicts between two important but opposing needs or desires.

Close Relationships Spark Dialectical Tensions

Have you ever felt as though you wanted to be closer to someone, but you also wanted to maintain your individuality? In your relationships, have you wished to have more self-disclosure but still wanted to keep some thoughts private? Maybe you enjoy novelty and surprise in your relationships, but you also want them to be stable and predictable. If you can relate to such feelings, you have experienced what relationship researchers call **dialectical tensions**—conflicts between two important but opposing needs or desires. Dialectical tensions are common in close relationships.[20] Within families, romantic relationships, and friendships, three dialectical tensions in particular often arise.

Outside of Class: Over the course of a week, have students make note of when and how they experience these three dialectical tensions in their own relationships.

AUTONOMY VERSUS CONNECTION. A common tension in intimate relationships is between *autonomy*—the feeling of wanting to be one's own person—and *connection*—the desire to be close to others. People often experience that tension with their children. Especially as children enter adolescence, it's natural for them to desire greater autonomy. After all, adolescence is the period of life when teenagers begin to develop independent identities and make decisions for themselves.[21] Many adolescents, however, still want to be emotionally close to their parents. Even as they are learning to behave like adults, they still need and crave the security of family closeness. In fact, it's not uncommon for parents and children to experience that dialectical tension for some time, even as the children grow into adulthood.

OPENNESS VERSUS CLOSEDNESS. Another common dialectical tension is the conflict between *openness*—the desire for disclosure and honesty—and *closedness*—the desire to keep certain facts, thoughts, or ideas to oneself. Suppose your brother asks you how your new relationship is going. On one hand, you might want to confide in him as a way of reinforcing your closeness to him. On the other hand, you might feel it's best to keep some of the details to yourself out of respect for your partner's privacy. In other words, part of you desires openness, and another part desires closedness.

PREDICTABILITY VERSUS NOVELTY.   In addition, many close relationships experience conflict between *predictability*—the desire for consistency and stability—and *novelty*—the desire for fresh, new experiences. After nearly 20 years of marriage, for instance, Pauline and Victor were so settled into their routines that their relationship had become highly predictable. Such predictability could be comforting, but at times it made their marriage feel stale and

Like being on a seesaw, negotiating dialectical tensions requires us to go back and forth between two opposing desires. © *Leland Bobbe/The Image Bank/Getty Images*

left them longing for new experiences. They found that trying something new—such as taking a foreign language class together or volunteering at a soup kitchen—provided a refreshing change from the predictability of their life together. By the same token, however, they recognized that predictability gave their relationship an orderliness and certainty that they both appreciated.

Managing Dialectical Tensions

Dialectical tensions are a normal part of any close, interdependent relationship, and they become problematic only when people fail to manage them properly. Let's suppose Moira has become engaged to marry Albee and she is experiencing the tension between autonomy and connection. Moira strongly desires to merge with Albee and be connected to him, yet she also adamantly wishes to retain her individuality and autonomy.

Researchers have identified eight strategies that people in intimate relationships use to manage dialectical tensions. None of these strategies is inherently positive or negative.[22] Rather, their effectiveness depends on the individual's goals for the relationship and the context in which he or she is using them.

To illustrate these strategies, let's look at how Moira might use them to manage this tension:

- *Denial:* This strategy involves responding to only one side of the tension and ignoring the other. Were Moira to adopt this strategy, for instance, she might deny her desire for autonomy and focus all her attention on being connected with Albee.

- *Disorientation:* This strategy involves escaping the tension entirely by ending the relationship. Moira may feel so disoriented by the tension between her desires for autonomy and those for connection, for example, that she calls off her engagement.

- *Alternation:* Alternation means going back and forth between the two sides of a tension. On some days, for example, Moira might act in ways that enhance her

Talking Point: One characteristic of all dialectical tensions is that the opposing forces are both desirable. Autonomy opposes connectedness because we really want some measure of autonomy *and* some measure of connectedness in our relationships with others. We don't necessarily want them at the same time, in the same way, or even to the same degree, but we generally want some of each. The same is true of the other tensions.

autonomy and individuality, such as spending time alone. On other days, she might act in ways that enhance her connection to Albee, such as sharing activities they both enjoy.

- *Segmentation:* This strategy involves dealing with one side of a tension in some aspects, or segments, of one's relationship, and dealing with the other side of the tension using other segments. Were Moira to select this strategy, she might emphasize her connection to Albee by sharing intimate disclosures, but she might emphasize her autonomy by keeping her finances separate or retaining her own last name when they marry. Rather than going back and forth between the two sides of the tension, as in alternation, she is addressing one side of the tension in some segments of her relationship and the other side in other segments.

- *Balance:* People who use balance as a strategy try to compromise, or find a middle ground, between the two opposing forces of a tension. For instance, Moira might disclose most of her feelings to Albee but keep some of her feelings to herself. This strategy might not make her feel as autonomous as she wants or as connected as she wants, but she might feel she is satisfying each desire to some degree.

- *Integration:* In this strategy, people try to develop behaviors that will satisfy both sides of a tension simultaneously. Moira feels connected to Albee when they spend their evenings together, but she also likes to choose how she spends her time. To integrate these needs, she often will read or do crossword puzzles while Albee watches television in the same room. This arrangement enables her to feel both autonomous and connected at the same time. Unlike the balance strategy, which focuses on compromising each desire, integration focuses on finding ways to satisfy both desires without compromising either one.

- *Recalibration:* Adopting this strategy means "reframing" a tension so that the contradiction between opposing needs disappears. Instead of feeling conflicted by their competing needs for autonomy and connection, Moira and Albee could agree, through discussion, to treat autonomy and connection as equally desirable. As a result, they might come to see autonomy and connection as complementary rather than opposing needs.

© Jack Hollingsworth/Getty Images, RF

- *Reaffirmation:* Finally, reaffirmation means simply embracing dialectical tensions as a normal part of life. Moira might come to realize that she will always feel torn between her needs for autonomy and connection. Instead of fighting the tension or struggling to resolve it, she simply accepts it as a normal feature of her relationship. Whereas reframing means eliminating the tension by seeing the opposing needs as complementary, reaffirmation means accepting the tension as normal.

It's not uncommon for family members, friends, and romantic partners to try several of these strategies. If you do so in your own close relationships, you may find some of these techniques more effective than others. Improving your communication in close relationships doesn't require you to adopt specific strategies and ignore others. Rather, if you're aware of the different options for managing dialectical tensions, then you can choose the ones that work best for you.

In the IM: In the out-of-class activity "What Makes a Romantic Relationship Work?" students will reflect on what they think are the most important characteristics of successful romantic relationships and then will collect responses on the same question from people in long-term relationships.

3 Forming and Maintaining Social Bonds

We've considered why relationships matter and how they reward us. In this section, we'll look at several theories that explain the various interpersonal forces that work to form and develop relationships, and what makes some relationships closer than others. Some of those theories help us to understand with whom we choose to form relationships, including

- Attraction theory, which describes why we are drawn to others
- Uncertainty reduction theory, which indicates why we initially interact with others
- Predicted outcome value theory, which details why we get to know some people and not others

Other theories explain why and how we maintain relationships once we form them, including

- Social exchange theories, which indicate how we compare our current relationships with our alternatives and how we count our costs and benefits
- Relational maintenance behaviors, which are the communication behaviors we use to sustain our relationships

Attraction Theory

The process of forming most relationships begins with **interpersonal attraction,** which is any force that draws people together. You're probably already familiar with the concept of **physical attraction,** or being drawn to someone because of his or her looks. There are at least two other ways to be attracted to a person, though. One is **social attraction,** which means being attracted to someone's personality. For example, you might like your new neighbor because of her positive attitude. Likewise, you might be drawn to a classmate in your

interpersonal attraction Any force that draws people together to form a relationship.

physical attraction Attraction to someone's physical appearance.

social attraction Attraction to someone's personality.

Most relationships are sparked by some type of attraction. That might include physical attraction (attraction to one's appearance), social attraction (attraction to one's personality), and task attraction (attraction to one's abilities). © 81a Productions/Masterfile, RF

task attraction Attraction to someone's abilities and dependability.

Some standards of beauty—such as the preferred body type—vary from culture to culture. © Lars A. Niki/The McGraw-Hill Education, © Bruce Yuanyue Bi/Getty Images

communication course because he has a great sense of humor. A third kind of attraction is **task attraction,** or being attracted to someone's abilities and dependability.[23] You might feel positively toward your co-worker because he shows up on time every day, rain or shine. Maybe you admire your romantic partner's excellent karaoke skills. Any or all of those types of attraction can draw us to others and make us want to get to know them better.

A variety of qualities in a new acquaintance can spark the forces of interpersonal attraction. However, research suggests four especially powerful factors: personal appearance, proximity, similarity, and complementarity.

WE ARE ATTRACTED BY APPEARANCE. When we say a person is attractive, we often mean that he or she *looks* attractive. Humans are highly visually oriented, so when we find someone to be physically attractive, we are often motivated to get to know that person better. There are at least two reasons why we behave that way. One reason is that we value and appreciate physical attractiveness, so we want to be around people we consider attractive.[24] Another reason is that, throughout history, humans have sought physically attractive persons as mates. Because attractive people often have particularly healthy genes, children produced with attractive people are likely to be healthy, because they will inherit those genes.[25]

A popular cultural saying is that "beauty is only skin deep." That maxim suggests that physical beauty or attractiveness is superficial, meaning that it reflects only people's outer appearance but offers no indication of who they are or how they behave. Indeed, perhaps you've heard someone assert that an individual is physically handsome or beautiful but that "it's what's on the inside that really counts." Despite the popularity of that belief, however, decades of research demonstrate that in reality we pay an enormous amount of attention to physical appearance when we're forming relationships.[26]

What makes one person more physically attractive than another is a combination of social and genetic characteristics. Some notions of beauty vary widely from culture to culture. Consider weight, for example. In North America and Western Europe, a thin, physically fit body type is generally considered the most attractive. In many African and Australian tribal cultures, however, an overweight body is considered the most attractive, at least for women.[27]

Cultures also vary in the ways in which they manipulate or mutilate the body to achieve physical attractiveness. One example is the practice of wearing lip plates. Girls in the Mursi of southern Ethiopia and the Mebêngôkre Indians of Brazil have their lips pierced at a young age and a large wooden or clay plate inserted into the hole. As the girls grow older, their lip plates are increased in size, and those with the largest plates are considered the most desirable as mates.[28] Similarly, women in the Padaung tribe of Myanmar often wear metal rings around their necks to make their necks appear longer than they are. Women with the longest necks are considered the most attractive and most desirable as mates.[29]

Other aspects of physical attractiveness are more cross-cultural. For instance, people around the world prefer bodies and faces that are symmetrical—similar on the left and right sides—and that have features that are proportional in size to one another. Across cultures, men are also attracted to women who appear healthy and young, because those characteristics signal their ability to produce healthy offspring.[30] Similarly, women across cultures are attracted to men who look powerful and appear to have resources, because those characteristics signal their ability to provide for a family.[31]

WE ARE ATTRACTED BY PROXIMITY.   Another important predictor of attraction is *proximity,* which refers to how closely together people live or work and how often they interact. We're more likely to form and maintain relationships with people we see often than with people we don't.[32] We tend to know our next-door neighbors better than the neighbors down the road, and we're more likely to become friends and maintain friendships with our classmates and co-workers than with people we rarely see.

In Everyday Life: We often find a person to be attractive to us in only one way. For instance, you may be drawn to someone's personality (social attraction) or talents (task attraction) even if you don't find that person physically attractive.

Focus on Scholarship: Ethnic groups within the same society can also differ in their satisfaction with their bodies and body types. One study, for instance, found that African American women are more satisfied with their looks than white American women.[iii]

[iii]Roberts, A., Cash, T. F., Feingold, A., & Johnson, B. T. (2006). Are black-white differences in females' body dissatisfaction decreasing? A meta-analytic review. *Journal of Consulting and Clinical Psychology, 74,* 1121–1131.

On the popular TV show *Scandal,* co-workers at the crisis management firm Pope & Associates form close friendships through their close proximity and shared interests despite their different backgrounds. © *Nicole Wilder / Getty images*

fact OR *fiction*? WHEN FORMING RELATIONSHIPS, OPPOSITES ATTRACT

You've probably heard the saying that "opposites attract." That cultural idea suggests that when we're forming relationships, we are more likely to be attracted to people we perceive as different from us than to people we see as similar to ourselves. Is that often-repeated notion fact or fiction?

The answer is that we are attracted both to similarity and to difference . . . but not to the same degree. Compared to difference—which researchers call *complementarity*—we find similarity to be much more attractive. Decades of research have shown that we are more likely to form relationships with people who are similar to, rather than different from, ourselves.

In one study, undergraduate students looked at photos of models and indicated how attracted they were to them. The models' physical attractiveness made a difference; students reported being more attracted to the physically attractive models. In addition, however, students were more attracted to models when they perceived, on the basis of their photos, that the models' physical traits (such as height or eye color), demographic traits (such as age or ethnicity), and character traits (such as intelligence or trustworthiness) were similar to their own. Beyond the effects of physical

appearance, that is, students were most attracted to those they perceived as most similar to themselves.

Notice that the students' reports of attraction were based on their *perceived similarity* to the models. When it comes to attraction, does it matter whether we are actually similar to someone else or only perceive that we are? Research indicates that actual similarity is more influential than perceived similarity when it comes to attraction, but both influences are powerful.

ASK YOURSELF

- What kinds of similarity do you most value in others? Why?

- Are certain types of similarity more attractive to you in romantic relationships than in friendships or professional relationships? If so, what are the differences?

Sources: Park, H., & Lennon, S. J. (2008). Beyond physical attractiveness: Interpersonal attraction as a function of similarities in personal characteristics. *Clothing & Textiles Research Journal, 26,* 275–289; Montoya, R. M., Horton, R. S., & Kirchner, J. (2008). Is actual similarity necessary for attraction? A meta-analysis of actual and perceived similarity. *Journal of Social and Personal Relationships, 25,* 889–922.

Some researchers have suggested that computer-mediated communication has reduced the influence of physical proximity on attraction. With chat rooms, instant messaging, and other forms of online interaction, we're free to develop relationships with virtually anyone, no matter how geographically distant they are. Indeed, research has shown that a vast majority of Internet users have developed social bonds with people they met online.[33]

WE ARE ATTRACTED BY SIMILARITY. You've probably had the experience of getting to know someone and marveling at how much you have in common. When we meet people with backgrounds, experiences, beliefs, and interests similar to our own, we find them to be comfortable and familiar; sometimes it's almost as if we already know them. Perhaps, however, you've heard the cultural adage that "opposites attract," which suggests that we are more drawn to people who are different from us. Is that idea true? Check out the "Fact or Fiction?" box to find out.

As the box explains, we generally see similarity as an attractive quality in others.[34] There are at least two reasons why. One reason is that we often find social validation in people who are similar to us. Liking people who are similar to us is, in a way, like liking ourselves. You might be especially drawn to people who share your hobbies, your sense of humor, or your way of seeing the world, for instance, because those people make you feel better about who you are.[35] We don't necessarily think about that at a conscious level, but it may nonetheless be one of the reasons we find similarity attractive.

A second reason we find similarity attractive is that it is in our genetic interests to do so.[36] For our primitive ancestors, similarity—particularly in physical appearance and behavior—was one of the most reliable ways to distinguish relatives from nonrelatives. That was important, because two people who look and behave similarly are more likely to share genetic material with each other than are two people who look and behave differently. And humans, like many other species, are motivated to help those with whom they share genetic material. That is why, for instance, we love our own children more than we love other people's children and why we give more of our resources to family members than to strangers.[37] When we help our genetic relatives, we help our own genes survive into future generations. Again, we don't do so consciously. Rather, researchers believe that over millennia, humans have developed the motivation to help their genetic relatives because it ensures the survival of their own genes.[38]

WE ARE ATTRACTED BY COMPLEMENTARITY.   Of course, no one is *exactly* like you—we all differ from one another in various ways. As the "Fact or Fiction?" box described, we may believe that opposites attract, but, in reality, similarity is often more attractive than difference. Even though we're attracted to similarity, however, we can also be attracted to people who are different from ourselves if we see their differences as *complementary*—that is, as beneficial to ourselves because they provide a quality we lack. Someone who's shy might be drawn to a more outgoing person because that friend can help him become more sociable. A person who prefers to plan activities ahead of time might be attracted to a friend who's more spontaneous.

The key to attraction based on complementarity is that the people involved have to see their differences as positive. We may not be drawn to people with religious beliefs or political orientations that are radically different from our own, for instance. If we are convinced our beliefs and orientations are correct, we may see such differences as negative. Because religious beliefs and political orientations often reflect our fundamental ways of viewing the world, we may look upon opposing viewpoints as threatening to our own, and that perspective may decrease our attraction to someone else. If we enjoy engaging in other ways of thinking, however, then we may see differences in beliefs and orientations as complementary, and we thus might view a person with dissimilar beliefs as attractive—and as a potential friend.[39]

Uncertainty Reduction Theory

A second major theory of why we form relationships focuses not on interpersonal attraction but on the uncertainty we feel when we don't know others very well. Let's say you meet someone and want to get to know the person better. What does it mean to get to know someone? According to communication scholars Charles Berger and Richard Calabrese, it means reducing our level of uncertainty about the person.[40]

When you first meet a new co-worker, for instance, you don't know much about her, so your uncertainty about her is high. Berger and Calabrese's **uncertainty reduction theory** suggests that you will find uncertainty to be unpleasant, so you'll be motivated to reduce your uncertainty by using communication behaviors to get to know her. At first, you'll probably talk about basic information, such as where she lives or what she likes to do in her spare time. As you get to know her better, she will probably disclose more personal information about herself. You may also learn about her by paying attention to nonverbal cues, such as her personal appearance, voice, and gestures. According to uncertainty reduction theory, each new piece of information you gain reduces your uncertainty more.

Focus on Scholarship: Research on college residence halls and apartment complexes shows that we are most likely to form friendships with the people who live closest to us.[iv] The reason is partly because we have more opportunities to interact with them and partly because we perceive similarity with them due to our shared living arrangements.

[iv]Marmaros, D., & Sacerdote, B. (2006). How do friendships form? *Quarterly Journal of Economics, 121,* 79–119.

In the IM: The out-of-class activity "Forming Friendships Online" engages students to develop new friendships online and to reflect on the ways they present themselves in an online context.

Outside of Class: You might challenge your students to get to know someone who is quite different from themselves. Suggest that they seek out someone whose values, beliefs, or background is substantially different from their own, and take note of the challenges—and also the rewards—of making an effort to get to know that person.

uncertainty reduction theory A theory suggesting that people are motivated to reduce their uncertainty about others.

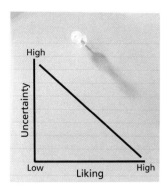

FIGURE 1 Uncertainty Reduction Theory According to uncertainty reduction theory, as uncertainty about a person goes down, liking for that person goes up.

 predicted outcome value theory A theory predicting that we form relationships when we think the effort will be worth it.

Importantly, uncertainty reduction theory also suggests that the less uncertain you are, the more you will like the person. Because we dislike being uncertain about people, we will like people more as our uncertainty about them is decreased. The relationship between liking and uncertainty, as reflected in uncertainty reduction theory, is illustrated in Figure 1.

Predicted Outcome Value Theory

You have just read that as your uncertainty about your new co-worker is reduced, you probably will like her more. What happens, however, if you don't like the information you learn about her? Will you still like her more or want to get to know her better? Communication professor Michael Sunnafrank offered a slightly different way to think about how we form relationships. In his **predicted outcome value theory,** he suggested that when we first communicate with others, we try to determine whether continued communication with them will be worth our effort.[41]

If we like what we learn about someone during our initial conversations, we predict positive outcomes for future communication with that person, meaning we will want to get to know the person better. In contrast, if we don't like what we learn about someone during our initial conversations, we predict negative outcomes for future communication, and we won't be motivated to continue to get to know him or her.[42]

There are many reasons why we might predict positive outcomes when we first communicate with a particular individual. We might find that we have many things in common with her or that she has a great sense of humor and is fun to be around. We might also find that she is very knowledgeable about something we're interested in, such as kayaking or designing web pages, so we can learn more about those hobbies by being around her. If we value those qualities, then Sunnafrank's theory predicts that we will engage in communication behaviors aimed at getting to know her better, such as increasing verbal communication and nonverbal immediacy around her.[43]

In other cases, we might predict negative outcomes when we first get to know someone. After spending time with a new acquaintance, for instance, we might discover that she's always criticizing people, she's boring, or she's very defensive. If we dislike those qualities, predicted outcome value theory proposes that we will reduce our verbal and nonverbal communication with her or avoid her altogether. Figure 2 illustrates the process of predicted outcome value theory.

Understanding Relationship Formation

Attraction theory, uncertainty reduction theory, and predicted outcome value theory all help us to understand how, and with whom, we form relationships. According to attraction theory, we want to get to know people when we feel some measure of physical, social, or task attraction to them. Any of those forms of

FIGURE 2 Predicted Outcome Value Theory Predicted outcome value theory says we project how positive our interactions with people will be in the future, and we behave toward them accordingly.

attraction will motivate us to engage in **approach behaviors,** which are communication behaviors that signal interest in another person. Approach behaviors include verbal statements, such as introducing yourself to someone and asking about him or her. They also include nonverbal actions, such as smiling and maintaining eye contact with the person. We use such communication behaviors to express our desire to get to know others, and attraction theory predicts that they are the result of physical, social, and/or task attraction.

According to uncertainty reduction theory, the primary purpose of engaging in approach behaviors is to collect information about the other person to reduce our uncertainty about him or her. The more our uncertainty is reduced, the more we will like the person. As we have seen, that assumption might be true if most of what we learn about the person is positive. What if we find out, however, that he or she is bigoted, obnoxious, or dull? According to uncertainty reduction theory, we may still like the person more because our uncertainty has been reduced.

According to predicted outcome value theory, however, we should like the person less, because the outcomes we'd predict from knowing him or her would seem less positive. As a result, we should no longer be motivated to engage in approach behaviors with the person. Rather, we would likely engage in **avoidance behaviors,** which are communication behaviors that signal a lack of interest in someone else. As with approach behaviors, avoidance behaviors include both verbal actions, such as saying "please leave me alone," and nonverbal behaviors, such as avoiding eye contact with the person and not spending time with him or her. According to predicted outcome value theory, therefore, we're motivated to form relationships with people only when the initial information we learn about them is positive.

Yet merely *forming* a relationship doesn't necessarily mean we'll want to *maintain* it. Not all relationships become close and meaningful. Some friendships start strong but fade over time, whereas others grow and flourish. Two theoretical traditions in particular—cost/benefit theories and the concept of relational maintenance behaviors—help us understand why and how we maintain relationships.

Theories about Costs and Benefits

Suppose you've been drawn to someone, you've gotten to know her, and the two of you have become friends. At that point, you've completed the process of forming a relationship. How will you decide whether you want to stay in the relationship or let it die out? One way is by examining the give-and-take of relational costs and benefits.

Recall that relationships carry costs as well as rewards. You invest certain resources in a friendship, such as your time, attention, and money. In return, you receive certain benefits from it, such as emotional support, entertainment, and help. Two specific theories—social exchange theory and equity theory—help us understand how those costs and benefits influence which relationships we are most likely to maintain.

SOCIAL EXCHANGE THEORY AND RELATIONSHIP FORMATION. The guiding principle of **social exchange theory** is that people seek to maintain relationships in which their benefits outweigh their costs.[44] Think of your relationship with a neighbor. There are costs involved in being neighborly. You have to be willing to help when needed, and you may experience a loss of privacy if your neighbor is aware of your comings and goings. There are also benefits to a neighborly relationship, such as knowing someone

approach behaviors
Communication behaviors that signal one's interest in getting to know someone.

Talking Point: Another theory—dialectics theory—suggests that uncertainty is not always negative. It points out that we have competing needs for openness (uncertainty reduction) and closedness (uncertainty maintenance) in our relationships; it's good to get to know someone well, but it's also good to preserve a little mystery.

CONNECT: Easily track any Connect assignment using reports such as assignment results and statistics.

avoidance behaviors
Communication behaviors that signal one's lack of interest in getting to know someone.

In the IM: The in-class activity "Write a Personal Ad for a Friend" encourages students to think about what they most look for when forming a friendship.

Talking Point: Point out to students that scientific theories (such as uncertainty reduction theory and predicted outcome value theory) often lead us to make different predictions about the same outcome. They do so because they draw attention to different characteristics, and researchers use empirical tests to determine the extent to which each theory is accurate.

social exchange theory
A theory predicting that people seek to form and maintain relationships in which the benefits outweigh the costs.

can watch your home when you're away and having someone close by whose company you enjoy. The question, according to social exchange theory, is whether you think the benefits outweigh the costs. If you do, then you're likely to maintain that relationship; if not, then you're less inclined to maintain it.

comparison level A person's realistic expectation of what the person wants and thinks he or she deserves from a relationship.

An important concept in social exchange theory is your **comparison level,** your realistic expectation of what you want and think you deserve from a relationship. Your expectations are based on both your experiences with relationships and the prevailing cultural norms for such relationships. Perhaps you think neighbors should be friendly and should help you out when you need it but otherwise should mind their own business. Those ideas would form part of your comparison level for your own neighborly relationships. Similarly, you might believe that relatives and friends should care about your well-being, always keep your secrets, and support you even when they disagree with your decisions. Those desires and expectations would be part of your comparison level for your own family and friendships.

comparison level for alternatives A person's assessment of how good or bad his or her current relationship is, compared with other options.

Equally important is your **comparison level for alternatives.** That concept refers to your assessment of how good or bad your current relationship is compared with your perceived options. Are you satisfied with your neighborly relationships, or do you think you could find better neighbors if you moved? Likewise, are you happy with your current friendships, or do you think you'd be better off finding new friends? Social exchange theory suggests that we maintain relationships when we believe that doing so is better than an alternative, such as ending the relationships or finding new ones. In contrast, we're most likely to end relationships if we believe staying in them is worse than our alternatives.

Research suggests that, in some relationships, your comparison level for a particular relationship will strongly influence how satisfied you are in that relationship.[45] Your comparison level for alternatives, however, will more strongly influence whether that relationship will last. Even satisfying relationships can end if the alternatives are more appealing. In comparison, sometimes unsatisfying relationships endure over time. Figure 3 shows the association between the comparison level and the comparison level for alternatives.

Let's say your friend Clarissa has a great sense of humor, enjoys many of the same activities you do, and is always willing to listen when you have a problem. To the extent that you value those characteristics, you would perceive your friendship with her as matching your comparison level for friendships. Perhaps Clarissa also has a tendency to gossip and speak badly of other people when she's around you. Not only do you find that behavior unappealing, but it makes you wonder what she says about you behind your back. You have also seen Clarissa behave dishonestly, such as when she accused one of her classmates of stealing even when she knew he hadn't. If you find dishonesty and a tendency to gossip to be unattractive qualities, you might perceive that your friendship doesn't meet your comparison level for friendships. Indeed, you might consider ending your friendship with Clarissa after you see her behave in those ways. Social

	Comparison Level	
	High	**Low**
Comparison Level for Alternatives — High	Your relationship is satisfying, but you may be inclined to end it if an even more satisfying relationship looks probable.	You're likely to be dissatisfied with this relationship and will probably look for opportunities to end it.
Comparison Level for Alternatives — Low	You'll probably be satisfied with this relationship and won't be likely to end it.	Although you won't find your relationship satisfying, you are unlikely to end it.

FIGURE 3 Comparison Level and Comparison Level for Alternatives in Social Exchange Theory Social exchange theory says four outcomes are possible when we cross our comparison level with our comparison level for alternatives.

exchange theory, however, argues that you'd first have to consider how attractive your alternatives are.

Suppose you ended your friendship with Clarissa. In that case, you'd no longer have to put up with her gossiping and dishonesty. At the same time, however, you would also lose what you value about her as a friend, including her good humor and her willingness to listen. If you have other friends who provide you with the same benefits—or if you believe you could make such friends—then you might decide it's worth ending your relationship with Clarissa. In that situation, you've decided that your comparison level for alternatives exceeds your comparison level. Because you think you'd be better off without having Clarissa as a friend, you would likely end that relationship, according to social exchange theory.

Conversely, suppose you don't have other friends who benefit you the way that Clarissa does. Maybe you've just moved to the area, and she's your only real friend. You might conclude that even though you dislike some of her behaviors, you're still better off maintaining your friendship than ending it. In that situation, you've decided that your comparison level exceeds your comparison level for alternatives. Because you believe you'd be better off keeping Clarissa as a friend, you would likely maintain that relationship.

One major contribution of social exchange theory is that it provides an explanation for why people maintain relationships that appear to be costly. For instance, people frequently wonder why anyone would stay in an abusive friendship. Any type of abuse—whether physical, psychological, or emotional—represents a cost, rather than a benefit, of being in a relationship. For the person being abused, however, the choice between maintaining or ending the abusive relationship is rarely as simple as it appears to outsiders. Some victims of abuse believe that the other person's positive qualities compensate for his or her negative ones; thus, they have a favorable comparison level. Other victims believe that the costs of ending the relationship—which might include loneliness, loss of other friends, and even the threat of violence—exceed the costs of staying in the relationship. In that case, their comparison level exceeds their comparison level for alternatives. They acknowledge that the relationship is bad, but they're convinced that the consequences of ending it would be worse.

EQUITY THEORY AND RELATIONSHIP FORMATION. If you think of relationships as having costs and rewards, then it's easy to see that both people in a given relationship might not benefit equally. Imagine your sister Chandra is always text messaging you about her problems but never has time to listen to you about yours. She's getting the benefit of your time and attention without the cost of giving her own time and attention to you. In contrast, you are putting more into the relationship than you're getting from it.

We invest time, emotional energy, and even physical energy in our close friendships. © *Randy Faris/Cardinal/Corbis, RF*

over-benefited The state in which one's relational rewards exceed one's relational costs.

under-benefited The state in which one's relational costs exceed one's relational rewards.

equity theory A theory predicting that a good relationship is one in which a person's ratio of costs and rewards is equal to that of the person's partner.

Focus on Ethics: In a peer relationship, such as between friends or co-workers, how ethical is it to be consistently over-benefited? If these are relationships among equals, is that fair?

In that situation, Chandra is **over-benefited** and you are **under-benefited.** According to **equity theory,** that arrangement is a recipe for trouble.[46] Equity theory borrows the concepts of cost and reward from social exchange theory and extends them by defining a good relationship as one in which your ratio of costs and rewards is equal to your partner's. It's fine if you're working harder on your relationship than your sister is, as long as you're getting more out of it than she does. For example, if you're doing all the cooking every night but Chandra is letting you share her apartment for free, you're probably getting more out of the relationship than Chandra is, even though you may be putting more effort into it.

If the two of you get the same level of benefit but your costs are greater than the other person's, equity theory predicts you won't want to maintain that relationship. That observation doesn't mean that relationships have to be equitable at every moment or in every instance. It does suggest, however, that they must be equitable in the long run.

To illustrate that point, let's say you meet your friend Braden regularly for dinner, and he picks up the check almost every time. Assuming you and he derive the same pleasure from each other's company, that would seem to be a friendship in which Braden is under-benefited and you are over-benefited. Let's also say, though, that you bought airplane tickets for his grandparents so they could attend his college graduation ceremony. Monetarily, that one contribution equaled the value of several dinners. Thus, your financial investments in your friendship are equal in the long run.

Relational Maintenance Behaviors

Social exchange theory and equity theory explain *why* we choose to maintain relationships. In contrast, the concept of relational maintenance behaviors explains *how* we maintain them. Let's imagine now that you've made friends with someone and you're both satisfied with the costs and benefits of your friendship. You'll want to maintain your relationship so that it continues to grow and thrive. How do you accomplish that? Communication researchers Laura Stafford and Dan Canary have found that we use five primary **relational maintenance behaviors:** positivity, openness, assurances, social networks, and sharing tasks.[47]

relational maintenance behaviors Behaviors used to maintain and strengthen personal relationships.

Media Note: The classic *Saturday Night Live* skit "Debbie Downer" illustrates how challenging it is to be around people who are consistently negative. Few people are cheerful and courteous all the time, but relationships are maintained by positive behaviors much more than by negative ones.

POSITIVITY. Behaviors that entail *positivity* make others feel comfortable around us. Positivity behaviors include acting friendly and cheerful, being courteous, and refraining from criticizing other people. People who engage in positivity behaviors smile frequently, express their affection and appreciation for others, and don't complain. In other words, they're pleasant and fun to be around. As you might guess, those types of behaviors tend to make people well liked.[48] In contrast, behaviors such as complaining, being critical of others, and pouting when things don't go one's way reflect low positivity. How much positivity do you generally express? Check out the "Assess Your Skills" box to find out.

Talking Point: The expression "too much information" (or "TMI") has developed as a way to indicate that someone is engaging in more disclosure than is appropriate.

OPENNESS. *Openness* describes a person's willingness to talk with his or her friend or relational partner about their relationship. People who use this relational maintenance strategy are likely to disclose their thoughts and feelings, ask how their friend feels about the relationship, and confide in their friend. Although it's possible to have too much openness in a relationship, an optimal amount will help maintain the relationship and keep it strong.[49] When people refuse to share their thoughts and feelings with others or don't reciprocate others' disclosures, they are displaying low amounts of openness.

assess your skills | HOW MUCH POSITIVITY DO YOU COMMUNICATE?

One of the most important ways to maintain close relationships is to communicate positivity. How much positivity do you express? Think of the way you communicate in one of your close relationships. On a scale of 1 to 7, indicate how much you agree with each of the following statements. Offer a lower number if you agree less, and a higher number if you agree more.

In this close relationship, I . . .

1. _____ Try to find positive topics of conversation to focus on.
2. _____ Express joy for my partner's good news.
3. _____ Enjoy laughing and sharing humor with my partner.
4. _____ Work hard to handle conflicts between us in a cooperative way.
5. _____ Try to be patient with my partner.
6. _____ Am willing to overlook my partner's shortcomings.
7. _____ Smile at my partner.
8. _____ Am rarely impolite.

When you're done, add up your responses. How's how to interpret the results:

- If you scored between 8 and 22, then you can probably increase your positivity. Learning more about this relational maintenance behavior may help you improve your relationship.

- If your score was between 23 and 38, you express a moderate level of positivity in this relationship. You're definitely on the right track, but even more positivity may be a benefit.

- If you scored between 39 and 56, you communicate a great deal of positivity in this relationship, which probably contributes to its stability and success.

Source: Items adapted from Stafford, L. (2011). Measuring relationship maintenance behaviors: Critique and development of revised relationship maintenance behavior scale. *Journal of Social and Personal Relationships, 28,* 278–303.

ASSURANCES. Stafford and Canary define *assurances* as verbal and nonverbal behaviors that people use to illustrate their faithfulness and commitment to others. A statement such as "Of course I'll help you; you're my best friend" sends the message that the communicator is committed to the relationship, and it reassures the other person that the relationship has a future.[50] In contrast, when individuals don't acknowledge the importance of their friendships, they convey the message that they aren't very committed to them. Practice your ability to give assurances by checking out the "Got Skills?" box on page 296.

SOCIAL NETWORKS. Today, some people use the term social networks to refer to social media, but in fact the term *social networks* refers to all of the relationships one has. An important relational maintenance behavior is to share one's social networks with another person. Two close friends, for instance, are likely to know each other's families, co-workers, and other friends. When that happens, we say that the friends' social networks have converged. Research shows that convergence is an important way to keep relationships stable and strong.[51] Individuals undermine that convergence when they speak poorly of the friends and relatives of their friends or actively avoid spending time with them.

got skills?   GIVING ASSURANCES

Verbal assurances can strengthen our close relationships.

WHAT?
Learn to provide verbal relational assurances.

WHY?
To help maintain important relationships, such as those with friends and co-workers.

HOW?
1. Through either verbal or nonverbal behaviors, stress your commitment to your relationship.
2. As you have the opportunity, assure your friend or relational partner that you value him or her and intend to stay in that relationship for the foreseeable future.

TRY!
1. Tell a good friend how much you care about him or her and how glad you are that you're friends.
2. Discuss something that would be fun to do with this friend in the future, such as going on a road trip together.

CONSIDER: *In what other ways can you assure your friend of his or her value to you?*

Talking Point: Many relationships depend on equal sharing of tasks. Neighbors, for instance, generally expect that their favors for each other will be reciprocated. When tasks are not equally shared in a relationship, then one party is over-benefited and the other is under-benefited.

SHARING TASKS.   As the term suggests, *sharing tasks* means performing one's fair share of the work in a relationship. If your brother gives you a ride to the airport whenever you need it, for example, then it's only fair that you help him paint his apartment when he asks. If your roommate cooks you dinner, it would be fair for you to do the dishes afterward. As we've seen, being in a relationship requires investments of energy and effort. One way of maintaining a relationship, then, is to make certain the two parties are contributing equally.[52] When you expect others to do favors for you without reciprocating, you are not sharing tasks equally.

The "At a Glance" box reviews the five primary relational maintenance behaviors.

Understanding Relationship Maintenance

To understand relationships, especially close relationships, we need to examine both *why* people maintain such relationships and *how* they maintain them. Social exchange theory and equity theory each explain why people maintain their relationships by focusing on the rewards and costs of those relationships. As we've considered, your

AT A GLANCE

The Five Primary Relational Maintenance Behaviors

Positivity	Acting friendly, being courteous, refraining from criticism
Openness	Being willing to discuss your relationship
Assurances	Expressing and stressing your faithfulness and commitment
Social Networks	Introducing one person to your other friends, family members, and co-workers
Sharing Tasks	Performing your fair share of the work in your relationship

relationships bring you certain rewards, such as pleasure, safety, and material help, and they also invoke certain costs, such as your time, attention, and financial resources. Are the rewards you get from a particular relationship worth the costs of that relationship? Social exchange theory and equity theory both help you answer that question, although they do so in slightly different ways.

SOCIAL EXCHANGE THEORY AND RELATIONSHIP MAINTENANCE.   Social exchange theory leads us to compare the costs and rewards of our current relationships with those of our alternatives. Suppose you are deciding whether to maintain a relationship with your friend Betsy. One alternative would be simply to end that friendship. Another option would be to replace her with a different friend. According to social exchange theory, whether you stick with Betsy or adopt one of those alternatives depends on your perception of the costs and rewards associated with each option. From the perspective of this theory, you ultimately will choose the option that benefits you most.

EQUITY THEORY AND RELATIONSHIP MAINTENANCE.   In contrast to social exchange theory, equity theory leads us to compare how much the current relationship costs and rewards ourselves with how much it costs and rewards our partner. If you're debating whether to stay friends with Betsy, you would therefore consider how your ratio of costs and rewards compares with hers. What you're striving for, according to equity theory, is a balance between your own cost/benefit ratio and Betsy's. From the perspective of this theory, we prefer relationships in which we receive benefits equal to—not greater than or less than—those of our partners.

SHIFTS IN COSTS AND BENEFITS.   Importantly, some of the characteristics we think of as benefits can turn into costs. At the beginning of a romantic relationship, for instance, one partner might experience the other's sense of humor as a benefit. If that person later develops a tendency to make inappropriate or offensive jokes in social situations, however, then his or her sense of humor can turn into a cost by making the person difficult to be

Although they started out on opposing sides of a war, shifting costs and benefits changed the nature of the relationship between Jaime and Brienne on *Game of Thrones.* © *HBO/Photos 12 / Alamy*

around. Costs can also turn into benefits. For example, you may regard a friend's political views to be a cost if they are radically different from yours, because you feel irritated and defensive when he expresses them. Over time, you may come to realize that his ideas have expanded your way of thinking and helped you to understand certain political issues. What you first regarded as a cost to your friendship may now seem like a benefit.

In summary, once we form relationships, we maintain them through our communication behaviors. Some of the most important types of relationship maintenance behaviors are behaving positively, being open, giving assurances, sharing social networks, and sharing tasks. These behaviors are especially important in maintaining close relationships. Additional ways of maintaining relationships include doing favors for a friend and always asking the friend about his or her day. Many people also maintain their relationships by participating together in their shared interests, such as watching sporting events, going to movies, and trying out new recipes.[53] In various ways, each of those behaviors conveys the message that you appreciate and value the other person, and enjoy his or her company. Because many relationships are voluntary, feeling appreciated and valued can motivate individuals to stay in them.

LEARN IT   What is the difference between physical, social, and task attraction? According to uncertainty reduction theory, how is uncertainty related to liking? According to predicted outcome value theory, when we predict positive relational outcomes, what are we motivated to do? What is a comparison level for alternatives? What does it mean to be under-benefited and to be over-benefited? What behaviors do people enact to maintain their relationships?

APPLY IT   Choose one of your friendships, and make a point of practicing the five relational maintenance behaviors—positivity, openness, assurances, social networks, and sharing tasks—with that friend over the next several weeks. In a journal entry, describe the ways in which you enacted each of those communicative behaviors and the responses they elicited from your friend.

REFLECT ON IT   Do you feel over-benefited in any of your relationships? Which relational maintenance behaviors are most important in your relationships?

Talking Point: At the initiating stage, the nature of the relationship to be formed isn't necessarily defined. Meeting someone for the first time might be the beginning of a romantic relationship, but it might also be the beginning of a friendship or even a professional relationship.

Focus on Scholarship: Joseph Walther's research has shown that people often engage the experimenting stage more rapidly when interacting online than when interacting face-to-face. Online interaction, he suggests, can encourage *hyperpersonal communication*, during which people disclose more intimate information earlier in the relationship than they would in face-to-face contexts.

 # 4 Stages of Relationship Development

Relationships don't materialize overnight. Rather, they evolve over time—and research shows that most relationships come together in stages. In this section, we examine one of the most widely used models of the stages of relationship development, and then explore a similar model of the stages of relationship dissolution. We'll also consider how individual and cultural differences affect relationship development, and we'll discover how people manage their personal relationships online.

Getting In: Relationship Formation

Researchers have found that people follow fairly consistent steps when they form new relationships. Communication scholar Mark Knapp, for instance, has suggested

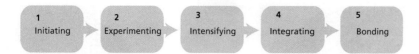

FIGURE 4 Relationship Formation Communication scholar Mark Knapp suggests that relationships form in five stages.

that relationship formation involves five stages: initiating, experimenting, intensifying, integrating, and bonding (see Figure 4).[54] These stages can describe the development of any kind of personal relationship, whether romantic, platonic, or professional, although they are often applied to romantic relationships, specifically.[55]

INITIATING.   The **initiating stage** occurs when people meet and interact for the first time. For instance, you may make eye contact with someone on the first day of class and decide to introduce yourself, or you might find yourself sitting next to someone on an airplane and strike up a conversation. "What's your name?" and "Where are you from?" are common questions people ask at this initial stage.

EXPERIMENTING.   Suppose you begin talking with someone you find interesting. You might then move to the **experimenting stage,** during which you have conversations to learn more about that person. Individuals at the experimenting stage ask questions such as "What kind of music do you like?" and "What do you do for fun?" to gain basic information about each other. This stage helps people decide if they have enough in common to continue getting to know each other.

INTENSIFYING.   During the **intensifying stage,** people move from being acquaintances to being friends. They spend more time together and might begin to meet each other's friends, co-workers, or relatives. They start to share more intimate information with each other, such as their fears, future goals, and secrets about the past. They also increase their commitment to each other and may express that commitment verbally through statements such as "You're really important to me."

INTEGRATING.   The **integrating stage** occurs when a deep commitment has formed, and people share a strong sense that the relationship has its own identity. At that stage, the partners' lives become integrated with each other, and they also begin to think of themselves as a pair—not just "you" and "I" but "we." Others start expecting to see the two individuals together and begin referring to the pair as close friends or as a romantic couple.

BONDING.   The final stage in Knapp's model of relationship development is the **bonding stage,** in which the partners make a public announcement of their commitment to each other. That might involve moving in together, getting engaged, or having a commitment ceremony. Beyond serving as a public expression of people's commitment, bonding also allows individuals to gain the support and approval of people in their social networks.

initiating stage The stage of relationship development when people meet and interact for the first time.

experimenting stage The stage of relationship development when individuals have conversations to learn more about each other.

intensifying stage The stage of relationship development when individuals move from being acquaintances to being close friends.

integrating stage The stage of relationship development when a deep commitment has formed, and there is a strong sense that the relationship has its own identity.

bonding stage The stage of relationship development when people publicly announce their commitment to each other.

The integrating stage occurs when the relationship begins to form its own identity.
© monkeybusinessimages/Getty Images, RF

A brief summary of the five stages of relationship development appears in the "At a Glance" box.

AT A GLANCE

Knapp's Stages of Relationship Development

Initiating	Meeting and interacting with each other for the first time
Experimenting	Having conversations to learn more about each other
Intensifying	Moving from being acquaintances to being friends
Integrating	Forming a deep commitment and developing a relationship with its own identity
Bonding	Making a public announcement of commitment to each other

Talking Point: Ask students to indicate how, in their own relationships, they know they have arrived at the integrating stage. What are the markers?

Talking Point: Entering the differentiating stage doesn't necessarily mean a relationship is coming to an end. Many long-term relationships experience differentiation from time to time.

differentiating stage The stage of relationship dissolution when partners begin to see their differences as undesirable or annoying.

Getting Out: Relationship Dissolution

Just as relationships develop over time, they can also come apart over time. Communication researcher Mark Knapp has described five stages that relationships go through when they end: differentiating, circumscribing, stagnating, avoiding, and terminating (see Figure 5).[56] Although these stages are often used to describe the dissolution of romantic relationships, they can characterize the end of any close relationship.

DIFFERENTIATING. People in any close relationship are similar to each other in some ways and different in other ways. In happy, stable relationships, people see their differences as complementary. At the **differentiating stage,** however, they begin to see their differences as undesirable or annoying.

FIGURE 5 **Relationship Dissolution** According to Knapp, relationships come apart in five stages.

CIRCUMSCRIBING. When partners in a close relationship enter the **circumscribing stage,** they begin to decrease the quality and the quantity of their communication with each other. Their purpose in doing so is to avoid dealing with conflicts.[57] At this stage, people start spending more time apart.[58] When they're together, they usually don't talk about problems, disagreements, or sensitive issues in their relationship and instead focus on safe topics and issues about which they agree.

circumscribing stage The stage of relationship dissolution characterized by decreased quality and quantity of communication between partners.

STAGNATING. If circumscribing progresses to the point where the partners are barely speaking to each other, the relationship enters the **stagnating stage,** at which time the relationship stops growing and people feel as if they are just "going through the motions." Partners avoid communicating about anything important because they fear it will only lead to conflict. Many relationships stay stagnant for long periods of time.

© MaxRiesgo/Getty Images, RF

AVOIDING. When people decide they are no longer willing to live in a stagnant relationship, they enter the **avoiding stage,** during which they create a physical and emotional distance between each other. Some people take a direct route to creating distance, such as by moving out of the house or saying "I can't be around you right now." Others create distance indirectly, such as by making up excuses for being apart ("I have company in town all next week, so I won't be able to see you") and curtailing availability to the other person by screening phone calls or not responding to text messages.

stagnating stage The stage of relationship dissolution when partners are barely communicating with each other.

avoiding stage The stage of relationship dissolution when partners create a physical and emotional distance between each other.

TERMINATING. The last stage in Knapp's model of relationship dissolution is the **terminating stage,** at which point the relationship is officially judged to be over. In romantic relationships, that usually involves one or both partners' moving out if the couple shared a residence. It also involves dividing property, announcing to friends and family that the relationship has ended, and negotiating the rules of any future contact between the partners. For legally married partners, relational termination means getting a **divorce,** the legal discontinuation of the marriage.

The decision to end a close relationship is a significant one. Particularly when a marriage or significant romantic bond ends, families require substantial reorganization, which can take an enormous mental and emotional toll, particularly on children. Research shows that children can be negatively affected by divorce well into their adulthood.[59] That isn't always the case, though. When the romantic partnership is highly conflicted, neglectful, or abusive, for instance, children and their parents are often better off after the relationship ends.[60]

The "At a Glance" box summarizes the five stages of relationship dissolution.

terminating stage The stage of relationship dissolution when the relationship is deemed to be officially over.

divorce The legal termination of a marriage.

Focus on Scholarship: Anthropologist Helen Fisher has determined that around the world, more couples divorce in their fourth year of marriage than in any other year.

Talking Point: Young couples are at greatest risk of divorce, particularly if their own parents have also divorced.[v]

[v]Amato, P. R. (2001). What children learn from divorce. *Population Today, 29*, 1, 4.

AT A GLANCE

Knapp's Stages of Relationship Dissolution

Differentiating	Finding differences with one's partner to be unpleasant and annoying
Circumscribing	Decreasing the quality and quantity of communication with the partner
Stagnating	"Going through the motions" of a relationship that is no longer satisfying
Avoiding	Creating physical and emotional separation from the partner
Terminating	Formally ending the relationship

CONNECT: Assigning students to complete the SmartBook chapter before class can help prepare them to participate in active class discussions and activities.

Individual and Cultural Variations in Relationship Development

Not every relationship goes through the stages of development in the same way. For instance, some potential friends or romantic partners may stay at the experimenting stage for a long time before moving into the intensifying stage. Others may progress through the stages very quickly. Still others may go as far as the integrating stage but put off the bonding stage.

When it comes to romantic relationships, in particular, researchers have found that gay and lesbian pairs follow stages of relationship development that are largely similar to those followed by opposite-sex pairs.[61] The intensifying and integrating stages may be experienced differently for same-sex couples, however, if the partners have to contend with discrimination or keep their relationship status private. If legal marriage isn't an option in their country, then same-sex pairs would also experience the bonding and terminating stages differently than legally married heterosexual couples.

The processes of relationship formation and dissolution can also vary across cultures. To the extent that cultures vary in their expectations about relationships—especially romantic relationships—they also differ in their ways of beginning and ending them. For instance, some countries practice *arranged marriage,* in which one's parents select a romantic partner for him or her. In such instances, the process of forming a marital relationship includes negotiation and decision making by the parents and less input (if any) from the children. Other countries allow the practice of *polygamy,* in which a person can have more than one spouse at a time. The integration and bonding stages, in particular, would look different in those cultures, because one person may be joining multiple spouses at once. We will learn more about arranged marriage and polygamy in the Interpersonal Communication in Close Relationships chapter.

Focus on Scholarship: In one study, nearly 2,200 people rated their online friendships as less satisfying than the friendships they maintained offline.[vi]

[vi]Antheunis, M. L., Valkenburg, P. M., & Peter, J. (2012). The quality of online, offline, and mixed-mode friendships among users of a social networking site. *Cyberpsychology: Journal of Psychosocial Research on Cyberspace, 6*(3). doi: 10.5817/CP2012-3-6.

Relationship Development and Maintenance via Online Social Networking

Online social networking is one of the primary contexts for relationship development and maintenance.[62] These days, many relationships are formed and maintained on Facebook and similar sites, and research suggests that people use many of the same communication behaviors to develop and sustain their relationships online and offline. Let's look specifically at how people deal with uncertainty, use relational maintenance behaviors, and manage dialectical tensions.

DEALING WITH UNCERTAINTY.   As you've seen, uncertainty reduction theory suggests that we dislike feeling uncertain about other people. While maintaining existing relationships—and especially while forming new ones—we are therefore motivated to reduce our uncertainty to the extent that we can. There's always some level of uncertainty when we get to know others. Our uncertainty can be especially high when we interact with people online, though. Because of "leanness," the online channel makes it easier for others to hide or misrepresent information about themselves.

Research shows that, for college students, using Facebook is one of the primary strategies for reducing uncertainty in the initial stages of a relationship. Communication scholars suggest that using Facebook makes the early stages of relationship development less effortful and anxiety-producing, because users can gather information about new or potential friends or romantic partners in an unobtrusive way. Specifically, researchers describe the process of *creeping*, which means checking out someone's information on Facebook without the person's knowledge.[63] Research indicates that, to reduce uncertainty, people pay the most attention to someone's relationship status, friends, and photographs.

Creeping is an example of a *passive strategy* for uncertainty reduction, because it involves gathering observations unobtrusively. To reduce their uncertainty, some people instead use an *active strategy,* which means asking for information about a person from his or her friends or acquaintances. For instance, suppose Garrett is interested in getting to know his classmate Angelique, and he notices from her Facebook page that they have three friends in common. Garrett might send instant messages to those friends, asking them about Angelique. He could also use an *interactive strategy,* which entails asking Angelique about herself directly. He might send her a friend request, for instance, and then start a conversation with her if she accepts.

Although people use passive, active, and interactive strategies when forming relationships online, research indicates that interactive strategies reduce uncertainty the most.[64] In fact, one study found that asking people about themselves directly increased social attraction, compared to adopting passive or active strategies for reducing uncertainty.[65]

USING RELATIONAL MAINTENANCE BEHAVIORS.
Even when people form relationships offline, they often use social networking to maintain them. We can examine that process by considering the relational maintenance behaviors of positivity, openness, assurances, social networks, and sharing tasks.

In an online environment, some of these behaviors are more relevant than others. Openness, for instance, helps us learn more about those with whom we have relationships. Through mutual self-disclosure, we share our lives with friends, colleagues, relatives, and romantic partners, and

Talking Point: A romantic couple "goes Facebook official" when both partners change their status on Facebook to announce their relationship. According to research, this move usually occurs after the couple has already become exclusive, and it signals increased commitment in the relationship.[vii]

[vii]Fox, J., Warber, K. M., & Makstaller, D. C. (2013). The role of Facebook in romantic relationship development: An exploration of Knapp's relational stage model. *Journal of Social and Personal Relationships, 30,* 771–794.

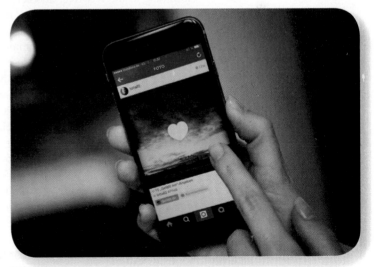

When friends positively acknowledge our postings on social media, our uncertainty is reduced. © AP Images/picture-alliance/dpa/Britta Pedersen

got skills?

EXPRESSING AFFECTION ONLINE

Use these behaviors to convey affection to others via Facebook.

WHAT?	WHY?	HOW?	TRY!
Learn to communicate affection via Facebook.	To enhance the quality of your relationships with Facebook friends.	1. Remember that personalized gestures on Facebook convey more affection than impersonal gestures, such as "liking" a post. 2. To express affection to Facebook friends, comment on their photos, include them in your status updates, tag them in pictures, and write messages on their wall.	1. Identify a Facebook friend for whom you care a great deal. 2. Find a photo that includes both of you, and post it on your wall with a caption indicating how much you value your relationship with that person. **CONSIDER:** *Why is it useful to use personalized gestures to convey affection on Facebook? How could you apply that advice to other online venues, such as Twitter or Instagram?*

we get to know those people better. According to communication scholars Erin Hollenbaugh and Amber Ferris, Facebook plays a key role in fostering openness online.[66] Their study found that people who use Facebook specifically to maintain relationships tend to self-disclose more information—and about a wider range of topics—than people who use Facebook for other reasons, such as to pass the time.

Communication plays a key role in people's abilities to maintain relationships online. Another study examined people's Facebook friends—a group that can include their platonic friends, romantic partners, family members, co-workers, roommates, and others. According to the research, another relational maintenance behavior—positivity—was a major predictor of which Facebook relationships developed and grew.[67] The researchers found that behaviors such as tagging people in photos and sending them private Facebook messages were instrumental in communicating positivity. In a separate study, communication experts Daniel Mansson and Scott Myers found that Facebook users also used tagging and messaging to convey affection to their relational partners.[68] You can practice Mansson and Myers's tips for expressing affection online by checking out the "Got Skills?" box.

Using social media allows people to converge their social networks in very efficient ways. When you become Facebook friends with a co-worker, for example, you can see the names and photos of his or her other friends immediately. You also have the option to invite those people to become friends of yours. Unsurprisingly, research finds that integrating social networks is another key relational maintenance behavior on social media sites.[69] Unlike in face-to-face relationships, however, the maintenance behaviors of assurances and task-sharing do not appear to enhance online relationships to a significant degree.[70]

MANAGING DIALECTICAL TENSIONS. As we've seen, people in relationships often encounter dialectical tensions—that is, conflicts between two important but opposing needs or desires. In many relationships, a key dialectical tension is between the desire to self-disclose (openness) and the desire to keep information private (closedness). Communication researchers Jesse Fox, Jeremy Osborn, and Katie Warber found that a conflict between openness and closedness is common for romantic partners who use Facebook as a way to maintain their relationship. That is, romantic partners often feel torn between wanting to share news about their relationship on Facebook and also wanting to keep that information to themselves.[71]

© M4OS Photos / Alamy

Recall that people use a variety of strategies to manage the dialectical tensions they experience. Fox and his colleagues discovered that some of those strategies are also common in online communication. To manage the openness-closedness tension, in particular, some couples use *denial* by refusing to discuss their relationship on Facebook. Others use *recalibration:* by considering Facebook disclosure a natural part of the modern relational process, they reframe the tension to make it less problematic. Still others use *segmentation* by negotiating with each other what is appropriate to share about the relationship on Facebook and what is not. Finally, some use *alternation* by focusing on disclosure at some times in the relationship and privileging privacy at other times.

Relationships don't come together—or come apart—randomly. Instead, forming, maintaining, and even ending relationships are all processes that unfold over time. People may vary in how they undertake these tasks, and they may not necessarily follow the stages exactly in order. Diversity in culture, sexual orientation, and other factors can make the processes of relationship development and dissolution different for different people. Whether we're interacting with people face-to-face or online, however, research suggests that we use many of the same strategies to do so.

In the IM: You can now access the end-of-chapter Discussion Questions and the Research Library in the Instructor's Manual for each chapter.

LEARN IT How are the integrating and bonding stages different from each other? What are the characteristics of the circumscribing stage? Which cultural differences likely influence the process of relationship development? Which relational maintenance behaviors are most influential online?

APPLY IT Do some "creeping" on your own Facebook page to find out exactly what a new Facebook friend would learn about you. Examine the information you post about yourself and your likes and dislikes. Pay particular attention to the photos to which your Facebook friends have access. Consider whether the image you present of yourself would help or hurt your ability to form new relationships with people who have friended you.

REFLECT ON IT Why do you suppose it is common for relationships to stay stagnant for long periods of time? In what ways do you think your own culture and sexuality affect how you form and maintain your close relationships?

MASTER the chapter

1 Why Relationships Matter (p. 275)

- Each of us has a need to belong that motivates us to seek, form, maintain, and protect strong relationships.
- Relationships bring us emotional, material, and health rewards.
- Relationships incur costs in our time, our energy, and other resources.

2 The Nature of Personal Relationships (p. 279)

- Relational commitment involves the desire to stay in a relationship and to take responsibility for another's well-being.
- Close relationships usually involve a high degree of interdependence.
- Close relationships also require the continuous investment of resources.
- Many dialectical tensions—including the tensions of autonomy versus connection, openness versus closedness, and predictability versus novelty—are common in close relationships.

3 Forming and Maintaining Social Bonds (p. 285)

- We value attraction in the form of physical appearance, proximity, similarity, and complementarity.

- Uncertainty reduction theory says we are driven to reduce uncertainty about others by getting to know them.
- According to predicted outcome value theory, we form relationships when we think there is value in doing so.
- Social exchange theory predicts that we form relationships in which the benefits equal or outweigh the costs.
- According to equity theory, a good relationship is one in which our ratio of costs and rewards is the same as our partner's.
- People use several relational maintenance behaviors, including positivity, openness, assurances, social networks, and shared tasks.

4 Stages of Relationship Development (p. 298)

- Many relationships develop according to the stages of initiating, experimenting, intensifying, integrating, and bonding.
- Relationships likewise dissolve according to the stages of differentiating, circumscribing, stagnating, avoiding, and terminating.
- Differences in sexual orientation, culture, and other factors can influence the processes of relationship development and dissolution.
- In online environments, people manage uncertainty, use relational maintenance behaviors, and deal with dialectical tensions.

KEY TERMS

Connect

To maximize your study time, check out CONNECT to access the SmartBook study module for this chapter, watch videos, and check out other resources.

10 Interpersonal Communication in Close Relationships

© Everett Collection Inc / Alamy

GOOD FRIENDS AND PRODUCTIVE WORK PARTNERS

Some people find it hard to balance a friendship with a working relationship, but that isn't the case for Benj Pasek and Justin Paul. The two met during a summer orientation for the musical theater program before their freshman year of college. Pasek recalls that he and Paul were the worst students in their dance class, so they would hide behind each other to avoid being seen by their instructor. The students became fast friends, and they soon started working together to write their first stage production. That effort became the start of a prolific collaboration. In the last decade, the Tony-nominated composers have contributed to multiple musical theater productions, including *James and the Giant Peach* and *A Christmas Story, The Musical.* The duo has also written original songs for the NBC musical drama *Smash* and has performed as singers in venues around the world.

For Pasek and Paul, a close friendship was the springboard to a productive working relationship. Says Pasek, "It's a marriage in a way: Sometimes it's rocky, [and] you have highs and lows. But we've been working together for more than 10 years. I think it's a cool thing to share that with someone."[1*]

*Koerner, A. F., & Fitzpatrick, M. A. (2004). Communication in intact families. In A. L. Vangelisti (Ed.), The Routledge Handbook of Family Communication (pp. 177–195). New York, NY: Routledge.

t's difficult to overstate the significance of our close relationships, such as those with friends, romantic partners, relatives, and co-workers. These are the people whose lives affect us the most and with whom we share our deepest sorrows and greatest joys. We usually invest more in, and feel more committed to, our close relationships than any others. Those bonds shape our lives in unique and important ways.

Our close relationships also influence each other. Growing up in a family gives most of us our first exposure to the concept of personal relationships and our first examples of romantic unions. Moreover, the romantic relationships we form in adulthood often serve as the basis for starting new families. Likewise, many of us develop close friendships with people we meet at work. Thus, although friendships, romantic pairs, families, and work relationships are different in some important respects, there is often an intimate connection between them. This chapter explores the types of interpersonal communication we share with our friends, romantic partners, relatives, and co-workers.

Writing Note: Ask students to reflect on what they think of when they hear the word *intimacy*. Use their answers to generate discussion about how even nonsexual relationships (such as family relationships and close friendships) can be intimate.

In Everyday Life: With a romantic partner, and especially with a relative, it's easy to feel that although you love the person, you may not necessarily always like him or her. One characteristic that often distinguishes these relationships from less intimate ones is that they can sustain this ambivalence.

Talking Point: Ask your students if they can think of any examples of friendships they're in that aren't voluntary.

1 Communicating in Friendships

Five common characteristics of friendships—such as the friendship between these two women—are that they are voluntary, usually develop between peers, are governed by rules, differ by sex, and have a life span. © *Masterfile, RF*

Your various friendships are likely as different and individual as your friends themselves. Some of those friendships are probably long-term and seem almost like family ties. Others may be specific to certain contexts, such as work, school, and the place where you volunteer. Even though each is unique in some ways, nearly all friendships have certain qualities in common that affect how people communicate. In this section, we take a look at five common characteristics of friendships.

Friendships Are Voluntary

One of the defining characteristics of friendship is that it is voluntary.[2] We choose our friends and they choose us, and we don't have to be friends with anyone we don't want to be. That's part of what makes a friendship so special: Both friends are in the relationship by choice.

Friendship is voluntary, but that doesn't mean we choose our friends arbitrarily. Indeed, as we learned in the Forming and Maintaining Personal Relationships chapter, attraction and the balance of costs and rewards both affect whom we pursue and maintain as friends. According to research, we are generally drawn to friends we see as similar to ourselves, as attraction

communication *LIGHT SIDE*

FACEBOOK FRIENDS: 302 IS THE MAGIC NUMBER

As valuable as friends are to us, research suggests it's possible to have *too many* friends—at least on Facebook.

That idea may seem counterintuitive to you. In *real life,* after all, having many friends signals that you are popular, admired, and well liked by others, all of which cast you in a positive light. It might therefore seem that having several hundred (or even several thousand) Facebook friends would make you appear especially impressive.

© IndianSummer/Alamy

Communication researchers at Michigan State University discovered otherwise, however, when they asked students to rate the likeability of a person depicted in a Facebook page with either 102, 302, 502, 702, or 902 friends. As you might expect, the person shown on the Facebook page was rated as least likeable when only 102 friends were advertised. However, likeability scores peaked at 302 friends and dropped continually after that. In other words, the experimental subject was seen as more likeable with 302 friends than with 502, 702, or even 902 friends. The researchers suggested that people who have several hundred Facebook friends or more might be perceived as shallow because it would be so difficult to maintain high-quality friendships with that many people. Their study indicates that to appear likeable but not shallow, the optimal number of Facebook friends to have is approximately 300.

Source: Tong, S. T., Van Der Heide, B., Langwell, L., & Walther, J. B. (2008). Too much of a good thing? The relationship between number of friends and interpersonal impressions on Facebook. *Journal of Computer-Mediated Communication, 13,* 531–549.

theory suggests,[3] and those who reciprocate the time and effort we put into the relationship, as social exchange theories suggest.[4]

The fact that friendships are voluntary also doesn't mean that they flourish on their own. On the contrary, they require communication behaviors on our part and on the part of our friends. Not only do we have to interact with others to form friendships in the first place, we also have to use relationship maintenance behaviors such as positivity, openness, assurances, network convergence, and sharing tasks to maintain them. Besides face-to-face communication, research shows that close friends engage in relational maintenance behaviors in a variety of ways, including through Facebook,[5] Xbox Live,[6] and via text messaging.[7]

Given that friendship is voluntary, does that mean we should strive to have as many friends as possible? Friends certainly bring us many benefits. In some contexts, however—such as on a Facebook page—it might be possible to have *too many* friends, as the "Communication: Light Side" box explains.

Friends Are Usually Peers

peer Someone of similar power or status to oneself.

A second important characteristic of friendship is that it is usually a relationship between equals. A **peer** is someone similar in power or status to oneself. Your instructors, boss, and parents aren't your peers because those people all exercise some measure of control over you, at least temporarily. Most of us conceive of friendship as a relationship with peers—that is, people who are our equals, no more or less powerful than we are.

Does that mean we can't become friends with our instructors, boss, and parents? Not at all—in fact, many of us consider those people to be very good friends. We can have satisfying friendships with individuals who have some type of power over us. Those relationships can also be complicated, however. When a friend exercises power over you, it can cause conflicts between the voluntary nature of your friendship and the involuntary nature of your parent–child, teacher–student, or employer–employee relationship. For instance, a professor who is also your friend may vacillate between giving you a good grade and giving you the poorer grade you might have earned. In such a situation, he may feel that the expectations of your friendship and the expectations of your professional relationship are in conflict.

Friendships Are Governed by Rules

In some ways, a friendship is like a social contract to which both parties agree. By being someone's friend, you acknowledge—at least implicitly—that you expect certain things from that person and that he or she can expect certain things from you. Those expectations are possible because friendships have rules. Even if the rules aren't explicitly stated, most people within a given society usually know and understand them.[8]

As you'll see in the "At a Glance" box, researchers have identified and studied many of the underlying rules of friendship. Some of these rules relate to specific communication behaviors, such as standing up for your friends to support them and being the kind of friend with whom others can share secrets. Perhaps you've been in a friendship in which one or more of those implicit rules was broken. For example, maybe a friend has been criticizing you behind your back or has failed to offer help when you needed it. Just as with communication rules in general—discussed in the About Communication chapter—friendship rules often become explicit only when someone violates them. As research tells us, most people agree there simply are right and wrong ways to treat friends.[9]

In the IM: The in-class activity "The Rules of My Friendships" asks students to identify the implicit and explicit rules guiding their own friendships.

Focus on Scholarship: Although physical attractiveness is generally noted as a desirable quality in romantic partners, research indicates that both men and women value physical attractiveness in their platonic friends, particularly in friends of the opposite sex.[i]

[i]Sprecher, S., & Regan, P. C. (2002). Liking some things (in some people) more than others: Partner preferences in romantic relationships and friendships. *Journal of Social and Personal Relationships, 19,* 463–481.

AT A GLANCE

Friendship Rules

Research by communication scholar Jeff Hall has confirmed that people have certain rules for friendships. When the parties to the relationship observe those rules, the friendships tend to be stronger. Here are some of the most important friendship rules that Hall's work has identified. What rules, if any, would you add to this list?

- Stand up for your friends and support them
- Offer resources to your friends
- Be enjoyable to be around
- Provide help even without being asked
- Share common interests and viewpoints
- Be the kind of person with whom friends can share thoughts and secrets

Source: Hall, J. A. (2012). Friendship standards: The dimensions of ideal expectations. *Journal of Social and Personal Relationships, 29,* 884–907.

Friendships Differ by Sex

You've probably noticed some differences between the friendships you have with women and the ones you have with men. In fact, researchers have written volumes about sex differences and similarities in friendships and friendship behaviors. In this section, we examine those differences and similarities separately for same-sex and opposite-sex friendships.

SAME-SEX FRIENDS. One of the most consistent findings concerning same-sex friendships is that women and men value different aspects of their respective friendships. Essentially, friendships among women tend to place greater emphasis on conversational and emotional expressiveness, whereas men's friendships focus on shared activities and interests.[10]

Best friends Juanita and Lindsay, for instance, frequently get together just to talk and catch up. Their visits often include sharing their feelings about what's going on in their lives. During those talks, Juanita and Lindsay listen to each other and express their support and affection for each other. Sometimes, they engage in an activity while they talk, such as attending Lindsay's daughter's basketball game or driving to the bus station to pick up Juanita's sister; sometimes, they simply talk. Juanita and Lindsay agree that their ability to share, disclose, and express feelings with each other is what makes their friendship satisfying.

In contrast, when Alex thinks about his closest male friends, he thinks of Jake, his golfing buddy, and Davin, his patrol partner on the police force. The time he spends with those friends almost always revolves around some type of activity. With Jake, it's usually playing a round of golf and then having nachos and beer at a sports bar. With Davin, it's working together during the many hours they spend on patrol. Alex feels close to each friend because he enjoys their company when they are engaged in these activities.

Significantly, Alex's time with Davin and Jake allows them to talk about what's happening in their lives. During a long patrol shift, for instance, Alex and Davin frequently talk about their children's activities and their plans for the future. Similarly, during a recent round of golf, Jake told Alex how much he missed his recently deceased father. Most often, though, Alex and his friends simply enjoy the time they spend together

Studies show that men's friendships often focus on shared activity, whereas women's friendships often center on shared conversation. © James Woodson/Digital Vision/Getty Images, RF, © Purestock/PunchStock, RF

doing activities, even if their time together doesn't involve much conversation. For Alex, it's the doing, not the talking, that makes a friendship close.

Although research has confirmed that those sex differences exist, it has also identified two important qualifications about these differences. First, as with nearly all sex differences in behavior, those differences in same-sex friendships are just averages. They don't characterize all friendships. Some women's friendships focus more on shared activities than on conversation, and some men routinely share personal conversations with their male friends even if they aren't engaged in an activity together.

Second, the fact that women's and men's relationships differ does not mean that friendships are more important to one sex than to the other. Some people believe that because women self-disclose more to one another than men do, women's friendships are closer and more satisfying than men's are. In fact, research has demonstrated that women and men report equal levels of closeness in their same-sex friendships.[11] What differs between the sexes is simply the characteristics that make those friendships close. For women, the key characteristic is shared conversation; for men, it's shared activity.

OPPOSITE-SEX FRIENDS.   What do we know about communication in opposite-sex friendships? Research suggests that both men and women value those relationships as a chance to see things from each other's perspective.[12] Opposite-sex friendships can provide opportunities for men to be emotionally expressive and for women to enjoy shared activities that their same-sex friendships do not.[13]

In addition, many opposite-sex friends feel some degree of physical or romantic attraction toward each other,[14] and they often communicate in ways that resemble romantic relationships, such as by flirting with each other and sharing sexual humor.[15] In fact, a study of American college students conducted by communication scientists Melissa Bisson and Timothy Levine found that 60 percent of the students reported having engaged in sexual activity with a nonromantic opposite-sex friend.[16] Although some research has suggested that sexual activity changes the fundamental nature of an opposite-sex friendship from platonic to romantic,[17] participants in Bisson and Levine's study reported avoiding such problems by not talking explicitly about the status of their relationship.

Whether they are attracted to each other or not, many opposite-sex friends have specific reasons for not wanting their friendship to evolve into a romantic relationship. In surveys of more than 600 American college students, communication scholars Susan Messman, Dan Canary, and Kimberly Hause discovered that people keep their opposite-sex friendships nonromantic for six primary reasons:[18]

- They aren't physically attracted to their friend.
- Their relatives and other friends wouldn't approve of a romantic relationship with the friend.
- They aren't ready to be in a romantic relationship.
- They want to protect their existing friendship.
- They fear being disappointed or hurt.
- They are concerned about a third party, such as a sibling, who is romantically interested in the friend.

Studies show that overall, both women and men consider their same-sex friends to be more loyal and helpful than their opposite-sex counterparts.[19] At the same time, however, opposite-sex friendships allow women and men to enjoy those aspects of friendship most valued by the other sex. Thus, it appears that same-sex and opposite-sex friendships offer unique rewards.

Talking Point: Many college students use the term "friends with benefits" to refer to friendships that are not romantic but do involve sexual activity.[ii]

[ii]Mongeau, P. M., Knight, K., Williams, J., Eden, J., & Shaw, C. (2013). Identifying and explicating variation among friends with benefits relationships. *Journal of Sex Research, 50,* 37–47.

Talking Points: Ask your students how many of their close friends from high school they still see on a regular basis. Even very close friendships are vulnerable when life circumstances change (such as graduating from high school and starting college).

Men and women often value opposite-sex friendships as opportunities to communicate in ways that are important to the other sex.
© ColorBlind Images/Blend Images LLC, RF

Friendships Have a Life Span

As important as friendships are to us, most are not permanent. Rather, as with most relationships, friendships have a life span: They are initiated, they are maintained, and eventually many of them end. In a now-classic work, communication scholar and friendship expert William Rawlins proposed that most friendships move through a life span consisting of six stages (as shown in Figure 1).[20]

Suppose two strangers, Naya and Emily, have been called for jury duty on the same day and they meet in the jurors' waiting lounge. Let's see how their relationship might progress through Rawlins's six stages.

- Role-limited interaction: At the *role-limited interaction* stage, Naya and Emily meet and interact for the first time. Because they are strangers at this stage, their communication follows social and cultural norms for interaction between strangers. They are civil and polite but share little personal information.

- Friendly relations: After chatting for a while, Naya and Emily may enter the *friendly relations* stage. At that point, their conversation becomes friendlier. For example, they may share personal stories or anecdotes. Naya and Emily may intend for their friendly interaction simply to make their wait in the jurors' lounge more enjoyable. However, it can also be an invitation for friendship.

- Moves toward friendship: Suppose Emily e-mails Naya the following week to ask if she'd like to go to an art gallery opening. Emily's invitation can signal progression to the *moves toward friendship* stage. At this stage, Naya and Emily's communication becomes more social and less bound by norms and rules.

- Nascent friendship: If Naya and Emily continue getting together and enjoying their interactions, they may enter the *nascent friendship* stage. At that point, they begin to think of themselves as friends. Their communication continues to become more personal and less prescribed.

- Stabilized friendship: Over time, Naya and Emily's relationship may progress to the *stabilized friendship* stage. At that point, they consider their friendship to be

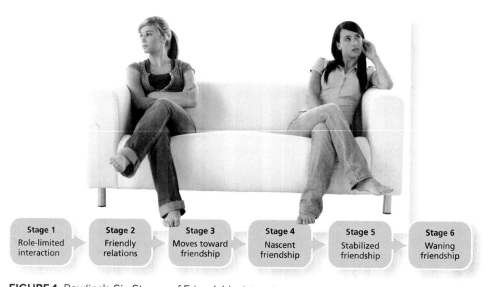

Stage 1	Stage 2	Stage 3	Stage 4	Stage 5	Stage 6
Role-limited interaction	Friendly relations	Moves toward friendship	Nascent friendship	Stabilized friendship	Waning friendship

FIGURE 1 Rawlins's Six Stages of Friendship © *Larry Williams/Cardinal/Corbis, RF*

fully established. They trust each other strongly and may even adjust their attitudes and opinions to be more in line with each other's.

- Waning friendship: After many years of close friendship, Naya and Emily may enter the *waning friendship* stage. That stage marks the decline of their friendship. Their friendship may simply become more distant and casual, or it may end altogether.

There are many reasons why a friendship comes to an end.[21] Research suggests that we can divide those reasons into two general categories: events that cause friends to dislike each other, and changes in life circumstances that decrease opportunities for communication and attention. Let's look at each situation.

FRIENDS CAN GROW TO DISLIKE EACH OTHER. Some friendships end because the friends no longer like each other. Although two people initially may have become friends because of their perceived similarity or their social attraction to each other, they can develop negative feelings toward each other that cause them to end their friendship. Studies have demonstrated that negative feelings are most likely to arise when one friend:

- Constantly nags or criticizes the other
- Betrays the other's confidence or trust
- Behaves in a hostile or physically violent way around the other
- Begins abusing alcohol or other drugs
- Fails to provide help or support when the other friend needs it
- Becomes intolerant of the other friend's romantic partner or other friends
- Feels he or she no longer has anything in common with the other friend

We don't necessarily terminate friendships on the basis of a single negative event. When a friend repeatedly wrongs us, however, we might grow to dislike him or her over time. That change in feelings can lead us to end the friendship.[22] In such cases, we might decide to confront the individual directly and make it clear that we no longer wish to be friends. In other cases, we might decide simply to reduce our communication with the person by avoiding him or her.

© Mixa/Getty Images, RF

FRIENDS' LIFE CIRCUMSTANCES CAN CHANGE. Although friendships sometimes end because of negative feelings, many friends simply "drift apart." As our lives change and evolve, we may have less opportunity to interact with particular friends. That doesn't necessarily mean we develop any negative feelings for them. It does mean, however, that some friendships end simply from lack of attention.

According to research, one of the most common life changes that can end a friendship is physical separation.[23] Recall that physical proximity is one of the main reasons we're attracted to potential friends. Friendships are relatively easy to maintain with people you see all the time. If one friend moves away, however, keeping up the friendship becomes more challenging.[24] Friends may keep in touch for a while after being separated, but their communication often declines over time, causing them to lose track of each other. To the extent that friends have access to Facebook or other social media, however, a lack of physical proximity doesn't necessarily prevent them from maintaining a close friendship.[25]

Other changes in life circumstances can also cause friendships to fade. When one friend gets married or has a baby, for instance, his or her attention is understandably diverted toward the new spouse or child. As a result, he or she has less time and opportunity to interact with friends. The demands of work or school can also make it difficult to spend time with friends. Experiencing a chronic illness can likewise limit opportunities to see friends. That may be particularly true with illnesses that impair social abilities, such as depression and chronic anxiety.

It is important to note that in those situations we don't necessarily *want* the friendship to end. Rather, we may simply no longer have the necessary time, energy, and attention to maintain it. If the friend is particularly important to us, however, we can use our communication and relational maintenance behaviors to keep the friendship going. It may take only an occasional phone call or e-mail message to maintain contact and let a friend know we still care about him or her. We can even use the Internet to help us restore communication with friends we've lost touch with.

LEARN IT   What does it mean to say that friendship is voluntary? What is a peer? Which rules are common for friendships in North America? Do people report feeling greater loyalty to same-sex or opposite-sex friends? Why do friendships come to an end?

APPLY IT   Working alone or in a small group, generate a list of what you consider to be the five most important rules for friendships, and rank them in terms of their importance. For each rule, identify one or two interpersonal communication behaviors that help you follow that rule in your own friendships.

REFLECT ON IT   Do you have any friendships that you feel are involuntary? What do you value differently about your same-sex and opposite-sex friendships?

2   Communicating in Romantic Relationships

The most intimate of relationships is often the one we share with a romantic partner. Romantic relationships—particularly, significant long-term ones—engage people mentally, emotionally, physically, financially, and even spiritually, and they often play a substantial role in people's social experiences. As noted earlier, they are also often the foundation for beginning new families. In this section, we survey the important characteristics of romantic relationships, examine different types of romantic bonds, and explore the communication behaviors that significantly influence romantic partners' satisfaction with their relationship.

Characteristics of Romantic Relationships

In April 2011, Prince William of Wales married his longtime girlfriend, Kate Middleton. As second in line to the British throne—and presumably a future king—William is expected by custom and social tradition to marry and produce children to ensure the continuation of his royal line. His obligations aside, however, the prince would most

Focus on Scholarship: Not all health behaviors are improved by marriage. Being married appears to have no effect on smoking,[iii] and it actually increases the risk of weight gain associated with a sedentary lifestyle.[iv]

[iii]Eng, P. M., Kawachi, I., Fitzmaurice, G., & Rimm, E. G. (2005). Effects of marital transitions on changes in dietary and other health behaviours in U.S. male health professionals. *Journal of Epidemiology and Community Health, 59,* 56–62.

[iv]Jeffrey, R. W., & Rick, A. M. (2002). Cross-sectional and longitudinal associations between body mass index and marriage-related factors. *Obesity Research, 10,* 809–815.

Although traditions vary around the world, forming romantic relationships is a practically universal human activity: 95 percent of us will get married. © *Thomas Cockrem/Alamy*, © *Steve Raymer/Asia Images/Getty Images*, © *Maria Teijeiro /Age Fotostock, RF*

likely have married anyway, as forming romantic relationships is a nearly universal human experience. Like William and Kate, some 95 percent of us will get married at least once in life, and many of those who don't marry will have at least one significant, marriagelike romantic relationship.[26]

Marriages and long-term relationships are very important to our health and well-being. Multiple studies have shown, for instance, that married people live longer[27] and healthier[28] lives than people who never marry. One reason for those findings is that marriage reduces a person's likelihood of engaging in risky health behaviors. In line with that idea, research demonstrates that married people, compared with unmarried people, drink less[29] and are less likely to use illicit drugs such as marijuana.[30] They are also less likely to suffer from mental illnesses such as depression.[31] Several studies have shown that the health benefits of marriage are greater for men than for women.[32] However, women are also healthier if married than if single, particularly if they are unemployed and lack the social support and financial resources employment provides.[33]

People in every known society form romantic unions, and although many romantic relationships share certain characteristics, there is also diversity among them. Let's look at variations in the extent to which romantic relationships are exclusive, voluntary, based on love, composed of opposite-sex partners, and permanent.

ROMANTIC RELATIONSHIPS AND EXCLUSIVITY. One common expectation for romantic relationships is that they are exclusive. Usually, exclusivity takes the form of **monogamy,** which means being in only one romantic relationship at a time and avoiding romantic or sexual involvement with people outside the relationship. Exclusivity is an expression of commitment and faithfulness that romantic partners share and trust each other to uphold. As a result, relational **infidelity,** which means having romantic or sexual interaction with someone outside of one's romantic relationship, is often an emotionally traumatic experience for the partner who is wronged.

Not all romantic partners expect their relationship to be exclusive, however. Instead, some couples choose to have "open" relationships in which romantic and/or sexual involvement with people outside the relationship is accepted.[34] Although it's difficult to know exactly how common that type of relationship is, research indicates that open relationships are observed between heterosexuals,[35] bisexuals,[36] gay men,[37] and lesbians alike.[38]

Not only are some romantic relationships not exclusive, but exclusivity isn't always an expectation for marriage. In fact, many countries—primarily in Africa and southern Asia—allow the practice of **polygamy,** in which one person is married to two or more

Talking Point: Every U.S. state forbids a person from having more than one legal spouse at a time and also provides that marital infidelity is grounds for divorce. In some U.S. states and foreign countries, marital infidelity is even illegal.[v] Most states categorize marital infidelity as a misdemeanor, but others—including Idaho, Massachusetts, Michigan, Oklahoma, and Wisconsin—consider it a felony.

[v]Statsky, W. P. (2012). *Family law* (6th ed.). Boston, MA: Cengage.

monogamy Being in only one romantic relationship at a time and avoiding romantic or sexual involvement with others outside the relationship.

infidelity Sexual involvement with someone other than one's romantic partner.

polygamy A practice in which one person is married to two or more spouses at the same time.

Polygamy is common in many countries. © AP Images/Mark Baker

spouses at the same time. Some people in open or polygamous relationships report that they appreciate the closeness and intimacy they share with multiple partners. Others indicate that feelings of jealousy and resentment can lead to increased conflict in such relationships.[39]

ROMANTIC RELATIONSHIPS AND VOLUNTARINESS. Another common expectation for romantic relationships is that they are voluntary, meaning that people choose for themselves whether to become romantically involved—and if they decide to, they, and not others, select their romantic partner. That expectation presumes that a relationship is strong and satisfying only if both partners have freely chosen to participate in it. One indicator of that expectation in the United States is the abundance of online and in-person dating services, which allow customers to browse the profiles of prospective partners and choose which ones they want to make contact with. In fact, one such service—Match.com—claims more than 75 million users in 40 countries.[40]

Even if people enter into romantic relationships voluntarily, they do not always stay in them voluntarily. Indeed, research shows that many people are unhappy in their relationships but stay in them anyway.[41] According to relationship scholars Denise Previti and Paul Amato, the most common reasons people stay in relationships involuntarily are

- They want to provide stability for their children.
- Their religious beliefs disallow separation or divorce.
- They are concerned about the financial implications of separating.
- They see no positive alternatives to their current relationship.[42]

In much of the world, however, it is common for other people—usually parents—to select a person's romantic partner. According to the practice of *arranged marriage* (which is most common in the Middle East and other parts of Asia and Africa), people are expected to marry the partner their parents select for them. Sometimes, children can reject their parents' selection of a spouse, in which case the parents look for someone else. In other cases, children may be pressured to marry the person their parents have chosen for them. In either situation, an arranged marriage is not entirely voluntary.[43]

The fact that arranged marriages aren't voluntary doesn't necessarily mean that people whose marriages are arranged are dissatisfied with the relationship. Indeed, people who expect their marriages to be arranged may prefer this practice to the task of choosing a spouse on their own.[44] For people who expect to choose their own romantic partner, however, the practice of arranged marriage would likely decrease their satisfaction with their relationships.

In cultures where arranged marriages are the norm, parents play an active role in choosing their children's spouses, just as their own parents did for them.

ROMANTIC RELATIONSHIPS AND LOVE. In much of the Western world, people think of marriage and other romantic relationships as being based on love. In individualist societies such as the United States and Canada, people tend to believe not only that they should get to choose their romantic partner but that their choice should be based on love and attraction.[45] Indeed, the typical American wedding ceremony (whether religious or civil) emphasizes the importance of love in the marital relationship, whereas losing love is frequently cited as a reason why relationships fail.[46]

Whether or not they love each other, however, some people enter into romantic relationships for other reasons. Some form relationships for financial stability.[47] Others establish relationships to gain, consolidate, or protect power,[48] such as when members of royal or politically powerful families intermarry.

Would you marry someone you didn't love? Many people in collectivistic societies would say yes. In countries such as China and India, for instance, the choice of a spouse has more to do with the wishes and preferences of family and social groups than it does with love, even if the marriage isn't arranged. One study found that only half of the participants in India and Pakistan felt that love was necessary for marriage, whereas 96 percent of the U.S. American participants did.[49] Sociologist Frances Hsu explained that when considering marriage, "an American asks, 'How does my heart feel?' A Chinese [person] asks, 'What will other people say?'"[50]*

As family studies scholar Stephanie Coontz points out, the connection between love and marriage is a historically recent trend, even in Western cultures.[51] She explains that although romantic love has existed throughout the ages, societies began thinking of love as a basis for marriage only within the last three centuries. Coontz indicates that before that time, some societies believed that love should develop after marriage, and many others thought love had no place at all in marriage. Thinking of marriage primarily as a romantic relationship is therefore a recent development.

ROMANTIC RELATIONSHIPS AND SEXUALITY. People form romantic relationships with others whether they are heterosexual or homosexual. In many ways, people often communicate similarly in same- and opposite-sex romantic relationships.[52] Both kinds of relationships value intimacy

© Thinkstock/Stockbyte/ Getty Images, RF

Focus on Scholarship: Research shows that divorce rates for arranged marriages are actually lower than for voluntary ones.[vi]

[vi]Allendorf, K. (2013). Determinants of marital quality in an arranged marriage society. *Social Science Research, 42,* 59–70; Xiaohe, X., & White, M. K. (1990). Love matches and arranged marriages: A Chinese replication. *Journal of Marriage and Family, 52,* 709–722.

Media Note: A feature article about arranged marriage is available online at: http://nymag.com/nymetro/news/culture/features/11621/

Media Note: On the student web page, the video clip "Gita and Karen Disagree" portrays a conversation about the merits of arranged marriage.

*Hsu, F. K. L. (1981). The self in cross-cultural perspective. In A. J. Marsella, B. De Vos, & F. L. K. Hsu (Eds.), Culture and Self (pp. 24–55). London, England: Tavistock. Quote is from p. 50.

People communicate in very similar ways in same- and opposite-sex romantic relationships. © amc / Alamy

and equality between partners.[53] They both experience conflict[54] and do so over similar topics.[55] They both benefit from receiving emotional support from family members and friends.[56] Further, they both negotiate how to accomplish mundane needs, such as everyday household chores.[57] Research indicates, in fact, that people in same-sex romantic relationships report levels of relationship satisfaction equal to those of opposite-sex dating, engaged, and married couples.[58]

Despite those similarities, same- and opposite-sex romantic relationships in most parts of the world differ with respect to their legal recognition. In the United States and abroad, the question of whether same-sex romantic partners should be allowed to marry has been socially and politically controversial for decades. Supporters of same-sex marriage argue that people should be permitted to marry whomever they love and that it is discriminatory to deny marriage rights to people based on their sex. Opponents say that marriage is inherently a reproductive relationship and that allowing same-sex couples to marry threatens the sanctity of marriage and the family. In June 2015, the Supreme Court of the United States ruled that denying same-sex couples the ability to marry violated the U.S. Constitution, thereby guaranteeing same-sex couples the right to marry in all fifty states. With this decision, the United States joined more than 20 other nations that have legalized same-sex marriage since 2000.

ROMANTIC RELATIONSHIPS AND PERMANENCE.   People often conceive of marriage and other long-term romantic relationships as permanent. That expectation is reflected in the fact that traditional wedding vows in many parts of the world emphasize the permanence of marriage. The vow "till death do us part" captures this sentiment by suggesting that once spouses are married, they will stay together for life. One survey of 300 marriage license applicants illustrates this idea. Even though respondents correctly noted that a large percentage of new marriages end in divorce, every single respondent said the likelihood that his or her own marriage would end in divorce was zero![59]

Many marriages do last for many years, thanks in part to the large number of ways in which societies promote, protect, and reward marriages. In the United States, for instance, federal law provides spouses a number of benefits that are often denied to couples who are not legally married. Many of those benefits relate to communication and the maintenance of marriage and family relationships.[60] Here are just a few:

- *Spousal privilege:* Communication between spouses is privileged and protected, just like doctor–patient and attorney–client communication.
- *Visitation:* Marriage gives spouses rights of visitation if one spouse is hospitalized or imprisoned.
- *Stepchildren:* Stepparents have legal status with stepchildren only if they are legally married to the children's parent.
- *Cohabitation on controlled properties:* Marriage allows spouses to live together on military bases and other controlled properties.
- *Inheritance and property rights:* Unless a person's will specifies otherwise, a spouse is entitled to receive a person's estate when he or she passes away.

Talking Point: Several traditions around the world illustrate the concept that marriage is more of an economic relationship than a romantic one. For example, a *dowry* consists of money or presents provided from the bride's family to the groom's, and a *bride price* consists of a cost paid by a groom to the bride's family. Even the practice of giving an engagement ring originated as a symbol of the prospective groom's ability to support his spouse financially.

Focus on Ethics: Many people have opined that denying same-sex couples the right to marry is an infringement of fundamental civil rights (similar to denying interracial couples the right to marry). What are the ethical issues surrounding this issue? Is it ethical to deny same-sex couples the right to marry? Do people have a fundamental right to marry in the first place?

fact OR fiction? HALF OF ALL MARRIAGES END IN DIVORCE

An often-quoted statistic about marriages is that half of them end in divorce. According to that idea, a given marriage has roughly a 50-50 chance of succeeding. Is that idea fact or fiction?

According to research, it's fiction. The idea seems to have come about in the 1970s and was based on census data that simply compared the number of marriages per year to the number of divorces. That comparison produces a false result, however, because it is not the same people getting married and divorced each year.

We can say with greater accuracy that the divorce rate—at least for first marriages—peaked at around 40 percent in the early 1980s and has been declining ever since. By the early 2000s, it was approximately 30 percent. A given person's likelihood of divorce is influenced by many factors, such as education level, religiosity, and age at first marriage. In fact, for college-educated women who earn their own income and marry after the age of 25, the likelihood of divorce is only 20 percent—meaning that their marriages have a 4-in-5 chance of succeeding.

ASK YOURSELF

- Why do you suppose factors such as education, age, and religious affiliation make a difference in a person's likelihood of divorcing?

- If you believed the U.S. divorce rate was actually increasing, rather than decreasing, on what did you base that belief?

Source: Heller, K. (2015). The myth of the high rate of divorce. *PsychCentral.* Retrieved April 6, 2015, from http://psychcentral.com/lib/the-myth-of-the-high-rate-of-divorce/00011473

- *Medical and burial decisions:* Spouses have the ability to make medical decisions for each other and to make burial or cremation decisions when one of them dies.

- *Domestic violence protection:* If one spouse is abusive or violent, the other spouse can request domestic violence protection orders from a court.

Many marriages and romantic relationships don't last, however. After a period of time together, romantic partners often find that they no longer share the same goals or feel the same level of attraction toward each other. They may also have developed romantic feelings for someone else and may choose to end their current relationship to develop a relationship with that person. No matter the cause, many romantic relationships end.

People often repeat the claim that, in the United States, half of all marriages end in divorce. Is that actually true? Check out the "Fact or Fiction?" box to find out.

Differing Relational Types among Romantic Couples

In the Forming and Maintaining Personal Relationships chapter, we explored the five stages—initiating, experimenting, intensifying, integrating, and bonding—that people often follow when developing close relationships, including romantic pairs. Even if people progress through the same steps, however, that doesn't necessarily mean they'll end up with the same type of relationship. Rather, research on marriage indicates that romantic couples embody distinct relational types. Communication researcher Mary Anne Fitzpatrick has spent many years studying patterns of marital communication. Her work suggests that people form and maintain marriages by relying on *marital schemata,* which represent their cognitive models for what marriage is and should be.[61] Fitzpatrick's research has found that three types of marriages are especially common: traditional, separate, and independent.[62]

Talking Point: Expectations about the permanence of marital relationships may be softening, and one indicator of that is the popularity of *prenuptial agreements,* or contracts that specify the division of property in the event that a marriage dissolves. All 50 U.S. states and the District of Columbia allow people to enter into prenuptial agreements before getting married or forming domestic partnerships.

Talking Point: Ask your students how many marriages or significant long-term romantic relationships they genuinely expect to have in their lifetimes. Some may say zero; many may say one; others may say more than one. Use their responses to generate a discussion about their own expectations regarding the permanence of marriage or other romantic relationships.

Even if we form relationships according to the same basic stages, we don't necessarily end up with the same type of relationship. According to marriage expert Mary Anne Fitzpatrick, three fundamental types of marriage are especially common: traditional, separate, and independent. © Image100/Alamy, RF

- *Traditional couples* take a culturally conventional approach to marriage. They believe in gender-typical divisions of labor in which wives are in charge of housework and childrearing and husbands are responsible for home repair and auto maintenance. When conflict arises, spouses in traditional couples engage in it rather than avoid it.

- *Separate couples* are similar to couples in traditional marriages except that the spouses are autonomous rather than interdependent. They often have their own interests and social networks, and they think of themselves as separate individuals rather than as one couple. Because of their lack of interdependence, spouses in separate couples generally don't engage in conflict. Even when they disagree, they tend to ignore conflict rather than deal with it directly.

- *Independent couples* see themselves as being independent of social expectations for marriage. They don't necessarily believe in conventional gender roles or divisions of labor, so the wife might support the family financially while the husband stays home with the children. Although these couples consider themselves to be independent of cultural norms, they are highly interdependent. As a result, they engage in conflict when it arises.

Fitzpatrick also found that in about half the couples she has studied, the husband and wife don't agree as to whether their marriage is traditional, separate, or independent. She refers to couples in which the two spouses have differing beliefs about their marriage as *mixed couples*. The most common type of mixed couple is one in which the wife's expectations match those of traditional couples and the husband's expectations match those of separate couples. Communication patterns in mixed couples most likely reflect the particular expectations each spouse holds.

Romantic relationships are as individual as the people who compose them, and several of the ways they differ are related to communication behaviors. In the next section, we'll take a brief look at various ways people communicate in their romantic relationships.

Talking Point: Ask students to guess which marital type reports the highest levels of commitment and love. Many will guess independent couples, but research has shown that traditional U.S. couples report the commitment and love of all four types (including mixed couples).[vii] The reason may be that traditional couples receive the most social support and validation (because they most closely adhere to society's expectations of marriage). The same has been found among Malaysian couples, but not those from India or China.[viii]

[vii]Weigel, D. J., & Ballard-Reisch, D. S. (1999). All marriages are not maintained equally: Marital type, marital quality, and the use of maintenance behaviors. *Personal Relationships, 6*, 291–303.

[viii]Mustafa, H., Hasim, M. J. M., Aripin, N., & Hamid, H. A. (2013). Couple types, ethnicity, and marital satisfaction in Malaysia. *Applied Research in Quality of Life, 8*, 299–317.

Interpersonal Communication in Romantic Relationships

We can learn about the quality of romantic relationships by looking at how partners communicate with each other. Four communication behaviors have particular influence on romantic partners' satisfaction with their relationship: conflict management, privacy management, emotional communication, and instrumental communication.

ROMANTIC RELATIONSHIPS VARY IN HOW THEY HANDLE CONFLICT. Conflict is a common characteristic of many romantic relationships. Communication scholars William Wilmot and Joyce Hocker define *conflict* as "an expressed struggle between at least two interdependent parties who perceive incompatible goals, scarce resources, and interference from the other party in achieving their goals."[63]* Partners in a romantic relationship can have conflicts about many issues, including how they spend their time and money, raise their children, manage their personal and professional obligations, and enact their sex life. Although conflict isn't fun, it isn't necessarily bad for a relationship. The way couples handle conflict—rather than the amount of conflict they experience—is what influences the success of their relationship.

Much of what we know about how romantic partners handle conflict comes from research on marriage. For instance, clinical psychologist and marital therapist John Gottman has spent many years studying how spouses communicate during conflict episodes.[64] His work suggests marital couples can be classified into four groups, depending on how they handle conflict:[65]

- *Validating couples* talk about their disagreements openly and cooperatively. In such couples, spouses communicate respect for each other's opinions even when they disagree with them. They stay calm, even when discussing hotly contested topics. They also use humor and expressions of positive emotion to defuse the tension that conflict can create.

- *Volatile couples* also talk about their disagreements openly, but in a way that is competitive rather than cooperative. That is, each spouse tries to persuade the other to adopt his or her point of view. Conflicts in such couples tend to be marked with expressions of negative rather than positive emotion. However, those conflicts are often followed by intense periods of affection and "making up."

- *Conflict-avoiding couples* deal with their disagreements indirectly rather than openly. To avoid the discomfort of engaging in conflict directly, these couples try to defuse negative emotion and focus on their similarities. They feel there is little to be gained by engaging in conflict directly, believing that most problems will resolve themselves. They often "agree to disagree," a tactic that allows them to sidestep conflict but that can leave their points of disagreement unresolved.

- *Hostile couples* experience frequent and intense conflict. During conflict episodes, hostile couples use negative emotion displays, such as harsh tones of voice and facial expressions of anger or frustration. They also engage in personal attacks that include insults, sarcasm, name calling, blaming, and other forms of criticism.

Although Gottman developed his categories with reference to married couples, more recent work by researchers Thomas Holman and Mark Jarvis has indicated that the same categories also apply to unmarried heterosexual couples.[66] Comparatively less research has been conducted on the conflict communication of lesbian, gay, bisexual, or transgender relationships. Gottman's studies have identified some differences in the conflict styles of homosexual and heterosexual couples, however.[67] Specifically, his research has found that compared with heterosexual couples, gay and lesbian couples:

- Use more humor and positive emotion during conflict conversations

In Everyday Life: Many married couples would say that there is "his marriage" and there is "her marriage," and the two are not necessarily the same. The mixed-couple type illustrates this idea that women and men often do not experience their marriage in the same way.

Focus on Scholarship: According to Gottman's work, volatile couples are the most communicative and expressive of all types of couples.

Gottman's research has found that same-sex couples deal with conflict slightly differently than do heterosexual couples.
© Stockbyte/Thinkstock, RF

*Hocker, J. L., & Wilmot, W. W. (2013). *Interpersonal Conflict* (9th ed.). New York, NY: McGraw-Hill. Quote is from p. 40.

- Are less likely to become hostile after a conflict
- Use fewer displays of dominance and power during a conflict episode
- Are less likely to take conflict personally
- Stay calmer emotionally and physiologically during conflict

For many romantic relationships, conflict is unpleasant but unavoidable. We will further probe successful strategies for managing it in the Interpersonal Conflict chapter.

Talking Point: One way researchers ascertain the privacy boundaries in a relationship is by examining topics of conversation that are commonly avoided in that relationship, since these indicate a high desire for privacy on these issues. Research suggests that particular topics are commonly avoided in personal relationships, among them failures and negative experiences, information about substance abuse or sexual behavior, financial concerns or debt, and trouble with the law.

communication privacy management (CPM) theory Theory that explains how people manage the tension between privacy and disclosure.

ROMANTIC RELATIONSHIPS VARY IN HOW THEY HANDLE PRIVACY. In every romantic relationship, the partners must choose for themselves how to manage information they consider to be private. When Kali and Neal were having difficulty conceiving a child, for instance, they carefully considered whom they were going to tell. Neal felt the information was no one's business but theirs and preferred to keep it private. Kali wanted to tell her family and close friends, because she needed their emotional support. Their problems conceiving were causing enough stress in the relationship already; disagreeing on whether to keep them private was only making matters more stressful.

Communication scientist Sandra Petronio believes we all experience tensions between disclosing certain information and keeping it private. She developed **communication privacy management (CPM) theory** to explain how individuals and couples manage those tensions.[68] CPM theory maintains that Kali and Neal *jointly own* the information about their problems. The information belongs to them, and so they must decide whether to keep it to themselves or share it with others.[69]

Individuals and couples vary in their approach to privacy. Some of us are "open books"—that is, uninhibited about disclosing private information to others. Others are discreet, sharing private information only with a select few. Research indicates that some of us are simply more inclined than others to disclose private information. In most cases, however, our decisions about sharing information are influenced by the people to whom we are disclosing it, by how much we trust them, and by how much they have disclosed to us.[70] No matter what our reasons for disclosing to others, we should always be cognizant of information that a romantic partner expects us to keep private.

ROMANTIC RELATIONSHIPS VARY IN HOW THEY HANDLE EMOTIONAL COMMUNI-CATION. Emotional communication is an important part of most romantic relationships. Research tells us that how romantic partners express emotion to each other can say a lot about the quality of their relationship.[71] Specifically, it reflects how satisfied the partners are with each other.[72]

Suppose for example that Anita and her husband Jonah have been married for 8 years. They co-own a home where they run a small pottery studio and raise Jonah's twin girls from his previous marriage. They have their challenges just like any couple, but they are both highly satisfied with their relationship. Now suppose that Brad and Lynne live across the street from Anita and Jonah. They have been together for almost 10 years but have separated twice in that time. Their most recent separation lasted 7 months and would have ended their relationship permanently were it not for pressure from Lynne's family for the couple to work out its differences. Both Brad and Lynne would describe their relationship as very unsatisfying.

According to research, one of the most noticeable differences in the communication patterns of these two couples will be in their expression of emotion. Over the course of several studies, social psychologists John Gottman and Robert Levenson have identified two patterns of emotional communication that differentiate happy from unhappy couples.

First, happy partners such as Anita and Jonah communicate more positive emotion and less negative emotion with each other than do unhappy partners such as Brad and Lynne.[73] In particular, people in satisfying relationships express more affection, use more humor, and communicate more assurances or verbal expressions of their commitment to the relationship. In contrast, people in dissatisfying relationships express more anger, contempt, sadness, and hostility.[74] Gottman and Levenson's work has found, specifically, that people in satisfying couples maintain a ratio of 5 positive behaviors for every 1 negative behavior.[75]

The second pattern of emotional communication Gottman and Levenson identified is that unhappy couples are more likely than happy couples to reciprocate expressions of negative emotion.[76] When Lynne criticizes or expresses anger toward Brad, for example, he often reciprocates her behavior by expressing criticism or anger back at her. That type of response escalates the negativity in their conversation. As a result, the partners often find it difficult to address the issues underlying their conflict because they are so focused on the negative emotions they're communicating. In comparison, people in happy couples are more likely to respond to negative expressions with positive or neutral ones. Check out the "Got Skills?" box for tips on generating neutral responses to negative emotional expressions.

ROMANTIC RELATIONSHIPS VARY IN HOW THEY HANDLE INSTRUMENTAL COMMUNICATION.

People in most romantic relationships communicate with each other about many instrumental, day-to-day topics, such as who's making dinner and who's taking the children to soccer practice.[77] The fact that instrumental communication addresses the necessary daily tasks couples face explains why it is one of the most common forms of communication between romantic partners.[78] It can also be one of the most contentious issues couples face, because romantic partners often disagree over the division of responsibilities for instrumental tasks.[79]

How partners negotiate the division of everyday tasks matters for their relationship for at least two reasons. First, day-to-day tasks such as cleaning, cooking, and childcare *need* to be completed, so most couples cannot leave decisions about who will do them to chance. Second, the way in which partners divide mundane, everyday tasks often reflects the balance of power within their relationship.[80] If one partner assumes greater power and control than the other, that partner is in a greater position to dictate how tasks will be divided. If instead both partners see themselves as equally powerful, the division of instrumental tasks can be more equitable.[81]

Romantic relationships vary greatly in how the partners communicate about the division of day-to-day tasks. In opposite-sex relationships, people who believe in traditional gender-role behaviors will often divide instrumental tasks along stereotypical gender lines.[82] Thus, men perform tasks such as yard maintenance and auto repair, whereas women

Talking Point: Ask students to identify specific behaviors people use to communicate positive and negative emotion in their relationships.

Focus on Scholarship: The 5:1 ratio of positive to negative behaviors in happy couples is sometimes referred to as "Gottman's Ratio."

Focus on Scholarship: Research illustrates that the more conflict spouses experience between the demands of home and the demands of work, the more physical stress they go through.[ix]

[ix]Hill, E. J. (2005). Work-family facilitation and conflict, working fathers and mothers, work-family stressors and support. *Journal of Family Issues, 26,* 793–819.

How partners divide mundane tasks such as childcare often reflects the balance of power in their relationship.
© Moodboard/Corbis, RF

got skills?

RESPONDING TO NEGATIVE EMOTIONAL EXPRESSIONS

Don't let negativity escalate.

WHAT?

Learn to respond to negative emotional expressions with neutral ones.

WHY?

To deescalate negativity in a conversation, such as a disagreement with a romantic partner, so that any issues underlying the conflict can be addressed.

HOW?

1. When someone expresses negativity to you, mentally identify the emotion(s) being conveyed. Remember that there are several forms of negative emotion, including anger, disgust, resentment, jealousy, sadness, and fear.

2. Consciously tell yourself not to respond to the expression right away. Instead, ignore the negativity and focus on *what the person is saying* rather than on the way he or she is saying it.

3. Paraphrase the person's words as calmly as you can, to ensure that you understand the person's comments and will focus attention on the issue, not the emotion.

4. Invite the person to discuss the issue calmly. If you encounter more negativity, stay calm and continue paraphrasing the person's statements until he or she has calmed down.

TRY!

1. With a partner, role-play a conversation in which the person expresses various forms of negativity to you. For instance, your partner might act sad and angry that you haven't spent much time with him or her lately.

2. Practice ignoring your partner's negativity and calmly paraphrasing his or her comments. For example, "What I hear you saying is that you're feeling hurt that I haven't been around more."

3. If your partner verifies your interpretation, then say, "I'm happy to talk with you about that." Listen to what the person has to say, but remain calm. If you don't reciprocate your partner's negativity, he or she will probably calm down and be able to talk rationally.

CONSIDER: *Why does reciprocating negativity often escalate it?*

take responsibility for meal preparation and childcare. In contrast, partners who do not necessarily adopt traditional gender-role behaviors frequently have conflict over how instrumental tasks should be divided.[83] Specifically, women often wish their partners would take greater responsibility for household tasks and childcare than they actually do.[84] Compared to men, women are more likely than men to feel that the division of instrumental tasks is unfair, and those feelings reduce their relational satisfaction.[85]

With regard to same-sex relationships, research shows that homosexual partners divide instrumental tasks more equitably than opposite-sex partners, with each same-sex partner sharing in both stereotypically masculine and stereotypically feminine responsibilities. In a survey of 113 same-sex romantic couples from around the United States, communication professor Justin Boren discovered that such a pattern was common, particularly among couples who were highly satisfied with their relationships.[86]

LEARN IT What is relational infidelity? Where is arranged marriage common? How are traditional, separate, independent, and mixed couples different from each other? What characterizes validating, volatile, and conflict-avoiding couples? How do satisfied and unsatisfied couples differ in their emotional communication?

APPLY IT Pick a couple who has been together for at least 10 years, and ask the partners (together or separately) how their communication patterns have changed during that time. Ask them what advice they would give to others about communicating successfully in their relationship. Document your findings in a journal entry.

REFLECT ON IT To what extent do you expect your own romantic relationships to be permanent, or monogamous, or based on love? Has your privacy ever been violated by a romantic partner? If so, how did you feel? If not, how do you imagine you would respond?

3 Communicating in Families

It's hard to overestimate the importance of families in our lives. For most of us, our first relationships are with our family members. Familial relationships can provide us with a feeling of belonging, a sense of our own history, and a measure of unconditional love and support we cannot find anywhere else. Growing up in a family also introduces us to the concept of relationships and can help us form mental models for how to engage in friendships and romantic relationships in adolescence and adulthood. Yet families can also be a source of great frustration and heartache—and many family relationships experience both peace and conflict. The depth of our engagement with families, and the fact that they can be both so positive *and* so negative, make families one of our most important intimate relationships.

In this section, we'll examine what makes a family a family and which characteristics familial relationships often share. We'll also survey types of family structures and discover what communication issues are common in family relationships.

What Makes a Family?

If you were asked to draw a picture of your family, whom would you choose to include? Some people might be obvious options, such as your parents, spouse, siblings, and children. How about your grandparents? Nieces and nephews? In-laws? What about your stepsiblings? Maybe there are close friends or longtime neighbors whom you think of as family—would you include them as well?

Even researchers have difficulty defining exactly what makes a family a family, yet many scholars agree that most family relationships have one or more of three important characteristics: genetic ties, legal obligations, and role behaviors.

GENETIC TIES. Many family members are related "by blood," meaning they share a specified proportion of their genetic material. For instance, you share about 50 percent

CONNECT: Insight reports provide visualized data to instructors, making it possible to quickly confirm early signals of success or identify early warning signs regarding student performance or concept mastery.

What makes a family a family? According to researchers, most family relationships have at least one of three fundamental characteristics: genetic ties, legal obligations, and role behaviors. © *Hill Street Studios/ Blend Images/Getty Images, RF*

of your genes with your biological mother, biological father, and each full biological sibling (or 100 percent if you're an identical twin or identical triplet). With your grandparents, aunts and uncles, and any half-siblings, you share about 25 percent of your genes, and with cousins, it's about 12.5 percent.

Although many family relationships include genetic ties, some do not. Consider that we typically share zero percent of our genes with our spouses, steprelatives, and adopted relatives, yet we generally consider them to be family. Moreover, although sharing a genetic tie makes two people biological relatives, it does not necessarily mean they share a social or an emotional relationship. People who were adopted as infants, for example, may not even know their genetic parents and may consider their adoptive parents to be their family. Social networking sites such as Facebook even help some adopted children reunite with their birth parents.[87] Clearly, however, a genetic tie is not the only element that defines family relationships. Rather, families share other characteristics as well.

LEGAL OBLIGATIONS. Another aspect of many family relationships is that they involve legal bonds. For example, parents have many legal obligations toward their minor children, and neglecting their responsibilities to house, feed, educate, and care for their children is a crime.[88] Furthermore, marriage is the most heavily regulated family relationship from a legal perspective—in the United States, well over a thousand different federal laws govern some aspect of marriage.[89]

The law also regulates adoptive relationships and domestic partnerships, and even stepfamily relationships are affected by the laws regulating the stepparents' marriages. The existence of a legal bond is therefore another characteristic of many family relationships. Family members often feel they have responsibilities to one another even without the laws saying so, but laws formalize those responsibilities and help ensure they are met.

ROLE BEHAVIORS.   Regardless of whether a relationship is bound by genetic or legal ties, many people believe the most important characteristic that defines it as familial is that the individuals in it *act* like a family.[90] According to that idea, there are certain behaviors or roles that family members are expected to enact. Those may include living together, taking care of and loving one another, and representing themselves as a family to outsiders. People who enact such behaviors and who think of themselves as family are therefore family, according to that definition.

The three fundamental dimensions of a family we've considered—genetic, legal, and role—are not mutually exclusive. In fact, some relationships, such as those between parents and their biological children, include all of them. Rather, they are characteristics that often help to define a relationship as familial. How researchers define family is important, because that definition determines, in part, which relationships family scholars study and which they do not. How *you* define family is also important, because that can influence your decisions about whom you invite to significant occasions in your life, with whom you will share resources, and to whom you will entrust secrets or sensitive information.

Types of Families

One of the reasons it can be tricky to talk about families is that they come in so many forms. Let's begin to sort those out by distinguishing between what researchers label the family of origin and family of procreation. **Family of origin** is the family one grows up in, so it typically consists of one's parents or stepparents and siblings. **Family of procreation** is the family one starts as an adult, and it consists of a spouse or romantic partner and/or any children raised as one's own. Most adults would say they belong to both a family of origin and a family of procreation; others, however, may identify with only one type of family or with neither type.

Both families of origin and families of procreation develop in many forms. Perhaps the most traditional profile consists of a married woman and man and their biological children. Researchers often call that configuration a *nuclear family,* and although it has been the traditional family form in the United States, research indicates that it is no longer the most common family form.[91] One family type that is becoming increasingly common is the *blended family,* with two adult partners (who may be married or cohabiting and of the same or opposite sex) raising children who are not the biological offspring of both partners. The children may be adopted, or they may be the biological offspring of one of the parents and the stepchildren of the other.

A third family form is the *single-parent family,* in which one adult raises one or more children. As in blended families, the children may be the parent's biological offspring or they may be adopted children or stepchildren. There are more than 11 million single-parent families in the United States, and nearly 10 million of those are headed by a single mother.[92] A fourth family form, the *extended family,* includes relatives such as grandparents, cousins, aunts and uncles, and other individuals whom a person considers to be part of his or her family. Individuals may or may not interact with their extended family on a regular basis, but research shows extended-family relationships can be a significant part of their family experience.[93]

Communication Issues in Families

As in all significant relationships, communication plays a big part in making or breaking family relationships. Let's examine four communication issues that families commonly deal with: roles, rituals, stories, and secrets.

family of origin The family in which one grows up (often consisting of one's parents and siblings).

family of procreation The family one starts as an adult (often consisting of one's spouse and children).

In Everyday Life: Laws in most U.S. states still favor the mother over the father in child custody disputes. That reality partly accounts for why single-parent families are overwhelmingly more likely to be headed by a mother than a father.

Writing Note: Have students identify, in writing, the roles they believe they play in their own families, as well as the roles played by others in the family. Reinforce the idea that roles are different from positions.

In the IM: In the out-of-class activity "Family Role-Play," students will write a script depicting their family's discussion of an issue and then analyze it with respect to the roles adopted by each family member.

Outside of Class: Ask your students to ask their parents and/or siblings for their perceptions of the family's rituals: what rituals the family has, and what functions they serve. Students may get varying answers about the same rituals depending on whom they ask.

rituals Repetitive behaviors that have special meaning for a group or relationship.

FAMILY ROLES.   Family *roles* embody the functions individuals serve in the family system. One person may be the problem solver; another might act as the family jokester or the family peacemaker. One sibling may be the troublemaker, whereas another may serve as the caregiver. Importantly, family roles are different from family *positions,* such as father and daughter, which are based on the structure of our relationships with others. Roles are based not on relationship structures but rather on the social and emotional functions an individual's behavior serves within the family.

Family roles often become particularly relevant when the family is in conflict. Expert family therapist Virginia Satir has suggested that four roles become especially common during conflict episodes.[94] The first role is the *blamer,* who holds others responsible for whatever goes wrong but accepts no responsibility for his or her own behaviors. A second role is the *placater,* the peacemaker who will go to any lengths to reduce conflict. That person may simply agree with whatever anyone says to keep others from getting angry. A third role is the *computer,* who attempts to use logic and reason—rather than emotion—to defuse the situation. Finally, there's the *distracter,* who makes random, irrelevant comments so that the rest of the family will forget about the conflict. Each role leads people to communicate in different ways. Some role behaviors, such as computing and placating, can be useful for resolving conflict or at least for preventing it from escalating. The behavior of blamers and distracters, on the other hand, might make conflict worse by taking attention away from the topic of the conflict.

FAMILY RITUALS.   Many families have their own important traditions. One family's tradition might be to spend every Thanksgiving serving turkey dinners at a shelter for homeless veterans. Another's tradition might be to attend drag races together every summer. We call those traditions family **rituals,** or repetitive behaviors that have special meaning. Rituals serve a variety of functions in family interactions, among them reinforcing a family's values and providing a sense of belonging.[95] A family ritual such as an annual road trip isn't just about the trip. It's also about spending time together, creating memories, and emphasizing how important family relationships are.

According to communication scholars Dawn Braithwaite, Leslie Baxter, and Anneliese Harper, rituals can be especially important in blended families comprising stepparents and stepchildren. Their research found that people often "import" rituals from their original family into their blended family.[96] Sometimes, the blended family retains or adapts these rituals; sometimes it does not. For instance, Braithwaite and her colleagues described one family in which a widowed mother and her children would have a pizza "picnic" in the living room on a regular basis. The children would cuddle with the mother on the couch, eat pizza, and talk, and everyone considered it to be a special time. When the mother remarried and acquired stepchildren, however, the ritual stopped, perhaps because the stepchildren would have been uncomfortable taking part.

Braithwaite and colleagues also found that it's important for blended families to develop their own rituals. In one such family, a young man described how his new stepfather began a ritual of watching the Super Bowl with his brother and him. According to this young man, that ritual served as a means of promoting communication with his stepfather: "It gave us something in common and we could talk about

A family ritual such as a road trip isn't just about the trip. It's also about spending time together, creating memories, and reinforcing family bonds.
© Jean Mahaux/The Image Bank/Getty Images

sports. It gave us a link. We both understood things, so we could eventually talk about other things more freely. . . . I almost started thinking of him as my dad."[97]*

FAMILY STORIES.   Many of us can think of particular stories we've heard over and over again from family members. Maybe your grandparents were fond of describing how they overcame hardships when they were first married, and your parents have a favorite story about your childhood antics. Even an event that was stressful or unpleasant at the time but turned out well, such as getting a flat tire during a vacation, can serve a reassuring or cautionary function when it becomes part of the family. Stories are common in families, and communication scholars Jody Koenig Kellas and Haley Kranstuber Horstman suggest that they do more than provide entertainment. Family stories, they explain, give families a sense of their history, express what family members expect of one another, and reinforce connections across different generations.[98]

Family stories tend to have at least two characteristics in common. First, they're told and retold, often over long periods of time. In that way, they become part of a family's collective knowledge: After a while, most everyone in the family has heard each story over and over. Second, family stories convey an underlying message about the family, such as "We are proud," "We overcome adversity," or "We stick together no matter what."

FAMILY SECRETS.   Many families have secrets they intentionally keep hidden. Those secrets often contain information the family considers private and inappropriate for sharing with outsiders, such as details of religious practices, health or legal issues, family conflicts, or financial information. Keeping family secrets doesn't just protect private family information, though; it also reinforces the family's identity and exclusivity, because only family members are allowed to know the secrets.[99]

Secrets can also be kept *within* families. For instance, Mario may not want his parents to know he has moved in with his girlfriend, so he swears his sister to secrecy. Erin and Tammy may not want their young children to know that Tammy has breast cancer, so they agree to keep it secret. Individuals choose to keep secrets from other family members for many reasons, such as avoiding embarrassment or conflict, protecting another person's feelings, and maintaining a sense of autonomy and privacy.[100]

When families also work together, as does *Duck Dynasty's* Robertson family, communication issues take on new dimensions. © *Genaro Molina/Los Angeles Times/Contour/Getty Images*

LEARN IT   How do genetic ties, legal obligations, and role behaviors matter to the definition of families? What is the difference between a family of origin and a family of procreation? What are family roles, and how may they affect communication within families?

APPLY IT   Recall a family ritual from your childhood or adolescence. What did that ritual reflect about your family's rules, values, and beliefs? How did it reinforce the strength of your family relationships? Document your thoughts in a journal entry.

REFLECT ON IT   If you had to come up with a definition of *family*, what would it be? What family stories do you remember hearing as a child?

Braithwaite, D. O., Baxter, L. A., & Harper, A. M. (1998). The role of rituals in the management of dialectical tensions of "old" and "new" in blended families. Communication Studies, 49, 105–120. Quote is from p. 113.

4 Communicating in the Workplace

Nearly all of us will be employed at some point in our lives, and our jobs will require us to interact with other people. It's therefore realistic to assume that most of us will have to relate to and communicate with people we know from work, whether they are co-workers, superiors, subordinates, or customers. In fact, many public agencies and private corporations expect their employees to communicate with one another in well-defined ways. Those expectations might include communicating honestly, treating people with dignity, listening to others, and being open to other people's opinions. All such communication behaviors contribute to a civil and respectful work environment. They can also make it easier for employees to form and maintain relationship in the workplace.[101]

As you may know already from personal experience, relationships at work can be a "dual-edged sword." On the one hand, having friends at work is great, because they can make the workday pleasant and help and support you when you need it. On the other hand, relational roles and work roles often conflict. For instance, you may have to keep certain information private from your co-workers but you may feel compelled to share that information with a co-worker with whom you are romantically involved.

Workplace relationships can also be more challenging to control than regular relationships. As a part of our job, we are usually required to see and interact with our supervisors, co-workers, and customers whether we want to or not. Interaction with our social network, in contrast, is usually voluntary and easier to control. If you have an argument with a regular friend, for example, you can choose to avoid him or her for a period of time while you both cool down. Because of your work responsibilities, however, you may not have that option with workplace friends.

To deal successfully with the challenges of workplace friendships, it's important to understand their dynamics. Let's examine those dynamics in three specific workplace relationships: between co-workers, between superiors and subordinates, and with clients. We'll also look carefully at workplace communication online and its implications for relationships.

Relationships with Co-workers

In the workplace, you are probably most likely to form close relationships with your immediate co-workers. One reason that is true is that co-workers are usually peers rather than superiors or subordinates, so their levels of power and responsibility are similar to yours.[102] Another reason is that immediate co-workers share with you some common experiences, such as working for the same company, the same department, and the same supervisor. In addition, you probably spend a great deal of time with your co-workers, perhaps even more than you spend with people outside work. Those characteristics can form a ready-made basis for relationships.[103] To understand social bonds between co-workers, it is instructive to examine both friendships and romantic relationships.

FRIENDSHIPS AMONG CO-WORKERS. Having close friends in the workplace can benefit people both personally and professionally. Research shows that the quality of people's friendships with their co-workers affects their job satisfaction.[104] All other things being equal, the closer you are to your co-workers, the happier you are at work. Perhaps as a result, research finds that managers in a wide variety of organizations generally welcome and promote the development of workplace friendships.[105]

Friendships in the workplace provide many benefits. For one, they can be a rich source of information. Co-workers commonly share information about the work organization, its activities, and its people; in fact, employees rely more on their co-workers for information than any other source.[106] When co-workers are also friends, however, they may be especially inclined to share. Research confirms, in fact, that exchanging information in an organization contributes to the development of close workplace friendships.[107] Another benefit of workplace friends is that they are often a reliable source of emotional support.[108] Because they understand the specific demands of their shared work environment, workplace friends can empathize with each other and provide support even in ways that relatives and external friends cannot.[109]

Research indicates that having high-quality workplace friendships is important to overall job satisfaction. In jobs where individuals must spend long stretches of time together, relationships can be very close.
© *Monkey Business / Getty Images Plus, RF*

Like regular friendships, workplace friendships follow a developmental path. One study found that workplace friendships go through three distinct phases: (1) acquaintance to friend, (2) friend to close friend, and (3) close friend to "almost best" friend.[110] Once formed, workplace friendships tend also to be managed in much the same way as regular relationships. Communication scholars Patricia Sias and her colleagues have discovered that co-workers use several communicative strategies to maintain close friendships with each other.[111] These include, among others:

- Helping each other
- Asking about each other's lives
- Being direct and open in their communication with each other
- Avoiding messages that would embarrass or offend each other
- Displaying a positive mood around each other

As beneficial as friendships with co-workers are, however, they can also be challenging. This is because the relationship has both a *social dimension* and a *task dimension,* and those different aspects of the friendship frequently come into conflict. The social dimension is your personal relationship with the co-worker, whereas the task dimension is your professional relationship. Let's say, for example, that you're friends with your co-worker Kellie, who's up for a promotion. As her friend, you want her to have the promotion, but as her co-worker, you don't believe she has really earned it. It's easy to see how those mixed feelings could be troublesome for your friendship.

Clearly, then, to maintain friendships with your co-workers, you need to balance the personal and professional sides of the relationships at all times. For instance, you might decide it's important to tell Kellie you support her, to voice enthusiasm if she receives the promotion, and to express disappointment if she doesn't, because she's your friend. Even though you don't feel she has earned the promotion, your friendship with Kellie may motivate you to be supportive of her anyway.

Alternatively, you might remind Kellie that the promotion is very competitive, that she is competing with employees who have more experience and seniority than she does, and that she shouldn't be surprised if she doesn't get it. You might even say "I'm telling you this as your co-worker" to make it clear that you are speaking from the perspective of your professional relationship rather than your personal one. Which

Romance sometimes blossoms in the workplace, as it did for actors and writers B. J. Novak and Mindy Kaling. Even though their romantic relationship ended, the pair maintains their close working friendship. © *Mark Sullivan/Getty Images*

approach you choose will probably depend on how close your friendship is and on what your experiences have been in similar situations.

ROMANTIC RELATIONSHIPS BETWEEN CO-WORKERS.

If you watched the television show *The Office,* you might have been amused by the on-again/off-again romance between co-workers Ryan Howard and Kelly Kapoor. But you may not have realized that the two actors who played them, B. J. Novak and Mindy Kaling, were also co-workers, as both actors and writers on the show, whose relationship vacillated from friends and co-workers to romantic partners and back again several times before settling into a long-term, working friendship. Because people spend so much time at work, it is not surprising that some form romantic relationships with colleagues. According to one survey, 38 percent of people have dated a co-worker at least once, and a third of those workplace romances led to marriage.[112]

People can derive several benefits from working with their romantic partners. For instance, the positive feelings associated with attraction can energize employees. Research shows that positive emotion—such as the emotion of being in love—can boost people's creativity and help them be more innovative, which can be useful in a range of careers.[113] When romantic partners work in different departments of an organization, their relationship can encourage greater communication and cooperation within the workplace and improve people's ability to work as a team.[114] Experiencing love can also lead people to be more open and cooperative with others, which can ease personality conflicts in the workplace.[115]

Like friendships, workplace romances also have both social and task dimensions, and these dimensions can sometimes conflict, leading to relationship problems. For instance, suppose Tina works in the human resources department of a credit union where her boyfriend Erik works as a teller. Due to her role, Tina frequently encounters sensitive information about employees, and one day she learns that Erik's manager is unhappy with his performance and wants to transfer him to another branch. As a human resources professional, Tina feels obligated to keep such sensitive information private—but as Erik's girlfriend, she also feels a strong desire to share the information with him, especially because it affects him directly. This leads Tina to experience a *conflict of interest,* in which her personal and professional motivations contradict each other.

Another downside of workplace romances is that, when they end, the breakup can cause turbulence for the organization. In a regular romantic relationship, partners who break up might choose never to see or communicate with each other again. That isn't always an option when the partners work together, however. Because of their work roles, they may have to continue communicating and cooperating for the good of their employer, even if they feel hurt by the demise of their relationship. According to research, seeing each other in the workplace after a failed relationship can stir resentment as well as remind people of their own shortcomings as a romantic partner.[116]

These potential problems have led some employers to prohibit their employees from becoming romantically involved with each other. Not all romances are bad for the workplace, however. What determines whether a workplace romance will have positive or negative effects on an organization? According to research, three factors are especially influential: (1) the perceived fairness with which the organization treats its employees, (2) the evaluations that others in an organization make of a couple's relationship, and (3) the adjustment of organizational norms to support a couple's involvement.[117] Specifically, when workplace couples believe that their organization supports them, treats them fairly, and evaluates them positively, their relationships are more likely to benefit the organization rather than cause it problems.

Relationships between Superiors and Subordinates

As challenging as relationships among co-workers can be, those between superiors and subordinates are considerably more complicated, because they include a power difference that co-worker relationships generally do not have. If a supervisor and an employee become friends—and particularly if they become romantic partners—the power difference between them introduces a task dimension that can complicate their communication.

As with co-workers, many people enjoy becoming friends with their boss. Indeed, research shows that having a positive, friendly relationship with your supervisor usually adds to your job satisfaction.[118] That makes sense: if you like your supervisor, you'll probably enjoy working for him or her.

Genuine friendships between superiors and subordinates certainly aren't impossible to form or maintain. The challenge arises because what's best for the superior–subordinate relationship isn't always what's best for the friendship. If you're the employee, you might dislike or disagree with your boss's decisions concerning the company's policies or future direction, particularly when those decisions affect you. Conversely, if you're the supervisor, you may agonize about such decisions because you realize that what's best for the company is not always what's best for each individual employee.

To understand those stresses, imagine that your supervisor announces that the company will reduce the clerical staff on whom you depend to get your work done. Now imagine that to accommodate a new business strategy, your boss cancels a promotional campaign you've been developing, including a photo shoot you were looking forward to. In such cases, it can be hard not to take your boss's actions personally, and that kind of response can strain your friendship. In a study of superior–subordinate friendships, communication scholar Theodore Zorn found that superiors commonly experienced those types of tensions between their work responsibilities and their friendships with subordinates.[119]

Superiors and subordinates can find it challenging to be friends. Becoming romantically involved is even more fraught with difficulty, however, because of the conflict of interest inherent in supervising one's romantic partner. Suppose Liam is a unit manager at a software company where his partner, Chad, is a designer. If Liam oversees and evaluates Chad's work, he may feel that it is in his own interest to give Chad positive marks. Because they are romantically involved, what benefits Chad—such as a glowing performance review and the possibility of a raise—benefits both of them. That could motivate Liam to evaluate Chad's work more positively than he should, which would be unfair to his other employees. Many organizations specifically prohibit such an arrangement by not allowing employees to report directly to their spouses or romantic partners.

Even for superiors and subordinates who don't have a social or romantic relationship, one situation that's extremely problematic is the case in which the subordinate feels he or she has been sexually harassed. In the United States, the Equal Employment Opportunity Commission (EEOC) defines *sexual harassment* as unsolicited, unwelcome behavior of a sexual nature. You might intend to be friendly or supportive by putting your arm around a subordinate, for instance, but if the subordinate feels uncomfortable by your behavior, it may constitute harassment.

In Everyday Life: How many of your students would say they are friends with at least one superior, such as a supervisor or teacher? Among those who are, what are the challenges in those friendships?

assess your skills   IDENTIFYING SEXUAL HARASSMENT IN THE WORKPLACE

How well could you identify instances of sexual harassment in the workplace if you encountered them? To find out, read each statement below and mark whether you believe it is true or false according to U.S. law.

		True	False
1.	To qualify as sexual harassment, the victim and the perpetrator must be of opposite sexes.	_____	_____
2.	Telling off-color jokes can qualify as sexual harassment.	_____	_____
3.	Only unwelcome conduct can be sexual harassment.	_____	_____
4.	Only a supervisor can create a hostile work environment.	_____	_____
5.	If a worker "voluntarily" has sex with a supervisor, he or she hasn't been sexually harassed.	_____	_____
6.	The victim can include people other than the person who was directly harassed.	_____	_____
7.	Sexual harassment can include repeatedly asking a co-worker out on a date.	_____	_____
8.	Only someone with supervisory authority over a worker can engage in quid pro quo harassment.	_____	_____

Statements 2, 3, 6, 7, and 8 are true. Statements 1, 4, and 5 are false: It is possible to harass someone of the same sex; anyone in an organization can create a hostile work environment; and having sex with a supervisor, even if it appears voluntary, doesn't mean the sex wasn't coerced. Identifying sexual harassment can be tricky, but knowing what interpersonal behaviors are okay and not okay in workplace relationships is essential for competent communicators.

FROM ME TO YOU

It can be hard to speak up if you feel you are being sexually harassed at school or at work. Ignoring the situation won't make it go away, however. Remember that sexual harassment is illegal and that you have the right not to be victimized. Sometimes all it takes to stop the harassment is for you to speak up and tell another person that his or her behavior offends you. If you're uncomfortable doing so, or if the offensive behavior continues after you've communicated your feelings, inform someone in your organization's human resources department or affirmative action office.

Source: www.eeoc.gov/types/sexual_harassment.html

Focus on Ethics: Friendships with customers can pose some ethical challenges. Is it okay to give someone a better deal on a product or a service if that person is a friend? Are you cheating your employer by doing that? The ethical problem can work in reverse as well: Knowing a customer as a friend may put you in a better position to take advantage of that person's business.

According to the EEOC, sexual harassment can occur in two forms. The first, known as *quid pro quo* (Latin for "this for that"), happens when a supervisor offers an employee rewards in exchange for sexual favors. A statement such as "I'll give you tomorrow off if you have a drink with me tonight" can qualify as quid pro quo harassment if it is directed at a subordinate. The second form, known as *hostile work environment,* occurs when work conditions are sexually offensive or intimidating. Telling sexually suggestive jokes when both men and women are present or making derogatory comments about a person's sexual orientation can qualify as hostile work environment harassment.

Sexual harassment is a serious and pervasive problem in many organizations, and its victims often suffer long-term emotional and psychological harm. Competent communicators must consider how other people might interpret their verbal and nonverbal behaviors in the organizational context. How well could you identify sexual harassment if you saw or heard about it? Check out the "Assess Your Skills" box to find out.

Relationships with Clients

In most professions, you'll interact with customers. For instance, you may sell your company's products to the same retail stores or medical office each month and get to know the buyers there. Likewise, you may work in a position that regularly fosters close relationships with clients, such as a personal trainer, financial consultant, or bartender. Depending on the nature of your job, you may have customers you see or talk to regularly, so it's reasonable to expect that you may form relationships with some of them. Those relationships can be highly rewarding personally, and they can also benefit your organization because they can be a major reason why your customers continue to buy from you or your company.[120] After all, most of us prefer dealing with a salesperson or a service provider with whom we have developed a comfortable and trusting relationship.

At the same time, friendly relationships with customers invoke some of the same task–social tensions that relationships with co-workers, employers, and employees do. Your customers may be your friends, but they still expect you to furnish a high-quality product or service, and you still expect them to provide full and prompt payment. If either party doesn't uphold its end of the bargain, then the customer–provider relationship can be disrupted, and the relationship can suffer.

To avoid such tensions, some companies encourage employees not to develop personal relationships with customers. Although it may be very important to treat customers in a friendly way, many businesses recognize that the feelings of loyalty and favor we often have for friends can interfere with the professional relationship. When Deion took a position as a sales representative for a cable television company, for instance, he became close friends with several of his clients. Because he liked them, he began giving them steep discounts on their cable service that other customers didn't receive. Because they liked him, they consistently gave him the highest possible scores on customer satisfaction surveys. Those special deals and preferential evaluations continued for almost a year before Deion's regional manager realized what was happening. She reprimanded Deion for allowing his friendships with his clients to compromise his professional relationships with them.

The separation of personal and professional relationships is particularly important in the health care setting. In the United States, ethical guidelines issued by the American College of Physicians discourage doctors from treating friends, relatives, intimate partners, and other individuals with whom they have close personal relationships.[121] The reasoning behind those guidelines is that a doctor's professional judgment and objectivity could be compromised by his or her personal feelings for the patient. If that

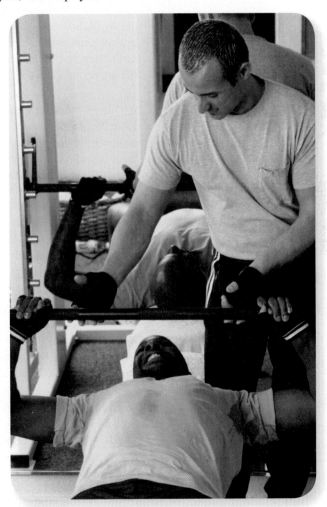

Relationships with clients can be highly rewarding if there are clear boundaries distinguishing the personal and professional dimensions of the relationship. © Doug Menuez/Getty Images, RF

happens, the doctor may not make proper decisions about the patient's condition or treatment, putting the patient's health at risk.

As with superiors and subordinates, relationships with customers need to have clear boundaries between personal and professional relationships. While conducting business, treat your customers equally, whether you feel personally close to them or not, and ask them to treat you as they would any other provider. A personal relationship with customers can be successful if the parties agree that their professional relationship is separate and should be treated professionally.

Online Communication in Workplace Relationships

No matter what kind of organization you work for, you will likely communicate with superiors, subordinates, and peers in electronically mediated ways, as well as face-to-face. As in any relationships, you want your communication in workplace relationships to be both appropriate and effective. Here are some tips to help you achieve high-quality communication:

- *Learn and follow your organization's policies for electronic communication.* Most employers have formal or informal policies regarding how electronically mediated communication should be used. These policies may specify what information can and cannot be communicated electronically and what forms of social media employees are permitted to use. Make sure you know what your organization expects.

- *Use electronic communication for convenience, not as a shield.* In many ways, the Internet makes communication in organizations more convenient and efficient. E-mail makes it possible to convey work-related messages quickly and to a broad audience. Teleconferencing allows people in geographically distant locations to meet in real time. When used in these ways, electronic forms of communication can enhance the effectiveness of workplace interaction. However, certain conversations—particularly those involving conflict or focusing on sensitive issues—are best conducted face-to-face. Because such conversations are often unpleasant, some people "hide behind" electronically mediated communication, expressing themselves through an e-mail or instant message instead of talking face-to-face. Using electronic communication for this purpose only separates people emotionally and risks leaving conflicts unresolved.

- *Don't write in an e-mail message what you wouldn't say in person.* In the workplace, employment law prohibits some types of communication, such as any communication that constitutes sexual harassment. Just as it would be illegal to harass a subordinate face-to-face, it is equally unlawful to do so in an e-mail message, a tweet, or a social media post.

- *Remember that electronic communication leaves a trail.* Anything you write to a co-worker in an e-mail message, an instant message, a Facebook post, or a tweet can be saved in its original form and shared with others, with or without your permission. Such messages can even be deliberately altered to make it appear that you've said something you haven't. Keep these observations in mind when deciding what to say to a co-worker in electronic form. Face-to-face conversations don't typically produce a permanent record of what is said, but electronic communication almost always does.

- *Take advantage of the communication trail when it helps you.* Of course, the fact that electronic communication leaves a trail can be extremely useful. When you're collaborating with someone on a joint project or working together to formulate a

got skills?

PRACTICING UPWARD, DOWNWARD, AND LATERAL COMMUNICATION

Learn to construct appropriate workplace messages.

WHAT?

Construct messages with the right tone and formality for your workplace audience.

WHY?

To communicate appropriately and effectively with superiors, subordinates, and peers.

HOW?

1. Messages to superiors should be the most formal. It is best to use clear, concise language and stay away from informalities, such as writing "U" when you mean "you."

2. Messages to subordinates and peers can sometimes be less formal and use more casual and personable language. Even with peers and subordinates, however, you want to communicate professionally.

TRY!

1. Suppose you want to ask your boss, your co-workers, and your subordinates for their feedback on a new parental leave policy.

2. Construct an e-mail message, directed at your supervisor, in which you ask if he or she would review the policy and offer you feedback.

3. Construct a similar e-mail message asking your peers and subordinates to provide feedback on the policy.

4. Compare your messages for their tone and formality. Pay attention to whether your language is appropriate for each audience.

5. Ask your instructor for feedback and/or share your messages with classmates in a small group.

CONSIDER: *What did you do to create differences in the tone and formality of your two messages?*

---

plan, for instance, the ability to consult previous e-mail messages or instant messages can be invaluable, because it helps to ensure that important ideas, deadline dates, and other details don't get lost. Thus, when it's to your advantage to create a running record of your communication, using electronic communication is a plus.

- *Know your audience.* Whether you're texting, tweeting, or composing an e-mail message, consider who is likely to read your words. In particular, pay attention to whether you are writing to a peer, a superior, or a subordinate, as each calls for a different approach with respect to the tone and formality of your message. When you communicate with people at higher levels of the organization, you are engaged in **upward communication,** and you want your language to be concise and respectful. Messages with subordinates constitute **downward communication,** and it's best if such messages use language that is clear and instructive. Finally, when you communicate with your peers, you are engaged in **lateral communication,** which can often be less formal than upward communication. Check out the "Got Skills?" box to practice using the right tone and formality for your workplace audience.

upward communication Messages sent to people at higher levels of an organization, such as superiors.

downward communication Messages sent to people at lower levels of an organization, such as subordinates.

lateral communication Messages sent to people at the same level of an organization, such as co-workers or peers.

In the IM: You can now access the end-of-chapter Discussion Questions and the Research Library in the Instructor's Manual for each chapter.

Whether with friends, romantic partners, relatives, or work colleagues, relationships enrich our lives in multiple ways. English poet Samuel Taylor Coleridge once wrote that "friendship is a sheltering tree"* to convey how friends can shield and protect us from the many stresses of life. The same can certainly be said of all positive relationships, as they make our lives safer, happier, and more meaningful.

LEARN IT   What is meant by the terms *social dimension* and *task dimension* in work relationships? How are superior–subordinate relationships different from co-worker relationships? Why are health care providers discouraged from treating friends and relatives? How are upward, downward, and lateral communication different from each other?

APPLY IT   Suppose the sales figures of your co-worker and close friend Kyle have been dismal recently. His manager has warned him that another month of poor sales performance will earn him a demotion. In contrast, you're having a successful year. One day, Kyle realizes that he is not going to make his sales quota for the month. In a panic, he asks you to let him take credit for some of your sales. That act would save his position—but also mean that your sales report would look unimpressive for the first time in months. You want to help Kyle but you worry about how your manager will feel about your performance.

With a friend or a classmate, role-play a conversation in which you discuss this situation and come to an agreement on how to resolve it. One of you should take your position in the conversation, and the other should take Kyle's. After your role-play, discuss alternative ways of responding to the situation. Identify how you think you would probably react in this situation, and why. Also, identify the ethical issues this situation raises.

REFLECT ON IT   Have you ever experienced tensions in your workplace friendships? If so, how were they resolved, and with what effects?

English poet Samuel Taylor Coleridge (21 October 1772–25 July 1834)

MASTER the chapter

1 Communicating in Friendships (p. 309)

- We generally expect friendships to be voluntary.
- Most friendships are between peers, or people of equal status.
- Friendships are governed by rules, many of which are implicit.
- Some characteristics of friendship differ according to the sexes of the friends involved.
- Friendships have a life span; they develop over time and we don't necessarily expect them to be permanent.

2 Communicating in Romantic Relationships (p. 316)

- Romantic relationships are often expected to be exclusive, voluntary, based on love, composed of opposite-sex partners, and permanent, although there are exceptions to each of these expectations.
- Couples come in traditional, separate, independent, and mixed forms.
- Romantic partners vary in how they handle conflict, privacy, emotional communication, and instrumental communication.

3 Communicating in Families (p. 327)

- Genetic ties, legal obligations, and role behaviors all influence whether a given relationship is considered to be familial.
- Families come in multiple forms, including natural families, blended families, single-parent families, and extended families.
- Family roles, rituals, stories, and secrets are all important aspects of how families communicate.

4 Communicating in the Workplace (p. 332)

- Having positive relationships with co-workers increases job satisfaction, although workplace friendships and romantic relationships can also be challenging.
- Relationships between superiors and subordinates can be very positive but are also complicated by the inherent power difference within them.
- Positive relationships with customers can be highly rewarding, both personally and professionally.
- Much professional communication occurs in electronically mediated formats, which calls for attention to the specific features of those communication channels.

KEY TERMS

communication privacy management (CPM) theory (p. 324)
downward communication (p. 339)
family of origin (p. 329)

family of procreation (p. 329)
infidelity (p. 317)
lateral communication (p. 339)
monogamy (p. 317)

peer (p. 310)
polygamy (p. 317)
rituals (p. 330)
upward communication (p. 339)

connect

To maximize your study time, check out CONNECT to access the SmartBook study module for this chapter, watch videos, and explore other resources.

CHAPTER 11 Interpersonal Conflict

© Christian Science Monitor/Getty Images

LEARNING TO MANAGE CONFLICT CONSTRUCTIVELY

Like many young adults, Damon Smith didn't feel comfortable handling conflict. "I didn't know how to express emotions with my mouth," said the 18-year-old student at Oakland, California's Bunche High School. "I knew how to hit people."* That is changing, however, with the help of an innovative new program designed to encourage young people to deal with their conflicts in constructive ways. School districts in several states are implementing "restorative justice" training, which teaches students critical conflict-management skills, such as listening to one another, practicing empathy, and apologizing for their wrongdoings. When conflicts arise inside or outside of school, faculty members bring together the students involved to work through the situation in a controlled and safe environment, where they can make their feelings known and discuss solutions. The goal of the program is to teach students alternatives to anger and violence that can help them address and manage interpersonal conflict in a positive manner.[1]

chapter preview

1 **The Nature of Interpersonal Conflict**

2 **Conflict in Personal Relationships**

3 **Power and Conflict**

4 **Managing Interpersonal Conflict**

*Brown, P. L. (2013, April 3). Opening up, students transform a vicious circle. The New York Times. Retrieved April 30, 2015, from http://nyti.ms/13RRgkh

Almost every relationship experiences conflict from time to time. Managing conflict can be productive, but it is also very challenging. As you'll see in this chapter, though, conflict management is a normal part of our interactions with others. You can learn to deal with conflict constructively if you have the appropriate skills. Several features of this chapter will help you develop those skills.

1 The Nature of Interpersonal Conflict

What exactly is conflict, and what is it like to experience conflict in relationships? In this section, we will define interpersonal conflict and identify the characteristics all conflicts have in common. Then we will take a look at some of the many ways people think about conflict in their relationships.

Defining Interpersonal Conflict

You may recall from the Interpersonal Communication in Close Relationships chapter that communication scholars William Wilmot and Joyce Hocker define **interpersonal conflict** as "an expressed struggle between at least two interdependent parties who perceive incompatible goals, scarce resources, and interference from the other party in achieving their goals."[2]* According to Wilmot and Hocker, an interaction must have all those elements to qualify as interpersonal conflict. Let's focus in on the key elements in their definition.

Writing Note: Ask students to describe, in writing, a recent conflict. Have them specifically identify how the conflict represented (1) an expressed struggle (2) between interdependent parties (3) who perceive incompatible goals and scarce resources as well as (4) interference from the other party.

interpersonal conflict An expressed struggle between interdependent parties who perceive incompatible goals, scarce resources, and interference from one another.

Conflict is often communicated verbally, but it can also be conveyed with nonverbal behaviors that express anger, concern, or disappointment. © *Stuart Jenner/iStock/Getty Images, RF*

Hocker, J. L., & Wilmot, W. W. (2013). Interpersonal Conflict (9th ed.). New York, NY: McGraw-Hill. Quote is from p. 40.

Talking Point: Help students understand that conflict is the *expression* of the disagreement, not the disagreement itself.

Talking Point: Point out that interdependence is always a matter of degree, so some relationships are more interdependent than others.

In Everyday Life: Students may think that to qualify as conflict, a disagreement has to be negative or mean-spirited. You might point out that most people experience multiple conflicts in everyday life that aren't necessarily negatively valenced.

CONFLICT IS AN EXPRESSED STRUGGLE. Having a conflict means more than just disagreeing. You may disagree with the president's foreign policies or your children's taste in music, but you don't really have a conflict until you've made the other person aware of your feelings. Conflict, therefore, is a *behavior*. Sometimes we express our disagreements verbally, but we can also express them through a nonverbal behavior such as a mean look or a harsh tone of voice.

CONFLICT OCCURS BETWEEN INTERDEPENDENT PARTIES. Although all conflicts involve disagreements, a disagreement becomes a conflict only if the parties depend on each other in some way—that is, if the actions of each party affect the well-being of the other. You may have noticed that conflict is particularly common in relationships with high degrees of interdependence, such as those you have with your parents, children, instructors, bosses, and close friends. However, suppose two parties are completely independent of each other, such as you and a celebrity you have never met. Even though you may disagree with that person, your disagreement isn't considered to be an interpersonal conflict, because your relationship is not interdependent.

It's possible to have conflicts within yourself as well. For example, you might occasionally feel conflicted about how you spend your time. Perhaps part of you thinks you should spend more time with your friends and family, but another part of you thinks you should devote more time to your schoolwork. This is conflict, but it isn't *interpersonal* conflict. Rather, it's *intrapersonal,* because it is occurring within yourself. Therefore, it operates outside the realm of interpersonal conflict.

CONFLICT IS ABOUT GOALS THE PARTIES SEE AS INCOMPATIBLE. Conflict stems from perceiving that our goals are incompatible with another person's goals. Labeling goals as "incompatible" doesn't simply mean that they are different. Rather, two goals are incompatible when it's impossible to satisfy both of them. You want to change lanes on the freeway, but the driver next to you won't let you in. You want to spend your tax refund on a new flat-screen television, but your spouse wants to spend it on a family trip.

Note that the first sentence in the previous paragraph explicitly refers to our *perceptions* that our goals are incompatible. In reality, it may be possible to resolve the conflict in a manner that allows both parties to achieve their goals. (See the discussion of conflict strategies later in the chapter.) The point here is that parties in a conflict perceive that their goals are mutually exclusive, even if that perception is not objectively true.

CONFLICT ARISES OVER PERCEIVED SCARCE RESOURCES. There's little sense in fighting over something one has in abundance. Rather, people tend to have conflict over resources they perceive to be limited. Many relational partners have conflict over money, for instance. When individuals feel they don't have enough money for everything they need and want, they can easily have conflict over how to spend the money they do have.

Time is another resource that people often perceive to be scarce. Therefore, people frequently engage in conflicts over how they should spend their time. Perhaps your romantic partner wants you to split your vacation time between hiking and being with his or her family. If you perceive that you don't have adequate time for both activities, then you can experience conflict over how you will spend your limited time off.

CONFLICT INCLUDES INTERFERENCE. Two parties might have opposing goals with respect to some issue, but they won't have genuine conflict until they act in ways that prevent each other from achieving their goals. You might disapprove of your roommate's smoking habit, for instance, but you won't have true conflict until you behave in ways that interfere with his habit. Complaining about his smoking, for instance, might diminish the enjoyment he derives from it. Hiding his cigarettes or throwing them out would make it more difficult for him to smoke. In either case, you are interfering with your roommate's ability to achieve his goal.

Thinking about Interpersonal Conflict

When you think about your own experiences with interpersonal conflict, what words or images come to mind? It turns out that people often think about conflict using figurative language, such as metaphors.[3] Researchers have identified a number of metaphors people use to describe conflict. Reflect on how well each of the following common metaphors about conflict describes the way you view your own conflict experiences:

- *Conflict is a war.* Conflict is a series of battles, with winners and losers.
- *Conflict is an explosion.* Conflict is like hearing a time bomb ticking and then watching something blow up.
- *Conflict is a trial.* Each side presents its arguments and evidence, and whoever argues best wins the conflict.
- *Conflict is a struggle.* Conflict is a difficult and ongoing part of life.
- *Conflict is an act of nature.* Conflict simply happens to people; it cannot be prevented or controlled.
- *Conflict is an animal behavior.* Only the strong survive; conflict is a natural part of all creatures' lives.
- *Conflict is a mess.* Conflict is messy, and it contaminates other aspects of life.
- *Conflict is miscommunication.* Conflict stems from misunderstandings and breakdowns in communication.
- *Conflict is a game.* Conflict is a fun competition in which participants test their skills against each other.
- *Conflict is a heroic adventure.* Conflict is about taking risks and conquering new territory.
- *Conflict is a balancing act.* Engaging in conflict is like juggling or walking a tightrope; one wrong move can spell disaster.
- *Conflict is a bargaining table.* Conflict brings people together for a collective purpose.
- *Conflict is a tide.* Conflict ebbs and flows; on the basis of experience, we can predict when it is likely to occur.
- *Conflict is a dance.* Partners learn how to "move" with each other through their conflict episodes.
- *Conflict is a garden.* Experiences of conflict represent seeds for the future; if cared for, they will result in a worthwhile harvest.

As you can see, those metaphors represent a wide variety of ideas. Some images are inherently negative, but others could be considered neutral or even positive. Can you imagine how the way you think about conflict might affect your experience of it? For instance, if you think of conflict as a game,

Two parties can be engaged in the same conflict but might frame the conflict quite differently. Do you think of conflict as a trial? As an animal behavior? As a dance? As a balancing act? As a war? As a game? © Comstock Images/ Alamy, RF

a dance, or a garden, might you experience it differently than if you think of it as a struggle, a mess, or a war?

Researchers have found that the way we interpret or "frame" a conflict can greatly affect the way we experience it and the communication choices we make to manage it.[4] While arguing with his co-worker Madison over use of the company car, for instance, Russell suddenly realized that Madison was smiling in the midst of their heated discussion. Her smiling made him even angrier, because he felt she wasn't taking him seriously. The angrier he got, however, the more she smiled. Only during a conversation weeks later did they learn that they frame conflict quite differently: Russell frames conflict as a war, but Madison frames it as a game.

One result of that difference is that Madison probably experienced less stress over the conflict than Russell did. Because Madison sees conflict as a fun competition rather than as a battle between winners and losers, she didn't necessarily feel threatened or distressed by what Russell said. Instead, she interpreted his comments as challenges that tested her interpersonal skills. In contrast, because Russell frames conflict as a war, he interpreted every statement from Madison as an attempt to defeat him. As a result, he finds interpersonal conflict to be stressful and threatening in a way that Madison does not.

Because the way we frame a conflict can influence our experience of it, many therapists encourage people to reframe their conflicts. **Reframing** means changing the way you think about an interpersonal situation.[5] For instance, a therapist or a counselor could help Russell think of his conflicts with his co-workers as an adventure, a balancing act, or a dance instead of as a war.

reframing Changing the way you think about an interpersonal situation.

LEARN IT What are the essential elements of interpersonal conflict? What does it mean to reframe a conflict?

APPLY IT For a period of time (say, three to five days), make note of every conflict you observe, whether it includes you or not. Note what each conflict was about, who was involved in it, and how (if at all) it was resolved. For each conflict, identify the expressed struggle, the interdependent parties, the incompatible goals, the scarce resources, and the interference that made it an interpersonal conflict.

REFLECT ON IT With whom do you have conflict most frequently? Which metaphors for conflict seem the most accurate to you?

2 Conflict in Personal Relationships

Conflict occurs at many social levels. Communities, organizations, and certainly nations have conflict with one another. Interpersonal conflict, however, often affects our lives more directly and more intimately than conflicts at those broader levels. In this section, we will examine several characteristics of interpersonal conflict and identify topics most likely to spur conflict in our personal relationships. Next, we will survey the ways that gender and culture influence conflict. We will conclude by considering why conflict seems to be especially common when we're communicating online.

Characteristics of Interpersonal Conflict

Although we have conflicts over different issues with different people, we can make some general observations that apply to all interpersonal conflict. In this section, we'll look at five basic characteristics of conflict in personal relationships.

CONFLICT IS NATURAL.   Most of us would be hard-pressed to think of a single important relationship in which we don't have conflict from time to time. Conflict is a normal, natural part of relating to others. Maybe you enjoy listening to music at night, whereas your housemates prefer quiet. Perhaps you feel you've earned a raise at work, but your boss disagrees. Almost every significant relationship—especially those with close friends, relatives, and romantic partners—is bound to experience conflict once in a while.

Having conflict with someone doesn't necessarily mean your relationship is unhealthy or distressed. Indeed, the presence of conflict indicates you have an interdependent relationship. It means you affect each other; if you didn't, you'd have no need for conflict in the first place. So, conflict itself isn't a bad thing. In fact, as we'll see later in this chapter, if we handle conflict productively, it can produce positive outcomes. What matters is how people handle their conflicts. Later in this chapter, we'll explore useful strategies for managing conflict.

CONFLICT HAS CONTENT, RELATIONAL, AND PROCEDURAL DIMENSIONS.   In personal relationships, conflicts often focus on a specific point of disagreement. On a deeper level, though, they can also have broader implications for the relationship itself. In fact, we can say that many conflicts have at least three different dimensions: content, relational, and procedural.

To understand that point, suppose Marc finds out that his teenage daughter Amber has been stealing his credit card out of his wallet to participate in online gaming. Let's see how their conflict unfolds along the three dimensions:

- Content: The *content dimension* of a conflict is the specific topic about which people disagree. When Marc confronts Amber about the dishonesty of stealing and the risks of gambling, they are engaging the content dimension by focusing on the particular issue that gave rise to their conflict.

- Relational: The *relational dimension* of a conflict consists of the implications the conflict has for the relationship. Even though Amber promises to change her behavior, Marc still feels that she has shown disrespect by stealing from him, and he worries about whether he can trust her. These concerns reflect the relational dimension of their conflict by raising questions about how this conflict will affect their feelings for each other in the future.

- Procedural: Finally, the *procedural dimension* of a conflict consists of the rules or expectations people follow

© BananaStock/PunchStock, RF

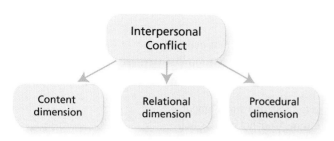

FIGURE 1 The Three Distinct Dimensions of Interpersonal Conflict

metaconflict Conflict about conflict.

direct conflict An open, straightforward approach to engaging in conflict.

indirect conflict The expression of conflict through negative behaviors that ignore the underlying disagreement.

when they argue. Suppose Marc believes conflict should be dealt with straightforwardly through open and honest discussion, whereas Amber prefers to avoid conflict, hoping that disagreements will resolve themselves. These different approaches to managing conflict reflect its procedural dimension.

When people adopt dramatically different procedures for managing conflict, they often wind up engaging in **metaconflict,** which is conflict about conflict itself. "You always run away from disagreements," Marc might say to Amber. She might respond, "Well, you want to have a fight about every little issue—sometimes you just have to let things go!" Notice here that Marc and Amber are no longer arguing about Amber's stealing and gambling but about *how they engage in conflict* in the first place. Their metaconflict is the result of approaching conflict with dramatically different expectations or rules. An illustration of the content, relational, and procedural dimensions of conflict appears in Figure 1.

CONFLICT CAN BE DIRECT OR INDIRECT.   In many instances, people deal with their conflicts openly, by engaging in **direct conflict.** When Maria and Sofie disagree on where to spend the holidays, for example, they have a series of arguments in which each one tries to persuade the other to adopt her point of view. When Rosemary grounds her son for using drugs, they argue openly about the seriousness of his behavior and the severity of his punishment.

People can also express conflict indirectly. Instead of dealing with their conflicts openly, for instance, individuals may behave in ways that are hurtful or vengeful toward others. Jade is upset with her boyfriend, so she deliberately flirts with other men in front of him. Tamir is angry at his wife for inviting her parents to dinner, so he spends the whole evening playing solitaire on his computer. Those **indirect conflict** behaviors express conflict, but in an indirect way that prevents the conflict from being resolved.

When you are experiencing conflict with another person, which is better: to deal with the conflict openly and directly, or to deal with it indirectly? That's a complex question, and the answer is that neither approach is better in every situation. Handling conflict directly can lead to quicker resolution, but it may also cause the conflict to escalate and become even more serious. Conversely, dealing with conflict indirectly may be easier and more comfortable, but it can also leave the conflict unresolved for a longer period of time. Which approach is better depends on the situation, what your goals are, with whom you're having the conflict, and how important the outcome of the conflict is to you. Later in this chapter, we'll discuss several strategies for engaging in conflict when you experience it.

CONFLICT CAN BE HARMFUL.   Experiencing conflict doesn't usually feel good, so it may not surprise you to learn that conflict can be harmful to your well-being when you don't manage it properly.

In fact, research shows that it can affect people negatively in a variety of ways.

- *Conflict can elevate stress.* One of the reasons conflict doesn't feel good is that it causes the body to produce a stress response. Specifically, the body reacts to conflict by increasing the levels of various stress hormones[6] and by causing the immune system to elevate natural killer cells in the bloodstream.[7] That stress can take its toll; one study even found that experiencing conflict can cause wounds to heal more slowly than they otherwise would.[8]

- *Conflict can cause health problems.* Engaging in conflict can harm people's physical health. In one study, for instance, psychologists videotaped 150 healthy married couples discussing a contentious topic for six minutes. Two days later, they took a CT scan of each spouse's chest. The researchers found that husbands who had been overly controlling during the conflict—and wives who had been overly hostile—had a greater degree of hardening of the arteries than spouses who didn't display those behaviors.[9]

- *Conflict can lead to aggressive behavior.* Conflict is especially harmful to personal well-being when it escalates into aggression and violence.[10] Researchers estimate that over the past two decades, as many as half of all marital, cohabiting, and dating relationships have involved some combination of verbal, physical, and/or sexual aggression.[11] Although the victims of such aggression are most likely to be women, men are also victimized, by both male and female romantic partners.[12] In fact, violence during conflict is approximately as common in gay and lesbian relationships as in heterosexual ones.[13] Alcohol use appears to play a key role in whether conflicts turn violent (see the "Communication: Dark Side" box for details).

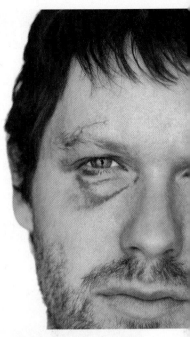

Although victims of relational violence are most likely to be women, men are also victimized, by both male and female romantic partners.
© Brad Wilson/Stone/Getty Images

CONFLICT CAN BE BENEFICIAL.   It's relatively easy to identify the negative features of conflict: it's stressful, it can damage health, and it can lead to aggression and violence. When conflict is managed well, however, it can have certain benefits. Working through a conflict in a positive, constructive manner can help two people learn more about each other and their relationship.[14] It may also lead them to a more satisfactory solution to the problem than either could have come up with alone. Those benefits may depend on whether only one party in an interpersonal conflict—or both parties—has the skills to manage it well.

Managing conflict constructively can also help to prevent small problems from escalating into larger ones. Let's say your co-worker complains to you constantly about his girlfriend while you're trying to get your work done. Instead of addressing the problem, however, you just let it annoy you day after day until you finally explode at him, yelling, causing a scene, and eventually being reprimanded by your boss. Simply addressing the situation when it first arose would likely have alleviated much of your frustration and prevented that small annoyance from turning into a conflict with your co-worker.

Over time, the ability to handle conflicts positively may give people more confidence in their communication skills and in the strength of their interpersonal relationships. Suppose Maya likes to keep her home spotlessly clean, whereas her new roommate Tamar is content with performing a light dusting now and then. Each finds the other's approach to housekeeping unreasonable, and a conflict ensues. Instead of allowing themselves to become hostile or defensive, they discuss their disagreement calmly. Each roommate listens respectfully while the other explains her point of view, and they focus their attention on resolving the problem instead of assigning blame. Ultimately, they come to the conclusion that hiring a cleaning service would give Maya the cleanliness she desires while relieving Tamar of the obligation to clean. Their constructive approach to handling conflict leaves them both satisfied with the outcome and optimistic about their ability to manage similar conflicts in the future.

Successful resolution of conflicts can be very beneficial, but can every conflict be resolved? Take a look at the "Fact or Fiction?" box to find out.

communication | *DARK SIDE*

ALCOHOL AND CONFLICT: A RISKY COMBINATION

Managing conflict can be challenging under the best of circumstances, but it appears to be even more problematic when people are under the influence of alcohol. Research has shown that excessive alcohol use leads to more aggressive behaviors and elevates the chances of violence within close relationships. It also represents a major public health risk: excessive use of alcohol is the third-leading preventable cause of death in the United States, after tobacco use and malnutrition.

Does consuming alcohol affect how people respond to conflict? The results of several studies indicate that it does. For instance, intoxication increases the likelihood of having conflict in the first place. When people have been drinking, that is, their disagreements are more likely to evolve into arguments. During conflict episodes, intoxicated people also rate both their own feelings and those of their partners as more negative than do sober individuals. In fact, conflict and alcohol use have a two-way relationship: not only does drinking exacerbate conflict, but having high levels of conflict can encourage people to drink more heavily.

These results suggest that people may benefit from avoiding conflict when they are under the influence of alcohol. Communicating in a sober state can help people pay attention to their disagreements instead of letting alcohol cloud their focus.

ASK YOURSELF

- Why do you think alcohol affects people's experiences with conflict?

- If you have ever engaged in conflict with an intoxicated person, how did you handle it? Which strategies for handling the conflict were more successful or less successful?

Alcohol often fuels interpersonal conflict on *The Real Housewives of Beverly Hills*. © *Evans Vestal Ward/Bravo/Getty Images*

Sources: Rodriguez, L. M., Neighbors, C., & Knee, C. R. (2014). Problematic alcohol use and marital distress: An interdependence theory perspective. *Addiction Research & Theory, 22,* 294–312; Mokdad, A. H., Marks, J. S., Stroup, D. F., & Gerberding, J. L. (2004). Actual causes of death in the United States, 2000. *Journal of the American Medical Association, 291,* 1238–1245.

The Most Common Sources of Conflict

Like relationships themselves, conflicts come in all shapes and sizes. What are some of the most typical issues people fight about? In one study, communication scholar Larry Erbert asked spouses to report the most common sources of conflict in their marriage.[15] You might be surprised to learn that men and women identified the same three leading sources of conflict. The most common was *personal criticisms,* or spouses' complaints or criticisms of each other's undesirable behaviors or bad habits (such as smoking or excessive drinking). Almost 20 percent of the couples Erbert interviewed mentioned personal criticisms as a common source of conflict.

The second-most-frequent answer, at 13 percent, was *finances,* or conflicts about money. It's not uncommon for spouses to disagree about how their money should be spent, saved, or invested. Further, because money is a scarce resource for many people, conflicts over finances can be particularly difficult.

Media Note: On the student web page, the video clip "Opposites Attract" portrays a series of conflicts involving a romantic couple engaged to be married.

fact OR fiction? | IF YOU TRY HARD ENOUGH, YOU CAN RESOLVE ANY CONFLICT

Conflict is a natural part of relationships, and there are multiple ways to manage it. The latter observation might lead you to believe that if you have the right skills and try hard enough, you can eventually resolve any conflict you encounter. It would be great if that were true, but it isn't.

The truth is that some conflicts are simply unsolvable. Let's say, for instance, that Juna and her brother Tom are arguing about abortion. As a conservative with strong religious beliefs, Juna cannot support a woman's right to choose abortion under any circumstances. Tom, whose political orientation is more liberal, feels that every woman has the right to choose whether to have a child or to terminate the pregnancy. In other words, Juna's and Tom's positions are diametrically opposed, meaning they share no common ground. As long as they hold those positions, Juna and Tom can argue forever, but they will never resolve their conflict.

When two positions are diametrically opposed, and when the people or groups holding those positions are unwilling or unable to change their positions in any way, the only real options are to avoid the conflict, to agree to disagree, and to try to minimize the effects of the conflict on other aspects of the relationship.

Third on the list was *household chores,* or conflicts over the division of labor. Spouses have to negotiate how to divide up tasks such as cleaning, cooking, gardening, and car maintenance, and many couples find it easy to disagree about who should take on which responsibilities. Conflict can also emerge when spouses fail to meet their responsibilities, because both spouses suffer when the laundry doesn't get washed or the lawn doesn't get mowed.

In his study, Erbert found that personal criticisms, finances, and household chores together accounted for approximately 42 percent of all the conflict topics mentioned. Other common sources of conflict for married couples were their children, employment, in-laws, sex, how they should spend holidays and vacations, how they should spend their time in general, and how they communicate with each other.[16] Studies have also shown that the major topics of conflict are nearly identical for gay, lesbian, and heterosexual couples.[17]

Many studies have focused on conflict in romantic relationships because of the high degree of interdependence that characterizes those relationships. We experience conflict in a host of relationships, however. Many of us routinely have conflict with superiors or subordinates, neighbors, parents or children, co-workers, instructors, and other people with whom we are interdependent. Like conflicts with romantic partners, many of those conflicts center on issues of power, respect, and the distribution of resources such as money and time.[18] We will look specifically at the central role of power in the next section.

In the IM: The in-class activity "Identifying Conflict Triggers" encourages students to identify their most common sources of conflict.

According to research, the major topics of conflict are nearly identical for gay, lesbian, and heterosexual couples. © *Davis Freeman/Queerstock, Inc./Alamy, RF*

How Sex and Gender Affect Conflict

It's almost cliché to say that sex and gender play an important role in conflict. Indeed, television shows such as *Modern Family* and *New Girl* and movies such as *The Other Woman* base much of their humor on the idea that women and men have difficulty understanding each other—a problem that creates situation after situation that is ripe for conflict. Although differences in their behaviors and ways of thinking can certainly be sources of conflict, women and men often have the added challenge of dealing with conflict in systematically different ways.

passive aggression A pattern of behaving vengefully while denying that one has aggressive feelings.

Sitcoms such as *New Girl* base much of their humor on the idea that men and women have trouble understanding each other. © *FOX/Getty Images*

As we saw in the Culture and Gender chapter, traditional gender socialization conflates sex and gender by teaching men to adopt masculine traits and behaviors and women to adopt feminine traits and behaviors. At least in North American societies, traditional gender socialization has encouraged women to "play nice" by avoiding conflict and sacrificing their own goals in order to accommodate the goals of others. Conversely, men are often encouraged to engage in conflict directly, using competitive or even aggressive behaviors to achieve victory. At the same time, however, men are often taught not to hurt women.[19]

Those messages about gender can create challenges for both women and men when it comes to managing conflict. Some women may feel that engaging in conflict overtly is contrary to the feminine gender role, so they adopt less direct tactics to achieve their goals. One such tactic is **passive aggression,** in which individuals behave vengefully while denying that they have aggressive feelings.

Consider the case of Chelsea, who becomes irritated when her boyfriend answers his cell phone whenever it rings, even while they're out to dinner. Instead of telling him how she feels, Chelsea expresses her irritation passively by sometimes failing to answer the phone when he calls. She then calls him back later and claims she hadn't heard the phone ring. In this way, Chelsea avoids overt conflict by behaving aggressively (ignoring her boyfriend's calls) but in a seemingly innocent manner (claiming she didn't hear the phone). As we'll see later in the chapter, however, women may also believe that they must fight for whatever resources are available to them, particularly when they feel they are in a less-powerful position than men.

Society's messages to men about conflict may encourage them to engage in conflict overtly—possibly aggressively—even in situations when a subtler, less direct approach could be just as effective. Because men are taught to engage in conflict directly but also not to hurt women, they may feel particularly conflicted about how to act during conflict episodes with women. Men often resolve that quandary by disengaging, thereby leaving the conflict unresolved. Psychologist John Gottman uses the term *stonewalling*

How you handle conflict may depend partly on your sex. Research shows that men are more likely than women to engage in direct conflict behaviors, which sometimes include being physically aggressive. Women are more likely than men to engage in passive-aggressive behaviors, such as running up the balance on a family member's credit card. © *Masterfile, RF;* © *Steve Cole/ Digital Vision/Getty Images, RF*

to describe that pattern of withdrawal. As we'll consider later in this chapter, stonewalling can be a particularly problematic behavior for couples.

In opposite-sex romantic relationships, traditional gender messages often encourage partners to adopt a **demand–withdraw pattern,** in which one partner (typically the woman) makes demands ("We need to talk about the problems in our relationship"), and the other partner (usually the man) responds by withdrawing ("I don't want to talk about it").[20] This pattern of behavior largely conforms to typical North American gender roles, and research indicates that those gender-related behavior differences are especially common in dissatisfied, distressed relationships.[21] One possible reason that demand–withdrawal is particularly common in distressed relationships is that if one partner usually withdraws from the conversation, then the conflict is unlikely to be resolved. Over time, unresolved conflict can lead to dissatisfaction.

Women and men appear to deal with conflict in much the same ways, whether they are heterosexual or homosexual. Research has found that lesbian and gay couples use strategies similar to those used by heterosexuals to deal with conflict.[22] As family communication researchers John Caughlin and Anita Vangelisti have suggested, however, gay and lesbian couples are also likely to experience potential sources of conflict that seldom afflict straight couples.[23] For one, lesbian and gay partners may have conflict over whom to tell, and how much to tell, about their sexual orientation.[24] If one partner is "out" to family and friends while the other partner conceals his or her sexual orientation, that discrepancy can lead to conflicts related to a couple's social relationships and their long-term plans. Gay and lesbian adults may also encounter discrimination and prejudice from their families, co-workers, or neighbors, which can cause considerable distress and make routine conflicts about other matters seem more substantial than they are.[25]

How Culture Affects Conflict

Just as gender messages encourage people to handle conflicts in particular ways, so do cultural messages. That is, the values and norms individuals learn from their culture can shape the way they respond to conflict with members of their own culture.

demand–withdraw pattern A pattern of behavior in which one party makes demands and the other party withdraws from the conversation.

Focus on Scholarship: Caughlin and Vangelisti's research, cited in the footnotes, has shown that although men sometimes play the demand role and women sometimes play the withdraw role, relationships in which the woman demands and the man withdraws are overwhelmingly more common.

Talking Point: What groups besides lesbians and gays might experience unique, group-specific conflicts?

Individualistic cultures teach people to stand up for themselves in the face of conflict. In contrast, collectivistic cultures teach people to maintain harmony by avoiding conflict. © BananaStock/ PunchStock, RF; © Jasper James/ moodboard - LBRF/Age Fotostock, RF

Focus on Scholarship: Research shows that people from collectivistic societies, such as Turkey's, often prefer to postpone or avoid conflict, rather than engage in it.[ii]

[ii]Cingöz-Ulu, B., & Lalonde, R. N. (2007). The role of culture and relational context in interpersonal conflict: Do Turks and Canadians use different conflict management strategies? *International Journal of Intercultural Relations, 31,* 443–458.

Let's look specifically at how cultural dimensions affect beliefs and behaviors about conflict and at how people from different cultures engage in conflict.

CULTURAL DIMENSIONS AND CONFLICT. As you will recall from the Culture and Gender chapter, cultures vary along several dimensions, and some of those differences affect how people think about and manage conflict. One example is whether a culture is individualistic or collectivistic. People raised in individualistic cultures are taught to value and nurture their individual rights, needs, and goals. They learn that it is acceptable to disagree with others, and they are encouraged to stand up for themselves in the face of conflict.[26] In contrast, people raised in collectivistic cultures are taught that the group's priorities take precedence over the individual's and that maintaining group harmony is more important than pursuing individual success. Thus, they are more likely to manage conflict through avoiding the disagreement, yielding to the other person's wishes, or asking a neutral party to mediate the conflict, because those strategies can help preserve harmony.[27] They would likely consider the direct, overt behaviors used by people in individualistic cultures to manage conflict to be insensitive or rude.

A second cultural dimension that influences how people manage conflict is whether the culture is low context or high context. People in low-context cultures (such as the United States) value communication that is explicit, direct, and literal. When they engage in conflict with one another, they therefore expect all parties to be clear about the source of the disagreement and upfront about their suggestions for resolution.[28] In comparison, people in high-context cultures (such as Japan or Thailand) value subtlety, deriving much of the meaning in their conversations from social conventions and nonverbal expressions. When they experience conflict with one another, they place a premium on saving face and not embarrassing the other party. As a result, they tend to discuss disagreements indirectly, without accusations or direct requests for action.[29]

CROSS-CULTURAL CONFLICT. When two people approach a conflict with dramatically different cultural values and norms, the likelihood is high that they will misinterpret each other's behaviors.[30] That misinterpretation can exacerbate their conflict, making it more challenging to come to a resolution.

Suppose that Gerry, who was raised in an individualistic culture, is having conflict with his co-worker Kenan, who grew up in a collectivistic culture. Kenan will likely try to manage the conflict in a way that preserves harmony in the relationship and avoids offending or embarrassing Gerry. On the contrary, Gerry may believe the best way to deal with their conflict is to raise his concerns with Kenan directly in a face-to-face encounter aimed at getting their disagreements "out in the open."

It's easy to imagine how Gerry's and Kenan's different styles of addressing conflict could be problematic. If Gerry approaches the conflict in the direct, adversarial way that is common in his culture, Kenan may feel personally attacked. Likewise, Kenan's more indirect way of engaging in conflict might imply to Gerry that Kenan doesn't care about the conflict or its outcome. In either case, Gerry and Kenan's working relationship can be damaged by their different approaches to conflict. By learning about the norms and behaviors of other cultures and interacting with people from different cultural backgrounds, however, individuals can improve their ability to handle intercultural conflict in constructive ways.

Managing Computer-Mediated Conflict

Conflict is common in face-to-face settings, but it can seem especially frequent when people communicate in computer-mediated ways. One reason is that online communication has a **disinhibition effect,** meaning that it invites people to say or do things that they wouldn't in person.[31] Online conflict frequently leads to *flaming,* which is the exchange of hostile and insulting messages.

For example, suppose that Saika's supervisor e-mails her to say he is not approving her vacation request for next month. Saika feels angry, particularly because she worked overtime last month while her supervisor was on vacation. Because she reads her supervisor's words online instead of hearing them in person, she feels less inhibited about expressing her anger. As a result of her disinhibition, she sends her supervisor an e-mail reply filled with angry, inflammatory statements that she would never make to him in person. Saika's behavior causes her supervisor great distress—and thus intensifies their conflict.

Researchers suggest several strategies for handling potential conflicts in online contexts.[32] First, *don't respond right away.* Instead, give yourself several hours to calm down and collect your thoughts. (Of course, that advice often applies to conflicts that occur in person as well.) Because e-mail puts your words in print right in front of another person, you may feel compelled to reply immediately, when instead you should take time to cool down first.

Second, *clarify anything that might be misunderstood* instead of assuming that you know what the other person meant by his or her statements. Third, *put yourself in the other person's shoes,* and think about how he or she would react to your response. Finally, *use emoticons and emoji to express your tone,* if appropriate, so that your reader knows when you're upset, when you're surprised, and when you're kidding.

Each of these suggestions is about being sensitive to the constraints of online communication. E-mailing, texting, tweeting, and other forms of computer-mediated messaging encourage communication that is quick and efficient but not always well thought out. During a conflict episode, it is easy to fire off a message in anger without having considered how others will receive and interpret our words. That doesn't necessarily mean we can't manage conflict constructively using computer-mediated communication. Rather, our success in managing conflict rests on our ability to think deliberately about what we want to say and how we want to say it. Instead of responding in an angry, disinhibited manner, Saika would have done better to craft her message calmly and compose her e-mail with her supervisor's perspective, rather than her own, in mind. Replying by e-mail gives her time to think about her response—instead of offering her

© Veer Incorporated, RF

disinhibition effect The tendency to say or do things in one environment (such as online) that one would not say or do in most other environments.

In Everyday Life: Ask your students for everyday examples of when they feel disinhibited during online interaction.

CONNECT: Insight reports let you easily compare time spent on an assignment with the assignment score to identify struggling students, as well as those who may need more of a challenge.

assess your skills | AVOID ONLINE DISINHIBITION

Computer-mediated communication can contribute to conflict because of disinhibition. When you receive an e-mail message, a text message, a Facebook post, or a tweet that makes you angry, consult this checklist before you write back to the person.

I . . .	✓
. . . realize that I may be misinterpreting the person's words.	_____
. . . bear in mind that I cannot see the person's facial expressions or hear the person's tone of voice.	_____
. . . will wait for at least an hour before writing a response.	_____
. . . will read the person's message again before writing a response, and consider whether I am misinterpreting it.	_____
. . . will write a response but not send or post it right away.	_____
. . . will wait for at least a few more hours—if not a day or two—before sending or posting my response.	_____
. . . will reread my response before sending or posting it, and consider revising it.	_____
. . . realize that the other person may misinterpret my words as well.	_____

FROM ME TO YOU

It takes a great deal of patience not to respond immediately to a message that angers you. Your instinct may be to strike back by making statements in the heat of the moment that you will later regret. Although doing so may feel satisfying in the short term, it often makes a bad situation even worse. A better approach is to gain control over the situation by following the checklist provided here.

words immediately, as she might in a face-to-face conversation—which can actually help her manage the conflict more constructively.

How well can you avoid the pitfalls of online disinhibition? Check out the "Assess Your Skills" box to find out.

LEARN IT In what ways can conflict be harmful? In what ways can it be beneficial? What are the most common topics of conflict in marital relationships? How do messages about gender affect us when we engage in conflict? Which cultural dimensions influence conflict behavior? What is the disinhibition effect?

APPLY IT The next time you receive an e-mail that's negative or aggressive, write a response right away, but then save it instead of sending it. Write a second response 24 hours later, and then compare it with the first response. Do you notice differences in your tone? Is your second response less aggressive and inflammatory? Which response would you choose to send? If it's the second one, then remember this lesson when you receive similar e-mails in the future.

REFLECT ON IT Why might you choose to engage in conflict indirectly rather than directly? When are you most likely to have conflict online?

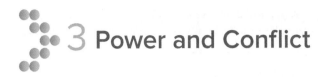 3 Power and Conflict

In the past few years, communities across the United States have experienced bitter conflicts over the actions of law enforcement personnel. Police officers in Albuquerque, New Mexico, fatally shot a mentally ill homeless man in a case they claimed was self-defense. In Tulsa County, Florida, a volunteer deputy sheriff shot and killed an unarmed man after mistakenly drawing his gun instead of his Taser. An officer in North Charleston, South Carolina, appears on a bystander's video shooting at, and killing, an unarmed man who was running away from him at the time. And in Ferguson, Missouri, a grand jury chose not to indict an officer who shot and killed an unarmed teenager. The fact that these victims were African American and charges were rarely brought against the shooters sparked accusations of institutional racism and fueled rallies, protests, and even riots in response. As these events became part of the national conversation, so did the relationship between power and conflict and what it means to properly use power.

© Chip Somodevilla/Getty Images

We have defined conflict as an expressed struggle between interdependent parties who perceive their goals as incompatible. Just because two parties are interdependent, however, doesn't mean that they are equally powerful. Indeed, conflict often occurs in relationships in which one person—say, a parent or a supervisor—has more power than the other—say, a child or an employee. Conflict often involves a struggle for power between two parties, with each party trying to exercise as much influence or control over the situation as possible. Power and conflict are thus inextricably linked.

In this section, we will define power and examine some of its characteristics, particularly as they relate to the experience of conflict. We will also consider various forms of power and probe how gender and culture influence the expression of power in personal relationships.

Characteristics of Power

Power is the ability to manipulate, influence, or control other people or events.[33] Certain people have more power than others. Nevertheless, we all possess some power, and we exercise it whenever we find ourselves in conflict with others. Let's look at five characteristics of power that will help us understand its relationship to conflict.

POWER IS CONTEXT-SPECIFIC. Most forms of power are relevant only in specific situations. Your boss has power over you at work, for instance, but he doesn't have the right to tell you what to do when you're at home. His influence over you is confined to the work environment. Similarly, your doctor has the power to give you medical advice and prescribe medical treatments, but she doesn't have the right to advise you

Talking Point: As with conflict itself, many students will think of power in negative ways, particularly when they think of power differences between people. You might preface your discussion of power by pointing out that it is inherently neither positive nor negative; rather, it is how people exercise their power that determines its valence.

power The ability to manipulate, influence, or control other people or events.

Media Note: In the instructor resources in the Online Learning Center, the video clip "Late to Class" portrays a clash of power and conflict in a context-specific relationship between teacher and student.

on your finances, education, or religious beliefs, because those areas are outside her sphere of influence. As such examples illustrate, power is almost always confined to certain realms or contexts.

symmetrical relationship A relationship between parties of equal power.

complementary relationship A relationship between parties of unequal power.

Talking Point: The Language chapter discusses persuasive language, which is another important example of how power and communication are interrelated.

one-up message A verbal message through which the speaker attempts to exert dominance or gain control over the listener.

one-down message A verbal message that reflects acceptance of, or submission to, another person's power.

one-across message A verbal message that seeks to neutralize relational control and power.

POWER IS ALWAYS PRESENT.   Even though power is context-specific, some form of power is relevant to every interpersonal interaction. When two people have roughly equal power in their relationship, such as friends, they have a **symmetrical relationship.** Conversely, when one person has more power than the other, such as a teacher and a student, the parties have a **complementary relationship.** The way two people interact with each other depends, in part, on whether their relationship is symmetrical or complementary. For instance, you might say or do things with a friend that you wouldn't say or do with a teacher. Keep in mind, though, that the power balance of a relationship can change over time. Parents and children usually have complementary relationships when the children are young, for example, but as the children become adults, their relationships often become more symmetrical.

POWER INFLUENCES COMMUNICATION.   The balance of power in a relationship—whether it is symmetrical or complementary—influences the way people in that relationship communicate. Many years ago, communication researchers Philip Ericson and L. Edna Rogers proposed that relational power is reflected in three specific types of verbal messages people use (Figure 2).[34]

- A **one-up message** expresses dominance and an attempt to control the relationship. One-up messages often take the form of commands, such as "Do the dishes," "E-mail me your itinerary," or "Stop making so much noise."

- A **one-down message** communicates submission to or acceptance of another person's decision-making ability. Examples include questions such as "Where would you like to go for dinner?" and statements of assent such as "Whatever you'd like is fine with me."

- Finally, a **one-across message** is neither dominant nor submissive, but instead conveys a desire to neutralize relational control. One-across messages often take the form of statements of fact, such as "Dad needs a new lawn mower" and "There are many brands to choose from."

⇧ **One-up message**   ⇩ **One-down message**   ⇔ **One-across message**

FIGURE 2 Relational Power and Verbal Messages
One-up messages convey dominance and control. One-down messages express submission or resignation. One-across messages communicate a desire to neutralize relational power. © Jose Luis Pelaez Inc/ Blend Images/Getty Images, RF; © Big Cheese Photo/SuperStock RF; © Boutet Jean-Pierre/Phototeque Oredia/Age Fotostock

Stop making so much noise!

Do you have any suggestions for what I should wear tonight?

Dad needs a new lawn mower.

got skills?   ONE-ACROSS MESSAGES

Maintain balanced power relations with one-across messages.

WHAT?
Learn to use one-across messages.

WHY?
To help neutralize relational power and control.

HOW?
1. Avoid statements that assert control over a situation, such as "I think we should see a movie tonight."
2. Similarly, avoid statements that concede control over a situation to another person, such as "I'm open to whatever you want to do."
3. Use statements that recognize facts affecting you both, such as "We have several options for something to do tonight."

TRY!
1. Role-play a conversation with a sibling or friend in which you discuss what gift to buy for your father's retirement. Let the other person begin the conversation.
2. Respond with a one-across message to as many of your partner's statements as you can, regardless of their form. Try to come to agreement on a gift selection. Afterward, switch roles and repeat the conversation.

CONSIDER: *How did using one-across messages neutralize power in your conversations?*

People in symmetrical relationships often communicate using the same types of messages.[35] They might both use one-up messages ("Put away the groceries." "I'll put them away in a moment"). They might both use one-down messages ("Do you have any suggestions for what to wear tonight?" "I'm sure whatever you choose will look great"). Finally, they might both use one-across messages ("There are so many good movies showing in town right now." "And several good plays as well"). In each case, their communication reflects the fact that neither party exercises power over the other. Check out "Got Skills?" for practice with one-across messages.

In contrast, people in complementary relationships frequently communicate using different types of statements. One person might use a one-up message ("Try searching for airfares online"), and the other might respond with a one-down message ("That's a great idea; thanks for the suggestion"). Alternatively, one partner might express a one-down message ("What should we get Grandma for her birthday?"), and the other might reply with a one-up message ("Let's get her some new DVDs"). In complementary relationships, one-up or one-down messages can also precede one-across messages. In response to a one-up message, for instance ("I think we should have pasta for dinner"), a partner might respond with a one-across message ("That's one option"). That move can signal that the partner doesn't wish to be dominated or controlled.

POWER CAN BE POSITIVE OR NEGATIVE.   There's nothing inherently good or bad about power. Rather, as with conflict, the way people handle power makes it positive or negative. Even complementary relationships in which there is a large difference

Talking Point: Agreeing on the power relationship doesn't mean agreeing with everything the more powerful person does. In other words, you might not like every decision your boss makes, but by continuing to work for him or her, you are agreeing to the power arrangement in which he or she has more power than you.

in power can be highly satisfying if they meet two conditions. First, the two parties must agree on the power arrangement. If the less-powerful person begins to question or challenge the other person's power (as when adolescents assert their independence from their parents), the relationship can become dissatisfying. Second, the powerful person should exercise his or her power ethically and responsibly, in ways that benefit both parties. When one party in a relationship abuses power by serving only personal needs or desires or improving his or her situation at the other party's expense, resentment and dissatisfaction can arise. For instance, charges that police officers have abused their power underlie many of the conflicts seen in communities around the United States.

POWER AND CONFLICT INFLUENCE EACH OTHER.   At their core, many conflicts are struggles for power. Siblings who fight over control of the television remote, neighbors who fight over their property boundaries, and drivers fighting for the few remaining spaces in a parking lot are all clashing over power: Who has the right to control resources?

Just as power influences conflict, conflict can also influence the balance and exercise of power. Let's say that after Shawn turns 15, he has conflict with his parents over household rules. As a result, his parents give him a later curfew and greater flexibility in deciding where he goes and with whom. That development changed the balance of power in the parent–child relationship, with Shawn acquiring more control over his own life and his parents having less control. This shift in power was the direct result of Shawn's conflict with his parents.

So far, we've talked about power as if it were a singular entity. In fact, power comes in many forms, as we'll see next.

Forms of Power

In the IM: The out-of-class activity "Power Diary" encourages students to take note of the forms of power they exercise with others over the course of a week.

People exercise influence or control over others in many ways. In a now-classic study, social psychologists John French and Bertram Raven classified power into five specific forms: reward, coercive, referent, legitimate, and expert power.[36] As we take a closer look at those forms, remember that they aren't mutually exclusive; rather, one person may exercise multiple forms of power in a given situation.

reward power Power that derives from the ability to reward.

Focus on Ethics: When is using coercive power unethical? When, if ever, is using reward power unethical?

REWARD POWER.   As its name implies, **reward power** operates when one party has the ability to reward the other in some way. Your supervisor has power over you, for instance, because she pays you and can promote you for doing what she says. In that case, your pay and the possibility for advancement are the rewards. Similarly, judges on talent shows such as *Dancing with the Stars* and *The Voice* have reward power because they determine who will advance in those contests.

coercive power Power based on the ability to punish.

COERCIVE POWER.   The opposite of reward power is **coercive power,** or power that derives from the ability to punish. When you go to court, for example, the judge has power over you because he can punish you with fines or imprisonment for not doing as he says. Parents and employers often have both reward power and coercive power over their children or their employees; they can provide rewards for good behavior and issue punishments for bad behavior.

referent power Power that derives from one's attraction to or admiration for another.

REFERENT POWER.   French and Raven used the term **referent power** to refer to the power of attraction, noting that people tend to comply with requests made by those whom they like, admire, or find attractive in some way. For instance, you might recognize that you work harder for instructors you like than for those you dislike. Similarly, you may be more receptive to messages from organizations such as People for the Ethical Treatment of Animals (PETA) when they are delivered by actors or music artists that you already admire, such as Ariana Grande or Common. Those examples involve complementary relationships. Referent power can also operate in symmetrical relationships, however. For instance, you might comply with requests from your friends because you like them and want to please them.

LEGITIMATE POWER.   People exercise **legitimate power** when their status or position gives them the right to make requests with which others must comply. If the moderator of an online forum deletes a comment you posted in anger, you may disagree with her decision but you recognize that she has a legitimate right to monitor the discussion. When you travel by air, you follow the instructions of the airport screeners, flight attendants, and pilots because you perceive that their positions give them certain authorities over you in that context.

EXPERT POWER.   The last form on French and Raven's list is **expert power,** which operates when we comply with the directions of people we perceive to be experts in a particular area. We follow the advice of a doctor, a professor, a stockbroker, or an electrician because we recognize that their training and experience give them expertise we ourselves don't have. A novice tennis player might admire his tennis coach because of her expertise in the sport. Like other forms of power, expert power is context-specific. You consult your stockbroker for financial advice, for example, but you wouldn't ask him how to fix your sink, because that goes beyond his expertise.

As we considered earlier, different forms of power often operate together. We've seen that parents have both reward and coercive power over their children, for instance, but they often have other forms of power as well. They have referent power if their children obey them out of respect or admiration. They have legitimate power when they exercise control on the basis of their position ("Because I'm your mother, that's why!"). Finally, they have expert power when they teach their children how to drive or balance a checkbook. The "At a Glance" box provides a quick reference to help you remember French and Raven's five forms of power.

Tennis players and fans might admire Serena Williams for her performance on the tennis court, which gives her expert power. But many people also admire her for her style, appearance, and confident nature, which give her referential power. © Karwai Tang/ Getty Images

legitimate power Power based on one's legitimate status or position.

expert power Power that derives from one's expertise, talent, training, specialized knowledge, or experience.

Talking Point: Expert power is probably more influential in high-power-distance cultures, in which experts are treated with greater deference, than in low-power-distance cultures.

AT A GLANCE

French and Raven's Forms of Relational Power

Reward	Power based on the ability to reward for compliance
Coercive	Power based on the ability to punish for noncompliance
Referent	Power based on liking, admiring, and being attracted to the powerful party
Legitimate	Power based on rightfully granted status or position
Expert	Power based on special knowledge, training, experience, and/or expertise

Once the exclusive domain of men, the Supreme Court of the United States was fully a third female by 2010. © *Steven Petteway/Supreme Court of the United States*

 patriarchy A social system in which men exercise a majority of the power.

Talking Point: Despite what students may have heard or been taught, researchers have yet to discover a single society that is legitimately matriarchal. Patriarchy is virtually universal as an organizing principle of societies.

In Everyday Life: According to the United Nations, the United States currently ranks 95th in the world for percentage of women in legislative positions.

Sex, Gender, and Power

Few factors influence the experience of power more than sex and gender. Across cultures and time periods, societies have defined male–female relationships largely in terms of men's power over women. The virtually universal practice of **patriarchy,** which structures social units such as families and communities so that men control the resources, has allowed men throughout history to exercise political, religious, and economic power over women.[37] As a result, women historically have experienced more limited access to education, lower-quality health care, fewer economic opportunities, and more-limited political involvement.

Those inequities persist in many parts of the world, including the United States. According to the United Nations, only 21.9 percent of elected political representatives in the United States are women.[38] Worldwide, the number is only slightly higher: 22 percent.[39] Women and men have equal employment rates in fewer than half the world's countries, and they have equal literacy rates in only a third of the countries. Finally, in a large majority of countries, women earn less than 70 percent of what men in comparable jobs earn.[40]

Traditional gender roles reinforce the inequitable division of power between women and men. As we saw in the Culture and Gender chapter, stereotypical femininity emphasizes characteristics such as passivity, submissiveness, and accommodation, whereas stereotypical masculinity prizes strength, control, and dominance. To the extent that men and women identify strongly with masculine and feminine gender roles, the inequitable distribution of power may be reflected in their interpersonal behavior. For instance, men may take for granted that what they say at work or at home will matter to those around them. They may also express dominance through verbal aggression, using words to attack or demean people around them.[41] In contrast, if women have less power than men or perceive they do, they may be less likely to assume that other people will take their words or ideas seriously.[42] They may also be inclined to exercise power in more covert ways, such as through passive-aggressive behavior.

As women gain positions of power and influence, gender inequities in power may be eroded. As of 2015, several nations had a female head of state, including Argentina, Norway, Liberia, South Korea, and the Central African Republic (Table 1). In the U.S. government, women have assumed unprecedented positions of power in the past three decades, including Secretary of State, Attorney General, Speaker of the House of Representatives, and Secretary of Homeland Security.

People who have studied the association between conflict and health have concluded that power affects women and men differently. In one study, a team of researchers led by human ecology professor Timothy Loving took a novel approach to measuring power relations in married couples.[43] The researchers selected 72 couples and instructed each spouse to complete measures indicating how much he or she loved the other. They then checked how closely each person's response matched that of his or her spouse. To determine the spouses' relative power, the researchers

TABLE 1

Countries with Female Heads of State

Country	Head of State	Title
Argentina	Cristina Fernández de Kirchner	President
Bangladesh	Sheikh Hasina Wajed	Prime Minister
Brazil	Dilma Rousseff	President
Central African Republic	Catherine Samba-Panza	President
Chile	Michelle Bachelet	President
Croatia	Kolinda Grabar-Kitarović	President
Cyprus (North)	Sibel Siber	Prime Minister
Germany	Angela Merkel	Chancellor
Jamaica	Portia Simpson Miller	Prime Minister
Kosovo	Atifete Jahjaga	President
Latvia	Laimdota Straujuma	Prime Minister
Liberia	Ellen Johnson Sirleaf	President
Lithuania	Dalia Grybauskaite	President
Malta	Marie-Louise Coleiro Preca	President
Norway	Erna Solberg	Prime Minister
Poland	Ewa Kopacz	Prime Minister
South Korea	Park Geun-hye	President
Switzerland	Simonetta Sommaruga	President
Trinidad and Tobago	Kamla Persad-Bissessar	Prime Minister

Note: This table includes elected and appointed heads of state but excludes monarchs. Information is current as of January 2015.

applied the *principle of least interest.* That principle states that the partner who is less invested in the relationship is the more powerful partner, because he or she has less to lose by leaving the relationship.[44]

In their study, the researchers used love as the measure of investment. If the wife and husband reported relatively equal love scores, the researchers considered them to have equal power. When the husband's love score was significantly higher than his wife's, the researchers concluded that the wife had more power. Conversely, when the wife's love score was significantly higher than her husband's, then the husband was more powerful.

The researchers then instructed each couple to engage in a conflict conversation while they monitored the stress hormone levels of all the participants. The results indicated that being in a power-balanced marriage benefited women and men by protecting them against an increase in the stress hormone ACTH. The same pattern was observed in marriages in which the wife was deemed more powerful. In marriages in which the husband was deemed more powerful, however, women's ACTH levels

Talking Point: ACTH (adrenocorticotropic hormone) is a stress hormone produced by the adrenal gland.

rose significantly, indicating increased stress. Among the same group, however, men's ACTH levels dropped significantly, indicating reduced stress.

In sum, then, men experienced no increase in stress as a result of marital conflict under any circumstances. Moreover, when men argued with less-powerful wives, their stress actually decreased. One possible explanation for those results is that because men historically have enjoyed power in social affairs and relationships, they may subconsciously not perceive marital conflict to be threatening and stressful, even when they have less power in the relationship.

Like men, women didn't experience increased stress as a result of conflict when they had equal power with or more power than their spouse. Unlike men, however, they did react stressfully to conflict when they had less power. Because of their less-powerful position, the wives in the study may have felt more threatened and insecure as a result of conflict, causing their stress to elevate. ACTH is only one hormone that reacts to stress, however, so the results might have been different had the researchers utilized other indicators of stress.

Culture and Power

Talking Point: What social groups in the United States have more power than the average citizen? What form(s) of power do they wield?

In India's caste system, people are born into social groups that largely dictate with whom they can associate. ©Amos Morgan/ Photodisc/Getty Images, RF

Cultural practices and beliefs also affect the ways in which people exercise power in personal relationships. Remember from the Culture and Gender chapter that one dimension along which cultures differ is their power distance. High-power-distance cultures are characterized by an uneven distribution of power. In those cultures, certain social groups—such as royalty, the upper class, and the ruling political party—have considerably more power than the average citizen. Moreover, people in high-power-distance cultures are socialized to view the unequal distribution of power as normal or even desirable. Upper-class citizens are treated with respect and privilege, whereas citizens of lesser status are taught to behave humbly.[45] In particular, lower-status citizens are not expected to question or challenge the decisions, opinions, or directions of the ruling class. When all social groups accept that arrangement, then the society can avoid many potential conflicts.[46] One example of that type of power division is India's caste system, in which people are born into social groups, or *castes,* that largely dictate with whom they can associate.

In contrast, low-power-distance cultures exhibit a more equal distribution of power among social groups. Although some social groups may have somewhat more power than others, the prevailing belief among citizens is that all people are inherently equal and that power differences between groups should be small. One result of that cultural belief is that people from low-power-distance cultures are more likely than their counterparts in high-power-distance cultures to question authority and to engage in conflict with teachers, supervisors, politicians, and others who exercise power over them.

Another difference is that people in low-power-distance cultures often believe they have greater control over the course of their life. Whereas people in high-power-distance cultures are often raised to believe their social class determines their life course, many people in low-power-distance cultures are socialized to believe they can achieve whatever they set their minds to. In the United States, for instance, there are many examples of people, such as Barack Obama and Oprah Winfrey, who have risen from humble beginnings to positions of great power and influence. As politician Adlai Stevenson, former U.S. ambassador to the United Nations, once noted, "In America, anyone can become president."

4 Managing Interpersonal Conflict

There are almost as many ways to handle conflict as there are topics about which to disagree. When you experience conflict in your personal relationships, you need to decide how to manage and resolve them. Sometimes you choose your behaviors wisely, and sometimes you choose poorly, but your actions almost always have an effect on your relationships. We'll begin this section by looking at some particularly problematic conflict behaviors. We'll then examine five general strategies you can use to manage conflict successfully.

Problematic Behaviors during Conflict

Earlier in this chapter, we learned that it isn't conflict itself that is necessarily damaging to our relationships; rather, it's the way we handle conflict that matters. Whereas some relational partners manage conflict maturely and constructively, others deal with it so poorly that it jeopardizes the relationship itself. Which behaviors are the problematic ones?

To find out, psychologist John Gottman has spent years studying how spouses and partners interact with each other during conflict episodes. Conventional wisdom might suggest that couples who fight frequently are most likely to split up. In fact, Gottman's research has found otherwise. According to Gottman, *how couples argue,* and not how frequently they argue, predicts their chances for staying together.[47] Gottman's work has identified four specific behaviors that are warning signs for separation or divorce: criticism, contempt, defensiveness, and stonewalling. Gottman refers to those behaviors as the "Four Horsemen of the Apocalypse" to indicate that they signal distress.[48] Let's take a closer look at each of those problematic behaviors.

CRITICISM. According to Gottman, the first warning sign occurs when partners engage in **criticism** or complaints about each other. Criticism isn't always bad, but it

Media Note: A video discussing John Gottman's laboratory research with couples is viewable at: www.youtube.com/watch?v=QEnVSrCCSw4

criticism The expression of complaints about another party.

becomes counterproductive when it focuses on people's personality or character rather than on their behavior. Statements such as "You always have to be right" and "You never listen" focus on attacking the person and assigning blame.

Criticisms also tend to be global statements about a person's value or virtue instead of specific critiques about the topic of the conflict. Instead of saying "You should be more attentive when I describe my feelings to you," for instance, a distressed partner might say "You never think of anyone but yourself." Because criticisms so often come across as personal attacks instead of as accurate descriptions of the sources of conflict, they tend to inflame conflict situations. At that point, criticism becomes a sign of a distressed relationship.

Criticism can also be counterproductive when partners engage in *gunnysacking*— that is, privately "saving up" their past grievances and then bringing them up all at once.[49] When Enrique criticized his wife Sonja for spending too much money on their children's school clothes, for example, Sonja responded by criticizing Enrique for past offenses she had not previously discussed with him. "You think *I'm* wasteful?" she replied. "What about all the money you wasted on that stupid fishing trip last year? And while we're on the subject, don't think I didn't notice that money you transferred out of our savings account last month without asking me. What'd you waste that on? Another piece of overpriced art for your office? You expect me to be careful with money while you've been wasting it ever since we got married!"

Each of Sonja's grievances may have merit. Nevertheless, her response to Enrique's criticism is unproductive. By bringing up all her criticisms at once, Sonja is deflecting attention from their current conflict, with the likely result that the current conflict will remain unresolved.

CONTEMPT. A second warning sign occurs when partners exhibit **contemptuous behaviors** toward each other by insulting each other and attacking each other's self-worth. Those behaviors can include calling each other names ("You stupid idiot"), using sarcasm or mockery to make fun of the other person, and using nonverbal behaviors that suggest a low opinion of the other person, such as eye rolling and sneering. They can also include ridiculing the person in front of others and encouraging others to do the same.

Regardless of its form, contempt functions to put down and degrade the other person. Research indicates that responding to conflict with this type of hostile behavior often increases physical stress in the partners, which can impair their health.[50]

DEFENSIVENESS. A third danger sign is that partners become defensive during their conflict. As you'll recall from the Language chapter, defensiveness is a feeling of excessive concern with guarding oneself against the threat of criticism. **Defensive behaviors** include casting oneself as a victim and denying responsibility for one's own role in a conflict. Instead of listening to their partners' concerns and acknowledging that they need to change certain

contemptuous behaviors
The expression of insults and attacks on another's self-worth.

defensive behaviors
Tactics that cast the self as a victim and deny responsibility for one's own role in a conflict.

Gottman has found that people stonewall when they feel emotionally and psychologically flooded. © *Steve Debenport/Getty Images, RF*

behaviors, defensive people whine ("It's not fair"), make excuses ("It's not my fault"), and respond to complaints with complaints ("Maybe I spend too much money, but you never make time for the kids and me"). People are particularly prone to feel defensive about criticisms when they recognize that the criticisms have merit but they don't want to accept the responsibility for changing their behaviors.

STONEWALLING.   The last of Gottman's "Four Horsemen" is **stonewalling,** or withdrawing from a conversation or an interaction. People who stonewall will often act as though they are "shutting down"; that is, they stop looking at their partners, they stop speaking, and they stop responding to what their partners are saying. In some cases, they even physically leave the room to end the conversation. The reason for their departure isn't to calm down, which might be an effective strategy. Rather, it is to shut off the conversation entirely.

Gottman's research has suggested that people stonewall when they feel emotionally and psychologically *flooded,* or incapable of engaging in the conversation any longer. Unfortunately, when one partner stonewalls, it becomes almost impossible for the couple to resolve its disagreements. Research has also shown that when husbands stonewall during a conflict, their wives often experience significant increases in the stress hormones cortisol and norepinephrine.[51]

Strategies for Managing Conflict Successfully

Gottman's work shows that criticizing, showing contempt, becoming defensive, and engaging in stonewalling aren't productive ways of handling conflict. Because you can't escape conflict, what alternatives do you have for managing it properly? According to researchers Robert Blake and Jane Mouton, your options for dealing with conflict are based on two underlying dimensions: your concern for your own needs and desires, and your concern for the other party's needs and desires.[52] When plotted on a graph (Figure 3), those dimensions give rise to five major strategies for engaging in conflict: competing, avoiding, accommodating, compromising, and collaborating.

As we look at each of those strategies in this section, keep in mind that conflict itself is neither inherently positive nor inherently negative. Rather, it is neutral. What determines whether it is good or bad is the strategy you adopt for handling it. Some of the strategies we examine here might seem more constructive to you than others, but none of them is the right choice in every situation. Instead, in a given set of circumstances, any particular strategy can be the best option.

COMPETING.   The **competing** style represents a high concern for your own needs and desires and a low concern for those of the other party. Your goal is to win the conflict while the other person loses. Engaging conflict in this style is much like playing football. There are no "tie games"—one team's win is the other team's loss.

The competing style might be appropriate in situations when there is a concrete outcome that cannot be shared, as when two people are competing for the same job. Ongoing competition can also enhance relationships, as long as relational partners view competition as a positive rather than negative aspect of their relationships.[53] Competition becomes problematic when it starts leading to feelings of resentment or desires to get even with the other person.[54]

In Everyday Life: Ask your students when, in everyday life, they get defensive about criticisms.

stonewalling Withdrawing from a conversation or an interaction.

Focus on Ethics: Gottman's extensive research has given him the ability to predict with a high degree of accuracy how likely a couple is to divorce after watching only a few minutes of their conflict conversation. Is it ethical for him to tell the partners if he thinks they are likely to divorce? Is it ethical for him *not* to tell them?

competing A strategy for managing conflict in which one's goal is to win while the other party loses.

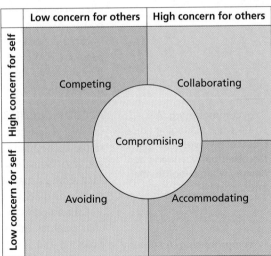

FIGURE 3 When concern for self and concern for others are juxtaposed, they give rise to five strategies for engaging in conflict: competing, avoiding, accommodating, collaborating, and compromising.

On *The Mindy Project*, Danny's strategies for dealing with his mother alternate between avoidance and accommodation. *Jennifer Clasen/ NBC/NBCU Photo Bank/Getty Images*

avoiding A strategy for managing conflict that involves ignoring or failing to deal with the conflict.

AVOIDING. A very different approach to conflict is the **avoiding** style, which involves a low concern for both the self and the other. Adopting this style means ignoring the conflict and hoping it will go away on its own. Whereas stonewalling means withdrawing from the conversation in the middle of a conflict episode, avoiding means failing to engage the conflict in the first place. Often, however, conflicts that are avoided simply become worse.

Some people choose avoidance because they are uncomfortable engaging in conflict; others choose it because they don't care enough about the outcome of the conflict to bother. Avoiding conflict isn't always the wrong choice; many people in satisfying relationships choose to ignore or avoid certain points of contention in order to maintain harmony.[55] When avoidance becomes the primary way of managing conflict, however, it often leaves important conflicts unresolved, a situation that leads to dissatisfying relationships.[56]

accommodating A strategy for managing conflict that involves giving in to the other party's needs and desires while subordinating one's own.

ACCOMMODATING. **Accommodating** is the opposite of competing. This style involves demonstrating a high concern for the other party but a low concern for the self. In the accommodating style, your goal is to sacrifice so that the other party wins and you lose. Sometimes people accommodate to "keep the peace" in their relationships. That strategy may work well in the short term. In the long term, continually accommodating the other party can make an individual feel resentful.

Culture plays an important role in the use of accommodation. In collectivistic societies (such as many Asian societies), accommodating in response to conflict is often expected and is viewed as respectful or noble.[57] In contrast, people in individualistic societies (such as the United States) may be seen as weak or spineless if they consistently accommodate others.

compromising A strategy for managing conflict in which both parties give up something they want so that both can receive something they want.

COMPROMISING. **Compromising** involves a moderate concern for everyone's needs and desires. In this strategy, both parties give up something in order to gain something. Neither party gets exactly what he or she wants, but all parties leave the conflict having gained something valuable.

got skills? COMPROMISING

Compromising gives both parties in a conflict something they value.

WHAT?
Learn to compromise when managing conflict.

WHY?
To help both parties in a conflict—such as a conflict over the selling price of a car—gain something of value.

HOW?
1. If it appears that neither party is going to "win" the conflict outright, say "Let's come up with a compromise."
2. Identify what's most important to you in the conflict ("I really need to sell this car for at least $6,500") and then ask the other party to do the same ("I want to get the best deal possible").
3. Propose solutions to the conflict that address each party's most pressing needs ("If you buy the car for $6,500, I'll throw in a mobile GPS unit and a year of satellite radio service").

TRY!
1. With a classmate pretending to be your roommate, practice a conversation in which you address his or her criticisms of your study habits or housecleaning practices at home.
2. Rather than accepting your partner's suggestions for change outright, identify what's most important to you and ask your partner to do the same.
3. Propose a solution that will give each of you something that you want. Continue proposing compromises until your partner accepts.

CONSIDER: *How does thinking about compromise force you to consider your partner's needs as well as your own?*

Let's say you're negotiating a job offer and you want a higher salary than the employer wants to pay. Through your negotiation, you agree to accept a lower salary than you originally wanted, and the employer agrees to give you an extra week of vacation in return. Neither of you got exactly what you wanted, but you each got something you valued in return for giving up something else.

Compromising takes time and patience, but it often leads to better outcomes than competing, avoiding, or accommodating. The "Got Skills?" box offers suggestions for practicing compromise during a conflict.

COLLABORATING.   The **collaborating** style represents a high concern for both your partner's needs and your own. The goal is to arrive at a win–win situation that maximizes both parties' gains. After they had their first child, for instance, Mick and Laura felt the strain of paying for day care while Mick worked and Laura went to school. Their collaborative solution was for Mick to reduce his work hours and for Laura to enroll in online courses so at least one of them would be home every day. The money they saved in day care made up for the income they lost because of Mick's reduced hours. Moreover, both Laura and Mick felt better because they were able to care for their child themselves.

Collaborating probably sounds like the ideal way to handle conflict—and in many situations, it is. It can also require a great deal of energy, patience, and imagination. Although it might seem like the best approach, it can also be the most difficult.

How might each of those strategies operate in real life? The "At a Glance" box highlights one conflict—two siblings fighting over who is going to get a new car—and illustrates how each of those approaches can be employed when engaging in the onflict.

collaborating A strategy for managing conflict that involves working toward a solution that meets both parties' needs.

Talking Point: Students may have difficulty distinguishing between compromising and collaborating. Point out that collaborating involves working together to determine how both parties can get what they want, whereas compromising involves both parties getting only a portion of what they want, after having given something else up.

AT A GLANCE

Five Approaches to Conflict

Carla and Ben, sister and brother, have each saved $1,500 to put toward a car. Their parents can add only enough money to buy one car, not two, so Carla is in conflict with Ben over who should get that money. Here are examples of five different approaches Carla might take when engaging this conflict:

Competing	Carla tries to get her parents to give all their saved-up money to her and none of it to Ben.
Avoiding	Carla doesn't bring up the conflict, hoping her parents will figure out a way to resolve it on their own.
Accommodating	Carla encourages her parents to give their saved-up money to Ben instead of to her.
Compromising	Carla suggests that she and Ben pool their money with their parents' money and buy one car that they will share.
Collaborating	Carla works with Ben and their parents to try to figure out how she and Ben can each get a car.

Talking Point: As you discuss each strategy, ask your students for examples about when that strategy would be preferred.

Talking Point: Gender roles may also be influential in accommodating, because putting the needs of others first is characteristic of the traditional feminine role.

CONNECT: Learning Resources in SmartBook provide additional hints and explanations to help break down complex topics and reach students with different learning styles.

LEARN IT How are criticism and contempt different? When might avoidance be a better conflict management strategy than accommodating?

APPLY IT Pair up with a classmate and watch an episode of your favorite reality TV show. Whenever conflict is portrayed in the program, help each other identify examples of any of Gottman's "Four Horsemen of the Apocalypse."

REFLECT ON IT How do you feel when someone stonewalls during a conflict with you? When do you find collaborating a challenge?

In the IM: You can now access the end-of-chapter Discussion Questions and the Research Library in the Instructor's Manual for each chapter.

MASTER the chapter

1 The Nature of Interpersonal Conflict (p. 343)

- Conflict is an expressed struggle between two or more interdependent parties who perceive incompatible goals, scarce resources, and interference.
- People often think about conflict using a variety of metaphors such as a trial, a game, a balancing act, and a garden.

2 Conflict in Personal Relationships (p. 346)

- Conflict is natural. It has content, relational, and procedural dimensions, and it can be direct or indirect. Conflict can be harmful, and it can also be beneficial.
- People have conflict about a range of issues. Some issues—such as personal criticism, finances, and household chores—are especially common in interpersonal relationships.

- Conflict is influenced by sex and gender role orientations, encouraging men to be competitive and women to be accommodating.

- How people manage conflict is affected by whether their culture is individualistic or collectivistic and also by whether it is high context or low context.

- Conflict is especially prevalent in online settings because of the disinhibition effect.

3 Power and Conflict (p. 357)

- Power is the ability to manipulate, influence, or control other people or events.

- Power is context-specific but always present. It can be positive or negative, depending on how it is exercised. Power and conflict influence each other.

- People exercise five general forms of power: reward, coercive, referent, legitimate, and expert.

- Power is influenced by sex and gender roles.

- The way people think about power is affected by whether they come from a high-power-distance culture or a low-power-distance culture.

4 Managing Interpersonal Conflict (p. 365)

- In romantic relationships, four conflict behaviors are reliable predictors of relationship dissolution: criticism, contempt, defensiveness, and stonewalling.

- People use five general strategies for managing conflict: competing, avoiding, accommodating, collaborating, and compromising. Which conflict management strategy is best depends on the situation and on the goals of the participants.

KEY TERMS

accommodating (p. 368)

avoiding (p. 368)

coercive power (p. 360)

collaborating (p. 370)

competing (p. 367)

complementary relationship (p. 358)

compromising (p. 368)

contemptuous behaviors (p. 366)

criticism (p. 365)

defensive behaviors (p. 366)

demand–withdraw pattern (p. 353)

direct conflict (p. 348)

disinhibition effect (p. 355)

expert power (p. 361)

indirect conflict (p. 348)

interpersonal conflict (p. 343)

legitimate power (p. 361)

metaconflict (p. 348)

one-across message (p. 358)

one-down message (p. 358)

one-up message (p. 358)

passive aggression (p. 352)

patriarchy (p. 362)

power (p. 357)

referent power (p. 360)

reframing (p. 346)

reward power (p. 360)

stonewalling (p. 367)

symmetrical relationship (p. 358)

McGraw Hill Education connect

To maximize your study time, check out CONNECT to access the SmartBook study module for this chapter, watch videos, and explore other resources.

12

Deceptive Communication

© Photos 12 / Alamy

FEELING THE PAIN
OF DISHONESTY

In the 2014 movie *Gone Girl,* Nick Dunne (played by Ben Affleck) returns home to find that his wife Amy (played by Rosamund Pike) has gone missing on their fifth wedding anniversary in what appears to have been a violent abduction. Suspicions quickly arise that Nick has murdered Amy, and he becomes the focus of intense scrutiny from the media and police. But as the story unfolds, with Amy's version told via diary entries and Nick's from his first-person account, it becomes clear that both Amy and Nick have been deceitful, and that their relationship was a complete sham. Nick is revealed to be a cheater, and Amy is revealed to be not merely manipulative and deceptive, but murderous. In the end, their marriage remains intact, bound almost entirely by lies and deception. Viewers are left to imagine their future unhappiness and distrust of each other in an empty relationship.

chapter preview

1 **The Nature of Interpersonal Deception**

2 **The Diversity of Deceptive Acts**

3 **Communication Behaviors and Deception**

4 **Detecting Lies in Different Contexts**

No one likes being lied to. When we find out someone has deceived us, we feel angry and taken advantage of. Although those feelings of betrayal and violation can occur in all relationships, they can be particularly strong—and painful—when the deception occurs in the context of a close relationship, as it did for Nick and Amy. Deception hurts us emotionally, and it erodes our trust in others, as the "Communication: Dark Side" box explains.[1]

Yet are you completely honest *all* the time? Do you ever pretend you're happy to see someone, just to avoid hurting that person's feelings? How about those times you say "Sorry, I have plans" when you don't really have plans, but you want to get out of something you don't want to do? Most of us would have to admit we don't always tell "the truth, the whole truth, and nothing but the truth." But being polite, tactful, or discreet isn't really the same thing as lying. Is it?

1 The Nature of Interpersonal Deception

You don't have to look far to find high-profile examples of deception. In 2015, NBC suspended news anchor Brian Williams after discovering that he had fabricated his account of being in a military helicopter that was forced to land after taking ground fire in 2003 in Iraq. The previous year, the U.S. Justice Department joined a lawsuit against professional cyclist Lance Armstrong after learning that the seven-time Tour de France champion had lied about using performance-enhancing drugs. From politicians to advertisers to celebrities, it seems that many people in our world attempt to benefit personally by deceiving others.

Whatever our personal feelings may be about the value of honesty, the reality is that most people conceal the truth on a regular basis.[2] To respect the privacy of a co-worker who is in treatment for alcohol addiction, for instance, you may tell her clients that she's away from work on a "special assignment." By the same token, you may tell your 12-year-old nephew that he did a "wonderful job" performing in his school musical, even though he can barely carry a tune, because you want to encourage him. Sometimes, in fact, we even reprimand people for telling the truth. When children make straightforward comments about other people ("You smell funny," "Your teeth are really yellow"), we usually teach them it is impolite to say such things, even though they are expressing honest opinions.

We might agree that lying is wrong if we do it to hurt someone, but what if we do it to *avoid* hurting

In Everyday Life: Many behaviors that we think of as tact or politeness involve being deceptive. When we take account of such behaviors, we realize that most of us are deceptive, to some degree, on a routine basis.

CONNECT: Learning Resources in SmartBook help students practice their skills by evaluating conversations and analyzing situations for communication competence.

Outside of Class: Ask students to keep a notebook for a week in which they record every instance in which they've been deceptive in any way, even in the service of politeness. For each deceptive act, have them record their motive. Discuss the aggregate findings with your class afterward.

© CBS Photo Archive/Getty Images

communication | *DARK SIDE*

LYING TO THE ONES WE LOVE: DECEPTION CAN CAUSE PAIN AND RUIN TRUST

A manda Broadband had always harbored suspicions about her husband Stuart's past. He claimed to have been faithful during their 15-year marriage, but in 2008 Amanda discovered—in a very public and humiliating way—that he had been lying. The spouses were contestants on Jerry Springer's British television game show *Nothing But the Truth,* in which participants are hooked up to a lie detector and asked a series of personal questions on the air. Those who answer every question truthfully can win the equivalent of $100,000, but one lie and all the money is lost. Faced with the chance to pocket significant cash, Stuart responded to a question about his marital fidelity by revealing that he had carried on an affair several years earlier. Although relieved to know the truth, Amanda felt hurt, betrayed, and deeply embarrassed—all the more so because her husband's deception had been exposed on national television.

Amanda's painful experience is not unique. As you have seen in this course, close personal relationships require the ability to trust. When you learn that someone you care about has lied to you, particularly about a matter of importance, that discovery often makes you less willing to believe other statements that person makes. In other words, it erodes your trust in the individual. Once truth is compromised in a close relationship, it may never fully recover, even if you forgive the person for lying. If you find yourself the victim of violated trust, think honestly about how that episode has affected your trust in that person.

ASK YOURSELF

- Where does trust come from? What makes you trust others?

- Has deception ever ruined your trust in another person? If so, how did your willingness to trust that person change over time, if at all?

Source: Nicholas, S. (2008, January 23). The couple who lost out by telling the truth to Jerry Springer. *MailOnline*. Retrieved May 14, 2015, from http://journalisted.com/article/5rdg

someone?[3] We may choose not to think of politeness or discretion as examples of lying, because words such as *lying* and *deception* have negative connotations. However, even when their intentions are admirable, people often misrepresent the truth to achieve them.[4] When we think of lying as a misrepresentation of the truth—no matter what the intention—we realize that deception is often a part of everyday social interaction.

Throughout this chapter, it's important to keep an open mind and think of deception as just one of many communication processes you're learning about in this class. That doesn't mean you should check your morals or beliefs at the door. On the contrary, how you think about the value of honesty, reliability, and integrity helps to define who you are as a human being. Many people believe that honesty is truly the best policy. Nearly all the major world religions promote the virtue of honesty and condemn deceptive behavior.

Remember, though, that *studying* something isn't the same as *condoning* it. Whether or not you

Talking Point: Students may equate studying deception with condoning it morally, so this is a good concern to address directly.

Religions are not the only organizations that promote honesty as a virtue. Many social groups like the Girl Scouts include values such as honesty, fairness, and personal responsibility into their laws and oaths as guidelines for members' actions. © AP Images/ Paul Sakuma

are ethically or morally opposed to lying, understanding deception helps you to become a better communicator.[5] In fact, the more you know about deception, the better you may become at detecting it.

Most of us would probably define deception as "making statements that aren't true," and we might associate it with actions such as fibbing, misleading, exaggerating, stretching the truth, concealing the truth, and telling white lies. None of those types of deception, however, represents a fully adequate definition. After all, people can be deceptive by leaving out parts of a story or by giving vague, ambiguous answers to questions. Neither of those scenarios requires saying anything that technically isn't true.

Defining Deception

According to communication researchers, **deception** occurs when a speaker transmits information knowingly and intentionally for the purpose of creating a false belief in the receiver. In other words, if you communicate in a way that is meant to make someone believe a fact or form an impression you know to be untrue, then you are engaging in deception. We can think of deceptive acts as falling along a continuum from high-stakes lies to low-stakes lies.

> **deception** The knowing and intentional transmission of information to create a false belief in the hearer.

HIGH-STAKES LIES.   High-stakes lies are those for which the penalties for getting caught are severe.[6] Many high-stakes lies are forms of *fraud,* which means they are misrepresentations of facts for the sake of material gain. Some types of fraudulent lies are (1) misrepresenting your identity by forging someone else's signature on checks or other documents; (2) impersonating a physician, a police officer, or some other licensed professional; (3) engaging in insider trading by using privileged information to make stock sales or purchases; (4) underreporting your income on your tax returns; and (5) filing false insurance claims. Each of those actions is a high-stakes lie because the penalty for getting caught can include steep fines and imprisonment. The same can be said for *perjury,* or lying under oath, which constitutes a felony.

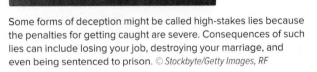

In addition to carrying legal penalties, high-stakes lies can carry significant personal penalties. For example, lying to your spouse to cover up an affair or lying to your boss about a substantial mistake you made would also qualify as a high-stakes lie because you could destroy your marriage or lose your job if your lie were to be revealed.[7]

Some forms of deception might be called high-stakes lies because the penalties for getting caught are severe. Consequences of such lies can include losing your job, destroying your marriage, and even being sentenced to prison. © *Stockbyte/Getty Images, RF*

LOW-STAKES LIES.   On the other end of the continuum are low-stakes lies, for which the penalties for getting caught are comparatively mild. Those lies, sometimes called "white lies," often serve to avoid embarrassing people and hurting their feelings. Some examples of low-stakes lies are (1) telling a friend you "love the graduation gift" she gave you when you actually don't like it; (2) assuring your brother and sister-in-law that helping them move "is no problem," even though it's inconvenient for you; (3) claiming that you arrived late to your haircut appointment because you "ran into heavy traffic on the way" when in fact you left your house late; and (4) saying "nice to meet you" to your newest co-worker even though he makes a bad first impression on you.

In many cases, the only real penalty for being caught in a low-stakes lie is emotional discomfort. If your hairdresser discovers you actually weren't late for your appointment because of traffic, for instance, you'll probably feel slightly guilty for having told the lie and slightly embarrassed at being discovered. Those emotions will probably be temporary, though, and it's unlikely that more serious consequences will follow.

MIDDLE-STAKES LIES. Many other deceptive acts fall somewhere along the continuum between high-stakes and low-stakes lies. Suppose, for instance, that while taking the midterm exam in your marketing class, you notice your friend Soren cheating on the test. After reading Soren's exam, the professor suspects him of cheating but doesn't have direct proof. She contacts several students—including you—to ask if you witnessed anyone cheating on the test. Because Soren is your friend, you say no. What penalties do you suffer if you are caught in that lie? Perhaps the professor gives you a failing grade on the exam, making it impossible for you to earn a grade higher than *C* in the class. That penalty is certainly more severe than just feeling guilty or embarrassed, but it isn't as severe as losing your job, your marriage, or your freedom. Lies of that sort might therefore be considered middle-stakes lies.

Students who cheat on exams risk failing grades or even automatic expulsion from class, making cheating a high-stakes lie. Failing to report someone else's cheating might be only a middle-stakes lie, though, depending on the expectations of the school. © PeopleImages .com/Getty Images, RF

In the IM: The in-class activity "Beliefs About Deception" encourages students to reflect on their ideas about deceptive behavior.

The Elements of Deception

In summary, to qualify as deception, a communicative act must have three basic elements:

- The sender must know the information is false.
- The sender must be transmitting the information on purpose.
- The sender must be attempting to make the receiver believe the information.

Importantly, a behavior must exhibit all three characteristics to be considered deceptive.

Our definition of deception excludes certain situations, which we now consider. You probably encounter such situations from time to time in your social interactions.

Talking Point: When people don't realize that the information they're giving is false, they usually don't exhibit any of the emotional or physiological signs of deception.

In Everyday Life: Joking, teasing, and sarcasm are three examples of common behaviors that would qualify as deception were it not for the speaker's lack of intention to be believed.

YOU AREN'T LYING IF YOU BELIEVE THAT WHAT YOU'RE SAYING IS TRUE. Suppose you ask me how long a nautical mile is, and I tell you it's 1,920 meters. That answer reflects what I honestly think. It's also untrue—a nautical mile is actually 1,852 meters. (You should know better than to ask a communication professor such questions.) So, I gave you false information. Did I transmit the information on purpose? Yes: You asked and I answered. Did I intend for you to believe the information? Of course. Nevertheless, according to our definition I wasn't being deceptive because I didn't know the information was false.

YOU AREN'T LYING IF YOU DON'T INTEND FOR OTHERS TO BELIEVE WHAT YOU'RE SAYING. Quite often, you make statements you don't mean for other people to take literally, such as "I'm so hungry I could eat a horse" and "I'm so tired I could sleep 'til Tuesday." You've probably never actually been that hungry or that tired—and if you say something like that, most people who hear you will understand that you don't literally mean what you're saying. If you say "It's raining cats and dogs," you know that felines and canines aren't actually falling from the sky; thus, the literal information is false. Nevertheless, you aren't being deceptive in that situation, because when you use such idioms you're not trying to make others believe the false information. Many forms of teasing and sarcasm also are not meant to be taken literally. We can usually tell by people's facial expressions or tone of voice when they are joking and don't expect us to believe them.

We can deceive others only if we try to make them believe something we know to be untrue. © Rick Gomez/Corbis, RF

YOU CANNOT LIE TO YOURSELF.   From time to time, you may try to make yourself believe facts or ideas that you know aren't true. When you realize such attempts didn't work, you may say, "I was just deceiving myself." According to our definition, however, it is *impossible* for people to deceive themselves. You certainly attempt to change your opinions or beliefs on various issues; sometimes you're successful and sometimes not. Recall, however, that for a communicative act to qualify as deception, the sender—knowing the information is false—must attempt to make the receiver believe it is true.

The problem with trying to deceive yourself is that the sender and the receiver are the same person—*you*—and you can't logically believe that something is true while at the same time knowing that it is false. The moment you believe your lie, in other words, it stops being a lie, because the sender now believes the information to be true. You might try to trick yourself from time to time; for example, you might set all your clocks and your watch 10 minutes fast so that you're never late. However, the process of deception requires that the sender and the receiver be *different* people.

Talking Point: At first, students may have a hard time understanding why it is technically impossible to lie to oneself.

Two additional observations deserve attention. First, deception involves the transmission of *information,* not just the transmission of *words.* Words convey information, of course, but, as we have discussed, so do nonverbal behaviors. Thus, it is possible to be deceptive without ever saying a word.

Imagine, for instance, that David and Aileen are living together as romantic partners but haven't yet told Aileen's family. Whenever her parents come to visit, David and Aileen therefore must alter their apartment to give the impression that they are simply roommates. Thus, they take down any photos showing the two of them together. David moves out of the master bedroom and into the guest room, which is referred to as "his" room. Through their actions, Aileen and David give the impression that they are simply two friends sharing an apartment. Even though they don't specifically say they aren't romantic partners, their actions convey that deceptive message.

Second, our definition of deception doesn't mention anything about motive. The reason someone is deceiving another person has nothing to do with whether that person is being deceptive. That point is important because we sometimes think lying isn't *really* lying if we do it for the "right" reasons. While treating an adolescent in critical condition after a car crash, for instance, a physician may choose not to tell him that his friend died in the accident because she's worried the stress and grief will compromise the victim's recovery. Similarly, a detective may give a homicide victim's relatives only a vague description of the crime, omitting details he believes they would find upsetting.

Focus on Ethics: In real life, many people do think the motive behind a lie is relevant to how ethical the lie is. Even people morally opposed to lying might nonetheless lie to save a life or property, believing those to be higher moral causes than honesty. Even though the motive behind a lie doesn't affect whether or not it is a lie, it may greatly affect people's evaluations of its ethicality.

In other circumstances, you may have deceived other people to help them—or, at least, to avoid hurting them—and felt justified in doing so.

In fact, people have several motives for engaging in deception, many of which are altruistic. Deception is deception, however, whether we consider it justified or not. Lying, even to save someone's life, is still lying.

Deception is relatively common in interpersonal communication. Research indicates that it is especially frequent when we are attempting to be polite and when we are communicating online. Let's take a closer look at each of those situations.

Interpersonal Deception Is a Common Component of Politeness

As several of our examples of deception have illustrated, one of the most common reasons people lie is to be polite and to avoid hurting others.[8] An important component of being polite, after all, is making others feel appreciated, whether one genuinely appreciates them or not.[9] Behaving politely therefore means trying not to cause offense.

In their attempts to be polite, people frequently make statements that express appreciation and steer clear of offense, even if those statements are misleading. For example, Ally is unimpressed the first time she hangs out with Rich, but she doesn't want to hurt his feelings, so she says, "I had fun; we should do this again," even though she doesn't mean it. Carma feels uncomfortable attending church with her mother-in-law whenever she visits, but she doesn't want to offend her, so she says, "I'd love to go," even though she doesn't want to.

Deceptions committed in the service of politeness help maintain social harmony and avoid disruptions in relationships. Imagine what interpersonal communication would be like if everyone told the complete, unedited truth about everything. People would no longer hold back their opinions about you or your behavior, no matter how hurtful those opinions would be to you. It's easy to imagine that such a situation would do more to damage relationships than to enhance them.

Even if we have moral objections to lying, some researchers believe that deception can serve as a "social lubricant" by decreasing friction between people and helping them get along.[10] Psychologist Leonard Saxe argues that people who are obsessed with being totally honest might become socially isolated because others would see them as impolite and lacking in social skill.[11]

Deception is Common When Communicating Online

Research indicates that deception also occurs frequently during electronically mediated communication. In three separate studies with business managers and graduate business students, for example, researchers compared participants' e-mail messages with messages they wrote using pen and paper.[12] The studies revealed two important trends:

- *First, participants lied more often in e-mail messages.* When they had the option of deceiving their partners, participants in the studies were 25 percent more likely to do so in e-mail than in a handwritten message.

Mild deception often acts as a social lubricant, helping people get along. Someone who is blatantly honest all the time would be considered impolite.
© Image Source/Getty Images, RF

Talking Point: Lies committed in the service of politeness may seem so benign and routine that people don't think of them as instances of deception at all.

Media Note: Jon Ronson's 2015 book, *So You've Been Publicly Shamed,* offers the observation that "Facebook is where you lie to your friends; Twitter is where you tell the truth to strangers."* You might ask your students what they make of this claim.

Media Note: Dateline NBC's series *To Catch a Predator III* focuses on how some adults use online communication to arrange sexual encounters with minors. The adults are often deceptive in their online communication and also in their face-to-face communication with the show's host after they are caught.

*Ronson, J. (2015). So you've been publicly shamed. *Macmillan*

- *Second, participants felt more justified lying in e-mail messages.* Specifically, e-mail communicators felt less guilty about lying than did those using hand-written messages.

E-mail isn't the only form of mediated communication that is susceptible to deception. Research has also found that lies are common in text-messaging[13] and on Twitter.[14]

Dishonesty may be even more common in forms of electronic communication that allow for anonymity. When participating in a chat room, for instance, or taking part in an online game, people have the ability to hide their true identities by using made-up screen names. That anonymity protects their privacy, but it also enables them to exaggerate or falsify aspects of their online identities, such as their age, educational level, ethnicity, and income.[15] Some online communicators even engage in *gender switching,* in which they pretend to be a member of the other sex.[16]

Some striking examples of online deception occur on dating websites, where subscribers post personal information with the hope of attracting potential romantic partners. Profiles on dating sites typically

Online avatars and screen names allow the opportunity for anonymity—and deception—on the Internet. © *Kubkoo/Getty Images, RF*

ask for information about the subscriber's height, weight, personal appearance, profession, education, hobbies, and preferences in a prospective partner. Perhaps not surprisingly, deception is common on such sites. In fact, research has found that as many as 20 percent of online daters admit to lying about some aspect of their personal profile. When people are asked *how many other people* they believe are being deceptive, however, that figure jumps to nearly 90 percent.[17] Recent research has found that deception is even more common when people share sexually explicit text messages, a behavior referred to as "sexting."[18]

What do online daters lie about? For women, the major areas of deception are age, weight, and physical appearance. For men, they are educational level, income, height, age, and even marital status. (Research suggests that at least 13 percent of men on dating websites are married.)[19] Why is such lying so common? The answer is that online daters are looking for a partner, and so they want their profile to be as attractive as possible, even if it isn't entirely accurate. Unfortunately, their belief that being completely truthful would hurt their chances may be justified. At least one study found that the more honest people were in describing themselves, the less success they had in finding dates online.[20]

Why, exactly, might someone choose to lie, either online or in person? We'll take a look at some of the most common reasons for deception in the next section.

Snapshots

Tall, Dark, and Handsome chats with Buxom Blonde.

www.CartoonStock.com

LEARN IT What is deception? Why can't people lie to themselves? What does it mean to call deception a "social lubricant"?

APPLY IT For two days, keep a journal in which you note every time you are deceptive with another person, no matter how or for what reason. Even deception done in the service of routine politeness should be recorded. For each entry, write down what you were deceptive about and what your intention was for deceiving.

REFLECT ON IT While keeping the deception diary, how did you feel when you caught yourself being deceptive to others? How do you feel when you think others are deceiving you, even if it's to spare your feelings?

2 The Diversity of Deceptive Acts

We've seen that lying can't occur by accident. Whenever people attempt to deceive others, they therefore must have a reason. In the examples we have considered thus far, people practiced deception for a number of reasons. Communication research confirms that people have many motivations for lying. You may view some of those motivations to be reprehensible—for example, lying to hurt someone. You may find others to be acceptable under some circumstances—for example, lying to avoid hurting someone.[21]

Some Reasons Why People Deceive

Let's consider some of the most common reasons why people engage in deception, and look at a brief example of each. Can you think of any other motives to add to this list?[22]

- *Some lies benefit the hearer.* To make your friend feel good, you say you like her new haircut even though you don't because it doesn't match her overall style.[23]

- *Some lies help you get to know someone.* You invent an excuse to interact with someone just so you can get to know the person.

- *Some lies protect your privacy.* Your co-worker asks how you are, and even though you're having problems at home, you say "fine" because you don't want to discuss your domestic situation with her.

- *Some lies help you avoid conflict.* Your romantic partner asks if you want to go with him to a party and you say that you do—even though you don't—to avoid a fight.

- *Some lies make you look better.* At your class reunion, you exaggerate facts about your education and income level to appear more successful than you are.[24]

- *Some lies help you avoid punishment.* You are stopped for speeding and tell the officer you didn't know what the speed limit was—when you actually did—hoping you won't get a ticket.

- *Some lies help you protect yourself from distress.* When your aunt invites you to Thanksgiving dinner, you make up a story about having other plans so that you don't have to listen to your uncle's inevitable criticisms of you.

- *Some lies help you get revenge on someone.* To get back at a former romantic partner for cheating on you, you spread false rumors about that person to his or her friends.

- *Some lies help you hurt someone for no reason.* Out of boredom one night, you make up a rumor about one of your classmates and begin posting it on various class listservs.

- *Some lies protect you or your livelihood.* Out of fear of social rejection or employment discrimination, you deny having a mental illness, even though you are currently being treated for one.

- *Some lies amuse you.* During a conversation with the stranger sitting next to you on a long flight, you tell her completely made-up stories about yourself.[25]

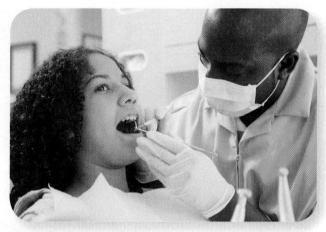

One of the many reasons people deceive is to make themselves look better in front of others. Are you ever less than honest with your dentist about how often you floss? If so, why? © *Lucidio Studio Inc/Flame/Corbis, RF*

Whatever people's motives for lying, there are many ways to deceive beyond simply making up information that is entirely untrue. For instance, telling your dentist you have been flossing regularly when in fact you haven't is one way to lie, but there are others as well. In fact, deceptive acts fall into two categories: acts of simulation and acts of dissimulation. Let's take a closer look at each.

Some Lies Falsify or Exaggerate

When people fabricate lies—that is, provide information that they know to be false or exaggerated—they are engaging in **acts of simulation.** Making up an excuse to break a date, telling a potential employer that you have a master's degree when you don't, and telling a friend you like his new car when you really think it's quite unattractive are all acts of simulation. In each of those examples, you're conveying a message you know isn't true for the purpose of getting your listener to believe it. People can engage in simulation through two different kinds of behaviors: falsification and exaggeration.

acts of simulation Forms of deception that involve fabricating information or exaggerating facts for the purpose of misleading others.

PEOPLE CAN LIE THROUGH FALSIFICATION. **Falsification** is outright lying—in other words, communicating false information as though it were true. Suppose, for example, that Ramón is applying for an apartment and he indicates on his application that he has rented before, when in fact he never has. In that case, Ramón has falsified his application; he has presented information that he knows to be false as though it were true. Similarly, if Sarah tells Annette that she is excited about the concert to which she is taking Annette for her birthday when she is actually dreading it, she is also falsifying. Even though Sarah has lied to benefit Annette—whereas Ramón has lied to benefit himself—they have both used falsification.

falsification A form of deception that involves presenting false, fabricated information as though it were true.

Studies have shown that falsification is one of the most common ways that people deceive others. In a diary study, for instance, communication scientist Sandra Metts found that people used falsification in almost half (48 percent) of their deception attempts.[26]

Job candidates sometimes exaggerate the details of their work history to appear more desirable to prospective employers. Research shows that exaggeration is a fairly common form of deception. © *Image Source/SuperStock, RF*

exaggeration A form of deception that involves inflating or overstating facts.

acts of dissimulation Forms of deception that involve omitting certain details that would change the nature of the story if they were known.

omission A form of deception that involves leaving consequential details out of one's story.

PEOPLE CAN LIE THROUGH EXAGGERATION. Another act of simulation is **exaggeration,** in which a person takes a fact that is true in principle and overstates it. Suppose, for example, you're interviewing for a job, and you exaggerate the level of responsibility you had at your last job to make it seem as though you're more qualified than you are. You may give completely true statements about what your responsibilities were, but you may overstate the level of those responsibilities to create a more favorable impression.[27] You might be tempted to think exaggeration isn't a form of deception. In fact, it does intentionally mislead others, so it is deceptive.

Some Lies Omit or Distort Information

When we engage in acts of simulation, we make statements or convey ideas that aren't true. In contrast, we engage in **acts of dissimulation** when we fail to convey information that, if known, would change the nature of our story. People can engage in dissimulation in two ways: through omission and through equivocation.

PEOPLE CAN LIE THROUGH OMISSION. **Omission** simply means leaving out consequential details of a story to create a false impression. Suppose Lukas is a salesperson who is attempting to sell a used car to Martha, an elderly woman living on a fixed income. While going over the details of the sale, Lukas tells Martha that "this car has 11,425 miles on it, it comes with a one-year limited warranty, and your car payment will be $185." He then indicates where she should sign to accept the agreement. Martha signs and takes the car home, only to discover later that her car payment is $185 *every two weeks.* When Lukas said her payment would be $185, she assumed that meant per month. Martha quickly realized she could not afford to keep the car, and she felt angry with Lukas for deceiving her.

Strictly speaking, everything Lukas told Martha was true—the car payment was, in fact, $185. Therefore, was Lukas being deceptive? Absolutely, because in all likelihood he knew Martha would assume that he was quoting the amount of her monthly payment and not her biweekly payment. Therefore, he knowingly created a false impression in Martha's mind, not by what he said but by what he did not say. Lukas may have told the truth, but he did not tell the *whole* truth, and the end effect was deceptive.

People can lie by omitting relevant information, such as by describing a car's positive features but failing to mention its limitations, or failing to define the terms of a loan. © *Barry Austin Photography/Photodisc/Getty Images, RF*

PEOPLE CAN LIE THROUGH EQUIVOCATION.   **Equivocation** means expressing information that is so vague or ambiguous that it creates the impression it has communicated a message it hasn't actually conveyed. Suppose Rena asks her waiter whether he thinks the pasta primavera is a good choice for dinner, and the waiter says, "It's one of our most popular dishes." Rena interprets that response to mean he thinks the pasta dish is a good choice. In fact, he never actually said that, did he?

Instead of answering Rena's question directly, her waiter gave an ambiguous response that he knew she would interpret as positive. That is an example of equivocation. Just like omission, equivocation deliberately creates a false impression, so it qualifies as a form of deception.

A brief review of the four primary forms of deception appears in the "At a Glance" box. Check out the "Got Skills?" box to practice your ability to identify those forms of deception in a conversation.

Finding out that you've been lied to can be distressing. You may feel as though the offender has violated your trust and irreparably harmed your relationship. You may also feel angry at being lied to—and perhaps even embarrassed that you believed the lie. Those negative feelings are probably magnified when the deceiver is someone to whom you are emotionally close, such as a family member, a good friend, or a romantic partner.

The distress generated by discovering they have been lied to makes many people eager to learn how to detect deception in others. Can *you* tell when you're being lied to? What are the best behaviors to look for as clues to deception? What makes certain people better liars than others? Let's explore each of those key questions.

equivocation A form of deception that involves giving vague, ambiguous answers to a question to create the false impression that one has answered it.

In Everyday Life: The courtroom oath to "tell the truth, the whole truth, and nothing but the truth" acknowledges that leaving out relevant details of a story can be as deceptive as falsifying information.

Talking Point: Many people would associate equivocation with the speech of politicians, who can be notorious for "talking around" a question without ever actually answering it.

Focus on Ethics: To discuss with the class: Are benevolent lies more ethical than malicious ones?

Media Note: In the instructor resources in the Online Learning Center, the video clip "Pulling the Weight of Work" illustrates some of the problems that acts of omission can create.

AT A GLANCE

Forms of Deception

Falsification	Passing off false or fabricated statements as though they were true
Exaggeration	Inflating or overstating information that is true in principle
Omission	Leaving out consequential pieces of information in one's story
Equivocation	Giving vague or ambiguous information to create a false impression

got skills?

IDENTIFYING DECEPTIVE FORMS

Practice crafting each form of deceptive message.

WHAT?	WHY?	HOW?	TRY!
Learn to generate the same deceptive message in multiple forms.	To identify the differences and similarities among forms of deception.	**1.** Review the four primary forms of deception (falsification, exaggeration, omission, and equivocation). **2.** For each form of deception, write out a question and then an answer that reflects that form. Identify the specific information you are including and excluding to make each answer deceptive.	**1.** Role-play a conversation with a classmate you don't know well, in which he or she asks you six to eight questions about your childhood. **2.** Respond to each question deceptively, using one of the four forms of deception. Use each form of deception at least once. **3.** After the conversation, ask your classmate to identify which form of deception was reflected in which answer, and correct any wrong responses. Repeat the process with you serving as questioner. **CONSIDER:** *How accurately could each of you identify the forms of deception your partner used?*

LEARN IT What are some common reasons why people deceive? How is exaggeration an act of simulation? What is the difference between omission and equivocation?

APPLY IT Revisit the list of reasons why people deceive that was presented at the beginning of this section. Select one reason, and then recall a situation when you used deception for that purpose. Write a short description of how you deceived the other person. Then write a description of how you may have served the same purpose *without* being deceptive.

REFLECT ON IT What motives for lying would you add to the list in this section? Whom do you most often notice exaggerating or equivocating?

3 Communication Behaviors and Deception

Psychologist Dr. Paul Ekman has spent much of his career identifying many of the verbal and nonverbal communication behaviors that are common in deceptive acts. In fact, he was the inspiration behind Tim Roth's character, Dr. Cal Lightman, on the Fox television series *Lie to Me*. As dramatized in the show, detecting deception successfully requires knowing what clues to look and listen for.

How good are *you* at distinguishing truth from deception? Before you answer, consider the following experiment. I put two average students, Machiko and Jody, in separate rooms. I go into the first room and tell Machiko how I spent my summer vacation. Meanwhile, Jody is alone in another room, doing nothing. Afterward, we all come back together, and I ask both Machiko and Jody whether I'm lying about my summer vacation.

Machiko could hear everything I said, listen to my tone of voice, and watch my body language to evaluate the believability of my story. Jody, however, was in another room and has no idea what I have said. Who will be more accurate in determining whether I have lied? Machiko, right? After all, Jody has no clue as to what I said and might as well flip a coin—at least that would provide a 50 percent chance of being right.

The truth is that Machiko would be more accurate, but not by much. Whereas Jody had a 50 percent chance of being right just by flipping a coin, Machiko's chance of being right—even after being in the room, hearing my story, and watching my body language—is only 55 percent, *just slightly better than if Machiko hadn't been there at all.* Research has shown that under normal conditions, the average person can detect deception about 55 percent of the time.[28] Even police interrogators, psychiatrists, customs officials, and polygraph examiners, whom you might expect to be good at detecting deception, typically do little better than the average person.[29]

Detecting Deception Is Difficult

Why don't we do any better than chance at detecting deception? One reason is that we often look for the wrong clues. How many times have you heard, for instance, that a lack of eye contact is the surest sign you're being lied to? In fact, that idea isn't true,

Focus on Scholarship: The names in this example—Machiko and Jody—are intentionally sex-neutral. Communication research has shown few, if any, systematic sex differences in the ability to detect deception or in the ability to deceive successfully.[i]

[i]See Burgoon, J. K., Blair, J. P., Buller, D. B., & Tilley, P. (2006). Sex differences in presenting and detecting deceptive messages. In K. Dindia & D. J. Canary (Eds.), *Sex differences and similarities in communication* (2nd ed., pp. 263–280). Mahwah, NJ: Lawrence Erlbaum Associates.

The character of Cal Lightman on the show *Lie to Me* was loosely based on the real-life psychologist Paul Ekman, whose research has identified behaviors related to deception. © *Isabella Vosmikova/Fox/Everett Collection*

One reason many of us aren't very good at detecting deception is that we want to believe that others are being honest with us. Unless we have a specific reason not to, we tend to believe most of what other people tell us. © Simon Jarratt/ Fancy/Corbis, RF

truth bias The tendency to believe what someone says, in the absence of a reason not to.

as we'll see shortly. Obviously, the more attention we focus on the wrong clues to deception, the less we focus on the *right clues.* Paying attention to the wrong clues will keep us from being accurate much of the time.[30]

A second reason we're not very good lie detectors is that most of us want to believe most of what we hear. Unless we have a reason not to, we tend to believe what other people tell us. Researchers call that tendency the **truth bias.**[31] Why is the truth bias our default position? One reason is that we generally expect our communication with others to be pleasant, and being lied to can be very unpleasant.[32] Another reason is that it takes a great deal of mental energy to question everything we hear, so it's much easier for us to believe what we're told, unless we have a specific reason not to.[33]

Even though the average ability to detect deception is around 55 percent, we might do better if we know what to look for and what not to look for in people's behaviors. What are the clues that best indicate someone is lying?

Some Behaviors Are Common during Acts of Deception

For a long time, scientists in various disciplines tried to discover a foolproof method for detecting lies. So far, research has identified only a small number of behaviors that show any consistent relationship with deception, and none of them characterizes every lie or every liar.[34] Let's now take a look at some of the verbal and nonverbal behaviors that show reliable associations with lying, and identify some behaviors that do not.

FALSE INFORMATION IS OFTEN INCONSISTENT. One of the most straightforward clues to deception is inconsistency in the information presented. Let's say you call in sick to work on Friday so you can leave town early for a weekend beach trip. While you're swimming on Saturday, however, your sunscreen washes off, and your boss sees you back at work on Monday with an obvious sunburn. That situation creates information inconsistency: The visual information provided by your appearance contradicts your story about being sick at home. Moreover, because it's hard to fake a sunburn, your boss correctly infers that you faked your illness.

Sometimes liars betray themselves with information inconsistency, and sometimes other people betray them. In fact, communication scholars Hee Sun Park, Timothy Levine, Steven McCornack, Kelly Morrison, and Merissa Ferrara have discovered that information provided by third parties is one of the most common ways people find out they've been lied to.[35] Referring to our previous example, suppose you didn't get sunburned, but your boss's daughter also happened to be at the beach and later innocently mentioned to her father that she had seen you. Clearly, she wasn't trying to get you into trouble. However, because her information was inconsistent with your story about being sick, the implication was that you did not tell the truth.

DECEIVERS OFTEN COMMIT SPEECH ERRORS. When people are telling lies, they often make more speech errors than usual. Speech errors include behaviors such as taking excessively long pauses in the middle of a conversation (while thinking up a story), using numerous vocal fillers such as "um" and "uh," starting to speak but then stopping abruptly, and taking an extra long time to respond to people's questions.[36]

If you call in sick when you're at the beach, inconsistencies between your story and your sunburn might alert your boss to the deception. © EyesWideOpen/Getty Images

Why are deceivers more prone to making those errors? The answer is that people often feel guilty or nervous (or both) when they are lying, and those emotions can cause their speech patterns to become less fluent than normal.[37] The key is knowing how smooth and fluent a person's speech *usually* is, so that you can discern when that person is making more speech errors than he or she typically does.

DECEPTION OFTEN INCREASES VOCAL PITCH. As discussed in the Nonverbal Communication chapter, vocal pitch describes how high or low a person's voice is. Sometimes, such as when you wake up in the morning, your pitch is lower than normal and your voice sounds deeper than usual. When you feel nervous, excited, or agitated, the opposite occurs: Your pitch sounds higher than normal.[38]

Because people often become stressed or nervous when they're being deceptive, their pitch tends to rise when they lie.[39] Moreover, because they may not even be aware they are speaking in a higher pitch than normal, increased vocal pitch can be a particularly good clue to deception. A now-classic study by communication researchers Joyce Bauchner, Elyse Kaplan, and Gerald Miller found that vocal characteristics such as pitch are more reliable clues to deception than any other nonverbal behavior.[40]

TWO EYE BEHAVIORS ARE ASSOCIATED WITH LYING. The "Fact or Fiction?" box explores how a lack of eye contact is a very poor clue that someone is lying. Much better indicators of deception are *eye blinking* and *pupil dilation* (or widening). If you are like the average person, you blink about 15 to 20 times per minute to keep a consistent layer of moisture on the surface of the eyes.[41] When you feel nervous or anxious, however—the way you might if you were lying to someone—you blink more often, as a way for your body to expend your nervous energy.[42] In addition, your pupils dilate when you get nervous or aroused.[43] Several studies have demonstrated that when people are telling lies, their pupils dilate more than usual.[44]

Talking Point: "Speech errors" is a good example of a behavior that shows a strong relationship with deception yet can also occur for reasons that have nothing to do with a speaker's honesty. This exemplifies that there is no foolproof behavioral clue to deception.

Talking Point: A technique called *voice stress analysis* analyzes the sound of the voice in an attempt to detect signs of distress, called vocal tremors, which may reflect deception. The accuracy of the procedure is still largely unknown.

fact **or** *fiction*? MOST PEOPLE CAN'T LOOK YOU IN THE EYE WHILE LYING

Ask almost anyone how to tell when you're being lied to, and the first response you are likely to get is: *Look for a lack of eye contact.* Furthermore, self-help books, websites, and even song lyrics repeat this common knowledge—after all, everyone knows that someone who's lying can't look you in the eye. Is that idea fact or fiction?

Although it may be a fact for children, it is absolutely a fiction for adults. Once we emerge from childhood, eye contact becomes a very *unreliable* clue to deception.

© Westend61/Getty Images, RF

Why? The answer is that eye contact is very easy to control. Much of what happens to us when we feel nervous—such as getting clammy hands or feeling dry in the mouth—is uncontrollable. Most of us, however, have a great deal of control over what we're looking at. Thus, many adults have little problem looking others in the eye while lying to them.

Moreover, because skilled communicators know that people equate the lack of eye contact with deception, they deliberately maintain normal eye contact when they lie so that the other person won't get suspicious. The eyes may be the windows to the soul, as the saying goes, but eye contact is no window to honesty!

FROM ME TO YOU

If you think someone is lying to you, be careful not to jump to conclusions. Remember that there is almost a 50 percent chance you are wrong. Even reliable clues to deception, such as speech errors and higher vocal pitch, can occur for reasons entirely unrelated to lying. If you notice these behaviors, pay attention to other characteristics that might also be clues to deception, such as information inconsistency. If you believe you've been lied to, talk to the person in private and convey the reasons for your suspicion.

Source: DePaulo, B. M., Lindsay, J. J., Malone, B. E., Muhlenbruck, L., Charlton, K., & Cooper, H. (2003). Cues to deception. *Psychological Bulletin, 129*, 74–118.

Talking Point: A genuine smile is also called a Duchenne smile.

Focus on Scholarship: Some researchers are currently studying *microexpressions*—fleeting expressions of emotion on the face, to try to discover a more foolproof method of detecting deception.[ii] As with voice stress analysis, research on the accuracy of microexpressions is ongoing but still inconclusive.

[ii] Porter, S., & ten Brinke, L. (2008). Reading between the lies: Identifying concealed and falsified emotions in universal facial expressions. *Psychological Science, 19*, 508–514.

LIARS OFTEN USE FALSE SMILES. On average, people don't smile any more or any less than normal when lying.[45] What tends to change, however, is the *type* of smile people use during deception. Specifically, deceivers are more likely than truth tellers to use a *false smile,* the kind of smile people wear when they want to look happier than they really are.[46] One of the distinctive features of genuine smiles is that they cause the skin at the sides of the eyes to wrinkle. In contrast, false smiles don't, so the upper and lower halves of the face seem inconsistent with each other. People often use false smiles when they're feeling distressed but are trying to hide it, as they might if they feel nervous or guilty about lying.

MANY LIARS USE MINIMAL BODY MOVEMENT. When we get nervous, many of us move around more—we may fidget or pace back and forth more than usual. That is our body's way of getting rid of nervous energy, so it might seem reasonable to expect that people exhibit more of such random movement when they're lying than when they're telling the truth. Surprisingly, research tells us just the opposite: Deceivers exhibit *fewer* body movements than truth tellers do. In particular, communication studies have found that compared with truth tellers, deceivers display fewer hand movements, less nodding, and fewer leg and foot movements.[47]

AT A GLANCE

Communication While Lying

Here's a review of how several behaviors tend to be affected by one's attempts to deceive. A "+" sign means the behavior usually increases during deception; a "–" sign means it usually decreases. "NC" means the behavior usually doesn't increase or decrease during deceptive acts.

Behavior	Typical Change, If Any
Information inconsistency	+
Speech errors	+
Blinking rate	+
Eye contact	NC
Pupil dilation	+
False smiles	+
Genuine smiles	NC
Vocal pitch	+
Body movement	–

Talking Point: Because no deception indicator is foolproof, people can act as though they're lying even when they aren't. In such cases, attempts to detect deception would produce false positives. The risk of false positives is one of the primary reasons why polygraph results are inadmissible in U.S. criminal trials.

In the IM: The out-of-class activity "Naive Theories of Deception" has students poll others about what clues they look for when they suspect deception.

Why do deceivers move less rather than more? One possible explanation is that to avoid getting caught, deceivers may try so hard to prevent themselves from pacing or fidgeting that they end up appearing rigid or tense. Another possible reason is that there are so many things to think about while lying (such as whether the story is believable and whether the hearer seems suspicious) that people simply don't pay as much attention to their nonverbal behaviors as they normally do.

The "At a Glance" box summarizes what research tells us about communication behaviors people use while lying. Before we move on, it's important to remember two things about this list of behaviors. The first is that these are not the only behaviors related to deception. Rather, they're just some of the behaviors that communication research has identified as reliable clues to lying. Second, none of these clues is foolproof. Even though people tend to make more speech errors, use more false smiles, blink more frequently, exhibit a higher vocal pitch, and move less when they lie, they may do all those behaviors for other reasons as well. Communication scientists have not yet discovered any foolproof clues to deception, and chances are good they never will.[48] Practice your ability to detect deception by doing the activity in the "Got Skills?" box.

Now that we've examined some of the behaviors to look for to detect deception, such as information inconsistency, and some of the behaviors to ignore, such as eye contact, let's take a look at the various factors that influence our skill at detecting lies when we communicate interpersonally.

 **got skills?**

DETECTING DECEPTION

Test your skill at separating deception from truth.

WHAT?

Practice your ability to detect deception in conversation.

WHY?

To improve your skill at distinguishing truthful and deceptive statements.

HOW?

1. Watch and listen to a classmate answer questions to determine if any of the answers are deceptive.

2. Focus your attention specifically on inconsistent information, speech errors, increased vocal pitch, body movement, false smiling, and increased blinking, because those are observable signs that deception may be occurring. Remember, however, that none of those signs is foolproof. Any of them could occur for reasons unrelated to deception.

TRY!

1. Tell your classmate that you are going to ask six questions and that you want him or her to provide deceptive answers to all, some, or none of them. Have your partner write down ahead of time which question(s), if any, he or she plans to answer deceptively.

2. Formulate six questions of roughly equal specificity to ask, such as "What did you do last Saturday?" "Whom do you most admire and why?" and "Why are you attending this school?" Ask the questions one at a time and note the answers.

3. Afterward, go through the questions with your classmate and indicate which answers, if any, you thought were deceptive. Identify the sign(s) that led you to believe certain answers were deceptive. Then have your classmate reveal which answers were indeed deceptive, if any.

CONSIDER: *What verbal or nonverbal behaviors made you suspicious of your classmate's answers?*

LEARN IT Why is deception so difficult to detect? Which verbal and nonverbal behaviors are reliable clues that someone is lying?

APPLY IT Conduct an informal survey of your friends and co-workers to see which communication behaviors they rely on the most to detect deception. How much consistency do you find in their answers? Do they identify primarily verbal or nonverbal behaviors?

REFLECT ON IT How would you rate your own ability to detect deception? With whom do you have the strongest truth bias?

4 Detecting Lies in Different Contexts

Is it really possible to tell if you're being lied to? Many characteristics of people or communication situations affect our ability to distinguish lies from the truth. We'll review a number of these characteristics in this section. Use this information in your interpersonal communication to improve your skill at detecting deceit.

Before reading this section, complete the short quiz in "Assess Your Skills." That exercise will help you identify your assumptions about deception detection so you can highlight what you learn in this section.

Familiarity Affects Our Ability to Detect Deception

Is it easier to detect deception when you are talking to strangers or to friends? On the one hand, you might be tempted to say "friends" because you know them better. You know how they normally speak and act, so it's easy to tell when they're not being themselves. On the other hand, we have a stronger truth bias for friends than for strangers,[49] so you might think you are more likely to believe what you hear from

In Everyday Life: If specific friends or family members have lied to us in the past, however, our truth bias—which would normally be quite strong in these close relationships—can actually become a *lie bias,* causing us to regard anything we hear from those persons with suspicion.

assess your skills | KNOWING THE TRUTH ABOUT LYING

It is easier to detect deception accurately in some situations than in others—but do you know which? *Before you read Section 4 of this chapter,* mark whether each statement below is true or false based on your best estimate.

True or False? T/F

1. It is easier to detect deception when you are talking to a stranger than to a friend. _____

2. Expressive people lie more often than unexpressive people. _____

3. Detecting deception is harder with people from other cultures than with people from your own culture. _____

4. We are usually more successful at lying when we are highly motivated to lie successfully. _____

5. Most people are better at detecting deception when they are suspicious than when they are not. _____

6. A lie communicated by e-mail is more likely to succeed than a lie communicated face to face. _____

Set aside your answers to this quiz until you have finished reading Section 4, "Detecting Lies in Different Contexts." Then come back to these questions and see which answers you got right. For any that you got wrong, write a short sentence indicating why you marked the answer you did. Doing so can help you identify any incorrect assumptions you may have about deception detection.

a friend than from a stranger. That would make it easier to detect deception from a stranger than from a friend. Depending on your perspective, then, *both* answers are plausible. So, which one is correct?

To solve this puzzle, communication scientists conducted an experiment in which individual participants made false or misleading statements to another person.[50] Half of the participants were paired with a close friend, and the other half with a stranger. After the conversations were concluded, the friends and the strangers were asked to report how truthful they thought the participants were being. The results showed that people were more accurate at detecting deception by strangers than by friends. In other words, the participants lied more successfully to their friends than they did to strangers. The researchers concluded that the truth bias prevented friends from noticing when they were being deceived.

Expressive People Are Better Liars

You probably know people who are very expressive; they tend to be outgoing, uninhibited, and very demonstrative of their emotions. According to several studies, expressive people are more successful at deception than unexpressive people, for at least two reasons.[51] First, expressive people tend to be more aware and in better control of their own communication behaviors than unexpressive people. Therefore, the conversational style they adopt when they are lying may appear to be more fluent and normal.[52]

Second, expressive communicators tend to be more aware of other people's behaviors, so they may be more skilled at anticipating a hearer's suspicion and correcting their behavior to allay those suspicions.[53] That doesn't necessarily mean that expressive people lie more often than unexpressive people.[54] But it does mean that they tend to be better at it when they do lie.

Highly expressive people don't necessarily lie more frequently than others—but their lies are often more believable. © *John Fedele/Blend Images, RF*

Talking Point: Highly expressive people are often high self-monitors, and research has shown that high self-monitors are better than low self-monitors at deceiving others successfully.

Culture Matters, but Only Sometimes

We've seen that the average person detects deception only about 55 percent of the time. Most studies of detection ability, however, have involved speakers and listeners who share the same cultural background. What if you're listening to someone whose culture is different from yours? Would that difference make it harder to detect deception?

Common sense suggests so, because you may not be familiar with another culture's communication practices. If you're not familiar with the way a person behaves when communicating under normal circumstances, then how can you identify changes in those behaviors when the person is lying? In line with that assumption, an early research study concluded that people are in fact much more accurate at detecting deception *within* cultures than *between* cultures.[55]

When we can both see and hear a speaker, that speaker's culture makes little difference in our ability to detect deception. © *AP Images/Cao haigen/Imaginechina*

In that study, however, participants were required to judge deception solely on the basis of *visual* cues. They watched videos of two people in a conversation but were unable to hear what those people were saying. As a result, they were unable to detect information inconsistency or listen for vocal cues. Rather, they had to base their judgments entirely on the behaviors they could *see*.

The researchers later repeated the study, but this time they allowed the participants to *hear* what the speakers were saying. When they did so, they discovered that the participants were equally able to detect deception by speakers of their own culture and speakers of other cultures.[56] We can likely conclude from those results that cultural differences can affect our ability to detect deception, but only when we have limited access to what the speaker is saying. In normal face-to-face conversation, culture appears to matter less.

Motivation Affects Our Ability to Deceive

Suppose you felt that you had to lie but the consequences of getting caught were severe, such as being expelled from school or going to jail. You'd probably be highly motivated to lie successfully—but would that help or hurt you? We often perform better when we're highly motivated. According to social psychologist Bella DePaulo, however, that observation doesn't apply to lying. Her hypothesis, called the **motivation impairment effect,** maintains that when people are engaged in high-stakes lies, their motivation to succeed will backfire by making their nonverbal performance *less* believable than normal.[57]

Why does that happen? The answer is that when the consequences of getting caught in a lie are severe, we experience a great deal of nervous energy, which we have to control if we are to succeed in being deceptive. The harder we try to

> **motivation impairment effect** A hypothesis that motivation to succeed in a high-stakes lie will impair a deceiver's nonverbal performance, making the lie less likely to be believed.

control our nervous energy, however, the more rigid, insincere, and unnatural we can end up looking and sounding. Put simply, when people tell high-stakes lies, their motivation to succeed ultimately will impair their ability to pass off deception as truth.[58] In contrast, because low-stakes lies don't produce the same degree of nervous arousal, DePaulo's theory does not predict that motivation to succeed will backfire when people attempt a low-stakes lie.

Suspicion May Not Improve Deception Detection

When we feel suspicious about what someone is telling us, we tend to scrutinize that person's behavior and message more than usual. Therefore, it seems logical to assume we are better able to detect deception when we're suspicious than when we aren't. That doesn't seem to be the case, however. Research tells us that even though suspicion causes people to think they're being lied to, it doesn't always make them any better at spotting deception.[59] In fact, some studies have shown that suspicion can actually make people *worse* at detecting lies, not better.[60]

One reason why suspicion might impair our detection ability is suggested by *interpersonal deception theory,* proposed by scholars David Buller and Judee Burgoon.[61] Interpersonal deception theory argues that skilled liars can detect when people are suspicious and then adapt their behavior to appear more honest.

Suppose, for instance, that Eliah's new doctor asks him how often he exercises. To make a good impression, Eliah exaggerates, saying he swims at least four times a week. He can immediately tell that his doctor is suspicious of his answer, so he adapts his behavior to make himself appear honest. He makes certain he is speaking with a normal vocal pitch and without committing excessive speech errors. He avoids nervous laughter, false smiles, and excessive blinking. He makes sure that he is moving and gesturing normally. Because he notices his doctor's suspicion, that is, he can make certain

Despite a history of deception that makes each of them highly suspicious of the other, research suggests that *Empire's* Cookie and Lucious may be unable to detect one another's lies. © *FOX/Getty Images*

he is communicating in ways that signal honesty rather than deception. As a result, his doctor eventually believes Eliah, even though he is being dishonest.

Another reason why suspicion can reduce our ability to detect deception is what researchers call the *Othello error.* That error occurs when a listener's suspicion makes a truthful speaker appear to be lying even though she or he isn't. Let's say Maggie is explaining to a school nurse that her 6-year-old son bruised the side of his face by falling off his bed. Because the nurse sees physically abused children frequently, she has suspicions about the truthfulness of Maggie's account. Maggie senses the nurse's suspicions and begins to feel defensive, which makes her appear nervous and flustered. She begins to fidget, makes speech errors, and uses false smiles. Noticing those behaviors, the nurse concludes that Maggie is lying. Maggie, however, is being completely truthful. She looks and sounds deceptive only because the nurse's obvious suspicion has made her nervous. In that instance, the nurse has been inaccurate in detecting deception—not by believing a lie but by failing to believe the truth.[62]

Context Affects Our Ability to Spot Lies

Suppose Stan's regional manager directed him to file a report about the company's quarterly earnings with the state auditor's office. He told Stan that the report wasn't due for six weeks but that it needed to be filed by the deadline or the company would incur financial penalties. With so much time before the deadline, Stan kept putting the assignment aside, focusing on more pressing projects. By the time he remembered it, it was three days overdue.

Fearing that his negligence might cost him his job, Stan chooses to lie to his manager about why the report was late. He has several options for how to deliver his lie: He could do it in person, over the telephone, by leaving a voice mail message, or by sending an e-mail. Which option gives him the best chance for success? On the one hand, we might say that an **interactive context,** such as a face-to-face or telephone conversation, helps Stan the most, because he can watch and listen for signs of suspicion from his manager and then adapt his behavior accordingly. On the other hand, a **noninteractive context,** such as voice mail or e-mail, may be best because it gives Stan the most control over his message.

Communication researchers have found that lies are more likely to succeed in an interactive context than in a noninteractive one—but only when the speaker is lying to a *stranger.*[63] Apparently, interacting directly with speakers makes people more likely to believe what those speakers are saying. One possible explanation for that finding is that interactivity helps create a sense of connection with someone else that is lacking in noninteractive contexts. In addition, when people are engaged in conversations, they pay more attention to their own communication behaviors than to the behaviors of others. Consequently, listeners might be less likely to notice any signs of deception displayed by the speaker.[64]

If, however, the speaker and the hearer are already friends, then the interactivity of the context doesn't seem to matter. In those cases, lies are equally successful in interactive and noninteractive contexts. Perhaps if friends already feel an emotional connection with each other, then communicating in interactive contexts no longer provides an advantage.

Familiarity, expressiveness, culture, motivation, suspicion, and interactivity certainly aren't the only characteristics that influence our detection skills. Yet each of those factors can play an important role in our ability to detect deception successfully.

CONNECT: SmartBook helps your students improve their comprehension of this chapter and boost their retention of that knowledge over time. You can even customize which sections of a SmartBook chapter are visible to students to help focus their study time.

interactive context A context for communicating in which participants can see and/or hear each other and react to each other in real time (for example, face-to-face conversation, telephone conversation).

noninteractive context A context for communicating in which the participants cannot react to each other in real time (for example, a voice mail message, an e-mail message).

In the IM: The in-class exercise "Detecting Prepared and Spontaneous Lies" lets students practice their abilities to detect deception.

When people communicate with strangers, they are less likely to be caught lying if they're talking face-to-face than if they're exchanging e-mail messages. Interactivity heightens our truth bias, but only with strangers. With friends, the mode of communication doesn't affect the ability to detect lying. © *Veer/ Somos Images/Getty Images, RF*

Although deception is relatively common in interpersonal communication, it can sometimes cause great distress. When deception is discovered in a personal relationship, it can lead to conflict and to feelings of anger and betrayal. We often find it difficult to forgive people who have lied to us, let alone to trust them again.

In this chapter, you've been introduced to many skills for detecting interpersonal deception, and previous chapters have introduced you to skills for managing conflict and maintaining your interpersonal relationships. Armed with those skills, you may find it easier to respond to the emotional distress of deception and to repair the emotional damage it can cause.

In the IM: You can now access the end-of-chapter Discussion Questions and the Research Library in the Instructor's Manual for each chapter.

LEARN IT Is it easier to detect deception from strangers or from friends? Why are expressive people better at lying than unexpressive people? How do cultural differences affect our ability to detect deception? What is the motivation impairment effect? How does suspicion affect our ability to detect deception? Are lies easier to detect in interactive or noninteractive contexts?

APPLY IT Sharpen your deception-detection skills by adopting an attitude of cautiously accepting information, particularly when it comes from highly expressive people. Train yourself to look beyond their expressive behaviors and to question the credibility of what you're hearing.

REFLECT ON IT When do you feel suspicious of others? With whom would you find it the most difficult to be deceptive?

MASTER the chapter

1 The Nature of Interpersonal Deception (p. 373)

- Deception occurs when a speaker knowingly and intentionally transmits false information to create a false belief in the hearer.
- Deceptive acts have three basic elements: the speaker knows the information is false, the speaker transmits the information on purpose, and the speaker tries to make the hearer believe that the information is true.
- Deception is especially common in the service of politeness and in computer-mediated communication.

2 The Diversity of Deceptive Acts (p. 380)

- People have several motives for lying, some of which are benevolent, some of which are malicious, and some of which are benign.
- Some deceptive acts are acts of simulation; these include falsification and exaggeration.
- Some deceptive acts are acts of dissimulation; these include omission and equivocation.

3 Communication Behaviors and Deception (p. 384)

- Detecting deception is often very difficult, partly because people often have a truth bias.
- Behaviors common during deceptive attempts include information inconsistency, speech errors, increased blinking, pupil dilation, false smiles, increased vocal pitch, and decreased body movement.

4 Detecting Lies in Different Contexts (p. 391)

- People are more accurate at detecting deception from strangers than from friends, on average.
- Expressive people are often more successful at lying than are unexpressive people.
- Cultural differences appear to matter only when the hearer has limited access to what the speaker is saying.
- Motivation to succeed at lying doesn't always help, and in the case of high-stakes deception it can actually impair an individual's ability to succeed.
- Suspicion does not necessarily improve a person's deception-detection ability.
- Deception detection is higher in noninteractive contexts than in interactive contexts, but only for strangers.

KEY TERMS

acts of dissimulation (p. 382)
acts of simulation (p. 381)
deception (p. 375)
equivocation (p. 383)

exaggeration (p. 382)
falsification (p. 381)
interactive context (p. 395)
motivation impairment effect (p. 393)

noninteractive context (p. 395)
omission (p. 382)
truth bias (p. 386)

connect

To maximize your study time, check out CONNECT to access the SmartBook study module for this chapter, watch videos, and explore other resources.

Glossary

A

accommodating A strategy for managing conflict that involves giving in to the other party's needs and desires while subordinating one's own.

action tendencies Motivations to act in a particular way when experiencing an emotion.

acts of dissimulation Forms of deception that involve omitting certain details that would change the nature of the story if they were known.

acts of simulation Forms of deception that involve fabricating information or exaggerating facts for the purpose of misleading others.

adaptor A gesture used to satisfy a personal need.

affect display A gesture that communicates emotion.

agreeableness One's tendency to be pleasant, accommodating, and cooperative.

alexithymia A personality trait limiting a person's ability to understand and describe emotions.

ambiguous language Language having more than one possible meaning.

amygdala A cluster of neurons in the brain that largely controls the body's fear response.

androgyny A gender role distinguished by a combination of masculine and feminine characteristics.

anger An emotional response to being wronged.

approach behaviors Communication behaviors that signal one's interest in getting to know someone.

artifact An object or a visual feature of an environment with communicative value.

asexuality A sexual orientation characterized by a general lack of interest in sex.

attribution An explanation for an observed behavior.

autonomy face The need to avoid being imposed upon by others.

avoidance behaviors Communication behaviors that signal one's lack of interest in getting to know someone.

avoiding A strategy for managing conflict that involves ignoring or failing to deal with the conflict.

avoiding stage The stage of relationship dissolution when partners create physical and emotional distance between each other.

B

bisexuality A sexual orientation characterized by sexual interest in both women and men.

bonding stage The stage of relationship development when people publicly announce their commitment to each other.

breadth The range of topics about which one person self-discloses to another.

C

channel A pathway through which messages are conveyed.

channel-lean context A communication context involving few channels at once.

channel-rich context A communication context involving many channels at once.

chronemics The use of time.

circumscribing stage The stage of relationship dissolution characterized by decreased quality and quantity of communication between partners.

closed-mindedness The tendency not to listen to anything with which one disagrees.

co-cultures Groups of people who share values, customs, and norms related to mutual interests or characteristics beyond their national citizenship.

coercive power Power based on the ability to punish.

cognitive complexity The ability to understand a given situation in multiple ways.

collaborating A strategy for managing conflict that involves working toward a solution that meets both parties' needs.

collectivistic culture A culture that places greater emphasis on loyalty to the family, workplace, or community than on the needs of the individual.

commitment A desire to stay in a relationship.

communication climate The emotional tone of a relationship.

communication codes Verbal and nonverbal behaviors, such as idioms and gestures, that characterize a culture and distinguish it from other cultures.

communication competence Communicating in ways that are effective and appropriate for a given situation.

communication privacy management (CPM) theory Theory that explains how people manage the tension between privacy and disclosure.

comparison level A person's realistic expectation of what the person wants and thinks he or she deserves from a relationship.

comparison level for alternatives A person's assessment of how good or bad his or her current relationship is, compared with other options.

competence face The need to be respected and viewed as competent and intelligent.

competing A strategy for managing conflict in which one's goal is to win while the other party loses.

competitive interrupting Using interruptions to take control of a conversation.

complementary relationship A relationship between parties of unequal power.

compromising A strategy for managing conflict in which both parties give up something they want so that both can receive something they want.

confirmation bias The tendency to pay attention only to information that supports one's values and beliefs while discounting or ignoring information that doesn't.

confirming messages Behaviors that indicate how much we value another person.

connotative meaning A word's implied or secondary meaning, in addition to its literal meaning.

contempt A feeling of superiority over, and disrespect for, others.

contemptuous behaviors The expression of insults and attacks on another's self-worth.

content dimension Literal information that is communicated by a message. See also *denotative meaning.*

context The physical or psychological environment in which communication occurs.

credibility The extent to which others find someone's words and actions trustworthy.

critical listening Listening with the goal of evaluating or analyzing what one hears.

criticism The expression of complaints about another party.

culture The system of learned and shared symbols, language, values, and norms that distinguish one group of people from another.

D

deception The knowing and intentional transmission of information to create a false belief in the hearer.

decode To interpret or give meaning to a message.

defamation Language that harms a person's reputation or image.

defensive behaviors Tactics that cast the self as a victim and deny responsibility for one's own role in a conflict.

defensiveness Excessive concern with guarding oneself against the threat of criticism.

demand–withdraw pattern A pattern of behavior in which one party makes demands and the other party withdraws from the conversation.

denotative meaning A word's literal meaning or dictionary definition.

depression A physical illness involving excessive fatigue, insomnia, changes in weight, feelings of worthlessness, and/or thoughts of suicide or death.

depth The intimacy of the topics about which one person self-discloses to another.

dialectical tensions Conflicts between two important but opposing needs or desires.

differentiating stage The stage of relationship dissolution when partners begin to see their differences as undesirable or annoying.

direct conflict An open, straightforward approach to engaging in conflict.

disconfirming messages Behaviors that imply a lack of regard for another person.

disgust A feeling of revulsion in reaction to something offensive.

disinhibition effect The tendency to say or do things in one environment (such as online) that one would not say or do in most other environments.

display rules Unwritten codes that govern the ways people manage and express emotions.

divorce The legal discontinuation of a marriage.

downward communication Messages sent to people at lower levels of an organization, such as subordinates.

dyad A pair of people.

E

egocentric Unable to take another person's perspective.

emblem A gesture with a direct verbal translation.

emoji Cartoon depictions of faces and other objects.

emoticons Textual representations of facial expressions.

emotion The body's multidimensional response to any event that enhances or inhibits one's goals.

emotional contagion The tendency to mimic the emotional experiences and expressions of others.

emotional intelligence The ability to perceive and understand emotions, use emotions to facilitate thought, and manage emotions constructively.

emotional reappraisal The process of changing how one thinks about the situation that gave rise to a negative emotion so that the effect of the emotion is diminished.

empathic listening Listening in order to experience what another person is thinking or feeling.

empathy The ability to think and feel as others do.

encode To put an idea into language or gesture.

envy The desire for something another person has.

equity theory A theory predicting that a good relationship is one in which a person's ratio of costs and rewards is equal to that of the person's partner.

equivocation A form of deception that involves giving vague, ambiguous answers to a question to create the false impression that one has answered it.

ethics A code of morality or a set of ideas about what is right.

ethnicity An individual's perception of his or her ancestry or heritage.

ethnocentrism Systematic preference for characteristics of one's own culture.

ethos A speaker's respectability, trustworthiness, and moral character.

F

euphemism A vague, mild expression that symbolizes something more blunt or harsh.

evaluative feedback A reply that offers an assessment of what the speaker has said or done.

exaggeration A form of deception that involves inflating or overstating facts.

experimenting stage The stage of relationship development when individuals have conversations to learn more about each other.

expert power Power that derives from one's expertise, talent, training, specialized knowledge, or experience.

explicit rule A rule about behavior that has been clearly articulated.

expressive talk Verbal communication whose purpose is to express emotions and build relationships.

extroversion One's tendency to be sociable and outgoing.

F

face A person's desired public image.

face needs Components of one's desired public image.

face-threatening act Any behavior that threatens one or more face needs.

facework The behaviors one uses to project one's desired public image to others.

facial display The use of facial expression for communication.

falsification A form of deception that involves presenting false, fabricated information as though it were true.

family of origin The family in which one grows up (often consisting of one's parents and siblings).

family of procreation The family one starts as an adult (often consisting of one's spouse and children).

fear The mind and body's reaction to perceived danger.

feedback Verbal and nonverbal responses to a message.

fellowship face The need to feel liked and accepted by others.

femininity A gender role, typically assigned to women, that emphasizes expressive, nurturing behavior.

fundamental attribution error The tendency to attribute others' behaviors to internal rather than external causes.

G

gender role A set of expectations for appropriate behavior that a culture typically assigns to an individual based on his or her biological sex.

gesticulation The use of arm and hand movements to communicate.

glazing over Daydreaming during the time not spent listening.

gossip The sharing of an individual's personal information with a third party without the individual's consent.

grief The emotional process of dealing with profound loss.

H

halo effect The tendency to attribute positive qualities to physically attractive people.

happiness A state of contentment, joy, pleasure, and cheer.

haptics The study of how people use touch to communicate.

hate speech A form of profanity meant to degrade, intimidate, or dehumanize groups of people.

heterosexuality A sexual orientation characterized by sexual interest in members of the other sex.

high-contact culture A culture in which people touch frequently and maintain little personal distance with one another.

high-context culture A culture in which verbal communication is often ambiguous, and meaning is drawn from contextual cues, such as facial expressions and tone of voice.

high-power-distance culture A culture in which much or most of the power is concentrated in a few people, such as royalty or a ruling political party.

homosexuality A sexual orientation characterized by sexual interest in members of one's own sex.

HURIER model A model of effective listening that involves hearing, understanding, remembering, interpreting, evaluating, and responding.

I

identity See *self-concept.*

illustrator A gesture that enhances or clarifies a verbal message.

image The way one wishes to be seen or perceived by others.

image management The process of projecting one's desired public image.

immediacy behavior Nonverbal behavior that conveys attraction or affiliation.

implicit rule A rule about behavior that has not been clearly articulated but is nonetheless understood.

indirect conflict The expression of conflict through negative behaviors that ignore the underlying disagreement.

individualistic culture A culture that emphasizes individuality and responsibility to oneself.

infidelity Sexual involvement with someone other than one's romantic partner.

information overload The state of being overwhelmed by the amount of information one takes in.

informational listening Listening to learn something.

in-group A group of people with whom one identifies.

initiating stage The stage of relationship development when people meet and interact for the first time.

instrumental needs Practical, everyday needs.

instrumental talk Verbal communication whose purpose is to solve problems and accomplish tasks.

integrating stage The stage of relationship development when a deep commitment has formed, and there is a strong sense that

the relationship has its own identity.

intensifying stage The stage of relationship development when individuals move from being acquaintances to being close friends.

interactive context A context for communicating in which participants can see and/or hear each other and react to each other in real time (for example, face-to-face conversation, telephone conversation).

interdependence A state in which each person's behaviors affect everyone else in the relationship.

interpersonal attraction Any force that draws people together to form a relationship.

interpersonal communication Communication that occurs between two people within the context of their relationship and that, as it evolves, helps them to negotiate and define their relationship.

interpersonal conflict An expressed struggle between interdependent parties who perceive incompatible goals, scarce resources, and interference from one another.

interpersonal perception The process of making meaning from the people in our environment and our relationships with them.

interpretation The process of assigning meaning to information that has been selected for attention and organized.

intimate distance The distance most people in Western cultures maintain with intimate partners; ranges from 0 to 1½ feet.

intrapersonal communication Communication with oneself.

investment The resources we put into our relationships.

I-statement A statement that claims ownership of one's thoughts or feelings.

J

jealousy The perception that an important relationship is being threatened by a third party.

Johari window A visual representation of components of the self that are known or unknown to the self and to others.

K

kinesics The study of movement.

L

language A structured system of symbols used for communicating meaning.

lateral communication Messages sent to people at the same level of an organization, such as co-workers or peers.

legitimate power Power based on one's legitimate status or position.

libel A defamatory statement made in print or in some other fixed medium.

liking A positive overall evaluation of another person.

listening The active process of making meaning out of another person's spoken message.

loaded language Terms that carry strongly positive or strongly negative connotations.

logos Listeners' ability to reason.

love The emotion of caring for, feeling attached to, and feeling deeply committed to someone.

low-contact culture A culture in which people touch infrequently and maintain relatively high levels of personal distance with one another.

low-context culture A culture in which verbal communication is expected to be explicit and is often interpreted literally.

low-power-distance culture A culture in which power is not highly concentrated in specific groups of people.

M

masculinity A gender role, typically assigned to men, that emphasizes strength, dominance, competition, and logical thinking.

mass communication Communication from one source to a large audience.

message Verbal and nonverbal elements of communication to which people give meaning.

metacommunication Communication about communication.

metaconflict Conflict about conflict.

meta-emotion An emotion about emotion.

model A formal description of a process.

monochronic A concept that treats time as a finite commodity that can be earned, saved, spent, and wasted.

monogamy Being in only one romantic relationship at a time and avoiding romantic or sexual involvement with others outside the relationship.

mood A feeling, often prolonged, that has no identifiable cause.

motivation impairment effect A hypothesis that motivation to succeed in a high-stakes lie will impair a deceiver's nonverbal performance, making the lie less likely to be believed.

N

nationality An individual's status as a citizen of a particular country.

need for affection One's need to give and receive expressions of love and appreciation.

need for control One's need to maintain a degree of influence in one's relationships.

need for inclusion One's need to belong to a social group and be included in the activities of others.

need to belong A hypothesis that says each of us is born with a fundamental drive to seek, form, maintain, and protect strong social relationships.

negativity bias The tendency to focus heavily on a person's negative attributes when forming a perception.

neuroticism One's tendency to think negative thoughts about oneself.

noise Anything that interferes with the encoding or decoding of a message.

non-evaluative feedback A reply that withholds assessment of what the speaker has said or done.

noninteractive context A context for communicating in which the participants cannot react to each other in real time (for example, a voice mail message, an e-mail message).

nonverbal channels The various behavioral forms that nonverbal communication takes.

nonverbal communication Behaviors and characteristics that convey meaning without the use of words.

norm of reciprocity A social expectation that resources and favors provided to one person in a relationship should be reciprocated by that person.

O

oculesics The study of eye behavior.

olfactics The study of the sense of smell.

omission A form of deception that involves leaving consequential details out of one's story.

one-across message A verbal message that seeks to neutralize relational control and power.

one-down message A verbal message that reflects acceptance of, or submission to, another person's power.

one-up message A verbal message through which the speaker attempts to exert dominance or gain control over the listener.

onomatopoeia A word formed by imitating the sound associated with its meaning.

organization The process of categorizing information that has been selected for attention.

out-group A group of people with whom one does not identify.

overattribution The tendency to attribute a range of behaviors to a single characteristic of a person.

over-benefited The state in which one's relational rewards exceed one's relational costs.

P

passion A secondary emotion consisting of joy and surprise, plus experiences of excitement and attraction for another.

passive aggression A pattern of behaving vengefully while denying that one has aggressive feelings.

pathos Listeners' emotions.

patriarchy A social system in which men exercise a majority of the power.

peer Someone of similar power or status to oneself.

perception The process of making meaning from the things we experience in the environment.

perceptual set A predisposition to perceive only what we want or expect to perceive.

personal distance The distance most people in Western cultures maintain with friends and relatives; ranges from 1½ to 4 feet.

personality The pattern of behaviors and ways of thinking that characterize a person.

physical attraction Attraction to someone's physical appearance.

polychronic A concept that treats time as an infinite resource rather than a finite commodity.

polygamy A practice in which one person is married to two or more spouses at the same time.

positivity bias The tendency to focus heavily on a person's positive attributes when forming a perception.

power The ability to manipulate, influence, or control other people or events.

predicted outcome value theory A theory predicting that we form relationships when we think the effort will be worth it.

primacy effect The tendency to emphasize the first impression over later impressions when forming a perception.

primary emotions Distinct emotional experiences not consisting of combinations of other emotions.

profanity A form of language considered vulgar, rude, or obscene in the context in which it is used.

proportionality The size of facial features relative to one another.

proxemics The study of spatial use.

pseudolistening Using feedback behaviors to give the false impression that one is listening.

public distance The distance most people in Western cultures maintain with public figures during a performance; ranges from 12 to 25 feet or more.

R

reason To make judgments about the world based on evidence rather than emotion or intuition.

rebuttal tendency The tendency to disrupt listening to internally debate a speaker's point and formulate a reply while the person is still speaking.

receiver The party who interprets a message.

recency effect The tendency to emphasize the most recent impression over earlier impressions when forming a perception.

reference groups The groups of people with whom one compares oneself in the process of social comparison.

referent power Power that derives from one's attraction to or admiration for another.

reflected appraisal The process whereby a person's self-concept is influenced by his or her beliefs concerning what other people think of the person.

reframing Changing the way you think about an interpersonal situation.

regulator A gesture that controls the flow of conversation.

relational dimension Signals about the relationship in which a message is being communicated.

relational maintenance behaviors Behaviors used to maintain and strengthen personal relationships.

reward power Power that derives from the ability to reward.

rituals Repetitive behaviors that have special meaning for a group or relationship.

S

sadness Emotion involving feeling unhappy, sorrowful, and discouraged, usually as a result of some form of loss.

Sapir-Whorf hypothesis The idea that language influences the ways that members of a culture see and think about the world.

secondary emotions Emotions composed of combinations of primary emotions.

selection The process of attending to a stimulus.

selective attention Listening only to what one wants to hear.

self-concept The set of stable ideas a person has about who he or she is; also known as *identity.*

self-disclosure The act of giving others information about oneself that one believes they do not already have.

self-esteem One's subjective evaluation of one's value and worth as a person.

self-fulfilling prophecy An expectation that gives rise to behaviors that cause the expectation to come true.

self-monitoring Awareness of one's behavior and how it affects others.

self-serving bias The tendency to attribute one's successes to internal causes and one's failures to external causes.

sexual orientation A characteristic determining the sex or sexes to which someone is sexually attracted.

similarity assumption One's tendency to presume that others think the same way he or she does.

skepticism The practice of evaluating the evidence for a claim.

slander A defamatory statement made aloud.

slang Informal, unconventional words that are often understood only by others in a particular group.

small group communication Communication occurring within small groups of three or more people.

social anxiety Fear of not making a good impression on others.

social attraction Attraction to someone's personality.

social comparison The process of comparing oneself with others.

social distance The distance most people in Western cultures maintain with casual acquaintances; ranges from 4 to 12 feet.

social exchange theory A theory predicting that people seek to form and maintain relationships in which the benefits outweigh the costs.

social penetration theory A theory that predicts that as relationships develop, communication increases in breadth and depth.

society A group of people who share symbols, language, values, and norms.

source The originator of a thought or an idea.

stagnating stage The stage of relationship dissolution when the relationship stops growing and the partners are barely communicating with each other.

stereotypes Generalizations about groups of people that are applied to individual members of those groups.

stigma A characteristic that discredits a person, making him or her be seen as abnormal or undesirable.

stonewalling Withdrawing from a conversation or an interaction.

supportiveness A person's feeling of assurance that others care about and will protect him or her.

symbol A representation of an idea.

symmetrical relationship A relationship between parties of equal power.

symmetry The similarity between the left and right sides of the face or body.

T

task attraction Attraction to someone's abilities and dependability.

terminating stage The stage of relationship dissolution when the relationship is deemed to be officially over.

truth bias The tendency to believe what someone says, in the absence of a reason not to.

turn-taking signal Nonverbal behavior that indicates when a person's speaking turn begins and ends.

U

uncertainty avoidance The degree to which people try to avoid situations that are unstructured, unclear, or unpredictable.

uncertainty reduction theory A theory suggesting that people are motivated to reduce their uncertainty about others.

under-benefited The state in which one's relational costs exceed one's relational rewards.

upward communication Messages sent to people at higher levels of an organization, such as superiors.

V

valence The positivity or negativity of an emotion.

vividness effect The tendency for dramatic, shocking events to distort one's perception of reality.

vocalics Characteristics of the voice that convey meaning in communication; also referred to as *paralanguage*.

Y

you-statement A statement that shifts responsibility for one's own thoughts or feelings to the listener.

Endnotes

CHAPTER 1

1. Talbot, M. (2012, January 1). Stumptown Girl: An indie-rock girl satirizes hipster culture, on "Portlandia." *The New Yorker,* retrieved March 10, 2015, from www.newyorker.com /magazine/2012/01/02/stumptown-girl

2. Walker, J., Illingworth, C., Canning, A., Garner, E., Woolley, J., Taylor, P., & Amos, T. (2014). Changes in mental state associated with prison environments: A systematic review. *Acta Psychiatrica Scandinavica, 129,* 427–436.

3. Gunther Moor, G., Bos, M. G. N., Crone, E. A., & van der Molen, M. W. (2014). Peer rejection cues induce cardiac slowing after transition into adolescence. *Developmental Psychology, 50,* 947–955.

4. Cacioppo, J. T., & Cacioppo, S. (2014). Social relationships and health: The toxic effects of perceived social isolation. *Social and Personality Psychology Compass, 8,* 58–72.

5. Perry, B. D. (2002). Childhood experience and the expression of genetic potential: What childhood neglect tells us about nature and nurture. *Brain and Mind, 3,* 79–100.

6. Field, T. (2014). *Touch* (2nd ed.). Cambridge, MA: MIT Press.

7. Holt-Lunstad, J., & Smith, T. B. (2012). Social relationships and mortality. *Social and Personality Psychology Compass, 6,* 41–53.

8. Eisenberger, N. I., & Cole, S. W. (2012). Social neuroscience and health: Neurophysiological mechanisms linking social ties with physical health. *Nature Neuroscience, 15,* 669–674.

9. Segrin, C., & Passalacqua, S. A. (2010). Functions of loneliness, social support, health behaviors, and stress in association with poor health. *Health Communication, 25,* 312–322.

10. Katz, I. (2014). *Stigma: A social psychological analysis* (3rd ed.). New York, NY: Psychology Press.

11. Herek, G. M., Saha, S., & Burack, J. (2013). Stigma and psychological distress in people with HIV/AIDS. *Basic and Applied Social Psychology, 35,* 41–54.

12. Barbato, C. A., Graham, E. E., & Perse, E. M. (2003). Communicating in the family: An examination of the relationship of family communication climate and interpersonal communication motives. *Journal of Family Communication, 3,* 123–148.

13. Baxter, L. A. (2004). Relationships as dialogues. *Personal Relationships, 11,* 1–22.

14. Korchmaros, J. D., Ybarra, M. L., & Mitchell, K. J. (2015). Adolescent online romantic relationship initiation: Differences by sexual and gender identification. *Journal of Adolescence, 40,* 54–64.

15. Tyyskä, V. (2013). Communication brokering in immigrant families: Avenues for new research. In S. S. Chuang & C. S. Tamis-LeMonda (Eds.), *Gender roles in immigrant families* (pp. 103–116). New York, NY: Springer.

16. Hartung, F.-M., & Renner, B. (2014). The need to belong and the relationship between loneliness and health. *Zeitschrift für Gesundheitspsychologie, 22,* 194–201.

17. Tay, L., Kuykendall, L., & Diener, E. (2015). Satisfaction and happiness—The bright side of quality of life. In W. Glatzer, L. Camfield, V. Møller, & M. Rojas (Eds.), *Global handbook of quality of life: Exploration of well-being of nations and continents* (pp. 839–853). Dordrecht, The Netherlands: Springer.

18. Mehl, M. R., Vazire, S., Holleran, S. E., & Clark, C. S. (2010). Eavesdropping on happiness: Well-being is related to having less small talk and more substantive conversations. *Psychological Science, 21,* 539–541.

19. Popenoe, D. (2007). *The state of our unions: The social health of marriage in America.* Piscataway, NJ: National Marriage Project.

20. Villeneuve, L., Trudel, G., Dargis, L., Préville, M., Boyer, R., & Bégin, J. (2014). Marital functioning and psychological distress among older couples over an 18-month period. *Journal of Sex & Marital Therapy, 40,* 193–208.

21. See Jenkins, R. (2014). *Social identity.* New York, NY: Routledge.

22. Astin, A. W., Astin, H. S., & Lindholm, J. A. (2010). *Cultivating the spirit: How college can enhance students' inner lives.* San Francisco, CA: Jossey-Bass.

23. Koltko-Rivera, M. E. (2006). Rediscovering the later version of Maslow's hierarchy of needs: Self-transcendence and opportunities for theory, research, and unification. *Review of General Psychology, 10,* 302–317.

24. Snyder, J., & Eng Lee-Partridge, J. (2013). Understanding communication channel choices in team knowledge sharing. *Corporate Communications: An International Journal, 18,* 417–431.

25. Walther, J. B., & Parks, M. R. (2002). Cues filtered out, cues filtered in: Computer-mediated communication and relationships. In M. L. Knapp & J. A. Daly (Eds.), *Handbook of interpersonal communication* (3rd ed., pp. 529–563). Thousand Oaks, CA: Sage.

26. Allwood, J. (2002). Bodily communication dimensions of expression and content. In B. Granström, D. House, & I. Karlsson (Eds.), *Multimodality in language and speech systems* (pp. 7–26). Dordrecht, The Netherlands: Kluwer Academic.

27. Nadin, M. (2001). One cannot not interact. *Knowledge-Based Systems, 14,* 437–440; Motley, M. T. (1990). On whether one can(not) communicate: An examination via traditional communication postulates. *Western Journal of Speech Communication, 54,* 1–20.

28. This position is usually attributed to Watzlawick, T., Beavin, J., & Jackson, D. (1967). *The pragmatics of human communication.* New York, NY: Norton.

29. See Motley, 1990.

30. See Knapp, M. L., Hall, J. A., & Horgan, T. G. (2014). *Nonverbal communication in human interaction* (8th ed.). Boston, MA: Cengage.

31. Richards, J. C., & Schmidt, R. W. (Eds.). (2013). *Language and communication.* New York, NY: Routledge.

32. National Communication Association. (1999). *How Americans communicate* [online]. Retrieved April 16, 2006, from www.natcom .org/research/Roper/how_americans_communicate.htm

33. Huston, T. L., & Melz, H. (2004). The case for (promoting) marriage: The devil is in the details. *Journal of Marriage and Family, 66,* 943–958.

34. For a classic text, see Katriel, T., & Philipsen, G. (1981). "What we need is communication": "Communication" as a cultural category in some American speech. *Communication Monographs, 48,* 300–317.

35. McDaniel, S. H., Beckman, H. B., Morse, D. S., Silberman, J., Seaburn, D. B., & Epstein, R. M. (2007). Physician self-disclosure in primary care visits: Enough about you, what about me? *Archives of Internal Medicine, 167,* 1321–1326.

36. Barrett, E. L., & Morman, M. T. (2012). Turning points of closeness in the father/daughter relationship. *Human Communication, 15,* 241–259.

37. National Communication Association, 1999.

38. Yoo, H., Bartle-Haring, S., Day, R. D., & Gangamma, R. (2014). Couple communication, emotional and sexual intimacy, and relationship satisfaction. *Journal of Sex & Marital Therapy, 40,* 275–293.

39. Jaremka, L. M., Glaser, R., Malarkey, W. B., & Kiecolt-Glaser, J. K. (2013). Marital distress prospectively predicts poorer cellular immune function. *Psychoneuroendocrinology, 38,* 2713–2719; Kiecolt-Glaser, J. K., & Newton, T. L. (2001). Marriage and health: His and hers. *Psychological Bulletin, 127,* 472–503.

40. Gouin, J.-P., Zhou, B., & Fitzpatrick, S. (2014). Social integration prospectively predicts changes in heart rate variability among individuals undergoing migration stress. *Annals of Behavioral Medicine,* [Epub, Sep 12] 1–9.

41. Beatty, M. J., Marshall, L. A., & Rudd, J. E. (2001). A twins study of communicative adaptability: Heritability of individual differences. *Quarterly Journal of Speech, 87,* 366–377.

42. Spitzberg, B. H. (2000). What is good communication? *Journal of the Association for Communication Administration, 29,* 103–119.

43. Spitzberg, B. H. (2013). (Re)introducing communication competence to the health professions. *Journal of Public Health Research, 2,* e23.

44. Alptekin, C. (2002). Towards intercultural communicative competence in ELT. *ELT Journal, 56,* 57–64.

45. Lou, H. C. (2015). Self-awareness—An emerging field in neurobiology. *Acta Paediatrica, 104,* 121–122.

46. Hwant, Y. (2011). Is communication competence still good for interpersonal media: Mobile phone and instant messenger. *Computers in Human Behavior, 27,* 924–934.

47. Khanjani, Z., Jeddi, E. M., Hekmati, I., Khalilzade, S., Nia, M. E., Andalib, M., & Ashrafian, P. (2015). Comparison of cognitive empathy, emotional empathy, and social functioning in different age groups. *Australian Psychologist, 50,* 80–85.

48. Curşeu, P. L., Janssen, S. E. A., & Raab, J. (2012). Connecting the dots: Social network structure, conflict, and group cognitive complexity. *Higher Education, 63,* 621–629.

49. Novak, C. (2008). *7 ways your e-mail can get you fired* [online]. Retrieved February 3, 2015, from: http://money.usnews.com/money/careers/articles/2008/08/04/7-ways-your-e-mail-can-get-you-fired

CHAPTER 2

1. Colangelo, L. L. (2009, July 12). Queens one of "most diverse places on Earth," new figures show. *Daily News.* Retrieved March 24, 2015, from www.nydailynews.com/new-york/queens/queens-diverse-places-earth-new-figures-show-article-1.430744

2. United States Census Bureau. (2015). State & county quick facts for Queens County, New York. Retrieved March 24, 2015, from http://quickfacts.census.gov/qfd/states/36/36081.html

3. Kosic, A., Mannetti, L., & Livi, S. (2014). Forming impressions of in-group and out-group members under self-esteem threat: The moderating role of the need for cognitive closure and prejudice. *International Journal of Intercultural Relations, 40,* 1–10.

4. Sirin, S. R., Ryce, P., Gupta, T., & Rogers-Sirin, L. (2013). The role of acculturative stress on mental health symptoms for immigrant adolescents: A longitudinal investigation. *Developmental Psychology, 49,* 736–748.

5. Rogers-Sirin, L., Ryce, P., & Sirin, S. R. (2014). Acculturation, acculturative stress, and cultural mismatch and their influences on immigrant children and adolescents' well-being. In R. Dimitrova, M. Bender, & F. van de Vijver (Eds.), *Global perspectives on well-being in immigrant families* (pp. 11–30). New York, NY: Springer.

6. See, e.g., Rushton, J. P. (2005). Ethnic nationalism, evolutionary psychology and genetic similarity theory. *Nations and Nationalism, 11,* 489–507.

7. Oswald, F. L., Mitchell, G., Blanton, H., Jaccard, J., & Tetlock, P. E. (2013). Predicting ethnic and racial discrimination: A meta-analysis of IAT criterion studies. *Journal of Personality and Social Psychology, 105,* 171–192.

8. The Economist. (2004, July 8). Danish immigration laws: Love bridge to Sweden. Retrieved February 6, 2015, from www.economist.com/node/2908031

9. Ethnologue. (2015). *Languages of the world.* Retrieved February 7, 2015, from http://ethnologue.com/world

10. Office of the New York State Comptroller: www.osc.state.ny.us/

11. Ethnologue, 2015.

12. Foundation for Endangered Languages: www.ogmios.org/home.htm

13. See Campbell, N., & Kean, A. (2012). *American cultural studies: An introduction to American culture* (3rd ed.). London, England: Routledge.

14. Holcomb, T. K. (2013). *Introduction to American deaf culture.* New York, NY: Oxford University Press.

15. Holcomb, S. K., & Holcomb, T. K. (2011). *Deaf culture, our way: Anecdotes from the deaf community* (4th ed.). San Diego, CA: DawnSign.

16. Digital Insights. (2015). *Social media 2014 statistics.* Retrieved February 7, 2015, from http://blog.digitalinsights.in./social-media-users-2014-stats-numbers/05205287.html

17. Leathers, D. G., & Eaves, M. (2008). *Successful nonverbal communication: Principles and applications* (4th ed.). Boston, MA: Pearson.

18. Hofstede, G. (2003). *Culture's consequences: Comparing values, behaviors, institutions, and organizations across nations* (2nd ed.). Thousand Oaks, CA: Sage.

19. Vargas, J. H., & Kemmelmeier, M. (2013). Ethnicity and contemporary American culture: A meta-analytic investigation of horizontal-vertical individualism-collectivism. *Journal of Cross-Cultural Psychology, 44,* 195–222.

20. Piot, C. (1999). *Remotely global: Village modernity in West Africa.* Chicago, IL: University of Chicago Press.

21. Hofstede, 2003.

22. Cai, D. A., & Fink, E. L. (2002). Conflict style differences between individualists and collectivists. *Communication Monographs, 69,* 67–87.

23. Martin, J., & Nakayama, T. (2012). *Intercultural communication in context* (6th ed.). New York, NY: McGraw-Hill.

24. Ruiz de Zarobe, L., & Ruiz de Zarobe, Y. (2012). *Speech acts and politeness across languages and cultures.* Bern, Switzerland: Peter Lang.

25. Hofstede, 2003.

26. Hofstede, G., & Hofstede, G. J. (2004). *Cultures and organizations: Software of the mind* (2nd ed.). Boston, MA: McGraw-Hill.

27. Martin & Nakayama, 2012.

28. Yook, E. L., & Albert, R. D. (1998). Perceptions of the appropriateness of negotiation in educational settings: A cross-cultural comparison among Koreans and Americans. *Communication Education, 47,* 18–29.

29. Hofstede & Hofstede, 2004.

30. Ibid.

31. Hall, E. T., & Hall, M. R. (1990). *Understanding cultural differences: Germans, French, and Americans.* Boston, MA: Intercultural.

32. Burgoon, J. K., Guerrero, L. K., & Floyd, K. (2010). *Nonverbal communication.* Boston, MA: Pearson.

33. van den Bos, K. (2009). Making sense of life: The existential self trying to deal with personal uncertainty. *Psychological Inquiry, 20,* 197–217.

34. Minkov, M., & Hofstede, G. (2014). A replication of Hofstede's uncertainty avoidance dimension across nationally representative samples from Europe. *Journal of Cross-Cultural Management, 14,* 161–171.

35. Lustig, M. W., & Koester, J. (2012). *Intercultural competence: Interpersonal communication across cultures* (7th ed.). Boston, MA: Pearson.

36. Pease, A., & Pease, B. (2004). *The definitive book of body language: The secret meaning behind people's gestures.* London, England: Orion.

37. Martey, R. M., Stromer-Galley, J., Banks, J., Wu, J., & Consalvo, M. (2014). The strategic female: Gender-switching and player behavior in online games. *Information, Communication & Society, 17,* 286–300.

38. Linde, J. A., & Edson, B. A. (2014). *The process of gender* (3rd ed.). Dubuque, IA: Kendall Hunt.

39. Connell, R. W., & Messerschmidt, J. W. (2005). Hegemonic masculinity: Rethinking the concept. *Gender & Society, 19,* 829–859.

40. See, e.g., Kimmel, M. (2011). *Manhood in America* (3rd ed.). New York, NY: Oxford University Press.

41. Galdas, P. M., Cheater, F., & Marshall, P. (2005). Men and health help-seeking behaviour: Literature review. *Journal of Advanced Nursing, 49,* 616–623.

42. U.S. Department of Justice, Bureau of Justice Statistics. *Victim characteristics.* Downloaded February 8, 2015, from: http://www.bjs.gov/index.cfm?ty=tp&tid=92

43. Kimmel, 2011.

44. Milestone, K., & Meyer, A. (2012). *Gender and popular culture.* Cambridge, England: Cambridge University Press.

45. Mangweth-Matzek, B., Hoek, H. W., Rupp, C. I., Lackner-Seifert, K., Frey, N., Whitworth, A. B., . . . Kinzi, J. (2014). Prevalence of eating disorders in middle-aged women. *International Journal of Eating Disorders, 47,* 320–324.

46. LaViolette, A. D., & Barnett, O. W. (2014). *It could happen to anyone: Why battered women stay* (3rd ed.). Thousand Oaks, CA: Sage.

47. Vafaei, A., Alvarado, B., Tomás, C., Muro, C., Martinez, B., & Zunzunegui, M. V. (2014). The validity of the 12-item Bem Sex Role Inventory in older Spanish population: An examination of the androgyny model. *Archives of Gerontology and Geriatrics, 59,* 257–263.

48. See Brettell, C. B., & Sargent, C. F. (2012). *Gender in cross-cultural perspective.* Boston, MA: Pearson.

49. Norton, A. T., & Herek, G. M. (2013). Heterosexuals' attitudes toward transgender people: Findings from a national probability sample of U.S. adults. *Sex Roles, 68,* 738–753.

50. Gooren, L. J. (2011). Care of transsexual persons. *The New England Journal of Medicine, 364,* 1251–1257.

51. Groth, K, A., Skakkebæk, A., Høst, C., Højbjerg Gravholt, C., & Bojesen, A. (2012). Klinefelter syndrome—A clinical update. *Journal of Clinical Endocrinology & Metabolism, 98,* 20–30.

52. Ono, M., & Harley, V. R. (2013). Disorders of sex development: New genes, new concepts. *Nature Reviews Endocrinology, 9,* 79–91.

53. Taskforce, A. L. C., Harper, A., Finnerty, P., Martinez, M., Brace, A., Crethar, H. C., . . . Hammer, T. R. (2013). Association for lesbian, gay, bisexual, and transgender issues in counseling competencies for counseling with lesbian, gay, bisexual, queer, questioning, intersex, and ally individuals. *Journal of LGBT Issues in Counseling, 7,* 2–43.

54. See, e.g., Savin-Williams, R. C., Joyner, K., & Rieger, G. (2012). Prevalence and stability of self-reported sexual orientation identity during young adulthood. *Archives of Sexual Behavior, 41,* 103–110; Savin-Williams, R. C., & Vrangalova, Z. (2013). Mostly heterosexual as a distinct sexual orientation group: A systematic review of the empirical evidence. *Developmental Review, 33,* 58–88.

55. Szymanski, D. M., & Moffitt, L. B. (2012). Sexism and heterosexism. In N. A. Fouad, J. A. Carter, & L. M. Subich (Eds.), *APA handbook of counseling psychology* (Vol. 2, pp. 361–390). Washington, DC: American Psychological Association.

56. Foucault, M. (1990). *The history of sexuality. Vol. 1: An introduction.* R. Hurley (Trans.). New York, NY: Vintage.

57. Rotundo, E. A. (1994). *American manhood: Transformations in masculinity from the revolution to the modern era.* New York, NY: Basic Books.

58. See Overby, L. M. (2014). Etiology and attitudes: Beliefs about the origins of homosexuality and their implications for public policy. *Journal of Homosexuality, 61,* 568–587.

59. Chandra, A., Mosher, W. D., Copen, C., & Sionean, C. (2011, March 3). *Sexual behavior, sexual attraction, and sexual identity in the United States: Data from the 2006–2008 National Survey of Family Growth.* Atlanta, GA: Centers for Disease Control and Prevention. Retrieved February 8, 2015, from www.cdc.gov/nchs/data/nhsr/nhsr036.pdf

60. Rosenthal, A. M., Sylva, D., Safron, A., & Bailey, J. M. (2011). Sexual arousal patterns of bisexual men revisited. *Biological Psychology, 88,* 112–115.

61. Burleson, B. E. (2005). *Bi America: Myths, truths, and struggles of an invisible community.* Binghamton, NY: Haworth.

62. Chandra et al., 2011.

63. Poston, D. L., & Baumle, A. K. (2010). Patterns of asexuality in the United States. *Demographic Research, 23,* 509–530.

64. Gray, J. (2012). Men are from Mars, women are from Venus: The definitive guide to relationships. London: Harper Element.

65. Gray, 1992, p. 5.

66. Tannen, D. (2007). *You just don't understand: Women and men in conversation.* New York, NY: William Morrow; Wood, J. T. (2000). Relational culture: The nucleus of intimacy. In J. T. Wood (Ed.), *Relational communication: Continuity and change in personal relationships* (2nd ed., pp. 76–100). Belmont, CA: Wadsworth.

67. See Wood, J. T. (2011). *Gendered lives: Communication, gender, & culture* (11th ed.). Stamford, CT: Cengage.

68. Burleson, B. R., & Kunkel, A. (2006). Revisiting the different cultures thesis: An assessment of sex differences and similarities in supportive communication. In K. Dindia & D. J. Canary (Eds.), *Sex differences and similarities in communication* (2nd ed., pp. 137–159). Mahwah, NJ: Lawrence Erlbaum Associates.

69. See, e.g., Leaper, C. (2012). Gender similarities and differences in language. In T. M. Holtgraves (Ed.), *The Oxford handbook of language and social psychology* (pp. 62–81). New York, NY: Oxford University Press; MacGeorge, E. L., Graves, A. R., Feng, B., Gillihan, S. J., & Burleson, B. R. (2004). The myth of gender cultures: Similarities outweigh differences in men's and women's provision of and responses to supportive communication. *Sex Roles, 50,* 143–175.

70. Dindia, K. (2006). Men are from North Dakota, women are from South Dakota. In K. Dindia & D. J. Canary (Eds.), *Sex differences and similarities in communication* (2nd ed., pp. 3–20). Mahwah, NJ: Lawrence Erlbaum Associates.

71. Floyd, K. (2014). Taking stock of research practices: A call for self-reflection. *Communication Monographs, 81,* 1–3; Canary, D. J., & Hause, K. S. (1993). Is there any reason to research sex differences in communication? *Communication Quarterly, 41,* 129–144; Wright, P. H. (1988). Interpreting gender differences in friendship: A case for moderation and a plea for caution. *Journal of Social and Personal Relationships, 5,* 367–373.

72. Mulac, A., Bradac, J. J., & Gibbons, P. (2001). Empirical support for the gender-as-culture hypothesis: An intercultural analysis of male/female language differences. *Human Communication Research, 27,* 121–152.

73. Athenstaedt, U., Haas, E., & Schwab, S. (2004). Gender role self-concept and gender-typed communication behavior in mixed-sex and same-sex dyads. *Sex Roles, 50,* 37–52. See also Hall, J. A. (2011). Sex differences in friendship expectations: A meta-analysis. *Journal of Social and Personal Relationships, 28,* 723–747.

74. Wood, J. T. (2011). *Gendered lives: Communication, gender, & culture* (11th ed.). Stamford, CT: Cengage.

75. Halim, M. L., Ruble, D., Tamis-LeMonda, C., & Shrout, P. E. (2013). Rigidity in gender-typed behaviors in early childhood: A longitudinal study of ethnic minority children. *Child Development, 84,* 1269–1284.

76. See, e.g., Martin, C., Fabes, R., Evans, S., & Wyman, H. (2000). Social cognition on the playground: Children's beliefs about playing with girls versus boys and their relations to sex segregated play. *Journal of Social and Personal Relationships, 17,* 751–771.

77. Lippa, R. A. (2000). Gender-related traits in gay men, lesbian women, and heterosexual men and women: The virtual identity of homosexual-heterosexual diagnosticity and gender diagnosticity. *Journal of Personality, 68,* 899–926.

78. Henley, N. (1995). Body politics revisited: What do we know today? In P. Kalbfleisch & M. Cody (Eds.), *Gender, power, and communication in human relationships* (pp. 27–61). Hillsdale, NJ: Lawrence Erlbaum Associates.

79. Kalbfleisch, P. J., & Herold, A. L. (2006). Sex, power, and communication. In K. Dindia & D. J. Canary (Eds.), *Sex differences and similarities in communication* (2nd ed., pp. 299–313). Mahwah, NJ: Lawrence Erlbaum Associates.

80. Litosseliti, L. (2013). *Gender & language: Theory and practice.* New York, NY: Routledge.

81. Mehl, M., & Pennebaker, J. (2002, January). *Mapping students' natural language use in everyday conversations.* Paper presented at the third annual meeting of the Society for Personality and Social Psychology, Savannah, GA; Anderson, K. J., & Leaper, C. (1998). Meta-analyses of gender effects on conversational interruption: Who, what, when, where, and how. *Sex Roles, 39,* 225–252.

82. Basow, S., & Rubenfeld, K. (2003). "Trouble talk": Effects of gender and gender-typing. *Sex Roles, 48,* 183–187.

83. Leaper, C., & Ayres, M. M. (2007). A meta-analytic review of gender variation in adults' language use: Talkativeness, affiliative speech, and assertive speech. *Personality and Social Psychology Review, 11,* 328–363.

84. Adetunji, A. (2010). Aspects of linguistic violence to Nigerian women. *Language, Society and Culture, 31,* 10–17.

85. Bemiller, M. L., & Zimmer Schneider, R. (2010). It's not just a joke. *Sociological Spectrum, 30,* 459–479.

86. Badgett, M. V. L., & Frank, J. (Eds.). (2007). *Sexual orientation discrimination: An international perspective.* New York, NY: Routledge.

87. Mulac, Bradac, & Gibbons, 2001.

88. Mulac, A. (2006). The gender-linked language effect: Do language differences really make a difference? In K. Dindia & D. J. Canary (Eds.), *Sex differences and similarities in communication* (2nd ed., pp. 219–239). Mahwah, NJ: Lawrence Erlbaum Associates.

89. Kulick, D. (2000). Gay and lesbian language. *Annual Review of Anthropology, 29,* 243–285.

90. Major, B., Schmidlin, A. M., & Williams, L. (1990). Gesture patterns in social touch: The impact of setting and age. *Journal of Personality and Social Psychology, 58,* 634–643.

91. Guerrero, L. K., & Floyd, K. (2006). *Nonverbal communication in close relationships.* Boston, MA: Allyn & Bacon.

92. Guerrero & Floyd, 2006.

93. Uzzell, D., & Horne, N. (2006). The influence of biological sex, sexuality and gender role on interpersonal distance. *British Journal of Social Psychology, 45,* 579–597.

94. Newport, F. (2001, February 21). Americans see women as emotional and affectionate, men as more aggressive. Retrieved February 8, 2015, from www.gallup.com/poll/1978/americans-see-women-emotional-affectionate-men-more-aggressive.aspx

95. Burgoon, J. K., & Bacue, A. E. (2003). Nonverbal communication skills. In J. O. Greene & B. R. Burleson (Eds.), *Handbook of communication and social interaction skills* (pp. 179–219). Mahwah, NJ: Lawrence Erlbaum Associates.

96. LaFrance, M., Hecht, M. A., & Levy Paluck, E. (2003). The contingent smile: A meta-analysis of sex differences in smiling. *Psychological Bulletin, 129,* 305–334.

97. Puce, A. (2013). Perception of nonverbal cues. In K. Ochsner & S. M. Kosslyn (Eds.), *The Oxford handbook of cognitive neuroscience* (Vol. 2, pp. 148–164). New York, NY: Oxford University Press.

98. Tossell, C. C., Kortum, P., Shepard, C., Barg-Walkow, L. H., Rahmati, A., & Zhong, L. (2012). A longitudinal study of emoticon use in text messaging from smartphones. *Computers in Human Behavior, 28,* 659–663.

99. A sex difference in anger expression was reported in Evers, C., Fischer, A. H., Rodriguez Mosquera, P. M., & Manstead, A. S. R. (2005). Anger and social appraisal: A "spicy" sex difference? *Emotion, 5,* 258–266. One study that failed to report such a difference was Burrowes, B. D., & Halberstadt, A. G. (1987).

Self- and family-expressiveness styles in the experience and expression of anger. *Journal of Nonverbal Behavior, 11,* 254–268.

100. See Bevan, J. L. (2013). *The communication of jealousy.* New York, NY: Peter Lang.

101. Nolen-Hoeksema, S. (2012). Emotion regulation and psychopathology: The role of gender. *Annual Review of Clinical Psychology, 8,* 161–187.

102. Kring, A. M., & Gordon, A. H. (1998). Sex differences in emotion: Expression, experience, and physiology. *Journal of Personality and Social Psychology, 74,* 686–703; see also Gross, J. J., & John, O. P. (1998). Mapping the domain of expressivity: Multimethod evidence for a hierarchical model. *Journal of Personality and Social Psychology, 74,* 170–191.

103. Kring & Gordon, 1998.

104. Gottman, J. M., Levenson, R. W., Gross, J., Frederickson, B. L., McCoy, K., Rosenthal, L., Ruef, A., & Yoshimoto, D. (2003). Correlates of gay and lesbian couples' relationship satisfaction and relationship dissolution. *Journal of Homosexuality, 45,* 23–43.

105. For a review, see Floyd, K. (2006). *Communicating affection: Interpersonal behavior and social context.* Cambridge, England: Cambridge University Press.

106. Floyd, K., & Voloudakis, M. (1999). Affectionate behavior in adult platonic friendships: Interpreting and evaluating expectancy violations. *Human Communication Research, 25,* 341–369.

107. Floyd, K. (2015). *The loneliness cure: Six strategies for finding real connections in your life.* Avon, MA: Adams Media.

108. Floyd, K., & Morman, M. T. (2000). Reacting to the verbal expression of affection in same-sex interaction. *Southern Communication Journal, 65,* 287–299.

109. See Taylor, S. E., Klein, L. C., Lewis, B. P., Gruenwald, T. L., Guring, R. A. R., & Updegraff, J. A. (2000). Biobehavioral responses to stress in females: Tend-and-befriend, not fight-or-flight. *Psychological Review, 107,* 411–429.

110. Floyd, K., & Morman, M. T. (2000). Affection received from fathers as a predictor of men's affection with their own sons: Tests of the modeling and compensation hypotheses. *Communication Monographs, 67,* 347–361; Floyd, K., & Tusing, K. J. (2002, July). *"At the mention of your name": Affect shifts induced by relationship-specific cognitions.* Paper presented at annual meeting of the International Communication Association, Seoul, South Korea.

111. Kurdek, L. A. (2006). Differences between partners from heterosexual, gay, and lesbian cohabiting couples. *Journal of Marriage and Family, 68,* 509–528.

112. Floyd, K., Sargent, J. E., & Di Corcia, M. (2004). Human affection exchange: VI. Further tests of reproductive probability as a predictor of men's affection with their fathers and their sons. *Journal of Social Psychology, 144,* 191–206; Floyd, K. (2001). Human affection exchange: I. Reproductive probability as a predictor of men's affection with their sons. *Journal of Men's Studies, 10,* 39–50.

CHAPTER 3

1. Cassidy, T. M. (2014, October). *Opening the window to lifelong learning: Applying the Johari Window framework in engineering communication curriculum.* Paper presented at the International Professional Communication Conference, Pittsburgh, PA.

2. Reported in Myers, D. G. (1980). *The inflated self.* New York, NY: Seabury.

3. Brown, J. D. (2014). Self-esteem and self-evaluation: Feeling is believing. In J. Suls (Ed.), *Psychological perspectives on the self* (Vol. 4, pp. 27–58). New York, NY: Psychology Press.

4. Steiger, A. E., Allemand, M., Robins, R. W., & Fend, H. A. (2014). Low and decreasing self-esteem during adolescence predict adult depression two decades later. *Journal of Personality and Social Psychology, 106,* 325–338; Orth, U., Robins, R. W., Widaman, K. F., & Conger, R. D. (2014). Is low self-esteem a risk factor for depression? Findings from a longitudinal study of Mexican-origin youth. *Developmental Psychology, 50,* 622–633.

5. See Swann, W. B. (2011). Self-verification theory. In P. A. M. Van Lange, A. W. Kruglanski, & E. T. Higgins (Eds.), *Handbook of theories of social psychology* (Vol. 2, pp. 23–42). Thousand Oaks, CA: Sage.

6. Swann, W. B., Rentfrow, P. J., & Guinn, J. S. (2003). Self-verification: The search for coherence. In J. P. Tangney & M. R. Leary (Eds.), *Handbook of self and identity* (pp. 367–383). New York, NY: Guilford.

7. Block, J., & Robins, R. W. (1993). A longitudinal study of consistency and change in self-esteem from early adolescence to early childhood. *Child Development, 64,* 909–923.

8. Roth, J. (2012). Changed for the worse: Subjective change in implicit and explicit self-esteem in individuals with current, past, and no posttraumatic stress disorder. *Psychotherapy and Psychosomatics, 81,* 64–66.

9. Church, A. T., Katigbak, M. S., Ibáñez-Reyes, J., de Jesús Vargas-Flores, J., Curtis, G. J., Tanaka-Matsumi, J., . . . Simon, J.-Y.R. (2014). Relating self-concept consistency to hedonic and eudaimonic well-being in eight cultures. *Journal of Cross-Cultural Psychology, 45,* 695–712.

10. Bornstein, M. H., Arterberry, M. E., & Lamb, M. E. (2013). *Development in infancy: A contemporary introduction* (5th ed.). Oxford, England: Taylor & Francis.

11. Dochtermann, N. A., Schwab, T., & Sih, A. (2015). The contribution of additive genetic variation to personality variation: Heritability of personality. *Proceedings of the Royal Society B; Biological Sciences, 282*(1798), 2014–2201.

12. Segal, N. L. (2012). *Born together—reared apart: The landmark Minnesota Twin Study.* Cambridge, MA: Harvard University Press.

13. Schwartz, C. E., Wright, C. I., Shin, L. M., Kagan, J., & Rauch, S. L. (2003). Inhibited and uninhibited infants "grown up": Adult amygdalar response to novelty. *Science* (June 20), 1952–1953.

14. See Samovar, L. A., Porter, R. E., McDaniel, E. R., & Roy, C. S. (2015). *Intercultural communication: A reader* (15th ed.). Boston, MA: Cengage.

15. See Stets, J. E., & Carter, M. J. (2011). The moral self: Applying identity theory. *Social Psychology Quarterly, 74,* 192–215.

16. Martey, R. M., & Consalvo, M. (2011). Performing the looking-glass self: Avatar appearance and group identity in *Second Life. Popular Communication: The International Journal of Media and Culture, 9,* 165–180.

17. Hergovitch, A., Sirsch, U., & Felinger, M. (2002). Self-appraisals, actual appraisals and reflected appraisals of pre-adolescent children. *Social Behavior and Personality, 30,* 603–612.

18. Ambert, A.-M. (2013). *The effect of children on parents* (2nd ed.). New York, NY: Routledge. See also Beatty, M. J., & Dobos, J. A. (1993). Adult males' perceptions of confirmation and relational

partner communication apprehension: Indirect effects of fathers on sons' partners. *Communication Quarterly, 41,* 66–76.

19. Mabe, A. G., Forney, K. J., & Keel, P. K. (2014). Do you "like" my photo? Facebook use maintains eating disorder risk. *International Journal of Eating Disorders, 47,* 516–523.

20. Emanuel, L., Neil, G. J., Bevan, C., Fraser, D. S., Stevenage, S. V., Whitty, M. T., & Jamison-Powell, S. (2014). Who am I? Representing the self offline and in different online contexts. *Computers in Human Behavior, 41,* 146–152.

21. See He, Q., Glas, C. A. W., Kosinski, M., Stillwell, D. J., & Veldkamp, B. P. (2014). Predicting self-monitoring skills using textual posts on Facebook. *Computers in Human Behavior, 33,* 69–78.

22. Centers for Disease Control and Prevention. (2012). Prevalence of autism spectrum disorders—Autism and developmental disabilities monitoring network, 14 sites, United States, 2008. Retrieved February 10, 2015, from www.cdc.gov/mmwr/preview/mmwrhtml /ss6103a1.htm

23. See, e.g., Birnie, C., McClure, M. J., Lydon, J. E., & Holmberg, D. (2009). Attachment avoidance and commitment aversion: A script for relationship failure. *Personal Relationships, 16,* 79–97.

24. Ridge, R. D., & Reber, J. S. (2002). "I think she's attracted to me": The effect of men's beliefs on women's behavior in a job interview scenario. *Basic and Applied Social Psychology, 24,* 1–14.

25. Sternberg, E., Critchley, S., Gallagher, S., & Raman, V. V. (2011). A self-fulfilling prophecy: Linking belief to behavior. *Annals of the New York Academy of Sciences, 1234,* 83–97.

26. Stets, J. E., & Burke, P. J. (2014). Self-esteem and identities. *Sociological Perspectives, 57,* 409–433.

27. Sommer, K. L., & Baumeister, R. F. (2002). Self-evaluation, persistence, and performance following implicit rejection: The role of trait self-esteem. *Personality and Social Psychology Bulletin, 28,* 926–938.

28. Murray, S. L., Rose, P., Bellavia, G., Holmes, J. G., & Kusche, A. (2002). When rejection stings: How self-esteem constrains relationship-enhancement processes. *Journal of Personality and Social Psychology, 83,* 556–573.

29. Baumeister, R. F., Campbell, J. D., Krueger, J. I., & Vohs, K. D. (2003). Does high self-esteem cause better performance, interpersonal success, happiness, or healthier lifestyles? *Psychological Science in the Public Interest, 4,* 1–44.

30. Baumeister, R. F. (2010). The self. In R. F. Baumeister & E. J. Finkel (Eds.), *Advanced social psychology: The state of the science* (pp. 139–176). Oxford, England: Oxford University Press.

31. Poikolainen, K., Tuulio-Henriksson, A., Aalto-Setälä, T., Marttunen, M., & Lönnqvist, J. (2001). Predictors of alcohol intake and heavy drinking in early adulthood: A 5-year follow-up of 15–19 year old Finnish adolescents. *Alcohol and Alcoholism, 36,* 85–88; McGee, R. O., & Williams, S. M. (2000). Does low self-esteem predict health compromising behaviours among adolescents? *Journal of Adolescence, 23,* 569–582.

32. Baumeister et al., 2003.

33. Tokunaga, R. S., & Rains, S. A. (2010). An evaluation of two characterizations of the relationships between problematic Internet use, time spent using the Internet, and psychosocial problems. *Human Communication Research, 36,* 512–545.

34. Lyubomirsky, S., Tkach, C., & DiMatteo, M. R. (2005). What are the differences between happiness and self-esteem? *Social Indicators Research, 52,* 1–43.

35. Uchida, Y., Norasakkunkit, V., & Kitayama, S. (2004). Cultural constructions of happiness: Theory and empirical evidence. *Journal of Happiness Studies, 5,* 223–239.

36. Orth, U., Robins, R. W., Trzesniewski, K. H., Maes, J., & Schmitt, M. (2009). Low self-esteem is a risk factor for depressive symptoms from young adulthood to old age. *Journal of Abnormal Psychology, 118,* 472–478.

37. Rey, L., Extremera, N., & Pena, M. (2011). Perceived emotional intelligence, self-esteem and life satisfaction in adolescents. *Psychosocial Intervention, 20,* 227–234.

38. Baumeister et al., 2003; Baumgardner, A. H., Kaufman, C. M., & Levy, P. E. (1989). Regulating affect interpersonally: When low esteem leads to greater enhancement. *Journal of Personality and Social Psychology, 56,* 907–921.

39. Ybarra, O. (1999). Misanthropic person memory when the need to self-enhance is absent. *Personality and Social Psychology Bulletin, 25,* 261–269.

40. D'Zurilla, T. J., Chang, E. C., & Sanna, L. J. (2003). Self-esteem and social problem solving as predictors of aggression in college students. *Journal of Social and Clinical Psychology, 22,* 424–440.

41. McGee, R., Williams, S., & Nada-Raja, S. (2001). Low self-esteem and hopelessness in childhood and suicidal ideation in early adulthood. *Journal of Abnormal Child Psychology, 29,* 281–291.

42. Sharaf, A. Y., Thompson, E. A., & Walsh, E. (2009). Protective effects of self-esteem and family support on suicide risk behaviors among at-risk adolescents. *Journal of Child and Adolescent Psychiatric Nursing, 22,* 160–168; Lewinsohn, P. M., Rohde, P., & Seeley, J. R. (1994). Psychosocial risk factors for future adolescent suicide attempts. *Journal of Consulting and Clinical Psychology, 62,* 297–305.

43. Forest, A. L., & Wood, J. V. (2012). When social networking is not working: Individuals with low self-esteem recognize but do not reap the benefits of self-disclosure on Facebook. *Psychological Science, 23,* 295–302.

44. Prickett, S. N. (2013, November 6). Sign of the times: Look out, it's Instagram envy. *The New York Times Blog.* Retrieved February 10, 2015, from http://tmagazine.blogs.nytimes.com/2013/11/06/ sign-of-the-times-look-out-its-instagram-envy/?_r=0

45. Krasnova, H., Wenninger, H., Widjaja, T., & Buxmann, P. (2013). Envy on Facebook: A hidden threat to users' life satisfaction? *Wirtschaftsinformatic Proceedings 2013,* paper 92.

46. For additional examples, see Twenge, J. (2006). *Generation me: Why today's young Americans are more confident, assertive, entitled—and more miserable than ever before.* New York, NY: Free Press.

47. Blais, R. R. (2005, January 27). School district cancels spelling bee (Check out the reason why they canceled it). *Free Republic,* retrieved February 12, 2015, from www.freerepublic.com/focus/ news/1330908/posts

48. Baumeister et al., 2003. (See note 29.)

49. See Twenge, J. M., & Campbell, W. K. (2009). *The narcissism epidemic: Living in the age of entitlement.* New York, NY: Free Press.

50. Forsyth, D. R., & Kerr, N. A. (1999, August). *Are adaptive illusions adaptive?* Paper presented at the annual meeting of the American Psychological Association, Boston, MA.

51. Baumeister et al., 2003. (See note 29.)

52. Wallace, H. M., & Baumeister, R. F. (2002). The performance of narcissists rises and falls with perceived opportunity for glory. *Journal of Personality and Social Psychology, 82,* 819–834.

53. Hall, J. A., Andrzejewski, S. A., & Yopchick, J. E. (2009). Psychosocial correlates of interpersonal sensitivity: A meta-analysis. *Journal of Nonverbal Behavior, 33,* 149–180.

54. Myers, D. G. (2011). *Psychology* (10th ed.). New York, NY: Worth.

55. Twenge, J. M., & Crocker, J. (2002). Race and self-esteem: Meta-analyses comparing whites, blacks, Hispanics, Asians, and American Indians and comment on Gray-Little and Hafdahl (2000). *Psychological Bulletin, 128,* 371–408; see also Gray-Little, B., & Hafdahl, A. R. (2000). Factors influencing racial comparisons of self-esteem: A quantitative review. *Psychological Bulletin, 126,* 26–54.

56. Bachman, J. G., O'Malley, P. M., Freedman-Doan, P., Trzesniewski, K. H., & Donnellan, M. B. (2011). Adolescent self-esteem: Differences by race/ethnicity, gender, and age. *Self and Identity, 10,* 445–473.

57. See Brown, R. (2010). *Prejudice: Its social psychology.* West Sussex, England: Wiley-Blackwell.

58. American Association of University Women. (1992). *The AAUW report: How schools shortchange girls.* Washington, DC: Author.

59. Twenge & Crocker, 2002.

60. Sidanius, J., & Pratto, F. (1999). *Social dominance.* Cambridge, England: Cambridge University Press.

61. Harris, S. R. (2006). *The meanings of marital equality.* Albany: State University of New York Press.

62. Iskender, M., & Akin, A. (2010). Social self-efficacy, academic locus of control, and Internet addiction. *Computers & Education, 54,* 1101–1106.

63. Cacioppo, J. T., & Patrick, W. (2009). *Loneliness: Human nature and the need for social connection.* New York, NY: W. W. Norton.

64. Zeigler-Hill, V., Besser, A., Myers, E. M., Southard, A. C., & Malkin, M. L. (2013). The status-signaling property of self-esteem: The role of self-reported self-esteem and perceived self-esteem in personality judgments. *Journal of Personality, 81,* 209–220.

65. For review, see Floyd, K. (2006). *Communicating affection: Interpersonal behavior and social context.* Cambridge, England: Cambridge University Press.

66. Floyd, K., & Deiss, D. M. (2012). Better health, better lives: The bright side of affection. In T. J. Socha & M. Pitts (Eds.), *The positive side of interpersonal communication* (pp. 127–142). New York, NY: Peter Lang.

67. McAdams, D. P., & Manczak, E. (2015). Personality and the life story. In M. Mikulincer, P. R. Shaver, L. M. Cooper, & R. J. Larsen (Eds.), *APA handbook of personality and social psychology* (Vol. 4, pp. 425–446). Washington, DC: American Psychological Association.

68. Bostwick, W. B., Boyd, C. J., Hughes, T. L., West, B. T., & McCabe, S. E. (2014). Discrimination and mental health among lesbian, gay, and bisexual adults in the United States. *American Journal of Orthopsychiatry, 84,* 35–45.

69. Meyer, I. H. (2003). Prejudice, social stress, and mental health in lesbian, gay, and bisexual populations: Conceptual issues and research evidence. *Psychological Bulletin, 129,* 674–697.

70. Hatzenbuehler, M. L., Bellatorre, A., Lee, Y., Finch, B. K., Muennig, P., & Fiscella, K. (2014). Structural stigma and all-cause mortality in sexual minority populations. *Social Science & Medicine, 103,* 33–41.

71. Cole, S., Kemeny, M., Taylor, S., Visscher, B., & Fahey, J. (1996). Accelerated course of HIV infection in gay men who conceal their homosexual identity. *Psychosomatic Medicine, 58,* 219–231.

72. King, M., Semlyen, J., Tai, S. S., Killaspy, H., Osborn, D., Popelyuk, D., & Nazareth, I. (2008). A systematic review of mental disorder, suicide, and deliberate self harm in lesbian, gay and bisexual people. *BMC Psychiatry, 8,* 70.

73. Russell, S. T., & Toomey, R. B. (2012). Men's sexual orientation and suicide: Evidence for U.S. adolescent-specific risk. *Social Science & Medicine, 74,* 523–529.

74. Huebner, D. M., & Davis, M. C. (2005). Gay and bisexual men who disclose their sexual orientations in the workplace have higher workday levels of salivary cortisol and negative affect. *Annals of Behavioral Medicine, 30,* 260–267.

75. Lewis, R. J., Derlega, V. J., Griffin, J. L., & Krowinski, A. C. (2003). Stressors for gay men and lesbians: Life stress, gay-related stress, stigma consciousness, and depressive symptoms. *Journal of Social and Clinical Psychology, 22,* 716–729.

76. Goldschmidt, M. M. (2004). Good person stories: The favor narrative as a self-presentation strategy. *Qualitative Research Reports in Communication, 5,* 28–33.

77. See Kim, W., Guan, Z., & Park, H. S. (2012). Face and facework: A cross-cultural comparison of managing politeness norms in U.S. and Korea. *International Journal of Communication, 6,* 19.

78. Goffman, E. (1959). *The presentation of the self in everyday life.* New York: Doubleday; see also Brown, P., & Levinson, S. C. (1987). *Politeness: Some universals in language usage.* Cambridge, England: Cambridge University Press.

79. Baiocchi-Wagner, E. (2011). "Facing threats": Understanding communication apprehensive instructors' face loss and face restoration in the classroom. *Communication Quarterly, 59,* 221–238.

80. Domenici, K., & Littlejohn, S. W. (2006). *Facework: Bridging theory and practice.* Thousand Oaks, CA: Sage.

81. Perkins, M. M., Ball, M. M., Whittington, F. J., & Hollingsworth, C. (2012). Relational autonomy in assisted living: A focus on diverse care settings for older adults. *Journal of Aging Studies, 26,* 214–225.

82. See, e.g., Schneider, B., & Remillard, C. (2013). Caring about homelessness: How identity work maintains the stigma of homelessness. *Text & Talk, 33,* 95–112.

83. Sprecher, S., Treger, S., & Wondra, J. D. (2013). Effects of self-disclosure role on liking, closeness, and other impressions in get-acquainted interactions. *Journal of Social and Personal Relationships, 30,* 497–514.

84. See Trepte, S., & Reinecke, L. (2013). The reciprocal effects of social network site use and the disposition for self-disclosure: A longitudinal study. *Computers in Human Behavior, 29,* 1102–1112.

85. Utz, S. (2015). The function of self-disclosure on social network sites: Not only intimate, but also positive and entertaining self-disclosures increase the feeling of connection. *Computers in Human Behavior, 45,* 1–10.

86. McKenna, K. Y. A., Green, A. S., & Gleason, M. E. J. (2002). Relationship formation on the Internet: What's the big attraction? *Journal of Social Issues, 58,* 9–31.

87. Walther, J. B., Van Der Heide, B., Ramirez, A., Burgoon, J. K., & Peña, J. (2015). Interpersonal and hyperpersonal dimensions of computer-mediated communication. In S. S. Sundar (Ed.), *The handbook of the psychology of communication technology* (pp. 3–22). Hoboken, NJ: John Wiley & Sons.

88. Gouldner, A. W. (1960). The norm of reciprocity: A preliminary statement. *American Sociological Review, 25,* 161–178.

89. Sprecher, S., Treger, S., Wondra, J. D., Hilaire, N., & Wallpe, K. (2013). Taking turns: Reciprocal self-disclosure promotes liking in initial interactions. *Journal of Experimental Social Psychology, 49,* 860–866.

90. Wu, J., & Lu, H. (2013). Cultural and gender differences in self-disclosure on social networking sites. In J. Petley (Ed.), *Media and public shaming: Drawing the boundaries of disclosure* (pp. 97–114). London, England: I. B. Tauris & Co.

91. See, e.g., Morman, M. T., Schrodt, P., & Tornes, M. J. (2013). Self-disclosure mediates the effects of gender orientation and homophobia on the relationship quality of male same-sex friendships. *Journal of Social and Personal Relationships, 30,* 582–605.

92. Dindia, K., & Allen, M. (1992). Sex differences in self-disclosure: A meta-analysis. *Psychological Bulletin, 112,* 106–124.

93. Wu & Lu, 2013.

94. Sprecher, Treger, Wondra et al., 2013.

95. Park, N., Jin, B., & Jin, S.-A.A. (2011). Effects of self-disclosure on relational intimacy in Facebook. *Computers in Human Behavior, 27,* 1974–1983.

96. Boldero, J. M., Robins, G. L., Williams, B. J., Francis, J. J., Hampton, A., & Fourie, A. J. (2009). Relational discrepancies and emotion: The moderating roles of relationship type and relational discrepancy valence. *Asian Journal of Social Psychology, 12,* 259–273.

97. Forgas, J. P. (2011). Affective influences on self-disclosure: Mood effects on the intimacy and reciprocity of disclosing personal information. *Journal of Personality and Social Psychology, 100,* 449–461.

98. See Afifi, T. D., & Steuber, K. (2010). The cycle of concealment model. *Journal of Social and Personal Relationships, 27,* 1019–1034.

99. Thoits, P. A. (2013). Self, identity, stress, and mental health. In C. S. Aneshensal, J. C. Phelan, & A. Bierman (Eds.), *Handbook of the sociology of mental health* (pp. 357–377). Dordrecht, The Netherlands: Springer.

100. Bender, J. L., Jimenez-Maroquin, M.-C., & Jadad, A. R. (2011). Seeking support on Facebook: A content analysis of breast cancer groups. *Journal of Medical Internet Research, 13,* e16.

101. Agne, R., Thompson, T. L., & Cusella, K. P. (2000). Stigma in the line of face: Self-disclosure of patients' HIV status to health care providers. *Journal of Applied Communication Research, 28,* 235–261.

102. Valkenburg, P. M., & Peter, J. (2011). Online communication among adolescents: An integrated model of its attraction, opportunities, and risks. *Journal of Adolescent Health, 48,* 121–127.

103. Valkenburg & Peter, 2011.

104. Hollenbaugh, E. R., & Everett, M. K. (2013). The effects of anonymity on self-disclosure in blogs: An application of the online disinhibition effect. *Journal of Computer-Mediated Communication, 18,* 283–302.

105. IKeepSafe blog. (2013, April 30). Real danger in sharing too much info online. Retrieved February 13, 2015, from www.ikeepsafe.org/cybersafety/real-danger-in-sharing-too-much-info-online/

CHAPTER 4

1. Stern, M. (2015, February 9). Kanye West blasts Beck's Album of the Year Grammys win. *The Daily Beast.* www.thedailybeast.com/articles/2015/02/09/kanye-west-blasts-beck-s-album-of-the-year-grammys-win-beck-needs-to-respect-artistry.html

2. Vazire, S., & Solomon, B. C. (2015). Self- and other-knowledge of personality. In M. Mikulincer, P. R. Shaver, M. L. Cooper, & R. J. Larsen (Eds.), *APA handbook of personality and social psychology* (Vol. 4, pp. 261–281). Washington, DC: American Psychological Association.

3. See, e.g., West, T. V. (2011). Interpersonal perception in cross-group interactions: Challenges and potential solutions. *European Review of Social Psychology, 22,* 364–401.

4. Goldstein, E. B. (2013). *Sensation and perception* (9th ed.). Belmont, CA: Wadsworth.

5. Floyd, K., Ramirez, A., & Burgoon, J. K. (2008). Expectancy violations theory. In L. K. Guerrero, J. A. DeVito, & M. L. Hecht (Eds.), *The nonverbal communication reader: Classic and contemporary readings* (3rd ed., pp. 503–510). Prospect Heights, IL: Waveland.

6. Tomita, A., Matsushita, K., & Morikawa, K. (2013). Mere exposure effect for amodally completed faces. *Perception, 42,* ECVP Abstract Supplement, 197.

7. Goldstein, 2013.

8. Burgoon, J. K., Guerrero, L. K., & Floyd, K. (2010). *Nonverbal communication.* Boston: Pearson/Allyn & Bacon.

9. Sowa, J. F. (2000). *Knowledge representation: Logical, philosophical, and computational foundations.* Pacific Grove, CA: Brooks/Cole.

10. See, e.g., Young, A. W., & Bruce, V. (2011). Understanding person perception. *British Journal of Psychology, 102,* 959–974.

11. Fiske, S. T., & Taylor, S. E. (2013). *Social cognition: From brains to culture* (2nd ed.). London, England: Sage.

12. Weiner, B. (2012). An attribution theory of motivation. In P. A. M. Van Lange, A. W. Kruglanski, & T. E. Higgins (Eds.), *Handbook of theories of social psychology* (Vol. 1, pp. 135–155). London, England: Sage.

13. Weiner, 2012.

14. See, e.g., Manusov, V. (2009). Attribution and interpersonal communication: Out of our heads and into behavior. In D. R. Roskos-Ewoldsen & J. L. Monahan (Eds.), *Communication and social cognition: Theories and methods* (pp. 141–170). New York, NY: Taylor & Francis.

15. Burgoon et al., 2010.

16. Harris, C. S. (Ed.). (2013). *Visual coding and adaptability.* New York, NY: Psychology Press.

17. Casini, L., Ramdani-Beauvir, C., Burle, B., & Vidal, F. (2013). How does one night of sleep deprivation affect the internal clock? *Neuropsychologia, 51,* 275–283.

18. Hartmann, A. S., Rief, W., & Hilbert, A. (2012). Laboratory snack food intake, negative mood, and impulsivity in youth with ADHD symptoms and episodes of loss of control eating. Where is the missing link? *Appetite, 58,* 672–678.

19. Ludy, M. J., & Mattes, R. D. (2011). Noxious stimuli sensitivity in regular spicy food users and non-users: Comparison of visual analog and general labeled magnitude scaling. *Chemosensory Perception, 4,* 123–133.

20. McClung, C. A. (2013). How might circadian rhythm control mood? Let me count the ways. *Biological Psychiatry, 74,* 242–249.

21. Gunn, H. E., Buysse, D. J., Hasler, B. P., Begley, A., & Troxel, W. M. (in press). Sleep concordance in couples is associated with relationship characteristics. *Sleep.*

22. Noguchi, K., Kamada, A., & Shrira, I. (2014). Cultural differences in the primacy effect for person perception. *International Journal of Psychology, 49,* 208–210.

23. Burgoon et al., 2010.

24. Kasabov, E., & Hain, T. (2014). Cross-generational perceptions and reactions during service recovery. *The Service Industries Journal, 34,* 71–87.

25. Kraus, M. W., Piff, P. K., Mendoza-Denton, R., Rheinschmidt, M. L., & Keltner, D. (2012). Social class, solipsism, and contextualism: How the rich are different from the poor. *Psychological Review, 119,* 546–572.

26. Ahler, D. J. (2014). Self-fulfilling misperceptions of public polarization. *The Journal of Politics, 76,* 607–620.

27. Sandberg, S. (2013). *Lean in: Women, work, and the will to lead.* New York, NY: Alfred A. Knopf.

28. Maeder, E. M., Wiener, R. L., & Winter, R. (2007). Does a truck driver see what a nurse sees? The effects of occupation type on perceptions of sexual harassment. *Sex Roles, 56,* 801–810.

29. Brand, R. J., Bonatsos, A., D'Orzcio, R. D., & DeShong, H. (2012). What is beautiful is good, even online: Correlations between photo attractiveness and text attractiveness in men's online dating profiles. *Computers in Human Behavior, 28,* 166–170.

30. Toma, C. L., & Hancock, J. T. (2012). What lies beneath: The linguistic traces of deception in online dating profiles. *Journal of Communication, 62,* 78–97.

31. Nowak, K. L., & Rauh, C. (2006). The influence of the avatar on online perceptions of anthropomorphism, androgyny, credibility, homophily, and attraction. *Journal of Computer-Mediated Communication, 11,* 153–178.

32. See Khan, S. R., Benda, T., & Stagnaro, M. N. (2012). Stereotyping from the perspective of perceivers and targets. *Online Readings in Psychology and Culture, 5*(1). Retrieved February 16, 2015, from http://scholarworks.gvsu.edu/orpc/vol5/iss1/1/

33. North, M. S., & Fiske, S. T. (2012). An inconvenienced youth? Ageism and its potential intergenerational roots. *Psychological Bulletin, 138,* 982–997.

34. See, e.g., Stangor, C., & Crandall, C. S. (Eds.). (2013). *Stereotyping and prejudice.* New York, NY: Psychology Press.

35. Ruble, R. A., & Zhang, Y. B. (2013). Stereotypes of Chinese international students held by Americans. *International Journal of Intercultural Relations, 37,* 202–211.

36. Todd, A. R., Galinsky, A. D., & Bodenhausen, G. V. (2012). Perspective taking undermines stereotype maintenance processes: Evidence from social memory, behavior explanation, and information solicitation. *Social Cognition, 30,* 94–108.

37. Allen, M., & Valde, K. S. (2006). The intersection of methodological and ethical concerns when researching a gendered world. In D. J. Canary & K. Dindia (Eds.), *Handbook of sex differences and similarities in communication* (2nd ed., pp. 97–110). Mahwah, NJ: Lawrence Erlbaum Associates.

38. Mickes, L., Walker, D. E., Parris, J. L., Mankoff, R., & Christenfeld, N. J. S. (2012). Who's funny: Gender stereotypes, humor production, and memory bias. *Psychonomic Bulletin & Review, 19,* 108–112.

39. Lee, Y.-T., McCauley, C., & Jussim, L. (2013). Stereotypes as valid categories of knowledge and human perceptions of group differences. *Social & Personality Psychology Compass, 7,* 470–486.

40. Forgas, J. P. (2011). Can negative affect eliminate the power of first impressions? Affective influences on primacy and recency effects in impression formation. *Journal of Experimental Social Psychology, 47,* 425–429.

41. Asch, S. (1946). Forming impressions of personality. *Journal of Abnormal and Social Psychology, 41,* 258–290.

42. Finnerty, J., Haywood, C., Ellis, J., Turnbull, I., Jones, D., & Bennett, P. (2013). You don't get a second chance to make a first impression. *BMJ Supportive & Palliative Care, 3,* A41.

43. Schiller, D., Breeman, J. B., Mitchell, J. P., Uleman, J. S., & Phelps, E. A. (2009). A neural mechanism of first impressions. *Nature Neuroscience, 12,* 508–514.

44. Ybarra, O. (2001). When first impressions don't last: The role of isolation and adaptation processes in the revision of evaluative impressions. *Social Cognition, 19,* 491–520.

45. Duffy, S., & Crawford, L. E. (2008). Primacy or recency effects in forming inductive categories. *Memory & Cognition, 36,* 567–577.

46. Bergeron, J., Fallu, J.-M., & Roy, J. (2008). A comparison of the effects of the first impression and the last impression in a selling context. *Recherche et Applications en Marketing, 23,* 19–36.

47. Biggs, A. T., Adamo, S. H., Dowd, E. W., & Mitroff, S. R. (2015). Examining perceptual and conceptual set biases in multiple-target visual search. *Attention, Perception, & Psychophysics,* 1–12.

48. Lewis, C., Scully D., & Condor, S. (1992). Sex stereotyping of infants: A re-examination. *Journal of Reproductive and Infant Psychology, 10,* 53–61.

49. Pascalis, O., de Haan, M., & Nelson, C. A. (2002). Is face processing species-specific during the first year of life? *Science, 296,* 1321–1323; Morton, J., & Johnson, M. H. (1991). CONSPEC and CONLERN: A two-process theory of infant face recognition. *Psychological Review, 98,* 164–181.

50. Balboni, M. J., Babar, A., Dillinger, J., Phelps, A. C., George, E., Block, S. D., . . . Balboni, T. A. (2011). "It depends": Viewpoints of patients, physicians, and nurses on patient-practitioner prayer in the setting of advanced cancer. *Journal of Pain and Symptom Management, 41,* 836–847.

51. Brantley-Hill, S. M., & Brinthaupt, T. M. (2014). Perceptions of affectionate communication among people with unfavorable and favorable attitudes toward homosexuality. *Journal of Homosexuality, 61,* 270–287.

52. Abrams, D. (2011). Wherein lies children's intergroup bias? Egocentrism, social understanding, and social projection. *Child Development, 82,* 1579–1593.

53. Piaget, J. (1930). *The child's conception of physical causality.* London, England: Routledge & Kegan Paul; Piaget, J. (1932). *The moral judgment of the child.* New York, NY: Harcourt, Brace & World.

54. Surtees, A. D. R., & Apperly, I. A. (2012). Egocentrism and automatic perspective taking in children and adults. *Child Development, 83,* 452–460.

55. Tritt, S. M., Page-Gould, E., Peterson, J. B., & Inzlicht, M. (2014). System justification and electrophysiological responses to feedback: Support for a positivity bias. *Journal of Experimental Psychology, 143,* 1004–1010.

56. Rim, S., Min, K. E., Uleman, J. S., Chartrand, T. L., & Carlston, D. E. (2013). Seeing others through rose-colored glasses: An affiliation goal and positivity bias in implicit trait impressions. *Journal of Experimental Social Psychology, 49,* 1204–1209.

57. Murray, S. L., Griffin, D. W., Derrick, J. L., Harris, B., Aloni, M., & Leder, S. (2011). Tempting fate or inviting happiness? Unrealistic idealization prevents the decline of marital satisfaction. *Psychological Science, 22,* 619–626.

58. Hibbing, J. R., Smith, K. B., & Alford, J. R. (2014). Differences in negativity bias underlie variations in political ideology. *Behavioral and Brain Sciences, 37,* 297–307.

59. Kanar, A. M., Collins, C. J., & Bell, B. S. (2010). A comparison of the effects of positive and negative information on job seekers' organizational attraction and attribute recall. *Human Performance, 23,* 193–212.

60. See Rozin, P., & Boyzman, E. B. (2001). Negativity bias, negativity dominance, and contagion. *Personality and Social Psychology Review, 5,* 296–320.

61. Spitzberg, B. H., & Manusov, V. (2014). Attribution theory: Finding good cause in the search for theory. In D. O. Braithwaite & P. Schrodt (Eds.), *Engaging theories in interpersonal communication: Multiple perspectives* (2nd ed., pp. 37–50). Thousand Oaks, CA: Sage.

62. Coombs, W. T. (2012). Attribution theory in communication research. In N. M. Seel (Ed.), *Encyclopedia of the sciences of learning* (pp. 375–379). New York, NY: Springer.

63. Weiner, B. (2012). An attribution theory of motivation. In P. A. M. Van Lange, A. W. Kruglanski, & E. T. Higgins (Eds.), *Handbook of theories of social psychology* (Vol 1., pp. 135–155). London, England: Sage.

64. Lefcourt, H. M. (2014). *Locus of control: Current trends in theory and research* (2nd ed.). New York, NY: Psychology Press.

65. Weiner, 2012.

66. Weiner, B. (2014). The attribution approach to emotions and motivation: History, hypotheses, home runs, headaches/heartaches. *Emotion Review, 6,* 353–361.

67. Loersch, C., & Payne, B. K. (2012). On mental contamination: The role of (mis)attribution in behavior priming. *Social Cognition, 30,* 241–252.

68. Sedikides, C. (2013). The self-serving bias in relationships: Case study on the evolution of a research program. In E. B. Baldursson (Ed.), *Experimental methods in psychology* (pp. 39–46). Aalborg, Denmark: Aalborg University Press.

69. Durtschi, J. A., Fincham F. D., Cui, M., Lorenz, F. O., & Conger, R. D. (2011). Dyadic processes in early marriage: Attributions, behavior, and marital quality. *Family Relations, 60,* 421–434.

70. Sedikides, C., & Alicke, M. D. (2012). Self-enhancement and self-protection motives. In R. M. Ryan (Ed.), *The Oxford handbook of human motivation* (pp. 303–322). New York, NY: Oxford University Press.

71. Moran, J. M., Jolly, E., & Mitchell, J. P. (2014). Spontaneous mentalizing predicts the fundamental attribution error. *Journal of Cognitive Neuroscience, 26,* 569–576.

72. Napolitan, D. A., & Goethals, G. R. (1979). The attribution of friendliness. *Journal of Experimental Social Psychology, 15,* 105–113.

73. Walther, J. B., Kashian, N., Jang, J. W., & Shin, S. Y. (in press). Overattribution of liking in computer-mediated communication: Partners infer the results of their own influence as their partners' affection. *Communication Research.*

74. Schweinle, W. E., Ickes, W., & Bernstein, I. H. (2002). Empathic accuracy in husband to wife aggression: The overattribution bias. *Personal Relationships, 9,* 141–158.

75. Schweinle et al., 2002.

76. Schweinle, W. E., & Ickes, W. (2007). The role of men's critical/rejecting overattribution bias, affect, and attentional disengagement in marital aggression. *Journal of Social and Clinical Psychology, 26,* 173–198.

77. See, e.g., Primi, C., & Agnoli, F. (2002). Children correlate infrequent behaviors with minority groups: A case of illusory correlation. *Cognitive Development, 17,* 1105–1131.

78. See Woolfolk, R. L., Doris, J. M., & Darley, J. M. (2006). Identification, situational constraint, and social cognition: Studies in the attribution of moral responsibility. *Cognition, 100,* 283–301.

79. McCabe, M. P., & Hardman, L. (2005). Attitudes and perceptions of workers to sexual harassment. *Journal of Social Psychology, 145,* 719–740; Fromuth, M. E., Holt, A., & Parker, A. L. (2002). Factors affecting college students' perceptions of sexual relationships between high school students and teachers. *Journal of Child Sexual Abuse, 10,* 59–73.

CHAPTER 5

1. Shipman, C., Smith, C., & Farran, L. (2009, February 6). "Man asks entire town for forgiveness for racism." ABC News/Good Morning America. http://abcnews.go.com/GMA/story?id=6813984

2. See Bickerton, D. (2009). *Adam's tongue: How humans made language, how language made humans.* New York, NY: Hill & Wang.

3. Boeckx, C. (2013). Biolinguistics: Fact, fiction, and forecast. *Biolinguistics, 7,* 316–328.

4. Van Orman Quine, W. (2013). *Word & object* (new ed.). Cambridge, MA: MIT Press.

5. See, e.g., Foreign Sound Effects Dictionary. (2015). Retrieved March 2, 2015, from http://comictranslation.wikia.com/wiki/English-French; http://comictranslation.wikia.com/wiki/English-German

6. Pinker, S. (2007). *The stuff of thought: Language as a window into human nature.* New York, NY: Viking.

7. Chianese, A., Fasolino, A. R., Moscato, V., Tramontana, P., & Caropreso, M. (2011). A novel approach for semantic interoperability in the web based on the Semantic Triangle communication model. *International Journal of Software Engineering and Knowledge Engineering, 21,* 1037.

8. Socyberty.com. (2008, February 21). The 50 most beautiful English words. Retrieved March 2, 2015, from http://socyberty.com/languages/the-50-most-beautiful-english-words/

9. Oxford University Press. (2013). *Paperback Oxford English Dictionary.* Oxford, England: Author.

10. Hayakawa, S. I., & Hayakawa, A. R. (1991). *Language in thought and action.* San Diego, CA: Harcourt.

11. Samovar, L. A., Porter, R. E., McDaniel, E. R., & Roy, C. S. (2015). *Intercultural communication: A reader* (14th ed.). Boston, MA: Cengage.

12. See Gudykunst, W. B., & Moody, B. (Eds.). (2002). *Handbook of international and intercultural communication* (2nd ed.). Thousand Oaks, CA: Sage.

13. Whorf, B. L., & Lee, P. (2012). *Language, thought, and reality: Selected writings of Benjamin Lee Whorf* (2nd ed.). Cambridge, MA: MIT Press.

14. Wolff, P., & Holmes, K. J. (2011). Linguistic relativity. *Wiley Inter-Disciplinary Reviews: Cognitive Science, 2,* 253–265.

15. For more detail on the Sapir-Whorf hypothesis, see Hussein, B. A.-S. (2012). The Sapir-Whorf hypothesis today. *Theory and Practice in Language Studies, 2,* 642–646.

16. Alter, A. (2013, May 29). The power of names. *The New Yorker.* Retrieved March 2, 2015, from www.newyorker.com/tech/elements/the-power-of-names

17. Steele, K. M., & Smithwick, L. E. (1989). First names and first impressions: A fragile relationship. *Sex Roles, 21,* 517–523.

18. Rubinstein, Y., & Brenner, D. (2014). Pride and prejudice: Using ethnic-sounding names and inter-ethnic marriages to identify labour market discrimination. *Review of Economic Studies, 81,* 389–425; see also Moss-Racusin, C. A., Dovidio, J. F., Brescoll, V. L., Graham, M. J., & Handelsman, J. (2012). Science faculty's subtle gender biases favor male students. *PNAS, 109,* 16474–16479.

19. U.S. Social Security Administration. Popular baby names. Retrieved March 2, 2015, from www.ssa.gov/OACT/babynames/

20. Forbes, G. B., Adams-Curtis, L. E., White, K. B., & Hamm, N. R. (2002). Perceptions of married women and married men with hyphenated surnames. *Sex Roles, 46,* 167–175; Foss, K. A., & Edson, B. A. (1989). What's in a name? Accounts of married women's name choices. *Western Journal of Speech Communication, 53,* 356–373.

21. Hoffnung, M. (2006). What's in a name: Marital name choice revisited. *Sex Roles, 55,* 817–825.

22. See Suter, E. A. (2004). Tradition never goes out of style: The role of tradition in women's naming practices. *The Communication Review, 7,* 57–87; Stafford, L., & Kline, S. L. (1996). Married women's name choices and sense of self. *Communication Reports, 9,* 85–92.

23. Smith, C. T., De Houwer, J., & Nosek, B. A. (2013). Consider the source: Persuasion of implicit evaluations is moderated by source credibility. *Personality and Social Psychology Bulletin, 39,* 193–205.

24. Shao, Y. (2013). Ethos, logos, pathos: Strategies of persuasion in social/environmental reports. *Social and Environmental Accountability Journal, 33,* 179–180.

25. Blankenship, K. L., & Craig, T. Y. (2011). Language use and persuasion: Multiple roles for linguistic styles. *Social & Personality Psychology Compass, 5,* 194–205.

26. See, e.g., Nabi, R. L. (2015). Emotional flow in persuasive health messages. *Health Communication, 30,* 114–124.

27. Soliz, J., & Giles, H. (2014). Relational and identity processes in communication: A contextual and meta-analytical review of Communication Accommodation Theory. *Communication Yearbook, 38,* 106–143.

28. Kline, S. L., Simunich, B., & Weber, H. (2009). The use of equivocal messages in responding to corporate challenges. *Journal of Applied Communication Research, 37,* 40–58.

29. Bull, P. (2008). "Slipperiness, evasion, and ambiguity": Equivocation and facework in noncommittal political discourse. *Journal of Language and Social Psychology, 27,* 324–332.

30. Daly, J. A., Diesel, C. A., & Weber, D. (1994). Conversational dilemmas. In W. R. Cupach & B. H. Spitzberg (Eds.), *The dark side of interpersonal communication* (pp. 127–156). Mahwah, NJ: Lawrence Erlbaum Associates.

31. Lakoff, R. T. (2004). *Language and woman's place: Text and commentaries.* Oxford, England: Oxford University Press.

32. Hosman, L. A., & Siltanen, S. A. (2006). Powerful and powerless language forms: Their consequences for impression formation, attributions of control of self and control of others, cognitive responses, and message memory. *Journal of Language and Social Psychology, 25,* 33–46.

33. Hosman, L. A., & Siltanen, S. A. (2011). Hedges, tag questions, message processing, and persuasion. *Journal of Language and Social Psychology, 30,* 341–349.

34. Huston, T. L., Caughlin, J. P., Houts, R. M., Smith, S. E., & George, L. J. (2001). The connubial crucible: Newlywed years as predictors of marital delight, distress, and divorce. *Journal of Personality and Social Psychology, 80,* 237–252.

35. Jorm, A. F., Dear, K. B. G., Rodgers, B., & Christensen, H. (2003). Interaction between mother's and father's affection as a risk factor for anxiety and depression symptoms. *Social Psychiatry and Psychiatric Epidemiology, 38,* 173–179.

36. See Floyd, K. (2006). *Communicating affection: Interpersonal behavior and social context.* Cambridge, England: Cambridge University Press.

37. Floyd, K., & Pauley, P. M. (2011). Affectionate communication is good, except when it isn't: On the dark side of expressing affection. In B. Spitzberg & W. R. Cupach (Eds.), *The dark side of close relationships* (2nd ed., pp. 145–174). New York, NY: Routledge.

38. Greeting Card Association. (2015). About the industry. Retrieved March 2, 2015, from www.greetingcard.org/AbouttheIndustry/tabid/58/Default.aspx

39. Forman, A. E., Kern, R., & Gil-Egui, G. (2012). Death and mourning as sources of community participation in online social networks: R.I.P. pages in Facebook. *First Monday, 17*(9). Retrieved March 6, 2015, from http://firstmonday.org/ojs/index.php/fm/article/view/3935/3288

40. See, e.g., Gillette, B. (2003). *Condolences & eulogies: Finding the perfect words.* New York, NY: Sterling Publishing.

41. See Pennebaker, J. W., & Evans, J. F. (2014). *Expressive writing: Words that heal.* Enumclaw, WA: Idyll Arbor.

42. Floyd, K., Mikkelson, A. C., Tafoya, M. A., Farinelli, L., La Valley, A. G., Judd, J., . . . Wilson, J. (2007). Human affection exchange: XIII. Affectionate communication accelerates neuroendocrine stress recovery. *Health Communication, 22,* 123–132.

43. Wiseman, R. (2008). *Quirkology: How we discover the big truths in small things.* New York, NY: Basic Books.

44. Mobbs, D., Greicius, M. D., Abdel-Azim, E., Menon, V., & Reiss, L. (2003). Humor modulates the mesolimbic reward centers. *Neuron, 40,* 1041–1048.

45. Martin, R. A. (2006). *The psychology of humor: An integrative approach.* New York, NY: Academic Press.

46. Deshpande, R. C. (2012). A healthy way to handle work place stress through yoga, meditation and soothing humor. *International Journal of Environmental Sciences, 2,* 2143–2154.

47. Hone, L. S., Hurwitz, W., & Lieberman, D. (2015). Sex differences in preferences for humor: A replication, modification, and extension. *Evolutionary Psychology, 13,* 167–181.

48. Greengross, G., & Miller, G. F. (2008). Dissing oneself versus dissing rivals: Effects of status, personality, and sex on the short-term and long-term attractiveness of self-deprecating and other-deprecating humor. *Evolutionary Psychology, 6,* 393–408.

49. Bucchianeri, M. M., Eisenberg, M. E., Wall, M. M., Piran, N., & Neumark-Sztainer, D. (2014). Multiple types of harassment: Associations with emotional well-being and unhealthy behaviors in adolescents. *Journal of Adolescent Health, 54,* 724–729.

50. Fernández, E. C. (2010). Euphemistic strategies in politeness and face concerns. *Pragmalingüística, 13,* 77–86.

51. Gladney, G. A., & Rittenburg, T. L. (2005). Euphemistic text affects attitudes, behavior. *Newspaper Research Journal, 26,* 28–41.

52. McGlone, M. S., Beck, G., & Pfiester, A. (2006). Contamination and camouflage in euphemisms. *Communication Monographs, 73,* 261–282.

53. Xiaoling, W., Zhang, M., & Hailin, D. (2012). Cross-cultural contrastive study of English and Chinese euphemisms. *Cross-Cultural Communication, 8,* 66–70.

54. Baar, J. (2014). *Spinspeak II: The dictionary of language pollution.* Bloomington, IN: AuthorHouse.

55. Gladney & Rittenburg, 2005.

56. See Haslam, N., & Loughnan, S. (2014). Dehumanization and infrahumanization. *Annual Review of Psychology, 65,* 399–423.

57. Kieffer, C. C. (2013). Rumors and gossip as forms of bullying: Sticks and stones? *Psychoanalytic Inquiry, 33,* 90–104.

58. Stephens, R., Atkins, J., & Kingston, A. (2009). Swearing as a response to pain. *NeuroReport, 20,* 1056–1060.

59. Waldron, J. (2012). *The harm in hate speech*. Cambridge, MA: Harvard University Press.

60. Tsesis, A. (2013, November 15). Inflammatory hate speech: Offense versus incitement. *Minnesota Law Review, 97*. Retrieved March 3, 2015, from http://papers.ssrn.com/sol3/papers.cfm?abstract_id=2234152

61. Gottman, J. M. (2006). Why marriages fail. In K. M. Galvin & P. J. Cooper (Eds.), *Making connections: Readings in relational communication* (4th ed., pp. 228–236). Los Angeles, CA: Roxbury.

62. Barbato, C. A., Graham, E. E., & Perse, E. E. (2003). Communicating in the family: An examination of the relationship of family communication climate and interpersonal communication motives. *Journal of Family Communication, 3,* 123–148.

63. Vangelisti, A. L., & Young, S. L. (2000). When words hurt: The effects of perceived intentionality on interpersonal relationships. *Journal of Social and Personal Relationships, 17,* 393–424.

64. Smidts, A., Pruyn, A. T. H., & van Riel, C. B. M. (2001). The impact of employee communication and perceived external prestige on organizational identification. *Academy of Management Journal, 49,* 1051–1062.

65. Ellis, K. (2000). Perceived teacher confirmation: The development and validation of an instrument and two studies of the relationship to cognitive and affective learning. *Human Communication Research, 26,* 264–291.

66. Akkirman, A. D., & Harris, D. L. (2005). Organizational communication satisfaction in the virtual workplace. *Journal of Management Development, 24,* 397–409.

67. Weger, H. (2005). Disconfirming communication and self-verification in marriage: Associations among the demand/withdraw interaction pattern, feeling understood, and marital satisfaction. *Journal of Social and Personal Relationships, 22,* 19–31.

68. See, e.g., Barbato et al., 2003.

69. Sachs-Ericsson, N., Verona, E., Joiner, T., & Preacher, K. J. (2006). Parental verbal abuse and the mediating role of self-criticism in adult internalizing disorders. *Journal of Affective Disorders, 93,* 71–78.

70. Bippus, A. M., & Young, S. L. (2005). Owning your emotions: Reactions to expressions of self- versus other-attributed positive and negative emotions. *Journal of Applied Communication Research, 33,* 26–45.

71. Haythornthwaite, C., & Kendall, L. (2010). Internet and community. *American Behavioral Scientist, 53,* 1083–1094.

CHAPTER 6

1. Miller, J. (2015, February 26). Scarlett Johansson defends John Travolta. *VanityFair.com,* www.vanityfair.com/hollywood/2015/02/john-travolta-scarlett-johansson-oscars

2. Nierenberg, G., Calero, H. H., & Grayson, G. (2011). *How to read a person like a book: Observing body language to know what people are thinking.* New Delhi, India: Rupa & Co.

3. Calero, H. H. (2005). *The power of nonverbal communication: How you act is more important than what you say.* Lansdowne, PA: Silver Lake.

4. Birdwhistell, R. L. (1970). *Kinesics and context.* Philadelphia: University of Pennsylvania Press; see also Philpott, J. S. (1983). The relative contribution to meaning of verbal and nonverbal

5. Burgoon, J. K., Guerrero, L. K., & Manusov, V. (2011). Nonverbal signals. In M. L. Knapp & J. Daly (Eds.), *The Sage handbook of interpersonal communication* (4th ed., pp. 238–282). Thousand Oaks, CA: Sage.

6. Burgoon, J. K., Guerrero, L. K., & Floyd, K. (2010). *Nonverbal communication.* Boston, MA: Allyn & Bacon.

7. See, e.g., Watkins, J. L., & Hall, J. A. (2014). The association between nonverbal sensitivity and flirting detection accuracy. *Communication Research Reports, 31,* 348–356.

8. Matsumoto, D., & Hwang, H. S. (2013). Facial expressions. In D. Matsumoto, M. G. Frank, & H. S. Hwang (Eds.), *Nonverbal communication: Science and applications* (pp. 15–52). Thousand Oaks, CA: Sage; but see Gendron, M., Roberson, D., van der Vyver, J. M., & Barrett, L. F. (2014). Perceptions of emotion from facial expressions are not culturally universal: Evidence from a remote culture. *Emotion, 14,* 251–262.

9. See Scherer, K. R., & Ekman, P. (Eds.). (2009). *Approaches to emotion.* Hillsdale, NJ: Lawrence Erlbaum Associates.

10. See Burgoon et al., 2010.

11. Elfenbein, J. A., & Ambady, N. A. (2003). When familiarity breeds accuracy: Cultural exposure and facial emotion recognition. *Journal of Personality and Social Psychology, 85,* 276–290; Elfenbein, H. A., & Ambady, N. (2002). On the universality and cultural specificity of emotion recognition: A meta-analysis. *Psychological Bulletin, 128,* 203–235.

12. Kappas, A., Hess, U., & Scherer, K. R. (1991). Voice and emotion. In R. S. Feldman & B. Rimé (Eds.), *Fundamentals of nonverbal communication* (pp. 200–237). Cambridge, England: Cambridge University Press.

13. Chong, D. S. F., van Eerde, W., Rutte, C. G., & Chai, K. H. (2012). Bringing employees closer: The effect of proximity on communication when teams function under time pressure. *Journal of Product Innovation Management, 29,* 205–215.

14. See, e.g., Meier, B. P., Robinson, M. D., Carter, M. S., & Hinsz, V. B. (2010). Are sociable people more beautiful? A zero-acquaintance analysis of agreeableness, extraversion, and attractiveness. *Journal of Research in Personality, 44,* 293–296.

15. Peters, C. (2005). Direction of attention perception for conversation initiation in virtual environments. *Lecture Notes in Computer Science, 3661,* 215–228.

16. Bavelas, J. B., & Gerwing, J. (2011). The listener as addressee in face-to-face dialogue. *International Journal of Listening, 25,* 178–198.

17. See Wiemann, J. M., & Knapp, M. L. (2008). Turn-taking in conversations. In D. C. Mortensen (Ed.), *Communication theory* (2nd ed., pp. 226–245). New Brunswick, NJ: Transaction.

18. Wiemann & Knapp, 2008; see also Burgoon et al., 2010.

19. Reisenzein, R., Studtmann, M., & Horstmann, G. (2013). Coherence between emotion and facial expression: Evidence from laboratory experiments. *Emotion Review, 5,* 16–23.

20. Cole, P. M., & Moore, G. A. (2015). About face! Infant facial expression of emotion. *Emotion Review, 7,* 116–120.

21. Bigelow, A. E., & Rochat, P. (2006). Two-month-old infants' sensitivity to social contingency in mother–infant and stranger–infant interaction. *Infancy, 9,* 313–325.

22. Scherer, K. R., Sundberg, J., Tamarit, L., & Salomão, G. L. (2015). Comparing the acoustic expression of emotion in the speaking and the singing voice. *Computer Speech & Language, 29,* 218–235.

23. Laukka, P., Juslin, P. N., & Bresin, R. (2005). A dimensional approach to vocal expression of emotion. *Cognition and Emotion, 19,* 633–653.

24. Bänziger, T., & Scherer, K. R. (2005). The role of intonation in emotional expressions. *Speech Communication, 46,* 252–267.

25. Hall, J. A., & Xing, C. (2015). The verbal and nonverbal correlates of the five flirting styles. *Journal of Nonverbal Behavior, 39,* 41–68.

26. Frisby, B. N., Dillow, M. R., Gaughan, S., & Nordlund, J. (2011). Flirtatious communication: An experimental examination of perceptions of social-sexual communication motivated by evolutionary forces. *Sex Roles, 64,* 682–694.

27. Floyd, K. (2006). *Communicating affection: Interpersonal behavior and social context.* Cambridge, England: Cambridge University Press.

28. Burgoon et al., 2010.

29. Porter, S., ten Brinke, L., & Wallace, B. (2012). Secrets and lies: Involuntary leakage in deceptive facial expressions as a function of emotional intensity. *Journal of Nonverbal Behavior, 36,* 23–37; Faragó, T., Andics, A., Devecseri, V., Kis, A., Gácsi, M., & Miklósi, Á. (2014). Humans rely on the same rules to assess emotional valence and intensity in conspecific and dog vocalizations. *Biology Letters, 10*(1), 2013–0926.

30. Heerey, E. A., & Kring, A. M. (2007). Interpersonal consequences of social anxiety. *Journal of Abnormal Psychology, 116,* 125–134.

31. Burgoon et al., 2011.

32. American Psychiatric Association. (2013). *Diagnostic and statistical manual of mental disorders* (5th ed.). Washington, DC: Author.

33. Girard, J. M., Cohn, J. F., Mahoor, M. H., Mavadati, S. M., Hammal, Z., & Rosenwald, D. P. (2014). Nonverbal social withdrawal in depression: Evidence from manual and automatic analyses. *Image and Vision Computing, 32,* 641–647.

34. Burgoon et al., 2010.

35. Guerrero, L. K., & Floyd, K. (2006). *Nonverbal communication in close relationships.* Mahwah, NJ: Lawrence Erlbaum Associates.

36. Awan, S. N. (2006). The aging female voice: Acoustic and respiratory data. *Clinical Linguistics & Phonetics, 20,* 171–180; Xue, S. A., & Deliyski, D. (2001). Effects of aging on selected acoustic voice parameters: Preliminary normative data and educational implications. *Educational Gerontology, 27,* 159–168.

37. Harnsberger, J. D., Shrivastav, R., Brown, W. S., Rothman, H., & Hollien, H. (2008). Speaking rate and fundamental frequency as speech cues to perceived age. *Journal of Voice, 22,* 58–69.

38. Brockmann, M., Drinnan, M. J., Storck, C., & Carding, P. N. (2011). Reliable jitter and shimmer measurements in voice clinics: The relevance of vowel, gender, vocal intensity, and fundamental frequency effects in a typical clinical task. *Journal of Voice, 25,* 44–53.

39. See Junger, J., Pauly, K., Bröhr, S., Birkholz, P., Neuschaefer-Rube, C., . . . Habel, U. (2013). Sex matters: Neural correlates of voice gender perception. *NeuroImage, 79,* 275–287.

40. Aliakbari, M., & Abdolahi, K. (2013). Does it matter what we wear? A sociolinguistic study of clothing and human values. *International Journal of Linguistics, 5,* 34–45; Ruetzler, T., Taylor, J., Reynolds, D., Baker, W., & Killen C. (2013). What is professional attire today? A conjoint analysis of personal presentation attributes. *International Journal of Hospitality Management, 31,* 937–943.

41. Pratt, M. G., & Rafaeli, A. (2004). Organizational dress as a symbol of multilayered social identities. In M. J. Hatch & M. Schultz (Eds.), *Organizational identity: A reader* (pp. 275–312). New York, NY: Oxford University Press.

42. Dunbar, N. E., & Segrin, C. (2012). Clothing and teacher credibility: An application of expectancy violations theory. *International Scholarly Research Notices,* article 140517; Chung, H., Lee, H., Chang, D.-S., Kim, H.-S., Lee, H., Park, H.-J., & Chae, Y. (2012). Doctor's attire influences perceived empathy in the patient-doctor relationship. *Patient Education and Counseling, 89,* 387–391.

43. Benkí, J., Broome, J., Conrad, F., Groves, R., & Kreuter, F. (2011). Effects of speech rate, pitch, and pausing on survey participation decisions. Retrieved March 10, 2015, from www.amstat.org/sections/srms/proceedings/y2011/Files/400189.pdf

44. Neal, T. M. S., & Brodsky, S. L. (2008). Expert witness credibility as a function of eye contact behavior and gender. *Criminal Justice and Behavior, 35,* 1515–1526; Maricchiolo, F., Gnisci, A., Bonaluto, M., & Ficca, G. (2009). Effects of different types of hand gestures in persuasive speech on receivers' evaluations. *Language and Cognitive Processes, 24,* 239–266.

45. Yokoyama, H., & Daibo, I. (2012). Effects of gaze and speech rate on receivers' evaluations of persuasive speech. *Psychological Reports, 110,* 663–676.

46. Sinclair, R. C., Moore, S. E., Mark, M. M., Soldat, A. S., & Lavis, C. A. (2010). Incidental moods, source likeability, and persuasion: Liking motivates message elaboration in happy people. *Cognition & Emotion, 24,* 940–961.

47. Debrot, A., Schoebi, D., Perrez, M., & Horn, A. B. (2013). Touch as an interpersonal emotion regulation process in couples' daily lives: The mediating role of psychological intimacy. *Personality & Social Psychology Bulletin, 39,* 1373–1385.

48. Viadis, D. C. F., & Halimi-Falkowicz, S. G. M. (2008). Increasing compliance with a request: Two touches are more effective than one. *Psychological Reports, 103,* 88–92.

49. Ramseyer, F., & Tschacher, W. (2011). Nonverbal synchrony in psychotherapy: Coordinated body movement reflects relationship quality and outcome. *Journal of Consulting and Clinical Psychology, 79,* 284–295.

50. Lutz-Zois, C. J., Bradley, A. C., Mihalik, J. L., & Moorman Eavers, E. R. (2006). Perceived similarity and relationship success among dating couples: An idiographic approach. *Journal of Social and Personal Relationships, 23,* 865–880; Morry, M. M. (2007). The attraction-similarity hypothesis among cross-sex friends: Relationship satisfaction, perceived similarities, and self-serving perceptions. *Journal of Social and Personal Relationships, 24,* 117–138.

51. See Levine, T. R. (Ed.). (2014). *Encyclopedia of deception.* Thousand Oaks, CA: Sage.

52. Villar, G., Arciuli, J., & Paterson, H. (2013). Vocal pitch production during lying: Beliefs about deception matter. *Psychiatry, Psychology and Law, 20,* 123–132.

53. Ekman, P., O'Sullivan, M., Friesen, W. V., & Scherer, K. R. (1991). Face, voice, and body in detecting deceit. *Journal of Nonverbal Behavior, 15,* 125–135.

54. Burgoon et al., 2010.

55. See Wang, R., Li, J., Fant, H., Tian, M., & Liu, J. (2012). Individual differences in holistic processing predict face recognition ability. *Psychological Science, 23,* 169–177.

56. Saxton, T. K., Debruine, L. M., Jones, B. C., Little, A. C., & Roberts, S. C. (2011). A longitudinal study of adolescents' judgments of the attractiveness of facial symmetry, averageness and sexual dimorphism. *Journal of Evolutionary Psychology, 9,* 43–55.

57. American Academy of Facial Plastic and Reconstructive Surgery. (2015). Nasal surgery: Understanding rhinoplasty. Retrieved March 11, 2015, from www.aafprs.org/patient/procedures/rhinoplasty.html

58. Calder, A. J., Keane, J., Manly, T., Sprengelmeyer, R., Scott, S., Nimmo-Smith, I., & Young, A. W. (2003). Facial expression recognition across the adult life span. *Neuropsychologia, 41,* 195–202.

59. Hampson, E., van Anders, S. M., & Mullin, L. I. (2006). A female advantage in the recognition of emotional facial expressions: Tests of an evolutionary hypothesis. *Evolution and Human Behavior, 27,* 401–416.

60. Hyde, J. S. (2014). Gender similarities and differences. *Annual Review of Psychology, 65,* 373–398.

61. Lieberman, M. D., & Rosenthal, R. (2001). Why introverts can't always tell who likes them: Multitasking and nonverbal decoding. *Journal of Personality and Social Psychology, 80,* 294–310.

62. Valli, C. (Ed.). (2006). *The Gallaudet dictionary of American Sign Language.* Washington, DC: Gallaudet University Press.

63. Bruce, S. M., Mann, A., Jones, C., & Gavin, M. (2007). Gestures expressed by children who are congenitally deaf-blind: Topography, rate, and function. *Journal of Visual Impairment & Blindness, 101,* 637–652.

64. Floyd, K., & Deiss, D. M. (2012). Better health, better lives: The bright side of affection. In T. J. Socha & M. Pitts (Eds.), *The positive side of interpersonal communication* (pp. 127–142). New York, NY: Peter Lang.

65. Stack, D. M. (2001). The salience of touch and physical contact during infancy: Unraveling some of the mysteries of the somesthetic sense. In G. Bremner & A. Fogel (Eds.), *Blackwell handbook of infant development* (pp. 351–378). Oxford, England: Blackwell.

66. See Blum, D. (2002). *Love at Goon Park: Harry Harlow and the science of affection.* New York, NY: Basic Books.

67. Del Prete, T. (1997). Hands off? A touchy subject. *The Education Digest, 62,* 59–61. Quote is from p. 59.

68. Field, T. (2001). *Touch.* Cambridge, MA: MIT Press. Quote is from p. 5.

69. For review, see Field, T. (2014). Massage therapy research review. *Complementary Therapies in Clinical Practice, 20,* 224–229.

70. Field, T. (2014). *Touch* (2nd ed.). Cambridge, MA: MIT Press.

71. Tjaden, P., & Thoennes, N. (2000). Prevalence and consequences of male-to-female and female-to-male intimate partner violence as measured by the National Violence Against Women Survey. *Violence Against Women, 6,* 142–161.

72. For example, see Kneidinger, L. M., Maple, T. L., & Tross, S. A. (2001). Touching behavior in sport: Functional components, analysis of sex differences, and ethological considerations. *Journal of Nonverbal Behavior, 25,* 43–62.

73. Kraus, M. W., Huang C., & Keltner, D. (2010). Tactile communication, cooperation, and performance: An ethological study of the NBA. *Emotion, 10,* 745–749.

74. Babel, M., McGuire, G., & King, J. (2014). Towards a more nuanced view of vocal attractiveness. *PLoS One, 9*(2), e88616.

75. Wolvin, A. (Ed.). (2010). *Listening and human communication in the 21st century.* Malden, MA: Blackwell.

76. Ephratt, M. (2008). The functions of silence. *Journal of Pragmatics, 40,* 1909–1938.

77. Wright, C. N., & Roloff, M. E. (2009). Relational commitment and the silent treatment. *Communication Research Reports, 26,* 12–21.

78. For further discussion, see Kamakura, W. A., Basuroy, S., & Boatwright, P. (2006). Is silence golden? An inquiry into the meaning of silence in professional product evaluations. *Quantitative Marketing and Economics, 4,* 119–141.

79. Hall, E. T. (1963). System for the notation of proxemic behavior. *American Anthropologist, 65,* 1003–1026.

80. Braithwaite, D. O., & Braithwaite, C. A. (2012). "Which is my good leg?" Cultural communication of persons with disabilities. In L. A. Samovar, R. E. Porter, & E. R. McDaniel (Eds.), *Intercultural communication: A reader* (11th ed., pp. 241–253). Boston, MA: Wadsworth.

81. Dovidio, J. F., Pagotto, L., & Hebl, M. R. (2011). Implicit attitudes and discrimination against people with physical disabilities. In R. L. Wiener & S. L. Wilborn (Eds.), *Disability and aging discrimination: Perspectives in law and psychology* (pp. 157–183). New York, NY: Springer.

82. Zebrowitz, L. A., & Franklin, R. G. (2014). The attractiveness halo effect and the babyface stereotype in older and younger adults: Similarities, own-age accentuation, and older adult positivity effects. *Experimental Aging Research, 40,* 375–393.

83. Rhodes, G,. Simmons, L. W., & Peters, M. (2005). Attractiveness and sexual behavior: Does attractiveness enhance mating success? *Evolution and Human Behavior, 26,* 186–201; Bale, C., & Archer, J. (2013). Self-perceived attractiveness, romantic desirability and self-esteem: A mating sociometer perspective. *Evolutionary Psychology, 11,* 68–84.

84. Devine, D. J., & Caughlin, D. E. (2014). Do they matter? A meta-analytic investigation of individual characteristics and guilt judgments. *Psychology, Public Policy, and Law, 20,* 109–134.

85. Smink, F. R. E., van Hocken, D., & Hoek, H. W. (2012). Epidemiology of eating disorders: Incidence, prevalence and mortality rates. *Current Psychiatry Reports, 14,* 406–414.

86. Elliot, A. J., & Maier, M. A. (2014). Color psychology: Effects of perceiving color on psychological functioning in humans. *Annual Review of Psychology, 65,* 95–120.

87. Küller, R., Mikellides, B., & Janssens, J. (2009). Color, arousal, and performance—A comparison of three experiments. *Color Research & Application, 34,* 141–152.

88. Burgoon et al., 2010.

89. Jandt, F. E. (2013). *An introduction to intercultural communication: Identities in a global community* (7th ed.). Thousand Oaks, CA: Sage.

90. See Matsumoto, D. (2006). Culture and nonverbal behavior. In V. L. Manusov & M. L. Patterson (Eds.), *The Sage handbook of nonverbal communication* (pp. 219–236). Thousand Oaks, CA: Sage.

91. Feghali, E. K. (1997). Arab cultural communication patterns. *International Journal of Intercultural Relations, 21,* 345–378.

92. Watson, O. M. (1970). *Proxemic behavior: A cross-cultural study.* The Hague: Mouton.

93. Adams, R. B., & Kleck, R. E. (2005). Effects of direct and averted gaze on the perception of facially communicated emotion. *Emotion, 5,* 3–11.

94. Matsumoto, 2006.

95. Ekman, P. (1993). Facial expressions and emotion. *American Psychologist, 48,* 384–392; Ekman, P., & Friesen, W. V. (1986). A new pan-cultural facial expression of emotion. *Motivation and Emotion, 10,* 159–168; Scherer, K. R., & Walbott, H. G. (1994). Evidence for universality and cultural variation of differential emotion response patterning. *Journal of Personality and Social Psychology, 66,* 310–328.

96. Matsumoto, D., Yoo, S. H., & Fontaine, J. (2008). Mapping expressive differences around the world: The relationship between emotional display rules and individualism versus collectivism. *Journal of Cross-Cultural Psychology, 39,* 55–74.

97. Malott, K. M. (2008). Achieving cultural competency: Assessment of US-based counselor educators instructing internationally. *International Journal for the Advancement of Counseling, 30,* 67–77.

98. Hall, E. T. (2012). Monochronic and polychronic time. In L. A. Samovar, R. E. Porter, & E. R. McDaniel (Eds.), *Intercultural communication: A reader* (11th ed., pp. 313–319). Boston, MA: Wadsworth.

99. Kemp, L. J., & Williams, P. (2013). In their own time and space: Meeting behaviour in the Gulf Arab workplace. *International Journal of Cross Cultural Management, 13,* 215–235.

100. Andersen, P. A. (2011). Tactile traditions: Cultural differences and similarities in haptic communication. In M. Hertenstein & S. J. Weiss (Eds.), *The handbook of touch: Neuroscience, behavioral, and health perspectives* (pp. 351–372). New York, NY: Springer.

101. Andersen, P. A. (2012). The basis of cultural differences in nonverbal communication. In L. A. Samovar, R. E. Porter, & E. R. McDaniel (Eds.), *Intercultural communication: A reader* (11th ed., pp. 293–312). Boston, MA: Wadsworth.

102. Kramsch, C. (1998). *Language and culture.* New York: Oxford University Press.

103. Sauter, D. A., Eisner, F., Ekman, P., & Scott, S. K. (2010). Cross-cultural recognition of basic emotions through nonverbal emotional vocalizations. *Proceedings of the National Academy of Sciences, 107,* 2408–2412.

104. See, e.g., Turpin, M., Demuth, K., & Campbell, A. N. (2014). Phonological aspects of Arandic baby talk. In R. Pensalfini, M. Turpin, & D. Guillemin (Eds.), *Language description informed by theory* (pp. 49–80). Amsterdam, The Netherlands: John Benjamins.

105. Wood, J. T. (2014). *Gendered lives: Communication, culture, and gender* (11th ed.). Belmont, CA: Cengage.

106. Floyd, K., Mikkelson, A. C., & Hesse, C. (2007). *The biology of human communication* (2nd ed.). Florence, KY: Cengage.

107. Burgoon, J. K., & Bacue, A. (2003). Nonverbal communication skills. In B. R. Burleson & J. O. Greene (Eds.), *Handbook of communication and social interaction skills* (pp. 179–219). Mahwah, NJ: Lawrence Erlbaum Associates.

108. Floyd, K. (2006). *Communicating affection: Interpersonal behavior and social context.* Cambridge, England: Cambridge University Press.

109. Kring, A. M., & Gordon, A. H. (1998). Sex differences in emotion: Expression, experience, and physiology. *Journal of Personality and Social Psychology, 74,* 686–703.

110. Else-Quest, N. M., Higgins, A., Allison, C., & Morton, L. C. (2012). Gender differences in self-conscious emotional experience: A meta-analysis. *Psychological Bulletin, 138,* 947–981.

111. Simpson, P. A., & Stroh, L. K. (2004). Gender differences: Emotional expression and feelings of personal inauthenticity. *Journal of Applied Psychology, 89,* 715–721.

112. Campbell, A., & Muncer, S. (2008). Intent to harm or injure: Gender and the expression of anger. *Aggressive Behavior, 34,* 282–293.

113. Mulac, A., Studley, L. B., Wiemann, J. W., & Bradac, J. J. (1987). Male/female gaze in same-sex and mixed-sex dyads: Gender-linked differences and mutual influence. *Human Communication Research, 13,* 323–344.

114. Wada, M. (1990). The effects of interpersonal distance change on nonverbal behaviors: Mediating effects of sex and intimacy levels in a dyad. *Japanese Psychological Research, 32,* 86–96.

115. Exline, R. V. (1963). Explorations in the process of person perception: Visual interaction in relation to competition, sex, and the need for affiliation. *Journal of Personality, 31,* 1–20.

116. Mulac et al., 1987.

117. Patterson, M. L., & Schaeffer, R. E. (1997). Effects of size and sex composition on interaction distance, participation, and satisfaction in small groups. *Small Group Behavior, 8,* 433–442.

118. Shaffer, D. R., & Sadowski, C. (1975). This table is mine: Respect for marked barroom tables as a function of gender of spatial marker and desirability of locale. *Sociometry, 38,* 408–419.

119. Marieb, E. N. (2011). *Essentials of human anatomy and physiology* (10th ed.). Boston, MA: Benjamin Cummings.

120. Bortfield, H., Leon, S. D., Bloom, J. E., Schober, M. F., & Brennan, S. E. (2001). Disfluency rates in conversation: Effects of age, relationship, topic, role, and gender. *Language and Speech, 44,* 123–147.

121. Major, B., Schmidlin, A. M., & Williams, L. (1990). Gesture patterns in social touch: The impact of setting and age. *Journal of Personality and Social Psychology, 58,* 634–643.

122. Major et al., 1990.

123. See Dortsch, S. (1997). Women at the cosmetics counter. *American Demographics, 19,* 4.

124. Bäzinger, T., Scherer, K. R., Hall, J. A., & Rosenthal, R. (2011). Introducing the MiniPONS: A short multichannel version of the Profile of Nonverbal Sensitivity (PONS). *Journal of Nonverbal Behavior, 35,* 189–204.

125. See, e.g., Bartlett, M. S., Littlewort, G. C., Frank, M. G., & Lee, K. (2014). Automatic decoding of facial movements reveals deceptive pain expressions. *Current Biology, 24,* 738–743.

126. Riggio, R. E. (2005). The Social Skills Inventory (SSI): Measuring nonverbal and social skills. In V. Manusov (Ed.), *The sourcebook of nonverbal measures: Going beyond words* (pp. 25–34). Mahwah, NJ: Lawrence Erlbaum Associates.

127. Riggio, R. E. (2006). Nonverbal skills and abilities. In V. L. Manusov & M. L. Patterson (Eds.), *The Sage handbook of nonverbal communication* (pp. 79–96). Thousand Oaks, CA: Sage.

128. Ilies, R., Curşeu, P. L., Dimotakis, N., & Spitzmuller, M. (2013). Leaders' emotional expressiveness and their behavioural and relational authenticity: Effects on followers. *European Journal of Work and Organizational Psychology, 22,* 4–14.

129. Kramer, A. D. I., Guillory, J. E., & Hancock, J. T. (2014). Experimental evidence of massive-scale emotional contagion through social networks. *Proceedings of the National Academy of Sciences, 111,* 8788–8790.

130. Liu, M. W., & Guan, Y. (2014). Consumer compliance in face-to-face interactions: The role of sensitivity and expressiveness. *Advances in Consumer Research, 42,* 584–585.

131. Fears, D. (2014, October 3). Teacher made bomb threat joke to escape meeting. *New York Post.* Retrieved March 13, 2015, from http://nypost.com/2014/10/03/bored-teachers-bomb-threat-joke-backfires-in-east-harlem/

132. Schade, L. C., Sandberg, J., Bean, R., Busby, D., & Coyne, S. (2013). Using technology to connect in romantic relationships: Effects of attachment, relationship satisfaction, and stability in emerging adults. *Journal of Couple & Relationship Therapy, 12,* 314–338.

133. Ling, R., & Baron, N. S. (2007). Text messaging and IM: Linguistic comparison of American college data. *Journal of Language and Social Psychology, 26,* 291–298.

CHAPTER 7

1. U.S. Department of Veterans Affairs. (2015). How common is PTSD? Retrieved March 16, 2015, from www.ptsd.va.gov/public/ PTSD-overview/basics/how-common-is-ptsd.asp

2. See McKay, H. (2013). *Why don't people listen?* Sydney, Australia: Macmillan.

3. Beard, D., & Bodie, G. (2015). Listening research in the communication discipline. In P. J. Gehrke & W. M. Keith (Eds.), *A century of communication studies: The unfinished conversation* (pp. 207–233). New York, NY: Routledge.

4. Bodie, G. D., & Worthington, D. L. (2010). Revising the Listening Styles Profile (LSP-16): A confirmatory factor analytic approach to scale validation and reliability estimation. *International Journal of Listening, 24,* 69–88.

5. Emanuel, R., Adams, J., Baker, K., Daufin, E. K., Ellington, C., Fitts, E., . . . Okeowo, D. (2008). How college students spend their time communicating. *International Journal of Listening, 22,* 13–28.

6. Dindia, K., & Kennedy, B. L. (2004, November). *Communication in everyday life: A descriptive study using mobile electronic data collection.* Paper presented at the annual conference of the National Communication Association, Chicago, IL.

7. Winsor, J. L., Curtis, D. B., & Stephens, R. D. (1997). National preferences in business and communication education: A survey update. *Journal of the Association for Communication Administration, 3,* 170–179.

8. See, e.g., Park, J.-K., Chung, T.-L., Gunn, F., & Rutherford, B. (2015). The role of listening in e-contact center customer relationship management. *Journal of Services Marketing, 29,* 49–58; Jagosh, J., Boudreau, J. D., Steinert, Y., MacDonald, M. E., & Ingram, L. (2011). The importance of physician listening from the patients' perspective: Enhancing diagnosis, healing, and the doctor–patient relationship. *Patient Education and Counseling, 85,* 369–374.

9. Brownell, J. (1990). Perceptions of effective listeners: A management study. *Journal of Business Communication, 27,* 401–415.

10. See, e.g., Floyd, K., Generous, M. A., Clark, L., Simon, A., & McLeod, I. (2015). Empathic communication by physician assistant students: Evidence of an inflation bias. *Journal of Physician Assistant Education, 26,* 94–98.

11. Rost, M., & Wilson, J. J. (2013). *Active listening.* New York, NY: Routledge.

12. Rider, E. A., & Keefer, C. H. (2006). Communication skills competencies: Definitions and a teaching toolbox. *Medical Education, 40,* 624–629.

13. Broome, B. J. (1991). Building shared meaning: Implications of a relational approach to empathy for teaching intercultural communication. *Communication Education, 40,* 235–249.

14. See Lindquist, J. D., & Kaufman-Scarborough, C. (2007). The Polychronic-Monochronic Tendency Model: PMTS scale development and validation. *Time & Society, 16,* 253–285.

15. Lustig, M. W., & Koester, J. (2012). *Intercultural competence: Interpersonal communication across cultures* (7th ed.). Boston, MA: Pearson.

16. Karakowsky, L., McBey, K., & Miller, D. L. (2004). Gender, perceived competence, and power displays: Examining verbal interruptions in a group context. *Small Group Research, 35,* 407–439; Anderson, K. J., & Leaper, C. (1998). Meta-analyses of gender effects on conversational interruption: Who, what, when, where, and how. *Sex Roles, 39,* 225–252.

17. van Straaten, I., Holland, R. W., Finkenauer, C., Hollenstein, T., & Engels, R. C. M. E. (2010). Gazing behavior during mixed-sex interactions: Sex and attractiveness effects. *Archives of Sexual Behavior, 39,* 1055–1062.

18. Sargent, S. L., & Weaver, J. B. (2003). Listening styles: Sex differences in perceptions of self and others. *International Journal of Listening, 17,* 5–18.

19. Brownell, J. (2012). *Listening attitudes, principles, and skills* (5th ed.). Boston, MA: Pearson.

20. Macrae, C. N., & Bodenhausen, G. V. (2001). Social cognition: Categorical person perception. *British Journal of Psychology, 92,* 239–255.

21. See Janusik, L. A. (2007). Building listening theory: The validation of the conversational listening span. *Communication Studies, 58,* 139–156.

22. Benoit, S. S., & Lee, J. W. (1986). Listening: It can be taught. *Journal of Education for Business, 63,* 229–232.

23. Brehmer, Y., Li, S.-C., Straube, B., Stoll, G., von Oertzen, T., Müller, V., & Lindenberger, U. (2008). Comparing memory skill maintenance across the life span: Preservation in adults, increase in children. *Psychology and Aging, 23,* 227–238.

24. Heyleyn, D., Bevacqua, E., Pelachaud, C., Poggi, I., Gratch, J., & Schröder, M. (2011). Generating listening behavior. In R. Cowie, C. Pelachaud, & P. Petta (Eds.), *Emotion-oriented systems* (pp. 321–347). Berlin, Germany: Springer.

25. Egan, G. (2013). *The skilled helper* (10th ed.). Belmont, CA: Brooks/Cole.

26. Floyd, K. (2014). Empathic listening as an expression of interpersonal affection. *International Journal of Listening, 28,* 1–12.

27. Surtees, A. D. R., & Apperly, I. A. (2012). Egocentrism and automatic perspective taking in children and adults. *Child Development, 83,* 452–460.

28. O'Brien, E., Konrath, S. H., Grühn, D., & Hagen, A. L. (2013). Empathic concern and perspective taking: Linear and quadratic effects of age across the adult life span. *Journal of Gerontology B: Psychological Sciences & Social Sciences, 68,* 168–175.

29. Tanis, M. (2007). Online social support groups. In A. Joinson, K. McKenna, T. Postmes, & U. D. Reips (Eds.), *The Oxford handbook of Internet psychology* (pp. 139–154). Oxford, England: Oxford University Press.

30. Bender, J. L., Jimenez-Marroquin, M.-C., & Jadad, A. R. (2011). Seeking support on Facebook: A content analysis of breast cancer groups. *Journal of Medical Internet Research, 13,* e16. Retrieved March 17, 2015, from www.ncbi.nlm.nih.gov/pmc/articles/ PMC3221337/

31. Alcoholics Anonymous Online Intergroup. (2015). Online meetings directory. Retrieved March 17, 2015, from www.aa-intergroup .org/directory.php

32. Han, J. Y., Shah, D. V., Kim, E., Namkoong, K., Lee, S.-Y., Moon, T. J., . . . Gustafson, D. H. (2011). Empathic exchanges in online cancer support groups: Distinguishing message expression and reception effects. *Health Communication, 26,* 185–197.

33. DeAndrea, D. C. (2015). Testing the proclaimed affordances of online support groups in a nationally representative sample of adults seeking mental health assistance. *Journal of Health Communication, 20,* 147–156.

34. Sun, N., Rau, P. P.-L., & Ma, L. (2014). Understanding lurkers in online communities: A literature review. *Computers in Human Behavior, 38,* 110–117.

35. van Mierlo, T. (2014). The 1% rule in four digital health social networks: An observational study. *Journal of Medical Internet Research, 16*(2).

36. Nielsen, J. (2006, October 9). The 90-9-1 rule for participation inequality in social media and online communities. *Nielsen Norman Group.* Retrieved March 21, 2015, from www.nngroup.com/articles/participation-inequality/

37. See Banbury, S. P., & Berry, D. C. (2005). Office noise and employee concentration: Identifying causes of disruption and potential improvements. *Ergonomics, 48,* 25–37.

38. Gailliot, M. T., Baumeister, R. F., DeWall, C. N., Maner, J. K., Plant, E. A., Tice, D. M., . . . Schmeichel, B. J. (2007). Self-control relies on glucose as a limited energy source: Willpower is more than a metaphor. *Journal of Personality and Social Psychology, 92,* 325–336.

39. Gazzaley, A., & Nobre, A. C. (2012). Top-down modulation: Bridging selective attention and working memory. *Trends in Cognitive Science, 16,* 129–135.

40. Media Dynamics, Inc. (2007, February 15). Our rising ad dosage: It's not as oppressive as some think. *Media Matters, XXI*(3), 1–2.

41. Toffler, A. (1970). *Future shock.* New York, NY: Random House.

42. Keller, E. (2007, July 19). Why you can't get any work done: Workplace distractions cost U.S. business some $650 billion a year. Retrieved November 23, 2007, from www.businessweek.com/careers/content/jul2007/ca20070719_880333.htm

43. MarketingCharts.com. (2013, March 21). 18–24-year-old smartphone owners send and receive almost 4K texts per month. Retrieved March 17, 2015, from www.marketingcharts.com/online/18-24-year-old-smartphone-owners-send-and-receive-almost-4k-texts-per-month-27993/

44. Lenhart, A. (2010, September). *Cell phones and American adults.* Washington, D.C.: Pew Research Center; Jones, Q., Ravid, G., & Rafaeli, S. (2004). Information overload and the message dynamics of online interaction spaces: A theoretical model and empirical exploration. *Information Systems Research, 15,* 194–210.

45. Wolvin, A. (2011). *Listening and human communication in the 21st century.* New York, NY: Wiley Blackwell.

46. Neal, K. L. (2014). *Six key communication skills for records and information managers.* Oxford, England: Elsevier.

47. Golen, S. (1990). A factor analysis of barriers to effective listening. *International Journal of Business Communication, 27,* 25–36.

48. Masicampo, E. J., & Baumeister, R. F. (2012). Committed but closed-minded: When making a specific plan for a goal hinders success. *Social Cognition, 30,* 37–55.

49. Profetto-McGrath, J. (2005). Critical thinking and evidence-based practice. *Journal of Professional Nursing, 21,* 364–371.

50. Farley, S. D. (2008). Attaining status at the expense of likeability: Pilfering power through conversational interruption. *Journal of Nonverbal Behavior, 32,* 241–260.

51. Kassin, S. M., Dror, I. E., & Kukucka, J. (2013). The forensic confirmation bias: Problems, perspectives, and proposed solutions. *Journal of Applied Research in Memory and Cognition, 2,* 42–52.

52. Guadagno, R. E., Rhoads, K. V. L., & Sagarin, B. J. (2011). Figural vividness and persuasion: Capturing the "elusive" vividness effect. *Personality and Social Psychology Bulletin, 37,* 626–638.

53. www.planecrashinfo.com/cause.htm

54. Federal Bureau of Investigation. (2015). Crime in schools and colleges. *FBI Uniform Crime Reports.* Retrieved March 19, 2015, from www.fbi.gov/about-us/cjis/ucr/nibrs/crime-in-schools-and-colleges/crime_in_schools_and_colleges#Analyses

55. Snyder, L. G., & Snyder, M. J. (2008). Teaching critical thinking and problem solving skills. *Delta Pi Epsilon Journal, 50,* 90–99.

56. Tannen, D. (1990). *You just don't understand: Women and men in conversation.* New York, NY: Ballantine.

57. Pollak, K. I., Arnold, R. M., Jeffreys, A. S., Alexander, S. C., Olsen, M. K., Abernethy, A. P., . . . Tulsky, J. A. (2007). Oncologist communication about emotion during visits with patients with advanced cancer. *Journal of Clinical Oncology, 25,* 5748–5752.

58. Floyd, K. (2006). *Communicating affection: Interpersonal behavior and social context.* Cambridge, England: Cambridge University Press.

CHAPTER 8

1. Lewis M., Haviland-Jones, J. M., & Barrett, L. F. (Eds.). (2010). *Handbook of emotions* (3rd ed.). New York, NY: Guilford.

2. See Austin, E. J. A. (2014). Changing the moods of others: The Mood Change Scale (MCS). *Personality and Individual Differences, 60,* S22–S23.

3. Kemeny, M. E., & Shestyuk, A. (2010). Emotions, the neuroendocrine and immune systems, and health. In M. Lewis, J. M. Haviland-Jones, & L. F. Barrett (Eds.), *Handbook of emotions* (3rd ed., pp. 661–675). New York, NY: Guilford.

4. Guerrero, L. K., & Floyd, K. (2006). *Nonverbal communication in close relationships.* Mahwah, NJ: Lawrence Erlbaum Associates.

5. Csikszentmihalyi, M., & Wong, M. M.-H. (2014). The situational and personal correlates of happiness: A cross-national sample. In M. Csikszentmihalyi (Ed.), *Flow and the foundations of positive psychology* (pp. 69–88). Dordrecht, The Netherlands: Springer.

6. Prado, C., Mellor, D., Byrne, L. K., Wilson, C., Xu, X., & Liu, H. (2014). Facial emotion recognition: A cross-cultural comparison of Chinese, Chinese living in Australia, and Anglo-Australians. *Motivation and Emotion, 38,* 420–428.

7. Carr, A. (2011). *Positive psychology: The science of happiness and human strengths.* New York, NY: Routledge.

8. Stins, J. F., Roelofs, K., Villan, J., Kooijman, K., Hagenaars, M. A., & Beek, P. J. (2011). Walk to me when I smile, step back when I'm angry: Emotional faces modulate whole-body approach-avoidance behaviors. *Experimental Brain Research, 212,* 603–611.

9. Seidel, E. -M., Habel, U., Kirschner, M., Gur, R. C., & Derntl, B. (2010). The impact of facial emotional expressions on behavioral tendencies in women and men. *Journal of Experimental Psychology: Human Perception and Performance, 36,* 500–507.

10. van Winkel, M., Peeters, F., van Winlek, R., Kenis, G., Collip, D., Geschwind, N., . . . Wichers, M. (2014). Impact of variation in the BDNF gene on social stress sensitivity and the buffering impact of positive emotions: Replication and extension of a gene-environment interaction. *European Neuropsychopharmacology, 24,* 930–938.

11. Sprecher, S., & Hatfield. E. (in press). The importance of love as a basis of marriage: Revising Kephart (1967). *Journal of Family Issues.*

12. Hatfield, E., Bensman, L., & Rapson, R. L. (2012). A brief history of social scientists' attempts to measure passionate love. *Journal of Social and Personal Relationships, 29,* 143–164.

13. Niehuis, S., Reifman, A., Feng, D., & Huston, T. L. (in press). Courtship progression rate and declines in expressed affection early in marriage: A test of the disillusionment model. *Journal of Family Issues.*

14. Fisher, H. E., Aron, A., & Brown, L. L. (2006). Romantic love: A mammalian brain system for mate choice. *Philosophical Transactions of the Royal Society B, 361,* 2173–2186.

15. Sprecher, S. (2014). Initial interactions online-text, online-audio, online-video, or face-to-face: Effects of modality on liking, closeness, and other interpersonal outcomes. *Computers in Human Behavior, 31,* 190–197.

16. See, e.g., Ray, G. B., & Floyd, K. (2006). Nonverbal expressions of liking and disliking in initial interaction: Encoding and decoding perspectives. *Southern Communication Journal, 71,* 45–65.

17. Gable, S. L., & Impett, E. A. (2012). Approach and avoidance motives and close relationships. *Social and Personality Psychology Compass, 6,* 95–108.

18. Bies, R. J., & Tripp, T. M. (2012). Negotiating the peace in the face of modern distrust: Dealing with anger and revenge in the 21st century workplace. In B. M. Goldman & D. L. Shapiro (Eds.), *The psychology of negotiations in the 21st century workplace: New challenges and new solutions* (pp. 181–210). New York, NY: Routledge.

19. Ronan, G. F., Dreer, L., Maurelli, K., Wollerman Ronan, D., & Gerhart, J. (2014). *Practitioner's guide to empirically supported measures of anger, aggression, and violence.* Cham, Switzerland: Springer International.

20. Player, M. S., King, D. E., Mainous, A. G., & Greesey, M. E. (2007). Psychosocial factors and progression from prehypertension to hypertension or coronary heart disease. *Annals of Family Medicine, 5,* 403–411.

21. Eaker, E. D., Sullivan, L. M., Kelly-Hayes, M., D'Agostino, R. B., & Benjamin, E. J. (2004). Anger and hostility predict the development of atrial fibrillation in men in the Framingham Offspring Study. *Circulation, 109,* 1267–1271.

22. Bleil, M. E., McCaffery, J. M., Muldoon, M. F., Sutton-Tyrrell, K., & Manuck, S. B. (2004). Anger-related personality traits and carotid artery atherosclerosis in untreated hypertensive men. *Psychosomatic Medicine, 66,* 633–639; Raikkonen, K., Matthews, K. A., Sutton-Tyrell, K., & Kuller, L. H. (2004). Trait anger and the metabolic syndrome predict progression of carotid atherosclerosis in healthy middle-aged women. *Psychosomatic Medicine, 66,* 903–908.

23. Eng, P. M., Fitzmaurice, G., Kubzansky, L. D., Rimm, E. B., & Kawachi, I. (2003). Anger expression and risk of stroke and coronary heart disease among male health professionals. *Psychosomatic Medicine, 65,* 100–110.

24. Wilcox, S., King, A. C., Vitaliano, P. P., & Brassington, G. S. (2000). Anger expression and natural killer cell activity in family caregivers participating in a physical activity trial. *Journal of Health Psychology, 5,* 431–440.

25. Gouin, J. P., Kiecolt-Glaser, J. K., Malarkey, W. B., & Glaser, R. (2008). The influence of anger expression on wound healing. *Brain, Behavior, and Immunity, 22,* 699–708.

26. See Segrin, C., & Flora, J. (2014). Marital communication. In C. R. Berger (Ed.), *Interpersonal communication* (pp. 443–466). Berlin, Germany: Walter de Gruyter.

27. Hutcherson, C. A., & Gross, J. J. (2011). The moral emotions: A social-functionalist account of anger, disgust, and contempt. *Journal of Personality and Social Psychology, 100,* 719–737.

28. Gottman, J. M. (2015). *Principia amoris: The new science of love.* New York, NY: Routledge.

29. Rozin, P., Haidt, J., & McCauley, C. (2010). Disgust. In M. Lewis, J. M. Haviland-Jones, & L. F. Barrett (Eds.), *Handbook of emotions* (3rd ed., pp. 757–776). New York, NY: Guilford.

30. Haidt, J. (2003). The moral emotions. In R. J. Davidson, K. R. Scherer, & H. H. Goldsmith (Eds.), *Handbook of affective sciences* (pp. 852–870). Oxford, England: Oxford University Press.

31. Curtis, V., de Barra, M., & Aunger, R. (2011). Disgust as an adaptive system for disease avoidance behaviour. *Philosophical Transactions of the Royal Society B: Biological Sciences, 366,* 389–401.

32. Russell, P. S., & Giner-Sorolla, R. (2013). Bodily moral disgust: What it is, how it is different from anger, and why it is an unreasoned emotion. *Psychological Bulletin, 139,* 328–351.

33. Eskine, K. J., Novreske, A., & Richards, M. (2013). Moral contagion effects in everyday interpersonal encounters. *Journal of Experimental Social Psychology, 49,* 947–950; see also Rozin, P., Markwith, M., & McCauley, C. R. (1994). The nature of aversion to indirect contacts with other persons: AIDS aversion as a composite of aversion to strangers, infection, moral taint, and misfortune. *Journal of Abnormal Psychology, 103,* 495–504.

34. Nemeroff, C., & Rozin, P. (1994). The contagion concept in adult thinking in the United States: Transmission of germs and of interpersonal influence. *Ethos, 22,* 158–186.

35. Buss, D. M. (2014). Evolutionary criteria for considering an emotion "basic": Jealousy as an illustration. *Emotion Review, 6,* 313–315; Schützwohl, A. (2008). The intentional object of romantic jealousy. *Evolution and Human Behavior, 29,* 92–99.

36. Parker, J. G., Nielsen, B. L., & McDonald, K. L. (in press). Sources and implications of maternal accuracy about young adolescents' vulnerability to friendship jealousy. *Journal of Research on Adolescence.*

37. van de Ven, N., Zeelenberg, M., & Pieters, R. (2012). Appraisal patterns of envy and related emotions. *Motivation and Emotion, 36,* 195–204.

38. Fiske, S. T. (2011). *Envy up, scorn down: How status divides us.* New York, NY: Russell Sage Foundation.

39. van de Ven, N., Zeelenberg, M., & Pieters, R. (2011). The envy premium in product evaluation. *Journal of Consumer Research, 37,* 984–998.

40. van de Ven, N., Zeelenberg, M., & Pieters, R. (2011). Why envy outperforms admiration. *Personality and Social Psychology Bulletin, 37,* 784–795.

41. Bonanno, G. A., Goorin, L., & Coifman, K. G. (2010). Sadness and grief. In M. Lewis, J. M. Haviland-Jones, & L. F. Barrett (Eds.), *Handbook of emotions* (3rd ed., pp. 797–810). New York, NY: Guilford.

42. Lopez-Duran, N. L., Kuhlman, K. R., George, C., & Kovacs, M. (2013). Facial emotional expression recognition by children at familial risk for depression: High-risk boys are oversensitive to sadness. *Journal of Child Psychology and Psychiatry, 54,* 565–574; Kotz, S. A., Kalberlah, C., Bahlmann, J., Friederici, A. D., & Haynes, J. D. (2013). Predicting vocal emotion expressions from the human brain. *Human Brain Mapping, 34,* 1971–1981.

43. American Psychiatric Association. (2013). *Diagnostic and statistical manual of mental disorders* (5th ed.). Washington, D.C.: Author.

44. See, e.g., Kendler, K. S., Gardner, C. O., & Prescott, C. A. (2006). Toward a comprehensive developmental model for major depression in men. *American Journal of Psychiatry, 163,* 115–124.

45. Leahy, R. L., Holland, S. J. F., & McGinn, L. K. (2011). *Treatment plans and interventions for depression and anxiety disorders* (2nd ed.). New York, NY: Guilford.

46. Carek, P. J., Laibstain, S. E., & Carek, S. M. (2011). Exercise for the treatment of depression and anxiety. *International Journal of Psychiatry in Medicine, 41,* 15–28.

47. Krpan, K. M., Kross, E., Berman, M. G., Deldin, P. J., Askren, M. K., & Jonides, J. (2013). An everyday activity as a treatment for depression: The benefits of expressive writing for people diagnosed with major depressive disorder. *Journal of Affective Disorders, 150,* 1148–1151.

48. Roth, A. J., Greenstein, M., Wiesel, T. W., & Schulberg, S. (2015). Depressive spectrum disorders and grief. In J. C. Holland, T. W. Wiesel, C. J. Nelson, A. J. Roth, & Y. Alici (Eds.), *Geriatric psycho-oncology: A quick reference on the psychosocial dimensions of cancer symptom management* (pp. 59–68). Oxford, England: Oxford University Press.

49. Kübler-Ross, E., & Kessler, D. (2005). *On grief and grieving: Finding the meaning of grief through the five stages of loss.* New York, NY: Scribner.

50. Öhman, A. (2010). Fear and anxiety: Overlaps and dissociations. In M. Lewis, J. M. Haviland-Jones, & L. F. Barrett (Eds.), *Handbook of emotions* (3rd ed., pp. 709–729). New York, NY: Guilford.

51. Mahan, A. L., & Ressler, K. J. (2012). Fear conditioning, synaptic plasticity and the amygdala: Implications for posttraumatic stress disorder. *Trends in Neurosciences, 35,* 24–35.

52. Amunts, K., Kedo, O., Kindler, M., Pieperhoff, P., Mohlberg, H., Shah, N. J., . . . Zilles, K. (2005). Cytoarchitectonic mapping of the human amygdala, hippocampal region and entorhinal cortex: Intersubject variability and probability maps. *Anatomy and Embryology, 210,* 343–352.

53. Adolphs, R., Gosselin, F., Buchanan, T., Tranel, D., Schyns, P., & Damasio, A. (2005). A mechanism for implied fear recognition in amygdala damage. *Nature, 433,* 68–72.

54. Duvarci, S., Popa, D., & Paré, D. (2011). Central amygdala activity during fear conditioning. *Journal of Neuroscience, 31,* 289–294.

55. Weinstein, A., Dorani, D., Elhadif, R., Bukovza, Y., Yarmulnik, A,. & Dannon, P. (2015). Internet addiction is associated with social anxiety in young adults. *Annals of Clinical Psychiatry, 27,* 4–9.

56. Xu, Y., Schneier, F., Heimberg, R. G., Princisvalle, K., Liebowitz, M. R., Wang, S., & Blanco, C. (2012). Gender differences in social anxiety disorder: Results from the national epidemiologic sample on alcohol and related conditions. *Journal of Anxiety Disorders, 26,* 12–19; Belzer, K. D., McKee, M. B., & Liebowitz, M. R. (2005). Social anxiety disorder: Current perspectives on diagnosis and treatment. *Primary Psychiatry, 12,* 40–53.

57. Schaefer, H. S., Larson, C. L., Davidson, R. J., & Coan, J. A. (2014). Brain, body, and cognition: Neural, physiological and self-report correlates of phobic and normative fear. *Biological Psychology, 98,* 59–69.

58. Larsen, J. T., Berntson, G. G., Poehlmann, K. M., Ito, T. A., & Cacioppo, J. T. (2010). The psychophysiology of emotion. In M. Lewis, J. M. Haviland-Jones, & L. F. Barrett (Eds.), *Handbook of emotions* (3rd ed., pp. 180–195). New York, NY: Guilford.

59. Roseman, I. J. (2013). Appraisal in the emotion system: Coherence in strategies for coping. *Emotion Review, 5,* 141–149.

60. See Steunebrink, B. R., Dastani, M., & Meyer, J.-J. C. (2009). A formal model of emotion-based action tendency for intelligent agents. In L. S. Lopes, N. Lau, P. Mariano, & L. M. Rocha (Eds.), *Progress in artificial intelligence* (pp. 174–186). Berlin, Germany: Springer.

61. Teatero, M. L., & Penney, A. M. (2015). Fight-or-flight response. In I. Milosevic & R. E. McCabe (Eds.), *Phobias: The psychology of irrational fear* (pp. 179–180). Santa Barbara, CA: ABC-CLIO.

62. Haidt, J. (2003). The moral emotions. In R. J. Davidson, K. R. Scherer, & H. H. Goldsmith (Eds.), *Handbook of affective sciences* (pp. 852–870). Oxford, England: Oxford University Press.

63. Paulus, A., & Wentura, D. (2014). Threatening joy: Approach and avoidance reactions to emotions are influenced by the group membership of the expresser. *Cognition & Emotion, 28,* 656–677.

64. Goddard, C. (2002). Explicating emotions across languages and cultures: A semantic approach. In S. R. Fussell (Ed.), *The verbal communication of emotions* (pp. 19–53). Mahwah, NJ: Lawrence Erlbaum Associates.

65. Woody, S. R., & Teachman, B. A. (2000). Intersection of disgust and fear: Normative and pathological views. *Clinical Psychology: Science and Practice, 7,* 291–311; see also Schwabe, C. W. (1988). *Unmentionable cuisine.* Charlottesville: University of Virginia Press.

66. Rosen, S. J. (2008). *Essential Hinduism.* Lanham, MD: Rowman & Littlefield.

67. Elison, J., Pulos, S., & Randy, L. (2006). Shame-focused coping: An empirical study of the compass of shame. *Social Behavior and Personality, 34,* 161–168.

68. Young, J. (2002). Morals, suicide, and psychiatry: A view from Japan. *Bioethics, 16,* 412–424.

69. Carter, C. S. (2014). Oxytocin pathways and the evolution of human behavior. *Annual Review of Psychology, 65,* 17–39.

70. Tsenkova, V. K., Carr, D., Coe, C. L., & Ryff, C. D. (2014). Anger, adiposity, and glucose control in nondiabetic adults: Findings from MIDUS II. *Journal of Behavioral Medicine, 37,* 37–46.

71. Kensinger, E. A., & Schacter, D. L. (2006). Processing emotional pictures and words: Effects of valence and arousal. *Cognitive, Affective, & Behavioral Neuroscience, 6,* 110–126.

72. Rainville, P., Bechara, A., Naqvi, N., & Damasio, A. R. (2006). Basic emotions are associated with distinct patterns of cardiorespiratory activity. *International Journal of Psychophysiology, 61,* 5–18; see also Damasio, A. (2003). Feelings of emotion and the self. *Annals of the New York Academy of Sciences, 1001,* 253–261.

73. Ekman, P., & Cordaro, D. (2011). What is meant by calling emotions basic. *Emotion Review, 3,* 364–370.

74. For a review of this work, see Matsumoto, D. (2006). Culture and nonverbal behavior. In V. Manusov & M. L. Patterson (Eds.), *The Sage handbook of nonverbal communication* (pp. 219–235). Thousand Oaks, CA: Sage.

75. See, e.g., Oishi, S. (2002). The experience and remembering of well-being: A cross-cultural analysis. *Personality and Social Psychology Bulletin, 28,* 1398–1406.

76. Rolls, E. T. (2015). Limbic systems for emotion and for memory, but no single limbic system. *Cortex, 62,* 119–157.

77. Hejmadi, A., Davidson, R. J., & Rozin, P. (2000). Exploring Hindu Indian emotion expressions: Evidence for accurate recognition by Americans and Indians. *Psychological Science, 11,* 183–187.

78. Metts, S., & Planalp, S. (2011). Emotion experience and expression: Current trends and future directions in interpersonal relationship research. In M. L. Knapp & J. A. Daly (Eds.), *The Sage handbook of interpersonal communication* (4th ed., pp. 283–315). Thousand Oaks, CA: Sage.

79. Becker-Asano, C., & Wachsmuth, I. (2010). Affective computing with primary and secondary emotions in a virtual human. *Autonomous Agents and Multi-Agent Systems, 20,* 32–49.

80. Koven, N. S. (2011). Specificity of meta-emotion effects on moral decision-making. *Emotion, 11,* 1255–1261.

81. Chen, F. M., Lin, H. S., & Li, C. H. (2012). The role of emotion in parent-child relationships: Children's emotionality, maternal meta-emotion, and children's attachment security. *Journal of Child and Family Studies, 21,* 403–410.

82. Katz, L. F., Maliken, A. C., & Stettler, N. M. (2012). Parental meta-emotion philosophy: A review of research and theoretical framework. *Child Development Perspectives, 6,* 417–422.

83. Gallois, C. (1993). The language and communication of emotion: Universal, interpersonal, or intergroup? *American Behavioral Scientist, 36,* 309–338.

84. Triandis, H. C. (1994). *Culture and social behavior.* New York, NY: McGraw-Hill.

85. Tsai, J. L., & Levenson, R. W. (1997). Cultural influences of emotional responding: Chinese American and European American dating couples during interpersonal conflict. *Journal of Cross-Cultural Psychology, 28,* 600–625.

86. Soto, J. A., Levenson, R. W., & Ebling, R. (2005). Cultures of moderation and expression: Emotional experience, behavior, and physiology in Chinese Americans and Mexican Americans. *Emotion, 5,* 154–165.

87. Montesquieu, C. de S. (1989). *The spirit of the laws.* Cambridge, England: Cambridge University Press. (Original work published 1748.)

88. Pennebaker, J. W., Rimé, B., & Blankenship, V. E. (1996). Stereotypes of emotional expressiveness of northerners and southerners: A cross-cultural test of Montesquieu's hypothesis. *Journal of Personality and Social Psychology, 70,* 372–380.

89. Andersen, P. A. (2005). The touch avoidance measure. In V. L. Manusov (Ed.), *The sourcebook of nonverbal measures: Going beyond words* (pp. 57–66). Mahwah, NJ: Lawrence Erlbaum Associates.

90. Hoge, C. W., Castro, C. A., Messer, S. C., McGurk, D., Cotting, D. I., & Koffman, R. L. (2004). Combat duty in Iraq and Afghanistan, mental health problems, and barriers to care. *New England Journal of Medicine, 351,* 13–22.

91. See Moran, C. M., Diefendorff, J. M., & Greguras, G. J. (2013). Understanding emotional display rules at work and outside of work: The effects of country and gender. *Motivation and Emotion, 37,* 323–334.

92. Churches, O., Nicholls, M., Thiessen, M., Kohler, M., & Keage, H. (2014). Emoticons in mind: An event-related potential study. *Social Neuroscience, 9,* 196–202.

93. Stelmaszewska, H., Fields, B., & Blandford, A. (2005, September). *Emotion and technology: An empirical study.* Paper presented at the Workshop on the Role of Emotion in Human-Computer Interaction, Edinburgh, Scotland.

94. Dimberg, U., & Thunberg, M. (2012). Empathy, emotional contagion, and rapid facial reactions to angry and happy facial expressions. *PsyCh Journal, 1,* 118–127.

95. Sy, T., Côté, S., & Saavedra, R. (2005). The contagious leader: Impact of the leader's mood on the mood of group members, group affective tone, and group processes. *Journal of Applied Psychology, 90,* 295–305.

96. Hancock, J. T., Gee, K., Ciaccio, K., & Lin, J. M.-H. (2008, November). *I'm sad you're sad: Emotional contagion in CMC.* Paper presented at the Association for Computing Machinery conference on computer-supported cooperative work, San Diego, CA.

97. Coviello, L., Sohn, Y., Kramer, A. D. I., Marlow, C., Franceschetti, M., Christakis, N. A., & Fowler, J. H. (2014). Detecting emotional contagion in massive social networks. *PLoS One, 9,* e90315.

98. Fisher, A. H., Rodriguez Mosquera, P. M., van Vianen, A. E. M., & Manstead, A. E. R. (2004). Gender and culture differences in emotion. *Emotion, 4,* 87–94.

99. See, e.g., Guerrero, L. K., Jones, S. M., & Boburka, R. R. (2006). Sex differences in emotional communication. In K. Dindia & D. J. Canary (Eds.), *Sex differences and similarities in communication* (2nd ed., pp. 241–261). Mahwah, NJ: Lawrence Erlbaum Associates.

100. Floyd, K. (2006). *Communicating affection: Interpersonal behavior and social context.* Cambridge, England: Cambridge University Press; Burgoon, J. K., & Bacue, A. E. (2003). Nonverbal communication skills. In J. O. Greene & B. R. Burleson (Eds.), *Handbook of communication and social interaction skills* (pp. 179–219). Mahwah, NJ: Lawrence Erlbaum Associates.

101. Chaplin, T. M., & Aldao, A. (2013). Gender differences in emotion expression in children: A meta-analytic review. *Psychological Bulletin, 139,* 735–765.

102. Hess, U., Adams, R. B., & Kleck, R. E. (2005). Who may frown and who should smile? Dominance, affiliation, and the display of happiness and anger. *Cognition & Emotion, 19,* 515–536.

103. Hess, U., Adams, R. B., & Kleck, R. E. (2004). Facial appearance, gender, and emotion expression. *Emotion, 4,* 378–388.

104. Edlund, J. E., Heider, J. D., Scherer, C. R., Fare, M. M., & Sagarin, B. J. (2006). Sex differences in jealousy in response to actual infidelity. *Evolutionary Psychology, 4,* 462–470; Mathes, E. W. (2005). Men's desire for children carrying their genes and sexual jealousy: A test of paternity uncertainty as an explanation of male sexual jealousy. *Psychological Reports, 96,* 791–798; Shackelford, T. K., Buss, D. M., & Bennett, K. (2002). Forgiveness or breakup: Sex differences in responses to a partner's infidelity. *Cognition & Emotion, 16,* 299–307.

105. Fernandez, A. M., Vera-Villarroel, P., Sierra, J. C., & Zubeidat, I. (2007). Distress in response to emotional and sexual infidelity: Evidence of evolved gender differences in Spanish students. *Journal of Psychology, 141,* 17–24; see also Buss, D. M., Shackelford, T. K., Kirkpatrick, L. E., Choe, J. C., Hang, K. L., Hawegawa, M., Hawegawa, T., & Bennett, K. (1999). Jealousy and the nature of beliefs about infidelity: Tests of competing hypotheses about sex differences in the United States, Korea, and Japan. *Personal Relationships, 6,* 125–150.

106. Takahashi, H., Matsuura, M., Yahata, N., Koeda, M., Suhara, T., & Okubo, Y. (2006). Men and women show distinct brain activations during imagery of sexual and emotional infidelity. *NeuroImage, 32,* 1299–1307.

107. Shackelford, T. D., Goetz, A. T., Buss, D. M., Euler, H. A., & Hoier, S. (2005). When we hurt the ones we love: Predicting violence against women from men's mate retention. *Personal Relationships, 12,* 447–463.

108. Ibid.

109. Harris, C. R. (2003). A review of sex differences in sexual jealousy, including self-report data, psychophysiological responses, interpersonal violence, and morbid jealousy. *Personality and Social Psychology Review, 7,* 102–128; DeSteno, D., Bartlett, M. Y., Braverman, J., & Salovey, P. (2002). Sex differences in jealousy: Evolutionary mechanism or artifact of measurement? *Journal of Personality and Social Psychology, 83,* 513–518.

110. Green, M. C., & Sabini, J. (2006). Gender, socioeconomic status, age, and jealousy: Emotional responses to infidelity in a national sample. *Emotion, 6*, 330–334.

111. Berman, M. I., & Frazier, P. A. (2005). Relationship power and betrayal experience as predictors of reactions to infidelity. *Personality and Social Psychology Bulletin, 31*, 1617–1627; Harris, C. R. (2002). Sexual and romantic jealousy in heterosexual and homosexual adults. *Psychological Science, 13*, 7–12.

112. Sagarin, B. J. (2005). Reconsidering evolved sex differences in jealousy: Comment on Harris (2003). *Personality and Social Psychology Review, 9*, 62–75.

113. Kring, A. M., & Gordon, A. H. (1998). Sex differences in emotion: Expression, experience, and physiology. *Journal of Personality and Social Psychology, 74*, 686–703.

114. Cleary, A. (2012). Suicidal action, emotional expression, and the performance of masculinities. *Social Science & Medicine, 74*, 498–505; Bennett, K. M. (2007). "No sissy stuff": Towards a theory of masculinity and emotional expression in older widowed men. *Journal of Aging Studies, 21*, 347–356.

115. See Addis, M. E. (2008). Gender and depression in men. *Clinical Psychology: Science and Practice, 15*, 153–168.

116. Yik, M. S. M., & Russell, J. A. (2001). Predicting the big two of affect from the big five of personality. *Journal of Research in Personality, 35*, 247–277.

117. Demir, M. (2008). Sweetheart, you really make me happy: Romantic relationship quality and personality as predictors of happiness among emerging adults. *Journal of Happiness Studies, 9*, 257–277.

118. Graziano, W. G., & Tobin, R. M. (2009). Agreeableness. In M. R. Leary & R. H. Hoyle (Eds.), *Handbook of individual differences in social behavior* (pp. 46–61). New York, NY: Guilford.

119. Lucas, R. E., Le, K., & Dyrenforth, P. S. (2008). Explaining the extraversion/positive affect relation: Sociability cannot account for extraverts' greater happiness. *Journal of Personality, 76*, 385–414.

120. Steel, P., & Ones, D. S. (2002). Personality and happiness: A national-level analysis. *Journal of Personality and Social Psychology, 83*, 767–781.

121. McNulty, J. K. (2008). Neuroticism and interpersonal negativity: The independent contributions of perceptions and behaviors. *Personality and Social Psychology Bulletin, 34*, 1439–1450.

122. Miller, D. J., Vachon, D. D., & Lynam, D. R. (2009). Neuroticism, negative affect, and negative affect instability: Establishing convergent and discriminant validity using ecological momentary assessment. *Personality and Individual Differences, 47*, 873–877.

123. Kokkonen, M., & Pulkkinen, L. (2001). Extraversion and neuroticism as antecedents of emotion regulation and dysregulation in adulthood. *European Journal of Personality, 15*, 407–424.

124. Brackett, M. A., Mayer, J. D., & Warner, R. M. (2004). Emotional intelligence and its relation to everyday behavior. *Personality and Individual Differences, 36*, 1387–1402. Quote is from p. 1389.

125. Mayer, J. D., Roberts, R. D., & Barsade, S. G. (2008). Human abilities: Emotional intelligence. *Annual Review of Psychology, 59*, 507–536.

126. Mayer, J. D., Salovey, P., Caruso, D. R., & Sitarenios, G. (2001). Emotional intelligence as a standard intelligence. *Emotion, 1*, 232–242.

127. Van Rooy, D. L., Alonso, A., & Viswesvaran, C. (2005). Group differences in emotional intelligence scores: Theoretical and practical implications. *Personality and Individual Differences, 38*, 689–700.

128. Spitzer, C., Siebel-Jürges, U., Barnow, S., Grabe, H. J., & Freyberger, H. J. (2005). Alexithymia and interpersonal problems. *Psychotherapy and Psychosomatics, 74*, 240–246.

129. Joukamaa, M., Taanila, A., Miettunen, J., Karvonen, J. T., Koskinen, M., & Veijola, J. (2007). Epidemiology of alexithymia among adolescents. *Journal of Psychosomatic Research, 63*, 373–376.

130. Swart, M., Kortekaas, R., & Aleman, A. (2009). Dealing with feelings: Characterization of trait alexithymia on emotion regulation strategies and cognitive-emotional processing. *PLoS One, 4*(6), e5751.

131. Vanheule, S., Desmet, M., Meganck, R., & Bogaerts, S. (2007). Alexithymia and interpersonal problems. *Journal of Clinical Psychology, 63*, 109–117.

132. Yelsma, P., & Marrow, S. (2003). An examination of couples' difficulties with emotional expressiveness and their marital satisfaction. *Journal of Family Communication, 3*, 41–62.

133. Iwamitsu, Y., Shimoda, K., Abe, H., Tani, T., Okawa, M., & Buck, R. (2005). The relation between negative emotional suppression and emotional distress in breast cancer diagnosis and treatment. *Health Communication, 18*, 201–215.

134. Mayne, T. J. (1999). Negative affect and health: The importance of being earnest. *Cognition & Emotion, 13*, 601–635.

135. Grewal, D., & Salovey, P. (2005). Feeling smart: The science of emotional intelligence. *American Scientist, 93*, 330–339.

136. Pond, R. S., Kashdan, T. B., DeWall, C. N., Savostyanova, A., Lambert, N. M., & Fincham, F. D. (2012). Emotion differentiation moderates aggressive tendencies in angry people: A daily diary analysis. *Emotion, 12*, 326–337.

137. Feinberg, M., Willer, R., Antonenko, O., & John, O. P. (2012). Liberating reason from the passions: Overriding intuitionist moral judgments through emotion reappraisal. *Psychological Science, 23*, 788–795.

138. John, O. P., & Gross, J. J. (2004). Healthy and unhealthy emotion regulation: Personality processes, individual differences, and lifespan development. *Journal of Personality, 72*, 1301–1334.

139. Bippus, A. M., & Young, S. L. (2005). Owning your emotions: Reactions to expressions of self- versus other-attributed positive and negative emotions. *Journal of Applied Communication Research, 33*, 26–45.

CHAPTER 9

1. Parks, M. R. (2007). *Personal relationships and personal networks.* Mahwah, NJ: Lawrence Erlbaum Associates. Quote is from p. 1.

2. Sutcliffe, A., Dunbar, R., Binder, J., & Arrow, H. (2012). Relationships and the social brain: Integrating psychological and evolutionary perspectives. *British Journal of Psychology, 103*, 149–168.

3. Chhuon, V., & Wallace, T. L. (2014). Creating connectedness through being known: Fulfilling the need to belong in U.S. high schools. *Youth & Society, 46*, 379–401; Baumeister, R. F., & Leary, M. R. (1995). The need to belong: Desire for interpersonal attachments as a fundamental human motivation. *Psychological Bulletin, 117*, 497–529.

4. Kapoor, R. (2014). Taking the solitary confinement debate out of isolation. *Journal of the American Academy of Psychiatry and the Law, 42*, 2–6.

5. Merolla, A. J. (2010). Relational maintenance during military deployment: Perspectives of wives of deployed U.S. soldiers. *Journal of Applied Communication Research, 38,* 4–26.

6. Perissinotto, C. M., Cenzer, I. S., & Covinsky, K. E. (2012). Loneliness in older persons: A predictor of functional decline and health. *JAMA Internal Medicine, 172,* 1078–1084.

7. Antheunis, M. L., Valkenburg, P. M., & Peter, J. (2012). The quality of online, offline, and mixed-mode friendships among users of a social networking site. *Cyberpsychology: Journal of Psychosocial Research on Cyberspace, 6*(3). doi: 10.5817/CP2012-3-6.

8. See, e.g., Siedlecki, K. L., Salthouse, T. A., Oishi, S., & Jeswani, S. (2014). The relationship between social support and subjective well-being across age. *Social Indicators Research, 117,* 561–576.

9. Yee, C. I., Gonzaga, G. C., & Gable, S. L. (2014). Positive emotions in close relationships. In M. M. Tugade, M. N. Shiota, & L. D. Kirby (Eds.), *Handbook of positive emotions* (pp. 215–228). New York, NY: Guilford.

10. Menéndez-Villalva, C., Gamarra-Mondelo, M. T., Alonso-Fachado, A., Naveira-Castelo, A., & Montes-Martínez, A. (2015). Social network, presence of cardiovascular events and mortality in hypertensive patients. *Journal of Human Hypertension, 29,* 417–423.

11. House, J. S., Landis, K. R., & Umberson, D. (1988). Social relationships and health. *Science, 241,* 540–545; see also Cacioppo, J. T., Cacioppo, S., Capitanio, J. P., & Cole, S. W. (2015). The neuroendocrinology of social isolation. *Annual Review of Psychology, 66,* 733–767.

12. See, e.g., Lupien, S. J., McEwen, B. S., Gunnar, M. R., & Heim, C. (2009). Effects of stress throughout the lifespan on the brain, behavior and cognition. *Nature Reviews Neuroscience, 10,* 434–445.

13. Hostinar, C. E., Sullivan, R. M., & Gunnar, M. R. (2014). Psychobiological mechanisms underlying the social buffering of the hypothalamic-pituitary-adrenocortical axis: A review of animal models and human studies across development. *Psychological Bulletin, 140,* 256–282.

14. Wills, T. A., & Ainette, M. G. (2012). Social networks and social support. In A. Baum, T. A. Revenson, & J. Singer (Eds.), *Handbook of health psychology* (2nd ed., pp. 465–492). New York, NY: Psychology Press.

15. Viner, R. M., Ozer, E. M., Denny, S., Marmot, M., Resnick, M., Fatusi, A., & Currie, C. (2012). Adolescence and the social determinants of health. *The Lancet, 379,* 1641–1652.

16. Bruening, M., Eisenberg, M., MacLehose, R., Nanney, M. S., Story, M., & Neumark-Sztainer, D. (2012). Relationship between adolescents' and their friends' eating behaviors: Breakfast, fruit, vegetable, whole-grain, and dairy intake. *Journal of the Academy of Nutrition and Dietetics, 112,* 1608–1613.

17. Fitzgerald, A., Fitzgerald, N., & Aherne, C. (2012). Do peers matter? A review of peer and/or friends' influence on physical activity among American adolescents. *Journal of Adolescence, 35,* 941–958.

18. Tang, T. S., Brown, M. B., Funnell, M. M., & Anderson, R. M. (2008). Social support, quality of life, and self-care behaviors among African Americans with type 2 diabetes. *The Diabetes Educator, 34,* 266–276.

19. See Oshio, T., Nozaki, K., & Kobayashi, M. (2013). Division of household labor and marital satisfaction in China, Japan, and Korea. *Journal of Family and Economic Issues, 34,* 211–223.

20. Fox, J., Osborn, J. L., & Warber, K. M. (2014). Relational dialectics and social networking sites: The role of Facebook in romantic relationship escalation, maintenance, conflict, and dissolution. *Computers in Human Behavior, 35,* 527–534.

21. Oudekerk, B. A., Allen, J. P., Hessel, E. T., & Molloy, L. E. (2015). The cascading development of autonomy and relatedness from adolescence to adulthood. *Child Development, 86,* 472–485.

22. Baxter, L. A. (2011). *Voicing relationships: A dialogic perspective.* Thousand Oaks, CA: Sage.

23. Powell, L., Richmond, V. P., & Cantrell-Williams, G. (2012). The "drinking buddy" scale as a measure of para-social behavior. *Psychological Reports, 110,* 1029–1037.

24. Eastwick, P. W., Eagly, A. H., Finkel, E. J., & Johnson, S. E. (2011). Implicit and explicit preferences for physical attractiveness in a romantic partner: A double dissociation in predictive validity. *Journal of Personality and Social Psychology, 101,* 993–1011.

25. See Perilloux, C., Cloud, J. M., & Buss, D. M. (2013). Women's physical attractiveness and short-term mating strategies. *Personality and Individual Differences, 54,* 490–495.

26. Li, N. P., Yong, J. C., Tov, W., Sng, O., Fletcher, G. J. O., Valentine, K. A., . . . Balliet, D. (2013). Mate preferences do predict attraction and choices in the early stages of mate selection. *Journal of Personality and Social Psychology, 105,* 757–776.

27. For an extended discussion, see Guerrero, L. K., & Floyd, K. (2006). *Nonverbal communication in close relationships.* Mahwah, NJ: Lawrence Erlbaum Associates.

28. Nialla Fayers-Kerr, K. (2012). *Miranda et les archives culturelles: Des plateaux-labiaux Mun (Mursi) aux peinture corporelles et retour en arrière* [The Miranda and the cultural archive: From Mun (Mursi) lip-plates, to body painting and back again]. *Paideuma, 58,* 245–259.

29. Stone, P. K. (2012). Binding women: Ethnology, skeletal deformations, and violence against women. *International Journal of Paleopathology, 2,* 53–60.

30. Little, A. C., Jones, B. C., Feinberg, D. R., & Perrett, D. I. (2014). Men's strategic preferences for femininity in female faces. *British Journal of Psychology, 105,* 364–381; Dixson, B. J., Grimshaw, G. M., Linklater, W. L., & Dixson, A. F. (2011). Eye-tracking of men's preferences for waist-to-hip ratio and breast size of women. *Archives of Sexual Behavior, 40,* 43–50.

31. Bryan, A. D., Webster, G. D., & Mahaffey, A. L. (2011). The big, the rich, and the powerful: Physical, financial, and social dimensions of dominance in mating and attraction. *Personality and Social Psychology Bulletin, 37,* 365–382.

32. See Buss, D. (2014). *Evolutionary psychology: The new science of the mind* (5th ed.). Boston, MA: Pearson.

33. See, e.g., Sheeks, M. S., & Birchmeier, Z. P. (2007). Shyness, sociability, and the use of computer-mediated communication in relationship development. *CyberPsychology & Behavior, 10,* 64–70; Yum, Y.-O., & Hara, K. (2005). Computer-mediated relationship development: A cross-cultural comparison. *Journal of Computer-Mediated Communication, 11,* 133–152.

34. Reid, C. A., Davis, J. L., & Green, J. D. (2013). The power of change: Interpersonal attraction as a function of attitude similarity and attitude alignment. *Journal of Social Psychology, 153,* 700–719.

35. Montoya, R. M., & Horton, R. S. (2013). A meta-analytic investigation of the processes underlying the similarity-attraction effect. *Journal of Social and Personal Relationships, 30,* 64–94.

36. Buss, 2014.

37. Salmon, C. A., Shackelford, T. K., & Michalski, R. L. (2012). Birth order, sex of child, and perceptions of parental favoritism. *Personality and Individual Differences, 52,* 357–362.

38. Mikkelson, A. C., Floyd, K., & Pauley, P. M. (2011). Differential solicitude of social support in different types of adult sibling relationships. *Journal of Family Communication, 11,* 220–236.

39. Kausel, E. E., & Slaughter, J. E. (2011). Narrow personality traits and organizational attraction: Evidence for the complementary hypothesis. *Organizational Behavior and Human Decision Processes, 114,* 3–14.

40. See, e.g., Antheunis, M. L., Valkenburg, P. M., & Peter, J. (2010). Getting acquainted through social network sites: Testing a model of online uncertainty reduction and social attraction. *Computers in Human Behavior, 26,* 100–109.

41. Ramirez, A., Sunnafrank, M., & Goei, R. (2010). Predicted outcome value theory in ongoing relationships. *Communication Monographs, 77,* 27–50.

42. Ramirez, A., Walther, J. B., Burgoon, J. K., & Sunnafrank, M. (2002). Information-seeking strategies, uncertainty, and computer-mediated communication: Toward a conceptual model. *Human Communication Research, 28,* 213–228.

43. Sunnafrank, M., & Ramirez, A. (2004). At first sight: Persistent relational effects of get-acquainted conversations. *Journal of Social and Personal Relationships, 21,* 361–379.

44. Stafford, L. (2015). Social exchange theories: Calculating the rewards and costs of personal relationships. In D. O. Braithwaite & P. Schrodt (Eds.), *Engaging theories in interpersonal communication: Multiple perspectives* (2nd ed., pp. 403–415). Thousand Oaks, CA: Sage.

45. Nakonezny, P. A., & Denton, W. H. (2008). Marital relationships: A social exchange theory perspective. *American Journal of Family Therapy, 36,* 402–412.

46. Guerrero, L. K., La Valley, A. G., & Farinelli, L. (2008). The experience and expression of anger, guilt, and sadness in marriage: An equity theory explanation. *Journal of Social and Personal Relationships, 25,* 699–724.

47. Stafford, L. (2011). Measuring relationship maintenance behaviors: Critique and development of revised relationship maintenance behavior scale. *Journal of Social and Personal Relationships, 28,* 278–303.

48. Ogolsky, B. G., & Bowers, J. R. (2013). A meta-analytic review of relationship maintenance and its correlates. *Journal of Social and Personal Relationships, 30,* 343–367.

49. Bauminger, N., Finzi-Dottan, R., Chason, S., & Har-Even, D. (2009). Intimacy in adolescent friendship: The roles of attachment, coherence, and self-disclosure. *Journal of Social and Personal Relationships, 25,* 409–428.

50. Goodboy, A. K., & Myers, S. A. (2008). Relational maintenance behaviors of friends with benefits: Investigating equity and relational characteristics. *Human Communication, 11,* 71–85.

51. See Tong, S. T., Kashian, N., & Walther, J. B. (2011). Relational maintenance and CMC. In K. B. Wright & L. M. Webb (Eds.), *Computer-mediated communication in personal relationships* (pp. 98–118). New York, NY: Peter Lang.

52. Braun, M., Lewin-Epstein, N., Stier, H., & Baumgärtner, M. K. (2008). Perceived equity in the gendered division of household labor. *Journal of Marriage and Family, 70,* 1145–1156.

53. See, e.g., Daniels, S., Glorieux, I., Minnen, J., & van Tienoven, T. P. (2012). More than preparing a meal? Concerning the meanings of home cooking. *Appetite, 58,* 1050–1056; Fehr, B. (2004). Intimacy expectations in same-sex friendships: A prototype interaction-pattern model. *Journal of Personality and Social Psychology, 86,* 265–284.

54. See Mongeau, P. M., & Henningsen, M. L. M. (2015). Stage theories of relationship development: Charting the course of interpersonal communication. In D. O Braithwaite & P. Schrodt (Eds.), *Engaging theories in interpersonal communication: Multiple perspectives* (2nd ed., pp. 389–402). Thousand Oaks, CA: Sage.

55. Fox, J., Warber, K. M., & Makstaller, D. C. (2013). The role of Facebook in romantic relationship development: An exploration of Knapp's relational stage model. *Journal of Social and Personal Relationships, 30,* 771–794.

56. Mongeau & Henningsen, 2015.

57. Welch, S.-A., & Rubin, R. B. (2002). Development of relationship stage measures. *Communication Quarterly, 50,* 24–40.

58. Avtgis, T. A., West, D. V., & Anderson, T. L. (1998). Relationship stages: An inductive analysis identifying cognitive, affective, and behavioral dimensions of Knapp's relational stages model. *Communication Research Reports, 15,* 280–287.

59. Larson, K., & Halfon, N. (2013). Parental divorce and adult longevity. *International Journal of Public Health, 58,* 89–97; Gilman, S. E., Kawachi, I., Fitzmaurice, G. M., & Buka, S. L. (2003). Family disruption in childhood and risk of adult depression. *American Journal of Psychiatry, 160,* 939–946.

60. See Duerr, H. P., Duerr-Aguilar, Y. A., Andritzky, W., Camps, A., Deegener G., Dum, C., . . . Hautzinger, M. (2014). Loss of child well-being: A concept for the metrics of neglect and abuse under separation and divorce. *Child Indicators Research,* 1–19.

61. Peplau, L. A. (2003). Lesbian and gay relationships. In L. Garnets & D. Kimmel (Eds.), *Psychological perspectives on lesbian, gay, and bisexual experiences* (pp. 395–419). New York, NY: Columbia University Press.

62. Tong, S. T., & Walther, J. B. (2011). Relational maintenance and computer-mediated communication. In K. B. Wright & L. M. Webb (Eds.), *Computer-mediated communication in personal relationships* (pp. 98–118). New York, NY: Peter Lang.

63. Fox et al., 2013.

64. Antheunis, M. L., Valkenburg, P. M., & Peter, J. (2010). Getting acquainted through social networking sites: Testing a model of online uncertainty reduction and social attraction. *Computers in Human Behavior, 26,* 100–109.

65. Ibid.

66. Hollenbaugh, E. E., & Ferris, A. L. (2014). Facebook self-disclosure: Examining the role of traits, social cohesion, and motives. *Computers in Human Behavior, 30,* 50–58.

67. Sosik, V. S., & Bazarova, N. N. (2014). Relational maintenance on social network sites: How Facebook communication predicts relational escalation. *Computers in Human Behavior, 35,* 124–131.

68. Mansson, D. H., & Myers, S. A. (2011). An initial examination of college students' expressions of affection through Facebook. *Southern Communication Journal, 76,* 155–168.

69. Fox, J., Osborn, J. L., & Warber, K. M. (2014). Relational dialectics and social networking sites: The role of Facebook in romantic relationship escalation, maintenance, conflict, and dissolution. *Computers in Human Behavior, 35,* 527–534.

70. Sosik & Bazarova, 2014.

71. Fox et al., 2014.

CHAPTER 10

1. Koerner, A. F., & Fitzpatrick, M. A. (2004). Communication in intact families. In A. L. Vangelisti (Ed.), *The Routledge handbook of family communication* (pp. 177–195). New York, NY: Routledge.
2. Cheung, S. K., & McBride-Chang, C. (2014). Friendship satisfaction. In A. C. Michalos (Ed.), *Encyclopedia of quality of life and well-being research* (pp. 2364–2366). Dordrecht, The Netherlands: Springer.
3. Selfhout, M., Denissen, J., Branje, S., & Meeus, W. (2009). In the eye of the beholder: Perceived, actual, and peer-rated similarity in personality, communication, and friendship intensity during the acquaintanceship process. *Journal of Personality and Social Psychology, 96,* 1152–1165.
4. Linden-Andersen, S., Markiewicz, S., & Doyle, A.-B. (2009). Perceived similarity among adolescent friends: The role of reciprocity, friendship quality, and gender. *Journal of Early Adolescence, 29,* 617–637.
5. McEwan, B. (2013). Sharing, caring, and surveilling: An actor-partner interdependence model examination of Facebook relational maintenance strategies. *Cyberpsychology, Behavior, and Social Networking, 16,* 863–869.
6. Ledbetter, A. M., & Kuznekoff, J. H. (2012). More than a game: Friendship relational maintenance and attitudes toward Xbox LIVE communication. *Communication Research, 39,* 269–290.
7. Brody, N., & Peña, J. (2015). Equity, relational maintenance, and linguistic features of text messaging. *Computers in Human Behavior, 49,* 499–506.
8. Felmlee, D., Sweet, E., & Sinclair, H. C. (2012). Gender rules: Same- and cross-gender friendship norms. *Sex Roles, 66,* 518–529.
9. Hall, J. A., Larson, K. A., & Watts, A. (2011). Satisfying friendship maintenance expectations: The role of friendship standards and biological sex. *Human Communication Research, 37,* 529–552.
10. Hall, J. A. (2011). Sex differences in friendship expectations: A meta-analysis. *Journal of Social and Personal Relationships, 28,* 723–747.
11. See, e.g., Parks, M. R., & Floyd, K. (1996). Meanings for closeness and intimacy in friendship. *Journal of Social and Personal Relationships, 13,* 85–107.
12. Monsour, M. (1997). Communication and cross-sex friendships across the life cycle: A review of the literature. In B. Burleson (Ed.), *Communication yearbook 20* (pp. 375–414). New York, NY: Routledge.
13. Reeder, H. M. (2003). The effect of gender role orientation on same- and cross-sex friendship formation. *Sex Roles, 49,* 143–152.
14. Bleske-Rechek, A., Somers, E., Micke, C., Erickson, L., Matteson, L., Stocco, C., . . . Ritchie, L. (2012). Benefit or burden? Attraction in cross-sex friendship. *Journal of Social and Personal Relationships, 29,* 569–596.
15. Lewis, D. M. G., Al-Shawaf, L., Conroy-Beam, D., Asao, K., & Buss, D. M. (2012). Friends with benefits II: Mating activation in opposite-sex friendships as a function of sociosexual orientation and relationship status. *Personality and Individual Differences, 53,* 622–628.
16. Bisson, M. A., & Levine, T. R. (2009). Negotiating a friends with benefits relationship. *Archives of Sexual Behavior, 38,* 66–73.
17. Bleske-Rechek et al., 2012; see also Owen, J., Fincham, F. D., & Manthos, M. (2013). Friendship after a friends with benefits relationship: Deception, psychological functioning, and social connectedness. *Archives of Sexual Behavior, 42,* 1443–1449.
18. Messman, S. J., Canary, D. J., & Hause, K. S. (2000). Motives to remain platonic, equity, and the use of maintenance strategies in opposite-sex friendships. *Journal of Social and Personal Relationships, 17,* 67–94.
19. Rose, S. M. (1985). Same- and cross-sex friendships and the psychology of homosociality. *Sex Roles, 12,* 63–74.
20. Rawlins, W. K. (1992). *Friendship matters: Communication, dialectics, and the life course.* New Brunswick, NJ: Transaction Publishers.
21. Card, N. A. (2007). "I hated her guts!": Emerging adults' recollections of the formation, maintenance, and termination of antipathetic relationships during high school. *Journal of Adolescent Research, 22,* 32–57.
22. Bleske-Rechek, A. L., & Buss, D. M. (2001). Opposite-sex friendship: Sex differences and similarities in initiation, selection, and dissolution. *Personality and Social Psychology Bulletin, 37,* 1310–1323.
23. Sekara, V., & Lehmann, S. (2014). The strength of friendship ties in proximity sensory data. *PLoS One, 9*(7), e100915.
24. Preciado, P., Snijders, T. A. B., Burk, W. J., Stattin, H., & Kerr, M. (2012). Does proximity matter? Distance dependence of adolescent friendships. *Social Networks, 34,* 18–31.
25. Craig, E., & Wright, K. B. (2012). Computer-mediated relational development and maintenance on Facebook. *Communication Research Reports, 29,* 119–129.
26. U.S. Census Bureau. (2011). Decennial census data on marriage and divorce. Retrieved April 6, 2015, from www.census.gov/hhes/socdemo/marriage/data/census/index.html
27. Kaplan, R. M., & Kronick, R. G. (2006). Marital status and longevity in the United States population. *Journal of Epidemiology and Community Health, 60,* 760–765.
28. Manzoli, M., Villarti, P., Pirone, G. M., & Boccia, A. (2007). Marital status and mortality in the elderly: A systematic review and meta-analysis. *Social Science & Medicine, 64,* 77–94.
29. Duncan, G. J., Wilkerson, B., & England, P. (2006). Cleaning up their act: The effects of marriage and cohabitation on licit and illicit drug use. *Demography, 43,* 691–710.
30. Bachman, J. G., Schulenberg, J., Johnston, L. D., Bryant, A. L., Merline, A. C., & O'Malley, P. M. (2002). *The decline of substance use in young adulthood: Changes in social activities, roles, and beliefs.* Mahwah, NJ: Lawrence Erlbaum Associates.
31. Lamb, K. A., Lee, G. R., & DeMaris, A. (2003). Union formation and depression: Selection and relationship effects. *Journal of Marriage and Family, 65,* 953–962.
32. Kiecolt-Glaser, J. K., & Newton, T. L. (2001). Marriage and health: His and hers. *Psychological Bulletin, 127,* 472–503.
33. See Waldron, I., Hughes, M. E., & Brooks, T. L. (1996). Marriage protection and marriage selection—Prospective evidence for reciprocal effects of marital status and health. *Social Science & Medicine, 43,* 113–123.
34. Matsick, J. L., Conley, T. D., Ziegler, A., Moors, A. C., & Rubin, J. D. (2014). Love and sex: Polyamorous relationships are perceived more favourably than swinging and open relationships. *Psychology & Sexuality, 5,* 339–348.
35. Taormino, T. (2008). *Opening up: A guide to creating and sustaining open relationships.* San Francisco, CA: Cleis Press.
36. McLean, K. (2004). Negotiating (non)monogamy: Bisexuality and intimate relationships. *Journal of Bisexuality, 4,* 83–97.

37. Parsons, J. T., Starks, T. J., DuBois, S., Grov, C., & Golub, S. A. (2013). Alternatives to monogamy among gay male couples in a community survey: Implications for mental health and sexual risk. *Archives of Sexual Behavior, 42,* 303–312.

38. Munson, M., & Stelboum, J. P. (2013). *The lesbian polyamory reader: Open relationships, non-monogamy, and casual sex.* New York, NY: Routledge.

39. See Esmaili, G., Sadrpushan, N., & Gorji, Y. (2012). Comparison of life quality for men in monogamy and polygamy families. *Journal of Sociological Research, 3,* 428–439.

40. Romano, E. (2015, March 5). Happy 20th birthday, Match.com! Inside the world's biggest dating service. Retrieved April 6, 2015, from www.datingsitesreviews.com/article.php?story=happy-20th-birthday--match-com--inside-the-world-s-biggest-dating-service

41. Hawkins, D. N., & Booth, A. (2005). Unhappily ever after: Effects of long-term, low-quality marriages on well-being. *Social Forces, 84,* 451–471.

42. Previti, D., & Amato, P. R. (2003). Why stay married? Rewards, barriers, and marital stability. *Journal of Marriage and Family, 65,* 561–573.

43. Buunk, B. P., Park, J. H., & Duncan, L. A. (2010). Cultural variation in parental influence on mate choice. *Cross-Cultural Research, 44,* 23–40.

44. Sandhya, S. (2009). The social context of marital happiness in urban Indian couples: Interplay of intimacy and conflict. *Journal of Marital and Family Therapy, 35,* 74–96.

45. Fletcher, G. J. O., Simpson, J. A., Campbell, L., & Overall, N. C. (2015). Pair-bonding, romantic love, and evolution: The curious case of *Homo sapiens. Perspectives on Psychological Science, 10,* 20–36.

46. See Hawkins, A. J., Willoughby, B. J., & Doherty, W. J. (2012). Reasons for divorce and openness to marital reconciliation. *Journal of Divorce & Remarriage, 53,* 453–463.

47. Smock, P. J., Manning, W. D., & Porter, M. (2005). "Everything's there except money": How money shapes decisions to marry among cohabitors. *Journal of Marriage and Family, 67,* 680–696.

48. Compton, J., & Pollak, R. A. (2007). Why are power couples increasingly concentrated in large metropolitan areas? *Journal of Labor Economics, 25,* 475–512.

49. Levine, R. B. (1993). Is love a luxury? *American Demographics, 15,* 27–28.

50. Hsu, F. K. L. (1981). The self in cross-cultural perspective. In A. J. Marsella, B. De Vos, & F. L. K. Hsu (Eds.), *Culture and self* (pp. 24–55). London, England: Tavistock. Quote is from p. 50.

51. Coontz, S. (2006). *Marriage, a history: How love conquered marriage.* New York, NY: Penguin.

52. Gotta, G., Green, R.-J., Rothblum, E., Solomon, S., Balsam, K., & Schwartz, P. (2011). Heterosexual, lesbian, and gay male relationships: A comparison of couples in 1975 and 2000. *Family Process, 50,* 353–376.

53. Peplau, L. A., Fingerhut, A. W., & Beals, K. P. (2004). Sexuality in the relationships of lesbians and gay men. In J. Harvey, A. Wenzel, & S. Sprecher (Eds.), *Handbook of sexuality in close relationships* (pp. 350–369). Mahwah, NJ: Lawrence Erlbaum Associates.

54. Kurdek, L. A. (2005). What do we know about gay and lesbian couples? *Current Directions in Psychological Science, 14,* 251–254.

55. Kurdek, L. A. (2006). Differences between partners from heterosexual, gay, and lesbian cohabiting couples. *Journal of Marriage and Family, 68,* 509–528.

56. Graham, J. M., & Barnow, Z. B. (2013). Stress and social support in gay, lesbian, and heterosexual couples: Direct effects and buffering models. *Journal of Family Psychology, 27,* 569–578.

57. Peplau, L. A., & Spalding, L. R. (2000). The close relationships of lesbians, gay men and bisexuals. In C. Hendrick & S. S. Hendrick (Eds.), *Close relationships: A sourcebook* (pp. 111–124). Thousand Oaks, CA: Sage.

58. Balsam, K. F., Beauchaine, T. P., Rothblum, E. D., & Solomon, S. E. (2008). Three-year follow-up of same-sex couples who had civil unions in Vermont, same-sex couples not in civil unions, and heterosexual married couples. *Developmental Psychology, 44,* 102–116; Roisman, G. I., Clausell, E., Holland, A., Fortuna, K., & Elieff, C. (2008). Adult romantic relationships as contexts of human development: A multimethod comparison of same-sex couples with opposite-sex dating, engaged, and married dyads. *Developmental Psychology, 44,* 91–101.

59. Barker, L. A., & Emery, R. E. (1993). When every relationship is above average: Perceptions and expectations of divorce at the time of marriage. *Law and Human Behavior, 17,* 439–450.

60. Human Rights Campaign. (2015). Overview of federal benefits granted to married couples. Retrieved April 7, 2015, from www.hrc.org/resources/entry/an-overview-of-federal-rights-and-protections-granted-to-married-couples

61. See, e.g., Givertz, M., Segrin, C., & Hanzal, A. (2009). The association between satisfaction and commitment differs across marital couple types. *Communication Research, 36,* 561–584.

62. Koerner, A. F., & Fitzpatrick, M. A. (2004). Communication in intact families. In A. L. Vangelisti (Ed.), *The Routledge handbook of family communication* (pp. 177–195). New York, NY: Routledge.

63. Hocker, J. L., & Wilmot, W. W. (2013). *Interpersonal conflict* (9th ed.). New York, NY: McGraw-Hill. Quote is from p. 40.

64. Cleary Bradley, R. P., Drummey, K., Gottman, J. M., & Gottman, J. S. (2014). Treating couples who mutually exhibit violence or aggression: Reducing behaviors that show a susceptibility for violence. *Journal of Family Violence, 29,* 549–558.

65. Gottman, J. M. (2015). *Principia amoris: The new science of love.* New York, NY: Routledge.

66. Holman, T. B., & Jarvis, M. O. (2003). Hostile, volatile, avoiding, and validating couple-conflict types: An investigation of Gottman's couple-conflict types. *Personal Relationships, 10,* 267–282.

67. See Gottman, J. M., Levenson, R. W., Swanson, C., Swanson, K., Tyson, R., & Yoshimoto, D. (2003). Observing gay, lesbian, and heterosexual couples' relationships: Mathematical modeling of conflict interaction. *Journal of Homosexuality, 45,* 65–91.

68. Petronio, S., & Durham, W. T. (2015). Communication privacy management theory: Significance for interpersonal communication. In D. O. Braithwaite & P. Schrodt (Eds.), *Engaging theories in interpersonal communication: Multiple perspectives* (2nd ed., pp. 335–347). Thousand Oaks, CA: Sage.

69. Petronio, S. (2010). Communication privacy management theory: What do we know about family privacy regulation? *Journal of Family Theory & Review, 2,* 175–196.

70. See Sprecher, S., Treger, S., Wondra, J. D., Hilaire, N., & Wallpe, K. (2013). Taking turns: Reciprocal self-disclosure promotes liking in initial interactions. *Journal of Experimental Social Psychology, 49,* 860–866.

71. Mirgain, S. A., & Cordova, J. V. (2007). Emotion skills and marital health: The association between observed and self-reported

emotion skills, intimacy, and marital satisfaction. *Journal of Social and Clinical Psychology, 26,* 983–1009.

72. Lawrence, E., Pederson, A., Bunde, M., Barry, R. A., Brock, R. L., Fazio, E., . . . Dzankovic, S. (2008). Objective ratings of relationship skills across multiple domains as predictors of marital satisfaction trajectories. *Journal of Social and Personal Relationships, 25,* 445–466.

73. See, e.g., Fredrickson, B. L. (2013). Updated thinking on positivity ratios. *American Psychologist, 68,* 814–822.

74. Gottman, J. M. (2011). *The science of trust: Emotional attunement for couples.* New York, NY: W. W. Norton.

75. Ibid.

76. Ibid.

77. Bianchi, S. M., Sayer, L. C., Milkie, M. A., & Robinson, J. P. (2012). Housework: Who did, does or will do it, and how much does it matter? *Social Forces, 91,* 55–63.

78. Alberts, J. K., Yoshimura, C. G., Rabby, M., & Loschiavo, R. (2005). Mapping the topography of couples' daily conversation. *Journal of Social and Personal Relationships, 22,* 299–322.

79. Dillon, L. M., Nowak, N., Weisfeld, G. E., Weisfeld, C. C., Shattuck, K. S., Imamoğlu, O. E., . . . Shen, J. (2015). Sources of marital conflict in five cultures. *Evolutionary Psychology, 13,* 1–15.

80. Kawamura, S., & Brown, S. L. (2010). Mattering and wives' perceived fairness of the division of household labor. *Social Science Research, 39,* 976–986.

81. Forste, R., & Fox, K. (2012). Household labor, gender roles, and family satisfaction: A cross-national comparison. *Journal of Comparative Family studies, 43,* 613–631.

82. Braun, M., Lewin-Epstein, N., Stier, H., & Baumgärtner, M. K. (2008). Perceived equity in the gendered division of household labor. *Journal of Marriage and Family, 70,* 1145–1156.

83. Mannino, C. A., & Deutsch, F. M. (2007). Changing the division of household labor: A negotiated process between partners. *Sex Roles, 56,* 309–324.

84. Kluwer, E. S., Heesink, J. A. M., & Van de Vliert, E. (2000). The division of labor in close relationships: An asymmetrical conflict issue. *Personal Relationships, 7,* 263–282.

85. Kawamura & Brown, 2010.

86. Boren, J. P. (2007, November). *Negotiating the division of household labor in same-sex romantic partnerships.* Paper presented at the annual meeting of the National Communication Association, Chicago, IL.

87. Luscombe, B. (2010, August 16). Finding Mom on Facebook. *Time,* pp. 45–46.

88. Statsky, W. P. (2012). *Family law* (6th ed.). Boston, MA: Cengage.

89. General Accounting Office. (1997). Memo B-275860. Retrieved April 9, 2015, from www.gao.gov/archive/1997/og97016.pdf

90. Floyd, K., Mikkelson, A. C., & Judd, J. (2006). Defining the family through relationships. In L. H. Turner & R. West (Eds.), *The family communication sourcebook* (pp. 21–39). Thousand Oaks, CA: Sage.

91. U.S. Census Bureau. (2009). *American community survey.* Retrieved April 10, 2015, from www.census.gov/acs/www/

92. U.S. Census Bureau. (2010). *Living arrangements of children: March 2010.* Washington, DC: Author.

93. Floyd, K., & Morman, M. T. (Eds.). (2014). *Widening the family circle: New research on family communication* (2nd ed.). Thousand Oaks, CA: Sage.

94. Satir, V. (1988). *The new peoplemaking.* Palo Alto, CA: Science and Behavior Books.

95. Crespo, C. (2012). Families as contexts for attachment: Reflections on theory, research, and the role of family rituals. *Journal of Family Theory & Review, 4,* 290–298.

96. Braithwaite, D. O., Baxter, L. A., & Harper, A. M. (1998). The role of rituals in the management of dialectical tensions of "old" and "new" in blended families. *Communication Studies, 49,* 105–120.

97. Ibid. Quote is from p. 113.

98. Koenig Kellas, J., & Horstman, H. K. (2015). Communicated narrative sense-making: Understanding family narratives, storytelling, and the construction of meaning through a communicative lens. In L. H. Turner & R. West (Eds.), *The Sage handbook of family communication* (pp. 76–90). Thousand Oaks, CA: Sage.

99. Afifi, T. D., Merrill, A., & Davis, S. M. (2015). Examining family secrets from a communication perspective. In L. H. Turner & R. West (Eds.), *The Sage handbook of family communication* (pp. 169–183). Thousand Oaks, CA: Sage.

100. See Orgad, Y. (2015). The culture of family secrets. *Culture & Psychology, 21,* 59–80.

101. Myers, K. K., Siebold, D. R., & Park, H. S. (2011). Interpersonal communication in the workplace. In M. L. Knapp & J. A. Daly (Eds.), *The Sage handbook of interpersonal communication* (4th ed., pp. 527–562). Thousand Oaks, CA: Sage.

102. Sias, P. M. (2014). Workplace relationships. In L. L. Putman & D. K. Mumby (Eds.), *The Sage handbook of organizational communication: Advances in theory, research, and methods* (pp. 375–400). Thousand Oaks, CA: Sage.

103. Venkataramini, Y., Labianca, G., & Grosser, T. (2013). Positive and negative workplace relationships, social satisfaction, and organizational attachment. *Journal of Applied Psychology, 98,* 1028–1039.

104. Mao, H.-Y., Hsieh, A.-T., & Chen, C.-Y. (2013). The relationship between workplace friendship and perceived job significance. *Journal of Management & Organization, 18,* 247–262.

105. Berman, E. M., West, J. P., & Richter, M. N. (2002). Workplace relationships: Friendship patterns and consequences (according to managers). *Public Administration Review, 62,* 217–230.

106. Sias, 2014.

107. Ellwardt, L., Steglich, C., & Wittek, R. (2012). The co-evolution of gossip and friendship in workplace social networks. *Social Networks, 34,* 623–633.

108. Ptacek, J. (2014). *I get by with a little help from my friends: A qualitative study of nurse close work friendship and social support.* Unpublished masters thesis, Department of Communication, Western Michigan University.

109. Sias, 2014.

110. Sias, P. M., & Cahill, D. J. (1998). From coworkers to friends: The development of peer friendships in the workplace. *Western Journal of Communication, 62,* 273–299.

111. Sias, P. M., Gallagher, E. B., Kopaneva, I., & Pedersen, H. (2012). Maintaining workplace friendships: Perceived politeness and predictors of maintenance tactic choice. *Communication Research, 39,* 239–268.

112. CareerBuilder. (2012, February 9). Nearly one-third of workers who had office romances married their co-worker, finds annual CareerBuilder Valentine's Day survey. Retrieved April 13, 2015, from www.careerbuilder.com/share/aboutus/pressreleasesdetail.aspx?sd=2%2F9%2F2012&id=pr678&ed=12%2F31%2F2012

113. Fredrickson, B. L. (2013). Positive emotions broaden and build. *Advances in Experimental Social Psychology, 47,* 1–53.

114. Mainiero, L. A. (1989). *Office romance: Love, power, and sex in the workplace.* New York, NY: Rawson Associates.

115. Ibid.

116. Pierce, C., & Aguinis, H. (2000). Effects of a dissolved workplace romance and rater characteristics on responses to a sexual harassment accusation. *Academy of Management Journal, 43,* 869–880.

117. See, e.g., Alder, G. S., & Quist, D. M. (2014). Rethinking love at the office: Antecedents and consequences of coworker evaluations of workplace romances. *Human Resource Management, 53,* 329–351.

118. Willemyns, M., Callois, C., & Callan, V. (2003). Trust me, I'm your boss: Trust and power in supervisor–supervisee communication. *International Journal of Human Resource Management, 14,* 117–127.

119. Zorn, T. E. (1995). Bosses and buddies: Constructing and performing simultaneously hierarchical and close friendship relationships. In J. T. Wood & S. Duck (Eds.), *Under-studied relationships: Off the beaten track* (pp. 122–147). Thousand Oaks, CA: Sage.

120. Gwinner, K. P., Gremler, D. D., & Bitner, M. J. (1998). Relational benefits in service industries: The customer's perspective. *Journal of the Academy of Marketing Science, 26,* 101–114.

121. American College of Physicians. (2005). *Ethics manual* (5th ed.). Philadelphia, PA: Author.

CHAPTER 11

1. Brown, P. L. (2013, April 3). Opening up, students transform a vicious circle. *The New York Times.* Retrieved April 30, 2015, from http://nyti.ms/13RRgkh

2. Hocker, J. L., & Wilmot, W. W. (2013). *Interpersonal conflict* (9th ed.). New York, NY: McGraw-Hill. Quote is from p. 40.

3. Adapted from Hocker & Wilmot, 2013.

4. Dewulf, A., & Bouwen, R. (2012). Issue framing in conversations for change: Discursive interaction strategies for "doing differences." *Journal of Applied Behavioral Science, 48,* 168–193.

5. Arora, P., Pössel, P., Barnard, A. D., Terjesen, M., Lai, B. S., Ehrlich, C. J., . . . Gogos, A. K. (2015). Cognitive interventions. In R. Flanagan, K. Allen, & E. Levine (Eds.), *Cognitive and behavioral interventions in the schools* (pp. 221–248). New York, NY: Springer.

6. Spies, L. A., Margolin, G., Susman, E. J., & Gordis. E. B. (2011). Adolescents' cortisol reactivity and subjective distress in response to family conflict: The moderating role of internalizing symptoms. *Journal of Adolescent Health, 49,* 386–392.

7. Dopp, J. M., Miller, G. E., Myers, H. F., & Fahey, J. L. (2000). Increased natural killer-cell mobilization and cytotoxicity during marital conflict. *Brain, Behavior, and Immunity, 14,* 10–26.

8. Kiecolt-Glaser, J. K., Loving, T. J., Stowell, J. R., Malarkey, W. B., Lemeshow, S., Dickinson, S. L., & Glaser, R. (2005). Hostile marital interactions, proinflammatory cytokine production, and wound healing. *Archives of General Psychiatry, 62,* 1377–1384.

9. Smith, T. W., Berg, C., Uchino, B. N., Florsheim, P., & Pearce, G. (2006, March). *Marital conflict behavior and coronary artery calcification.* Paper presented at annual meeting of the American Psychosomatic Society, Denver.

10. See, e.g., Finkel, E. J., & Eckhardt, C. I. (2013). Intimate partner violence. In J. A. Simpson & L. Campbell (Eds.), *The Oxford handbook of close relationships* (pp. 452–474). New York, NY: Oxford University Press.

11. Lloyd, S. A., & Emery, B. C. (2000). The context and dynamics of intimate aggression against women. *Journal of Social and Personal Relationships, 17,* 503–521.

12. Drijber, B. C., Reijnders, U. J. L., & Ceelen, M. (2013). Male victims of domestic violence. *Journal of Family Violence, 28,* 173–178.

13. Baker, N. L., Buick, J. D., Kim, S. R., Moniz, S., & Nava, K. L. (2013). Lessons from examining same-sex intimate partner violence. *Sex Roles, 69,* 182–192.

14. Ubinger, M. E., Handal, P. J., & Massura, C. E. (2013). Adolescent adjustment: The hazards of conflict avoidance and the benefits of conflict resolution. *Psychology, 4,* 50–58.

15. Erbert, L. A. (2000). Conflict and dialectics: Perceptions of dialectical contradictions in marital conflict. *Journal of Social and Personal Relationships, 17,* 638–659.

16. Roloff, M. E., & Chiles, B. W. (2011). Interpersonal conflict: Recent trends. In M. L. Knapp & J. A. Daly (Eds.), *The Sage handbook of interpersonal communication* (4th ed., pp. 423–442). Thousand Oaks, CA: Sage.

17. Kurdek, L. A. (2005). What do we know about gay and lesbian couples? *Current Directions in Psychological Science, 14,* 251–254.

18. See, e.g., Weaver, C. M., Shaw, D. S., Crossan, J. L., Dishion, T. J., & Wilson, M. N. (2015). Parent–child conflict and early childhood adjustment in two-parent low-income families: Parallel developmental processes. *Child Psychiatry & Human Development, 46,* 94–107.

19. Wood, J. T., & Fixmer-Oraiz, N. (2015). *Gendered lives: Communication, gender, & culture* (11th ed.). Stamford, CT: Cengage.

20. Schrodt, P., Witt, P. L., & Shimkowski, J. R. (2014). A meta-analytical review of the demand/withdraw pattern of interaction and its associations with individual, relational, and communicative outcomes. *Communication Monographs, 81,* 28–58.

21. Donato, S., Parise, M., Pagani, A. F., Bertoni, A., & Iafrate, R. (2014). Demand-withdraw, couple satisfaction and relationship duration. *Procedia/Social and Behavioral Sciences, 140,* 200–206.

22. Kurdek, 2005.

23. Caughlin, J. P., & Vangelisti, A. L. (2006). Conflict in dating and marital relationships. In J. G. Oetzel & S. Ting-Toomey (Eds.), *The Sage handbook of conflict communication: Integrating theory, research, and practice* (pp. 129–157). Thousand Oaks, CA: Sage.

24. Legate, N., Ryan, R. M., & Weinstein, N. (2011). Is coming out always a "good thing"? Exploring the relations of autonomy support, outness, and wellness for lesbian, gay, and bisexual individuals. *Social Psychology & Personality Science, 3,* 145–152.

25. Etengoff, C., & Daiute, C. (2014). Family members' uses of religion in post-coming-out conflicts with their gay relative. *Psychology of Religion and Spirituality, 6,* 33–43.

26. Komarraju, M., Dollinger, S. J., & Lovell, J. L. (2008). Individualism-collectivism in horizontal and vertical directions as predictors of conflict management styles. *International Journal of Conflict Management, 19,* 20–35.

27. Gudykunst, W. B., & Kim, Y. Y. (2003). *Communicating with strangers: An approach to intercultural communication* (4th ed.). New York, NY: McGraw-Hill.

28. Croucher, S. M., Bruno, A., McGrath, P., Adams, C., McGahan, C., Suits, A., & Huckins, A. (2012). Conflict styles and high-low context cultures: A cross-cultural extension. *Communication Research Reports, 29,* 64–73.

29. Ibid.

30. Liddicoat, A. J. (2009). Communication as culturally contexted practice: A view from intercultural communication. *Australian Journal of Linguistics, 29,* 115–133.

31. Lapidot-Lefler, N., & Barak, A. (2012). Effects of anonymity, invisibility, and lack of eye-contact on toxic online disinhibition. *Computers in Human Behavior, 28,* 434–443.

32. Suler, J. R. (2004). The online disinhibition effect. *CyberPsychology and Behavior, 7,* 321–326.

33. See Sturm, R. E., & Antonakis, J. (2015). Interpersonal power: A review, critique, and research agenda. *Journal of Management, 41,* 136–163.

34. Ericson, P. M., & Rogers, L. E. (1973). New procedures for analyzing relational communication. *Family Process, 12,* 245–267.

35. Bennett, M. S., Erchul, W. P., Young, H. L., & Bartel, C. M. (2012). Exploring relational communication patterns in preferral intervention teams. *Journal of Educational and Psychological Consultation, 22,* 187–207.

36. French, J. P. R., & Raven, B. (1959). The bases of social power. In D. Cartwright & A. Zander (Eds.), *Group dynamics* (pp. 607–623). New York, NY: Harper & Row.

37. Brown, R. (1991). *Human universals.* Philadelphia, PA: Temple University Press.

38. Center for American Women and Politics. (2015). *Women in elective office 2015.* New Brunswick, NJ: Eagleton Institute of Politics. Figure cited is average of percentage of women in elected positions in federal government (19.4%) and state government (24.5%).

39. United Nations Inter-Agency Network on Women and Gender Equality. (2015, January). *Facts and figures: Leadership and political participation.* Washington, DC: Author.

40. Ibid.

41. Schumacher, J. A., & Leonard, K. E. (2005). Husbands' and wives' marital adjustment, verbal aggression, and physical aggression as longitudinal predictors of physical aggression in early marriage. *Journal of Consulting and Clinical Psychology, 73,* 28–37.

42. Spender, D. (1990). *Man made language.* London, England: Pandora.

43. Loving, T. J., Heffner, K. I., Kiecolt-Glaser, J. K., Glaser, R., & Malarkey, W. B. (2004). Stress hormone changes and marital conflict: Spouses' relative power makes a difference. *Journal of Marriage and Family, 66,* 595–612.

44. Sprecher, S., Schmeeckle, M., & Felmlee, D. (2006). The principle of least interest: Inequality in emotional involvement in romantic relationships. *Journal of Family Issues, 27,* 1255–1280.

45. Moran, R. T., Abramson, N. R., & Moran, S. V. (2014). *Managing cultural differences* (9th ed.). New York, NY: Routledge.

46. See Madlock, P. E. (2012). The influence of power distance and communication on Mexican workers. *International Journal of Business Communication, 49,* 169–184.

47. Gottman, J. M., & Silver, N. (2015). *The seven principles for making marriage work: A practical guide from the country's foremost relationship expert.* New York, NY: Harmony Books.

48. Gottman, J. M., & Silver, N. (2012). *What makes love last? How to build trust and avoid betrayal.* New York, NY: Simon & Schuster.

49. Rancer, A. S. (2012). *Understanding aggressive communication.* Boston, MA: Holt, Rinehart, & Winston.

50. Jaremka, L. M., Glaser, R., Malarkey, W. B., & Kiecolt-Glaser, J. K. (2013). Marital distress prospectively predicts poorer cellular immune function. *Psychoneuroendocrinology, 38,* 2713–2719.

51. Kiecolt-Glaser, J. K., Loving, T. J., Stowell, J. R., Malarkey, W. B., Lemeshow, S., Dickinson, S. L., & Glaser, R. (2005). Hostile marital interactions, proinflammatory cytokine production, and wound healing. *Archives of General Psychiatry, 62,* 1377–1384.

52. Blake, R. R., & Mouton, J. S. (2005). *The new managerial grid.* New Delhi, India: Jaico Publishing.

53. See Urban, W. (2005). Competition and interpersonal conflict in same-sex platonic friendships. *The Hilltop Review, 1,* 3.

54. Olson, L. N., & Braithwaite, D. O. (2004). "If you hit me again, I'll hit you back": Conflict management strategies of individuals experiencing aggression during conflicts. *Communication Studies, 55,* 271–285.

55. Tjosvold, D., & Sun, H. F. (2002). Understanding conflict avoidance: Relationship, motivations, actions, and consequences. *International Journal of Conflict Management, 13,* 142–164.

56. Wilmot, W. W., & Hocker, J. L. (2013). *Interpersonal conflict* (9th ed.). New York, NY: McGraw-Hill.

57. Oetzel, J. G., & Ting-Toomey, S. (2003). Face concerns in interpersonal conflict: A cross-cultural empirical test of the face negotiation theory. *Communication Research, 30,* 599–625.

CHAPTER 12

1. Tyler, J. J., Feldman, R. S., & Reichert, A. (2006). The price of deceptive behavior: Disliking and lying to people who lie to us. *Journal of Experimental Social Psychology, 42,* 69–77.

2. Serota, K. B., Levine, T. R., & Boster, F. J. (2010). The prevalence of lying in America: Three studies of self-reported lies. *Human Communication Research, 36,* 2–25.

3. See Levine, E. E., & Schweitzer, M. E. (2015). Prosocial lies: When deception breeds trust. *Organizational Behavior and Human Decision Processes, 126,* 88–106.

4. Levine, T. R., Serota, K. B., Carey, F., & Messer, D. (2013). Teenagers lie a lot: A further investigation into the prevalence of lying. *Communication Research Reports, 30,* 211–220.

5. Plante, T. G. (2004). *Do the right thing: Living ethically in an unethical world.* Oakland, CA: New Harbinger.

6. Porter, S., & ten Brinke, L. (2010). The truth about lies: What works in detecting high-stakes deception? *Legal and Criminological Psychology, 15,* 57–75.

7. Roggensack, K. E., & Sillars, A. (2014). Agreement and understanding about honesty and deception rules in romantic relationships. *Journal of Social and Personal Relationships, 31,* 178–199.

8. Agosta, S., Pezzoli, P., & Sartori, G. (2013). How to detect deception in everyday life and the reasons underlying it. *Applied Cognitive Psychology, 27,* 256–262.

9. Johnson, D., & Tyler, L. (2013). *Modern manners: Tools to take you to the top.* New York, NY: Potter Style/Random House.

10. Vrij, A. (2007). Deception: A social lubricant and a selfish act. In K. Fiedler (Ed.), *Social communication* (pp. 309–342). New York, NY: Psychology Press.

11. Saxe, L. (1991). Lying: Thoughts of an applied social psychologist. *American Psychologist, 46,* 409–415.

12. Naquin, C. E., Kurtzberg, T. R., & Belkin, L. Y. (2010). The finer points of lying online: E-mail versus pen and paper. *Journal of Applied Psychology, 95,* 387–394.

13. Smith, M. E., Hancock, J. T., Reynolds, L., & Birnholtz, J. (2014). Everyday deception or a few prolific liars? The prevalence of lies in text messaging. *Computers in Human Behavior, 41,* 220–227.

14. Giatsoglou, M., Chatzaou, D., Shah, N., Faloutsos, C., & Vakali, A. (2015). Retweeting activity on Twitter: Signs of deception. In T. Cao, E.-P. Lim, Z.-H. Zhou, T.-B. Ho, D. Cheung, & H. Motoda (Eds.), *Advances in knowledge discovery and data mining* (pp. 122–134). Cham, Switzerland: Springer International.

15. Cho, D., Kim, S., & Acquisti, A. (2012, January). Empirical analysis of online anonymity and user behaviors: The impact of real name policy. *Proceedings of the 45th Hawaii International Conference on System Science,* 3041–3050.

16. Huh, S., & Williams, D. (2010). Dude looks like a lady: Gender swapping in an online game. In W. S. Bainbridge (Ed.), *Online worlds: Convergence of the real and the virtual* (pp. 161–175). London, England: Springer.

17. See Frost, J. (2006). *Impression formation in the information age: A study of and design for online dating.* Unpublished doctoral dissertation, Massachusetts Institute of Technology. *Dissertation Abstracts International: Section B: The Sciences and Engineering, 67*(5-B), 2875.

18. Drouin, M., Tobin, E., & Wygant, K. (2014). "Love the way you lie": Sexting deception in romantic relationships. *Computers in Human Behavior, 35,* 542–547.

19. Epstein, R. (2007, February/March). The truth about online dating. *Scientific American Mind,* 28–35.

20. Gibbs, J. L., Ellison, N. B., & Heino, R. D. (2006). Self-presentation in online personals: The role of anticipated future interaction, self-disclosure, and perceived success in Internet dating. *Communication Research, 33,* 152–177.

21. See Johnson, C. E. (2001). *Meeting the ethical challenges of leadership.* Thousand Oaks, CA: Sage.

22. Knapp, M. L. (2008). *Lying and deception in human interaction.* Boston, MA: Pearson/Allyn & Bacon.

23. Regier, W. G. (2007). *In praise of flattery.* Lincoln: University of Nebraska Press.

24. Feldman, R. S., Forrest, J. A., & Happ, B. R. (2002). Self-presentation and verbal deception: Do self-presenters lie more? *Basic and Applied Social Psychology, 24,* 163–170.

25. Ruedy, N. E., Moore, C., Gino, F., & Schweitzer, M. E. (2013). The cheater's high: The unexpected affective benefits of unethical behavior. *Journal of Personality and Social Psychology, 105,* 531–548.

26. Metts, S. (1989). A preliminary investigation of deception in close relationships. *Journal of Social and Personal Relationships, 6,* 159–179.

27. Shulman, D. (2007). *From hire to liar: The role of deception in the workplace.* Ithaca, NY: Cornell University Press.

28. DePaulo, B. M., & Morris, W. L. (2004). Discerning lies from truths: Behavioural cues to deception and the indirect pathway of intuition. In P. A. Granhag & L. A. Strömwall (Eds.), *The detection of deception in forensic contexts* (pp. 15–40). New York, NY: Cambridge University Press; but see Levine, T. R. (2015). New and improved accuracy findings in deception detection research. *Current Opinion in Psychology, 6,* 1–5.

29. Vrij, A. (2008). *Detecting lies and deceit: Pitfalls and opportunities* (2nd ed.). New York, NY: Wiley.

30. See Kaufmann, G., Drevland, G. C. B., Wessel, E., Goverskeid, G., & Magnussen, S. (2003). The importance of being earnest: Displayed emotions and witness credibility. *Applied Cognitive Psychology, 17,* 21–34; O'Sullivan, M. (2003). The fundamental attribution error in detecting deception: The boy-who-cried-wolf effect. *Personality and Social Psychology Bulletin, 29,* 1316–1327.

31. Street, C. N. H., & Masip, J. (2015). The source of the truth bias: Heuristic processing? *Scandinavian Journal of Psychology, 56,* 254–263.

32. See Xia, S. (2013). *An investigation about relationship maintenance strategies after the discovery of deception about infidelity.* Unpublished master's thesis, Texas Tech University; Jang, S. A. (2008). The effects of attachment styles and efficacy of communication on avoidance following a relational partner's deception. *Communication Research Reports, 25,* 300–311.

33. Rapp, D. N., Hinze, S. R., Kohlhepp, K., & Ryskin, R. A. (2014). Reducing reliance on inaccurate information. *Memory & Cognition, 42,* 11–26.

34. DePaulo, B. M., Lindsay, J. J., Malone, B. E., Muhlenbruck, L., Charlton, K., & Cooper, H. (2003). Cues to deception. *Psychological Bulletin, 129,* 74–118.

35. Park, H. S., Levine, T. R., McCornack, S. A., Morrison, K., & Ferrara, M. (2002). How people really detect lies. *Communication Monographs, 69,* 144–157.

36. Sporer, S. L., & Schwandt, B. (2006). Paraverbal indicators of deception: A meta-analytic synthesis. *Applied Cognitive Psychology, 20,* 421–446.

37. See Battigalli, P., Charness, G., & Dufwenberg, M. (2013). Deception: The role of guilt. *Journal of Economic Behavior & Organization, 93,* 227–232.

38. Giddens, C. L., Barron, K. W., Byrd-Craven, J., Clark, K. F., & Winter, A. S. (2013). Vocal indices of stress: A review. *Journal of Voice, 27,* e21–e29.

39. Villar, G., Arciuli, J., & Paterson, H. (2013). Vocal pitch production during lying: Beliefs about deception matter. *Psychiatry, Psychology and Law, 20,* 123–132.

40. Bauchner, J. E., Kaplan, E. P., & Miller, G. R. (1980). Detecting deception: The relationship of available information to judgmental accuracy in initial encounters. *Human Communication Research, 6,* 251–264.

41. See Barbato, G., De Padova, V., Paolillo, A. R., Arpaia, L., Russon, E., & Ficca, G. (2007). Increased spontaneous eye blink rate following prolonged wakefulness. *Physiology & Behavior, 90,* 151–154.

42. DePaulo et al., 2003; DePaulo, B. M., Stone, J. I., & Lassiter, G. D. (1985). Deceiving and detecting deceit. In B. R. Schlenker (Ed.), *The self and social life* (pp. 323–370). New York, NY: McGraw-Hill; Zuckerman, M., & Driver, R. E. (1985). Telling lies: Verbal and nonverbal correlates of deception. In A. W. Siegman & S. Feldstein (Eds.), *Multichannel integrations of nonverbal behavior* (pp. 129–148). Hillsdale, NJ: Lawrence Erlbaum Associates.

43. Jomier, J., Rault, E., & Aylward, S. R. (2004). Automatic quantification of pupil dilation under stress. *IEEE International Symposium on Biomedical Imaging, 1,* 249–252.

44. Webb, A. K., Honts, C. R., Kircher, J. C., Bernhardt, P., & Cook, A. E. (2009). Effectiveness of pupil diameter in a probable-lie comparison question test for deception. *Legal and Criminological Psychology, 14,* 279–292.

45. Burgoon, J. K., Guerrero, L. K., & Floyd, K. (2010). *Nonverbal communication.* Boston, MA: Allyn & Bacon.

46. Ekman, P. (2003). Darwin, deception, and facial expression. *Annals of the New York Academy of Sciences, 1000,* 205–221; Ekman, P., Friesen, W. V., & O'Sullivan, M. (1988). Smiles when lying. *Journal of Personality and Social Psychology, 54,* 414–420;

Scharlemann, J. P. W., Eckel, C. C., Kacelnik, A., & Wilson, R. K. (2001). The value of a smile: Game theory with a human face. *Journal of Economic Psychology, 22,* 617–640.

47. Sporer, S. L., & Schwandt, B. (2007). Moderators of nonverbal indicators of deception: A meta-analytic synthesis. *Psychology, Public Policy, and Law, 13,* 1–34.

48. Burgoon, J. K., & Buller, D. B. (2015). Interpersonal deception theory: Purposive and interdependent behavior during deceptive interpersonal interactions. In D. O. Braithwaite & P. Schrodt (Eds.), *Engaging theories in interpersonal communication: Multiple perspectives* (2nd ed., pp. 349–362). Thousand Oaks, CA: Sage; but see Frank, M. G., & Ekman, P. (2004). Appearing truthful generalizes across different deception situations. *Journal of Personality and Social Psychology, 86,* 486–495.

49. Burgoon, J. K., Buller, D. B., Ebesu, A., & Rockwell, P. (1994). Interpersonal deception: V. Accuracy in deception detection. *Communication Monographs, 61,* 303–325.

50. Burgoon, J. K., & Floyd, K. (2000). Testing for the motivation impairment effect during deceptive and truthful interaction. *Western Journal of Communication, 64,* 243–267; see also Millar, M., & Millar, K. (1995). Detection of deception in familiar and unfamiliar persons: The effects of information restriction. *Journal of Nonverbal Behavior, 19,* 69–84.

51. Weiss, B., & Feldman, R. S. (2006). Looking good and lying to do it: Deception as an impression management strategy in job interviews. *Journal of Applied Social Psychology, 36,* 1070–1086; Feldman, R. S., Tomasian, J. C., & Coats, E. J. (1999). Non-verbal deception abilities and adolescents' social competence: Adolescents with higher social skills are better liars. *Journal of Nonverbal Behavior, 23,* 237–249.

52. DePaulo, B. M., Lindsay, J. J., Malone, B. E., Muhlenbruck, L., Charlton, K., & Cooper, H. (2003). Clues to deception. *Psychological Bulletin, 129,* 74–118.

53. Buller, D. B., & Burgoon, J. K. (1996). Interpersonal deception theory. *Communication Theory, 6,* 203–242.

54. For an exception, see Feldman, R. S., Forrest, J. A., & Happ, B. R. (2002). Self-presentation and verbal deception: Do self-presenters lie more? *Basic and Applied Social Psychology, 24,* 163–170.

55. Bond, C. F., Omar, A., Mahmoud, A., & Bonser, R. N. (1990). Lie detection across cultures. *Journal of Nonverbal Behavior, 14,* 189–204.

56. Bond, C. F., & Atoum, A. O. (2000). International deception. *Personality and Social Psychology Bulletin, 26,* 385–395.

57. For review, see Burgoon & Floyd, 2000; see also DePaulo, B. M., & Kirkendol, S. E. (1989). The motivational impairment effect in the communication of deception. In J. Yuille (Ed.), *Credibility assessment* (pp. 51–70). Deurne, Belgium: Kluwer.

58. Bond, C. F., & DePaulo, B. M. (2006). Accuracy of deception judgments. *Personality and Social Psychology Review, 10,* 214–234.

59. Kim, R. K., & Levine, T. R. (2011). The effect of suspicion on deception detection accuracy: Optimal level or opposing effects? *Communication Reports, 24,* 51–62.

60. Burgoon et al., 1994.

61. Buller & Burgoon, 1996.

62. See Bond, C. F., Thomas, B. J., & Paulson, R. M. (2004). Maintaining lies: The multiple-audience problem. *Journal of Experimental Social Psychology, 40,* 29–40; Ekman, P., & Yamey, G. (2004). Emotions revealed: Recognising facial expressions. *British Medical Journal, 328,* 75–76.

63. Burgoon, J. K., Buller, D. B., & Floyd, K. (2001). Does participation affect deception success? A test of the interactivity principle. *Human Communication Research, 27,* 503–534.

64. Dunbar, N. E., Ramirez, A., & Burgoon, J. K. (2003). The effect of participation on the ability to judge deceit. *Communication Reports, 16,* 23–33.

Index

expertise
in communication, 17
vs. experience, 239
and power, 361
explicit rules, 16–17
expressed struggle, conflict as, 344
expressive talk
and deception, 391
definition of, 59
gender differences in, 59–60
extended families, 329
Extremely Loud and Incredibly Close (film), 251, 251*f*
extroversion, 266
eye behaviors, 191–192
in deception, 387
types of, 191–192
eye contact, 191–192
in conversation management, 183
cultural differences in, 203, 208
in deaf co-culture, 41
in deception, 385–386, 387, 388
in empathic listening, 242
functions of, 191–192
gender differences in, 204

F

face
definition of, 92
saving, 92
face needs, 91–94
definition of, 92
threats to, 93–94
types of, 92–93
Facebook
development of, 88
emotional contagion on, 264
number of friends on, 310
relationship development and maintenance on, 302–303, 304
support groups on, 227
tribute pages on, 157, 158
face-threatening acts, 93
facework
definition of, 92
strategies for improving, 92
facial expressions or displays, 189–191
cultural differences in, 203
in deceptive communication, 188
definition of, 189
of emotion, 181–182, 184, 190–191, 203
smiles, 188, 388, 387*f*

ubiquity of nonverbal communication through, 178
facial primacy, principle of, 189
facial recognition, 118, 119*f*
factual claims
vs. interpretations, 133, 171
vs. opinions, 171–173
false smiles, 188, 388, 387*f*
falsification, 381, 383
familiarity, and deception detection, 391
families, 327–331
characteristics defining, 327–329
communication issues in, 329–331
types of, 329
family of origin, 329
family of procreation, 329
The Fault in Our Stars (film), 75*f*
FBI (Federal Bureau of Investigation), 238
fear, 252
action tendencies associated with, 255
appeals to, 152*t*
definition of, 252
intensity of forms of, 257
in jealousy, 249
Federal Bureau of Investigation (FBI), 238
feedback
in communication climates, 169–170
definition of, 10
evaluative vs. non-evaluative, 169–170
in listening, 223–224
in models of communication, 9–12
fellowship face, 92–93
feminine cultures, 46, 54
feminine gender role
definition of, 52–53
and emotional expression, 265, 266
and interpersonal conflict, 352–353
and nonverbal communication, 66, 67
and power, 362
and self-disclosure, 99
Ferrara, Merissa, 386
Ferris, Amber, 304
Field, Tiffany, 4, 194
figurative language, about conflict, 345–346
filler words, 197
filters, perceptual, 13–14
finances, interpersonal conflict over, 344, 350

financial commitment, 280
Fink, Edward, 44
first impressions
names in, 150
primacy effect in, 116–117
Fitzpatrick, Mary Anne, 321–322
flaming, 355
flooded feeling, 367
Fonda, Jane, 274
food
and cultures, 38
and eating disorders, 200
football, Deflate-gate in, 121
Foss, Karen, 151
Fox, Jesse, 305
framing
of conflict, 346
of negative emotions, 270
fraud, 375
Frederick II (German emperor), 4
free speech, hate speech as, 165
French, John, 360–361
Fresh Off the Boat (TV show), 36*f*
Friedman, Rachelle, 280
friendly relations stage, 314
Friends (TV show), 13–14
friendships, 309–316
common characteristics of, 309–316
among co-workers, 332–334
deception detection in, 391, 395
end of, 315–316
rules for, 311
stages of, 314–315, 314*f*, 333
between superiors and subordinates, 335
Friesen, Wallace, 261, 262
fundamental attribution error, 126–128
fundamental frequency, 197
furniture arrangement, 201
Future Shock (Toffler), 232

G

Gallup, 65
Game of Thrones (TV show), 297*f*
gaming, gender-switching in, 49–50
Gandolfini, James, 224*f*
gays, 55–56
See also homosexuality; same-sex romantic relationships

gender, 49–68
of avatars, 49–50, 379
components of, 50–57
definition and use of term, 51, 51*f*
and domestic violence, 349
influence on communication, 57–68
influence on perception, 132
and power, 362–364
in self-concept, 76–77
gender clash, 57–58
gender cultures, 57–58
gender differences, 57–68
in conflict, 351–353
in decoding facial expressions, 190
in emotions, 65–66, 204, 264–265
in friendships, 312–313
as gender cultures, 57–58
in listening, 221
in nonverbal communication, 64–68, 204–205
in perception, 132
in self-disclosure, 99
in self-esteem, 85–86
in verbal communication, 59–64, 155
gender roles, 52–54
in concept of gender, 50–51
and conflict, 351–353
cultural differences in, 52–54
definition and use of term, 51, 51*f*, 52
and emotional expression, 265, 266
and nonverbal communication, 66, 67
and perceptual accuracy, 112–113
and power, 362
and self-disclosure, 99
types of, 52–53
See also specific types
gender stereotypes, 62, 65, 266
gender-switching, online, 49–50, 379
generalizations
in stereotypes, 115–116
weasel words in, 155
generalized complaints, 166
genetic ties, in families, 327–328
geography, in emotional expression, 260–261
gesticulation, 193
gestures, 192–193
in conversation management, 183